T.O. 21M-HGM25A-1-1

TITAN I
MISSILE WEAPON SYSTEM
OPERATION AND ORGANIZATIONAL MAINTENANCE MANUAL

TECHNICAL MANUAL

OPERATION AND ORGANIZATIONAL
MAINTENANCE

USAF MODEL

HGM-25A

MISSILE WEAPON SYSTEM
OPERATION

AF 04(645)-56
AF 04(694)-395

LATEST CHANGED PAGES SUPERSEDE
THE SAME PAGES OF PREVIOUS DATE

Insert changed pages into basic publication.
Destroy superseded pages

PUBLISHED UNDER AUTHORITY OF THE SECRETARY OF THE AIR FORCE

©2011 Periscope Film LLC
ISBN #978-1-937684-94-5
All Rights Reserved
www.PeriscopeFilm.com

1 AUGUST 1963
CHANGED 19 MARCH 1964

*This book has been digitally watermarked
to prevent illegal duplication.*

DISCLAIMER:
This manual is sold for historic research purposes
only, as an entertainment. It contains obselete
information and is not intended to be used as part
of an actual training program. The material
in this book has been declassified.

T.O. 21M-HGM25A-1-1 (21-SM68-1)

Reproduction for nonmilitary use of the information or illustrations contained in this publication is not permitted without specific approval of the issuing service. The policy for use of Classified Publications is established for the Air Force in AFR 205-1.

INSERT LATEST CHANGED PAGES, DESTROY SUPERSEDED PAGES.

LIST OF EFFECTIVE PAGES

NOTE: The portion of the text affected by the changes is indicated by a vertical line in the outer margin of the page.

TOTAL NUMBER OF PAGES IN THIS PUBLICATION IS 581 CONSISTING OF THE FOLLOWING:

Page No.	Issue	Page No.	Issue
*Title	19 Mar 64	3-17	13 Mar 64
*A thru C	19 Mar 64	3-18 thru 3-21	Original
i thru iii	Original	3-22	3 Jan 64
iv	3 Jan 64	3-23 thru 3-30	Original
v	18 Dec 63	3-31	17 Jan 64
vi	Original	3-31A Added	17 Jan 64
vii	18 Dec 63	3-32	17 Jan 64
viii thru ix	Original	3-32A thru 3-32E Added	17 Jan 64
*x thru xA	19 Mar 64	3-33	Original
xi thru xii	18 Dec 63	3-34	18 Dec 63
xiii	31 Jan 64	3-35	17 Jan 64
xiv	18 Dec 63	3-36	Original
xv thru xxxi	Original	3-37	17 Jan 64
xxxii	18 Dec 63	3-38	Original
xxxiii	20 Feb 64	3-39	17 Jan 64
1-1	5 Nov 63	3-40 thru 3-41	Original
1-1A Added	5 Nov 63	3-42	13 Mar 64
1-2 thru 1-16	Original	3-43 Deleted	13 Mar 64
1-17	18 Dec 63	3-44 thru 3-51	Original
1-18	Original	3-52	13 Mar 64
1-19	18 Dec 63	3-53 Deleted	13 Mar 64
1-19A Added	18 Dec 63	3-54 thru 3-58	13 Mar 64
1-20	18 Dec 63	3-58A Deleted	13 Mar 64
1-21 thru 1-33	Original	3-59 thru 3-63	13 Mar 64
1-34 thru 1-35	16 Jan 64	3-64 thru 3-65	Original
1-36 thru 1-39	Original	3-66	18 Dec 63
1-40	16 Jan 64	3-67	20 Feb 64
1-41	Original	3-67A Added	20 Feb 64
1-42	18 Dec 63	3-68	17 Jan 64
1-43 thru 1-50	Original	3-69 thru 3-71	Original
1-51	18 Dec 63	*3-72 thru 3-77	19 Mar 64
1-52 thru 1-57	Original	*3-77A Deleted	19 Mar 64
1-58	3 Jan 64	*3-78 thru 3-82	19 Mar 64
1-59	17 Jan 64	*3-82A Deleted	19 Mar 64
1-60	18 Dec 63	*3-83	19 Mar 64
1-61 thru 1-143	Original	*3-83A Deleted	19 Mar 64
2-1 thru 2-2	Original	*3-84 thru 3-86	19 Mar 64
3-1 thru 3-16	Original		

*The asterisk indicates pages changed, added, or deleted by the current change.

ADDITIONAL COPIES OF THIS PUBLICATION MAY BE OBTAINED AS FOLLOWS:
USAF ACTIVITIES.—In accordance with T.O. 00-5-2.

Changed 19 March 1964   TOCN 1-1 (DEN-12)

USAF
A

T.O. 21M-HGM25A-1-1 (21-SM68-1)

Page No.	Issue	Page No.	Issue
3-86A thru 3-86G Added	13 Mar 64	4-18 thru 4-24	Original
3-87 thru 3-89	Original	4-25	17 Jan 64
3-90	17 Jan 64	4-26 thru 4-29	Original
3-91 thru 3-101	Original	4-30	31 Jan 64
3-102	17 Jan 64	4-31	18 Dec 63
3-103 thru 3-128	Original	4-32 thru 4-34 Deleted	18 Dec 63
3-129	7 Oct 63	4-35 thru 4-36	Original
3-130	20 Feb 64	4-37	18 Dec 63
3-130A	13 Mar 64	4-38 thru 4-39 Deleted	18 Dec 63
3-131 thru 3-132	20 Feb 64	4-40 thru 4-45	Original
3-133	18 Dec 63	4-46	17 Jan 64
3-134 thru 3-135	20 Feb 64	4-47	18 Nov 63
3-136 thru 3-138	17 Jan 64	4-48	17 Jan 64
3-138A Added	17 Jan 64	4-49	13 Mar 64
3-139	17 Jan 64	4-50	Original
3-140	Original	4-51 thru 4-52	18 Nov 63
3-141	31 Jan 64	4-53 thru 4-58	Original
3-142 thru 3-143	13 Mar 64	4-59	3 Jan 64
3-144 thru 3-145	Original	4-60	18 Dec 63
3-146	3 Jan 64	4-61	5 Nov 63
3-147	17 Jan 64	4-62 thru 4-63	Original
3-147A Added	3 Jan 64	5-1 thru 5-2	3 Jan 64
3-148 thru 3-151	Original	5-3 thru 5-4	18 Dec 63
3-152 thru 3-154	18 Dec 63	5-5 Deleted	18 Dec 63
3-154A Added	18 Dec 63	5-6	18 Dec 63
3-155 thru 3-157	Original	*5-7	19 Mar 64
3-158 thru 3-164	18 Dec 63	5-8 thru 5-10	18 Dec 63
3-164A thru 3-164B Added	18 Dec 63	5-11 Deleted	18 Dec 63
3-165 thru 3-168	Original	5-12	17 Jan 64
3-169	18 Dec 63	5-13	18 Dec 63
3-170	Original	5-14 thru 5-15	Original
3-171	18 Dec 63	5-16 thru 5-20	17 Jan 64
3-171A Added	18 Dec 63	5-20A Added	17 Jan 64
3-172 thru 3-176	Original	5-21 thru 5-22	Original
3-177	18 Dec 63	5-22A Added	18 Dec 63
3-178 thru 3-185	Original	5-23 thru 5-25	Original
3-186	18 Dec 63	5-26	31 Jan 64
3-187 thru 3-232	Original	5-27	Original
4-1	3 Jan 64	5-28	31 Jan 64
4-1A Added	3 Jan 64	5-29 thru 5-30	Original
4-2 thru 4-3	Original	5-31 thru 5-33	31 Jan 64
4-4 thru 4-5	18 Dec 63	5-34 thru 5-35	Original
4-6 thru 4-11	Original	5-36	31 Jan 64
4-12 thru 4-13	18 Dec 63	5-37 thru 5-38	Original
4-13A Added	18 Dec 63	5-39	13 Mar 64
4-14 thru 4-17	17 Jan 64	5-40 thru 5-43	Original
		5-44	17 Jan 64
		5-45 thru 5-46	Original

*The asterisk indicates pages changed, added, or deleted by the current change.

T.O. 21M-HGM25A-1-1 (21-SM68-1)

Page No.	Issue
5-47 thru 5-48	31 Jan 64
5-49	17 Jan 64
5-50	5 Nov 63
5-51 thru 5-52	17 Jan 64
5-52A Added	17 Jan 64
5-53 thru 5-54	5 Nov 63
6-1 thru 6-7	Original
7-1 thru 7-3	Original
GLOSSARY-1 thru GLOSSARY-9	Original
INDEX-1 thru INDEX-2	Original
*INDEX-3 thru INDEX-3A	19 Mar 64
INDEX-4	17 Jan 64
INDEX-5 thru INDEX-10	Original

*The asterisk indicates pages changed, added, or deleted by the current change.

TABLE OF CONTENTS

I GENERAL DESCRIPTION

1-1	Introduction.	1-1
1-3	SM68 Missile.	1-1
1-4	Leading Particulars	1-1
1-6	Countdowns.	1-1
1-14	Post Launch and Shutdown Operations	1-4
1-16	Propellants	1-4
1-18	External Cable Conduits	1-4
1-20	Access Panels	1-4
1-22	Ordnance.	1-4
1-28	Vernier Nozzles	1-6
1-30	Launch Complex.	1-6
1-31	Leading Particulars	1-6
1-34	Missile Silo.	1-6
1-49	Equipment Terminal.	1-17
1-60	Propellant Terminal	1-27
1-64	Control Center.	1-27
1-79	Power House	1-42
1-82	Antenna Terminal.	1-42
1-87	Fuel Terminal	1-48
1-98	Portal.	1-51
1-100	Tunnels	1-51
1-106	Local Control Stations.	1-53
1-111	Pump House and Spray Ponds (VAFB)	1-53
1-114	Facility Systems.	1-53
1-116	Facility Air Conditioning, Heating, and Ventilating System.	1-57

Section		Page
1-123	Portal and Antenna Silo Environmental Seal Heating Systems	1-58
1-125	Power Generation System	1-58
1-127	Power Distribution System	1-58
1-129	Water Supply, Distribution, and Waste Systems	1-58
1-136	Sanitary Sewage System	1-59
1-138	Non-sanitary Waste System	1-59
1-140	Sensing, Warning, and Blast Protection Systems	1-59
1-142	Utility Compressed Air System	1-59
1-144	Plant Compressed Air System	1-59
1-148	Portal Hydraulic System	1-62
1-151	Instrument and TV Camera Mount Elevators	1-62
1-153	Antenna Silo Personnel Elevators (Operational bases)	1-62
1-155	Subsystems	1-62
1-158	Guidance System	1-62
1-192	Flight Control System	1-86
1-212	Electrical System	1-96
1-236	Engine System	1-98
1-282	Propellant System	1-107
1-302	Missile Launcher System	1-113
1-334	Re-Entry Vehicle System	1-117
1-346	Launch Sequencer	1-118
1-348	Control Center Circuits	1-118
1-363	Time Display Board	1-121
1-369	Hydraulic System	1-121
1-397	Missile Air Conditioning System	1-127
1-405	Communication System	1-129
1-407	Instrumentation and Range Safety System Facilities (VAFB)	1-129
1-410	Mobile Telemeter Station	1-131

Section			Page
	1-412	Command Destruct Facilities	1-131
	1-414	Radar Tracking Facilities	1-131
	1-416	AME-Cotar Fields	1-131
	1-418	Radar Surveillance System AN/TPS-39(v)	1-131
	1-419	Purpose	1-131
	1-421	Description	1-133
	1-426	Maintenance Plan	1-133
	1-428	Organizational Level and Field Level Maintenance	1-133
	1-437	Depot Maintenance	1-142
	1-441	Scheduled and Unscheduled Maintenance	1-143
	1-445	Commodity Servicing	1-143
	1-446	Diesel Fuel	1-143
	1-448	Liquid Oxygen, Liquid Nitrogen, Gaseous Nitrogen, Helium and Rocket Fuel (RP-1)	1-143
II	RECEIPT THROUGH LAUNCH		
	2-1	Scope	2-1
	2-3	Missile and Re-Entry Vehicle Installation and Checkout	2-1
	2-5	Alert Status Monitoring	2-1
	2-7	System Exercises	2-1
	2-9	Tactical Launch (EWO)	2-1
	2-11	Post Launch	2-1
III	NORMAL OPERATING PROCEDURES		
	3-1	Scope	3-1
	3-3	Crew Administrative Procedures	3-1
	3-5	Crew Inspection	3-1
	3-7	Pre-Departure Crew Briefing	3-1
	3-9	Complex Entry Procedures (Operational bases)	3-1
	3-11	Crew Shift Change Briefing	3-1

Section		Page
3-13	Crew Operations Briefing	3-4
3-15	Individual Changeover	3-4
3-17	Activity Coordination Briefing	3-4
3-33	Special Activities Briefing	3-15
3-35	Personnel Control	3-16
3-39	Contingency Procedures	3-16
3-44	Seven High/Redskin Notification System	3-20
3-48	Serious Illness or Injury	3-22
3-50	Servere Weather Report Procedure	3-22
3-52	Deleted	
3-54	Exit Procedures (Operational Bases)	3-22
3-56	Radar Surveillance System (Anti-intrusion)	3-22
3-71	Security Procedures	3-27
3-83	Alert Status Monitoring	3-30
3-85	Weather Information	3-30
3-87	Index of Refraction	3-30
3-94	Launch Site Targeting Procedure	3-89
3-96	Launch and Exercise Countdowns	3-89
3-98	Alert Procedures	3-89
3-109	Fast Reaction Message	3-123
3-111	Launch, Exercise, and Guidance Countdown Procedures	3-123
3-113	Power House Countdown Procedure	3-124
3-115	Launch Countdown System Functions	3-124
IV	EMERGENCY PROCEDURES	
4-1	General	4-1
4-5	Boil-off Procedure	4-1
4-7	OSBV Lox Dump	4-1

Section			Page
	4-10	Recycle of Electrical System and PLPS	4-2
	4-12	Verification of Lox Tanks Empty	4-2
	4-14	Hazard Procedures	4-2
	4-16	Radar Surveillance System (Anti-Intrusion)	4-2
	4-17	Alarm Indication	4-2
	4-19	Primary Power Failure	4-3
	4-21	Jamming and Anti-Jamming	4-3
V	COMBAT CREW MALFUNCTION ISOLATION		
	5-1	Scope	5-1
	5-3	Malfunction Isolation	5-1
	5-5	Malfunction Isolation of Propellant Loading and Pressurization System	5-1
	5-7	Malfunction Isolation of Electrical System	5-1
	5-9	Malfunction Isolation of Flight Control System	5-1
	5-11	Malfunction Isolation of RVS and GMTS	5-1
	5-12A	Malfunction Isolation for Launcher	5-2
	5-13	Malfunction Isolation for Guidance	5-2
	5-15	Malfunction of Power House	5-2
VI	OPERATING LIMITATIONS		
	6-1	Scope	6-1
	6-3	Weather Limitations	6-1
	6-6	Power House	6-1
	6-7	One Generator Operation	6-1
	6-9	Diesel Fuel Oil Supply	6-2
	6-11	Ice Banks	6-2
	6-13	Countdown Limitations	6-2
	6-14	First Hold Period	6-2
	6-17	Second Hold Period	6-2

Changed 18 December 1963 TOCN-1 (DEN-5)

Section			Page
	6-20	Launch Platform Raising and Lowering.	6-4
	6-28	Launcher Platform Operating Weight Limits	6-5
	6-32	Target Selection.	6-7
	6-34	GGS Malfunction or Not-Ready.	6-7
	6-36	Handover or Shutdown.	6-7
	6-38	Radar Surveillance System	6-7
VII	CREW DUTIES		
	7-1	Scope	7-1
	7-3	General	7-1
	7-5	Missile Combat Crew Commander (MCCC).	7-1
	7-7	Missile Launch Officer (MLO).	7-1
	7-9	Guidance Electronics Officer (GEO).	7-2
	7-11	Ballistic Missile Analyst Technician (BMAT)	7-2
	7-13	Missile Maintenance Technician (MMT).	7-3
	7-15	Electrical Power Production Technicians (EPPT).	7-3
GLOSSARY			GLOSSARY-1
ALPHABETICAL INDEX			INDEX-1

LIST OF ILLUSTRATIONS

Number	Title	Page
1-1	Missile Configuration	1-2
1-2	Table of Leading Particulars.	1-3
1-3	Access Panels	1-5
1-4	Operational Base Launch Complex (Sheet 1 of 3).	1-7
1-5	VAFB Launch Complex (Sheet 1 of 2).	1-10
1-6	Missile Silo.	1-12
1-7	Silo Doors.	1-14

T.O. 21-SM68-1　　　　　　　　　　　　　　　　List of Illustrations

Number	Title	Page
1-8	Crib Structure	1-15
1-9	Launcher Platform	1-16
1-10	Umbilical Tower	1-18
1-11	Launcher Platform Drive System (Operational Bases)	1-19
1-11A	Launcher Platform Drive System (VAFB)	1-19A
1-12	Umbilical Lines and Support Mechanism	1-20
1-13	Equipment Terminal, Level I	1-21
1-14	Typical Power Pack Room and Electrical Room	1-23
1-15	Equipment Terminal, Level II	1-24
1-16	Equipment Terminal, Level III	1-25
1-17	Equipment Terminal, Level IV	1-26
1-18	Propellant Terminal Lower Level	1-28
1-19	Propellant Terminal Upper Level	1-29
1-20	Control Center (VAFB)	1-30
1-21	Control Center (Operational Bases)	1-31
1-22	Control Center Operations Room Equipment Location (Sheet 1 of 2)	1-32
1-23	Launch Control Console (Operational Bases)	1-34
1-24	Launch Control Console (VAFB)	1-35
1-25	Missile Guidance Console	1-38
1-26	Launch Complex Facilities Console (Operational Bases)	1-40
1-27	Launch Complex Facilities Console (VAFB)	1-41
1-28	Power House (VAFB)	1-43
1-29	Power House Lower Level Typical Equipment Location (Operational Bases)	1-44
1-30	Power House Mezzanine Typical Equipment Location (Operational Bases)	1-45
1-31	Antenna Terminal (VAFB)	1-46
1-32	Antenna Terminal (Operational Bases)	1-47

Changed 18 December 1963　TOCN-1 (DEN-5)

T.O. 21-SM68-1 List of Illustrations

Number	Title	Page
1-33	Tunnel Junction 10 (VAFB)	1-49
1-34	Tunnel Junction 12 (Operational Bases)	1-50
1-35	Tunnels and Blast Locks Location Diagram	1-52
1-36	Ground Level Control Station	1-54
1-37	Tunnel Entrance Control Station	1-55
1-38	Pump House and Spray Ponds (VAFB)	1-56
1-39	Table of Sensing, Warning, and Blast Protection Systems (Sheet 1 of 2)	1-60
1-40	Table of Missile Subsystems	1-63
1-41	Guidance System	1-64
1-42	Control Center Operations Room Equipment Functions (Sheet 1 of 3)	1-66
1-43	Control Center Electrical Equipment Room, Radar Equipment	1-69
1-44	Antenna Terminal Equipment Location	1-70
1-45	Antenna Terminal Equipment Functions	1-71
1-46	Antenna Silo Equipment Location	1-72
1-47	Antenna Silo Equipment Functions (Sheet 1 of 2)	1-73
1-48	Missile Guidance Set	1-75
1-49	Missile Guidance Set Equipment Functions	1-77
1-50	Antenna-Mast Group OA-2903A/GRW-5 or Collimation Antenna-Mast Group (GS-58128)	1-78
1-51	Optical Camera-Telescope Target RR-101/GRW-5	1-78
1-52	Radar Transmitting Units, Block Diagram	1-81
1-53	Missile Guidance Set AN/DRW-18, AN/DRW-19, AN/DRW-20, AN/DRW-21, or AN/DRW-22, Block Diagram	1-83
1-54	Azimuth and Elevation Error Detection	1-84
1-55	Radar Receiving Units Block Diagram	1-85
1-56	Digital Data Printer RO-144/GSK-1, Printout Data (Sheet 1 of 6)	1-87

Number	Title	Page
1-57	Missile Axes and Movement Diagram	1-93
1-58	Stage I Engine	1-99
1-59	Stage II Engine	1-100
1-60	Stage I Rocket Engine Subassembly	1-102
1-61	Stage II Rocket Engine Subassembly	1-104
1-62	Propellant System Flow Diagram	1-108
1-63	Table of Propellant System Control Assemblies	1-111
1-64	Water Spray Equipment	1-116
1-65	Time Display Board (Operational Bases)	1-122
1-66	Stage I Hydraulic Equipment Location	1-124
1-67	Stage II Hydraulic Equipment Location	1-126
1-68	Missile Air Conditioning System (Operational Bases)	1-128
1-69	Conditioned Air Flow	1-130
1-70	Typical Radar Surveillance System AN/TPS-39(V)	1-132
1-71	Class D Transmitter Set	1-134
1-72	Class D Receiver Set (Receiver Group Cover Removed)	1-135
1-73	Class A Antenna Group (Receiver or Transmitter Set)	1-136
1-74	Receiver Group	1-137
1-75	Annunciator	1-138
1-76	Annunciator Power Supply	1-139
1-77	Table of Radar Surveillance System AN/TPS-39(V) Capabilities	1-140
3-1	Crew Inspection	3-2
3-2	Crew Changeover Briefing Procedures	3-3
3-3	Individual Changeover, Abbreviated Checklist Procedures (Sheet 1 of 2)	3-5
3-4	Individual Changeover, Amplified Checklist Procedures (Sheet 1 of 8)	3-7

T.O. 21M-HGM25A-1-1 (21-SM68-1) List of Illustrations

Number	Title	Page
3-5	Broken Arrow, Bent Spear, and Dull Sword Procedures (Sheet 1 of 3)	3-17
3-6	Seven High/Redskin Notification Procedures	3-21
3-7	Serious Injury or Illness Checklist Procedure (Sheet 1 of 2)	3-23
3-8	Severe Weather Report Procedure	3-25
3-9	Guidance Electronics Officer Alert Status Monitoring (Standby) Procedure (Sheet 1 of 2)	3-31
3-9A	Guidance Electronics Officer Alert Status Monitoring (Power On) Procedure (Sheet 1 of 5)	3-32A
3-10	Ballistic Missile Analyst Technician Alert Status Monitoring Procedure (Operational Bases) (Sheet 1 of 11)	3-33
3-11	Ballistic Missile Analyst Technician Alert Status Monitoring Procedure (VAFB) (Sheet 1 of 10)	3-44
3-12	Missile Maintenance Technician Alert Status Monitoring Procedure (Operational Bases) (Sheet 1 of 9)	3-54
3-13	Missile Maintenance Technician Alert Status Monitoring Procedure (VAFB) (Sheet 1 of 9)	3-63
3-13A	Electrical Power Production Technician Alert Status Monitoring Procedure (LAFB 724TH/725TH SQDN) (Sheet 1 of 7)	3-72
3-14	Electrical Power Production Technician Alert Status Monitoring Procedure (EAFB, BAFB, LAFB, MHAFB) (Sheet 1 of 8)	3-79
3-14A	Facility Technician Alert Status Monitoring Procedure (Operational Bases) (Sheet 1 of 4)	3-86A
3-14B	Facility Technician Alert Status Monitoring Procedure (VAFB) (Sheet 1 of 3)	3-86E
3-15	Typical Weather Chart	3-87
3-16	Index of Refraction Calculation Procedure	3-88
3-17	Retargeting Flow Diagram	3-90
3-18	Inventory Targeting Package Procedure (Sheet 1 of 2)	3-91
3-19	Install and Verify Guidance Program Tape and Target Tape Procedure (Sheet 1 of 6)	3-93
3-20	Digital Guidance Simulation Procedure (Sheet 1 of 5)	3-99
3-21	Printed Record from Digital Guidance Simulation	3-104

Changed 19 March 1964 TOCN 1-1 (DEN-12)

T.O. 21M-HGM25A-1-1 (21-SM68-1) List of Illustrations

Number	Title	Page
3-22	R/V Cards and Launch Console Label Installation Procedure (Sheet 1 of 4)	3-105
3-23	Verify Target Procedure	3-109
3-24	Handover Target Compatibility Procedure	3-110
3-25	Fast Retargeting, Install and Verify Target Tape and Verify Guidance Program Tape Procedure (Sheet 1 of 5)	3-111
3-26	Fast Retargeting Verify Target Procedure	3-116

Number	Title	Page
3-27	Fast Retargeting Post Retargeting Procedure (Sheet 1 of 2)	3-117
3-28	Fast Retargeting R/V Card and Launch Console Label Installation Procedure (Sheet 1 of 4)	3-119
3-29	Launch Countdown Procedure (Sheet 1 of 5)	3-125
3-30	Lox or CSE Countdown Procedure (Sheet 1 of 6)	3-130
3-31	Guidance Countdown Procedure (Sheet 1 of 8)	3-136
3-32	Powerhouse Countdown Procedure (Sheet 1 of 4)	3-144
3-33	Launch Countdown System Functions (Operational Bases) (Sheet 1 of 39)	3-148
3-34	Launch Countdown System Functions (VAFB) (Sheet 1 of 44)	3-187
3-35	Launch Countdown System Functions Launcher Control System Lower Launcher (Sheet 1 of 2)	3-231
4-1	Hazard Condition Chart (Sheet 1 of 2)	4-4
4-2	Gox Hazard in Missile Silo (Sheet 1 of 3)	4-6
4-3	Gox Hazard in Propellant Terminal (Sheet 1 of 3)	4-9
4-4	Lox Hazard in Propellant Terminal Lox Vent (Operational Bases) (Sheet 1 of 2)	4-12
4-5	Lox Spillage in Missile Silo (Sheet 1 of 4)	4-14
4-6	Missile Silo Fire (Sheet 1 of 4)	4-18
4-7	Propellant Terminal Fire (Sheet 1 of 3)	4-22
4-8	Equipment Terminal Fire (Sheet 1 of 3)	4-25
4-9	Hydraulic Fire, Equipment Terminal (Sheet 1 of 4)	4-28
4-10	Deleted.	
4-11	Fire in Fuel Terminal (Sheet 1 of 3)	4-35
4-12	Deleted.	
4-13	Missile Silo Explosion (Sheet 1 of 2)	4-40
4-14	Lox Empty Propellant Terminal	4-42
4-15	Battery Power, Equipment Terminal	4-43
4-16	Power House Emergency (Sheet 1 of 2)	4-44

Number	Title	Page
4-17	Loss of All AC Power (Sheet 1 of 3)	4-46
4-18	Loss of One of Two Generators During Alert Status Monitoring (EAFB, BAFB, LAFB, MHAFB) (Sheet 1 of 2)	4-49
4-19	Loss of One of Two Generators During Alert Status Monitoring (LAFB 724TH/725TH SQDN)	4-51
4-20	Loss of One of Three Generators During Countdown (LAFB 724TH/725TH SQDN)	4-52
4-21	Two Generator Countdown (LAFB 724TH/725TH SQDN)	4-53
4-22	Loss of Launcher Feeder AC Power	4-54
4-23	Loss of Power House Feeder AC Power	4-55
4-24	Loss of Control Center Feeder AC Power	4-56
4-25	Loss of Power House Intake Fan	4-57
4-26	Loss of Power House Exhaust Fan	4-58
4-27	Diesel Engine Run-Away (Sheet 1 of 2)	4-59
4-28	Power House Fire	4-61
4-29	Single Generator Operation	4-62
4-30	Standby Diesel Engine Manual Start (LAFB 724TH/725TH SQDN)	4-63
5-1	PLPS Red (LCFC) at TSI	5-3
5-2	No LOX LOADING White (LCC)	5-4
5-3	Deleted.	
5-4	PLPS Red at LOX LOADING or T-700	5-6
5-5	LOX EMPTY Red (LCFC)	5-7
5-6	PLPS Red at T-280 (Sheet 1 of 3)	5-8
5-7	Deleted.	
5-8	GROUND POWER Red at T-870	5-12
5-9	GROUND POWER Red Prior to T-280	5-13
5-10	BATTERY POWER Red	5-14
5-11	GROUND POWER Red at T-280	5-15

T.O. 21M-HGM25A-1-1 (21-SM68-1)　　　　List of Illustrations

Number	Title	Page
5-12	FLIGHT CONTROLS Red on LCFC (T-280) and Assembly 3A2 (Sheet 1 of 6)	5-16
5-13	RVS Red (LCFC) T-280 or RVS Red (LCFC) T-280 and CONTROL CENTER CIRCUITS Red (Sheet 1 of 2)	5-21
5-13A	LOWER LAUNCHER Pressed White and Launcher Remains in the Intermediate Position	5-22A
5-14	TSI to T-280 GUIDANCE Red	5-23
5-15	LAUNCHER Red, Power Pack Not Operating at T-281	5-24
5-16	All Guidance Indicators Not Lighted	5-25
5-17	CONSTANTS REGISTER 6 Inoperative	5-26
5-18	POWER ON Not White	5-27
5-19	GUID X NOT RDY Does Not Go Out (Before START GUID X Green)	5-28
5-20	GUID X NOT RDY Does Not Go Out (After START GUID X Green)	5-29
5-21	START CD Indicator Does Not Light	5-30
5-22	POWER ON Not Green (Sheet 1 of 3)	5-31
5-23	TARGET GATED Not Green and No Gated Pulse when START GUID X is Initiated	5-34
5-24	MAG RDY Not White	5-35
5-25	MAG ON Not Green (Before LIFT OFF White)	5-36
5-26	START GUID X Not Green	5-37
5-27	RAISE ANT Not White	5-38
5-28	ANT RAISE Not Green	5-39
5-29	MISSILE READY Not White	5-40
5-30	ACQ MISSILE Not Green	5-41
5-31	LIFT OFF Not White	5-42
5-32	GUID IN PROGRESS Not Green	5-43
5-33	GGS FAULT Lighted	5-44
5-34	ABORT Red (During GUID X Run)	5-45
5-35	ABORT Red (During Missile Flight)	5-46

Changed 31 January 1964　TOCN 1-1 (DEN-9)

Number	Title	Page
5-36.	MAG I Not Indicating Between 1.5 to 1.9 MA	5-47
5-37	Erratic MAG I Indication	5-48
5-38	Table of Power House Malfunction Isolation (Sheet 1 of 6)	5-49
6-1	Maximum Allowable Hold Time, First Hold	6-3
6-2	Launcher Platform Operating Weight Limits	6-6

LIST OF RELATED MANUALS

T.O. 21-SM68-1FJ-1-2   Operation and Organizational Mainte-
                                                    nance -- Radio-Inertial Guidance System,
                                                    Launch and Guidance Operations.

SAC CEM 21-SM68-2-20-1 (VAFB)   Organizational Maintenance -- Air Con-
SAC CEM 21-SM68-2-20-2 (LAFB 724TH SQDN)   ditioning, Heating, and Ventilating
SAC CEM 21-SM68-2-20-3 (LAFB 725TH SQDN)   Systems.
SAC CEM 21-SM68-2-20-4 (EAFB)
SAC CEM 21-SM68-2-20-5 (BAFB)
SAC CEM 21-SM68-2-20-6 (LAFB)
SAC CEM 21-SM68-2-20-7 (MHAFB)

SAC CEM 21-SM68-2-21-1 (VAFB)   Organizational Maintenance -- Power
SAC CEM 21-SM68-2-21-2 (LAFB 724TH SQDN)   Generation and Distribution Systems.
SAC CEM 21-SM68-2-21-3 (LAFB 725TH SQDN)
SAC CEM 21-SM68-2-21-4 (EAFB)
SAC CEM 21-SM68-2-21-5 (BAFB)
SAC CEM 21-SM68-2-21-6 (LAFB)
SAC CEM 21-SM68-2-21-7 (MHAFB)

SAC CEM 21-SM68-2-24-1 (VAFB)   Organizational Maintenance -- Water
SAC CEM 21-SM68-2-24-2 (LAFB 724TH SQDN)   Supply, and Waste Systems.
SAC CEM 21-SM68-2-24-3 (LAFB 725TH SQDN)
SAC CEM 21-SM68-2-24-4 (EAFB)
SAC CEM 21-SM68-2-24-5 (BAFB)
SAC CEM 21-SM68-2-24-6 (LAFB)
SAC CEM 21-SM68-2-24-7 (MHAFB)

SAC CEM 21-SM68-2-25-1 (VAFB)   Organizational Maintenance -- Sensing,
SAC CEM 21-SM68-2-25-2 (LAFB 724TH SQDN)   Warning, and Blast Protection Systems.
SAC CEM 21-SM68-2-25-3 (LAFB 725TH SQDN)
SAC CEM 21-SM68-2-25-4 (EAFB)
SAC CEM 21-SM68-2-25-5 (BAFB)
SAC CEM 21-SM68-2-25-6 (LAFB)
SAC CEM 21-SM68-2-25-7 (MHAFB)

SAC CEM 21-SM68-2-26-1 (VAFB)   Organizational Maintenance -- Mech-
SAC CEM 21-SM68-2-26-2 (LAFB 724TH SQDN)   anical Specialties.
SAC CEM 21-SM68-2-26-3 (LAFB 725TH SQDN)
SAC CEM 21-SM68-2-26-4 (EAFB)
SAC CEM 21-SM68-2-26-5 (BAFB)
SAC CEM 21-SM68-2-26-6 (LAFB)
SAC CEM 21-SM68-2-26-7 (MHAFB)

T.O. 21-SM68-2D-2-1   Operation and Organizational Main-
                                                    tenance -- Missile

List of Related Manuals

T.O. 21-SM68-2D-3-1 (Post update) T.O. 21-SM68-2D-3-2 (Prior update)	Operation and Organizational Maintenance -- Rocket Engine System.
T.O. 21-SM68-2D-6-1	Organizational Maintenance -- Radio-Inertial Guidance System Computer Data Flow Diagrams.
T.O. 21-SM68-2D-6-2	Organizational Maintenance -- Radio-Inertial Guidance System, Computer Schematic and Power Distribution Diagrams.
T.O. 21-SM68-2D-6-3	Organizational Maintenance -- Radio-Inertial Guidance System, Computer Equation File, A-U.
T.O. 21-SM68-2D-6-4	Organizational Maintenance -- Radio-Inertial Guidance System, Computer Equation File, V-Z.
T.O. 21-SM68-2D-6-5	Organizational Maintenance -- Radio-Inertial Guidance System, Computer Equation File Simulator.
T.O. 21-SM68-2D-6-6-1 T.O. 21-SM68-2D-6-6-2 T.O. 21-SM68-2D-6-6-3	Organizational Maintenance -- Radio-Inertial Guidance System, Computer Wire Tabulations-Computer and Peripheral Equipment (Part I), (Part II), and (Part III).
T.O. 21-SM68-2D-6-7	Organizational Maintenance -- Radio-Inertial Guidance System, Computer Wire Tabulations, Power.
T.O. 21-SM68-2D-6-8	Organizational Maintenance -- Radio-Inertial Guidance System, Computer, Wire Tabulations, MGE.
T.O. 21-SM68-2D-6-9	Organizational Maintenance -- Radio-Inertial Guidance System, Computer, Maintenance Tape Records.
T.O. 21-SM68-2D-6-10	Organizational Maintenance -- Radio-Inertial Guidance System, Computer Command Timing.
T.O. 21-SM68-2D-8-1 (VAFB) T.O. 21-SM68-2D-8-2 (except VAFB)	Organizational Maintenance -- Launcher System.
T.O. 21-SM68-2D-10-1 (Post update) T.O. 21-SM68-2D-10-2 (Prior to update)	Operation and Organizational Maintenance -- Electrical System.

T.O. 21-SM68-1   List of Related Manuals

T.O. 21-SM68-2D-11-1 (Post update) T.O. 21-SM68-2D-11-2 (Prior to update)	Operation and Organizational Maintenance -- Flight Control System.
T.O. 21-SM68-2D-12-1 T.O. 21-SM68-2D-12-2	Operation and Organizational Maintenance -- Propellant System.
T.O. 21-SM68-2D-13-1 (VAFB)	Operation and Organizational Maintenance -- Instrument and Range Safety System.
T.O. 21-SM68-2D-15-1 T.O. 21-SM68-2D-15-2	Operation and Organizational Maintenance -- Launch Control and Status System.
T.O. 21-SM68-2D-16-1 T.O. 21-SM68-2D-16-2	Operation and Organizational Maintenance -- Launch Control and Checkout Equipment.
T.O. 21-SM68-2F-3-1	Operation and Organizational Maintenance -- Rocket Engine System.
T.O. 21-SM68-2F-6-1	Organizational Maintenance -- Radio-Inertial Guidance System, Computer, Computer and Peripheral Equipment.
T.O. 21-SM68-2F-6-2	Organizational Maintenance -- Radio-Inertial Guidance System, Computer, MAE.
T.O. 21-SM68-2F-6-3	Organizational Maintenance -- Radio-Inertial Guidance System, Computer, Power.
T.O. 21-SM68-2F-6-4	Organizational Maintenance -- Radio-Inertial Guidance System, Computer Simulator.
T.O. 21-SM68-2F-6-5	Organizational Maintenance --Radio-Inertial Guidance System, Computer, Maintenance Routine Analysis.
T.O. 21-SM68-2F-7-1-1	Operation and Organizational Maintenance -- Missile Guidance Set AN/GRW-5.
T.O. 21-SM68-2F-7-1-2	Operation and Organizational Maintenance -- Missile Guidance Set AN/GRW-5, Guidance Conditioning and Status Command Guidance, Tracking, and Monitoring Loops.

T.O. 21-SM68-2F-7-1-3	Operation and Organizational Maintenance -- Missile Guidance Set AN/GRW-5, Guidance Exercise, Timing, and Maintenance, Test, and Alignment Loops (Function Manual);
T.O. 21-SM68-2F-7-1-4	Operation and Organizational Maintenance -- Missile Guidance Set AN/GRW-5, Power Loop.
T.O. 21-SM68-2F-8-1 (VAFB) T.O. 21-SM68-2F-8-2 (except VAFB)	Organizational Maintenance -- Launcher System.
T.O. 21-SM68-2F-10-1	Operation and Organizational Maintenance -- Electrical System.
T.O. 21-SM68-2F-11-1	Operation and Organizational Maintenance -- Flight Control System.
T.O. 21-SM68-2F-12-1	Operation and Organizational Maintenance -- Propellant System.
T.O. 21-SM68-2F-15-1	Operation and Organizational Maintenance -- Launch Control and Status System.
T.O. 21-SM68-2FJ-7-1	Operation and Organizational Maintenance -- Missile Guidance Set AN/DRW-18, AN/DRW-19, AN/DRW-20, AN/DRW-21, AN/DRW-22, and Guided Missile Test Set AN/DRM-5B(V).
T.O. 21-SM68-2FJ-7-2	Operation and Organizational Maintenance -- Missile Guidance Set AN/GRW-5, Antenna Protecting and Elevating Set.
T.O. 21-SM68-2FJ-9-1 (Post update) T.O. 21-SM68-2FJ-9-2 (Prior to update)	Operation and Organizational Maintenance -- Hydraulic System.
T.O. 21-SM68-2FJ-13-1 (VAFB)	Operation and Organizational Maintenance -- Instrument and Range Safety System.
T.O. 21-SM68-2FJ-14-1 (Post update) T.O. 21-SM68-2FJ-14-2 (Prior to update)	Operation and Organizational Maintenance -- Missile Air Conditioning System.
T.O. 21-SM68-2FJ-18-1	Operation and Organizational Maintenance -- Intra site Communications Systems.

T.O. 21-SM68-2FJ-28-1	Operation and Organizational Maintenance -- Combined Systems Exerciser.
T.O. 21-SM68-2J-2-1	Operation and Organizational Maintenance -- Missile Handling.
T.O. 21-SM68-2J-3-1	Operation and Organizational Maintenance -- Rocket Engine System.
T.O. 21-SM68-2J-5-3	Operation and Organizational Maintenance -- Re-Entry Vehicle System, Checkout and Trouble Analysis, Launch Site.
T.O. 21-SM68-2J-6-1	Organizational Maintenance -- Radio-Inertial Guidance System, Computer Checkout.
T.O. 21-SM68-2J-6-2	Organizational Maintenance -- Radio-Inertial Guidance System, Computer, Trouble Analysis, Computer and Peripheral Equipment.
T.O. 21-SM68-2J-6-3	Organizational Maintenance -- Radio-Inertial Guidance System, Computer, Trouble Analysis, Power.
T.O. 21-SM68-2J-6-4	Organizational Maintenance -- Radio-Inertial Guidance System, Computer, Trouble Analysis, MGE.
T.O. 21-SM68-2J-6-5	Organizational Maintenance -- Radio-Inertial Guidance System, Computer Servicing and Repair, Computer and Peripheral Equipment.
T.O. 21-SM68-2J-6-6	Organizational Maintenance -- Radio-Inertial Guidance System, Computer Servicing and Repair Power.
T.O. 21-SM68-2J-6-7	Organizational Maintenance -- Radio-Inertial Guidance System, Computer Servicing and Repair, MGE.
T.O. 21-SM68-2J-7-1-1	Operation and Organizational Maintenance -- Missile Guidance Set AN/GRW-5, Checkout and Trouble Analysis.
T.O. 21-SM68-2J-7-1-2	Operation and Organizational Maintenance -- Missile Guidance Set AN/GRW-5.
T.O. 21-SM68-2J-8-1 (VAFB) T.O. 21-SM68-2J-8-4 (except VAFB)	Organizational Maintenance -- Launcher System, Checkout and Trouble Analysis.

T.O. 21-SM68-2J-8-2 (VAFB) T.O. 21-SM68-2J-8-5 (except VAFB)	Organizational Maintenance -- Launcher System, Handling, Servicing, and Repair.
T.O. 21-SM68-2J-8-3	Operation and Organizational Maintenance -- Launcher System, Structural Repair.
T.O. 21-SM68-2J-10-1 (Post update) T.O. 21-SM68-2J-10-2 (Prior to update)	Operation and Organizational Maintenance -- Electrical System.
T.O. 21-SM68-2J-11-1 (Post update) T.O. 21-SM68-2J-11-2 (Prior to update)	Operations and Organizational Maintenance -- Flight Control System.
T.O. 21-SM68-2J-12-1 (Post update) T.O. 21-SM68-2J-12-4 (Prior to update)	Operation and Organizational Maintenance -- Propellant System.
T.O. 21-SM68-2J-12-2 (Post update) T.O. 21-SM68-2J-12-5 (Prior to update)	Operation and Organizational Maintenance -- Propellant System Checkout and Trouble Analysis.
T.O. 21-SM68-2J-12-3 (Post update) T.O. 21-SM68-2J-12-6 (Prior to update)	Operation and Organizational Maintenance -- Propellant System Handling, Servicing, and Repair.
T.O. 21-SM68-2J-15-1	Operation and Organizational Maintenance -- Launch Control and Status System.
T.O. 21-SM68-3	Operation and Organizational Maintenance -- Missile Airframe Structural Repair.
T.O. 21-SM68-4-1	Illustrated Parts Breakdown -- Missile Assembly Complete.
T.O. 21-SM68-4-2	Illustrated Parts Breakdown -- Missile Weapon System, Launch Complex.
T.O. 21-SM68-4-3	Illustrated Parts Breakdown -- Missile Guidance Set AN/GRW-5 and Missile Guidance Computer Set AN/GSK-1, Launch Complex.

SAFETY PRECAUTIONS

Personnel safety and warning devices are designed to indicate safe conditions, dangerous conditions, and degrees of danger. Areas and equipment that might be dangerous to personnel are clearly posted.

At all bases, each person will be familiar with the safety program. This program consists of training classes, posters, protective enclosures around dangerous areas, and planned procedures for the performance of hazardous operations. Job and function manuals contain safety precautions that supplement the safety program, listing safety precautions applicable to specific areas and jobs. Warnings and cautions are inserted as necessary throughout the manuals and have the following significance:

WARNING

* Indicates a hazardous condition that could result in injury or death.

CAUTION

* Indicates a hazardous condition that could result in damage to equipment.

There are basically three types of fires (class A, B, and C) that can be encountered within a launch complex. If personnel should detect a fire, notify the control center immediately, then proceed to combat the fire as follows:

Class A: The burning of any combustible fiber is to be combated with water or portable CO_2 fire extinguishers.

WARNING

* Water is not to be used to combat class B or class C fires. Water will not extinguish these fires and aid in the spreading of them.

Class B: The burning of any petroleum product is to be combated with foam or CO_2 fire extinguishers.

Class C: A fire within any electrically charged device or equipment will be combated with CO_2 fire extinguishers only.

Various type of color coding are utilized throughout the launch complex for safety purposes with the following significance:

RED: Red is the basic color used to denote danger or to indicate immediate stops.

ORANGE: Orange is the basic color used for marking dangerous parts of machines or electrical equipment.

YELLOW: Yellow is the basic color used to indicate the need for caution.

GREEN: Green is the basic color used to denote safety, first aid equipment, safety devices, and facilities directly related to safety.

General hazards associated with the operation and maintenance of the weapon system are listed in the following table of safety precautions.

T.O. 21-SM68-1

ITEM	HAZARD		SAFEGUARDS	CORRECTIVE ACTION
	CONDITION	RESULT		
			ELECTRICAL	
Electrical circuits	Personal contact	Burns, shocks, or electrocution of personnel.	Use protective and safety approved test equipment or tools. Remove all personal jewelry or other metal objects prior to working on electrical circuitry. Do not touch personnel in contact with electrical equipment.	Remove power. Remove injured personnel from conductor. Administer first aid. Obtain medical care for the injured.
			CHEMICAL	
Sulfuric acid (H_2SO_4)	Handling and storage.	Severe irritant to all skin tissues.	Wear protective clothing. Use caution at all times.	Wash affected area with bicarbonate of soda solution.
Sodium hydroxide (NaOH) and potassium hydroxide (KOH)	Handling and storage	Severe irritant to all skin tissue.	Wear protective clothing. Use caution at all times.	Wash affected area with vinegar or any other acetic acid solution. Flush with copious amounts of water.
Refrigerants Rl1 and Rl2	Handling and storage	Irritant to skin and eyes.	Wear protective clothing.	Treat affected area for frost bite. Flush eyes with copious amounts of water.

Safety Precautions (Sheet 1 of 9)

ITEM	HAZARD		SAFEGUARDS	CORRECTIVE ACTION
	CONDITION	RESULT		
			CHEMICAL (CONT.)	
Cleaning solvents	Handling and storage.	Skin irritant.	Wear protective clothing. Do not enter a heavily vapored area without using a self-contained breathing apparatus, wearing a safety harness, and having an outside attendant. Do not allow trichloroethylene to come in contact with strong alkalies. Trichloroethylene reacts with strong alkalies to form explosive mixtures. Treat all cleaning solvents as flammable agents.	Use water to flush affected areas. Administer first aid. Secure medical attention. Isolate the area.
Fuels and lubricants	Storage and handling.	Injury to personnel. Damage to equipment.	Do not smoke, weld, or generate sparks in the vicinity. Maintain area in a clean, combustion-free condition. Do not vent fumes into a closed area.	Use water to flush fuel spills and absorbent compounds or rags for lubricant spills.
			Prevent contact with any oxidizer.	Use dry chemical or carbon dioxide fire extinguishers to combat fires.
			Do not allow spills to remain unattended.	
Tricresyl phosphate	Ingestion or inhaling fumes.	Illness or death.	Wear the prescribed protective clothing. Respirator required when vapor present.	Apply first aid and secure medical attention.

Safety Precautions (Sheet 2 of 9)

ITEM	HAZARD		SAFEGUARDS	CORRECTIVE ACTION
	CONDITION	RESULT		
			MECHANICAL	
Operation of maintenance equipment	Entanglement and structural failure. Falling objects. Swinging load hooks.	Injury to personnel.	Wear appropriate protective equipment such as hard hats, safety-toe shoes, and goggles or face shields when required. Stay clear of hoisting and loading operations. Do not remove protective covers or guards while equipment is operating. Do not wear loose clothing or jewelry when working around operating machinery and electrical equipment. Observe all safety precautions pertaining to the proper operation and maintenance of equipment.	Administer first aid; secure medical attention.
Environmental pressures	Pressure differential between rooms, and/or areas.	Doors slam or will not open.	Use extreme caution when opening or closing all doors.	If possible, shut down equipment to equalize pressures.

Safety Precautions (Sheet 3 of 9)

T.O. 21-SM68-1

ITEM	HAZARD		SAFEGUARDS	CORRECTIVE ACTION
	CONDITION	RESULT		
			MECHANICAL (CONT.)	
Pneumatics	High pressures.	Sudden release of pressure from containers may cause serious injury to personnel and/or damage to equipment.	Do not perform maintenance on pressurized lines prior to relieving pressure.	Administer first aid to injured personnel.
Equipment in a maintenance status	Improper handling.	Damage to equipment and/or injury to personnel.	Use AF Form 267 and locking devices, if applicable.	Do not attempt to operate or tamper with tagged devices without proper clearance.
			PHYSIOLOGICAL	
High frequency vibrations and noises	Performance of duty in power house and other high level noise areas.	Pain, a feeling of fullness, and/or ringing or burning of the ears. Dizziness, impairment of mental concentration, and/or occasional nausea.	The use of approved ear muffs and/or ear plugs. Post hazard areas with warning signs.	Remove affected individual from the noise area immediately, and obtain medical attention.
High humidity and temperatures	Improper air-conditioning.	Adverse attitude, poor manual dexterity, and exhaustion.	Limit the length of tours of duty in areas of this nature.	Maintain proper temperature and humidity.

Safety Precautions (Sheet 4 of 9)

ITEM	HAZARD		SAFEGUARDS	CORRECTIVE ACTION
	CONDITION	RESULT		
			GASES	
Helium and gaseous nitrogen (He, GN_2)	Leakage, high pressure lines and containers, concentrated vapors.	Personnel injuries.	Do not vent into closed areas (Gases will displace oxygen in the air). Do not enter areas likely to contain vapor concentration without using a self-contained breathing apparatus, wearing a safety harness, and having an outside attendant. Do not pressurize tanks and lines in excess of recommended pressures. Open valves with caution. Vent pressures from system before performing maintenance.	Isolate area, administer first aid and secure medical attention.
Hydrogen (H_2)	Caused by excessive charging of lead acid batteries.	Explosion, asphyxiation.	No flaming or sparking devices near battery banks. Adhere to all warning signs. Keep area well ventilated.	Administer first aid. Secure medical attention.

Safety Precautions (Sheet 5 of 9)

ITEM	HAZARD		SAFEGUARDS	CORRECTIVE ACTION
	CONDITION	RESULT		
			GASES (CONT.)	
Phosgene Gas ($COCl_2$)	Created by heating freon, R-11 refrigerant, and R-12 liquids.	Respiratory irritation.	Evacuate the affected area. Do not allow freon R-11 or R-12 to become heated.	Remove personnel from affected area and administer first aid. Obtain medical attention.
			CRYOGENICS	
Liquid Oxygen (lox) handling and storage.	Low temperature		Wear clean cotton clothing, asbestos or neoprene gloves, face shield, apron, and rubber boots or cotton shoe socks.	If lox should come in contact with the skin or eyes, use safety shower or eyewash fountain to flush with running water. Obtain medical aid immediately.
	Gaseous oxygen fire and explosion.	Injury or death to personnel.	Do not smoke, weld, or generate sparks in the vicinity of lox.	Isolate the area and allow lox to boil off. Use only water, dry chemical, or carbon dioxide fire extinguishers on lox fires.
			Maintain area in a clean, combustion-free condition.	
			Allow lox-cooled equipment to stand for at least 2 hours after purging before performing maintenance on malfunctioning components.	
			Avoid contact with lines carrying lox.	Treat affected part of body for frost bite.
			Do not store or use lox in unvented tanks or systems. Do not vent lox into closed areas.	

Safety Precautions (Sheet 6 of 9)

T.O. 21-SM68-1

Safety Precautions

ITEM	HAZARD		SAFEGUARDS	CORRECTIVE ACTION
	CONDITION	RESULT		
			CRYOGENICS (CONT.)	
			Do not allow organic substances particularly oil or grease, to contact lox. Use only lox-compatible lubricants, valve packing, and gasket material when assembling equipment for use with lox. Do not store lox equipment until it has been cleaned.	
			Avoid contaminating clothing with lox. If contamination occurs, remove all such clothing immediately.	
Liquid nitrogen (LN2)	Low temperature.	Serious injury to personnel.	Wear clean cotton clothing, asbestos or neoprene gloves, face shield, apron, and rubber boots or cotton shoe socks.	If liquid nitrogen should come in contact with the skin or eyes, use safety shower or eyewash fountain to flush contaminated skin areas or eyes with running water. Obtain medical aid immediately.
	Fire.	Serious injury to personnel.	Do not smoke, weld, or generate sparks in the vicinity of liquid nitrogen. (Because of its low temperature, liquid nitrogen will liquify oxygen from the ambient air creating a lox hazard.)	Isolate area and allow lox to boil off. Use only water, dry chemical, or CO2 fire extinguishers on lox fires.
			Maintain area in a clean, combustion-free condition.	

Safety Precautions (Sheet 7 of 9)

T.O. 21-SM68-1

ITEM	HAZARD		SAFEGUARDS	CORRECTIVE ACTION
	CONDITION	RESULT		
			CRYOGENICS (CONT.)	
			Allow nitrogen-cooled equipment to warm up to near ambient temperature before performing maintenance on malfunctioning components. Avoid contact with lines carrying liquid nitrogen. Do not store or use liquid nitrogen in unvented tanks or systems.	
	Displaced oxygen.	Asphyxiation of personnel.	Do not vent liquid nitrogen into closed areas. When entering a tank that has contained nitrogen, use a self-contained breathing apparatus, a safety harness, and have an outside attendant.	Remove personnel from affected area and administer first aid. Secure medical attention.
			ORDNANCE	
Separation bolts, hold down bolts, engine igniters	Inadvertent activation.	Injury to personnel. Damage to equipment.	Do not smoke, weld, or generate sparks in the vicinity of ordnance items. Do not place ordnance items near an open flame, electrical circuits, or ground cables. Do not subject ordnance items to impact, excessive heat, or radio frequency radiation.	Evacuate victims to hazard free area, and apply first aid. Summon medical assistance and fire fighting equipment.

Safety Precautions (Sheet 8 of 9)

ITEM	HAZARD		SAFEGUARDS	CORRECTIVE ACTION
	CONDITION	RESULT		
			ORDNANCE (CONT.) Do not handle ordnance items unless authorized to do so. Do not enter the affected area without breathing apparatus.	

Safety Precautions (Sheet 9 of 9)

INTRODUCTION

This manual is provided for missile combat crews (MCC) at SM68 missile weapon system operational and training facilities. All information contained in this manual is based on the latest released engineering data and missile operation concepts. Deviation from the specified procedures shall not be made except for reasons of safety or when directed by proper authority.

The primary purpose of this manual is to support the related procedures contained in T.O. 21-SM68-CL-14-1, T.O. 21-SM68-CL-17-1, T.O. 21-SM68-CL-19-1, and T.O. 21-SM68-CL-21-1 with sufficient procedural and descriptive data to provide an overall concept of the missile weapon system operation.

Section I contains a general description of the over all weapon system including the launch complex, integral structures, and various subsystems.

Section II contains a brief coverage of the receipt through launch operation plan.

Section III contains the normal operating procedures of the missile combat crew including personnel briefing, training, crew functions and individual responsibilities. These normal procedures cover all requirements, exclusive of emergencies and malfunctions, for maintaining an alert condition, countdown, launch, post launch, and contingency actions.

Section IV contains a brief description of each of the accepted emergency procedures, including the action to be taken by the missile combat crew, to safe the weapon system when confronted with a hazardous situation.

Section V contains the procedures to be used by the missile combat crew to analyze and isolate malfunctions which may occur during a launch countdown.

Section VI contains the operating limitations that must be observed when running the equipment, whether for a training exercise or an actual EWO launch. Limitations include those of the individaul subsystems, alert status, and environmental conditions.

Section VII contains a description of the responsibilities of each missile combat crew member as related to the operation of the missile launch complex. Information is categorized in accordance with the title of each member of the combat crew.

Operation and organizational maintenance procedures for the functional systems are covered in the dash one (-1) and dash two (-2) series of the 21-SM68 technical orders. Frequency and sequence of jobs not directly associated with missile launch operations are contained in T.O. 21-SM68-6.

T.O. 21M-HGM25A-1-1 (21-SM68-1) Introduction

Time Compliance Technical Orders applicable to this Technical Order are as follows:

TCTO NUMBER	DATE
21M-HGM25A-759	27 June 1963
21M-HGM25A-763	16 September 1963
21M-HGM25A-790	1 November 1962
21M-HGM25A-833	21 May 1963
21M-HGM25A-834	23 May 1963
21M-HGM25A-853	8 June 1963
21M-HGM25A-859	10 September 1963
31X3-10-11-613	16 January 1963
31X3-10-11-617	18 December 1962
31X3-10-11-621	16 January 1963
31X3-10-11-621A	1 February 1963
31X3-10-11-622	17 January 1963
31X3-10-11-625	15 October 1963
31X3-10-11-626	8 March 1963
31X3-10-11-627	29 August 1963
31X3-10-11-630	30 September 1963
31X3-10-12-543	31 May 1963
31X3-10-12-545	14 May 1963
31X3-10-12-545A	25 June 1963
31X3-10-17-546	26 February 1963
31X3-10-26-514	17 July 1963
31X3-10-27-511	18 October 1963
35M3-2-4-529	25 July 1963
31X7-2-11-512	21 June 1963
31X3-10-11-634	Not released

SECTION I

GENERAL DESCRIPTION

1-1. **INTRODUCTION.**

1-2. The SM68 Missile Weapon System consists of a radio inertially guided, liquid fueled missile and the associated ground equipment necessary to maintain and launch the missile. The weapon system is capable of destroying enemy targets over 5500 nautical miles distant. The missile complex is designed to maintain an operational readiness condition with no outside support after sustaining an attack that destroys all nonhardened facilities. For maximum safety and effectiveness, individual launch sites are widely separated. All in-commission missiles are maintained in a constant alert condition and may be counted down individually or simultaneously.

1-3. **SM68 MISSILE.**

1-4. **LEADING PARTICULARS.**

1-5. The SM68 missile consists of three sections: Stage I and Stage II, both powered by rocket engines, and a re-entry vehicle. Provisions are included for inflight separation (staging) of Stage II from Stage I and separation of the re-entry vehicle from Stage II. The Stage I and Stage II vehicles each contain a rocket engine and hydraulic equipment; the two stages together contain flight control equipment and electrical equipment; Stage II contains guidance equipment. Figure 1-1 outlines the external missile configuration and identifies the major parts of the SM68 missile. Figure 1-2 provides a table of leading particulars.

1-6. **COUNTDOWNS.**

1-7. Basically the SM68 missile countdown capability can be limited to EWO launch and exercise countdowns.

1-8. The EWO launch countdown may be initiated within a matter of minutes on any missile that is on EWO alert, provided that a valid execution order is received by the missile combat crews. Prompt and efficient reaction to this order is the primary responsibility of a missile combat crew.

1-9. Combined systems exercise (CSE) countdown is an integrated weapon system operation wherein a missile countdown in a non-launch mode parallels a guidance system countdown in an exercise mode. The CSE countdowns are basically identical to an actual launch type countdown. The receipt of a launch exercise enable signal is indicated by the START LCH EXERCISE indicator on the missile guidance console. Pressing of the LAUNCH EXERCISE pushbutton indicator on the missile guidance console enables the ground guidance system and the launch system to perform a combined systems exercise. The CSE countdown proceeds from start countdown through the simulated function of missile liftoff to the end of guidance. A series of steering orders and discrete commands, generated by a CSE guidance program in the computer, are transmitted from the ground guidance system to the missile during the plus time portion of the CSE countdown.

1-10. Three modes of CSE can be accomplished: dry CSE, fuel CSE, and lox CSE. These modes of operation will accomplish a weapon system checkout through functional use of the missile facility and aerospace operating equipment (AOE).

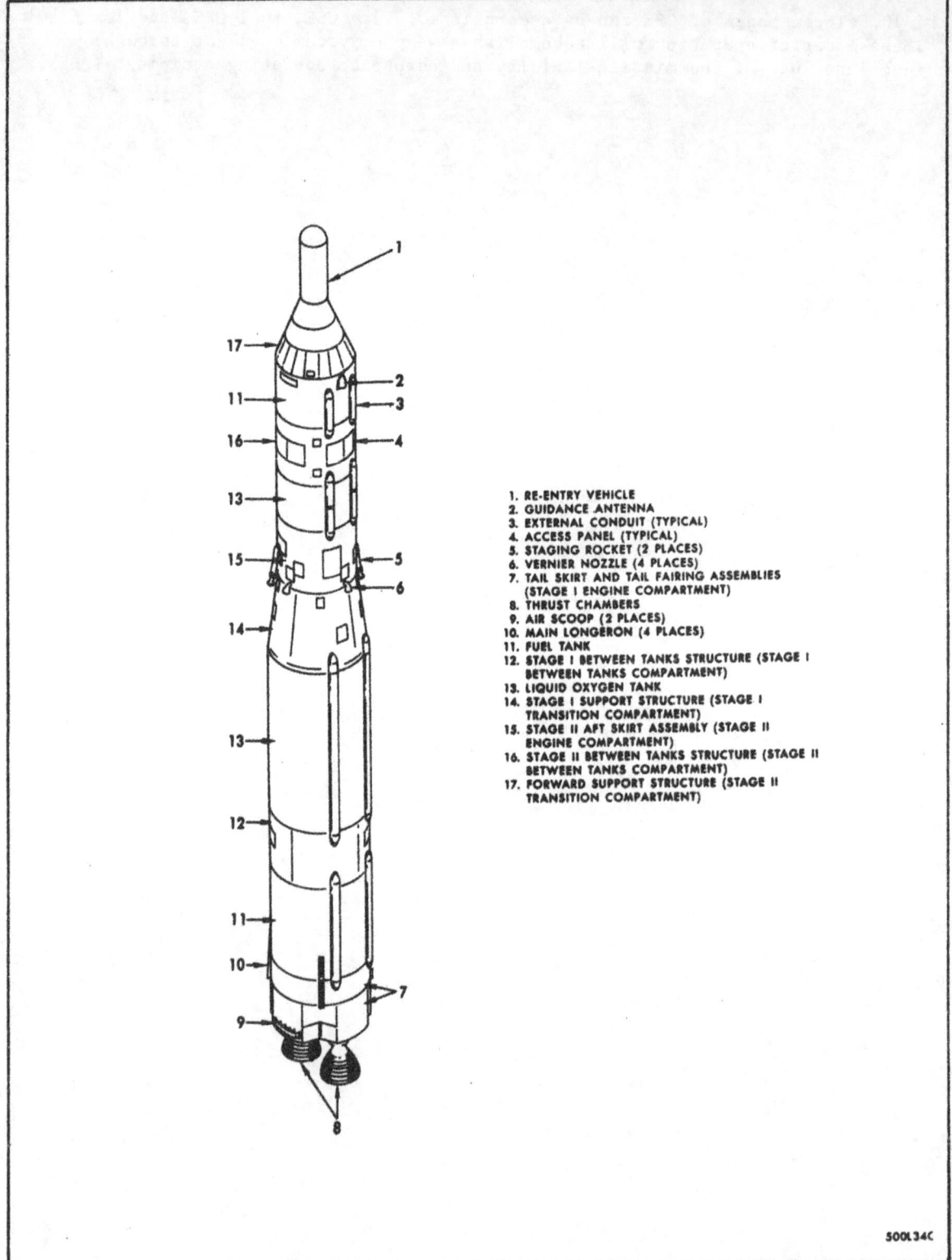

Figure 1-1. Missile Configuration

FACILITIES OR EQUIPMENT	PARTICULARS
SM-68 MISSILE Length	Overall, including air frame and component extensions, 98 feet, 10 inches. Stage I - 10 feet, Stage II - 8 feet, R/V - 2 feet 9 inches.
PROPELLANT Fuel Oxidizer	 Rocket propellant number one (RP-1) Liquid oxygen (lox)
PROPELLANT CAPACITIES: (Approximately) Fuel tank Liquid oxygen tank	 Stage I - 7750 Gallons, Stage II - 2027 Gallons Total - 9,777 Gallons. Stage I - 12,400 Gallons, Stage II - 2985 Gallons Total - 15,385 Gallons.
PROPULSION: Stage I engine Stage II engine Vernier thrust	 300,000 pounds thrust at sea level. 80,000 pounds thrust at 250,000 feet altitude. 900 pounds at 250,000 feet altitude.
GUIDANCE SYSTEM	Radio inertial guidance
RANGE	5,500 nautical miles.

Figure 1-2. Table of Leading Particulars.

1-11. DRY CSE. The purpose of the dry CSE mode is to exercise the applicable subsystems during a countdown without transfer of propellants or gases. This is done with a minimum of preparation and can be performed and recycled on short notice. Dry CSE is performed with no launcher movement, with or without fuel aboard the missile. The entire exercise can be performed with the complex in the hardened condition.

1-12. FUEL CSE. The fuel CSE mode enables the weapon system to be exercised through a countdown and simulated nose cone release without transferring propellants or helium gases. The fuel mode is performed with only fuel loaded and with launcher movement. During countdown the fuel tanks are pressurized with N_2 while the lox and helium pressure switches are simulated. The launcher platform is raised and guidance is initiated. Shutdown occurs after simulated nose cone release.

1-13. LOX CSE. The lox CSE mode enables the weapon system to be exercised through a countdown and simulated re-entry vehicle release. The lox and helium systems are pressurized and the fuel pressure switches are simulated. The launcher platform is raised and guidance is initiated. Shutdown occurs after simulated nose cone release.

1-14. POST LAUNCH AND SHUTDOWN OPERATIONS.

1-15. Post launch and shutdown operations return the missile complex to a hardened configuration. Missiles and facilities are safed and any shutdown missiles are recycled to a readiness condition.

1-16. PROPELLANTS.

1-17. Liquid oxygen (lox) and RP-1 (processed kerosene) are the propellants used by the rocket engines. The walls of the tanks in which the propellants are stored serve also as skin for the missile.

1-18. EXTERNAL CABLE CONDUITS.

1-19. External cable conduits on the exterior of each propellant tank wall provide for the routing of electrical cables and pressurization lines. At VAFB these conduits also provide routing for the range safety system, consisting of instrumentation cables and primacord lines.

1-20. ACCESS PANELS.

1-21. Access panels provide missile entrances for inspection, replacement, and repair of systems and equipment. Access panels are (figure 1-3) are located in the between-tanks, support, engine, and transition areas. There are no external access panels on the propellant tanks. Manholes on tank domes are provided in order to enter the propellant tanks for repair or cleaning.

1-22. ORDNANCE

1-23. STAGING ROCKETS. The two staging rockets are mounted 180 degrees apart on the outside of the Stage II engine compartment. At separation, they provide 9600 pounds of thrust for approximately 3 seconds, producing a minimum separation distance of 10 feet between the first and second stages.

1-24. STAGING SEPARATION BOLTS. The four staging separation bolts are located at four restraining points around the missile. They are used to secure Stage II to

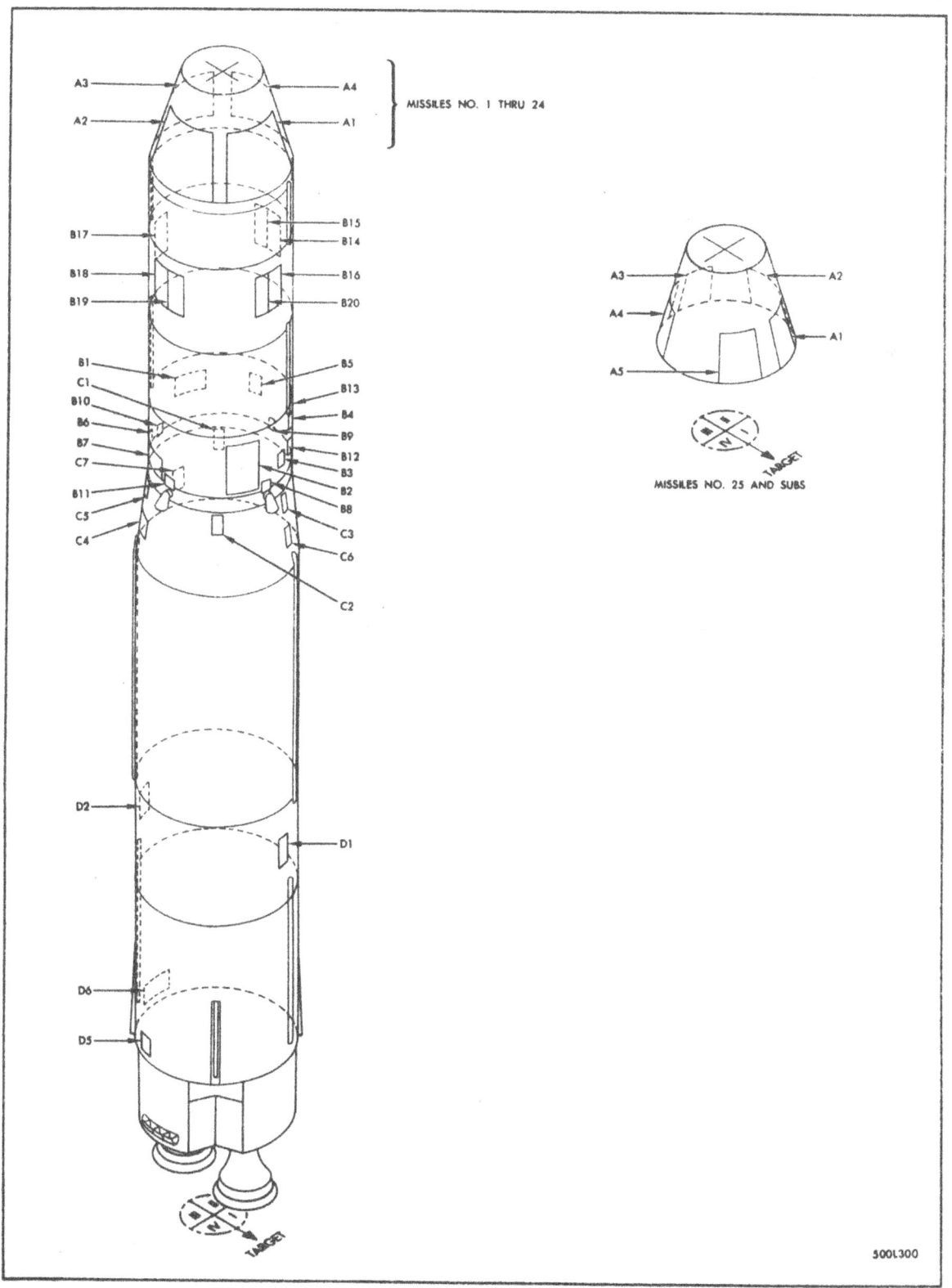

Figure 1-3. Access Panels

Stage I. Each staging separation bolt consists of one stud, two nuts, and two nut squibs. At separation, the squibs disengage the nuts from the studs, allowing Stage I and Stage II to separate.

1-25. STAGING ROCKET RELEASE SQUIBS. One staging rocket release squib is mounted in each of the two piston and cylinder assemblies at the forward end of the staging rockets. After the staging rockets have burned out, the release squibs fire to jettison the staging rockets.

1-26. IGNITERS. Two pyrotechnic igniters are used to start fuel and lox burning in the combustion chamber. Power to the igniters is supplied by the engine control system (ECS) aerospace operating equipment, and applied to the igniters through the thrust chamber valve switch. Each thrust chamber igniter assembly consists of a cluster of 8 single pyrotechnic igniters mounted on an igniter holder.

1-27. MISSILE RELEASE BOLTS. Hold-down clamps, secured by explosive bolts, hold the missile to the launcher until sufficient engine thrust is attained for missile launching. The explosive bolts are electrically detonated to release the missile hold-down clamps, and explosive bolts within the umbilical tower are fired to enable tower retraction. The electrical system arms and fires the explosive bolts.

1-28. VERNIER NOZZLES.

1-29. The four vernier nozzles are small uncooled thrust chambers on Stage II that control Stage II attitude during staging and assist in controlling Stage II powered flight. After Stage II sustainer engine shutdown, the nozzles make final trajectory and velocity corrections before the re-entry vehicle is released. The nozzles are spaced 90 degrees apart around the aft end of Stage II.

1-30. LAUNCH COMPLEX.

1-31. LEADING PARTICULARS.

1-32. The launch complex consists of three missile launchers, a power house, antenna terminal and antenna silo, fuel terminal, portal, tunnels, and local control stations. Each launcher contains a missile silo, equipment terminal, and propellant terminal. At VAFB, the launch complex also contains a pump house.

1-33. The launch complexes are similar in function and physical layout. Differences between certain areas at VAFB and the operational bases are shown in figures 1-4 and 1-5. All of the structures are of reinforced concrete construction and have structural grounding networks, ventilation systems, drainage systems, weather protection, and complete utilities such as water, heat, sewage disposal, and electric power. All structures at the operational bases are underground; at VAFB, the structures are combination underground and reinforced surface structures. Equipment is designed to provide maximum accessibility of components and to allow repair of malfunctioning equipment by removal and replacement of components with a minumum of calibration and adjustment.

1-34. MISSILE SILO.

1-35. The missile silo (figure 1-6) stores and protects the missile underground. A launcher platform in the silo supports the missile and raises it above ground for launching.

(Text continued on page 1-13.)

T.O. 21-SM68-1 Section I

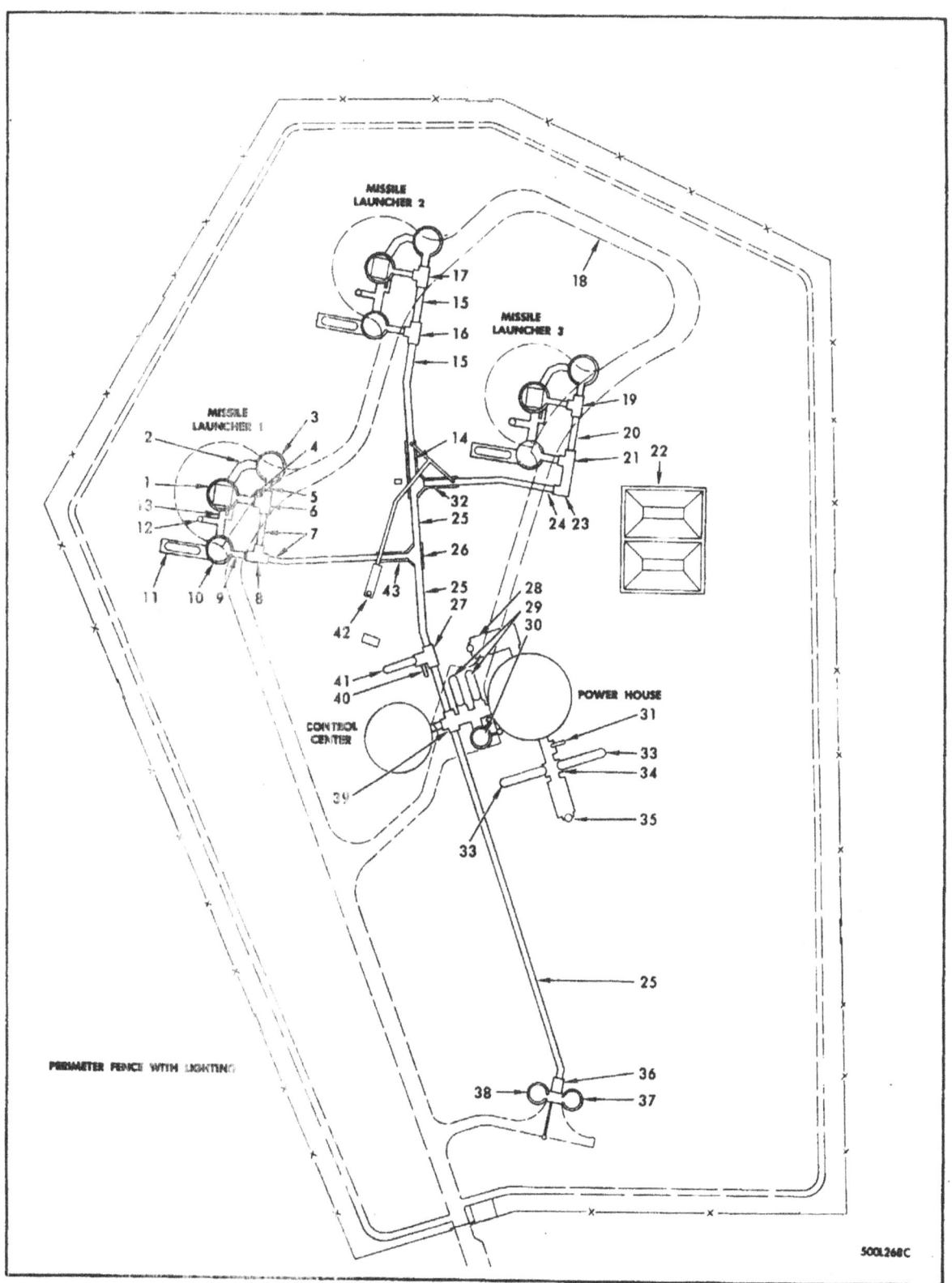

Figure 1-4. Operational Base Launch Complex (Sheet 1 of 3)

1. Missile Silo
2. Utilities Tunnel
3. Equipment Terminal
4. Missile Silo Branch Tunnel
5. Equipment Terminal Branch Tunnel
6. Tunnel Junction 1
7. Missile Launcher 1 Branch Tunnel
8. Tunnel Junction 2
9. Propellant Terminal Branch Tunnel
10. Propellant Terminal
11. Lox Storage Area
12. Lox Fill and Vent Shaft
13. Lox Tunnel
14. Blast Lock 2
15. Missile Launcher 2 Branch Tunnel
16. Tunnel Junction 5
17. Tunnel Junction 4
18. Service Road
19. Tunnel Junction 7
20. Missile Launcher 3 Branch Tunnel
21. Tunnel Junction 9
22. Sewage Stabilization Pond
23. Tunnel Junction 8
24. Missile Launcher 3 Branch Tunnel
25. Main Tunnel
26. Tunnel Junction 13
27. Tunnel Junction 12
28. Power House Air Filtration Facility
29. Water Storage Tanks
30. Portal
31. NO. 2 Diesel Oil Tank
32. Blast Lock 3
33. NO. 4 Diesel Oil Tank
34. Tunnel Junction 11
35. Power House Exhaust
36. Antenna Terminal
37. Antenna Silo 2
38. Antenna Silo 1
39. Tunnel Junction 10
40. Nitrogen Blanket Tank
41. Missile Fuel Storage Tank
42. Launcher Area Air Filtration Facility
43. Blast Lock 1

Figure 1-4. Operational Base Launch Complex (Sheet 2 of 3)

Figure 1-4. Operational Base Launch Complex (Sheet 3 of 3)

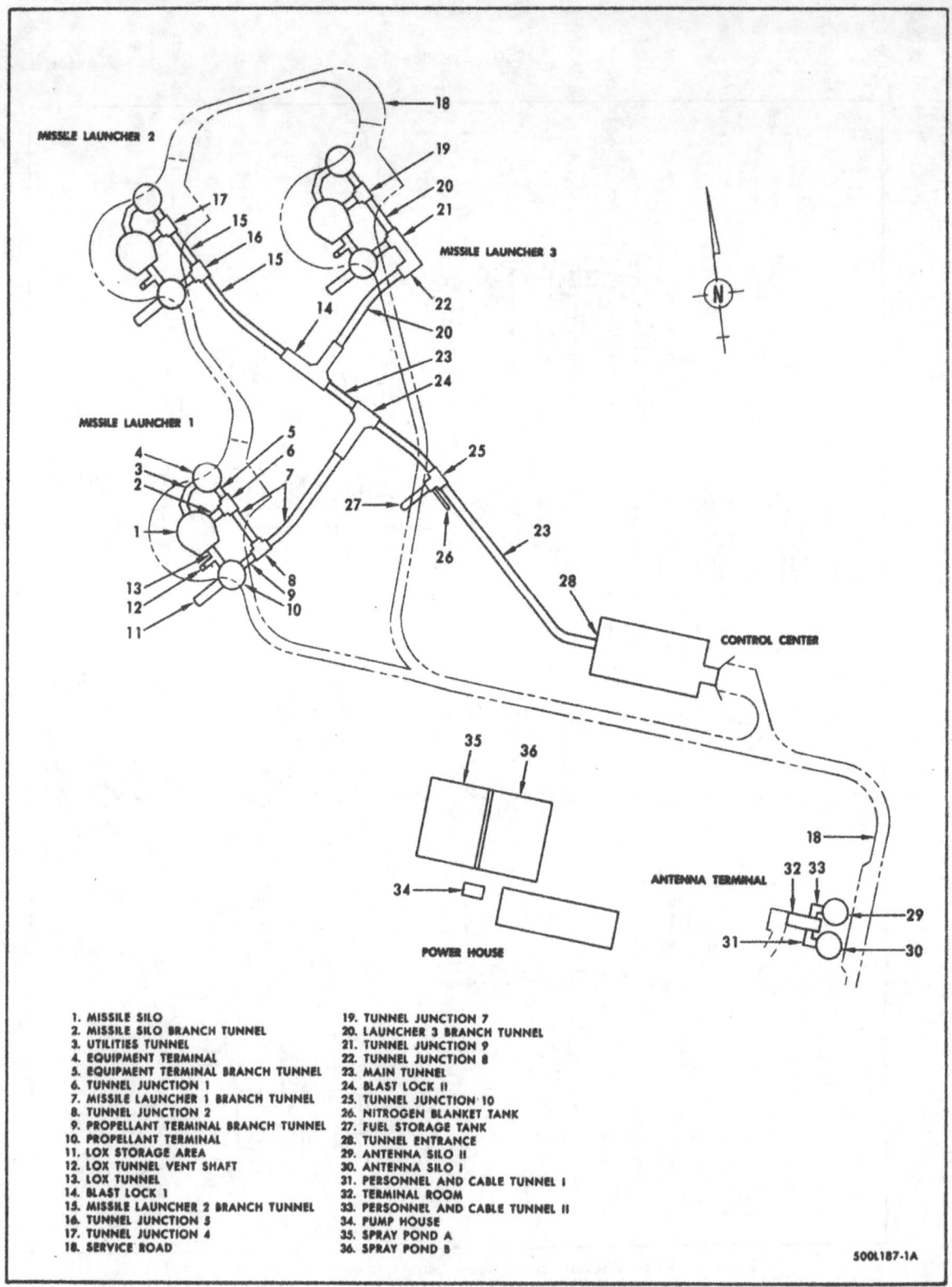

Figure 1-5. VAFB Launch Complex (Sheet 1 of 2)

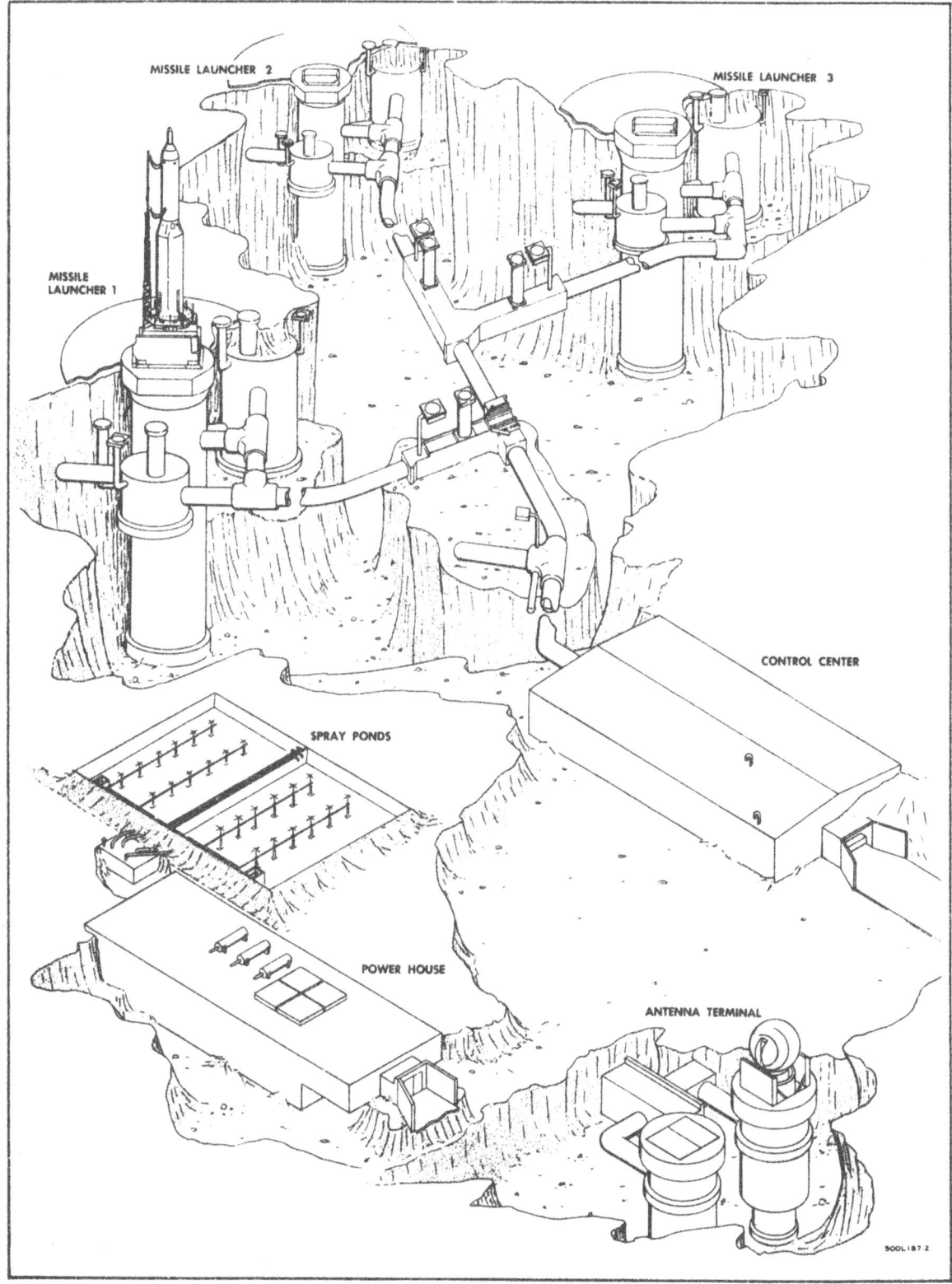

Figure 1-5. VAFB Launch Complex (Sheet 2 of 2)

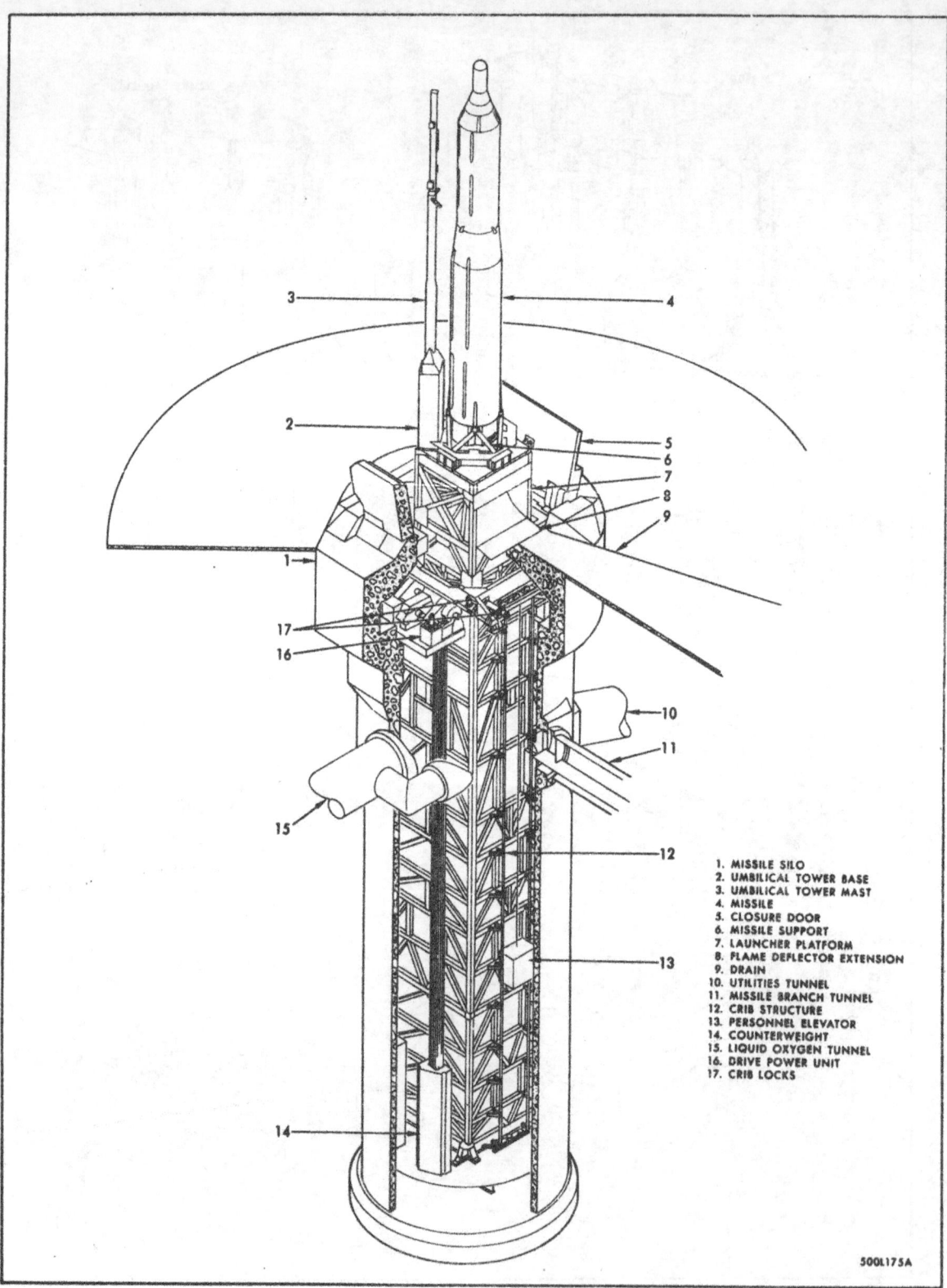

Figure 1-6. Missile Silo

(Text continued from page 1-6.)

1-36. The missile silo, including the door foundation, forms a cylindrical reinforced concrete structure approximately 158 feet in depth and 40 feet in diameter. A pair of reinforced concrete silo doors (figure 1-7), each weighing about 230,000 pounds, cover the silo mouth. The silo doors protect the missile from weather, overpressures due to nuclear blast, and contamination from nuclear attack. Structural isolation of the door foundation minimizes the transmission of surface shock to the missile silo. The doors are opened hydraulically by double-acting actuating cylinders.

1-37. Equipment in the silo includes the crib structure, launcher platform, launch platform drive system, umbilical lines and their support mechanisms, hydraulic plumbing, water plumbing, electrical circuitry, fire fighting, and sensing devices.

1-38. CRIB STRUCTURE. The crib structure (figure 1-8) is constructed of vertical steel framework which functions as a support frame for maintenance, protection, and launch of the missile. The crib structure is suspended by spring supports within the silo, which protect the missile against violent ground shocks. The crib supports all the maintenance platforms and control stations. The maintenance platforms provide work areas at various heights within the silo. The crib structure also supports the personnel elevator as well as ladders and stairways. Personnel safety devices, such as eyewash and shower stations, railings, and nets, are positioned about the crib. Hydraulic and electrical lines are routed along the crib structure for the actuation and control of crib mechanisms and maintenance equipment.

1-39. The personnel elevator, supported by the crib structure, carries personnel and equipment to the five maintenance platforms, the missile service platform, the rail access platform, and crib bottom. The elevator is driven by an electric hoist and is controlled from a self-service panel inside the car. There are call stations located at each elevator stop and at the self-service panel inside the car.

1-40. Five maintenance platforms are mounted on the crib. The main platform sections at each level are extended and retracted hydraulically. Platform sideleaves are extended manually to provide a continuous walkway and working area completely encircling the missile, except at the fifth level. The platforms are retractable to allow the launcher platform to pass without interference. Work platforms at each level may be controlled from the personnel elevator when it is at that level.

1-41. A crib-to-silo bridge is provided at the end of the missile silo branch tunnel to bridge the space between the silo wall and the crib structure and is the primary elevator stop. A gate protects personnel on the bridge.

1-42. LAUNCHER PLATFORM. The launcher platform (figure 1-9) is a shell structure that supports the missile in the silo during storage and launch operation. The launcher platform consists of the missile support structure (A-frame mounts), flame deflector, water spray equipment, umbilical tower base, guide rollers, platform-to-crib locks, platform-to-crib seal, and service platform.

1-43. The launcher platform converts the tension of the wire ropes into vertical movement of the missile within the crib structure. Vertical and lateral platform-to-crib locks secure the launcher platform in the launching position. At the silo-mouth, the support structure provides a level, stable platform from which the missile is released when engine thrust is sufficient for lift off. Engine exhaust is deflected by the flame deflector, and the water spray equipment protects the

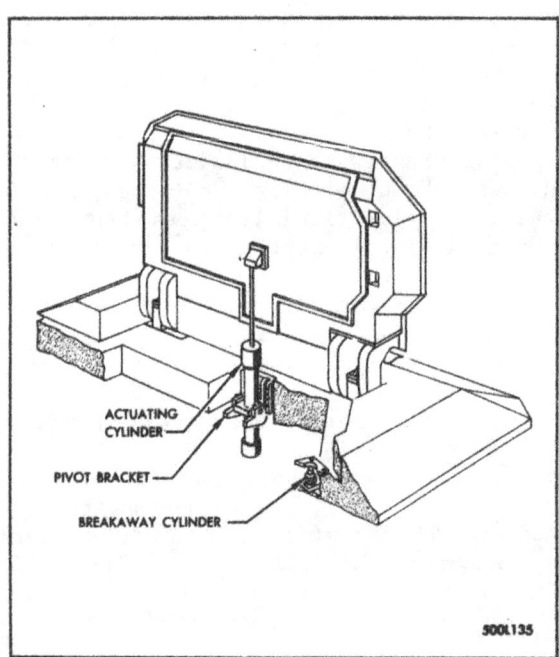

Figure 1-7. Silo Doors

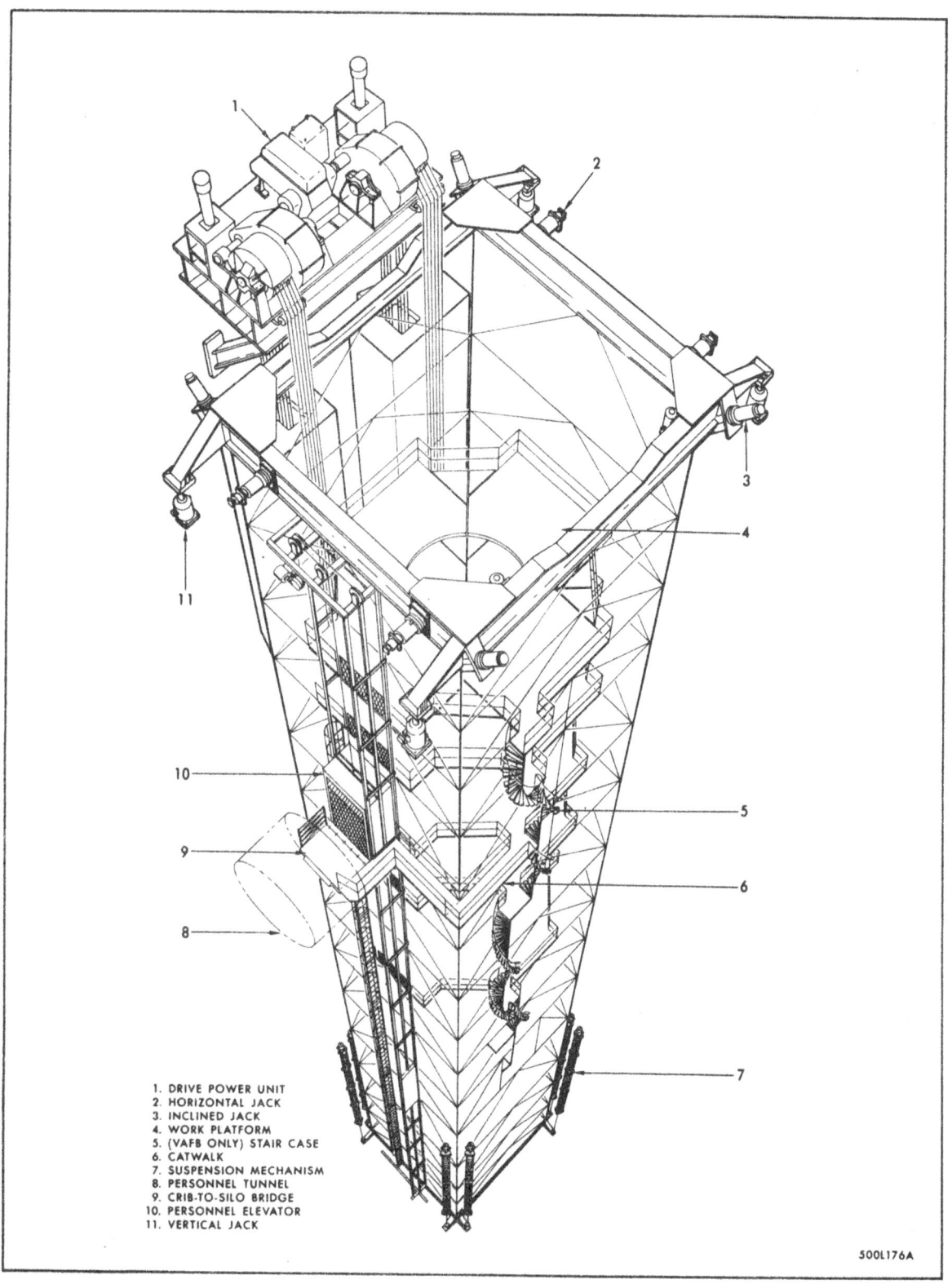

Figure 1-8. Crib Structure

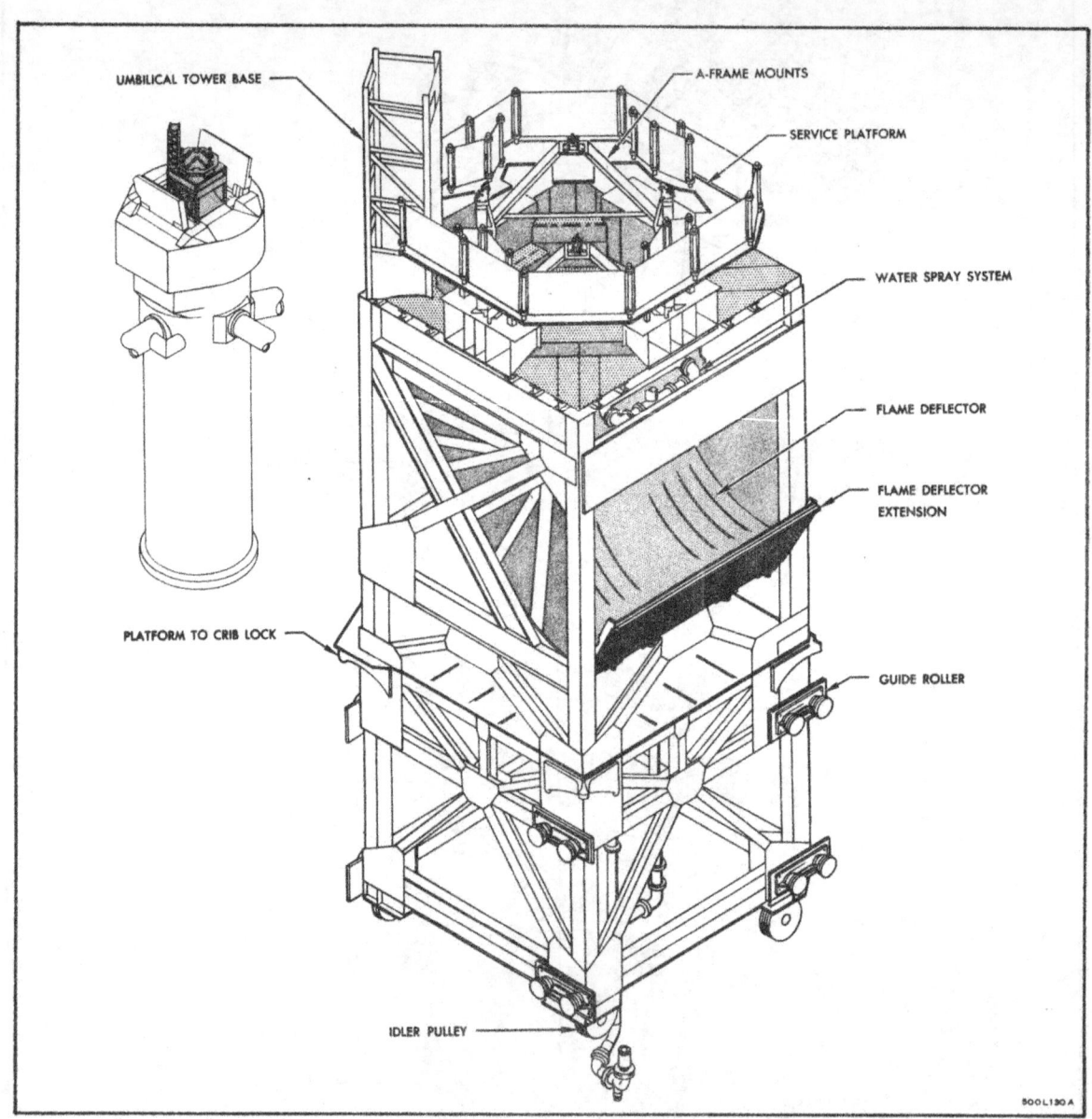

Figure 1-9. Launcher Platform

missile and launcher platform from engine exhaust heat damage. The platform-to-crib seals prevent the entrance of engine exhaust, water, fuel, or liquid oxygen into the silo.

1-44. The umbilical tower (figure 1-10) is located at one corner of the launcher platform and consists of a pivoting boom and stationary tower base. The tower supports three groups of umbilical lines: group one, Stage I engine compartment; group two, Stage II engine compartment; and group three, Stage II transition compartment. At launch, the umbilical tower is tilted away from the missile by detonating explosive bolts. The tower tilt disconnects all umbilical connectors mechanically by lanyards.

1-45. The service platform provides a work area for personnel performing maintenance on the missile support system and the Stage I engine. The service platform is covered with metal decking and has removable guard rails.

1-46. LAUNCHER PLATFORM DRIVE SYSTEM. The launcher platform drive system (figure 1-11) raises and lowers the launcher platform and can hold it at any level in the silo. Two sets of wire ropes are attached to tension equalizers and are routed over idler pulleys located under the launcher platform. Tension equalizers mounted on the crib structure maintain tension on the wire ropes to keep the platform level and to minimize rope damage from unequal loading. The tension equalizers slacken a portion of the wire ropes, and allow the crib to move freely in the event of ground shock.

1-47. UMBILICAL LINES AND SUPPORT MECHANISM. Umbilical lines with associated support mechanism (figure 1-12) connect service and power facilities to the missile when it is on the launcher platform. The umbilical lines not required for missile launching are routed within the silo and connected to the crib. These lines extend from the crib to the missile-mounted umbilical connectors and are disconnected prior to the raising of the launcher platform.

1-48. (Prior to incorporation of TCTO 21-SM68-763.) Upon receipt of a signal from the logic circuitry an electrically controlled umbilical retraction mechanism pivots the umbilical lines away from the missile. When the umbilicals are fully retracted a retracted-and-latched signal is received by the logic circuitry from each retraction mechanism. (After incorporation of TCTO 21-SM68-763.) The crib umbilicals will be disconnected by lanyard upon positive launcher movement.

1-49. EQUIPMENT TERMINAL.

1-50. The equipment terminal is composed of four levels containing aerospace operating equipment (AOE) and aerospace ground equipment (AGE) termination racks, and amplification equipment for the missile and facility systems as follows: Level I, launcher control floor; Level II, air conditioning and hydraulic floor; Level III, checkout and launch floor; and Level IV, power floor. At operational bases all levels are serviced by an elevator. Actual layouts vary at different bases.

1-51. LEVEL I. Level I of the equipment terminal (figure 1-13) is divided into a power pack room and an electrical room. The power pack room contains the cycling control station and power pack equipment which supplies hydraulic pressure for operating the launcher system. The electrical room contains the motor control center and the logic racks for the launcher hydraulic equipment.

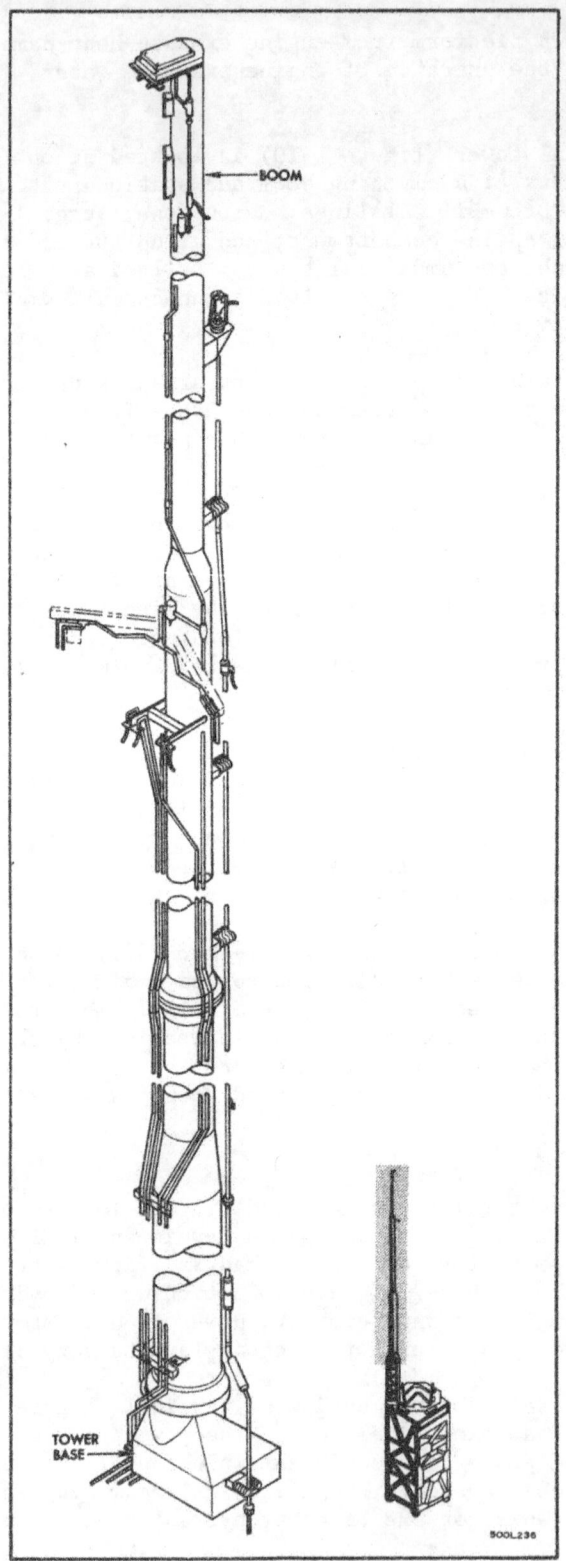

Figure 1-10. Umbilical Tower

T.O. 21-SM68-1   Section I

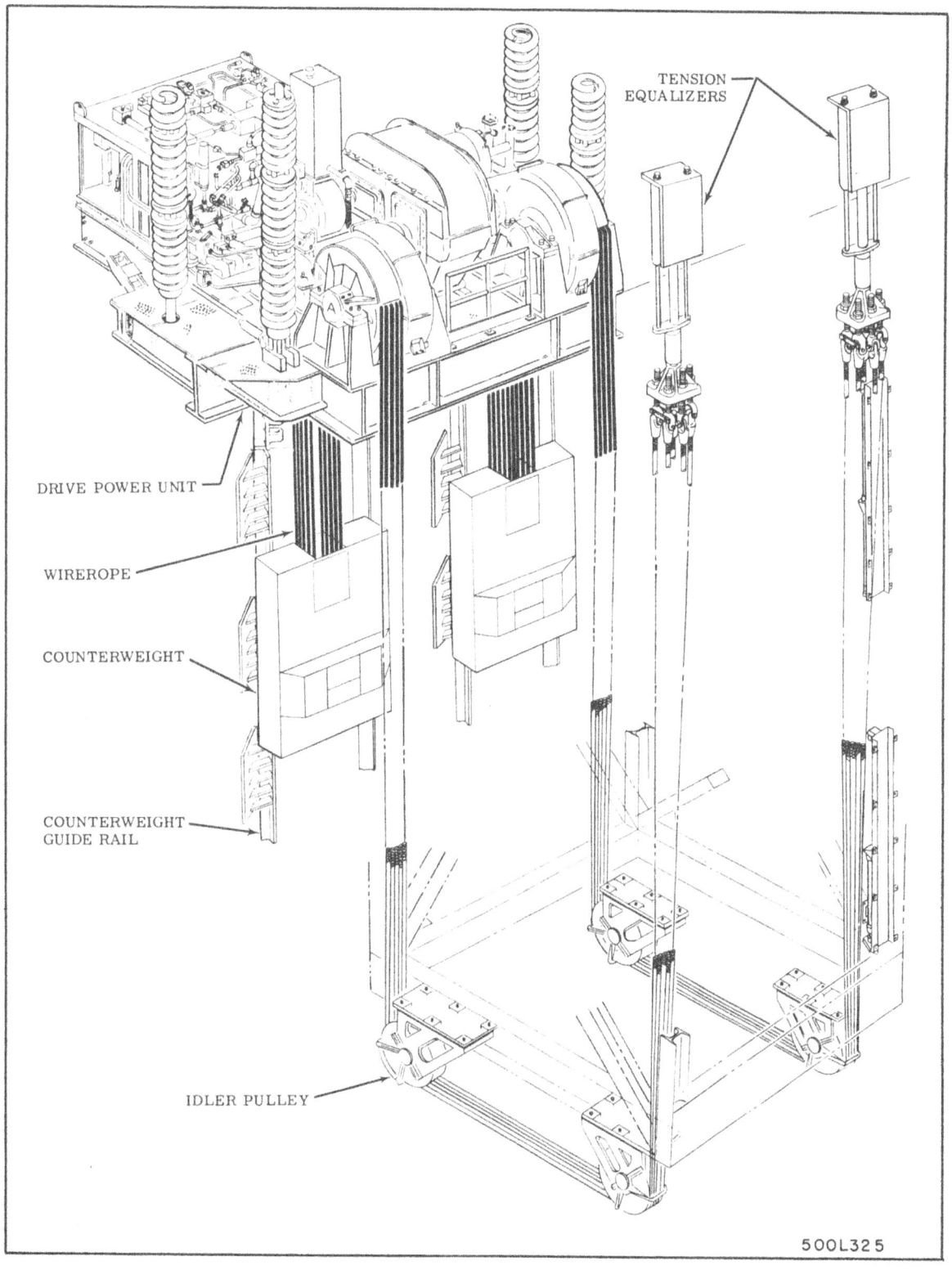

Figure 1-11. Launcher Platform Drive System (Operational Bases)

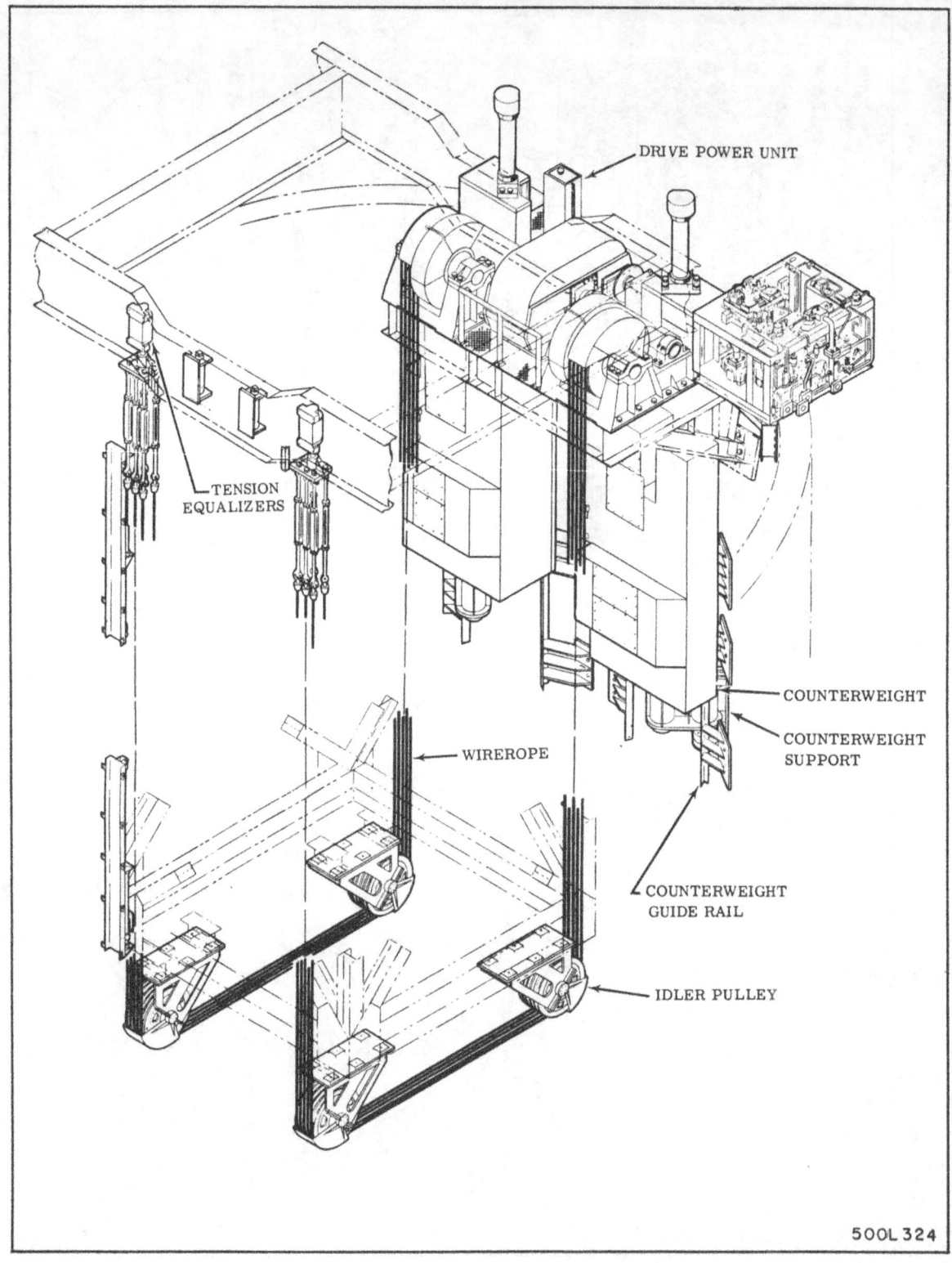

Figure 1-11A. Launcher Platform Drive System (VAFB)

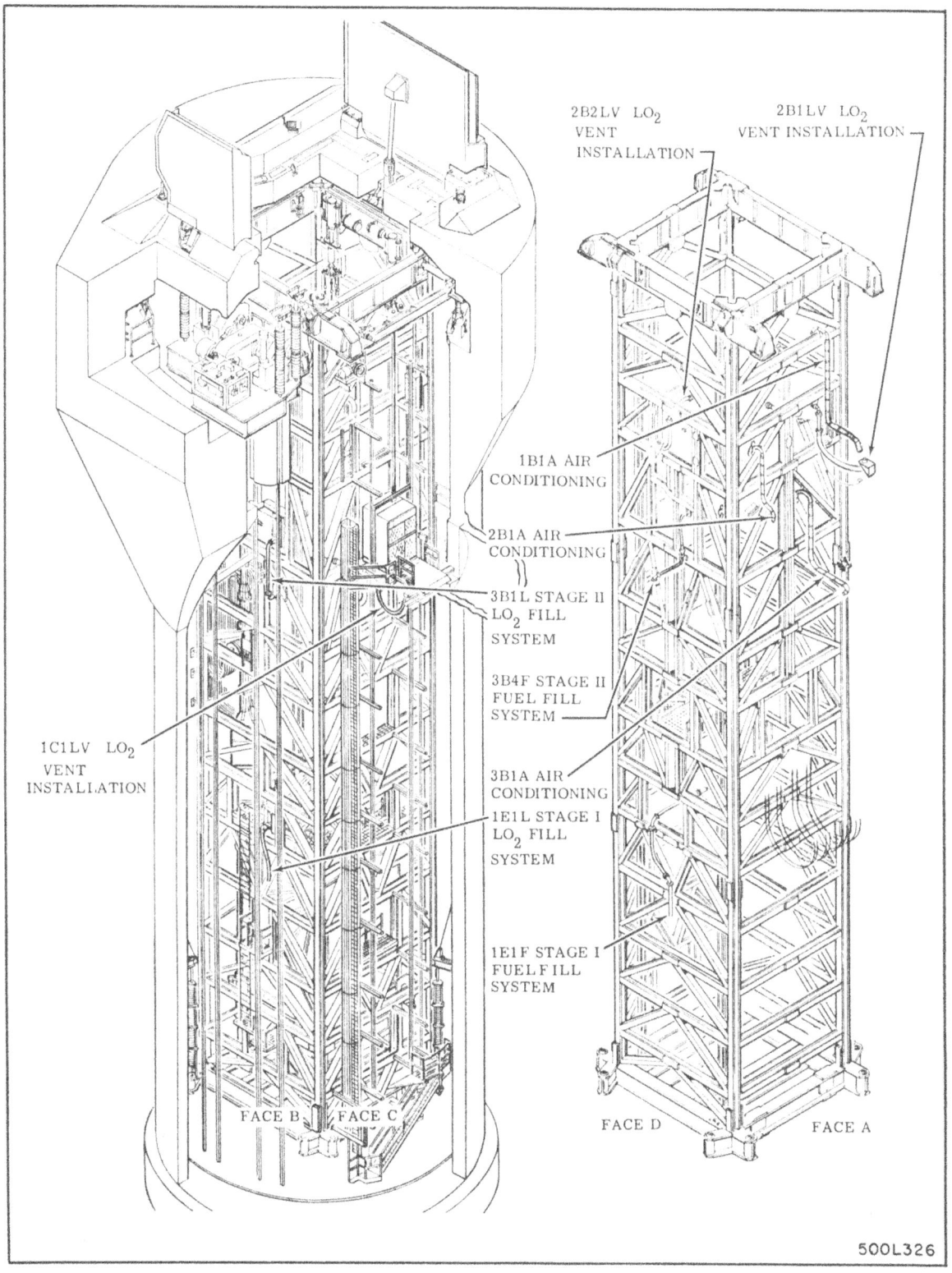

Figure 1-12. Umbilical Lines and Support Mechanism

T.O. 21-SM68-1

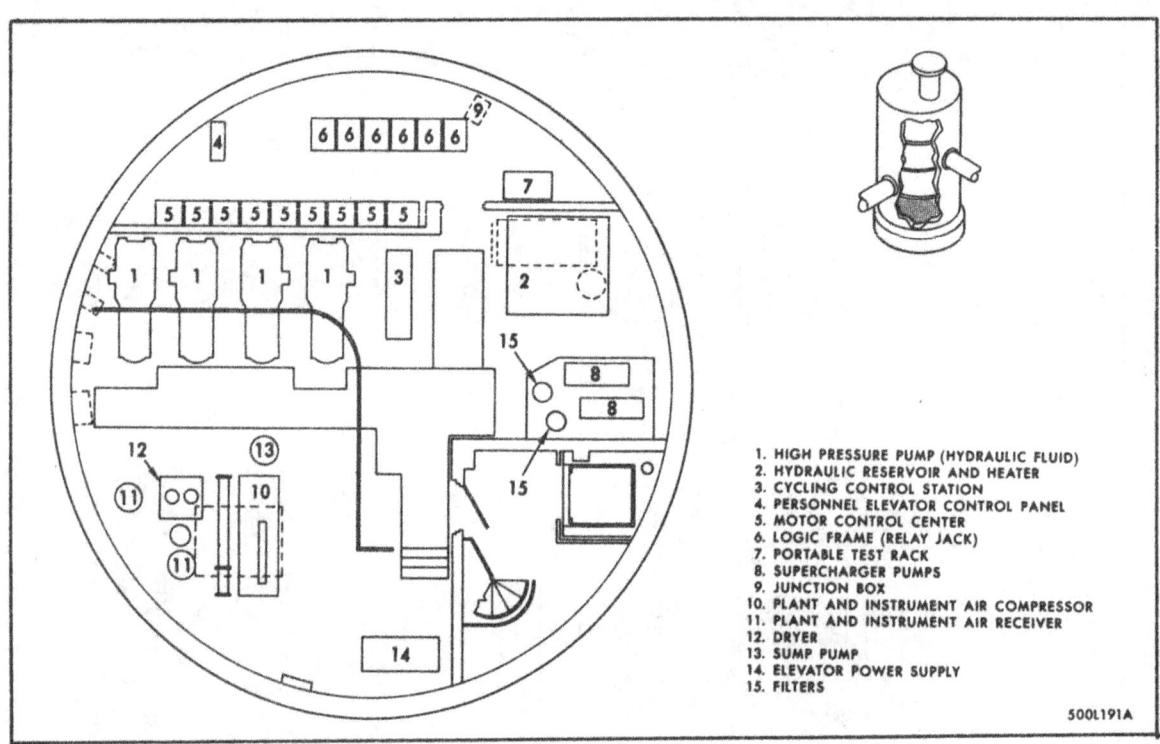

Figure 1-13. Equipment Terminal, Level I

1-52. A typical power pack room and electrical room are shown in figure 1-14. The power pack consists of a storage reservoir, supercharger pumps, high pressure pumps, heating facilities and heat exchangers, a filter system, and a cycling control station with shutoff valves permitting sectional isolation of the system during checkout and maintenance. The power pack consists of two major circuits: the main power pack and the auxiliary standby system. The hydraulic reservoir stores system fluid and maintains it at the required temperature for proper operation by means of an integral heating system. Sludge and contaminants are removed by the filtering system to prevent foreign objects from clogging the launcher mechanism.

1-53. The cycling control station provides manual control of the hydraulic power pack for purposes of checkout. It contains gages and an annunciator circuit. The annunciator circuit sounds a warning horn and lights the appropriate indicator on the annunciator panel when a loss of pressure in either the main line or the return line, or abnormally high temperature in the hydraulic storage reservoir occur.

1-54. The motor control center receives 480 V 60 CPS from the launcher unit substation and provides a centralized power supply and control station for the launcher system motors and heaters.

1-55. The launcher logic circuitry within the logic racks determines the status of the launcher system and controls the operation of various drives and actuators. The launcher logic circuitry is so arranged that the operation of the actuators of each launcher component is in proper sequence to perform a complete function. Groups of these functions, performed in proper sequence for missile firing, are sequenced by logic circuitry. These groups of functions are initiated upon receipt of a command signal from either the launch controller for automatic operation, or by maintenance personnel for local operation or equipment checkout.

1-56. LEVEL II. Level II of the equipment terminal (figure 1-15) contains the missile air conditioner and the missile silo air conditioning equipment. The missile air conditioner supplies heated or cooled air to maintain the proper temperature in the Stage II transition compartment, between-tanks compartment, and Stage II engine compartment. The missile silo air conditioning equipment supplies conditioned air to the missile silo. Level II also contains a hydraulic pumping unit that supplies hydraulic fluid to fill, bleed, and pressurize the hydraulic equipment in both missile stages.

1-57. LEVEL III. Level III of the equipment terminal (figure 1-16) contains launch and checkout equipment necessary to launch a missile or perform checkout of the following subsystems: engine control, flight control, launch sequencer, re-entry vehicle, electrical, missile guidance, and propellant loading and pressurization systems.

1-58. LEVEL IV. Level IV of the equipment terminal (figure 1-17) contains the equipment that supplies and distributes electrical power to the launcher area. This level contains motor control centers, a power switchboard, a 400 CPS motor-generator, two 28 VDC power supplies, a battery power supply, a 9 KVA transformer, and transformer substations.

1-59. The motor control centers and power switchboard distribute electrical power from the generator and power transformer substations to the equipment in the missile silo and launcher. The 400 CPS motor-generator supplies regulated power for missile systems until the airborne power supplies are used. A transformer rectifier furnishes the 28 VDC power supply for the ground checkout and launch control equipment.

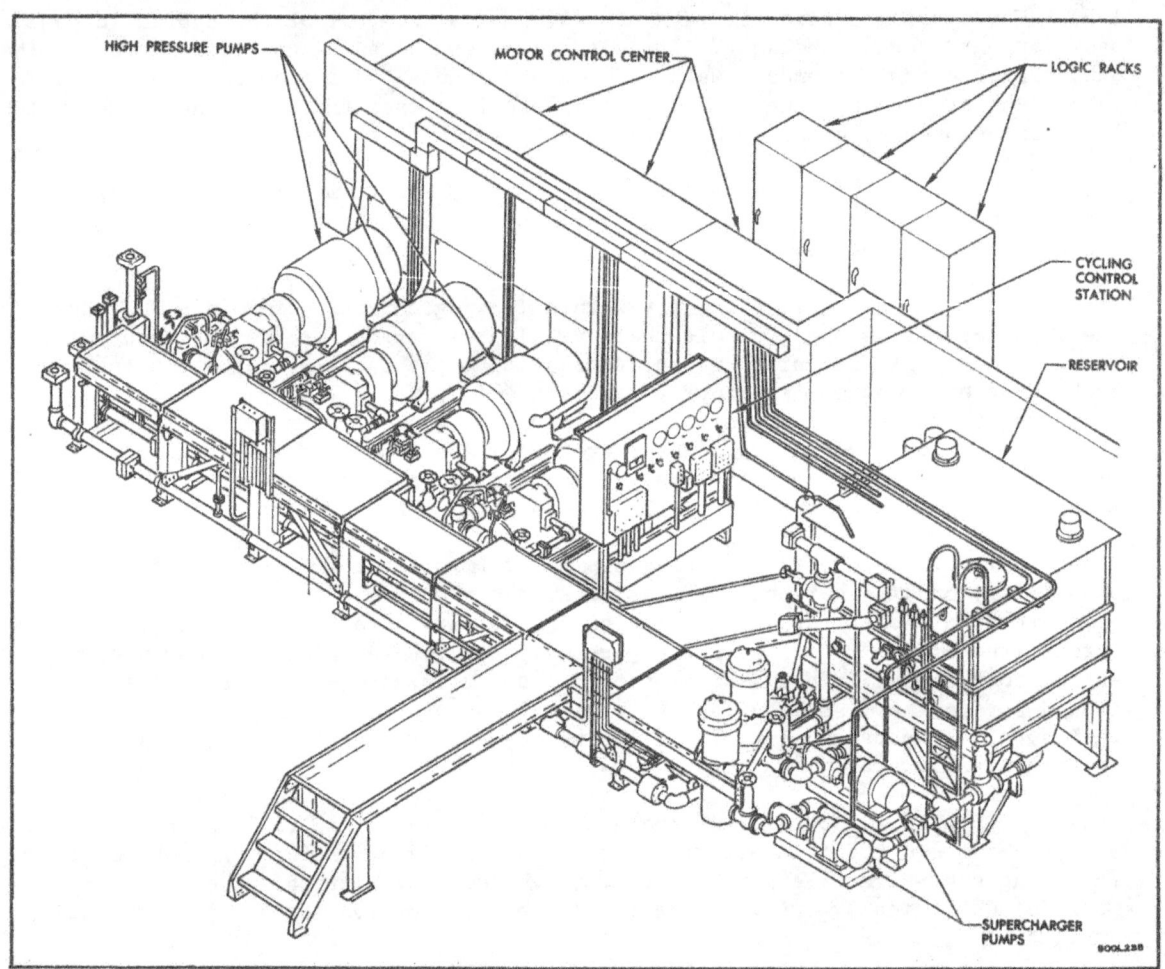

Figure 1-14. Typical Power Pack Room and Electrical Room

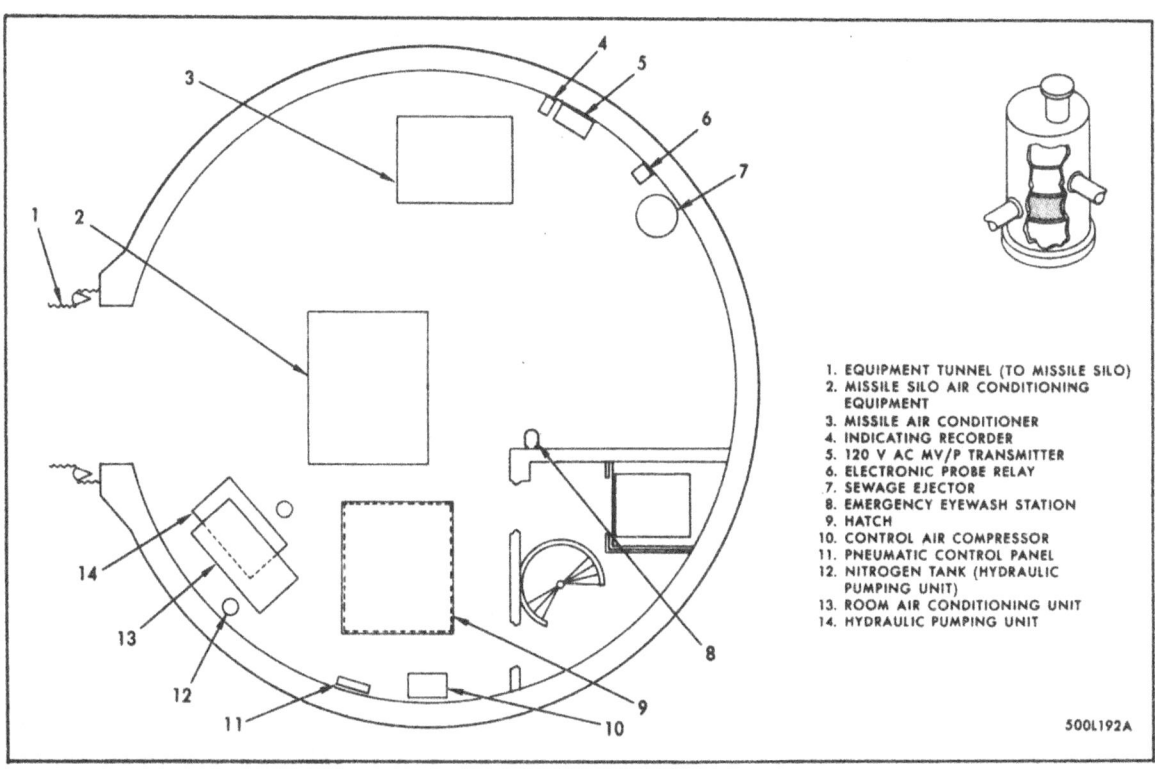

Figure 1-15. Equipment Terminal, Level II

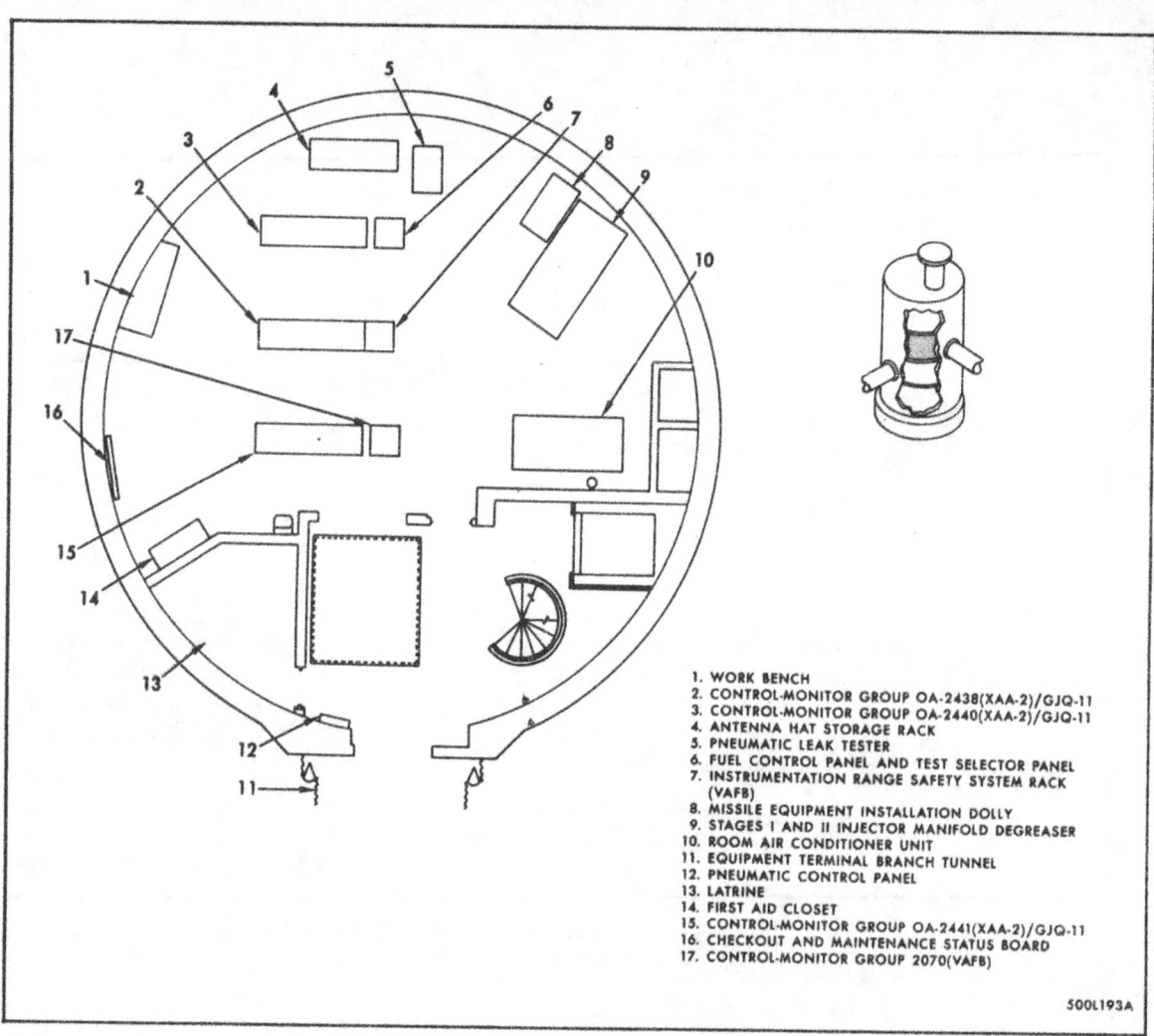

Figure 1-16. Equipment Terminal, Level III

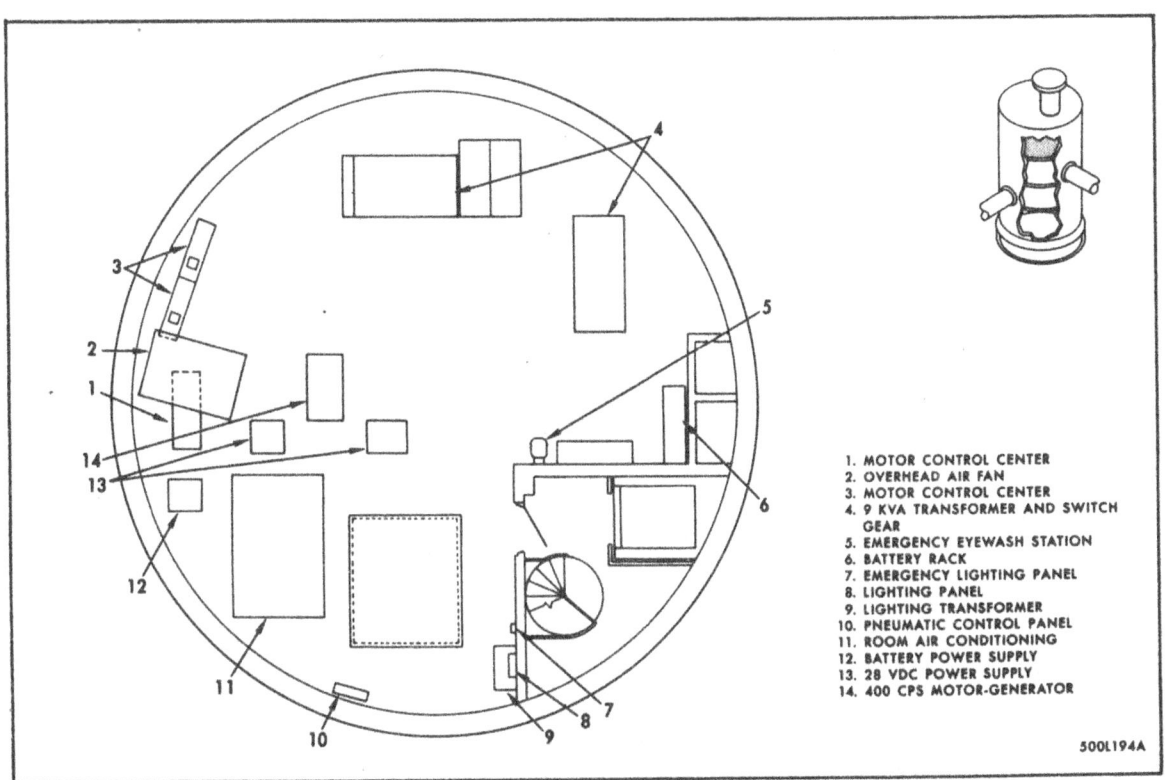

Figure 1-17. Equipment Terminal, Level IV

The battery power supply permits a safe shutdown of checkout and launch control equipment if a malfunction occurs in the 28 VDC power supply. The 9 KVA transformer supplies electrical power to the substations for distribution to the motor control centers and the power switchboard.

1-60. PROPELLANT TERMINAL.

1-61. The propellant terminal contains storage tanks for liquid oxygen, liquid nitrogen, gaseous nitrogen, and helium. Equipment and plumbing associated with the transfer of the liquids and fluids are also contained in the propellant terminals and in the liquid oxygen vent shaft tunnels that connect the propellant terminals to the missile silos. The propellant terminal has two levels; a lower level (figure 1-18), with an entrance to the liquid oxygen tunnel, and an upper level (figure 1-19), connecting the liquid oxygen storage tank access room with the propellant terminal branch tunnel.

1-62. LOWER LEVEL. The lower level of the propellant terminal (figure 1-18) contains helium storage tanks, nitrogen storage tanks, a helium cooler, a liquid oxygen subcooler, vacuum pumps, and an emergency eyewash and shower station. A liquid oxygen catchpot is provided to catch liquid oxygen spillage during transfer operations.

1-63. UPPER LEVEL. The upper level of the propellant terminal (figure 1-19) contains an emergency eyewash and shower station and the propellant transfer panels. The propellant transfer panels consist of the following: a liquid oxygen transfer panel, a nitrogen transfer panel, and a helium transfer panel. These panels provide a central location for pressure and level indicators that display liquid levels, storage bottle pressures, and system pressures. These panels also consist of pressure switches that relay status information to the launch control and checkout equipment in the equipment terminal.

1-64. CONTROL CENTER.

1-65. The control center contains the launch control console (LCC), missile guidance console, launch complex facility console (LCFC), display equipment, guidance computer, and radar equipment. The equipment and consoles monitor the status of the missile systems, and control the launcher equipment, the guidance antennas, and the missile during standby activities and launch operations. The control center at VAFB is shown in figure 1-20. At the operational bases, the control center is an underground, dome-shaped structure divided into an upper level and a lower level (figure 1-21). The two levels are divided into 14 rooms.

1-66. The control center operations room (figure 1-22) contains the equipment necessary to monitor the weapon system. The equipment initiates the launching of the missiles and includes components of the launch control and status system, and guidance system.

1-67. LAUNCH CONTROL CONSOLE (LCC). The launch control console (figure 1-23 and 1-24) (control-monitor group OA-2437) is a desk type console with a base and a combined control-display panel. The console serves as the primary center for initiating and monitoring an actual launch or exercise countdown for any one of the three missile launchers in the launch complex. The launch console base contains a working surface for the operator, two equipment drawers, a telephone dial, and two telephone jacks for the console operator's headset. Launch console operation is controlled

(Text continued on page 1-36)

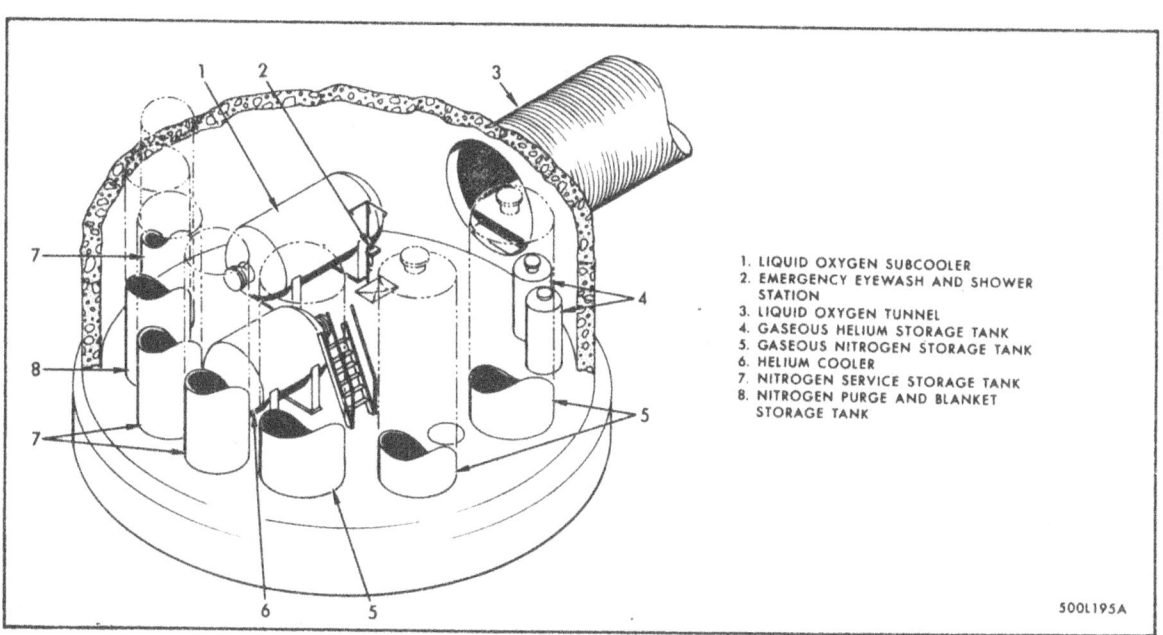

Figure 1-18. Propellant Terminal Lower Level

1. LIQUID OXYGEN SUBCOOLER
2. EMERGENCY EYEWASH AND SHOWER STATION
3. LIQUID OXYGEN TUNNEL
4. GASEOUS HELIUM STORAGE TANK
5. GASEOUS NITROGEN STORAGE TANK
6. HELIUM COOLER
7. NITROGEN SERVICE STORAGE TANK
8. NITROGEN PURGE AND BLANKET STORAGE TANK

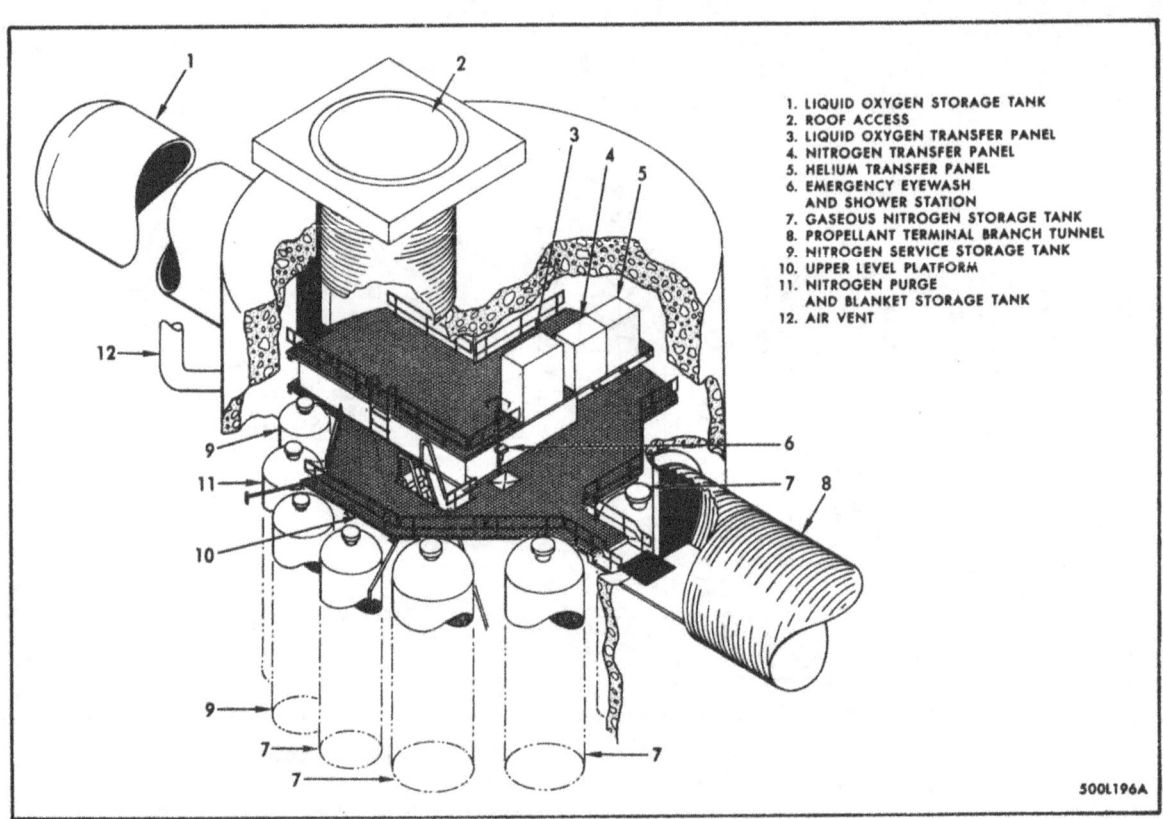

Figure 1-19. Propellant Terminal Upper Level

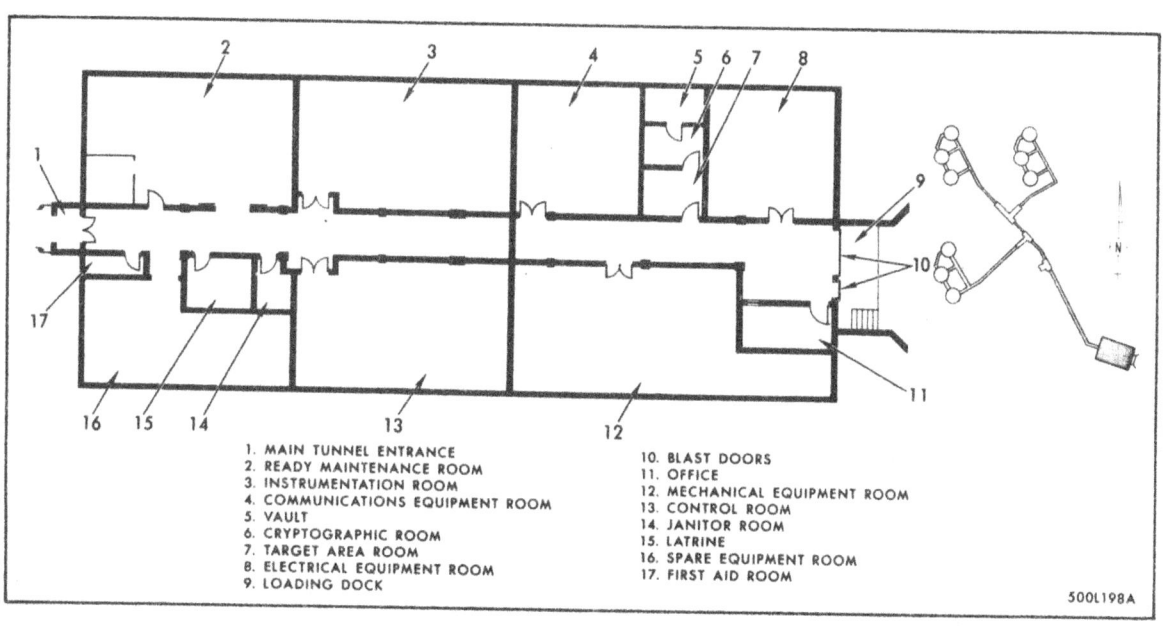

Figure 1-20. Control Center (VAFB)

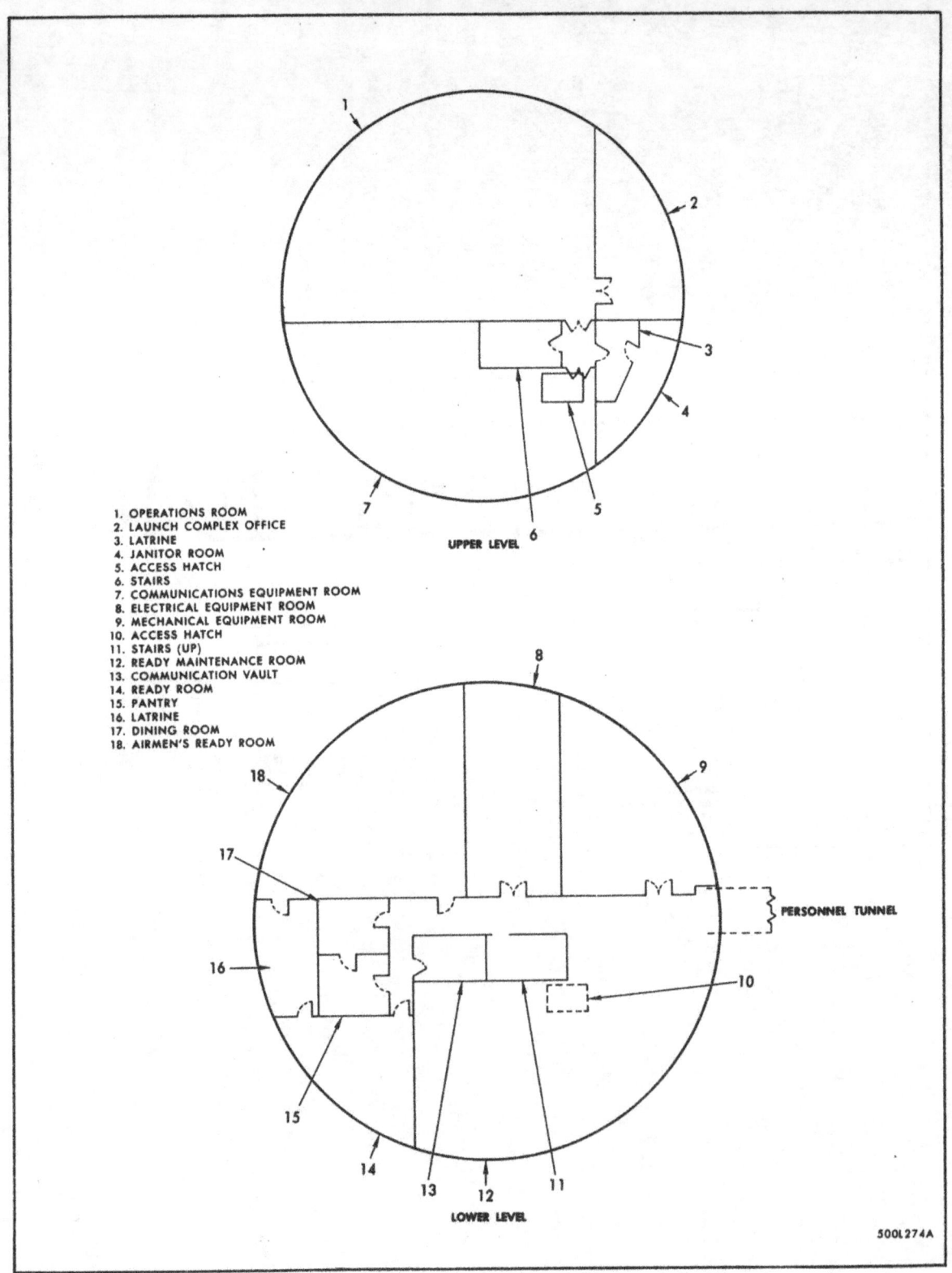

Figure 1-21. Control Center (Operational Bases)

T.O. 21-SM68-1

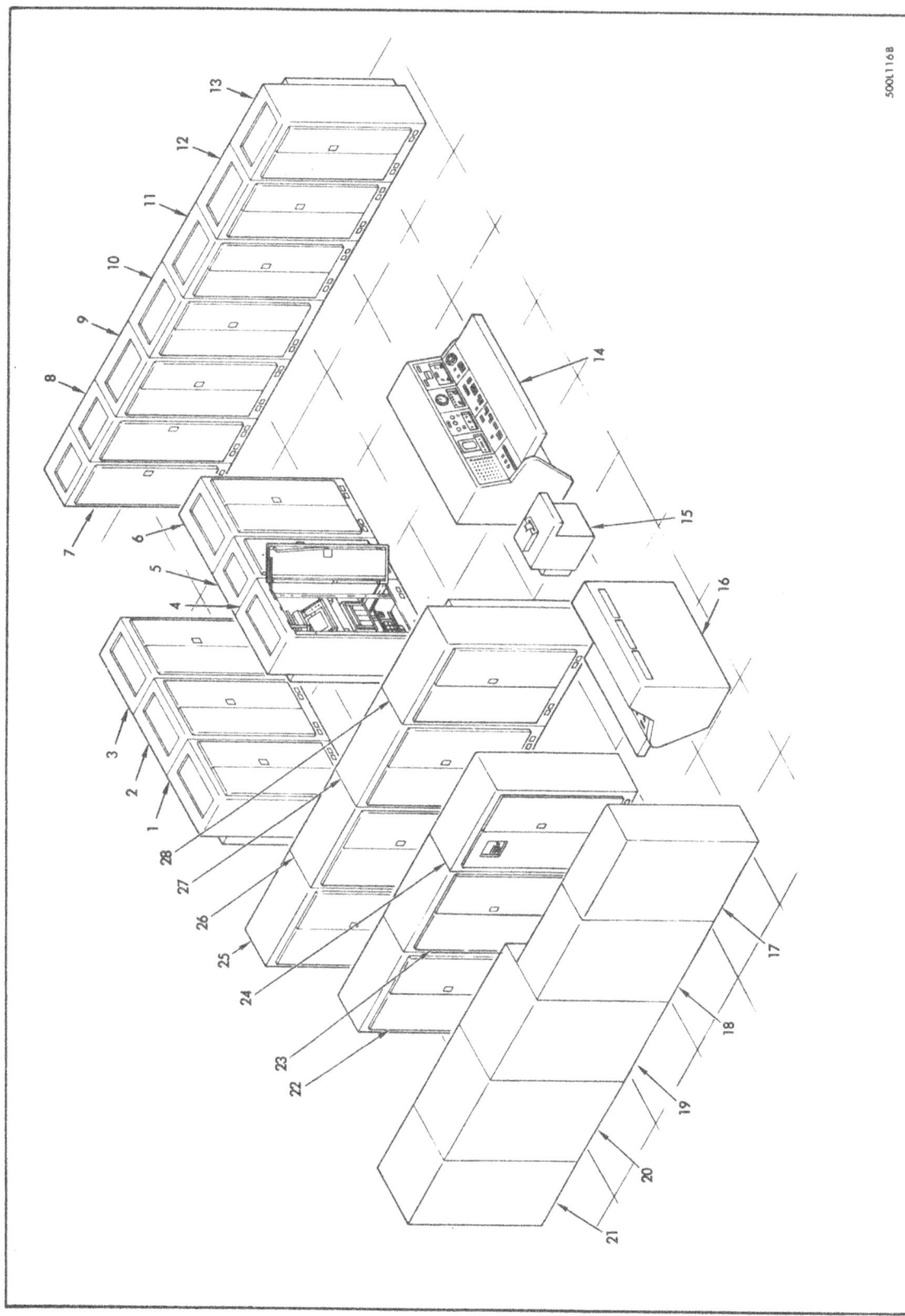

Figure 1-22. Control Center Operations Room Equipment Location (Sheet 1 of 2)

MISSILE GUIDANCE SET AN/GRW-5

1. Power supply set OA-2902C/GRM-40
2. Signal data converter CV-968B/GRM-40
3. Computer-signal data generator CP-561B/GRM-40
4. Signal data recorder RO-146/GRW-5
5. Power switchboard SB-1168/GRW-5
6. Power supply set OA-2898/GRW-5
7. Command signals decoder KY-344A/GRW-5
8. Reference signal generator TD-409A/GRW-5
9. Signal data converter CV-967C/GRW-5
10. Range computer CP-560A/GRW-5
11. Antenna Control C-3360C/GRW-5
12. Receiver group OA-3034B/GRW-5
13. Antenna position programmer C-3362B/GRW-5
14. Missile guidance console OA-3101/GRW-5 or OA-2897/GRW-5

MISSILE GUIDANCE COMPUTER SET AN/GSK-1

15. Digital data printer RO-144/GSK-1
16. Computer set console OA-2656/GSK-1
17. Signal data recorder group OA-2660/GSH-4 (VAFB)
18. Simulator-verifier SM-203/GSK-1
19. Signal data reproducer group OA-2658/GSK-1
20. Power distribution group OA-2656/GSK-1
21. Power supply group OA-2656/GSK-1
22. Data storage magnetic drum MU-422/GSK-1
23. Data input processor-verifier CM-166/GSK-1
24. Recording set control C-3206/GSH-4 (VAFB)
25. Core memory unit MU-423/GSK-1
26. Computer control C-3205/GSK-1
27. Computer arithmetic unit CP-539/GSK-1
28. Digital to digital converter CV-929/GSK-1

Figure 1-22. Control Center Operations Room Equipment Location (Sheet 2 of 2)

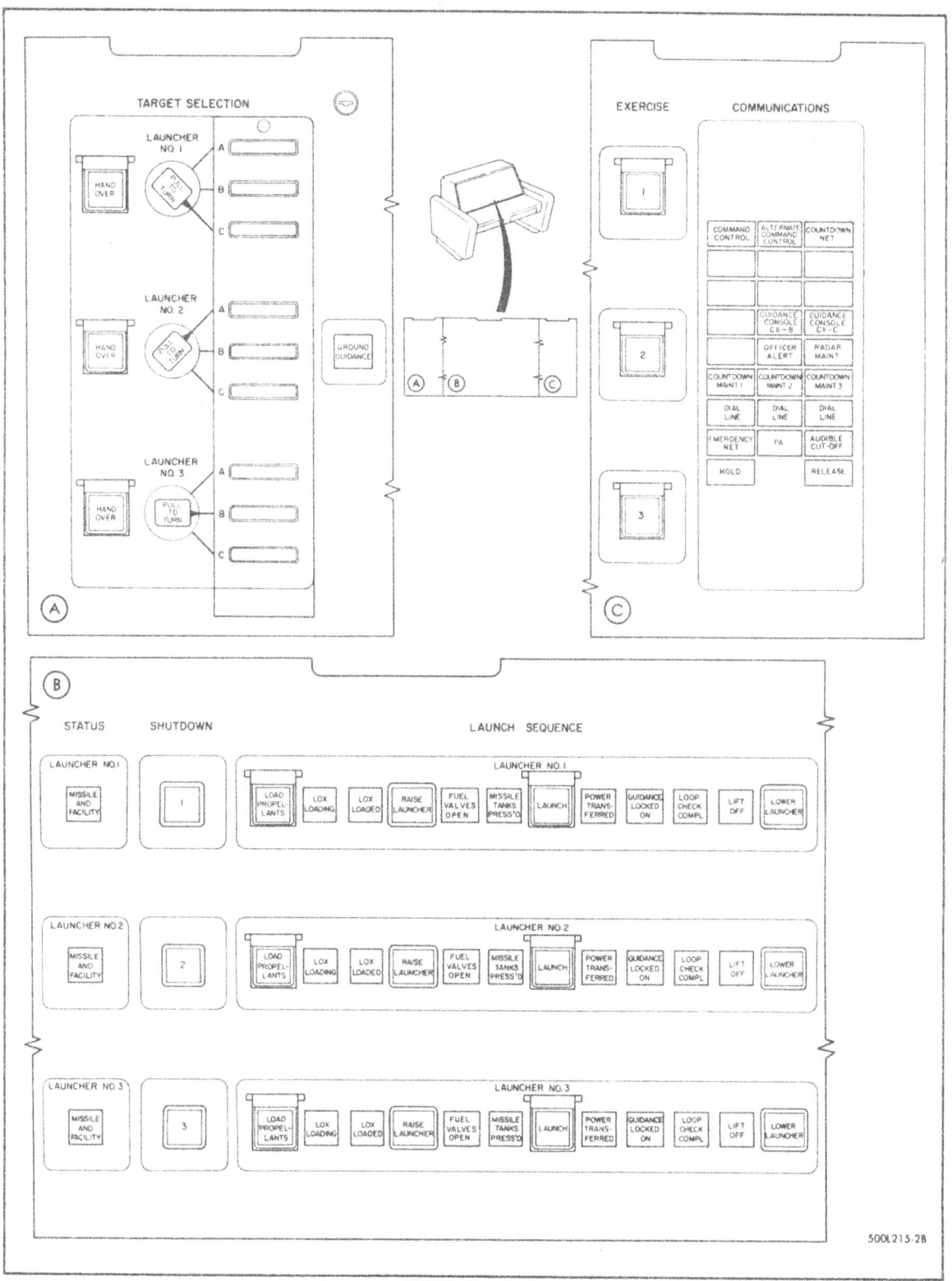

Figure 1-23. Launch Control Console (Operational Bases)

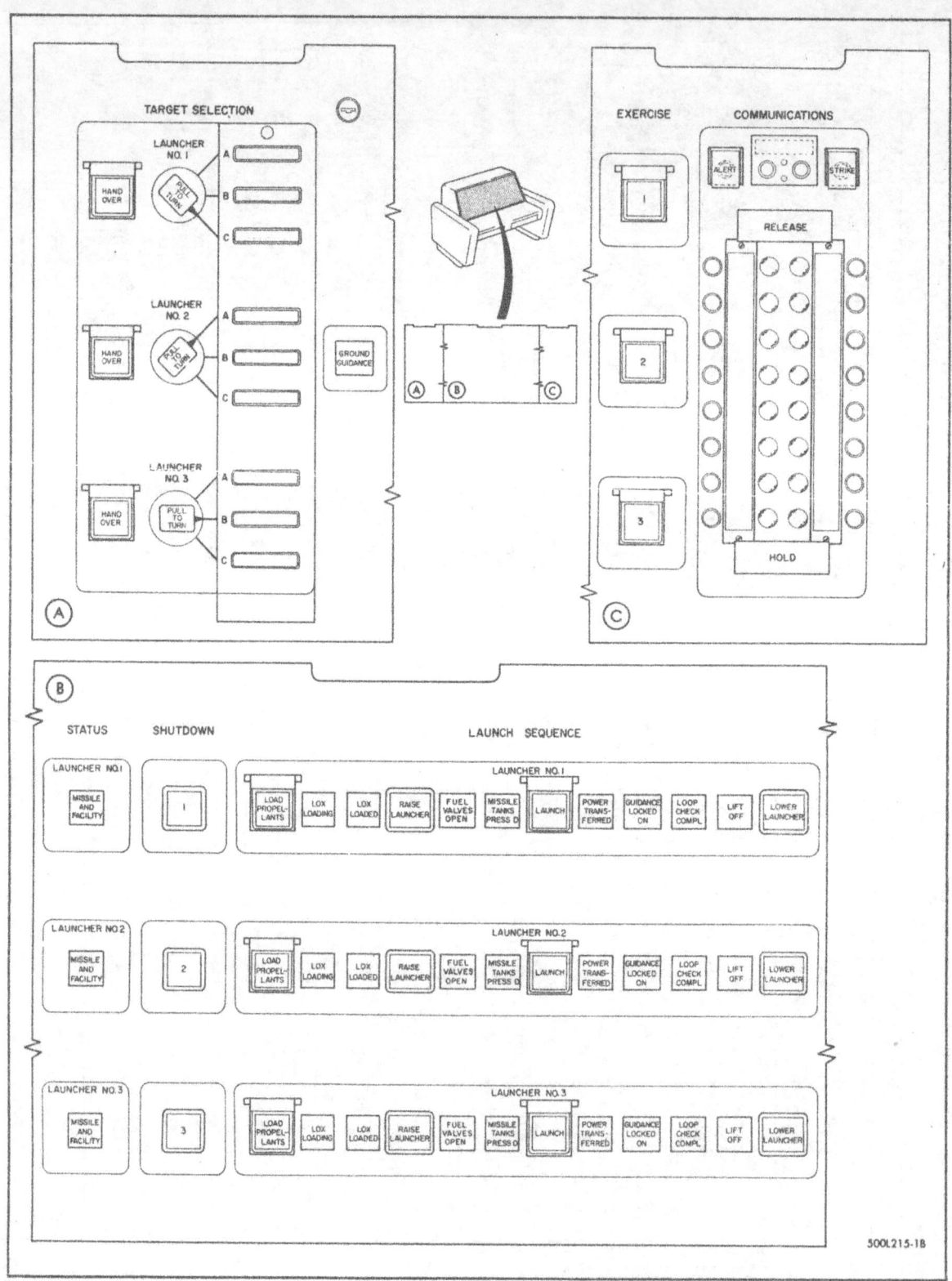

Figure 1-24. Launch Control Console (VAFB)

(Text continued from page 1-27.)
from the control-display panel, which contains three rows of controls and indicators (one row for each launcher). The controls consist of pushbutton indicators that are actuated manually by the missile launch officer to start the semiautomatic sequenced events of a countdown. The indicators provide visual monitoring of the ground guidance station, the three missile launchers, and the major sequenced events that occur during countdown. Transparent guards over the HANDOVER, LOAD PROPELLANTS, LAUNCH, and EXERCISE pushbutton indicators prevent the accidental pressing of these pushbuttons. The guards are hinged and must be raised before the pushbuttons can be pressed. The launch console panel is divided into six sections: TARGET SELECTION, STATUS, SHUTDOWN, LAUNCH SEQUENCE, EXERCISE, COMMUNICATIONS.

1-68. The TARGET SELECTION section of the LCC contains three HANDOVER push-pushbutton indicators, which select missile guidance control for each of the three missile launchers. When the HANDOVER pushbutton indicator is pressed, the indicator lights white, indicating the guidance control has been transferred to another launch complex. The indicator remains lighted white until the HANDOVER pushbutton indicator is pressed a second time to return guidance control to the original launch complex. The TARGET SELECTION section also contains three rotary switches (one for each launcher) and nine target identification display windows (three windows for each switch). When the switch is rotated to the desired target, the target identification display window lights green, indicating the proper target has been selected by the aerospace operating equipment (AOE). At T-80 the target identification display window changes from green to white, indicating the target selection is locked in the target card reader and logic assemblys of control-monitor group OA-2439. The target display windows are mounted on a hinged panel that allows access to the back of each window for the insertion of an eight digit target identification tab. To prevent unauthorized access to the target identification tabs, the hinged panel is secured with a lock.

1-69. The STATUS section of the LCC contains one GROUND GUIDANCE and three MISSILE AND FACILITY indicators that display the alert status of the ground guidance and of the missile and facility systems prior to and during a countdown. After launch, these indicators display the status of the ground guidance, aerospace operating equipment, and facility systems. For the ground guidance system, green indicates ready, red indicates not ready, and white indicates the station is operating and is locked on the desired missile. For the missile and faciliy systems, green indicates ready, and red indicates not ready for the corresponding missile launcher.

1-70. The SHUTDOWN section of the LCC contains three pushbutton indicators that initiate and indicate a shutdown. Pressing the 1, 2, or 3 pushbutton indicator terminates the countdown for the corresponding missile launcher and lights the indicator red. The indicator also lights red when the countdown is shut down automatically. Manual shutdown is possible throughout the countdown. If a malfunction should occur after the RAISE LAUNCHER pushbutton indicator is pressed, the countdown is automatically stopped.

1-71. The LAUNCH SEQUENCE section of the LCC contains three rows (one for each launcher) of three pushbutton indicators and eight status indicators that initiate and display the sequenced events of a countdown for each of the three missile launchers. To control countdown, the pushbutton indicators are pressed in the following order: LOAD PROPELLANTS, RAISE LAUNCHER, and LAUNCH. When the pushbutton indicators are pressed, the indicators light as each automatic operation initiated by the pushbutton indicators starts. The progress of each automatic operation is displayed by the eight status indicators. The completion of each automatic

T.O. 21-SM68-1

Section I
Paragraphs 1-72 to 1-74

operation is displayed by a green lamp in the pushbutton indicator that controls the next sequence of events. The LAUNCH SEQUENCE section also contains three LOWER LAUNCHER pushbutton indicators (one for each missile launcher) that display and initiate the lower-launcher phase after completion of the launch or shutdown phases. The LOWER LAUNCHER pushbutton indicator lights green when the launch phase is completed or if a shutdown is initiated after T-41. Pressing the pushbutton indicator changes the indication from green to white, indicating that the launcher platform is being lowered. When the missile launcher is returned to a hardened condition, the white lamp in the pushbutton indicator goes out.

1-72. The EXERCISE section of the LCC contains pushbutton indicators 1, 2, and 3 that are used to perform launch control system checkout for each of the corresponding missile launchers. During an exercise countdown, the sequenced events occur in the same order as for an actual launch with the following exceptions: fuel prevalves are not opened, batteries are not activated, power from the ground power source is not transferred to the airborne power supplies, Stage I rocket engine is not ignited, and explosive bolts for the missile release mechanism are not detonated. When an exercise is initiated by pressing LOAD PROPELLANTS, the EXERCISE indicator changes from green to white indicating that the exercise countdown is in progress. At the completion of the exercise, the indicator changes from white to green. (The pushbutton indicator will change from white to red if the exercise is not completed successfully.) If the EXERCISE pushbutton indicator is pressed again, the green light will go out. At this time, the launch control system is returned to launch capability.

1-73. The COMMUNICATIONS section of the LCC enables the missile launch officer to communicate by telephone or public address to all areas of the launch complex. A direct line to COMMAND CONTROL and DIAL LINE for off-site calls is also provided. The communication section for the operational bases is shown in figure 1-23 and the section for VAFB is shown in figure 1-24. Although the physical layouts of the two sections differ, the actual operation of each is similar. Pressing of any COMMUNICATIONS pushbutton indicator will connect the launch control console to the called station and simultaneously light the pressed pushbutton indicator. The RELEASE pushbutton indicator will break the circuit to the called station and return the indicator to not lighted. Once a station is connected and a hold is desired in order to connect another station, the HOLD pushbutton indicator is pressed; then by pressing the new station pushbutton indicator, the new station is connected. To break a station that has been held, the station pushbutton indicator must be re-pressed; then pressing of the RELEASE pushbutton indicator breaks the circuit and returns the indicator to not lighted. Line circuits are indicated by a white light and hold circuits are indicated by a yellow light. The DIAL LINE incoming signal is indicated by a flashing white light. The EMERGENCY NET indicates flashing red. By pressing this pushbutton indicator, any other network in use is automatically placed in HOLD and the EMERGENCY NET is connected.

1-74. MISSILE GUIDANCE CONSOLE. (Figure 1-25) Launch countdown operations of the guidance radar and computer in the launch complex are effected from the missile guidance console OA-3101G/GRW-5 or OA-2897G/GRW-5. Three rows of indicators and pushbutton indicators located on the two middle sloping panels are used to control the guidance system during countdown. The color coding of the pushbutton indicators is used to identify the following conditions: white, information or function in progress; green, function completed; yellow, caution; and red, warning. The lower or countdown row of pushbutton indicators is used for initiating the countdown function. Pressing a lower row pushbutton indicator initiates a function and a white indication that signifies the particular function is in progress. Completion of the

1-37

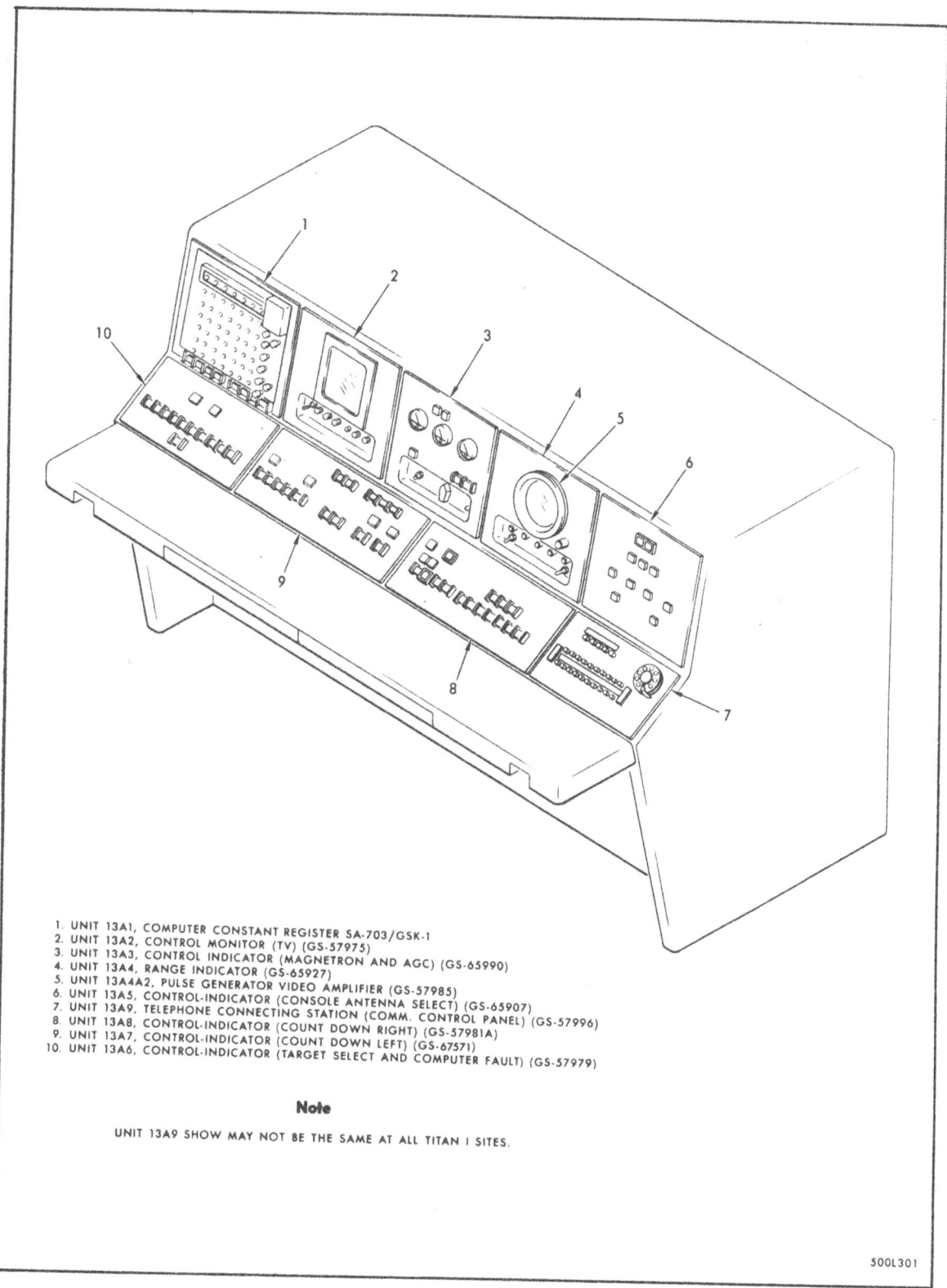

1. UNIT 13A1, COMPUTER CONSTANT REGISTER SA-703/GSK-1
2. UNIT 13A2, CONTROL MONITOR (TV) (GS-57975)
3. UNIT 13A3, CONTROL INDICATOR (MAGNETRON AND AGC) (GS-65990)
4. UNIT 13A4, RANGE INDICATOR (GS-65927)
5. UNIT 13A4A2, PULSE GENERATOR VIDEO AMPLIFIER (GS-57985)
6. UNIT 13A5, CONTROL-INDICATOR (CONSOLE ANTENNA SELECT) (GS-65907)
7. UNIT 13A9, TELEPHONE CONNECTING STATION (COMM. CONTROL PANEL) (GS-57996)
8. UNIT 13A8, CONTROL-INDICATOR (COUNT DOWN RIGHT) (GS-57981A)
9. UNIT 13A7, CONTROL-INDICATOR (COUNT DOWN LEFT) (GS-67571)
10. UNIT 13A6, CONTROL-INDICATOR (TARGET SELECT AND COMPUTER FAULT) (GS-57979)

Note

UNIT 13A9 SHOW MAY NOT BE THE SAME AT ALL TITAN I SITES.

Figure 1-25. Missile Guidance Console

function is signified by the change in indication from white to green. Pushbutton indicators in the lower row may not be pressed to initiate a countdown phase until the associated indicator in the middle row is lighted white. The indicators and pushbutton indicators in the upper row indicate abnormal or emergency conditions when lighted yellow or red. The console panel to the far left is associated with the target selected and computer fault function and the panel to the far right contains the telephone communication controls. The upper panels are primarily indicators with associated controls. A constants register at the extreme left is used to introduce azimuth, elevation, and range data, and index of refraction into the computer. The adjoining panel contains the television monitor with kinescope and camera controls. The camera, mounted on the antenna, relays to the kinescope a view of the missile as it is launched and started on its flight. Meters and controls for the high frequency transmitter and receiver are located on the center panel. The fourth panel contains a cathode-ray tube range indicator and associated controls. During a missile flight, the cathode-ray tube displays a visual indication of the return pulse from the missile as gated by the range unit. The panel at the extreme right contains pushbutton indicators that indicate handover mode and antenna status, and also permit switching of handover mode and of antennas.

1-75. LAUNCH COMPLEX FACILITIES CONSOLE (LCFC). The launch complex facilities console (figures 1-26 and 1-27) (control-monitor group OA-2436) is a desk type console consisting of a base and display panel. The facilities console indicates the status of the airborne equipment, aerospace operating equipment (AOE), and aerospace ground equipment (AGE) at each of the three missile launchers. The console also displays guidance system status and monitors the launch complex damage control system. The facilities console base contains a working surface for the operator, two equipment drawers, a telephone dial, two telephone jacks for the console operator's headset, and a hazard-alert buzzer for the launch complex damage control system. The display panel contains indicators for the visual indications of the equipment status and facility status, and pushbutton controls that initiate or terminate corrective functions of the launch complex damage control system. The display panel is divided into three sections: EQUIPMENT STATUS, FACILITY STATUS & CONTROL, and COMMUNICATIONS.

1-76. The EQUIPMENT STATUS section of the LCFC indicates the alert status of the ground guidance system, missile equipment, and AOE. The status of the launch complex ground guidance station is indicated by one GROUND GUIDANCE indicator that lights green for ready, white for in-operation (guidance locked on the desired missile), and red for malfunction or hold. The functional status of the missile and associated facilities for each missile launcher is indicated by three MISSILE AND FACILITY pushbutton indicators. These pushbutton indicators (one for each missile launcher) are lighted green when normal conditions prevail within the launch complex. During a countdown, the MISSILE AND FACILITY pushbutton indicator that corresponds to the operating launcher lights green for ready and red for malfunction. During a checkout, the pushbutton indicator is lighted red. When pressed, the pushbutton indicator initiates a no-go signal to the launch control and checkout equipment at the corresponding missile launcher. The other indicators in the equipment status section present the status of the placarded equipment or system for each missile launcher as follows: not lighted for ready, amber for in-checkout, and red for malfunction. The status of the complex security fence gate (operational bases) is initiated and indicated by a FENCE GATE pushbutton indicator which is lighted green for locked and red for unlocked. The PORTAL ACCESS blast door status is indicated by two pushbutton indicators, green for LOCK and red for UNLOCK.

1-77. The FACILITY STATUS & CONTROL section of the LCFC indicates conditions or hazards in the launch complex, grouped by major areas. Hazards such as fire,

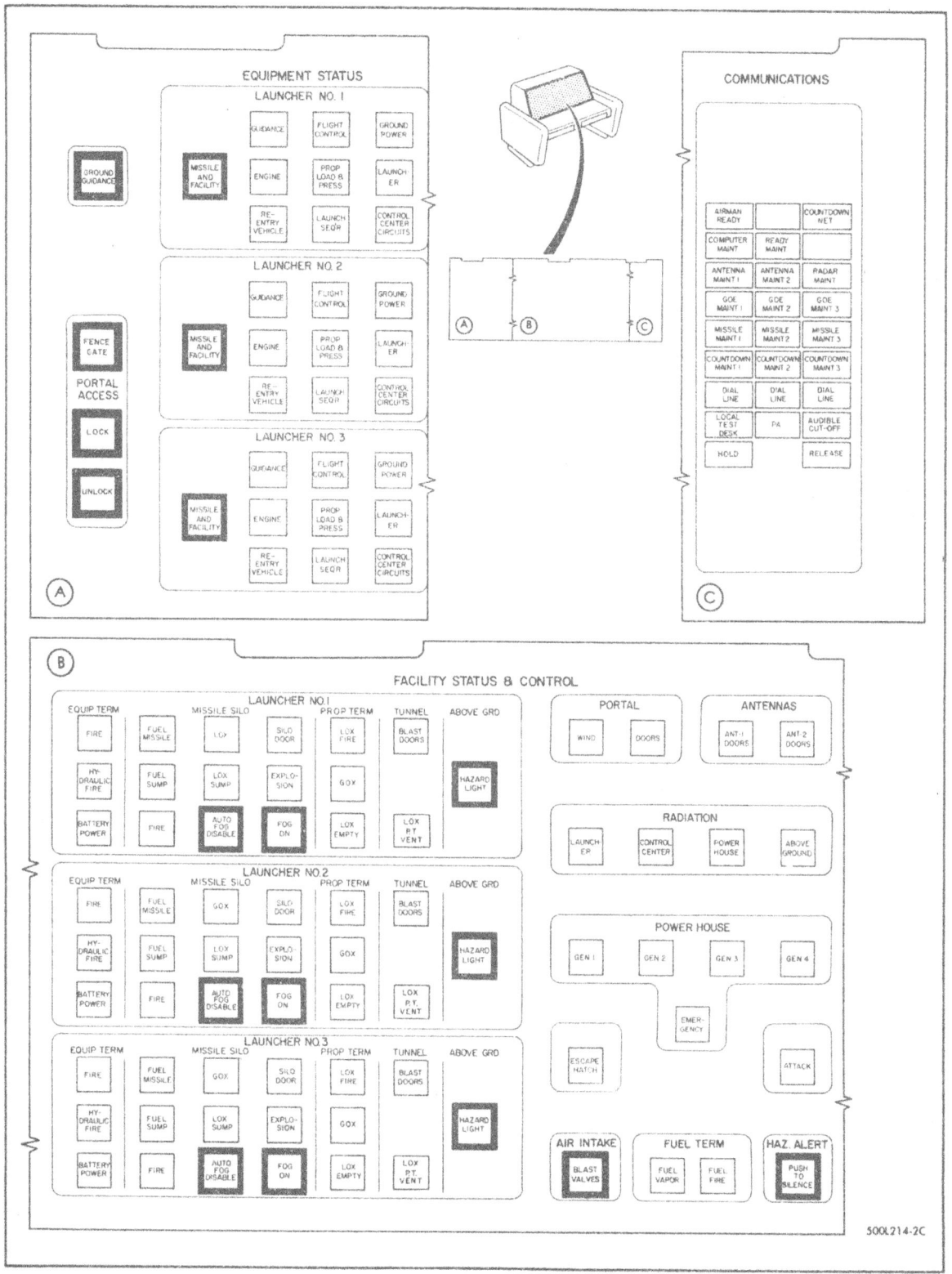

Figure 1-26. Launch Complex Facilities Console (Operational Bases)

T.O. 21-SM68-1 Section I

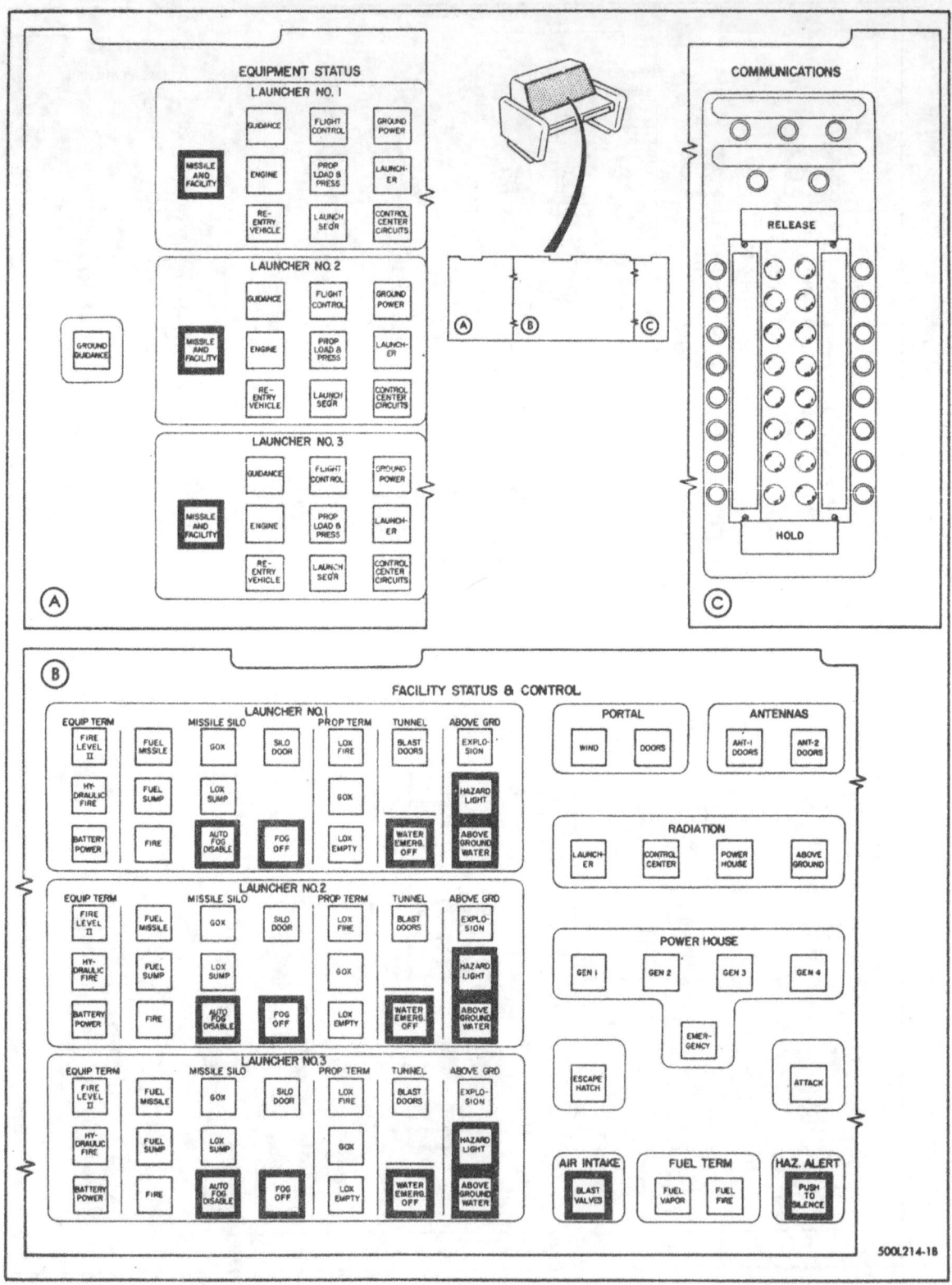

Figure 1-27. Launch Complex Facilities Console (VAFB)

1-41

radiation, and liquid oxygen vapors are indicated by flashing red lights. Corrective actions are initiated automatically by sensors in the launch complex damage control system or are controlled from the console. Corrective action in progress is indicated by a flashing white light that alternates with a flashing red light. Pushbutton indicators in the FACILITY STATUS & CONTROL section provide each launcher with manual control of the missile silo water fog equipment, the above ground hazard lights, and the hazard-alert buzzer on the facilities console. At VAFB, the above ground water equipment and the main water valve are also manually controlled at the facilities console by ABOVE GROUND WATER and WATER EMERG. OFF pushbutton indicators.

1-78. The COMMUNICATIONS section of the LCFC enables the console operator to communicate by telephone or public address to all areas of the launch complex.

1-79. POWER HOUSE.

1-80. The power house is the electrical power generating and distribution center for the launch complex. The power house contains generating equipment, transformers, electrical power distribution equipment, and water treatment equipment for the launch complex. The power house at VAFB (figure 1-28) is a two level subsurface structure. The roof of the power house supports the exhaust mufflers for the diesel generators and has four removable precast concrete covers over the generator room. Personnel and trucks enter the power house through a blast door located on the upper level at the south end of the structure. The blast door opens onto a loading dock next to the generator room. A stairwell next to the loading dock provides access to the lower level. In addition to the loading dock and generator room the power house contains a transformer room, pump room, compressor room, boiler room, office, storage area, and a shop area. The operational base power house (figures 1-29 and 1-30) is an underground, dome-shaped structure. The illustrations in this section concerning the power house show a typical layout for the equipment although the actual layout of the equipment from base to base may vary. Entry into the power house is through the personnel tunnel which opens into the power house through the launch complex main tunnel. Large diesel fuel storage tanks are located on each side of exhaust tunnel. Two water storage tanks are located adjacent to the portal entrance tunnel to the power house. The power house supplies all utilities, electrical power, water, and heat, for operation of the launch complex.

1-81. The power house mezzanine (figure 1-30) provides access to the air intake and exhaust tunnels. A water chlorinator, water pumps, water tanks, back wash tank, air receivers, air compressors, fuel oil day tanks, lube oil storage tanks, compression tanks, and a motor control center are located on the mezzanine. The power house lower level (figure 1-29) consists of an office, a shop area, a latrine, and a generator room. The equipment located in the generator room consists of four generators, ice banks, switch gear, water chillers, pumps of various types, heat exchangers, and motor control centers.

1-82. ANTENNA TERMINAL.

1-83. The antenna terminal is a subsurface structure and is composed of a terminal room and two silos. Entrance to the VAFB antenna terminal (figure 1-31) is through a blast door on the exposed side of the terminal room. The terminal room is connected to the two silos by tunnels. Entrance to the operational bases antenna terminal (figure 1-32) is through a personnel passage tunnel. The terminal room is connected directly to the silos. The silos are entered through blast doors.

(Text continued on page 1-48.)

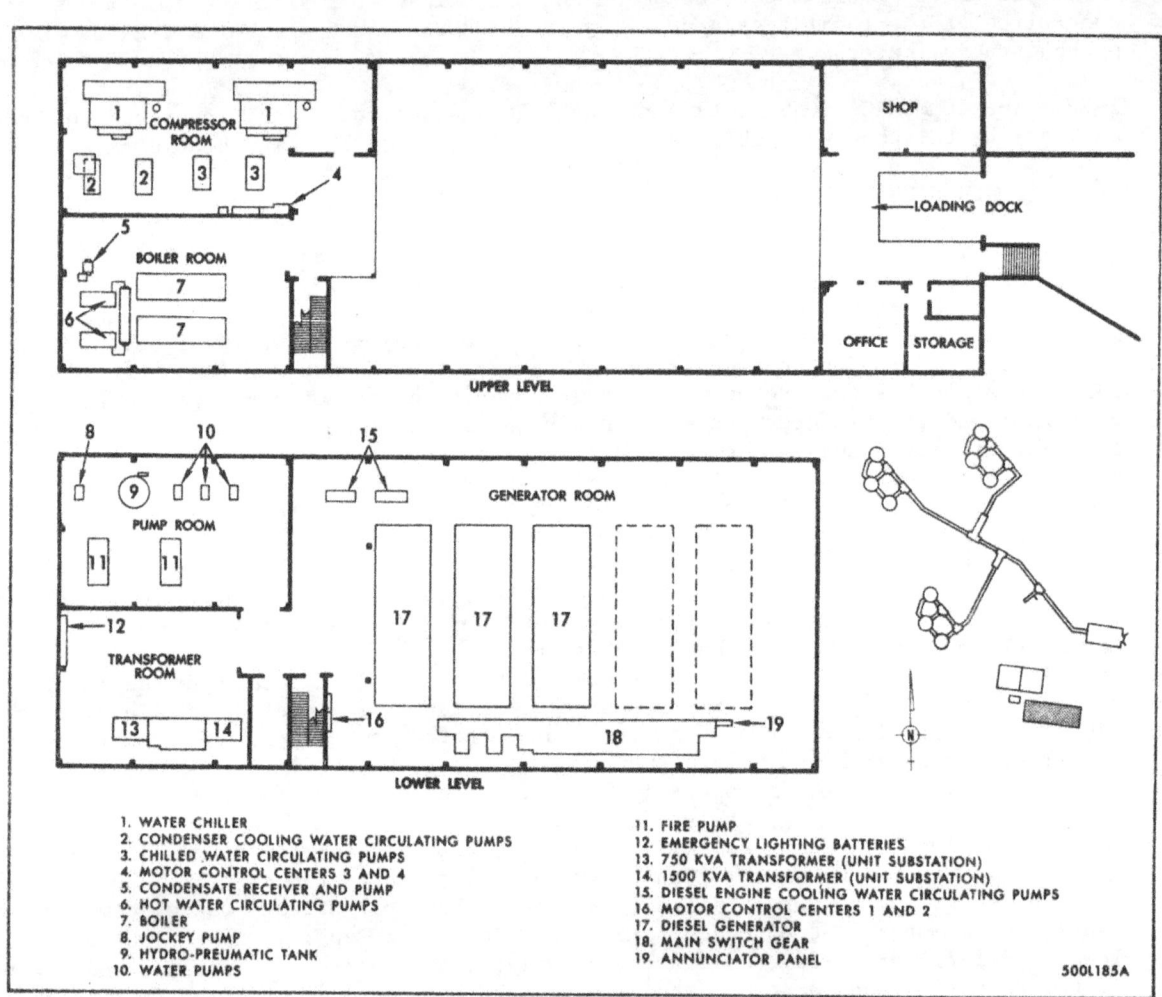

Figure 1-28. Power House (VAFB)

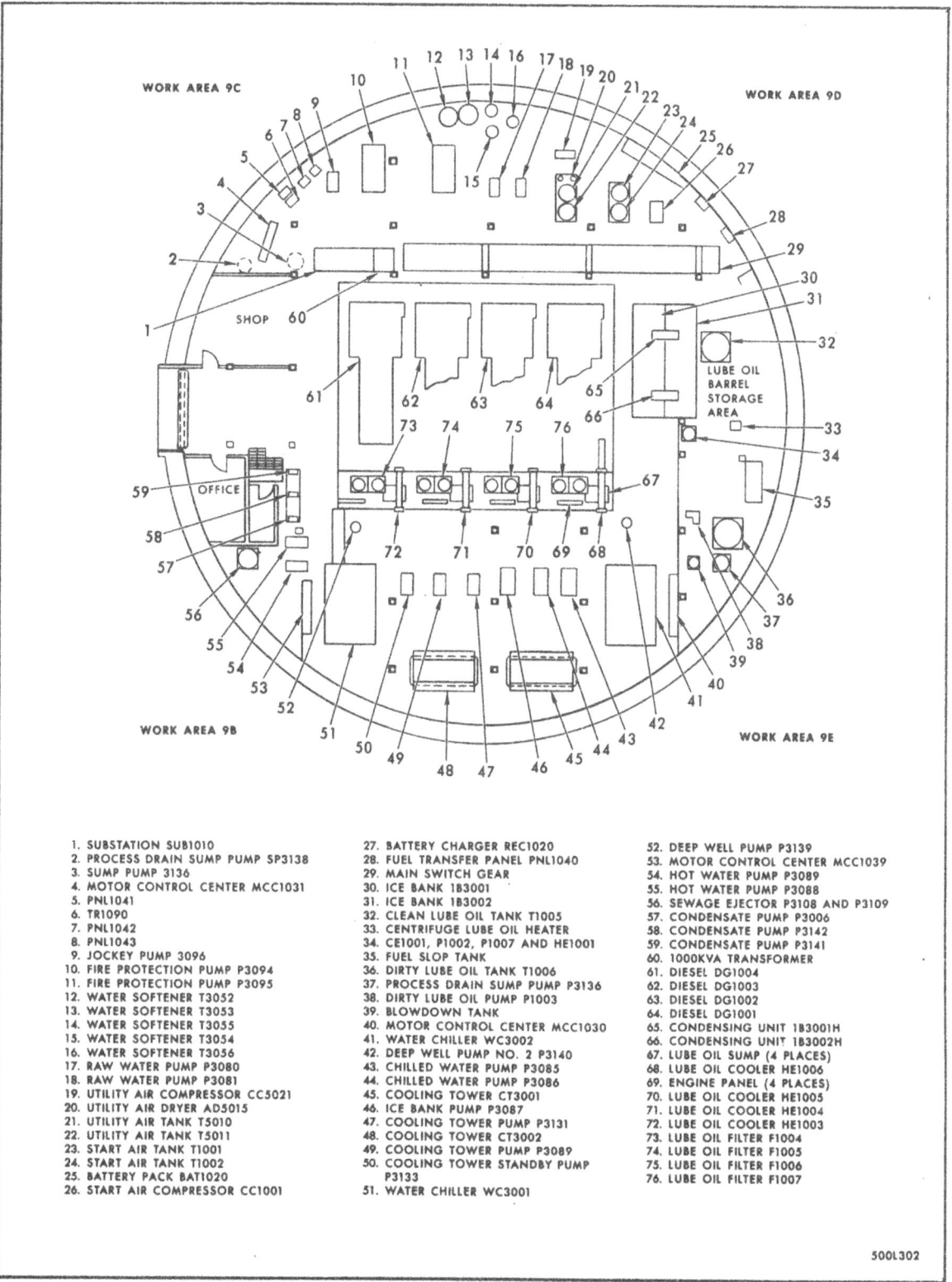

Figure 1-29. Power House Lower Level Typical Equipment Location (Operational Bases)

T.O. 21-SM68-1 Section I

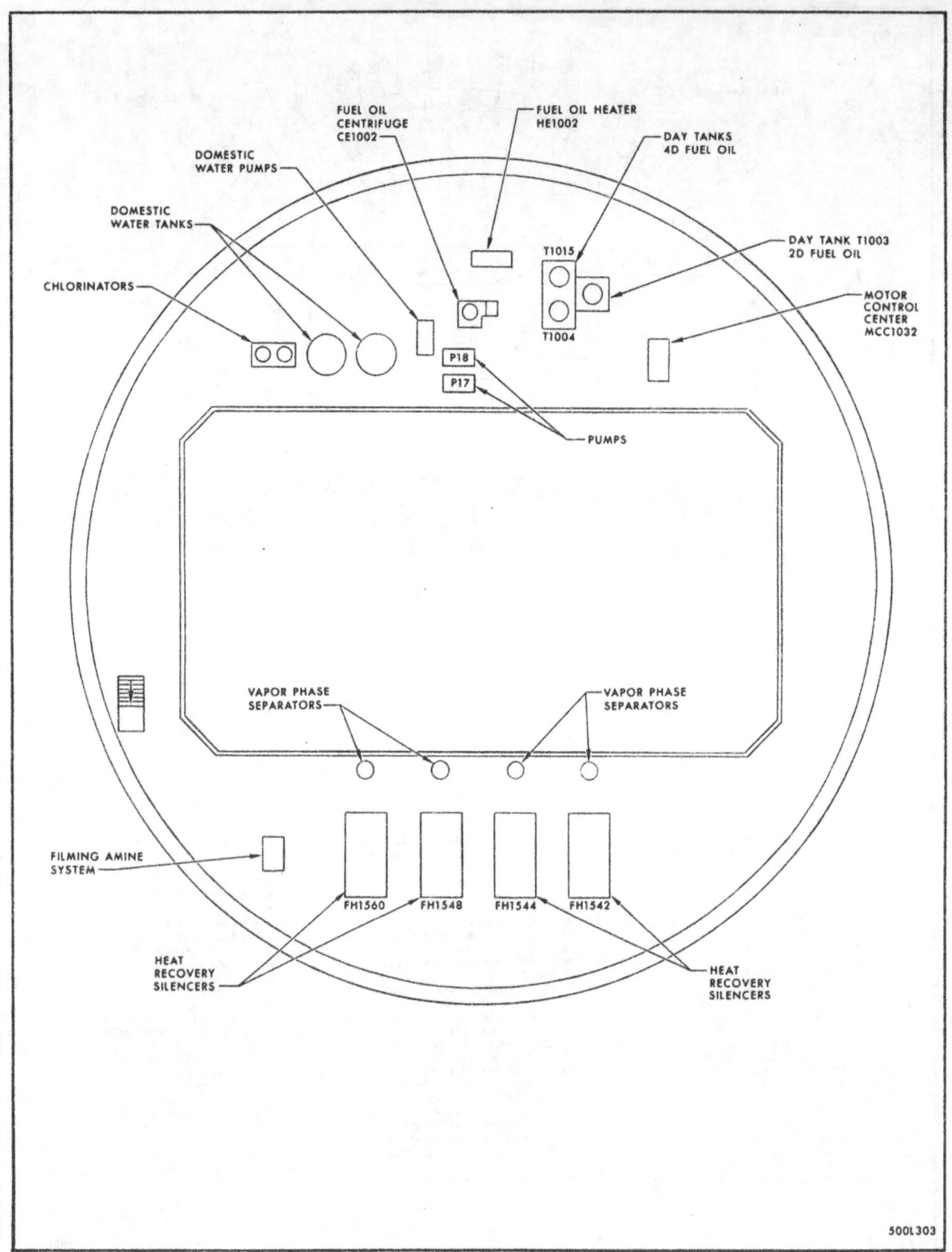

Figure 1-30. Power House Mezzanine Typical Equipment
Location (Operational Bases)

1-45

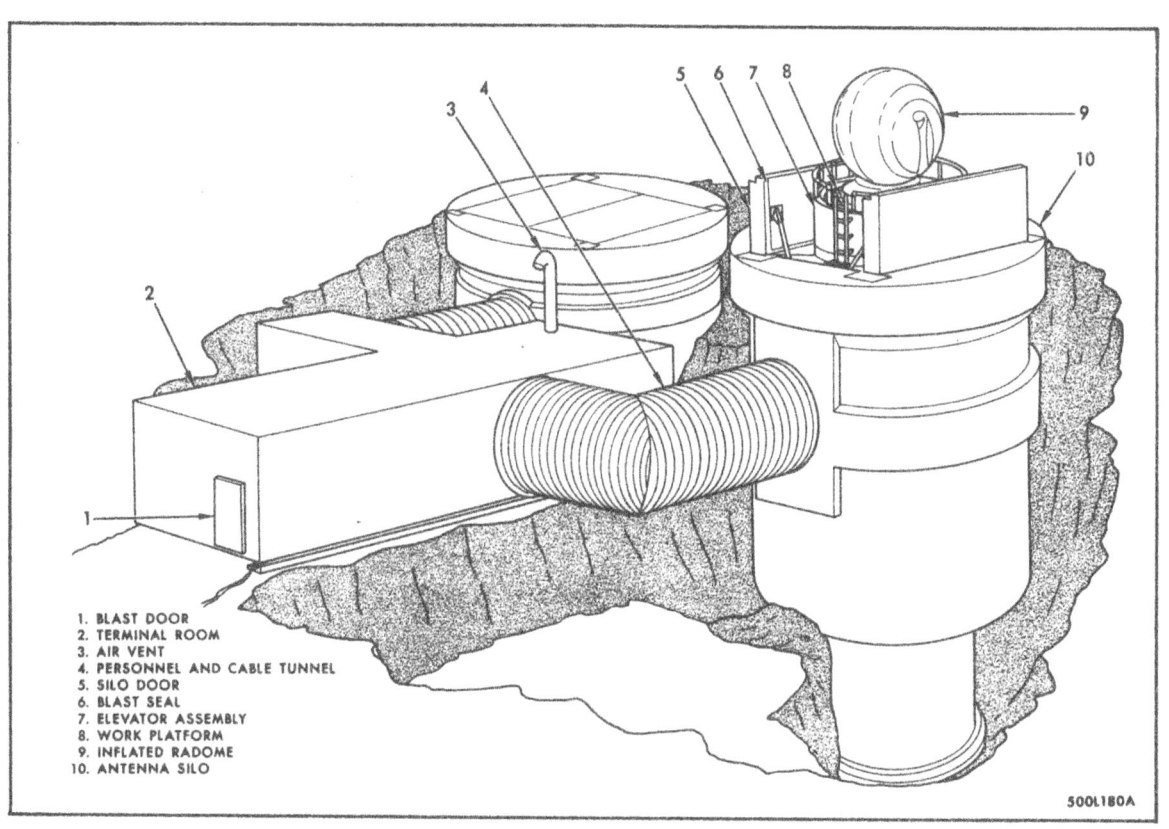

Figure 1-31. Antenna Terminal (VAFB)

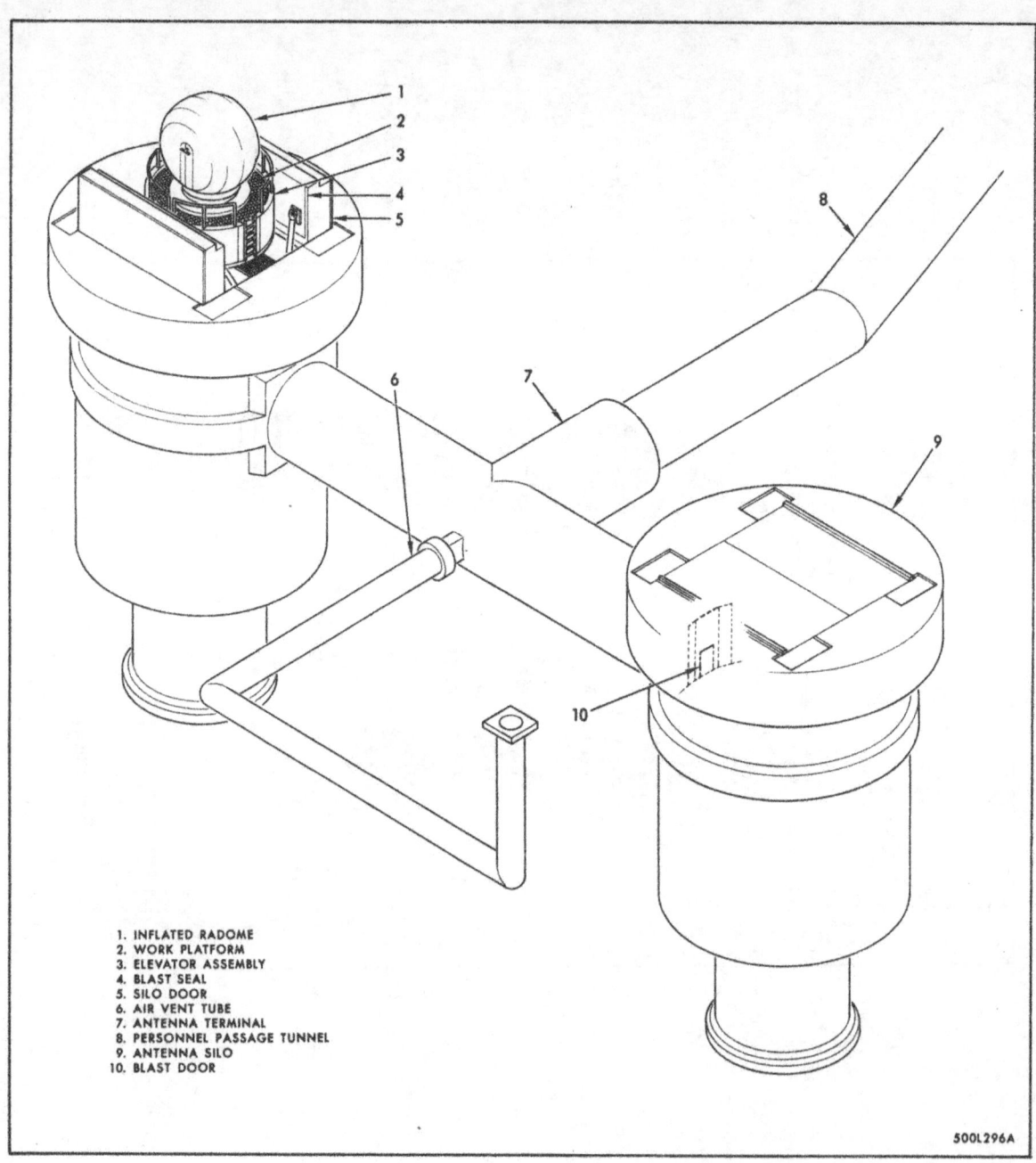

Figure 1-32. Antenna Terminal (Operational Bases)

(Text continued from page 1-42.)

1-84. The antenna terminal contains electrical and air conditioning equipment for control of two separate radar guidance antennas. Two complete systems are provided; one to be used for standby and one to be used for back-up or maintenance.

1-85. TERMINAL ROOM. The terminal room contains a motor control center, missile guidance equipment, antenna elevator control equipment, lighting control equipment, electrical receptacles, sump pump, air compressor, de-icer controls, and air conditioning equipment for the terminal room and silos.

1-86. ANTENNA SILOS. Each antenna silo contains an elevator assembly that raises the antenna to the above ground operating position. The operation of the elevator assembly is controlled by equipment in the terminal room. This equipment responds to signals received from the guidance station in the control center. Above ground equipment is used for the orientation and alignment of the antennas.

1-87. FUEL TERMINAL.

1-88. The fuel terminal contains the fuel storage tank and necessary controls for handling fuel. The area is connected to each launcher through the tunnel network and supplies fuel for each of the three missiles in the launch complex. The fuel terminal is located underground adjacent to tunnel junction 10 (figure 1-33) at VAFB and adjacent to tunnel junction 12 (figure 1-34) at the operational bases. The storage area contains a ground level valve box, fuel storage tank, a nitrogen blanket tank, a fuel filter, a fuel transfer pump, a fuel transfer panel, fuel transfer valves, and a carbon dioxide fire fighting system. Fuel servicing is accomplished through above ground fill lines.

1-89. GROUND LEVEL VALVE BOX. The ground level valve box is located above the fuel terminal area. The box contains terminal caps and fittings for the fuel recirculating, fuel fill, and nitrogen charge pipe lines. The ground level valve box is accessible from the road network and the fuel fill pad.

1-90. ACCESS ROOM. A circular section of tunnel forms the access room to the fuel storage tank and the nitrogen blanket tank. A fuel transfer pump in the access room transfers fuel to each launcher.

1-91. Ventilation is provided by a fan mounted above the fire door which pulls air from the tunnel junction into the access room. This fan is equipped with a fire damper which closes automatically in the event of a fire.

1-92. FUEL STORAGE TANK. The fuel storage tank is located lateral to the tunnel junction, with one end of the tank entering the access room. The tank serves as the main fuel storage tank for the three launchers. Fuel in the storage tank is blanketed with gaseous nitrogen. Three fuel lines are connected to the storage tank; one for initial fill, the second for unloading to the surface and transferring fuel to and from the launchers, and a third line is used for a fuel drain line from the launchers back to the storage tank.

1-93. NITROGEN BLANKET TANK. The nitrogen blanket tank is located lateral to the fuel storage tank. The nitrogen tank supplies gaseous nitrogen for blanketing the fuel tank and lines.

1-94. FUEL TRANSFER CONTROL PANEL. (See figures 1-33 and 1-34.) The fuel transfer control panel is located inside the tunnel junction. The panel contains controls

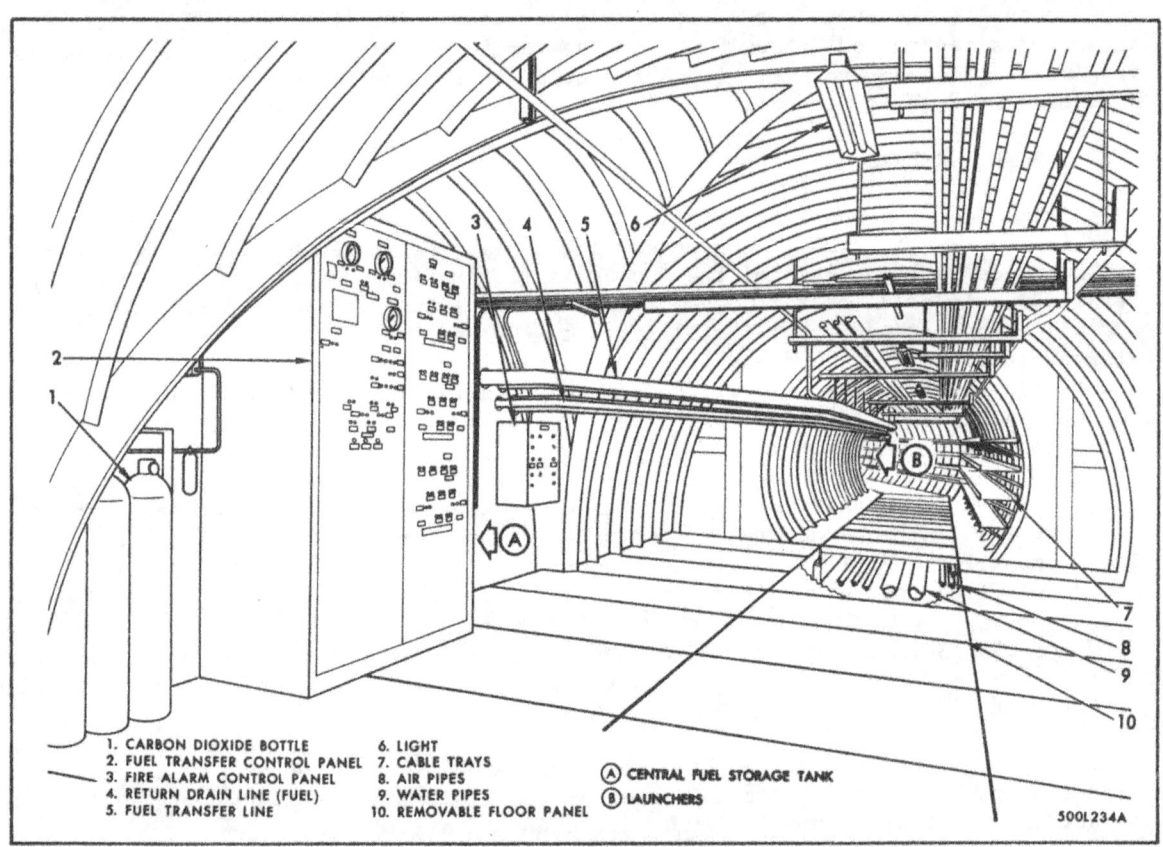

Figure 1-33. Tunnel Junction 10 (VAFB)

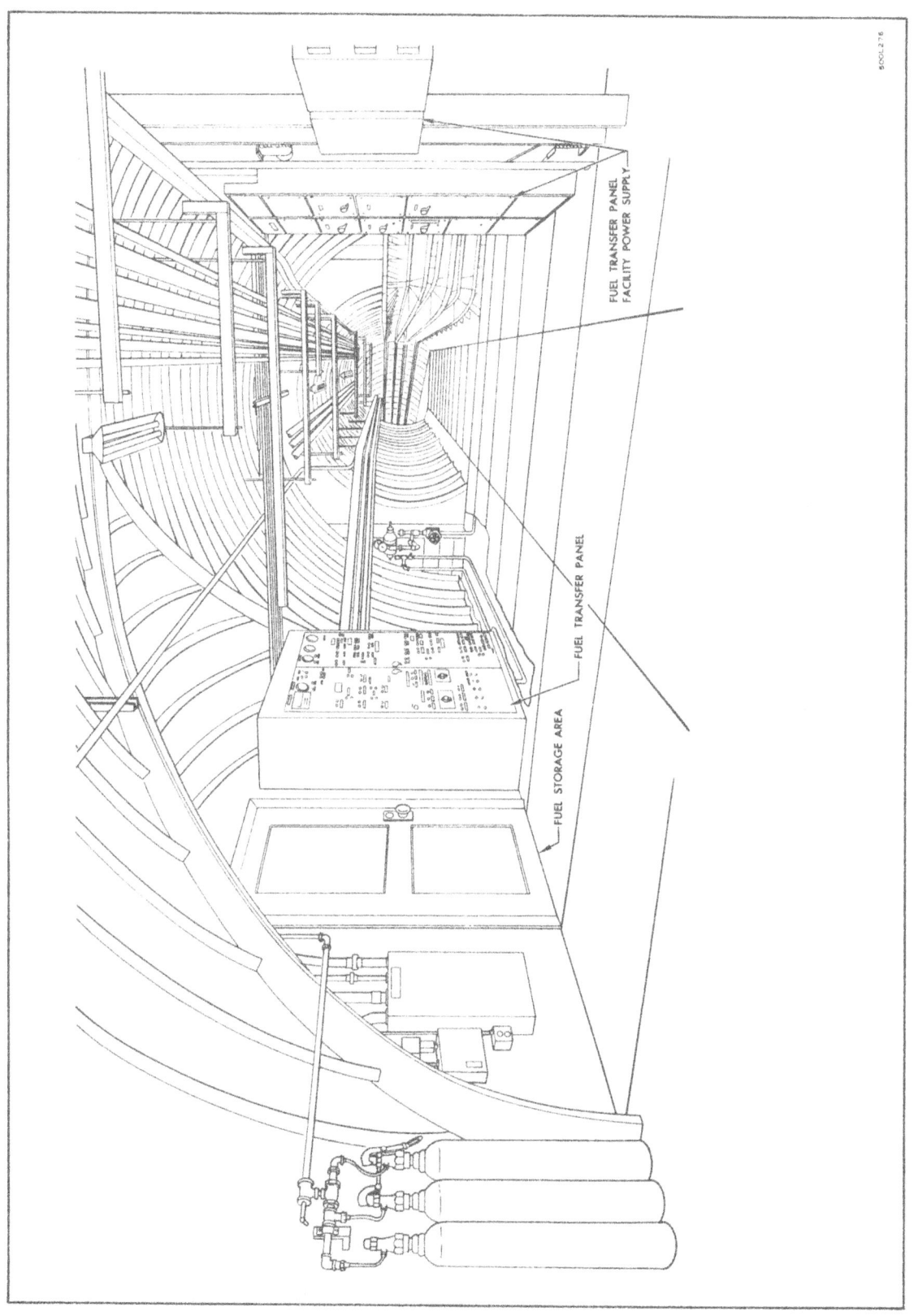

Figure 1-34. Tunnel Junction 12 (Operational Bases)

that effect fuel transfer operations to each missile launcher. Fuel transfer consists of loading and unloading fuel from the missile tanks and loading and recirculating fuel in the fuel storage tank.

1-95. FIRE FIGHTING SYSTEM. The fire fighting system for the fuel storage area consists of three 75-pound carbon dioxide cylinders (in the tunnel junction) connected to four distribution nozzles (in the access room). A fuel fire alarm control panel, located adjacent to the access room in the tunnel junction, controls the cylinders and the warning devices. The panel contains automatic relays; indicators for visual indications of safe, corrective, or unsafe conditions; and pushbuttons for silencing the alarm devices. The panel also contains a reset button for resetting the fire alarm electrical system.

1-96. There are two fuel fire sensors installed on the ceiling of the access room. These sensors are connected electrically to a relay in the alarm panel and respond to a predetermined temperature setting.

1-97. The alarm panel warns of an unsafe condition in the access room by causing an alarm horn and bell to sound simultaneously for fire.

1-98. PORTAL.

1-99. The portal provides access to the launch complex. At the operational bases, the portal contains a freight elevator for handling heavy equipment.

1-100. TUNNELS.

1-101. The tunnels at VAFB (figure 1-5) connect the control center with each of the three launchers. At operational bases (figure 1-4) the tunnels connect each missile launcher with the control center, power house, and antenna terminal. At VAFB the antenna terminal contains a separate tunnel system to connect the terminal room to the two antenna silos. The main tunnel system includes tunnel junctions, blast locks, and branch tunnels for each launcher, propellant terminal, and equipment terminal. The branch tunnels are connected to the main tunnel at tunnel juctions. In each missile launcher there is a liquid oxygen tunnel from the propellant terminal to the missile silo, and a utilities tunnel from the equipment terminal to the missile silo.

1-102. BLAST LOCKS. Each of the three launchers is isolated from the main tunnel system and the control center by reinforced concrete blast locks, as shown in figure 1-35. The blast locks are designed to provide continuous safety to the personnel in the tunnel system by having double blast doors leading to each launcher branch tunnel. The doors are equipped with safety devices which prevent personnel from opening both doors at the same time. At VAFB each blast lock has an overhead escape hatch at surface level. Personnel may leave the blast lock by means of an overhead ladder in the shaft of the escape hatch. Blast lock tunnels are vented to the surface with each air vent terminating in a blast valve at the surface. The blast valves close automatically when subjected to surface overpressures. Cables and utilities are routed through the locks into the branch tunnels.

1-103. Hazard warning lights located at the tunnel entrance to the missile silo, equipment terminal (Level III), propellant terminal, and blast locks indicate

T.O. 21-SM68-1
Section I

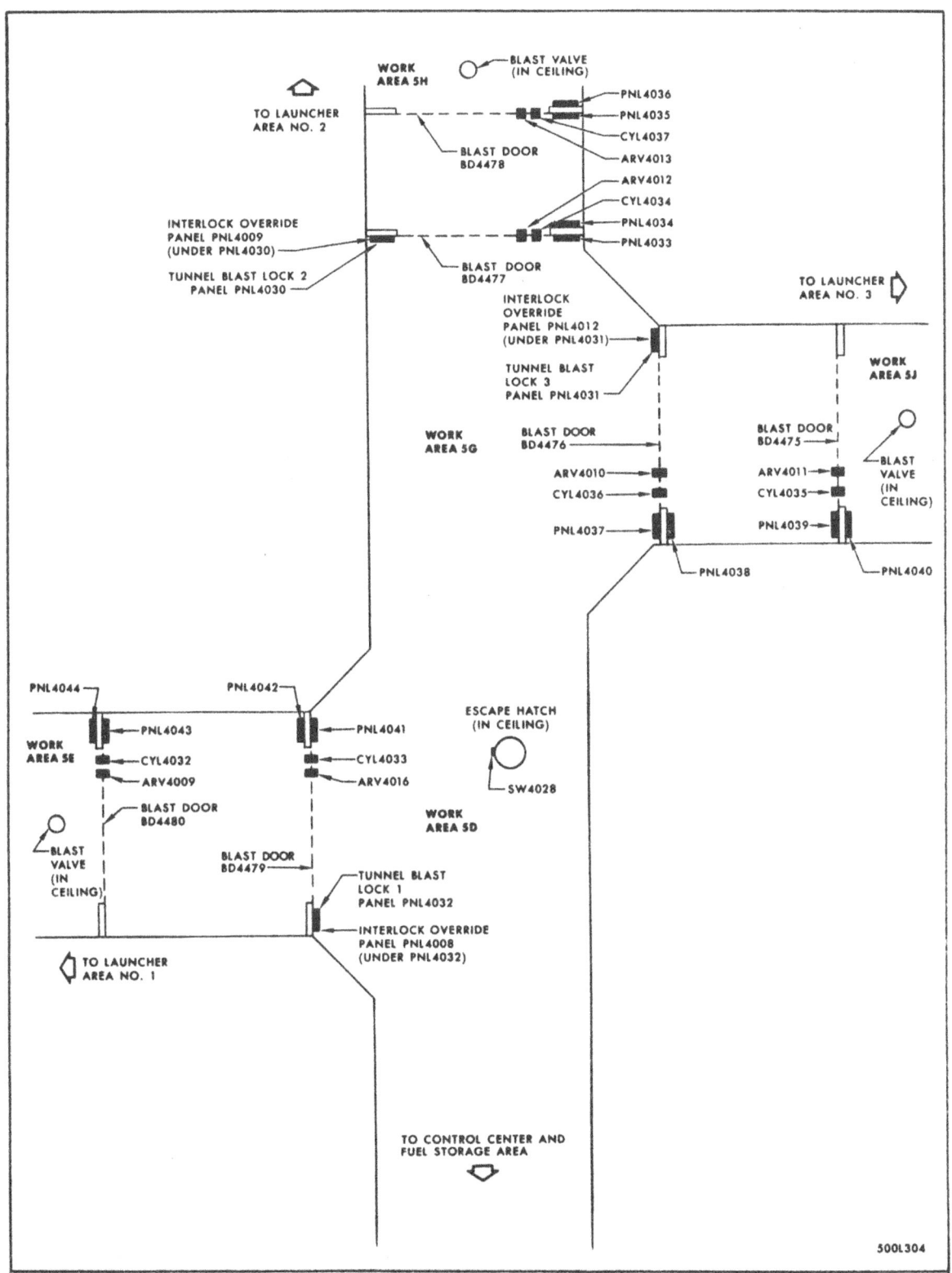

Figure 1-35. Tunnels and Blast Locks Location Diagram

conditions in those areas at all times. Red indicates a hazard, do not enter; amber (missile silo entrance only) indicates caution, permission required before entering; green indicates that normal conditions exist, access is permitted.

1-104. UTILITIES TUNNEL. The utilities tunnel located in each launcher connects the second floor of the equipment terminal to the missile silo. Missile and silo air conditioning, water, hydraulics, air, and electricity are routed through the utilities tunnel to the missile silo.

1-105. LIQUID OXYGEN TUNNEL. A liquid oxygen tunnel connects each propellant terminal to its respective missile silo. This tunnel contains the lines that supply liquid oxygen, helium, and nitrogen to the missile. Fuel lines are not routed through the liquid oxygen tunnel, but are routed to the missile silo through the missile silo branch tunnel.

1-106. LOCAL CONTROL STATIONS.

1-107. Missile installation and maintenance of the missile launcher systems and the missile are simplified by local controls operating through a logic rack. The ground level control, the tunnel entrance control, and the local pushbuttons and key switches can be used only when the power pack is in the remote operating condition.

1-108. The ground level control station (figure 1-36) is a portable console used to control the launcher platform operation from outside the missile silo during the installation or removal of a missile.

1-109. The tunnel entrance control station (figure 1-37) is used to control the silo doors, power pack, crib locks, and the launcher platform. This control station operates through a logic rack and all safety interlocks must be closed before the equipment will operate.

1-110. Local control pushbuttons are positioned about the crib structure to facilitate the operation of launcher equipment during maintenance operations. Key switches are used to operate the work platforms.

1-111. PUMP HOUSE AND SPRAY PONDS (VAFB).

1-112. The pump house and spray ponds (figure 1-38) are located adjacent to the power house and are connected to the power house by various water lines. The spray ponds serve as water reservoirs for the fire pumps and as cooling units for the diesel generators.

1-113. Water for the launch complex is piped through a 12-inch fresh water main located near the pump house. The water main supplies the domestic plumbing system and the spray ponds. The domestic water is distributed to the launch complex through the power house pump room. In the power house, makeup water from the domestic water system services the cooling system of the diesel generators, chilled water system, boilers, hot water system, blow down tank, and condensate pump.

1-114. FACILITY SYSTEMS.

1-115. The facility systems consist of various support systems located throughout the launch complex. These systems include:

  a. Facility air conditioning, heating, and ventilating system.

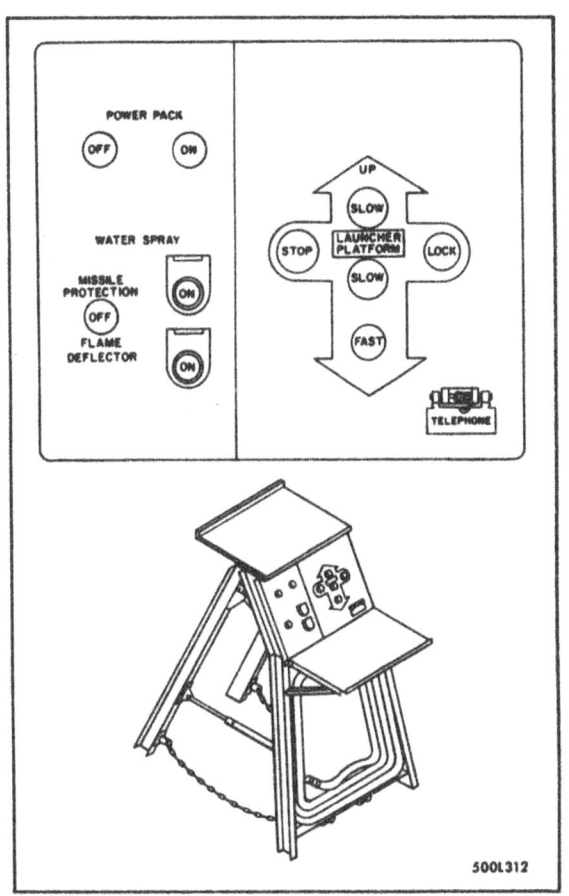

Figure 1-36. Ground Level Control Station

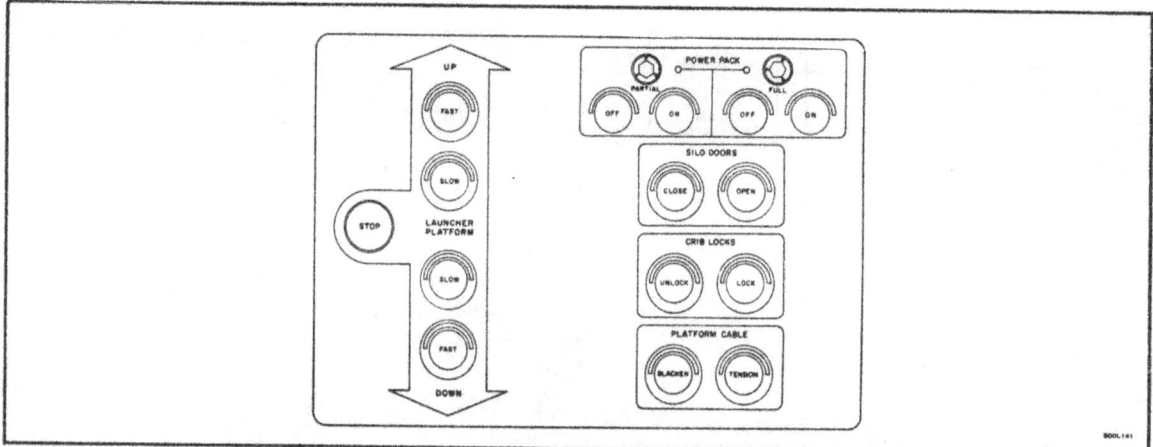

Figure 1-37. Tunnel Entrance Control Station

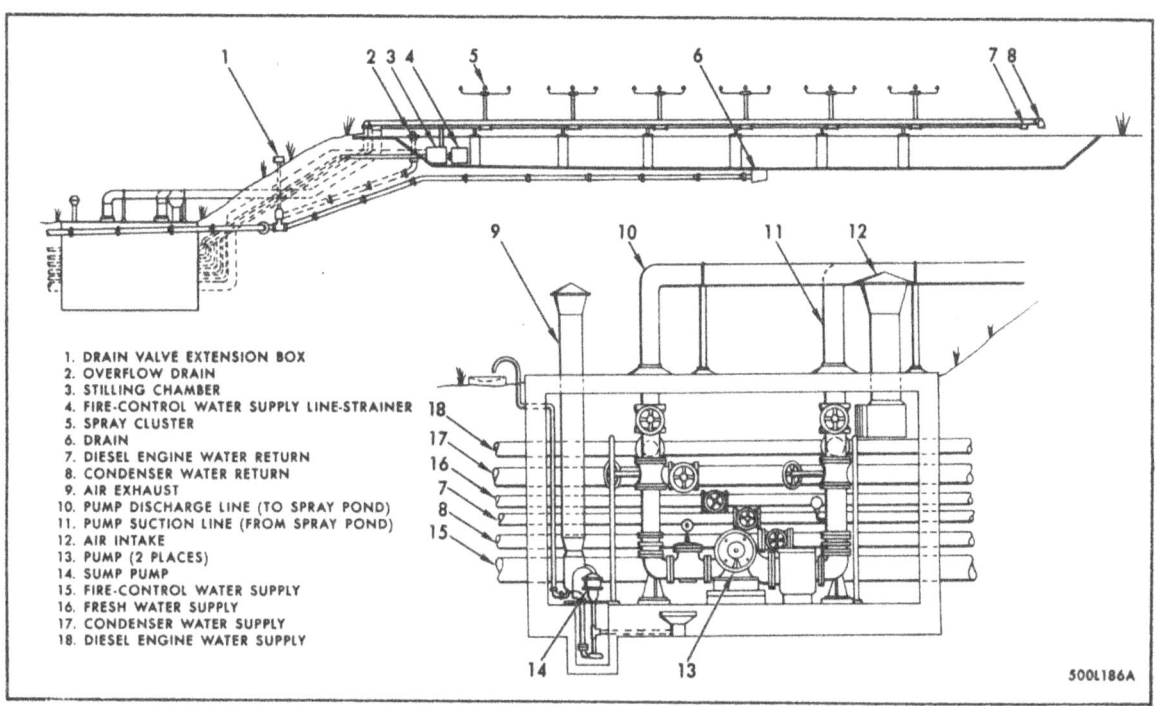

Figure 1-38. Pump House and Spray Ponds (VAFB)

b. Power generation system.

c. Power distribution system.

d. Water supply, distribution, and waste system.

e. Sensing, warning, and blast protection system.

f. Utility compressed air system.

g. Plant compressed air system.

h. Portal hydraulic system.

i. Instrument and TV camera mount elevators.

j. Antenna silo personnel elevators (operational bases only).

1-116. FACILITY AIR CONDITIONING, HEATING, AND VENTILATING SYSTEM.

1-117. The facility air conditioning, heating, and ventilating system consists of supply fans, dust collector, heat exchanger, hot water coil, circulating pump, and air compressor. The launcher air filtration facility supplies filtered and preheated air to the launcher area, fuel terminal, control center, antenna terminal and antenna silos, launcher (missile silo), equipment terminals, and propellant terminals.

1-118. EQUIPMENT TERMINAL AND MISSILE SILO AIR CONDITIONING, HEATING, AND VENTILATING SYSTEM. The equipment terminal and missile silo air conditioning, heating, and ventilating system consists of air conditioning units, exhaust fans, methylene chloride degreasing fan, transfer air fan, recirculating fan, circulating pump and an air compressor. This system controls temperature, humidity, and ventilation throughout the equipment terminals and missile silos.

1-119. PROPELLANT TERMINAL AIR CONDITIONING, HEATING, AND VENTILATING SYSTEM. The propellant terminal air conditioning, heating, and ventilating system consists of air conditioning units, circulating fans, exhaust fan, unit heater, and circulating pump. This system controls temperature, humidity, and ventilation in the propellant terminals and lox tunnel.

1-120. FUEL TERMINAL AIR CONDITIONING, HEATING, AND VENTILATING SYSTEM. The fuel terminal air conditioning, heating, and ventilating system consists of air conditioning units, circulating fans, exhaust fan, unit heater, and circulating pump. This system controls temperature, humidity, and ventilation in the fuel terminal.

1-121. CONTROL CENTER AIR CONDITIONING, HEATING, AND VENTILATING SYSTEM. The control center air conditioning, heating, and ventilating system consists of air conditioning units, centrifugal fans, exhaust fan, outside air fan, return air fan, transfer air fan, hot water circulating pump, and an air compressor. This system controls temperature, humidity, and ventilation throughout the control center.

1-122. ANTENNA TERMINAL/SILOS AIR CONDITIONING, HEATING, AND VENTILATING SYSTEM. The antenna terminal/silos air conditioning, heating, and ventilating system consists of air conditioning units, hot water circulating pumps, and an air compressor.

T.O. 21-SM68-1

Section I
Paragraphs 1-123 to 1-133

This system controls the temperature and humidity and cools the ground guidance operating equipment in the antenna terminal and antenna silos.

1-123. PORTAL AND ANTENNA SILO ENVIRONMENTAL SEAL HEATING SYSTEMS.

1-124. The three environmental seal heating systems consist of glycol circulating pumps and heat exchangers. These systems control the temperature of the ground level door seals to prevent the formation of ice. These systems are located in the portal and antenna silos.

1-125. POWER GENERATION SYSTEM.

1-126. At operational bases the power generation system supplies all of the electrical power required for the complex. This power is supplied by four diesel-driven generators located in the power house, each producing 1000 KW, 2400 V, 3-phase, 60 CPS power. The output of three generators in parallel will supply all the necessary electrical power for a missile launching. At VAFB power is generated by three diesel generators located in the power house, each producing 1000 KW, 4160 V, 3-phase, 60 CPS power.

1-127. POWER DISTRIBUTION SYSTEM.

1-128. Power is distributed at various voltages and phases throughout the complex by main switchgear feeders, unit substations, motor control centers, and lighting and power panels to individual equipment items. The 120 VDC power is provided by battery packs located throughout the complex and distributed by DC power panels and emergency lighting panels.

1-129. WATER SUPPLY, DISTRIBUTION, AND WASTE SYSTEMS.

1-130. RAW WATER SYSTEM. The raw water system supplies, stores, and distributes water to the fire water, domestic water, hot water, and chilled water systems. The raw water system normally consists of deep well pumps, raw water storage tanks, raw water pumps, and a water softener or demineralizer. Components of the raw water system are located in the power house and in tunnel junction 10.

1-131. The fire water system draws water from the raw water storage tank and distributes the raw water to fire hydrants and standpipes at ground level, and to the fog spray system, flame deflector, and engine compartment spray chamber in the missile silo for each launcher area. This system consists of a jockey pump, two fire water pumps, and the fire water distribution system and its necessary control panels. Components of the fire water system are located in the power house, tunnels and blast locks in each missile silo, and at ground level.

1-132. The treated water system distributes water to the diesel equipment. This system demineralizes and softens raw water to protect equipment.

1-133. Domestic water is provided for human consumption and use. The domestic water system consists of pressure regulating valves, chlorination system, domestic accumulator tank, domestic water pump, hydro-pneumatic tank, instantaneous water heaters, excess flow valves, pressure relief and associated valves, and piping, and indicators located throughout the launch complex.

Changed 3 January 1964 TOCN-1 (DEN-6)

1-134. Hot water is provided for personal use and for air conditioning throughout the complex. The hot water system consists of heat exchangers, hot water pumps, compression tanks, flow control valves, pressure differential controllers, and pressure differential valves. Components of the hot water system are located in the power house, tunnels and blast locks, control center, antenna terminal, launcher air filtration facilities, and propellant and equipment terminals of each complex.

1-135. Chilled water is used for air conditioning throughout the complex. The chilled water system furnishes chilled water for the heating and ventilation system, diesel engine lube oil coolers, and utility air after-cooler. This system consists of two cooling towers and/or a flash tank, water chillers, chilled water compression tank, chilled water pumps, ice banks, ice bank booster pumps, chilled and condensing water pumps, and differential pressure controller. The system can be operated either manually or automatically.

1-136. SANITARY SEWAGE SYSTEM.

1-137. A sanitary sewage system is provided to pump sewage topside to the sewage stabilization ponds. This system consists of sump pumps, controllers, injectors, and stabilization ponds. The major components are located in the control center, power house, equipment terminal, and at ground level.

1-138. NON-SANITARY WASTE SYSTEM.

1-139. Non-sanitary waste such as wash down, spillage, equipment drainage, and seepage water, is picked up by sump pumps and pumped directly to sealed chambers at ground level. The major components of this system are located in the power house, missile silo, propellant terminal, tunnels, and blast locks.

1-140. SENSING, WARNING, AND BLAST PROTECTION SYSTEMS.

1-141. Sensing and detection devices are located throughout the missile complex to detect hazardous situations and to relay such information to the control center and/or initiate automatic corrective action. Hazard indications are provided by lights, bells, and horns. Figure 1-39 lists sensing, warning, and blast protection indications for various systems throughout the complex.

1-142. UTILITY COMPRESSED AIR SYSTEM.

1-143. The utility compressed air system supplies compressed air for instrument operation and valve actuation throughout the facility systems. The major components of the utility compressed air system are located in the power house.

1-144. PLANT COMPRESSED AIR SYSTEM.

1-145. The plant compressed air supply system compresses, stores, and supplies unfiltered, undried compressed air to the pneumatic sewage ejector, utility outlets in the missile silo, propellant terminal, equipment terminal, and the filtered portion of the filtered compressed air system.

1-146. The filtered compressed air supply system supplies dry filtered air to the propellant loading system to operate control devices and valves and to the sensing, warning, and blast protection system to operate the blast valve in the propellant terminal access tunnel in sub-area 3B.

Changed 17 January 1964   TOCN-1 (DEN-8)

T.O. 21-SM68-1 Section I

HAZARD	LCFC						ET AP		FT AP				MS AP			PT AP		BLAP	CC AP		C-216			Analyzer	Reset	Bells in silo
Note: There are no bells at VAFB	Flashing red	Red	Flashing white	Amber	White	Buzzer	Red	Horn	Red	White	Horn	Bell	Red	White	Horn	Red	Horn	Red	Red	Amber	Red	White	Horn	Red		
Fire equipment terminal	X					X	X	X																	X	
Hydraulic fire C-216	X		X			X															X	X	X		X	
Fuel fire fuel terminal	X		X			X			X	X	X	X													X	
Fire missile silo	X		X			X							X	X	X	X									X	X
Gox vapor missile silo	X		X			X							X	X	X	X								X	X	
Lox sump missile silo	X		X			X							X	X												
Explosion silo (No reset at VAFB)	X					X							X		X		X	X							X	
Lox fire propellant terminal	X					X										X	X	X							X	
Gox vapor propellant terminal	X					X										X	X	X						X	X	
Lox empty		X																								
Power House emergency	X					X																			X	
Attack (Except VAFB)	X					X													X	X						
Radiation-launcher, CC, P.H. & above Gnd (Except VAFB)	X					X														X						
Battery power		X																								

Figure 1-39. Table of Sensing, Warning, and Blast Protection Systems (Sheet 1 of 2)

Changed 18 December 1963 TOCN-1 (DEN-5)

HAZARD	LCFC						ET AP		FT AP				MS AP			PT AP		BLAP	CC AP		C-216			Analyzer Reset	Bells in silo
Note: There are no bells at VAFB	Flashing red	Red	Flashing white	Amber	White	Buzzer	Red	Horn	Red	White	Horn	Bell	Red	White	Horn	Red	Horn	Red	Red	Amber	Red	White	Horn	Red	
Lox P.T. vent (Except VAFB)	Indicates "flashing red" on lox P.T. vent indicator																						
Launcher antenna #1 or #2		X																						
Oepn and blast door open		X																						
Antenna #1 or #2 open only			X																					
Blast door to antenna #1 or #2 open only		X																						
Wind above 60 MPH		X																						
Escape hatch		X																						
Auto-fog disables			X																					
Fog-on		X																						
Blast valve air intake																				X				
Hazard light	X	X	X																					
Portal doors open only			X																					
Portal doors and blast door open		X																						

Figure 1-39. Table of Sensing, Warning, and Blast Protection Systems (Sheet 2 of 2)

1-147. The plant compressed air system consists of a plant compressed air supply system and a filtered compressed air supply system. The plant compressed air supply system has components located in the equipment terminal, propellant terminal, missile silo, and adjacent personnel tunnels. The filtered compressed air supply system is located on Level I of the equipment terminal with other major components in the propellant terminal.

1-148. PORTAL HYDRAULIC SYSTEM.

1-149. The portal hydraulic system consists of a hydraulic power unit, accumulators, valve panels, hydraulic actuating cylinders, door control panels, and limit switches.

1-150. The hydraulic power unit supplies and maintains hydraulic pressure to the portal hydraulic system accumulators. The portal hydraulic system accumulators supply a working pressure to the hydraulic actuating cylinders to raise or lower the portal doors. Operation of the portal doors is controlled by the door control panels and the limit switches. The flow of hydraulic fluid in the system is controlled at the valve panels.

1-151. INSTRUMENT AND TV CAMERA MOUNT ELEVATORS.

1-152. The instrument and TV camera mount elevators are hydropneumatically operated by compressed air from the utility compressed air system. The major components are located in the portal work area. Controls are located in the control center and consist of an accumulator, filter, pressure reducing valves, solenoid operated valves, pneumatic operating cylinders, spring latches, and gate valves necessary to operate the system.

1-153. ANTENNA SILO PERSONNEL ELEVATORS. (Operational bases)

1-154. Antenna silo personnel elevators consist of two separate elevator systems. Each elevator is individually operated by a drive unit, governor, controller, and roller guides. The elevators provide a rapid means of transporting personnel and small items of equipment from the base of the antenna silos to the equipment level of the antenna elevator and to the upper catwalk of the antenna.

1-155. SUBSYSTEMS.

1-156. The missile subsystems (figure 1-40) consist of aerospace operating equipment (AOE), aerospace ground equipment (AGE) and airborne equipment. The AOE and airborne equipment contain all equipment required to launch a missile including rocket engine system, propellant system, electrical system, hydraulic system, air conditioning system, flight control system, guidance system, launch sequencer, launch control system, control center circuits, instrumentation and range safety systems (VAFB only), and re-entry vehicle system. This equipment is utilized to monitor status and checkout of the subsystems.

1-157. The AGE is utilized during missile handling, repair, adjustment, and calibration of missile systems and components.

1-158. GUIDANCE SYSTEM.

1-159. The guidance system (figure 1-41) of the SM68 missile weapon system is comprised of ground equipment that contains ground-based radar (missile guidance set

SYSTEM	COMPONENTS	FUNCTION
Rocket engine system	Stage I booster engine, Stage II sustainer engine, and engine control system.	Boosts the complete missile to stage separation altitude, and sustains Stage II flight to re-entry vehicle separation.
Propellant system	Stage I and Stage II propellant equipment and PLPS.	Supplies fuel and liquid oxygen to the rocket engines during flight.
Hydraulic system	Stage I and Stage II hydraulic equipment and hydraulic pump unit.	Supplies hydraulic power to the missile.
Missile air conditioning system	Air conditioning ducting.	Supplies conditioned air to the missile.
Electrical system	Distribution circuits, accessory power supply, and Stage II hydraulic pump batteries.	Provides electrical power for the missile.
Flight control system	Movement sensing devices, amplifiers, hydraulic actuators, and control assemblies.	Maintains the missile on its proper flight path and accepts control signals from the guidance system.
Guidance system	Ground guidance station, airborne receiving equipment, and GMTS.	Guides the missile on an exact trajectory that will enable the re-entry vehicle to hit the target area.
Instrumentation and range safety system (VAFB)	Airborne data sensing transmitting devices, airborne command destruct components, and ground receiving and transmitting stations.	Gathers missile flight data and, in an emergency, ruptures the propellant tanks to terminate powered flight.
Re-entry vehicle	Ablative structure, payload, and RVS.	Contains and protects the payload during re-entry into the earth's atmosphere.
Launch sequencer	Launch sequential timer, two launch sequence controller assemblies, and a filter assembly.	Sequences and monitors related systems during countdown operations.
Missile launcher system	Crib structure and suspension, launcher platform, criblocks, silo doors, and operating hydraulic system.	Provides structural support for the missile, positions missile for launch and protects personnel and components from nuclear attack.
Control center circuits	Launcher assemblies for each launcher, common assembly, and hazard warning assembly.	Distributes signals between the control center and other parts of the complex.

Figure 1-40. Table of Missile Subsystems

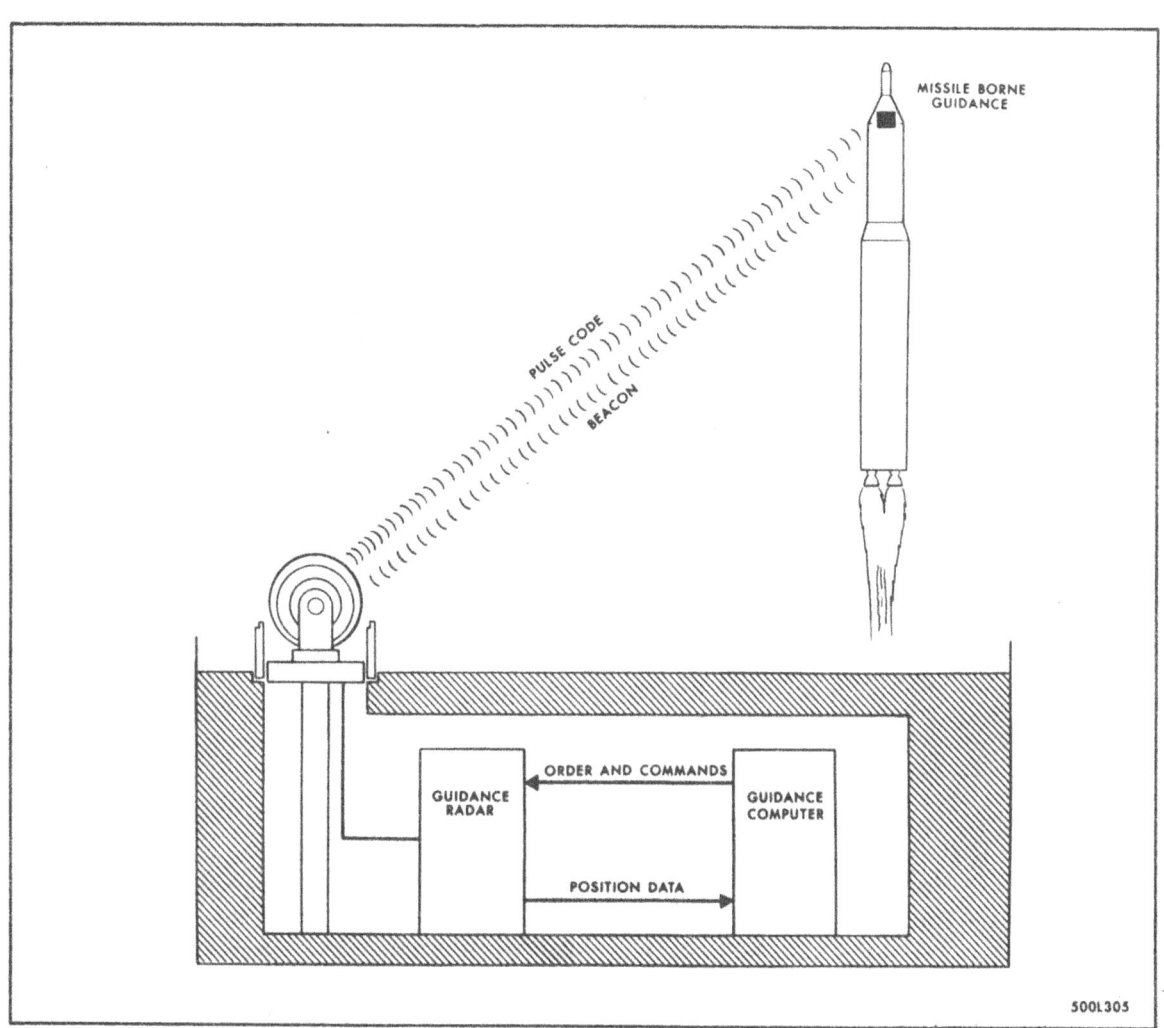

Figure 1-41. Guidance System

AN/GRW-5) and a computer (missile guidance computer set AN/GSK-1), missileborne equipment (missile guidance set AN/DRW-18, AN/DRW-19, AN/DRW-20, AN/DRW-21, or AN/DRW-22), and miscellaneous equipment. The guidance system controls the missile during the guidance phase of flight in order to project the re-entry vehicle to the selected target. The guidance system continuously determines the precise missile position and from this data determines missile velocities in three coordinates. Position and velocity data are compared to predetermined information stored in the ground equipment, and coded steering orders based upon this comparison are continuously issued to correct missile attitude. Commands to accomplish non-steering functions are issued as programmed by the computer. Steering orders and commands are transmitted by the ground-based radar, in the form of coded signals, to the airborne equipment. The airborne equipment decodes the signals and transmits a beacon signal to the ground-based radar for use in tracking.

1-160. GROUND EQUIPMENT. The ground equipment for the guidance system is located in the control center, antenna terminal, and antenna silos.

1-161. The control center operations room (figure 1-22) contains most of missile guidance set AN/GRW-5 and all of missile guidance computer set AN/GSK-1. The equipment is housed in air conditioned cabinets. Excessively high temperatures within the cabinets are thermostatically detected by an over-temperature alarm. Figure 1-42 lists the operations room equipment functions.

1-162. The power conversion equipment for the missile guidance set and missile guidance computer set is located in the electrical equipment room of the control center (figure 1-43). The equipment supplies 3-phase, 120 V 400 CPS power to the ground guidance radar equipment. An additional power plant is used to supply the 3-phase, 208 V 420 CPS power to the computer equipment.

1-163. Operational and checkout equipment associated with the antennas is located in the antenna terminal. (See figure 1-44.) Control equipment for the antenna elevators is also located in the antenna terminal. Construction of the antenna terminal is similar to that of the operations room, permitting interconnecting cables and air conditioning ducts to be routed beneath a false floor. Figure 1-45 lists antenna terminal equipment and functions of the equipment.

1-164. The antenna silo (figure 1-46) contains two antennas (primary and alternate back-up) and associated equipment. Figure 1-47 lists antenna silo equipment and functions of the equipment. The antennas are emplaced so that either one can guide any of three missiles in the complex. Each antenna and maintenance platform for the missile guidance set is mounted on an elevator in a silo-lift enclosure similar to that used for the missile. This affords protection against nuclear attack for the entire antenna assembly. To protect the antenna from shock effects while in the hardened condition, the entire assembly is nested in a crib suspended by shock mounts from the silo wall. Concrete doors over the antenna silo provide overpressure and radiation protection. The operating antenna is elevated during the final phase of countdown and throughout the guidance portion of missile flight. Precise orientation of the elevated antenna is provided by locking the elevator platform rigidly with respect to the silo.

1-165. MISSILEBORNE EQUIPMENT. The missile guidance set (figure 1-48) consists of a radio transmitter, a coordinate data receiver, a command signals decoder, a waveguide group, a dorsal antenna, and a ventral antenna. The missile guidance set is mounted below the re-entry vehicle in Stage II and is accessible through access

(Text continued on page 1-76.)

EQUIPMENT	FUNCTION
Missile guidance system exercise set AN/GRM-40	Simulates a missile on a reference trajectory during checkout and countdown. It consists of three cabinets containing circuitry for distribution of power throughout the exercise set, generation of typical in-flight signals, and conversion of these signals for input to the radar equipment.
Signal data recorder RO-146/GRW-5	Records system functions during checkout or guidance operation for later study and evaluation.
Power switchboard SB-1168/GRW-5	Controls and routes 3-phase, 120 V 400 CPS power from the electric power plant to ground radar equipment.
Power supply set OA-2898/GRW-5	Supplies regulated DC power to radar equipment in the operations room.
Command signals decoder KY-344A/GRW-5	Monitors and decodes radar transmitter signals and supplies the decoded orders and commands to the signal data recorder and guidance exerciser.
Reference signal generator TD-409A/GRW-5	Supplies timing signals for radar and computer equipment.
Signal data converter CV-967C/GRW-5	Processes azimuth, elevation, and range data for the computer and changes computer orders and commands into pulse code groups which serve as the radar trigger.
Range computer CP-560A/GRW-5	Generates missile range data in binary form for the computer and center tracking gates, in time, about the missile return signal.
Antenna control C-3360C/GRW-5	Generates antenna positioning signals that keep the feedhorns of the antenna-receiver-transmitter group positioned on the missile.
Receiver group OA-3034B/GRW-5	Covers azimuth and elevation IF signals into DC error signals for the antenna control, and converts the sum IF signal into range video signals for the missile guidance console and the range computer.

Figure 1-42. Control Center Operations Room Equipment Functions (Sheet 1 of 3)

EQUIPMENT	FUNCTION
Antenna position programmer C-3362B/GRW-5	Provides preset antenna position signal to enable the antenna-receiver-transmitter group to slew to the above-ground missile launch positions and designated test positions.
Missile guidance console OA-3101G/GRW-5 or OA-2897G/GRW-5	Controls and monitors guidance operation during countdown and missile flight.
Digital data printer RO-144/GSK-1	Supplies a printed record of computer calculated results for reference or maintenance purposes.
Signal data recorder group OA-2660/GSH-4(VAFB)	Records magnetically, computer equipment operation for postflight evaluation, and presents a readout (on paper tape) of computer instructions for verification.
Computer set console OA-2654/GSK-1	Operates and controls the computer during checkout maintenance and the loading and verification of computer programs.
Simulator-verifier SM-203/GSK-1	Generates programmed signals approximately equivalent to an in-flight missile, used for computer checkout.
Signal data reproducer group OA-2658/GSK-1	Converts computer instructions, which are inserted on punched paper tape, into electrical impulses for magnetic drum storage.
Power distribution group OA-2655/GSK-1	Rectifies AC power into DC power for computer equipment.
Power supply group OA-2656/GSK-1	Controls and routes 208 V 420 CPS power for the electric power plant to computer equipment.
Data storage magnetic drum MU-422/GSK-1	Stores computer information and instructions in the form of magnetized areas on the surface of a cylinder.
Data input processor-verifier CM-166/GSK-1	Controls functions of the perforated tape photoelectric reader assembly.
Recording set control C-3206/GSH-4(VAFB)	Processes and routes data used by the magnetic and perforated tape recorder assembly.

Figure 1-42. Control Center Operations Room Equipment Functions (Sheet 2 of 3)

EQUIPMENT	FUNCTION
Computer control C-3205/GSK-1	Controls the computations and routing of computer data as instructed by the magnetic drum control.
Core memory unit MU-423/GSK-1	Stores computer information in small magnetic cores; used by the computer arithmetic unit as a scratch pad.
Computer arithmetic unit CP-539/GSK-1	Performs the computations for the computer.
Digital to digital converter CV-929/GSK-1	Stores and routes all input for computer equipment; also stores and routes steering orders and discrete commands of the computer for the radar equipment.

Figure 1-42. Control Center Operations Room Equipment Functions (Sheet 3 of 3)

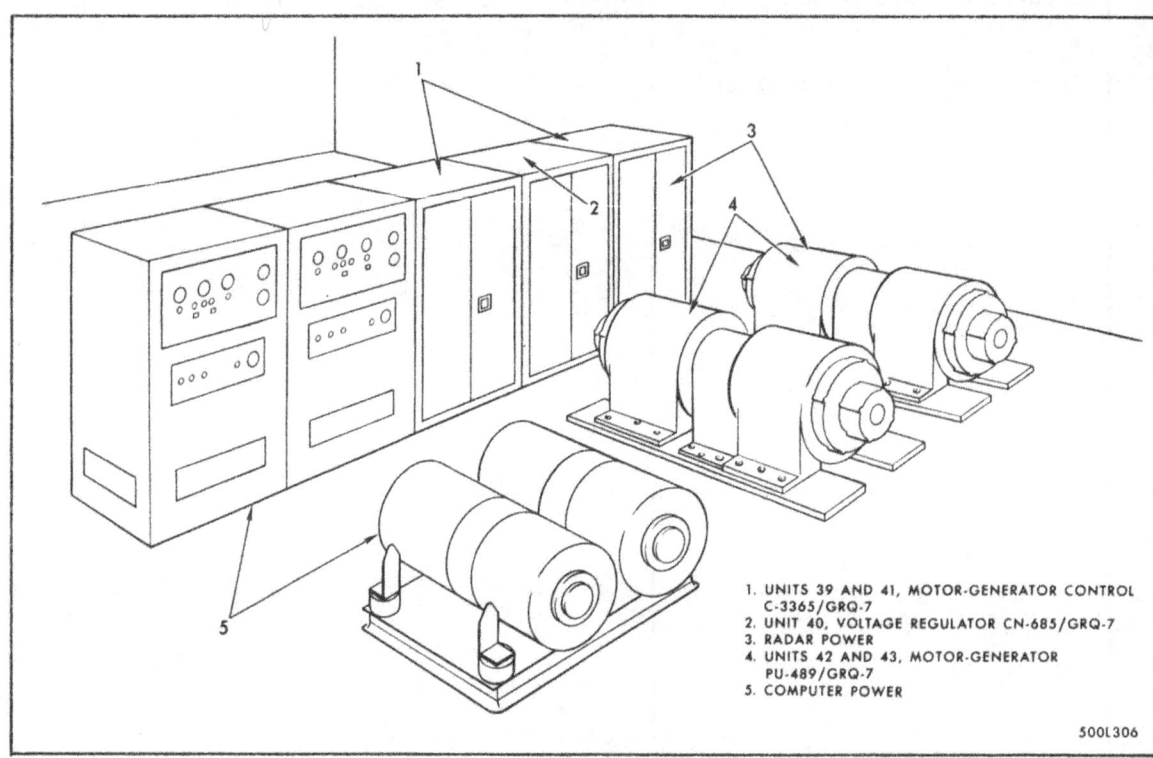

Figure 1-43. Control Center Electrical Equipment Room, Radar Equipment

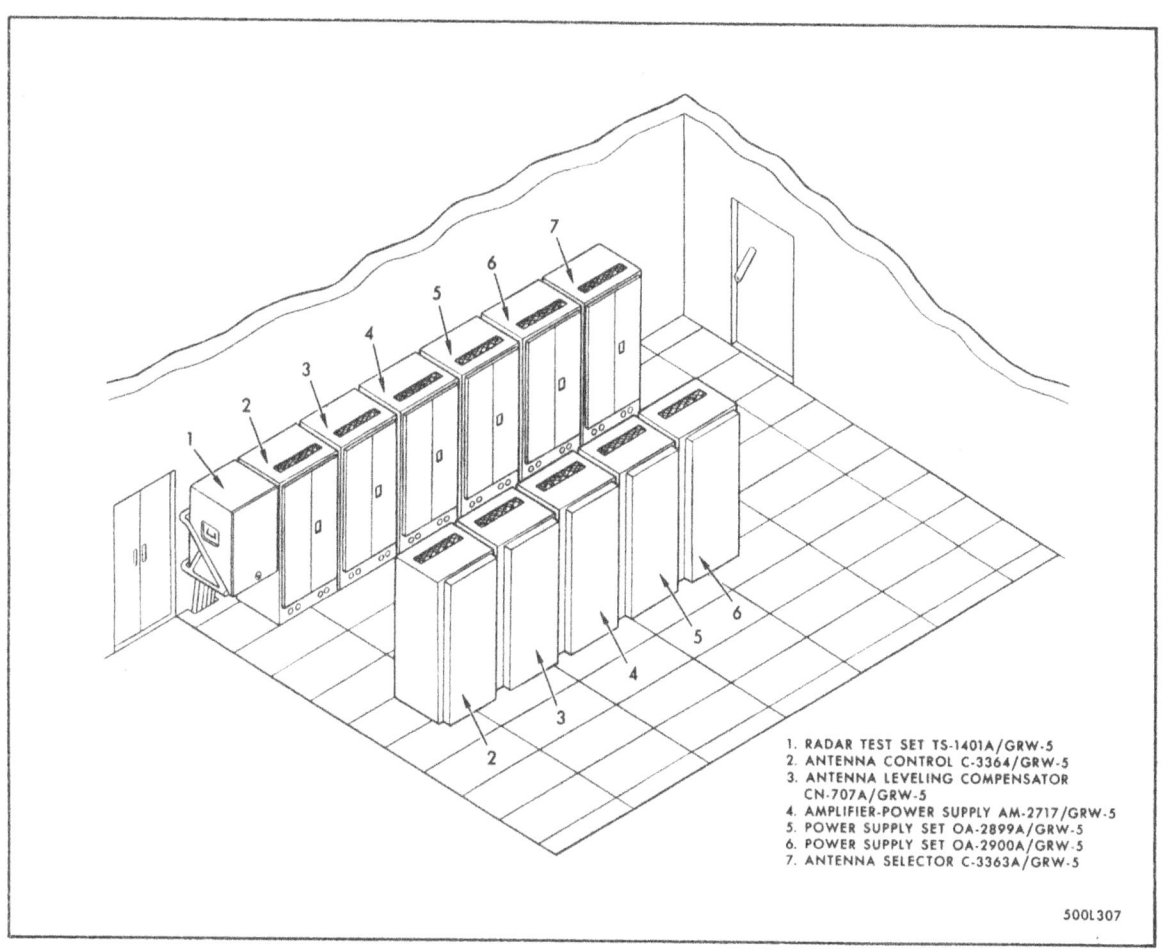

Figure 1-44. Antenna Terminal Equipment Location

EQUIPMENT	FUNCTION
Antenna selector C-3363A/GRW-5	Couples signals from the operations room to the appropriate antenna terminal and antenna silo equipment, and indicates operation, standby, or maintenance of the antenna silo.
Power supply set OA-2899A/GRW-5 and OA-2900A/GRW-5	Supplies AC and DC power to antenna terminal equipment.
Amplifier-power supply AM-2717/GRW-5	Amplifies servo drive signals for the antenna positioning circuits and supplies high voltage to the antenna-receiver-transmitter group.
Antenna leveling compensator CN-707A/GRW-5	Senses antenna tilt error in the event of a nuclear blast.
Antenna control C-3364/GRW-5	Controls, locally and remotely, the raising and lowering of the antenna-receiver-transmitter group.
Radar test set TS-1401A/GRW-5	Performs system tests while the antenna is lowered.

Figure 1-45. Antenna Terminal Equipment Functions

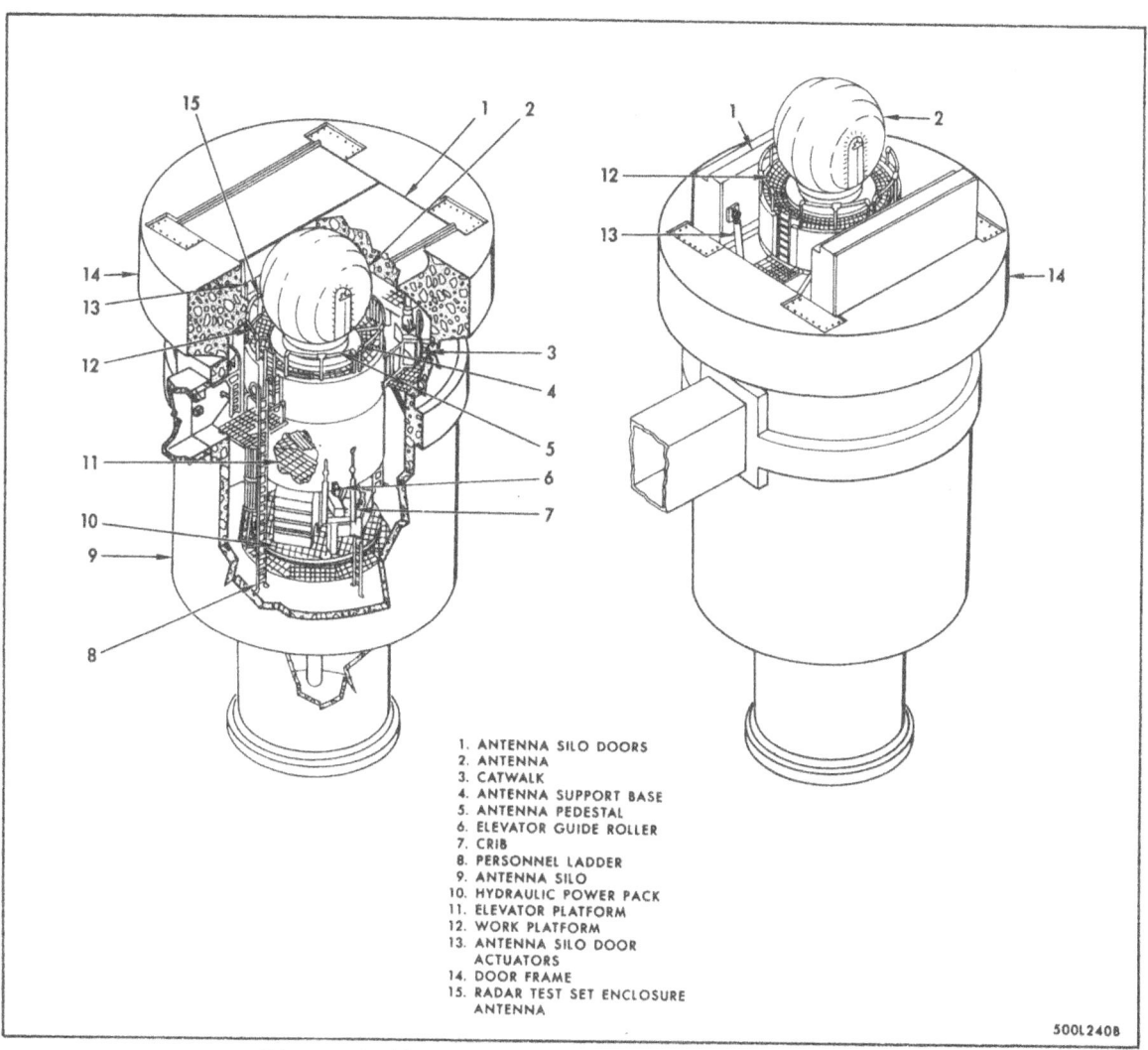

Figure 1-46. Antenna Silo Equipment Location

EQUIPMENT	FUNCTION
Lid assembly	Protects antenna silo equipment when the silo is in the lower (hard) position. It consists of the silo doors, the hydraulic antenna silo door actuators, and the door foundation.
Missile tracking antenna-receiver-transmitter group OA-2896A/GRW-5	Radiates RF guidance signals to the missile guidance set and receives RF tracking pulses. Receiving and transmitting equipment for the antenna is housed immediately behind the antenna feedhorns and reflector. The antenna is covered with an inflated cloth radome.
Catwalk	Allows passage around the interior of the antenna silo.
Antenna support base	In conjunction with the antenna pedestal, the antenna support base supports the antenna.
Antenna pedestal	In conjunction with the antenna support base, the antenna pedestal supports the antenna.
Crib	Supports the elevator assembly. Mechanical crib suspension springs act as shock absorbers for the elevator assembly. Elevator guide rollers are used to center the crib within the silo.
Elevator guide roller	Maintain the elevator within its crib.
Personnel ladder	Provides personnel access between work levels in the antenna silo.
Antenna silo	Houses the antenna and provides the necessary protection from static overpressures and nuclear radiation.
Power pack	Supplies hydraulic pressure for the antenna silo door actuators, the crib positioners, and the elevator platform.
Elevator assembly	To raise the antenna and its receiving and transmitting equipment (antenna-receiver-transmitter group) to the above-ground (soft) position. It is supported by the crib and consists of a hydraulic elevator, which raises the assembly, an elevator platform, and a work platform.

Figure 1-47. Antenna Silo Equipment Functions (Sheet 1 of 2)

EQUIPMENT	FUNCTION
Radar test set enclosure antenna	In conjunction with radar test set TS-1401A/GRW-5 used to check system operation in the "hard" condition.

Figure 1-47. Antenna Silo Equipment Functions (Sheet 2 of 2)

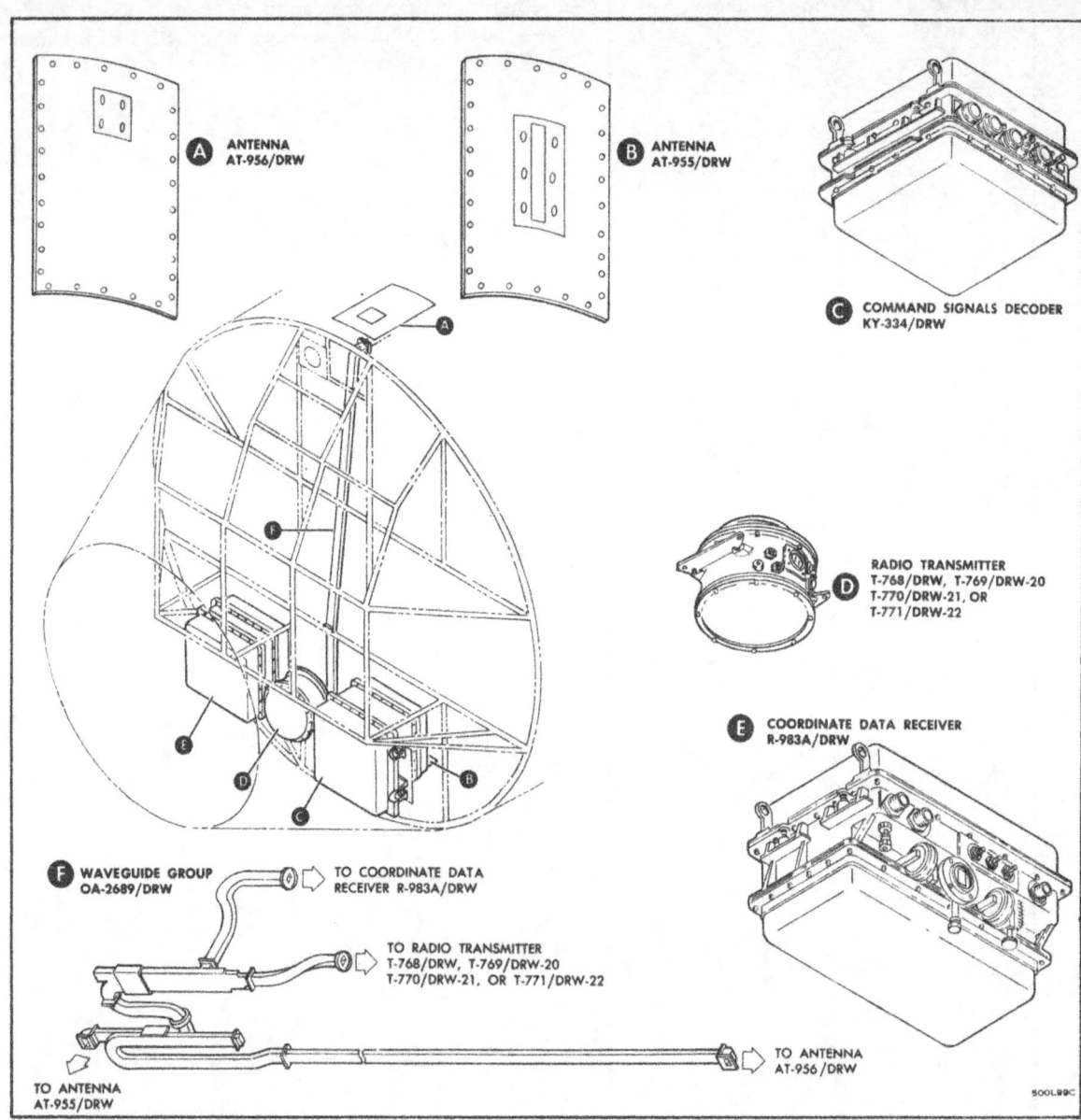

Figure 1-48. Missile Guidance Set

T.O. 21-SM68-1

Section I
Paragraphs 1-166 to 1-171

(Text continued from page 1-65.)
panels on the missile. The two antennas are mounted opposite each other on the missile skin and are connected to the radio transmitter and coordinate data receiver by the waveguide group. Power and signal cables interconnect the command signals decoder with the receiver and transmitter. Figure 1-49 lists missile guidance set equipment and functions of the equipment.

1-166. MISCELLANEOUS EQUIPMENT. The miscellaneous equipment of the guidance system consists of the antenna-mast group OA-2903A/GRW-5 or collimation antenna-mast group GS-58128, and a target assembly (orientation) GS-58156L1, L3 or optical camera-telescope target RR-101/GRW-5. These units are located on the surface of the launch complex.

1-167. The antenna-mast group (figure 1-50), located at each launch complex, is a soft test mast used to test and align the radar equipment and to boresight the antenna-receiver-transmitter group. The mast is 60 feet high and contains two feed horns, test flags, and a radar RF test set. Lamps mounted at the top of the mast are used to light the antenna-mast group during night testing operations.

1-168. The target assembly (orientation) or optical camera-telescope target (figure 1-51) is mounted on two cement pillars. An access platform is built around each of the pillars. The target is used to test and align the orientation and position of the radar antenna, using the antenna-mounted telescope and television camera. Three targets may be mounted: the optical azimuth (telescope) target, television camera target, and motion picture camera target. Only the telescope and television targets are normally installed. Floodlights, mounted on the pillars, are used to light the television target during night operations.

1-169. GROUND EQUIPMENT SYSTEM FUNCTIONS. System operation is divided into five phases: prelaunch, launch (countdown), Stage I guidance, Stage II guidance, and post launch. The phases cover the mission of the system beginning with the initial programming of the computer equipment and ending with the analysis of system performance.

1-170. During the prelaunch phase of system operation, periodic performance checks of the ground guidance equipment and missile guidance set are performed. A prepared program of instructions for solving the guidance equations and specific constants which differentiate one target from another are stored in the computer's memory sections. These instructions, once stored, remain in the computer until the complex target assignments or the ballistic equations are changed. During this period, numerical quantities representing systematic corrections for variables such as range, azimuth, and elevation reference, in addition to the latest index of refraction, are stored in the computer by means of electrically operated switches on the missile guidance console OA-3101G/GRW-5 or OA-2897G/GRW-5. These constants, with the exception of index of refraction, are checked periodically with the aid of computer programs and changed as required.

1-171. When an order to launch is received, preparation to fire a missile is started. Operation of the ground guidance system is keyed to match the missile countdown and to include the necessary functions required to prepare the guidance system for successful guidance. Countdown of the guidance system is subdivided into five phases: Start countdown, raise antenna, missile ready, lift-off, and end of guidance. The guidance electronics officer (GEO) positioned at the missile guidance console initiates the functions required for each phase in response to the information received from the launch control system. Completion of each phase is a

EQUIPMENT	FUNCTION
Coordinate data receiver R-983A/DRW	Receives the RF guidance signals transmitted by the guidance radar and inspects the codes for specified missile address.
Radio transmitter T-768/DRW, T-769/DRW-20, T-770/DRW-21, or T-771/DRW-22	Transmits the RF pulse used by the guidance radar for tracking.
Waveguide group OA-2689A/DRW	Routes RF guidance signals from the antennas to coordinate data receiver and routes RF tracking pulses from radio transmitter to the antennas.
Antenna AT-955/DRW or AT-955A/DRW and AT-956/DRW or AT-956A/DRW	Receives RF guidance signals and radiates RF tracking signals.
Command signal decoder KY-334/DRW	Decodes the orders and commands from the guidance signal and routes them to the applicable missile systems.
Band pass filter F-440/DRW-18, F-441/DRW-19, F-442/DRW-20, F-443/DRW-21, or F-444/DRW-22	Passes assigned frequency to coordinate data receiver.

Figure 1-49. Missile Guidance Set Equipment Functions

T.O. 21-SM68-1

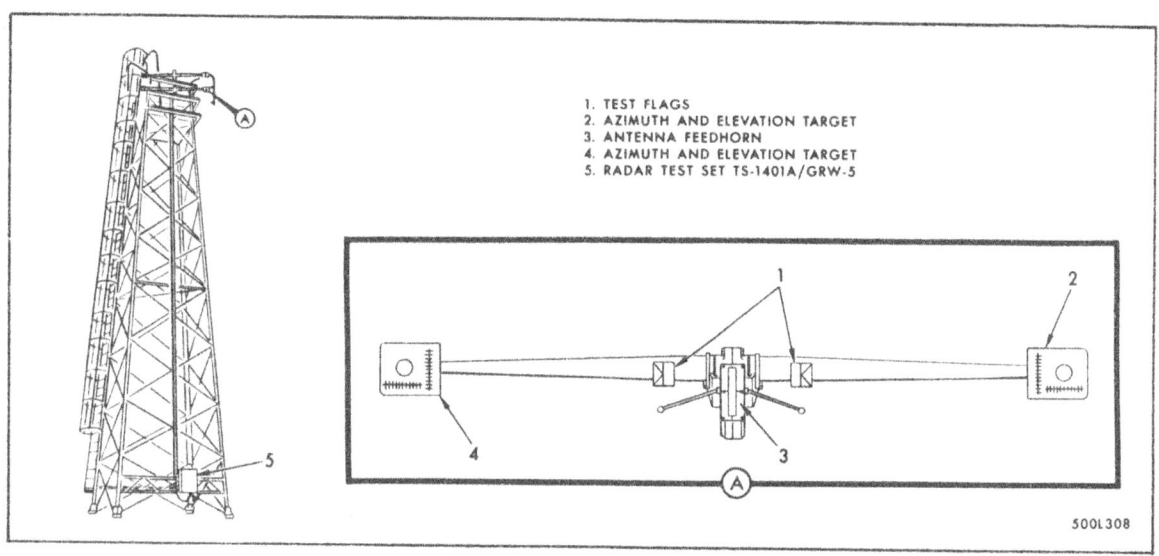

Figure 1-50. Antenna-Mast Group OA-2903A/GRW-5 or Collimation Antenna-Mast Group (GS-58128)

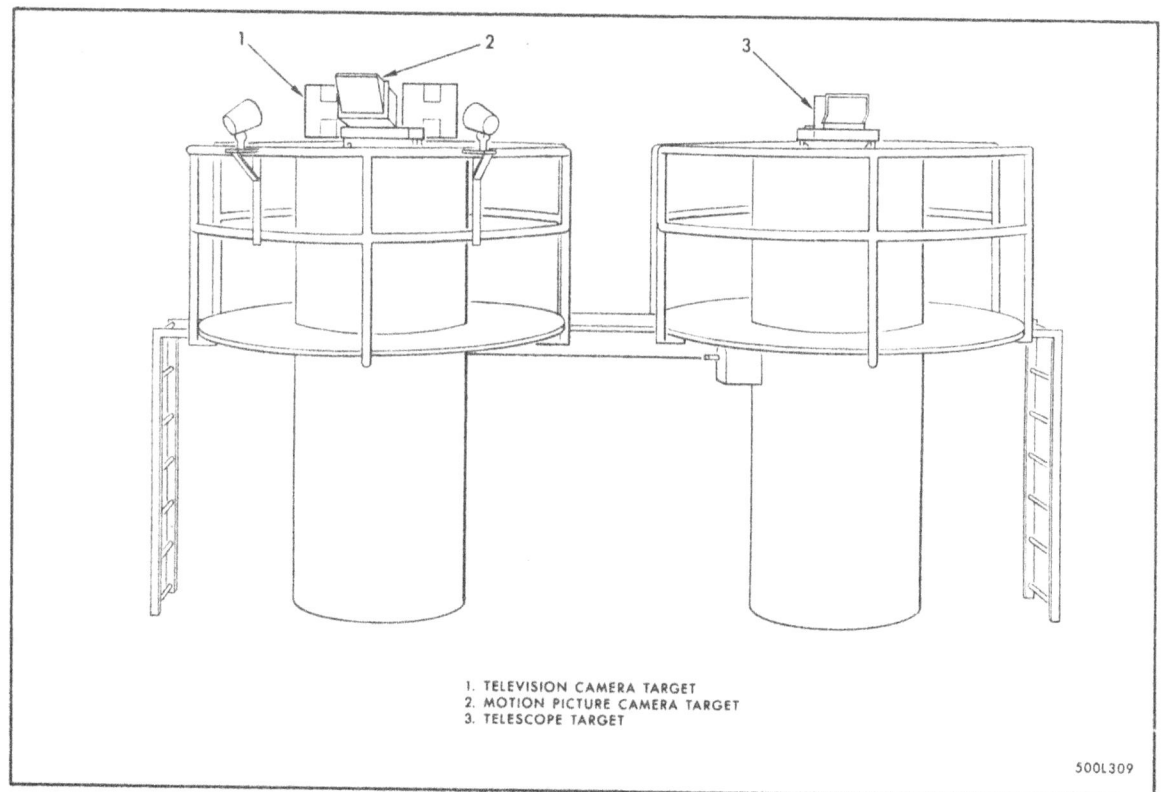

Figure 1-51. Optical Camera-Telescope Target RR-101/GRW-5

prerequisite to initiation of the next phase. The orderly progression of the countdown includes the procedures required to confidence-check the guidance system. These procedures include: Applying all ground guidance equipment power, performing a simulated guidance system exercise, raising the antenna, and acquiring the designated missile in its above-ground launch position. During this period, power to the missile guidance set is monitored with the guided missile test set AN/DRM-58(V) located in the equipment terminal. During the last few seconds of countdown, a combined guidance system/flight control system loop test is conducted to verify proper system performance. Emergency procedures, if required, can be initiated at the missile guidance console. If at any time the emergency procedures do not clear the fault in the ground guidance system, and countdown cannot be restored, the GEO advises the missile launch officer (MLO) to request handover.

1-172. A combined systems exercise (CSE) is an integrated weapon system operation wherein a missile and guidance system are counted down in an exercise mode. The CSE countdowns are identical to an actual launch as far as the MLO and GEO are concerned. Accidental use of a CSE program in the computer during a normal countdown is prevented by safeguards within the CSE program which will cause a GGS hold and prevent launching of a missile.

1-173. Handover is a mode of operation that retains within a squadron the capability of launching and guiding missiles of a complex which has lost the use of its guidance system. Handover is accomplished by using the guidance system of a complex which has completed its own countdowns to guide the missile of the complex requiring assistance.

1-174. The possible combinations of launchers and guidance system that can be used for handover, within the restrictions of the intervening terrain and targets, are specified in the handover target kit identification sheet which is parts of the targeting package.

1-175. The mechanics of operation consist of opening the interface signals between the launch control system and the ground guidance system of the two complexes involved by placing the appropriate systems in the handover mode and verifying the prerequisites of the handover launch countdown. Verbal communications are then used for pacing the launch control system and ground guidance system countdown. Only one function, lift-off, is electrically transmitted over the communications link. Electrically transmitting the lift-off signal over the communications link is necessitated by the guidance requirement for counting time to accurately generate acquisition and roll order functions during early stages of flight.

1-176. After the complete missile inventory has been fired and guidance completed, an analysis and interpretation is made of information recorded by signal data recorder RO-146/GRW-5 and digital data printer RO-144/GSK-1. Functions recorded by these units are, in general, initiated in other sections of the guidance system. The information recorded is used to analyze the quantitative and qualitative performances of the guidance system.

1-177. Ground control of the missile originates in a digital guidance computer that utilizes 23-bit input words from the guidance radar. The data contained in these binary words are the range, azimuth, and elevation positions of the missile as determined by the radar. Additional data required by the computer is the position of the target and various meteorological constants. This data is fed into the computer prior to launch. Using this information, the computer solves the ballistic flight problem and subsequently determines the corrections which will maintain the missile on an effective trajectory.

T.O. 21-SM68-1

Section I
Paragraphs 1-178 to 1-183

1-178. The antenna-maintenance key is used to afford proper operational control of the antenna and to insure the safety of personnel. The keys are normally in the ANTENNA A and ANTENNA B key switches located on the rear of the missile guidance console. The two keys issued for use in a given complex are different for each antenna. The key switches are located as follows: on the rear of the missile guidance console; in the elevator control cabinet in the antenna terminal; on the control box at the entrance to the silo; and on the handrail of the antenna work platform.

1-179. Each key switch at the missile guidance console has two positions, identified MAINT and STBY. The key cannot be removed from the switch unless it is in the MAINT position. Removal of the key from the missile guidance console will cause the respective ANTENNA A FACILITY - MAINT or ANTENNA B FACILITY - MAINT indicator to light yellow. Turning the key to STBY position will restore the indicator to green. When the selected antenna is in a maintenance status, the ANTENNA A or B FACILITY - MAINT, and MAINT pushbutton indicator on the front panel of the missile guidance console will be lighted yellow. After maintenance has been completed, the key is inserted (if it has been removed), then turned to the STBY position. The STBY pushbutton indicator on the front panel of the missile guidance console is pressed to complete the change of status from maintenance to standby. The ANTENNA A or B FACILITY - MAINT indicator, and MAINT pushbutton indicator will now be lighted green.

1-180. When the antenna system is in a maintenance status the antenna cannot be raised by signals originated at the missile guidance console. In order to operate the antenna in the maintenance status, the key is inserted in the key switch located on the antenna control C-3364/GRW-5 at the entrance of the silo and turned to the desired position (OFF REMOVE KEY or ON-OPERATE AUTOMATIC). When personnel working on the antenna maintenance platform desire to raise or lower the elevator, the key is inserted in the control box (OFF position) and is turned to the OPERATE position. The key should be retained by personnel when working in the antenna silo to prevent movement of the antenna without their knowledge. The key can be removed from a key switch located in the antenna area only when the key switch is in the OFF position.

1-181. The computer set console may be operated only when the computer set is in the maintenance or hold maintenance condition.

1-182. MISSILEBORNE EQUIPMENT SYSTEM FUNCTIONS. The missile guidance set completes a link between the ground guidance equipment and the missile control devices. During flight operation, the missile guidance set receives RF guidance signals from the ground guidance station to provide the missile with commands and steering orders. The missile guidance set sends an RF beacon signal to the ground guidance station to indicate the position of the missile and to acknowledge acceptance and decoding of the RF guidance signal. Steering orders are issued by ground guidance to correct the missile course. Commands to accomplish non-steering functions are issued as programmed by the guidance computer. Both steering orders and commands are transmitted in the form of coded signals to the guidance set in the missile. The missile guidance set receives and decodes the signals, passes them on to the applicable missile system, and transmits a beacon signal to the ground based radar for use in tracking.

1-183. THEORY OF OPERATION. Tracking of the missile is accomplished by transmitting a coded signal over the ground-to-missile data link. As each signal is decoded, the missile guidance set transmits an RF signal (tracking pulse) from the radar transmitting units (figure 1-52) to the ground radar. The beacon system is

1-80

T.O. 21-SM68-1

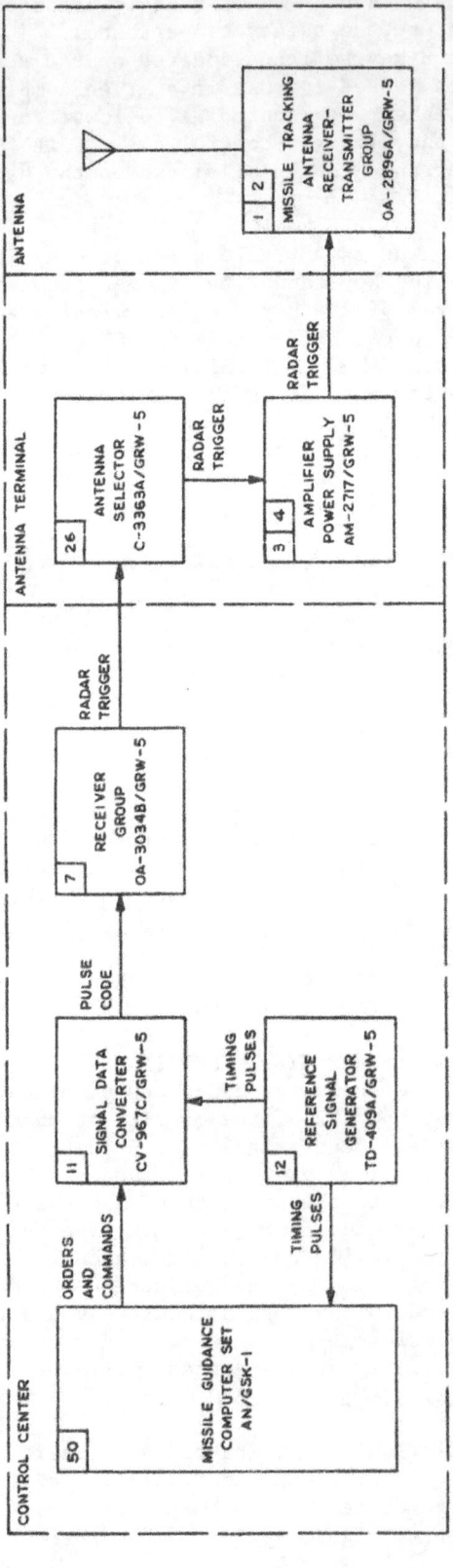

Figure 1-52. Radar Transmitting Units, Block Diagram

1-81

used in preference to an echo system to increase the tracking range and insure strong return signals from the missile. As the computer-generated steering orders and commands are issued, the ground guidance radar encodes this information. On receipt of the signal, the missile guidance set converts the coded signal into the steering orders (figure 1-53) and commands that actuate the missile flight control system. A stable reference along the pitch and yaw axis is provided by reference gyros in the flight control system. The steering orders from the missile guidance set are applied to the pitch and yaw gyros to adjust their reference axes. Deviations (error correction signals) from the established reference cause the thrust chambers of the missile rocket engines to gimbal to correct the missile attitude. Commands decoded by the missile guidance set complete the circuit in the flight control system corresponding to the particular command.

1-184. RF pulses from the missile guidance set are received by the missile tracking antenna-receiver group OA-2896A/GRW-5. The antenna is movable in azimuth and elevation and is kept locked on the missile by antenna positioning signals. The antenna contains four feedhorns, identified as A, B, C, and D which are mounted in a modified Cassegrainian reflector (figure 1-54). With each pulse received, azimuth and elevation information is determined by comparing the sum and difference of the energy received at the feedhorns. Range information is derived from the receiver sum signal compared with time.

1-185. The azimuth position of the missile is determined by the amount of energy received at horns AB in relation to horns CD, and antenna elevation position by the amount of energy received at horns AC in relation to horns BD. This energy difference is detected and converted to an IF signal by the receiver portion of the antenna-receiver-transmitter group (figure 1-55). The IF signals are routed to the receiver group in the operations room. The receiver group converts the azimuth and elevation IF signals to DC error signals and sends them to the antenna control. There, the signals are converted to antenna positioning signals and sent to the antenna servo drive motors via the antenna group in the antenna terminal. The drive motors, in turn, position the antenna in azimuth and elevation to reduce the error signals to zero.

1-186. The sum of the energy received by the four feedhorns (A+B+C+D) is detected and converted to a sum IF signal and is sent to the receiver group along with the azimuth and elevation IF signals. The receiver group converts the sum IF signal to range video signals for range computer CP-560A/GRW-5 and the missile guidance console. The range video signal is used in the range computer to center the tracking gates, in time, about the return signal from the missile guidance set. The range computer calculates target range and sums ten successive values of the target range. This summation, in the form of a binary number, is transmitted to signal data converter CV-967C/GRW-5 for presentation to the guidance computer equipment. The missile guidance console receives the range video signals and presents them in visual form for the operator.

1-187. As the antenna moves in response to the antenna positioning signals, digital signals representing azimuth and elevation positions are generated by code wheels mounted on the antenna and sent to the signal data converter. The signal data converter relays binary azimuth, elevation, and range data to the guidance computer equipment on a time-shared basis.

1-188. The azimuth, elevation, and range data sent to the guidance computer equipment is used in the guidance equations to solve the ballistic flight problem in real time. On the basis of these computations, the computer generates data in the form of steering orders and commands to guide and control the missile in flight.

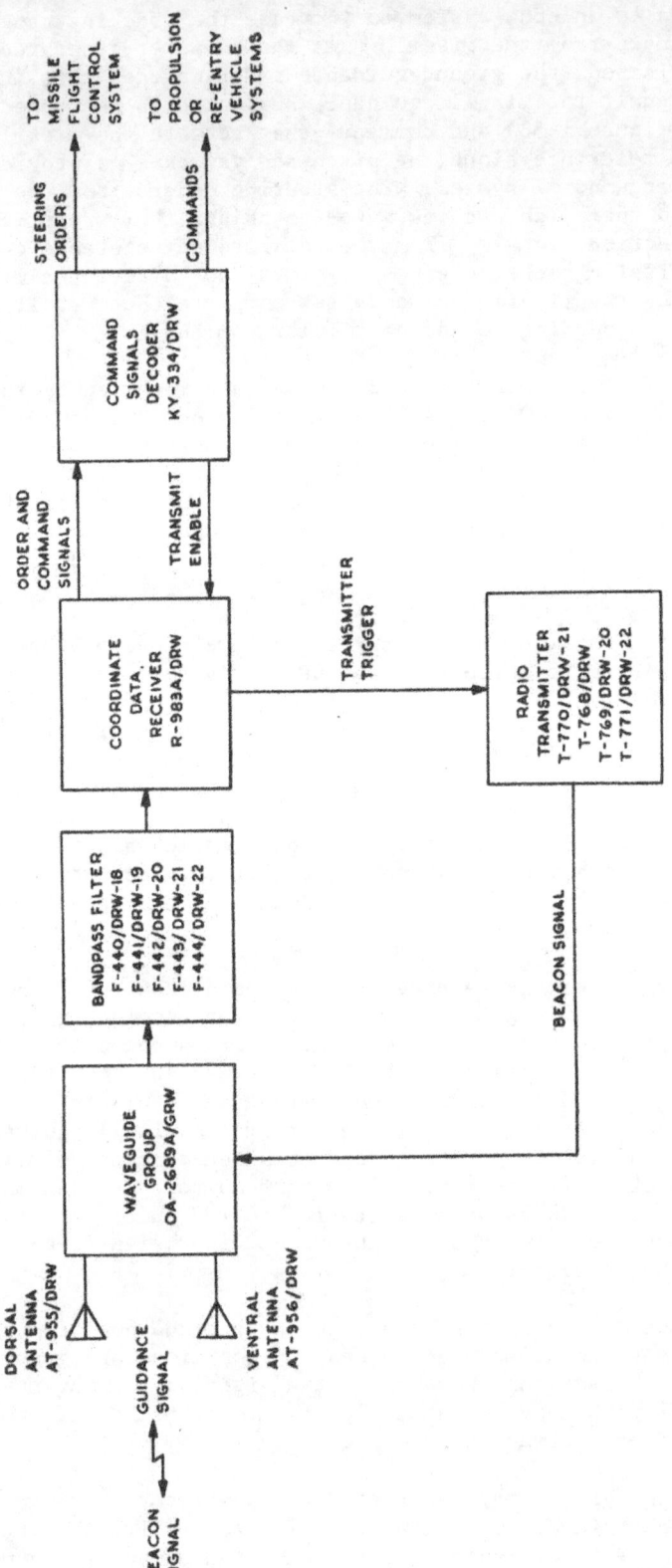

Figure 1-53. Missile Guidance Set AN/DRW-18, AN/DRW-19, AN/DRW-20, AN/DRW-21, or AN/DRW-22, Block Diagram

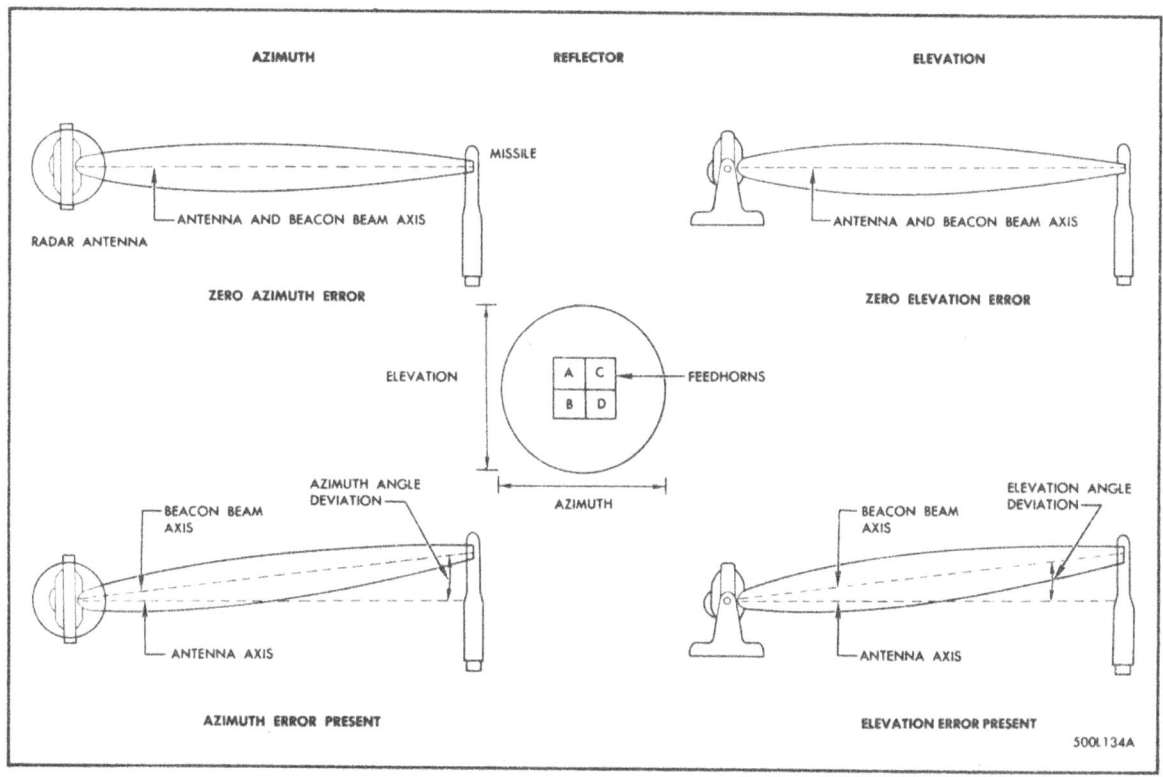

Figure 1-54. Azimuth and Elevation Error Detection

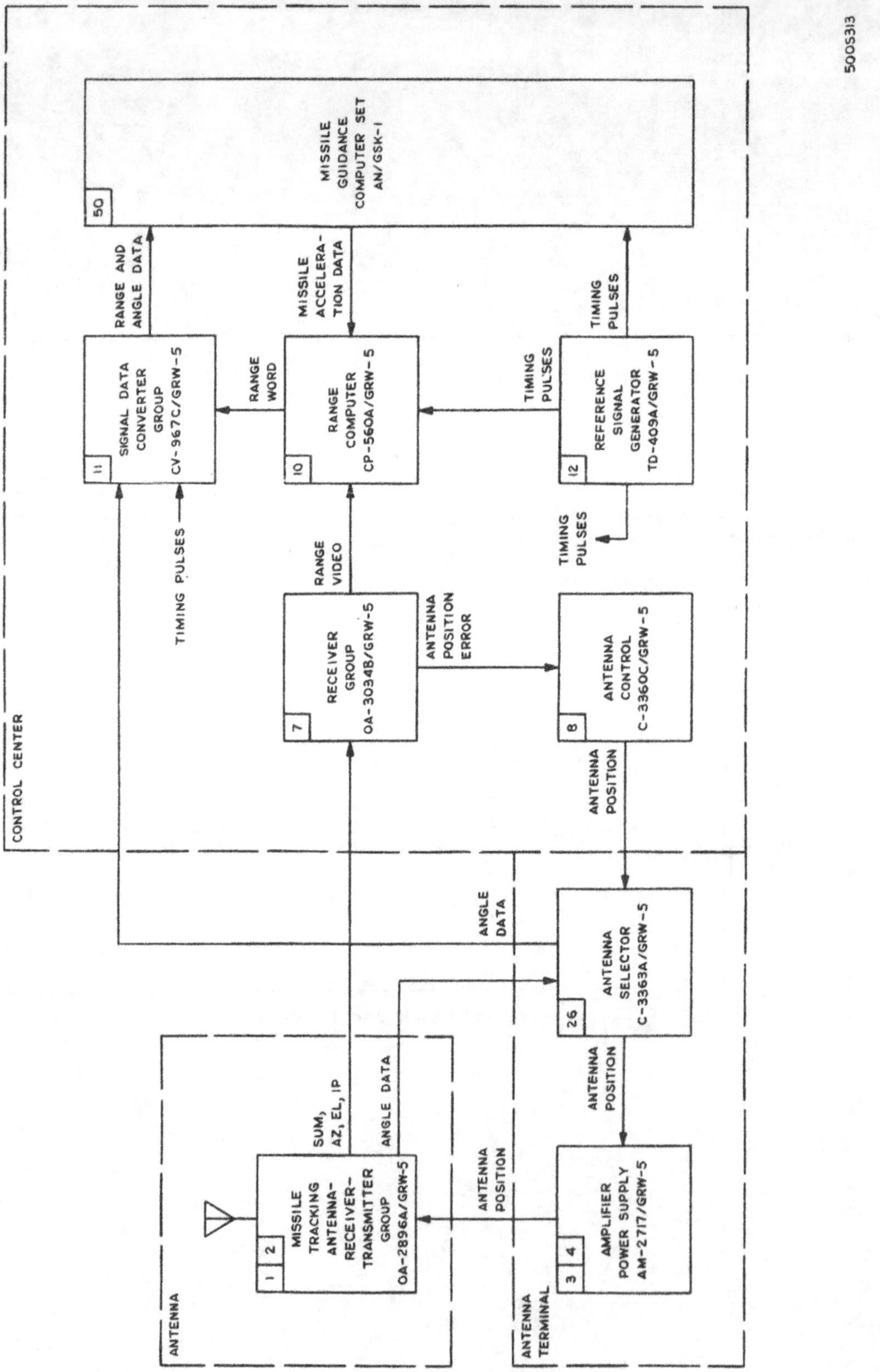

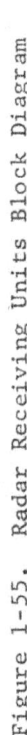

Figure 1-55. Radar Receiving Units Block Diagram

Several type of program constants are used by the computer during system operation. These include target constants which define the targets, prearm area, and trajectory shape. Eleven sets of these constants can be stored in the computer memory. These are known as the reference target and targets 1 through 10. The reference target constants will be used with the guidance exerciser. One of the other ten sets of target constants will be designated for use with an in-flight missile. Another type of constant describes the characteristics of the missile used in the launch complex. Other constants are guidance site constants which give the geographical location of the system.

1-189. The data representing the actual missile position is sent from the signal data converter to the digital-to-digital converter and then transferred into other computer circuitry; likewise, signals from other computer circuitry are sent to the digital-to-digital converter, then transferred to the radar.

1-190. The signal data recorder RO-146/GRW-5 provides a photographic record of important data, related to time, which reflects circuit operation and equipment performance during a data run or mission. The recorder has provisions for 24 channels; however, only 18 are used with this system. Each channel signal is recorded by means of a mirrored galvanometer which deflects when a signal current is applied. An optical system causes a light beam to be deflected from the galvanometer mirror onto a moving light-sensitive paper. The trace on the paper develops after exposure to fluorescent light. The 12-inch wide recorder paper is on a 200-foot roll and moves at variable speeds.

1-191. Digital data printer RO-144/GSK-1 located to the left of the missile guidance console is a parallel operation, eight-column printer. During countdown procedures, this unit prints data that is useful in evaluating the performance of the entire guidance system. The information printed may vary dependent on the portion of the operational program involved as shown in figure 1-56.

1-192. FLIGHT CONTROL SYSTEM.

1-193. The flight control system consists of ground and airborne equipment. The ground equipment checks and monitors airborne components during a system checkout and before launch. The airborne equipment consists of components that provide a programmed flight path during Stage I flight, stabilize the missile, and accept guidance commands to change missile attitude.

1-194. The ground equipment is located in control-monitor group OA-2441. During a system checkout, this equipment automatically and semiautomatically checks flight control equipment; during a launch countdown, it checks the airborne components on a go/no-go basis.

1-195. The airborne flight control components control missile attitude about the pitch, yaw, and roll axes during both stages of powered flight (figure 1-57). These components send electrical signals to airborne hydraulic equipment servo-actuators, which position the thrust chambers, and they also receive signals from the missile guidance set to correct or refine the missile flight path or attitude.

1-196. GROUND EQUIPMENT. The flight control system ground equipment consists of one equipment rack in control-monitor group OA-2441. The rack contains a signal analyzer assembly, command assembly, programmer check assembly, comparator assembly, signal generator assembly, signal selector assembly, power supply assembly,

(Text continued on page 1-94)

LINE NO.	DATA PRINTED	WHEN PRINTED	PRINTED
	Note		
	1. If level correction guidance program is used, word 1 below will be 55555555. 2. Plus (+) sign equals north or east miss-distance. 3. For guidance exercise, lines 12 and 13 will print guidance exerciser code (+0111111). 4. Refer to target tape contents sheet contained in the guidance control target trajectory kit folder. 5. If a zero appears in the program codes in the applicable last three digits, emergency action listed in T.O 21-SM68-1FJ-1-2 should be taken when TEST FAULT lamp lights.		
	COMBINED SYSTEMS EXERCISE PROGRAM - GUIDANCE EXERCISE		
1	Guidance program code	After ACQ MISSILE pushbutton indicator lighted green; or after START GUID X pushbutton indicator pressed; or if 02 bit of the azimuth data word in the BDR is set. (Pressing LAUNCH EXERCISE pushbutton indicator to yellow sets azimuth 02 bit.)	
2	Space		
3	Constant register 0	Following line 2	Eight digit octal number
4	Constant register 1	Following line 2	Eight digit octal number
5	Constant register 2	Following line 2	Eight digit octal number
6	Constant register 3	Following line 2	Eight digit octal number
7	Constant register 4	Following line 2	Eight digit octal number
8	Constant register 5	Following line 2	Eight digit octal number

Figure 1-56. Digital Data Printer RO-144/GSK-1, Printout Data (Sheet 1 of 6)

T.O. 21-SM68-1 Section I

LINE NO.	DATA PRINTED	WHEN PRINTED	PRINTED
COMBINED SYSTEMS EXERCISE PROGRAM - GUIDANCE EXERCISE			
9	Constant register 6	Following line 2	Sign and seven digit decimal number
10	Constant register 7	Following line 2	Sign and seven decimal number
11	Space		
12	Miss-distance	At end of evaluation	Sign and latitude miss-distance in tenths of miles (Refer to notes 2 and 3)
13	Miss-distance	At end of evaluation	Sign and longitude miss-distance in tenths of miles. (Refer to notes two and three)
1 thru 13	Abort code (may occur on any line printout listed above)	Azimuth 02 bit not set Note Normal ABORT code will be printed on unsuccessful GX run if AZ 02 is lighted.	00777700
COMBINED SYSTEMS EXERCISE PROGRAM - NORMAL FLIGHT			
	Note Lines 1 thru 11 as above if 02 bit of the azimuth data word in the BDR is set (LAUNCH EXERCISE pushbutton indicator lights yellow).		Refer to note 1 for line 1
12	BDR range to missile	End of fixed sequence program	Eight digit octal number
13	BDR azimuth to missile	End of fixed sequence program	Eight digit octal number
14	BDR elevation missile	End of fixed sequence program	Eight digit octal number

Figure 1-56. Digital Data Printer RO-144/GSK-1, Printout Data (Sheet 2 of 6)

LINE NO.	DATA PRINTED	WHEN PRINTED	PRINTED
COMBINED SYSTEMS EXERCISE PROGRAM - ABORTED FLIGHT			
(Lines 1-13 as above)			
1 thru 13	Abort code	At anytime Azimuth 02 bit is not set (after ACQ MISSILE pushbutton-indicator lighted green)	00777700
1 thru 13	Abort code	At anytime after ACQ MISSILE pushbutton indicator lights green if average elevation data word between two successive computer cycles differs by more than 2.5 degrees	00666600
COMBINED SYSTEMS EXERCISE PROGRAM - TARGET VERIFY PROGRAM			
1	Target verify program code	At target verify, or when ACQ MISSILE pushbutton-indicator is pressed	33333333 (Refer to note 5)
2	Sector number	At target verify, or when ACQ MISSILE pushbutton indicator is pressed	Two digit number
3	SAC control number	At target verify, or when ACQ MISSILE pushbutton indicator is pressed	Six digit number
4	SAC target island number	At target verify, or when ACQ MISSILE pushbutton indicator is pressed	Four digit number or five digit number (Refer to note 4)
5	SAC designated ground zero number	At target verify, or when ACQ MISSILE pushbutton indicator is pressed	Three digit number

Figure 1-56. Digital Data Printer RO-144/GSK-1, Printout Data (Sheet 3 of 6)

T.O. 21-SM68-1 Section I

LINE NO.	DATA PRINTED	WHEN PRINTED	PRINTED
COMBINED SYSTEMS EXERCISE PROGRAM - LEVEL MEASUREMENT PROGRAM			
1	Level measurement program code	ANT RAISE pushbutton indicator is pressed (blast detected)	22222222 (Refer to note 5)
2	Radial axis tilt	After program completion	Decimal value
3	Tangential axis tilt	After program completion	Decimal value
4	Space		
COMBINED SYSTEMS EXERCISE PROGRAM - LOOP TEST PROGRAM			
	Test Fault Code	Azimuth 02 bit not set when computer receives start loop test signal	00777700
GUIDANCE PROGRAM - EXERCISE OR NORMAL FLIGHT			
1	Guidance program code	After ACQ MISSILE pushbutton indicator START GUID X pushbutton indicator is pressed	11111111 (Refer to notes 1 and 5)
2	Space		
3	Constant register 0	Following line 2	Eight digit octal number
4	Constant register 1	Following line 2	Eight digit octal number
5	Constant register 2	Following line 2	Eight digit octal number
6	Constant register 3	Following line 2	Eight digit octal number
7	Constant register 4	Following line 2	Eight digit octal number
8	Constant register 5	Following line 2	Eight digit octal number
9	Constant register 6	Following line 2	Sign and seven digit decimal number

Figure 1-56. Digital Data Printer RO-144/GSK-1, Printout Data
(Sheet 4 of 6)

LINE NO.	DATA PRINTED	WHEN PRINTED	PRINTED
GUIDANCE PROGRAM - EXERCISE OR NORMAL FLIGHT			
10	Constant register 7	Following line 2	Sign and seven digit decimal number
11	Space		
12	Miss-distance	At end of evaluation	Sign and latitude miss-distance in tenths of miles (Refer to notes 2 and 3)
13	Miss-distance	At end of evaluation	Sign and longitude miss-distance in tenths of miles (Refer to notes 2 and 3)
GUIDANCE PROGRAM - ABORTED EXERCISE OR ABORTED NORMAL FLIGHT			
(Lines 1 thru 11 as above)			
12	Miss-distance	At end of evaluation	+0099999
13	Miss-distance	At end of evaluation	+0099999
GUIDANCE PROGRAM - EXERCISE OR NORMAL FLIGHT			
(SUCCESSFUL - NO TERMINAL EVALUATION)			
(Lines 1 thru 11 as above)			
12	Miss-distance	No evaluation	+0070000
13	Miss-distance	No evaluation	+0070000
TARGET VERIFY PROGRAM			
1	Target verify program code	At target verify, or when ACQ MISSILE push-button indicator pressed	33333333 (Refer to note 5.)
2	Sector number	At target verify, or when ACQ MISSILE push-button indicator pressed	Two digit number

Figure 1-56. Digital Data Printer RO-144/GSK-1, Printout Data (Sheet 5 of 6)

LINE NO.	DATA PRINTED	WHEN PRINTED	PRINTED
TARGET VERIFY PROGRAM			
3	SAC control number	At target verify, or when ACQ MISSILE pushbutton indicator pressed	Six digit number
4	SAC target data inventory number	At target verify, or when ACQ MISSILE pushbutton indicator pressed	Five digit number
5	SAC designated ground zero number	At target verify, or when ACQ MISSILE pushbutton indicator pressed	Three digit number
LEVEL MEASUREMENT PROGRAM			
1	Level measurement program code	ANT RAISE pushbutton indicator pressed (blast detected)	22222222 (Refer to note 5.)
2	Radial axis tilt	After program completion	Decimal value
3	Tangential axis tilt	After program completion	Decimal value
4	Space		

Figure 1-56. Digital Data Printer RO-144/GSK-1, Printout Data (Sheet 6 of 6)

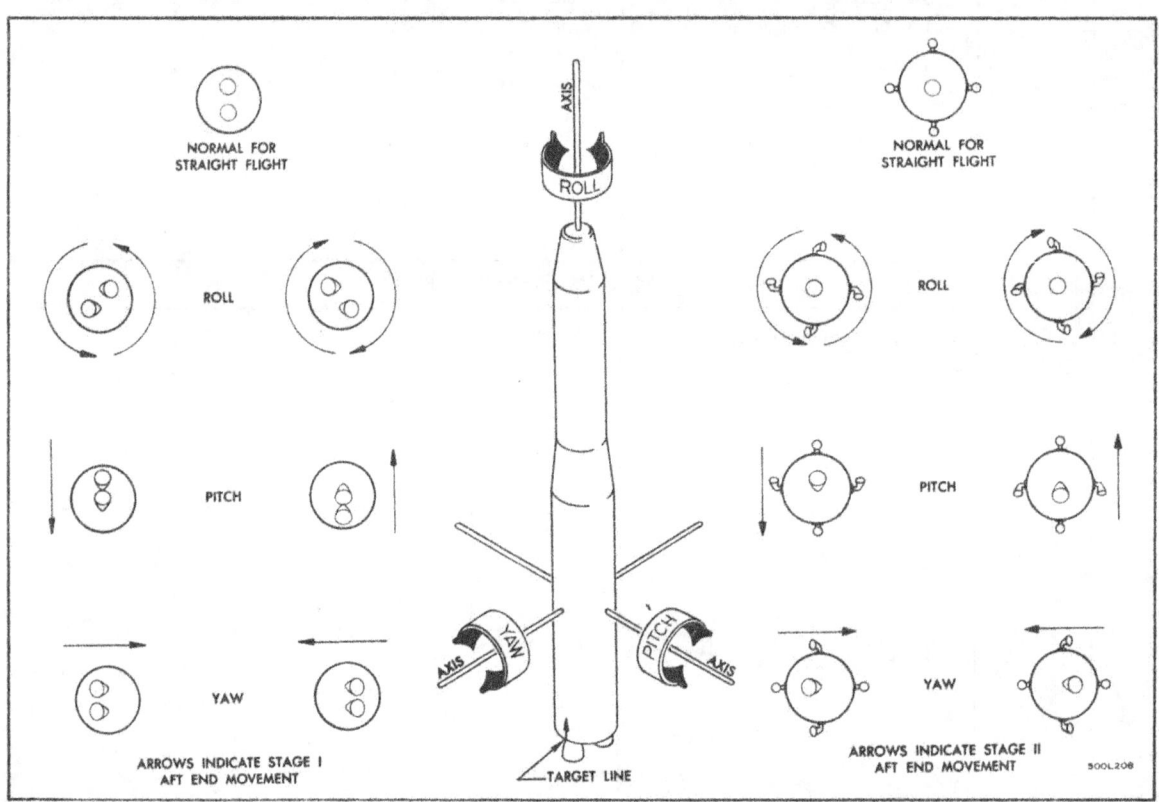

Figure 1-57. Missile Axes and Movement Diagram

(Text continued from page 1-86.)
and a blower assembly. These assemblies automatically perform self-tests and test flight control airborne components, evaluate system response, and verify operation of the pre-set pitch program. During system checkout, the gyro drift check is performed manually and a series of detailed automatic tests are performed in checking the flight control system. One test, performed during launch exercise, checks the flight control system in one complete operation. During launch operations, the flight control system is remotely controlled by the launch control and status system.

1-197. AIRBORNE EQUIPMENT. Components of the flight control system airborne equipment maintain correct missile attitude during powered flight. During Stage I powered flight the missile is directed on a preset flight path by the pitch programmer. Guidance is also provided by the ground guidance system during Stage I powered flight, Stage II powered flight, and vernier engine power flight. Missile steering and attitude control are accomplished by signals from the airborne components, applied to the servo-actuators, which in turn position the thrust chambers.

1-198. The Stage I airborne components consist of a Stage I rate gyroscope assembly, a Stage I autopilot amplifier package (magnetic amplifier), and four servo valves. The Stage I rate gyroscope assembly and the autopilot amplifier package are located in the Stage I transition compartment. The servo valves are in the Stage I engine compartment on the thrust chamber servo-actuators.

1-199. The Stage I rate gyroscope assembly senses missile deviation rates and produces proportional rate signals. The rate gyroscope assembly contains three rate gyroscopes, three heater circuits, and control circuits. Each rate gyroscope is positioned to measure the rate of missile deviation about one of the three missile control axes (pitch, yaw, and roll). (See figure 1-57.) Each rate gyroscope contains a gyroscope, a gimbal, a torsion bar, a signal generator, and a heater. The gyroscope is mounted in the gimbal and the gimbal is supported by the torsion bar and signal generator. As the missile moves around a control axis, the respective gyroscope precesses, causing the gimbal to exert a force on the torsion bar proportional to the angular rate of missile movement, and the signal generator produces an electrical output signal proportional to rate of missile deviation. The gimbal completely encloses the gyroscope and is immersed in high viscosity oil. The oil dampers gimbal oscillations and also reduces gimbal bearing friction. The heater maintains the damping oil at the proper operating temperature. The control circuits pitch rate signals from the signal generator to the Stage I autopilot amplifier package.

1-200. The Stage I autopilot amplifier package (magnetic amplifier) converts mixed rate signals, Stage I rate gyro rate signals, Stage II rate gyro displacement signals, and 3-axis reference gyro assembly displacement signals into correction signals, which are then transmitted to servo valves on the Stage I thrust chamber servo-actuators. The Stage I autopilot amplifier package has a gain change relay, three channel amplifiers, four mixer amplifiers, and four servo amplifiers as integral parts.

1-201. The Stage II airborne components consist of a 3-axis reference gyro assembly, a Stage II rate gyroscope assembly, a Stage II autopilot amplifier package (magnetic amplifier), a servo amplifier assembly, a transformer rectifier converter, a servo trim potentiometer box, a frequency converter, and six servo valves. Except for the servo valves, the airborne components are located in the transition compartment of Stage II. The servo valves are on the sustainer engine and vernier nozzle servo-actuators in the Stage II engine compartment.

1-202. The 3-axis reference gyro assembly establishes the missile attitude reference, senses missile deviations from this reference, and produces correction signals. The attitude reference is altered by pitch program signals and guidance signals to control the missile flight path. Guidance signals produce a roll program during the first 24 seconds of flight, superimpose an incremental pitch program on the pitch program generated in the 3-axis reference gyro assembly, and accomplish pitch and yaw steering during Stage I powered flight. During Stage II powered flight, there is no pitch program, guidance pitch and yaw signals only are used to control the missile flight path. Guidance signals control the missile in the yaw axis only during vernier powered flight. The 3-axis reference gyro assembly contains three displacement gyroscopes, three guidance amplifiers, three operational heaters, three standby heaters, three heater amplifiers, one time base, one time summing matrix, a pitch program power supply, and control stages.

1-203. Each displacement gyroscope is mounted so it will measure the angle of missile deviation about one of three control axes (pitch, yaw, or roll). (See figure 1-57.) Each displacement gyroscope contains a gyroscope, a gimbal, a torque generator, and a signal generator. Each gyroscope is mounted in a gimbal which is supported by the torque and signal generators. Just before launch, the signal generators are set to a zero error signal output by caging the gyroscopes. The zero error signal provides the missile with a zero reference during powered flight. If the missile deviates from the desired course during flight, the gyroscopes sense the angle and direction of deviation. As the missile moves off course, the gyroscopes precess, causing the gimbals to rotate and move the signal generator armature which generates an error signal. This error signal is sent to servo-actuators which change thrust chamber position and correct missile attitude.

1-204. To change the missile flight path a program or guidance signal is sent to a torque generator. The torque generator rotates the gimbal, which changes the gyroscope spin axis position in respect to the prelaunch position. The rotation of the gimbal causes the signal generator to produce an error signal. This error signal causes the missile to change attitude until the airframe control axis corresponds to the gyroscope reference.

1-205. The gimbal completely encloses the gyroscope and is immersed in high viscosity oil. The oil dampers gimbal oscillations and reduces gimbal bearing friction. The heaters and heater amplifiers keep the oil at the proper operating temperature. Guidance amplifiers demodulate and amplify signals from the guidance system before they are sent to the torque generators. The time base, time matrix, control stages, and pitch program power supply are utilized in supplying the pitch program to the torque generators.

1-206. The Stage II rate gyroscope assembly is identical to the Stage I rate gyroscope assembly.

1-207. The Stage II autopilot amplifier package (magnetic amplifier) amplifies and converts rate signals (from the rate gyroscope assembly) and displacement error signals (from the 3-axis reference gyroscope assembly) into correction signals. After amplification in the servo amplifier assembly, these signals reposition the Stage II thrust chamber and vernier nozzles. Signals are also sent to the Stage I autopilot amplifier package to position the Stage I thrust chambers.

1-208. The servo amplifier assembly amplifies the difference in voltage between the signals sent from the autopilot amplifier package and this voltage is fed to the servo-actuators to move the thrust chamber until the followup potentiometer

T.O. 21-SM68-1

Section I
Paragraphs 1-209 to 1-218

voltage sent from the autopilot amplifier package. This insures that the thrust chamber is positioned according to the command from the autopilot amplifier package.

1-209. The transformer rectifier converter supplies regulated 25 VDC power within the airborne flight control components.

1-210. The servo trim potentiometers provide a zero reference for the autopilot amplifier package. Adjustment of the individual servo trim potentiometers (one each for Stage I and Stage II thrust chamber servo actuators, excluding vernier actuators) assures that the thrust chambers are in the neutral position when there are zero error signals.

1-211. GUIDED MISSILE TEST SET. The test set consists of eight test units mounted in drawers within a cabinet and a waveguide assembly mounted to the rear of the cabinet. In addition, the test set employs a test board which couples the test set waveguide to the guidance set. Periodically, a checkout of the guidance set is performed to insure proper operation. This checkout is performed by the guided missile test set AN/DRM-5B(V). The test set performs the checkout by sending RF guidance signals, similar to those used during actual flight operation, to the guidance set. The test set verifies reception and decoding of the RF guidance signals by checking monitor signals from the guidance set.

1-212. ELECTRICAL SYSTEM.

1-213. The electrical system consists of ground and airborne electrical equipment. The electrical system converts facility power to 400 CPS, 60 CPS, and DC power; supplies AC and DC power for AOE and airborne equipment; controls ground hydraulic power and air conditioning for the missile; distributes electrical signals to the launcher system.

1-214. GROUND EQUIPMENT. The electrical system ground equipment consists of power switchboard JEU-7, power supply A/E24A, battery power supply A/E24A-5, power supply ECU-16, motor-generator A/E24A-3, launch and checkout circuits in control-monitor group OA-2438/GJQ-11, electrical umbilical disconnects, and launcher platform electrical AOE.

1-215. The power switchboard distributes 60 CPS facilities power to the electrical system units, the missile air conditioning system, the ground hydraulic equipment, and the instrumentation system. The unit is located on Level IV of the equipment terminal. It contains rack mounted removable assemblies which include remote-start and local-start enable circuits for the missile air conditioning system and the ground hydraulic system.

1-216. Power supply A/E24A-4 converts 480 V 60 CPS facilities power to 28 VDC. The unit is a skid-mounted transformer-rectifier, located on Level IV of each equipment terminal.

1-217. The battery power supply is a backup 28 VDC power source for power supply A/E24A-4. The battery power supply is a skid-mounted unit comprised of storage batteries and battery chargers. The unit is located on Level IV of the equipment terminal.

1-218. Power supply ECU-16 converts 480 V 60 CPS facilities power to 28 VDC. This power is used in starting and operating the airborne battery inverter-accessory power supply (BI-APS) and the Stage II hydraulic pump motor until the airborne battery power is transferred. The skid-mounted unit, located on Level IV of the equipment terminal, is a transformer-saturable reactor power supply.

1-219. Motor-generator A/E24A-3, driven by 60 CPS facilities power, produces 400 CPS power. The skid-mounted unit is located on Level IV of the equipment terminal.

1-220. Control-monitor group OA-2438 on Level III of the equipment terminal contains the electrical system launch and checkout equipment. The electrical system assemblies include the following: circuit breaker panels, prelaunch checkout assembly number 1, prelaunch checkout and control indicator assembly, voltage monitor, launch control assembly number 1, launch control assembly number 2, prelaunch checkout assembly number 3, time and cycle recorder, and centrifugal fan assemblies.

1-221. The circuit breaker panels contains circuit breakers and power contactors for protection and control of the 28 VDC, 117 V 400 CPS and 120 V 60 CPS circuits. These circuits supply power to the AOE and missile buses.

1-222. The prelaunch checkout assembly number 1 contains electrical system readiness-monitoring circuits and part of the control circuits for an automatic checkout stepper circuit. The front panel contains ten dual-lamp indicators that display equipment readiness condition as follows: Green for normal and red for malfunction.

1-223. Prelaunch checkout and control indicator assembly contains an electrical system operating mode selector, a lamp verification selector, manual checkout power pushbutton indicators, a system checkout-initiate pushbutton indicator, a system-checkout-step-digital readout indicator, and part of the electrical system checkout control circuits.

1-224. The voltage monitor chassis contains AC and DC voltage meters, selectors, and a frequency meter that permit monitoring of primary electrical system power during system checkout and service operation.

1-225. The launch control assembly number 1 contains remotely controlled circuits that sequence approximately the first half of the electrical system launch operations. The assembly has no front panel controls or indicators.

1-226. The launch control assembly number 2 contains remotely controlled circuits that sequence approximately the last half of the electrical system launch operations. The assembly has no front panel controls or indicators.

1-227. The prelaunch checkout assembly number 3 contains electrical system checkout circuits. The assembly has no front panel control or indicators.

1-228. The time and cycle recorder assembly contains the run-time monitor circuits for the electrical system. Run-time is recorded during both checkout and launch operations.

1-229. The centrifugal fan assemblies contain squirrel cage blowers that cool their associated rack of launch and checkout assemblies. Each assembly has a front panel fuse that protects the blower motor circuit.

1-230. ELECTRICAL UMBILICAL DISCONNECTS. The AOE electrical circuits are connected to the missile equipment through seven electrical umbilical disconnect plugs. The missile umbilical disconnect jacks are recessed in the missile skin and terminate the missile wiring. During launch, the plugs and jacks are mechanically disconnected by lanyards located on the umbilical tower and launcher platform.

1-231. LAUNCHER PLATFORM ELECTRICAL AOE. The launcher platform electrical AOE consists of junction boxes, a transition box, and wiring for all explosive bolts located on the launcher platform. The explosive bolts are electrically detonated to free the missile release mechanisms, and tower tilting mechanism. The electrical system arms and fires the explosive bolts.

1-232. AIRBORNE EQUIPMENT. During flight, the electrical airborne equipment supplies both AC and DC power at required voltages to the airborne equipment.

1-233. Stage I electrical equipment consists of DC power distribution bus panels located in the transition, between tanks, and engine compartments. These power panels are supplied with 28 VDC from the accessory power supply (APS) battery located in the Stage II engine compartment.

1-234. Stage II electrical equipment consists of a 117 400 CPS battery inverter-accessory power supply (BI-APS), a 28 VDC nickel-cadmium accessory power supply (APS) battery, main power control relays, AC power distribution bus panels, and DC power distribution panels. The BI-APS battery, and main power control relays are located in the Stage II transition compartment and are supplied with 117 V 400 CPS power from the BI-APS. The DC power distribution buses are located in the transition, between tanks, and engine compartments of Stage II. The DC buses are supplied with 28 volts by the APS battery.

1-235. Command signals from the launch sequencer to the electrical system control-monitor group OA-2438 initiate the start sequence of the electrical system. The sequence is started when the missile launch officer presses the launch control console LOAD PROPELLANTS pushbutton indicator. The airborne electrical equipment is placed in operation at different times during the countdown. During the countdown, airborne electrical equipment is powered by ground operating equipment power supplies until the airborne equipment is transferred to the airborne batteries. The APS battery and Stage II hydraulic pump motor battery are activated during the countdown. The batteries are activated when a squib ruptures a bag (in each battery) containing the electrolyte. The electrolyte is under gas pressure and is forced into the battery when the bag is ruptured.

1-236. ENGINE SYSTEM.

1-237. The rocket engine system includes the Stage I and Stage II engines (figures 1-58 and 1-59) and the associated aerospace operating equipment (AOE). The engines are physically and functionally complete and separate assemblies, and are installed in their respective missile stages. The rocket engines are connected to the ground operating equipment through the missile umbilicals.

1-238. The engines burn liquid oxygen and RP-1 fuel, and exhaust the resulting hot gases at supersonic velocities. The AOE starts the Stage I engine after checking that both engines are ready to fire. The Stage I engine (booster engine) is started on the ground and provides the thrust for missile lift off and initial acceleration. The Stage II engine is started at altitude and sustains the acceleration and establishes the programmed final velocity. The total operating time of both engines approaches 6 minutes for maximum range.

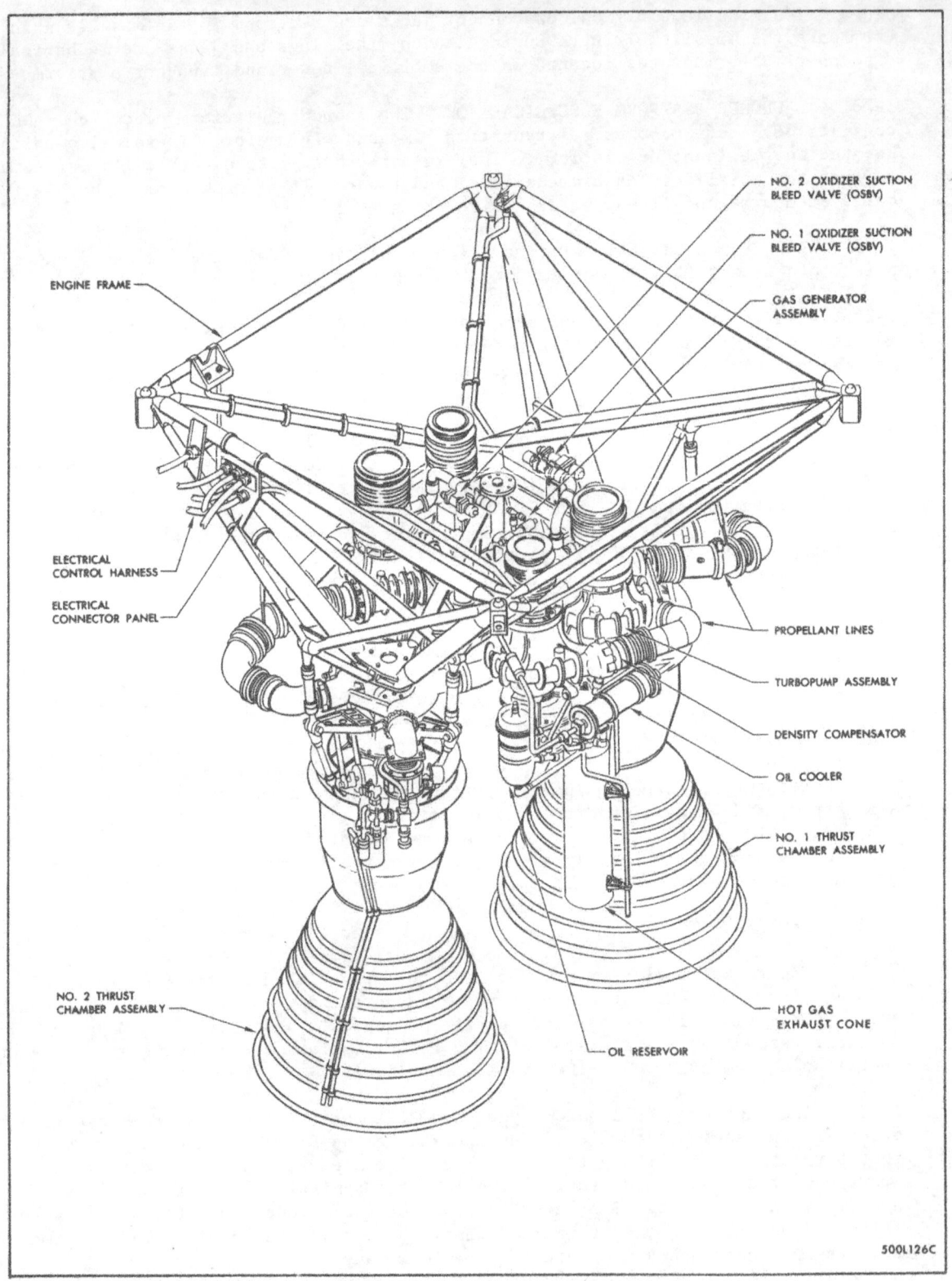

Figure 1-58. Stage I Engine

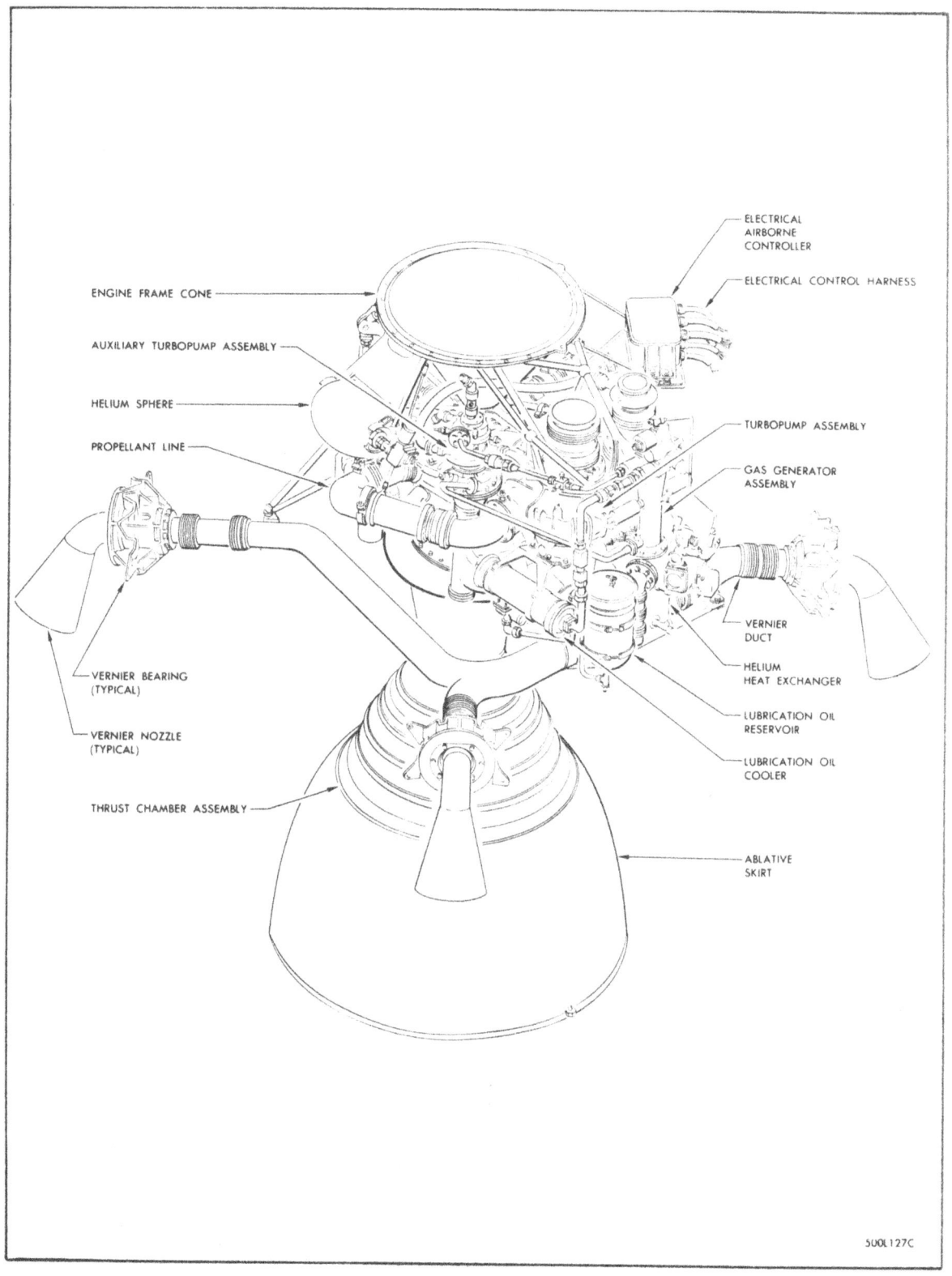

Figure 1-59. Stage II Engine

1-239. GROUND EQUIPMENT. The ground equipment for the engines consists of AOE and aerospace ground equipment (AGE).

1-240. The rocket engine AOE consists of an engine control system (ECS) and engine start equipment. This equipment fires the Stage I engine and arms the Stage II engine upon receipt of proper countdown commands from the launch sequencer. The rocket engine AOE is basically the same for all missiles. Differences will be covered in the text when necessary.

1-241. The ECS is contained in control-monitor group OA-2441 located on Level III of the equipment terminal. The checkout portions of the ECS are used in performing scheduled checkout and maintenance on the engines. The checkout and self check portions of the ECS are completely isolated from the control portion.

1-242. The engine start equipment is used to initiate operation of the Stage I engine. The start equipment includes two banks of nitrogen K-bottles pressurized to 3000 PSI. There is a 3-way hand valve (CV-505) that provides a capability for selecting either of the two banks before re-servicing becomes necessary. Other components include a nitrogen start valve (SOV 530), and a supply line equipped with a quick disconnect that is connected to the Stage I nitrogen start umbilical (1E1N). When the nitrogen is released by the start valve, the turbine of the turbopump assemblies of the Stage I engine subassemblies are accelerated and drive the turbopump. The flow of nitrogen to the turbines is cut off when the gas generators fire and provide sufficient power to sustain operation of the turbopump assemblies.

1-243. STAGE I ROCKET ENGINE. The Stage I rocket engine, designated LR87-AJ-3, consists of two engine subassemblies. (See figure 1-60.) The two subassemblies develop a total of 300,000 pounds of thrust and are mounted on a common engine frame that transfers the thrust to the missile airframe. The subassemblies are similar and are interconnected by instrumentation and electrical components. The subassemblies are started and shut down simultaneously, and each must reach 77 percent of its rated thrust before the missile is released from the launcher platform. Each engine subassembly includes a thrust chamber assembly, a turbopump assembly (TPA), a gas generator assembly, and propellant lines and valves. One subassembly also contains a helium heat exchanger.

1-244. The turbopump assembly (TPA) in each engine subassembly includes propellant pumps, a hot gas turbine, and lubrication equipment.

1-245. The gas generator assembly generates hot gases to drive the turbopump assembly. The gas generator assembly is bolted to the hot-gas inlet of the turbopump turbine. The gas generator includes a combustion chamber and injector, a valve assembly, and igniters. Two pyrotechnic igniters are used to start the burning of propellants in the combustion chamber.

1-246. The helium heat exchanger is installed on the trubine of the turbopump assembly of engine subassembly number two, and uses hot gases exhausted from the turbine to raise the temperature and expand the helium used to pressurize the propellant tanks. The helium flows from the storage spheres in the Stage I liquid oxygen tanks to the heat exchanger, circulates through a coil of tubing, and flows back to pressurize both propellant tanks of Stage I. The hot gases are exhausted from the heat exchanger through an exhaust duct and add approximately 600 pounds to the engine thrust.

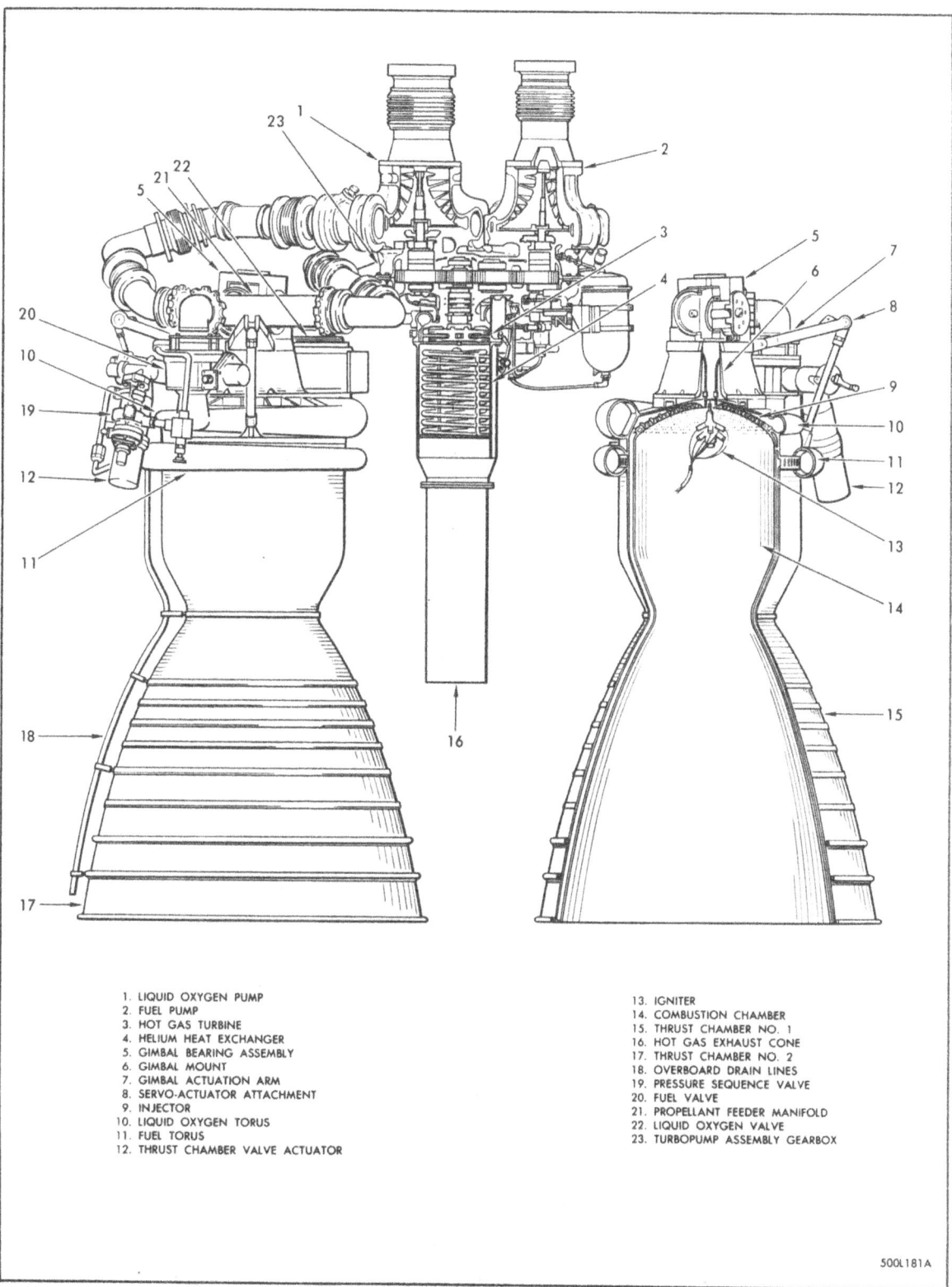

Figure 1-60. Stage I Rocket Engine Subassembly

1-247. STAGE II ROCKET ENGINE. The Stage II rocket engine subassembly (figure 1-61), designated LR91-AJ-3, consists of a single thrust chamber assembly and an integrated hot-gas vernier assembly. The thrust chamber operates as the sustainer engine and develops 80,000 pounds of thrust at an altitude of 250,000 feet. The sustainer engine operates after stage separation and accelerates and directs the missile along a programmed trajectory. The verniers provide attitude control during stage separation, roll control during sustainer engine operation, and final trimming control of missile velocity and attitude after sustainer engine shutdown.

1-248. The components that make up the Stage II rocket engine include a thrust chamber assembly, a turbopump assembly (TPA), a gas generator assembly, a hot-gas diversion valve assembly, an auxiliary turbopump assembly (ATPA), vernier components, helium heat exchanger, propellant lines, altitude start components, an airborne controller, and an electrical harness.

1-249. The engine frame is a stainless steel cone with a welded structure of steel tubes. The base of the steel cone is attached to the support structure of the liquid oxygen tank, and the apex of the cone is attached to the thrust chamber assembly. The welded steel tubes support the turbopump and auxiliary turbopump assemblies. Removable rods support the vernier ducts and propellant lines.

1-250. The engine assembly has a thrust chamber assembly which is gimbal mounted and allows directional control of the thrust to provide pitch and yaw control of the missile. The major components of the thrust chamber assembly include a combustion chamber and ablative skirt, an injector, propellant valves, a gimbal assembly, a gimbal manifold and swivel assembly, and an igniter assembly.

1-251. The turbopump assembly (TPA) supplies propellants to the thrust chamber at the flow rates required to develop rated thrust. Incorporated in the turbopump assembly are propellant pumps, a hot-gas turbine, and lubrication equipment.

1-252. The gas generator assembly burns a mixture of liquid oxygen and fuel to develop the hot-gas driving force used by the turbopump assembly, an auxiliary turbopump assembly, vernier components, and a helium heat exchanger. The gas generator assembly consists of a combustion chamber and injector, propellant valves, and igniters.

1-253. The operation of the diversion valve initiates the switching between vernier solo phase and thrust chamber phase during Stage II engine operation. The diversion valve is a three-way poppet valve located at the outlet of the gas generator. The hot gas diversion valve assembly directs hot gas from the gas generator to the turbopump assembly during thrust chamber operation, and by-passes hot gases through the hot-gas bypass line to the helium heat exchanger during vernier solo operation.

1-254. The auxiliary turbopump assembly (ATPA) supplies the gas generator with propellants. The assembly includes an oxidizer pump, a fuel pump, and a hot-gas turbine mounted on a common shaft. The liquid oxygen and fuel pumps are single stage, centrifugal pumps. The housing for the fuel pump forms the main body of the assembly and includes mounting pads, bearing supports, and internal bearing lubrication passages. The turbine is a single stage unit with one rotor and two gas inlets.

1-255. Vernier components include four nozzles, four bearings, and stainless steel hot-gas ducts. The nozzles are placed 90 degrees apart on the outside of the

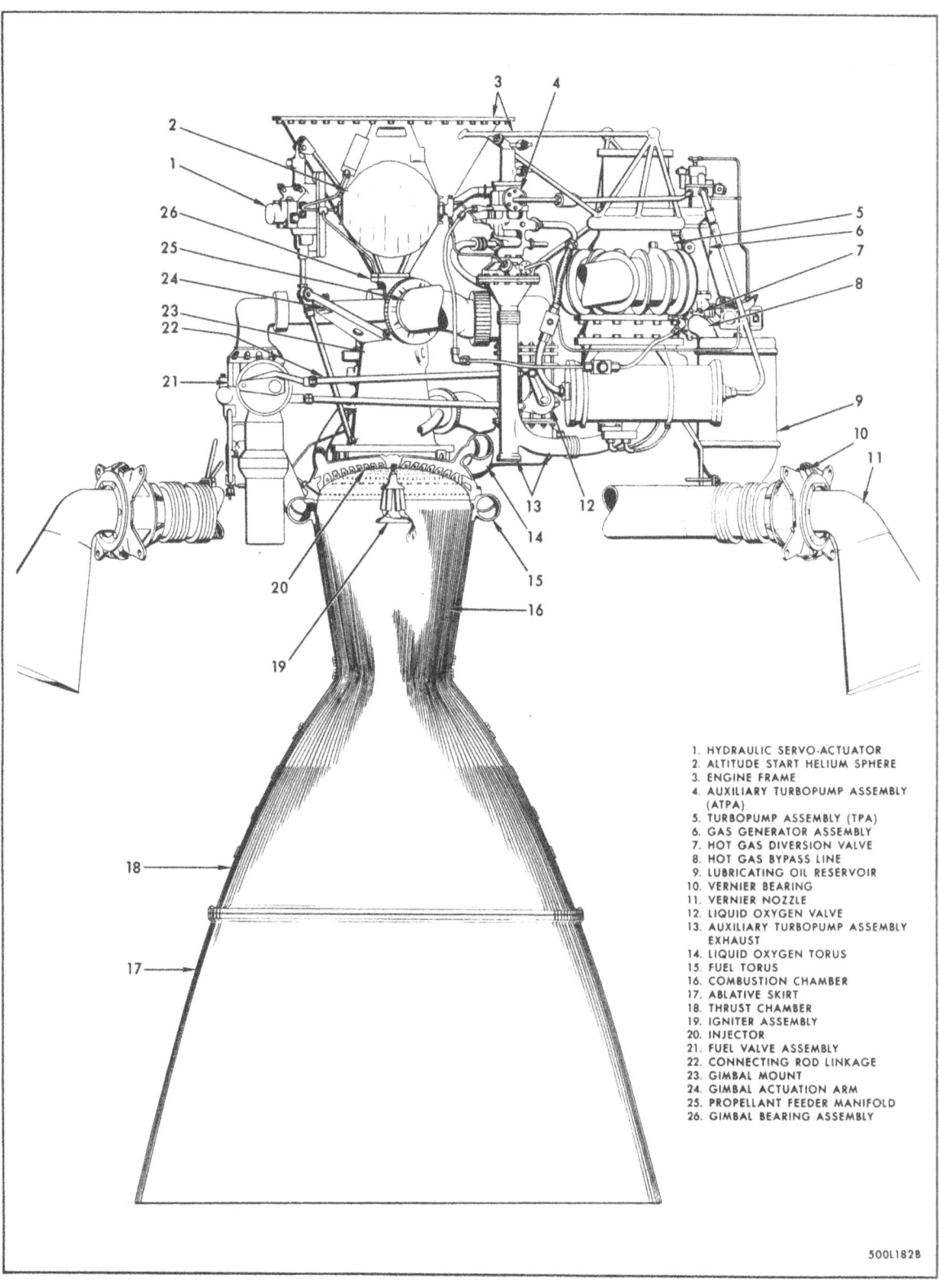

Figure 1-61. Stage II Rocket Engine Subassembly

Stage II engine compartment and are controlled by four hydraulic actuators. The nozzles are fastened to the engine compartment framework by bearings that allow a hydraulic servo-actuator to rotate each nozzle through an arc of 140 degrees. The hot-gas ducts conduct hot gases from the helium heat exchanger to the nozzles. During thrust chamber operation, the hot-gas is used after it is exhausted from the turbopump and auxiliary turbopump assemblies into the helium heat exchanger. During vernier solo operation, the hot-gas from the gas generator passes through the bypass line to the helium heat exchanger.

1-256. The helium heat exchanger is installed in the TPA turbine exhaust duct and uses hot gases exhausted from the turbine, or directly from the gas generator. Operation is the same as Stage I.

1-257. The propellant lines are the discharge and suction lines for both the turbopump assembly and the auxiliary turbopump assembly.

1-258. Altitude start components include a spherical helium start bottle and a start valve. The helium start bottle supplies helium at 3000 PSI. The start valve is installed at the outlet of the helium tank, and is solenoid operated. A helium line routes helium from the start valve to the turbine inlet on the auxiliary turbopump assembly. An electrical signal opens the start valve at the same time that the gas generator pilot valve is opened and the gas generator igniters are energized. The high pressure helium starts the auxiliary turbopump assembly and propellants are admitted to the gas generator and ignited. Hot gases from the generator sustain the operation of the auxiliary turbopump assembly, and the start valve is closed.

1-259. The airborne controller is mounted on the engine frame behind the turbopump assembly and relays electrical signals from AGE and the flight controls auto pilot to sequence and control Stage II engine operation.

1-260. The electrical harness connects the engine electrical components to the controller. The harness is completely enclosed in a molded silicon rubber cover that is highly resistant to fuel, extreme temperatures, and abrasion.

1-261. Checkout and maintenance activities associated with the rocket engine system are performed at control-monitor group OA 2441.

1-262. OPERATION. During countdown, the liquid oxygen tanks of both missile stages are filled and pressurized, and both engines are bled and checked. If both engines, the ground start system, and the other missile systems fulfill the go requirements, the Stage I engine is fired. The missile is released from the launcher when both subassemblies of the Stage I rocket engine reach 77 percent thrust. The engine control system signals the launch sequencer for shutdown if both thrust chambers of the Stage I engine do not reach 77 percent thrust within a specified period of time.

1-263. During the countdown prior to firing the Stage I engine, the final preparations are made to ready the Stage II engine for operation. The engine control system initiates the bleeding of gaseous oxygen from the Stage II engine propellant lines and checks the continuity of the electrical system. The gaseous oxygen bleed of the Stage II engine continues during first stage operation.

1-264. The Stage I engine subassemblies operate independently; however, their starting and shutdown sequences are closely synchronized by the electrical system and the single gas generator valve pilot valve.

1-265. The gas generator valve pilot valve is opened at T-279.9 to bleed actuation fuel into the gas generator valve actuators at static tank pressure. The pilot valve is closed 35 seconds before firing and a nitrogen purge is applied to the liquid oxygen manifold of the gas generator injector through a purge valve. The purge valve closes when the gas generator is started.

1-266. When the fire-switch-one (87FS1) signal is received to start the rocket engine, the ground based nitrogen start valve is opened and the thrust chamber igniters are energized. With the opening of the nitrogen start valve, nitrogen at 3000 PSI enters the turbines of the turbopump assembly to start the propellant pumps rotating to supply the propellants to the thrust chamber.

1-267. The rising fuel pressure from the turbopump assembly positions the thrust chamber valve pressure sequencing valve to the open position, admitting actuation fuel to the actuator. The actuator initiates the opening of the fuel valve and the fuel fills the combustion chamber cooling jacket.

1-268. The connecting rod from the fuel valve opens the oxidizer valve to admit liquid oxygen to the thrust chamber injector. The fuel enters the injector from the combustion chamber cooling jacket. The propellants are sprayed into the combustion chamber and ignited.

1-269. The position switch on the thrust chamber fuel valve assembly is actuated as the fuel valve opens, providing an electrical signal to open the gas generator valve pilot valve and energize the gas generator igniters. The pilot valve admits actuation fuel to the actuator to open the propellant valves. Propellants from the turbopump assembly are admitted to the injector and sprayed into the gas generator combustion chamber where they are ignited.

1-270. The position switch on the gas generator valve assembly is actuated as the valve opens, providing an electrical signal for closing the nitrogen start valve and de-energizing the thrust chamber and gas generator igniters. The hot gases developed by the gas generator continue to accelerate and drive the turbopump assembly. The turbopump assembly supplies propellants to the thrust chamber and gas generator. The rising pressure in the combustion chamber closes the thrust chamber pressure switch to complete the start missile release circuit.

1-271. The hot gas expelled by the gas generator drives the turbopump assembly. The hot gas developed by the thrust chamber provides the thrust for missile lift-off and initial acceleration.

1-272. The hydraulic servo-actuators pivot the thrust chamber to vary the direction of the thrust in accordance with signals received from the flight control system. Directional control of the thrust provides directional and orientation control of the missile.

1-273. The thrust control transducer and amplifier assembly monitors the pressure in the thrust chamber, and signals the gas generator valve control valve when a variation in chamber pressure is detected. The thrust is kept constant by varying the operation of the gas generator to maintain a constant chamber pressure.

1-274. To terminate the operation of the Stage I rocket engine, the fire-switch-two (87FS2) signal is initiated by low level sensors in the propellant tanks. The gas generator valve pilot valve is closed, draining the actuation fuel from the actuator. The propellant valve is closed, terminating the operation of the gas generator.

1-275. The position switch on the gas generator valve assembly is actuated as the gas generator propellant valves close. The position switch provides a signal to the pilot valve on the thrust chamber valve pressure sequencing valve.

1-276. The pilot valve returns the pressure sequencing valve to the closed position, draining the actuation fuel from the actuator. The actuator closes the propellant valves, terminating thrust chamber operation.

1-277. During the countdown (prior to Stage I firing), ground power is supplied to the oxidizer pump bearing heaters (TPA and ATPA) to prevent the lubricant from freezing. When Stage I fires, this heater power is transferred to airborne 28 VDC for missile flight. The auxiliary turbopump assembly and gas generator bleed valves are opened 35 seconds prior to Stage I firing and closed when the Stage I engine fires. The auxiliary turbopump assembly (ATPA) oxidizer suction bleed valve is opened at the start of the countdown launch phase, and will remain open until gas generator operation is initiated.

1-278. The gas generator is started approximately 7 seconds prior to shutdown of Stage I. The gas generator start signal opens the altitude start valve, gas generator pilot valve, and energizes the gas generator igniters. Pressurized helium is released to accelerate the turbine of the auxiliary turbopump assembly. The propellants pressurized by the auxiliary turbopump assembly are sprayed into the combustion chamber of the gas generator and ignited. The hot gases are by-passed the hot-gas diversion valve directly into the helium heat exchanger and exhausted to the vernier. Hot gases are used to sustain operation of the auxiliary turbopump assembly. The verniers operate solo for approximately 4 seconds to provide missile orientation while separation of stages occurs.

1-279. Approximately 11 seconds after the gas generator starts, the thrust chamber-start signal is received. The hot gases are diverted to the turbopump assembly, accelerating the turbopump. The rising fuel pressure opens the thrust chamber propellant valves and propellants are forced into the injector. During the steady-state operation, the verniers provide roll control and the servo-actuators pivot the thrust chamber to compensate for flight path error detected by the missile guidance system. The thrust control transducer and amplifier assembly controls the gas generator control valve to maintain constant thrust.

1-280. With the receipt of the shutdown signal, the hot-gas diversion valve is returned to the bypass position, terminating the turbopump assembly operation. The pilot valve closes and vents actuation fuel, which allows the propellant valves to close, terminating thrust chamber operation. The gas generator and auxiliary turbopump assembly continue to operate and provide vernier thrust for final missile velocity and orientation trimming.

1-281. When the signal for vernier shutdown is received, the gas generator valve pilot valve closes. The actuation fuel is vented, allowing the gas generator propellant valves to close. The gas generator is shut down and this terminates the operation of the auxiliary turbopump assembly and shut down the Stage II rocket engine.

1-282. PROPELLANT SYSTEM.

1-283. The propellant system (figure 1-62) includes ground and airborne equipment. Storage tanks in and adjacent to the propellant terminal contain liquid oxygen, helium, and nitrogen. Fuel is stored in the fuel terminal and is loaded in the

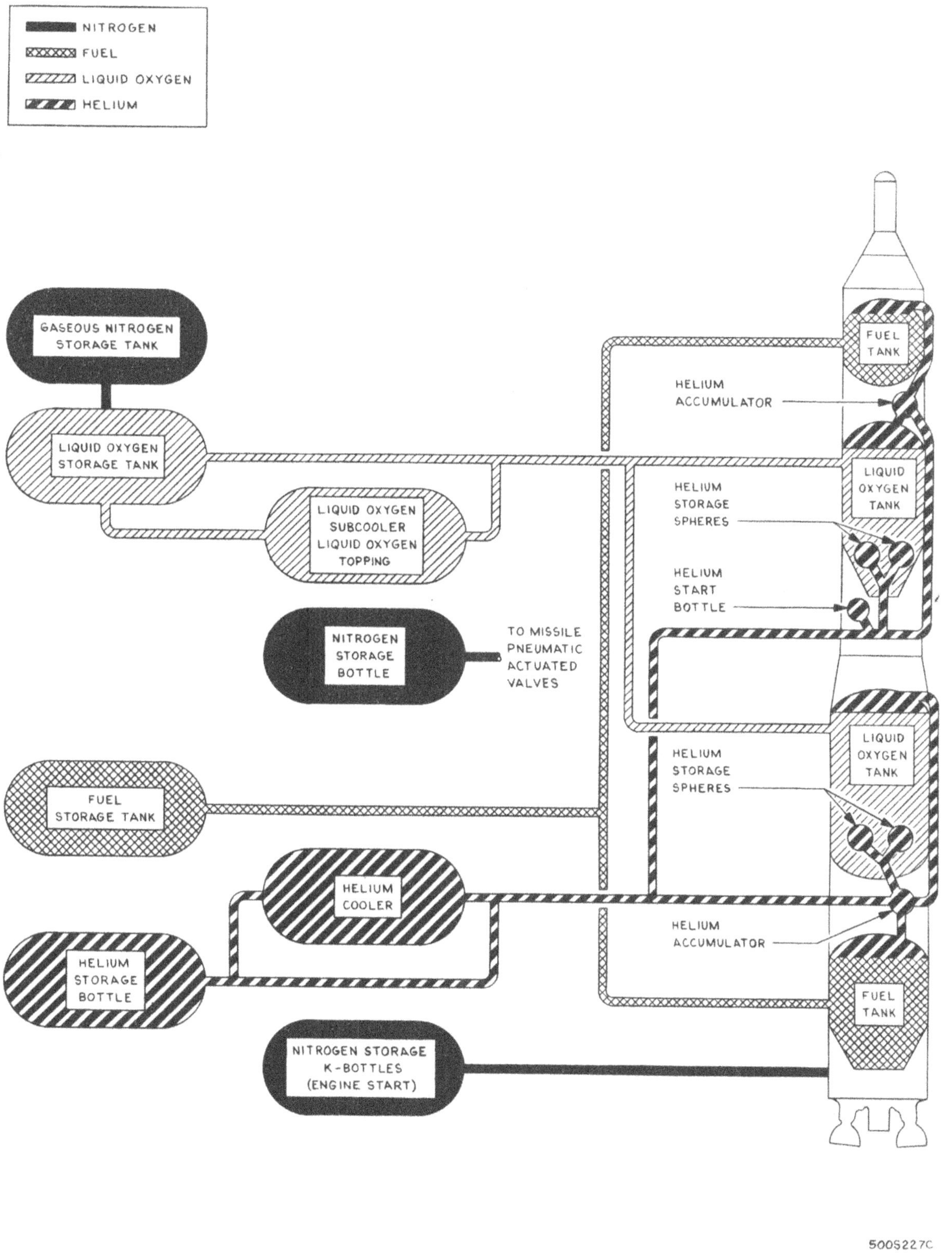

T.O. 21-SM68-1 Section I

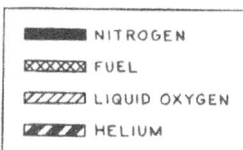

Figure 1-62. Propellant System Flow Diagram

missile fuel tanks during post installation system checkout. During countdown, liquid oxygen and pressurizing gas (helium) are transferred from the propellant terminal to the missile. The propellant system equipment includes features for stopping transfer safely at any time during countdown, for returning the liquid oxygen to the propellant terminal, and for returning fuel to the fuel terminal.

1-284. GROUND EQUIPMENT. The propellant system ground equipment consists of aerospace operating equipment (AOE) and aerospace ground equipment (AGE). The AOE consists of the equipment for handling liquid oxygen, helium, nitrogen, liquid nitrogen and fuel. The AGE consists of a liquid fuel water separator, a reciprocating power-driven compressor, a pumping method liquid oxygen-liquid nitrogen converter, a specimen examining ultraviolet light, a dew point indicator, and a liquid dispensing portable tank and converter unit.

1-285. LIQUID OXYGEN HANDLING EQUIPMENT. The liquid oxygen storage tank is a doubled-walled fabricated pressure vessel consisting of a stainless steel inner cylinder within a carbon steel outer cylinder. The annular space between the inner and outer tank walls is packed with insulation and the air is evacuated by a vacuum pump. Taps provided on the tank permit the measurement of the liquid and the ullage pressure.

1-286. Liquid oxygen catchpots are provided to catch spillage during transfer operations. The catchpots are closed stainless steel vessels located below and connected to the umbilical line drain connections. Before the umbilical lines are disconnected from the missile, their contents are drained into the catchpots so that spills will be eliminated during umbilical line retraction.

1-287. A liquid oxygen subcooler supplies a flow of subcooled liquid oxygen for topping operations. The subcooler consists of a doubled-walled tank having heat transfer coils inside the inner tank. A vacuum pump mounted on the tank maintains the vacuum in the annular space.

1-288. Transfer of liquid oxygen from the storage tank to the missile is accomplished by using nitrogen gas pressure to force the liquid oxygen through the transfer components and piping to the missile. The transfer piping to the Stage I and Stage II liquid oxygen tanks is sized so that transfer operations are completed at approximately the same time. The missile liquid oxygen tanks are unloaded through the Stage I liquid oxygen transfer piping by means of a pump located near the base of the missile silo.

1-289. HELIUM HANDLING EQUIPMENT. The helium handling equipment consists of helium storage tanks and a helium cooler. This equipment provides helium to pressurize the helium storage spheres located within the missile liquid oxygen tanks, and to pressurize the missile fuel and liquid oxygen tanks during and after elevation of the missile. During flight, helium pressure is applied from the helium spheres to operate the lox and fuel tank vent-relief valves.

1-290. The helium cooler consists of a doubled-walled tank with heat transfer coils inside the inner tank. The insulating annular space between the two tanks is evacuated, and a pump maintains the required vacuum. The cooler contains liquid nitrogen for lowering the temperature of the gaseous helium before it enters the missile helium storage spheres.

1-291. NITROGEN HANDLING EQUIPMENT. Nitrogen handling equipment consists of five high pressure nitrogen tanks. One storage tank (T502) supplies nitrogen gas pressure for the unloading of liquid nitrogen from the helium cooler, purging of the missile fuel tanks, and for blanketing the missile helium, lox, and fuel tanks during standby. One storage tank (T503) supplies nitrogen gas for the operation of leak detection and leak test equipment. One storage tank supplies nitrogen gas pressure for the pneumatically operated airborne valves prior to launch. One storage tank (T505) supplies nitrogen gas for purging of the missile liquid oxygen tanks after liquid oxygen has been unloaded. The same tank supplies nitrogen pressure for the blanketing of the liquid oxygen fill-drain transfer and topping lines, and for the pressure unloading of liquid nitrogen from the liquid oxygen subcooler. One storage tank (T301A,B,C) supplies nitrogen pressure for transferring liquid oxygen from the propellant terminal liquid oxygen tank (T201) to the missile liquid oxygen tanks.

1-292. FUEL HANDLING EQUIPMENT. The fuel terminal components include the storage tanks (nitrogen T510, RP1T110), and necessary lines and valves required to perform fueling operations. The tank and lines are blanketed with low-pressure nitrogen, which minimizes explosion hazards and excludes air and moisture. A fuel transfer pump, located in the central fuel storage access room, is controlled from the fuel transfer panel. Totalizing flowmeters register the transfer of the fuel and prevent overfilling of the missile fuel tanks. Fuel unloading and line drain pumps, located in each missile silo, are used for unloading fuel from the missile and for draining fuel lines.

1-293. CONTROL AND CHECKOUT EQUIPMENT. The propellant system AOE is controlled and checked out by control-monitor group OA-2440 located on Level III of the equipment terminal. The master launch and checkout assembly (6A2) performs readiness checkout, selects modes of system operation, and controls emergency unloading operations. The functions of the other propellant system control and checkout assemblies, located within control monitor group OA-2440, are listed in figure 1-63. Valve position pushbutton indicators are located on the panels of the assemblies. These indicators have the letters C and O engraved in them. The letters, in combination with colored lamps under the translucent indicator face, indicate valve positions.

1-294. AIRBORNE EQUIPMENT. During missile flight, liquid oxygen and fuel are supplied to the rocket engines by the airborne propellant equipment. Both stages rely upon pressurized tanks (fuel and liquid oxygen) and turbopump assemblies for the transfer of propellants. The propellant tanks are pressurized by helium gas from the helium storage spheres in the liquid oxygen tanks. The helium passes through the helium heat exchangers on the rocket engines; then, it passes through the primary regulators, accumulators, and secondary regulators into the propellant tanks.

1-295. STAGE I PROPELLANT EQUIPMENT. The Stage I propellant equipment includes a liquid oxygen tank, a liquid oxygen tank vent-relief valve, a liquid oxygen tank secondary regulator, a liquid oxygen high level sensor, a liquid oxygen fill-drain line and quick disconnect, a liquid oxygen tank pressure switch, two helium storage spheres, a helium accumulator and related components, a helium fill line and quick disconnect, a fuel tank, a fill-drain disconnect, a fuel tank secondary regulator, a fuel tank pressure switch, a fuel tank vent-relief valve, two fuel storage shutoff valves, and a gaseous nitrogen ground start line and quick disconnect.

1-296. STAGE II PROPELLANT EQUIPMENT. The Stage II propellant equipment is comprised of a liquid oxygen tank, two liquid oxygen tank vent-relief valves, a liquid oxygen tank secondary regulator, a liquid oxygen high level sensor, a liquid oxygen fill-drain line and quick disconnect, a liquid oxygen tank pressure switch, a

CHASSIS	FUNCTION
Missile fuel load and launch assembly 5A1	Enables the facility fuel control unit to load and unload fuel from the missile, monitors the fuel system airborne valves, and performs automatic checkout of fuel system airborne valves.
Facility liquid oxygen checkout assembly 5A2	Monitors liquid oxygen system facilities components.
Missile liquid oxygen checkout assembly 5A3	Performs automatic checkout of the liquid oxygen system, and monitors the liquid oxygen system airborne valves.
Missile liquid oxygen launch control assembly 5A7	Contains circuit components for the liquid oxygen checkout assembly 5A3.
Facility liquid oxygen control launch assembly 5A8	Contains circuit components for facility liquid oxygen checkout assembly 5A2.
Propellant quantity monitor assembly 6A1	Contains indicators to read out percent of desired level of liquid oxygen for Stage I and Stage II.
Master launch and checkout assembly 6A2	Serves as the master control panel for the propellant system AGE, selects mode of system checkout, performs readiness checkout, and controls emergency unloading operations.
Gas launch and checkout assembly 6A3	Performs automatic checkout of the helium and nitrogen systems and monitors the helium and nitrogen systems facility and airborne valves.
Propellant quantity control checkout assembly 6A4	Checks the operation of Stage I liquid oxygen propellant quantity control assembly 6A7 and Stage II liquid oxygen propellant quantity control assembly 6A8.

Figure 1-63. Table of Propellant System Control Assemblies

helium storage sphere, a helium accumulator and related components, a helium fill line and quick disconnect, an ATPA liquid oxygen container, a fuel tank, a fuel fill-drain quick disconnect, a fuel tank secondary regulator, a fuel tank pressure switch, a fuel tank vent-relief valve, a fuel storage shutoff valve, and a 3-way valve.

1-297. OPERATION. During alert status monitoring the PLPS monitors the missile vent valves, and fill and drain valves for preset condition; and that CV-537, CV-607, and CV-608 are not closed. When the countdown is initiated the PLPS automatically controls the loading of liquid oxygen and helium aboard the missile by controlling the applicable valves throughout the launcher area and within the missile. In the event of an abort the PLPS automatically returns the missile and propellant loading valves to a safe condition. After shutdown, missile helium and lox unloading is initiated manually at the appropriate pushbutton indicator and controlled automatically by the PLPS logic circuits.

1-298. FUEL TRANSFER. The transfer of fuel to the missile fuel tanks is a manual operation and is controlled at the fuel transfer panel and assembly 5A1 in control-monitor group 2440. For simplicity of control and safety of operation, the two missile stages are loaded sequentially rather than simultaneously. Flowmeters, one mounted at the end of each fill line, monitor the flow of fuel. The flowmeter will automatically shut off the fuel flow when the missile fuel tanks are full. The pump is stopped manually by a pushbutton at the fuel transfer panel or automatically upon the closing of the flowmeter. When fuel transfer operations are complete, the fuel system is manually returned to the standby condition.

1-299. LIQUID OXYGEN TRANSFER. The missile liquid oxygen tanks are filled automatically during launch operations. When a start-propellant-loading signal is received, the propellant system AOE automatically operates remote-controlled valves to start liquid oxygen loading. Liquid oxygen is transferred to the missile by pressurizing the liquid oxygen storage tank with nitrogen. Some liquid oxygen is routed into the fill lines to reduce boil-off of liquid oxygen as it is transferred. During lox loading subcooled liquid oxygen is routed into the tanks at a topping flow rate to balance boil-off and maintain the liquid oxygen tanks at a specific level.

1-300. HELIUM TRANSFER. Helium is transferred to the missile automatically during launch operations. The helium storage cylinder pressure regulating valve and the cold line valve open to let helium flow through the helium cooler, the line filter, and the umbilical connections to the airborne helium storage spheres. The helium storage spheres are charged to a pressure of 3100 PSI. The cold helium supply is maintained until the stop-topping signal is received. At that point, the cold line valve closes, the warm line end valve opens, and uncooled helium at 3100 PSI is transferred directly to the missile for propellant tank pressurization. The warm line valve and the transfer pressure regulating valve close when the start-Stage-I-engine signal is received.

1-301. PNEUMATIC OPERATION. Compressed air from the facility instrument air supply system is used to operate facility components. Nitrogen gas pressure is supplied to the missile during countdown to actuate pneumatic valves and umbilical disconnects and to purge the missile gas generator valve just prior to engine firing. The flow of gas is automatically controlled by flow control and pressure regulating valves.

1-302. MISSILE LAUNCHER SYSTEM.

1-303. The launcher system provides structural support for the missile during launching, positions the missile in a launch (soft) or static (hard) configuration, and positions the support equipment for launch or checkout. In addition, the launcher system supplies propellants, liquid nitrogen, and helium to the missile during countdown, transmits electrical and hydraulic power to the missile, provides protection for personnel and equipment from environmental conditions and nuclear attack, and incorporates monitoring checkout equipment.

1-304. SILO DOOR INSTALLATIONS. The silo doors provide access to the silo for missile emplacement and protect the silo equipment from environmental conditions and nuclear blast. The doors are electrically controlled and hydraulically actuated. Automatic operation is sequenced, controlled, and checked out by the launcher logic circuitry. The doors may be operated locally for maintenance and checkout at the tunnel entrance control station.

1-305. When the doors are closed, the upper door lip overlaps the lower door lip. This overlapping, together with the compression of the environmental seal around the edges of the doors, provides environmental protection for the silo.

1-306. Two hydraulic actuator cylinders operate the silo doors. Each cylinder is mounted on a pivot bracket located on the door foundation.

1-307. SILO DOOR FOUNDATION FITTING INSTALLATION. The silo door foundation fitting installation consists primarily of the breakaway cylinders and hinge coverplates.

1-308. The breakaway cylinders are installed in recesses in the door foundation. There are two cylinders for each door. The breakaway cylinders help raise the doors in the initial stages of the opening cycle and also help overcome loads caused by ice or debris.

1-309. SILO DOOR HYDRAULIC SYSTEM. The power pack supplies hydraulic pressure to the actuator and breakaway cylinders. Manual shutoff valves are located at various points on the supply lines to permit total or partial isolation of the supply system for trouble analysis and maintenance. The hydraulic circuit for both doors is the same. The system operates on 3000 PSI on the pressure side and 75 PSI on the return side.

1-310. CRIB STRUCTURE AND ASSOCIATED EQUIPMENT. The crib structure and associated equipment provide a rigid connection between the launcher platform, and the door foundation and the missile silo during the launch sequence. When the launcher system is hard, the crib structure is flexibly suspended to protect the missile from ground shock.

1-311. The crib structure is a steel framework mounted vertically within the missile silo. The crib structure consists of three main components: top support members, crib sections, and crib base.

1-312. The crib suspension and locking mechanisms lock the crib in a level position during tactical exercise, missile emplacement, and maintenance. When the silo is soft and the launcher platform is to be raised, the crib locks secure the crib rigidly in place to provide a stable platform for moving the launcher platform and launching the missile. The crib suspension and locking mechanisms contain the spring assemblies, crib locks, and all the electrical and hydraulic equipment that control and operate the crib locks.

1-313. LAUNCHER PLATFORM AND ASSOCIATED EQUIPMENT. The launcher platform and associated equipment consist of the following major units: the launcher platform assembly, the launcher platform drive power unit, and the launcher platform counterweight assembly. Each assists in raising or lowering the missile for launcher maintenance, exercise, or launch.

1-314. The launcher platform assembly supports the missile in the silo, and carries and supports the missile during ascent to the launch position. When the system is in the hard condition, the launcher platform assembly is held in position by its own weight and by that of the missile. The launcher platform assembly consists of the following major components: launcher platform-to-crib locks and seals, missile support installation, idler pulleys, flame deflectors, flame deflector extension, flame deflector safety net, flame shielding, guide rollers, service platforms and guard rails, water spray, and a base for the umbilical tower.

1-315. Four vertical and four lateral load locks secure the launcher platform to the crib when the launcher platform has reached the upper end of its travel. The locks absorb wind loads and engine thrust, and help support the weight of the launcher platform and fueled missile.

1-316. Each vertical load lock consists of a T-shaped locking key, a hydraulic motor, and a worm gear assembly. When the actuator motor is energized, the worm gear assembly rotates the locking key to engage two lugs mounted on the crib.

1-317. Each lateral load lock consists of wedge blocks and hydraulic cylinders. When energized, the cylinders pull the wedges vertically against stationary wedges on the launcher platform, completing the locking cycle.

1-318. When the launcher platform is raised to the launch position, the seals shield the gap between the launcher platform and crib and between the crib and silo.

1-319. Three sections guard against the entrance of exhaust gases, water, and propellants to the crib area. The launcher platform is sealed by a horizontal deck located directly under the flame deflector. The deck is pitched slightly from center to permit liquid run-off. A flange mounted at the outer edge of the deck mates with a compression seal when the flange is engaged.

1-320. The area between the launcher platform and the crib is sealed by the crib deck. The crib deck is mounted to the top of the crib and contains the flange with a strip of silicone sponge rubber on its outer edge. The flange on the deck meets the flange on the launcher platform, forming a compression seal. Also located on the crib deck are two clearance areas for the closure door cylinders. These act as sumps and contain drains to carry liquids away. The pitch of the crib deck guides the liquid to the sumps.

1-321. The area between the top of the crib and the bottom of the door foundation is sealed by a silicone rubberized glass fabric which is secured to the outer edge of the crib supports and to the outer edge of the door foundation opening. The gasket is flexible and can withstand ground shock.

1-322. The support installation consists of four A-shaped support assemblies with a missile release mechanism mounted on each support assembly. To permit missile emplacement, the missile release mechanism hold-down arm is removed. Once the missile is emplaced the hold-down arm is installed and tightened against the missile longeron fittings. During the launch cycle, the explosive bolts mounted on the missile release mechanism free the hold-down arm, permitting the missile to rise from the support assemblies.

1-323. A screw and spring mechanism extends the supports during missile emplacement and retracts them at missile lift-off. The retract mechanism contains lead washers that absorb the shock of support retraction.

1-324. An idler pulley assembly includes support and guard brackets, support blocks, a pulley, and an idler shaft and bearing. The idler pulleys, located at each bottom corner of the launcher platform, guide the wire rope cables (part of the drive mechanism) under and around the launcher platform. Each pulley has five grooves, one for each wire rope. A guard bracket prevents the wire ropes from slipping out of the grooves.

1-325. When the Stage I engines fire, the flame deflector acts as a scoop to direct the exhaust flames and gases horizontally.

1-326. The flame deflector extension prevents fuel, liquid oxygen, and water from entering the gap between the flame deflector and the ground line concrete. The deflector extension and retraction mechanisms are hydraulically actuated.

1-327. The flame shielding includes the launcher platform flame shielding and the tower base shielding. The launcher platform shielding consists of flame plates, shields, and supports mounted on the platform structure. It protects the launcher platform and structurally-mounted equipment from the effects of Stage I engine exhaust. The tower base flame shielding consists of a plate and bracket arrangement mounted on the umbilical tower base. The flame shielding extends from approximately 1 foot above the top of the launcher platform to 17 feet above the top of the launcher platform. The flame shielding protects the tower base from Stage I exhaust.

1-328. The safety net is built of a flexible, non-combustible material. It is secured to the pedestals by safety snap hooks and vibration-proof plate rings. The safety net may be removed to provide access to the Stage I engines from the flame deflector.

1-329. The water spray equipment (figure 1-64) consists of the flame deflector spray, engine compartment spray, and associated nozzles.

1-330. The flame deflector spray cools the flame deflector before the descent of the launcher platform and prevents damage to wiring and other components. The manifold, which contains nozzles and orifices, spans the width of the flame deflector.

1-331. The engine compartment spray cools the Stage I engines compartment in the event of an abort after engine firing before lift-off. The spray manifold is on a plane immediately above the engine exhaust and is protected by the flame shielding.

1-332. Both the engine compartment and the flame deflector spray manifold with their associated piping, fittings, and valves are secured to the launcher platform structure. Both manifolds are connected to a common water supply by a coupling, consisting of two self-aligning halves. The mechanism also includes an automatic valve which automatically turns the flow of water on or off. The service disconnect automatically engages and disengages with the raising and lowering of the launcher platform.

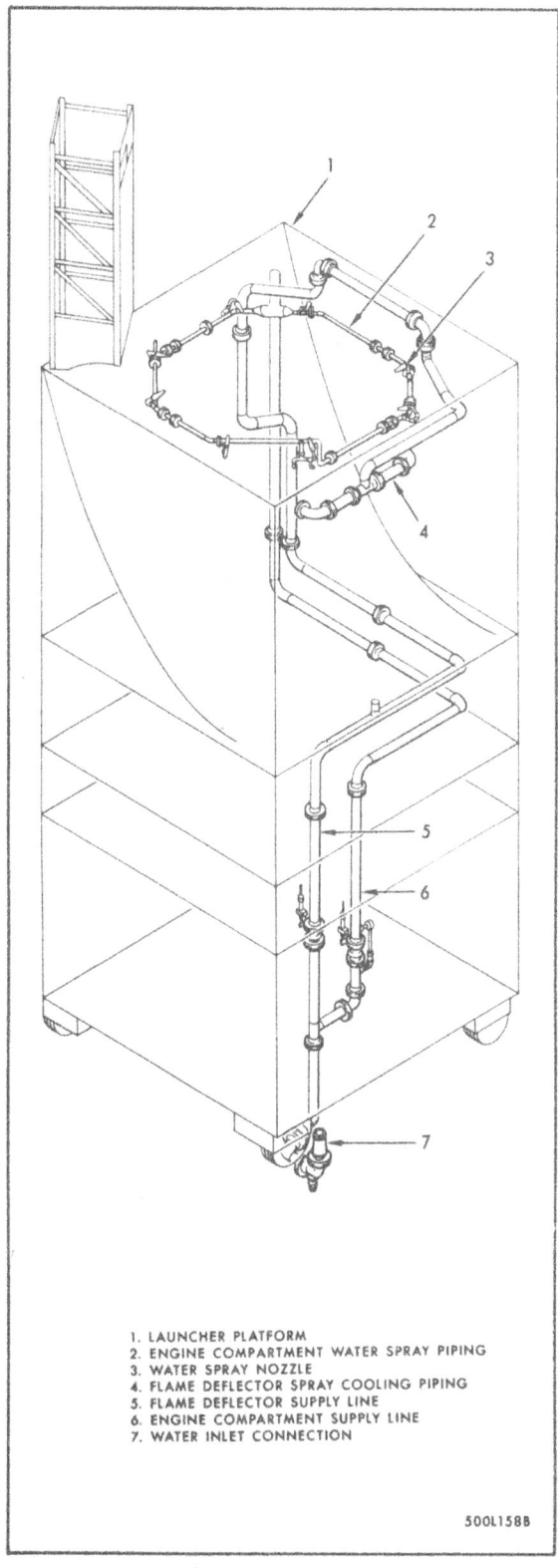

Figure 1-64. Water Spray Equipment

1-333. The guide roller assemblies enable the launcher platform to raise or lower smoothly, counteracting any forces due to wind, sheave friction, or center of gravity eccentricity. The assemblies consist of four large and one small guide rollers. They are mounted on the launcher platform structure. Both large and small guide roller assemblies consist of a mounting bracket, two guide roller shafts, two spherical roller bearings, and various bearing and shaft retainers.

1-334. RE-ENTRY VEHICLE SYSTEM.

1-335. The Mark 4 re-entry vehicle system consists of a re-entry vehicle and its associated ground equipment. The re-entry vehicle is connected to the ground equipment through the missile electrical cabling and connectors (interfaces).

1-336. The external contour of the re-entry vehicle is designed so that an aerodynamic righting moment occurs at the start of the re-entry regardless of the angle of attack. Spin fins impart a rotating moment to the vehicle to maintain the desired trajectory. The external surface of the re-entry vehicle is covered with an ablative type heat shielding material.

1-337. The re-entry vehicle houses the missile payload, protects it during re-entry into the atmosphere, fuses and arms the warhead, and transports the payload to the target area during the final portion of flight. The structure consists of a nose section, center section, and after section. Functional systems include a separation system and an arming-fuzing system. Prearming of the warhead occurs at a predetermined position during flight upon receipt of a signal from the ground guidance system.

1-338. The re-entry vehicle is held in place on the second stage airframe by tension applied through the separation mechanism to a tension cone. The cone firmly grasps the flare of the re-entry vehicle and provides for electrical interface with the missile airframe. When the separation command is received the separation mechanism releases the tension on the cone, causing it to spring apart and free the re-entry vehicle. The electrical interface is broken at this time.

1-339. GROUND EQUIPMENT. The re-entry vehicle ground equipment consists of aerospace operating equipment (AOE) and aerospace ground equipment (AGE). The AOE is used to program re-entry vehicle operation and to monitor re-entry vehicle operational readiness. The re-entry vehicle AGE includes both mechanical and electrical equipment. The mechanical equipment is used to handle components of the re-entry vehicle during transport, assembly, checkout, disassembly, and installation. The electrical equipment is used to check out the components of the re-entry vehicle during assembly and installation.

1-340. The re-entry vehicle aerospace operating equipment (AOE) sets the airburst switch in the re-entry vehicle for the programmed burst altitude and to establish airburst range. The AOE also monitors the ready or fault status of selected circuits within the re-entry vehicle system.

1-341. The AOE is mounted in one rack of control-monitor group OA-2440 located on Level III of each equipment terminal. This rack contains five AOE assemblies, three blank assemblies, and a blower assembly for cooling the operative assemblies.

1-342. The five AOE assemblies include a control indicator, a monitor indicator, a self-test indicator, a fuze-set programmer, and a digital-to-decimal converter. The five assemblies operate as a unit; each one is dependent on the other four assemblies for normal performance of its specific functions. The equipment has self-test capability for isolating malfunctions to the assembly level.

1-343. The burst selection function of the AOE selects groundburst and airburst in the re-entry vehicle and, if airburst, selects a burst altitude and range. The signals that actuate the fuze-setting mechanism of the re-entry vehicle originate from the target control system of control-monitor group OA 2439 in the control center and are transmitted to the AOE in the equipment terminal. There are no provisions in the AOE for introducing a fuze-setting signal other than through the launch control system. The signals transmitted from the target control system are in modified digital form. Appropriate circuits in the AOE convert the digital input to the decimal form that can be used by the re-entry vehicle for setting the airburst switch.

1-344. The monitoring function of the AOE includes monitoring the continuity of safety circuits within the re-entry vehicle. Continuity within the safety circuits results in a go (ready) indication appearing in the appropriate re-entry vehicle indicators. The fuze setting is monitored during the fuze-setting operation and is a representation of the chronological order of the setting procedure and the continued integrity of the fuze-setting circuit. These monitors function during both the readiness checkout and countdown.

1-345. The monitoring and burst-setting circuits of the re-entry vehicle AOE are provided with self-test circuits. Self-testing is divided into two related operations. The first is a functional test in which the fuze setting mechanism is exercised and the second is a fault recognition test in which simulated fault conditions are introduced into the circuits. An associated panel light identifies the assembly in which a fault condition exists.

1-346. LAUNCH SEQUENCER.

1-347. The launch sequencer contains four launch control and status system assemblies. They are the launch sequential timer assembly, launch sequence controller assemblies number 1 and 2, and the launch sequencer filter assembly. The launch sequencer controls, sequences, and monitors the related systems during launch countdown, exercise, and shutdown operations. It monitors the maximum time allowed for the above operations, the go/no-go status of the associated missile and facility, and controls the lower launcher operation. Detailed operation of the assemblies is classified and can be found in the launch control and status system function manual, T.O. 21-SM68-2J-15-1 or T.O. 21-SM68-2J-15-2.

1-348. CONTROL CENTER CIRCUITS.

1-349. The control center circuits consist of circuit assemblies in control-monitor group OA-2439. The assemblies function as a unit to distribute signals between equipment in the control center and equipment in other parts of the launch complex. Command and status signals generated by the functional systems at each of the three missile launchers, the facility damage control system, and the ground guidance station are distributed by the control center circuits to the corresponding indicators on the panels of the launch control console and the launch complex facilities console. The control center circuits include the logic circuitry for isolation of signals from the ground guidance station, for the interlock of the launcher raising and lowering sequence for each of the three missile launchers, for control of the manual missile and facility no-go signal from the facilities console to the corresponding missile launcher, and for the actuation of the hazard-alert buzzer in the facilities console.

1-350. The control center circuit assemblies consist of three control center circuits launcher assemblies (designated as 1, 2, and 3) and a control center circuits common assembly.

1-351. Control monitor group OA-2439 contains a control center circuit hazard warning assembly in addition to the other control center circuits assemblies. The control center circuits hazard warning assembly receives signals from the LCFC. The assembly sends signals to the facility above ground hazard lights to change color for appropriate above ground hazard conditions. It also sends coded signals to the facility warning horns located above ground and lights the respective indicators on the LCFC.

1-352. CONTROL CENTER CIRCUITS LAUNCHER ASSEMBLY. The control center circuits launcher assembly controls the energizing and de-energizing of the indicators on the launch console and on the facilities console in accordance with the status signals generated by the three control-monitor groups at each equipment terminal, the ground guidance station, and the launch complex damage control system. Command and status signals generated by the functional systems at each of the three missile launchers, the facility damage control system, and the ground guidance station are distributed by the control center circuits to the corresponding indicators on the panels of the LCC and the LCFC. The control center circuits also control the manual missile and facility no-go signal from the facilities console to the corresponding missile launcher, and control actuation of the facilities console hazard alert buzzer.

1-353. CONTROL CENTER CIRCUITS COMMON ASSEMBLY. The control center circuits common assembly contains the interlock circuits that prevent raising and lowering of more than one launcher platform at a given time. This assembly also distributes ground guidance no-go, handover, not-ready, loop-check complete, and in-progress signals between the launch control and status equipment in the control center and the launch sequencer in the equipment terminal and ground guidance station.

1-354. The control center circuits common assembly is equipped with pushbutton indicators and selector switches that display, select, and initiate a system checkout for each vital circuit of the launch control and status equipment. The vital circuits include circuitry which inter-changes information between the launchers and circuitry which applies launch sequence information to the ground guidance system during countdown. In addition to initiating system checkout of the vital control center circuits, the pushbutton indicators provide go/no-go displays of the status of the vital control center circuits for each missile launcher.

1-355. TARGET CONTROL. The target control in control-monitor group OA-2439 consists of three target card reader and logic assemblies (one for each missile launcher). These assemblies receive target selection signals from the launch console. Each assembly consists of a card reader and logic circuits that select, read out, and verify (by coded punch-hole type cards) the target information for the re-entry vehicle AOE. The target information contained on the card must be compatible with the target information in the guidance system. The three target card reader and logic assemblies are identical, and each assembly is supplied with three target cards. The cards are color coded blue, white, or yellow for association with missiles in launchers 1, 2, and 3 and target card reader and logic assemblies 1, 2, and 3 respectively. A corresponding color strip identifies target card reader and logic assembly and the associated target selector knob on the launch console. A target card is inserted in each of the three card readers, which are located on the front panel of the assembly. The target card is locked in place by pressing a PUSH TO CLOSE pushbutton actuator on the front of each card reader. Pressing the actuator also closes electrical contacts to complete the necessary circuitry for targeting control. When the proper target card is inserted correctly and locked, the card status indicator for that card lights green. The card status indicator lights red if a card is inserted improperly. White lamps behind the target cards light when the corresponding target is selected from the launch console. A spring-loaded key lock is provided to unlock each PUSH TO CLOSE pushbutton actuator for removal of the target cards.

1-356. CONTROL CENTER POWER SUPPLY. The control center power supply in control-monitor group OA-2439 consists of three assemblies that function as a unit to develop 28 VDC power. The 28 VDC power is provided for launch control and status system equipment in control room 2 (VAFB); indicator lamp verification circuits of launch consoles and facilities consoles; checkout of control center circuits; launch complex damage control system sensors, logic circuits, and associated equipment; and for contact closure signals from the guidance equipment to its corresponding control and checkout equipment. The three assemblies that make up the control center power supply include a 28 VDC power supply, a 28 VDC standby battery, and a power control assembly.

1-357. 28 VDC POWER SUPPLY ASSEMBLY. The 28 VDC power supply assembly is a transformer-rectifier power supply that converts 115 V, 60 CPS, 3-phase power to 28 VDC power. A temperature sensing device to detect overheating is included in the power supply assembly.

1-358. 28 VDC STANDBY BATTERY ASSEMBLY. The 28 VDC standby battery assembly serves as a source for 28 VDC power if a failure occurs in the 28 VDC power supply assembly. The standby battery assembly includes a sensing circuit, a nickel cadmium storage battery, and a battery charger.

1-359. The sensing circuit controls the application of voltage from the 28 VDC power supply assembly to the load bus. The sensing circuit transfers the load from the power supply assembly to the standby battery assembly when the sensing circuit detects a failure or out of tolerance condition in the power supply assembly output voltage. The power supply assembly DC output is out of tolerance when it is less than 27.5 V or more than 32.5 V.

1-360. The nickel cadmium storage battery is a chargeable storage battery that is capable of withstanding a minimum of 100 cycles of charge and discharge. The battery supplies the load bus with an output of from 27 V to 30 VDC at 25 amperes for 30 minutes. A BATTERY OUTPUT circuit breaker on the front of the standby battery assembly protects the battery from overloads.

1-361. The battery charger maintains the nickel cadmium storage battery in a fully charge condition when the battery is not connected to the load bus. The charger can fully charge a discharged battery in 8 hours. The rate of charge is controlled to maintain the battery in a non-gassing condition. A STORE-USE switch inside the standby battery assembly, when manually actuated, connects or disconnects the charger and the battery.

1-362. POWER CONTROL ASSEMBLY. The power control assembly controls the operation of the 28 VDC power supply assembly and the 28 VDC standby battery assembly. The power control assembly contains the controls and indicators to regulate input and output power to check the operation of the 28 VDC power supply assembly. The power control assembly also contains manually operated circuit breakers for the control center 28 VDC power distribution circuits. A LOAD TRANSFER RECT ON LINE pushbutton indicator, when pressed, connects the 28 VDC power supply to the load bus. At this time, the pushbutton indicator lights white and remains on until the power supply is disconnected from the load bus or until the BAT ON LINE pushbutton indicator is pressed. When the BAT ON LINE pushbutton indicator is pressed, the 28 VDC power supply is disconnected from the load bus and the 28 VDC standby battery is connected. The BAT ON LINE pushbutton indicator lights red and remains on until the standby battery is disconnected from the load bus.

1-363. TIME DISPLAY BOARD.

1-364. The control center time display board (figure 1-65) includes one standard 24-hour military clock, one residual time indicator for each launcher, one direct reading clock for each launcher, three control assemblies, and ENABLE/DISABLE indicators that indicate if it is possible to launch a missile.

1-365. RESIDUAL TIME INDICATOR. The residual time indicator is a 1000-second clock with primary and secondary sweep hands. The primary hand makes one revolution of the dial in 1000 seconds and the secondary hand makes one revolution of the dial in 10 seconds. The residual time indicator is started by the launch sequencer at the start of the countdown when the launch control console LOAD PROPELLANTS pushbutton indicator is pressed. At each countdown hold point, the residual time indicator is stopped and restarted when the countdown is resumed.

1-366. DIRECT READING CLOCK. The direct reading clock is a digital clock with three digits for minutes and two digits for seconds. The clock is started, stopped, and reset to zero by the launch sequencer. At each countdown hold point, the clock is automatically started and runs until the countdown is resumed.

1-367. CONTROL ASSEMBLIES. The three control assemblies, one for each residual time indicator and direct reading clock, are located inside the time display board. These assemblies contain relay logic circuits which couple control signals from the launch sequencer and power distribution panel of the control-monitor groups to each residual time indicator and direct reading clock.

1-368. ENABLE AND DISABLE INDICATORS. The ENABLE and DISABLE indicators indicate if a missile may or may not be launched. These indicators are part of a remotely controlled system designed to prevent the inadvertent or unauthorized launch of a missile. The DISABLE indicator is normally lighted, indicating that a missile cannot be launched. If the ENABLE indicator is lighted a missile may be launched.

1-369. HYDRAULIC SYSTEM.

1-370. The hydraulic system includes ground and airborne hydraulic equipment. The ground hydraulic equipment supplies filtered and demulsified hydraulic fluid under pressure to the airborne equipment during checkout and countdown. During flight, the airborne equipment provides the hydraulic power to position the Stage I and Stage II thrust chambers and to rotate the vernier nozzles at the command of the flight control system.

1-371. GROUND EQUIPMENT. The ground equipment consists of hydraulic pumping unit A/E27A-2 and the plumbing that connects the unit to the missile. The ground operating equipment supplies hydraulic fluid to both missile stages for filling and flushing the airborne equipment and maintains a continuous flow of hydraulic fluid to the airborne equipment during hydraulic system checkout and countdown.

1-372. Hydraulic pumping unit A/E27A-2 is a console type unit located on Level II of the equipment terminal. The unit may be operated either remotely by the electrical system or locally from its own control panel. During electrical system check-

T.O. 21-SM68-1

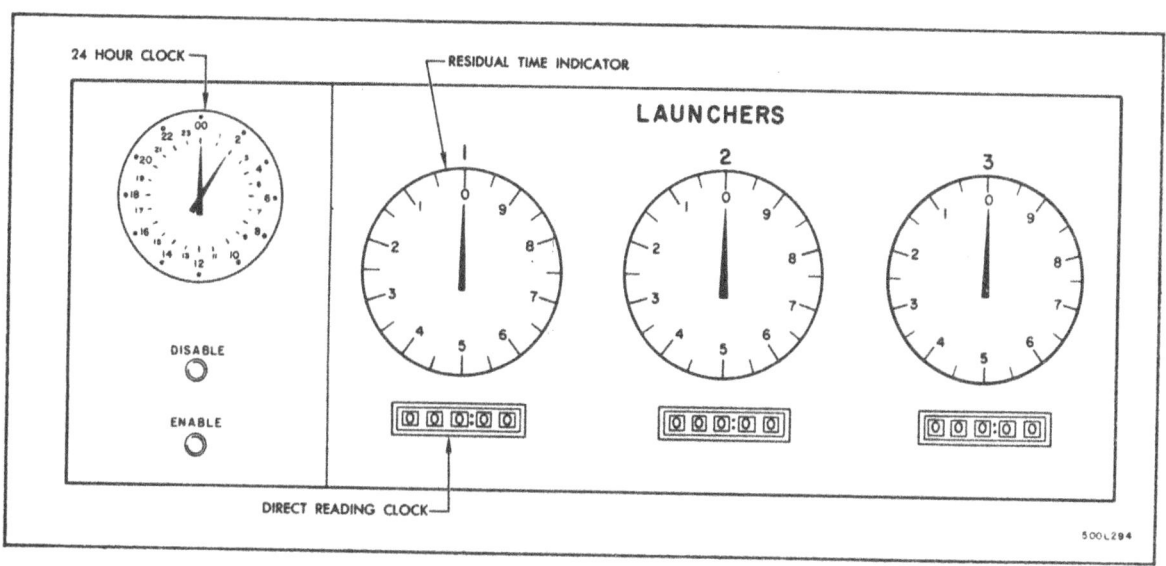

Figure 1-65. Time Display Board (Operational Bases)

out and launch countdown, the unit starts automatically in responce to signals from the launch sequencer. In addition to a reservoir, pressure gages, a temperature gage, flow direction valves, and a fire extinguisher, the unit contains a main fluid circuit and an auxiliary fluid circuit.

1-373. The main fluid circuit supplies hydraulic fluid at regulated flows of approximately 10 GPM to Stage I and 5 GPM to Stage II, at a pressure of 3250 PSI. A suction filter in the main circuit, between the reservoir and the main pump, removes 40-micron size particles from the fluid. The outlet line from the main pump contains two high pressure filters in series.

1-374. The main hydraulic pump is an axial-piston, variable volume, pressure compensated unit capable of delivering hydraulic fluid at a flow rate of 18 GPM at a pressure of 3250 PSI.

1-375. The auxiliary fluid circuit contains a filter pump and a demulsifier filter. The auxiliary fluid circuit is used to break up water emulsions within the hydraulic fluid.

1-376. The ground equipment plumbing directs pressurized hydraulic fluid to the missile in both the stored (in-silo) and raised (launch) positions for Stage I and in the stored position only for the Stage II. A pressure and a return line for each missile stage is routed from the hydraulic pumping unit through the utilities tunnel to an interface at the missile silo wall.

1-377. The hydraulic umbilical disconnects are mechanical self-sealing units that are disconnected from the missile by lanyards. The Stage II hydraulic umbilical disconnects are released as the launcher platform raises the missile to the launch position. The Stage I hydraulic umbilical disconnects are released at missile lift off.

1-378. AIRBORNE EQUIPMENT. The airborne hydraulic equipment provides a continuous flow of hydraulic fluid during flight. Pressurized hydraulic fluid is supplied to the servo-actuators, which position the rocket engine thrust chambers and vernier nozzles in accordance with signals received from the flight control system. Each stage of the missile contains a separate grouping of hydraulic components.

1-379. All components of the Stage I hydraulic equipment (figure 1-66) are located in the Stage I engine compartment. These components consist of a hydraulic pump, an accumulator and reservoir unit, four booster engine servo-actuators, a fluid level switch, and a pressure transducer.

1-380. The hydraulic pump is mounted on the turbopump accessory drive pad of rocket engine subassembly number 2. The pump is capable of supplying 15 GPM at a pressure of 3000 PSI.

1-381. The accumulator and reservoir unit consists of an accumulator, a reservoir, and a reservoir level switch. The unit maintains the required fluid level within the Stage I hydraulic components, dampens pressure fluctuations, maintains return pressure, and provides a means of measuring fluid level.

1-382. The regulator assures an ample supply of fluid to the pump and absorbs pressure surges during actuator motion. If the hydraulic pump fails, the accumulator portion of the regulator will supply pressure for the servo-actuators so that thrust chamber positioning control will be maintained for a short time.

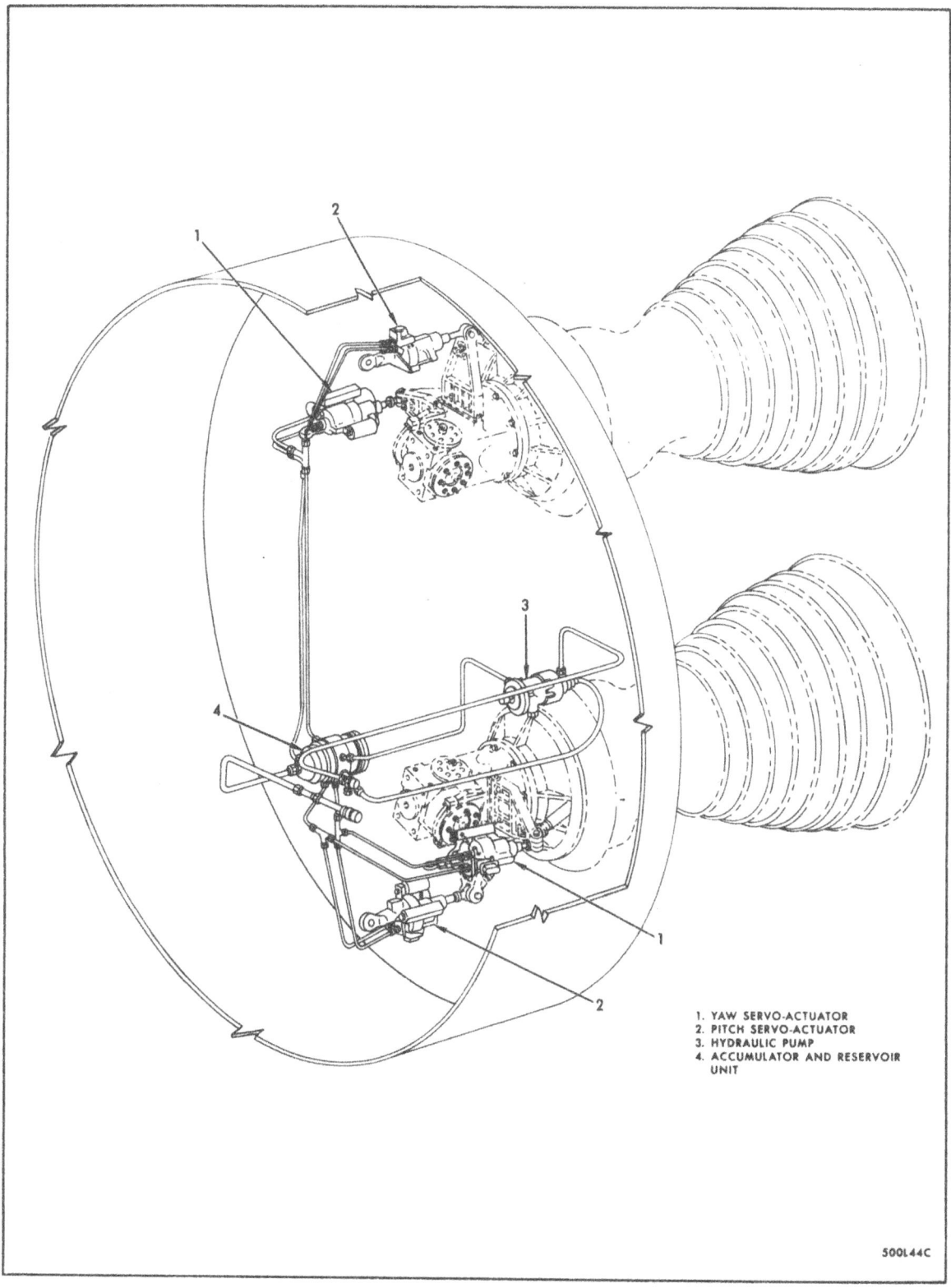

Figure 1-66. Stage I Hydraulic Equipment Location

1-383. The Stage I rocket engine (booster engine) requires four hydraulic servo-actuators to position the two thrust chambers. Each thrust chamber has one servo-actuator for yaw control and one for pitch control. Each servo-actuator contains a cylinder and piston, a servo valve, and a linear follow-up potentiometer.

1-384. The cylinder is attached to the engine frame and the piston is connected to the thrust chamber gimbal actuation arm. As the piston moves, due to the pressure differential within the cylinder, the thrust chamber is positioned by the gimbal actuation arm.

1-385. The servo valve controls the flow of hydraulic fluid into the cylinder. Signals from the flight control system actuate the valve, which restricts the flow of fluid to one side of the piston. This restriction in fluid flow creates a pressure differential within the cylinder and results in piston movement in the direction of the lower pressure. As the piston moves, it positions an internal wiper arm on the linear follow-up potentiometer. When the movement called for by the flight control system is made, the potentiometer balances an electrical circuit and the servo valve returns to neutral. At this time, the flow of hydraulic fluid to both sides or the piston is equal and piston movement ceases.

1-386. The level switch is mounted on the bottom of the regulating unit and sends a regulating unit level in-limit or out-of-limit signal to the hydraulic pumping unit panel and the electrical system.

1-387. All components of the Stage II hydraulic equipment (figure 1-67) are located in the Stage II engine compartment. These components consist of a hydraulic pump and motor, two sustainer engine servo-actuators, four vernier nozzle servo-actuators, an accumulator and reservoir unit, pressure switches, and a fluid level switch.

1-388. The functions of the Stage II accumulator and reservoir unit, pressure switches, and level switch are identical to the corresponding components used on Stage I.

1-389. The hydraulic pump in Stage II is an electric motor-driven variable-displacement, axial-piston pump. The pump motor is powered by a 28 VDC airborne battery and is coupled to the pump through a speed-reducer gear train. The pumping mechanism of the hydraulic pump consists of a drive shaft, pistons, and a block assembly. A spring-loaded pilot valve pressure-controller is mounted externally on the pump. Fluid delivery is 5 GPM at 3000 PSI. A pressure transducer (mounted as part of the IRRS kit on VAFB missiles only) monitors pump outlet pressure for telemetering instrumentation.

1-390. The Stage II rocket engine thrust chamber (sustainer engine) requires two hydraulic servo-actuators to position the thrust chamber. One servo-actuator for yaw movement and one for pitch movement are mounted between the thrust chamber and the engine frame. The sustainer engine servo-actuators are similar to the booster engine servo-actuators and operate in the same manner.

1-391. A vernier nozzle servo-actuator positions each vernier nozzle in accordance with signals received from the flight control system. Each servo-actuator consists of two cylinders and two pistons, a servo valve, and two linear potentiometers. The pistons are connected to a common drive cable, which is rigged over a cable drum on the vernier nozzle. When the servo valve restricts the flow of fluid to one cylinder of the servo-actuator, the piston in the other cylinder retracts and pulls the drive cable, causing the vernier nozzle cable drum to rotate and position the

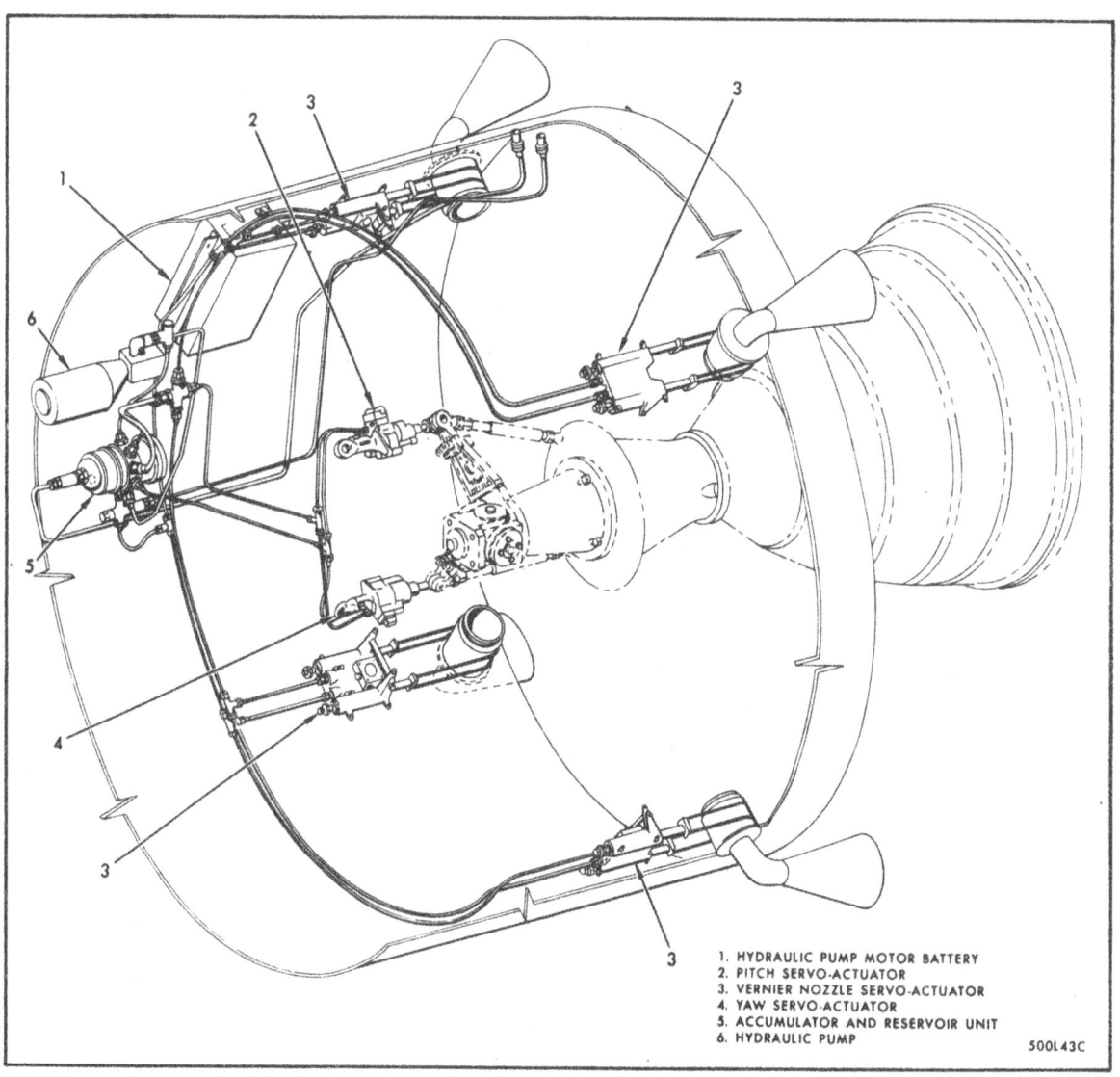

Figure 1-67. Stage II Hydraulic Equipment Location

vernier nozzle to the proper angle for attitude correction. Simultaneously, the opposite end of the drive cable extends the other piston of the servo-actuator. As the pistons move, they position a wiper arm on each linear follow-up potentiometer. When the vernier nozzle movement called for by the flight control system is made, the potentiometers balance an electrical circuit, and the servo-valve returns to neutral. At this time, the flow of hydraulic fluid is equalized to both cylinders, and piston movement ceases.

1-392. OPERATION. The hydraulic pumping unit is started during the countdown when a start-hydraulics signal is sent from the launch sequencer. The signal is received by the electrical system which starts the hydraulic pumping unit after the missile air conditioner has started and power has been applied to the missile electrical buses. The start-hydraulics signal is automatically initiated by the launch sequencer 180 seconds after the missile launch officer presses the launch control console LOAD PROPELLANTS pushbutton indicator.

1-393. After the RAISE LAUNCHER pushbutton indicator has been pressed, the Stage II hydraulic pump motor is started, the launcher platform is raised, the Stage II hydraulic umbilical disconnects are released, and the hydraulic pump motor battery is activated.

1-394. When the LAUNCH pushbutton indicator is pressed, ground power is removed from the missile buses, missile power is applied, the Stage I engine starts, and the engine operates the Stage I hydraulic pump. As the missile leaves the launcher platform, the Stage I hydraulic umbilical disconnects are released.

1-395. During Stage I flight operation, a turbine in the number 2 thrust chamber turbopump assembly drives the hydraulic pump through an accessory-drive gear train. Hydraulic fluid from the pump enters the accumulator portion of the regulating unit, which dampens pressure surges. The fluid is then routed to the booster hydraulic actuators. A servo valve in each actuator responds to signals from the flight control system and controls hydraulic fluid flow through the actuator. From the actuators, the fluid is returned to the regulating unit reservoir and then recycled by the hydraulic pump.

1-396. During Stage I and Stage II flight, the Stage II hydraulic pump motor is powered by the hydraulic pump motor battery. During Stage I operation, the sustainer engine servo-actuators are electrically locked in a neutral position by the flight control system. At stage separation the servo-actuators are unlocked, allowing them to position the sustainer thrust chamber in accordance with signals from the flight control system. In addition to the sustainer engine servo-actuators, Stage II has four vernier nozzle servo-actuators that position the vernier nozzles in response to signals from the flight control system.

1-397. MISSILE AIR CONDITIONING SYSTEM.

1-398. The missile air conditioning system (figure 1-68) provides conditioned air to the Stage II transition, between tanks, and engine compartments. The conditioned air maintains environmental temperatures necessary to the accuracy and reliability of the guidance, control, electrical, and propulsion components during checkout and launch operations. The system consists of the missile air conditioner A/F32C-5, the air conditioning ducting, and the air conditioning disconnects.

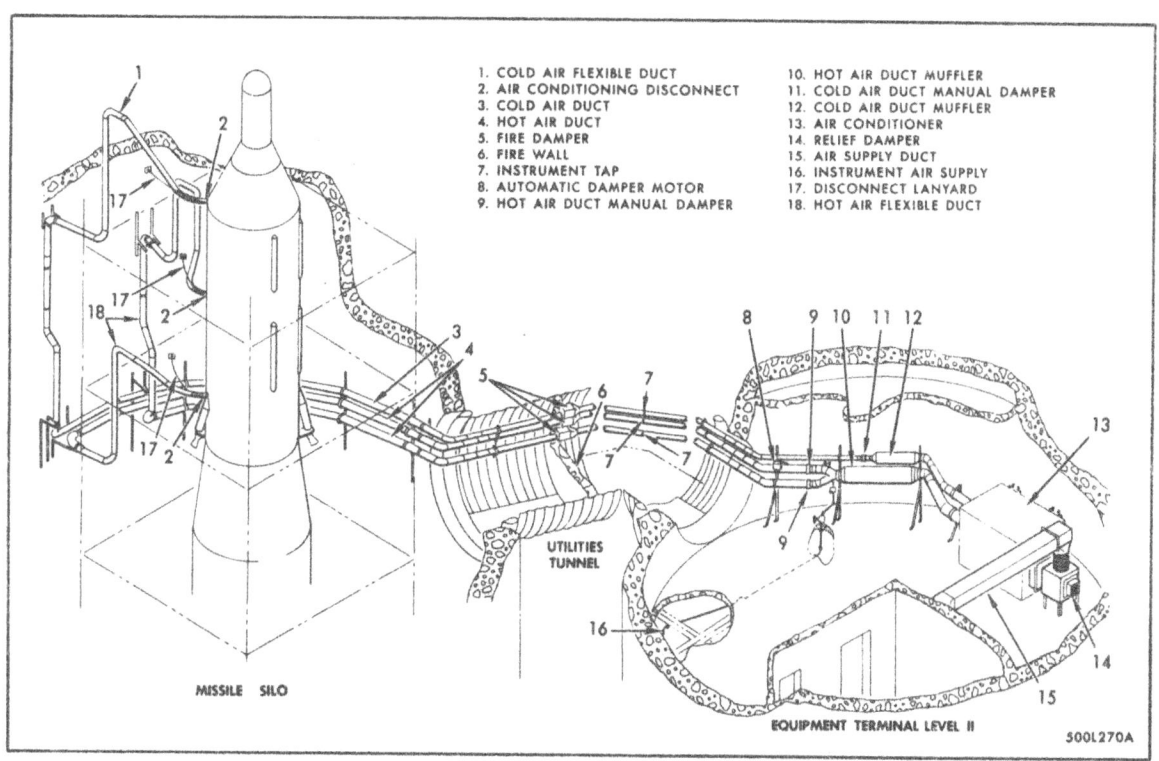

Figure 1-68. Missile Air Conditioning System (Operational Bases)

1-399. MISSILE AIR CONDITIONER. The missile air conditioner is located on Level II of the equipment terminal. Flush mounted hinged doors and panels cover the operating controls. The refrigeration, chilled water, hot water, and air flow components are enclosed and protected by removable access panels.

1-400. The chilled water circuit supplies water to a chilled water coil for cooling and dehumidifying incoming air and to the condenser for the condensation of high pressure gas. The chilled water coil is constructed of copper tubes and fins. The cooling capacity of the coil is 237,600 BTU/HR.

1-401. The hot water circuit supplies water to a hot water coil for the heating of conditioned air. The hot water coil is constructed of copper tubes and aluminum fins. The heating capacity of the coil is 205,000 BTU/HR.

1-402. The air flow circuit consists of a blower and the ducting required to induct air from the atmosphere, direct it through the air conditioner, and distribute it to the missile. Electrical controls maintain the proper volumes of discharged conditioned air.

1-403. ELECTRICAL CONTROL CIRCUITS. Six electrical control circuits operate and check the missile air conditioning system. Some of the electrical controls are located on the air conditioner control panel and the missile air conditioner control panel. Other electrical controls are located on control-monitor group OA-2438 on Level III of the equipment terminal. The remaining electrical controls are located on power switchboard JEU-7 on Level IV of the equipment terminal.

1-404. OPERATION. The missile air conditioning system is placed in operation automatically when the missile launch officer presses the LOAD PROPELLANTS pushbutton indicator on the launch control console. Intake air is blown through the chilled water coil and the evaporator where it is dehumidified and cooled. Part of the cold, dry air is then discharged through the cold air outlet. The remaining cold air is reheated at the hot water coil. The hot, dry air is then discharged through the hot air outlet. The conditioned air flow is illustrated in figure 1-69.

1-405. <u>COMMUNICATION SYSTEM.</u>

1-406. The communications system within the Titan I missile weapon system provides a means for integrating communications activities, such as command communications vital to launch functions, and maintenance communications required for location and repair of weapons system malfunctions as well as coordinating maintenance activities. This system also integrates security communications for visitor control and for movement of personnel and material, administrative communications for routing administrative operations, and emergency communications for reporting accidents and other emergencies. The communications system consists of communications paths and communications equipment. The primary alerting system provides alert and strike commands from SAC to all launch sites.

1-407. <u>INSTRUMENTATION AND RANGE SAFETY SYSTEM FACILITIES (VAFB).</u>

1-408. Instrumentation and range safety requirements are satisfied by a ground receiving station etc. The ground receiving station receives telemetered flight performance data from the airborne instrumentation system and a range safety system, which tracks the missile during flight and initiates command destruct signals if missile performance is erratic. The system includes an instrumentation control center building, a mobile telemetry station, a command destruct building, radar

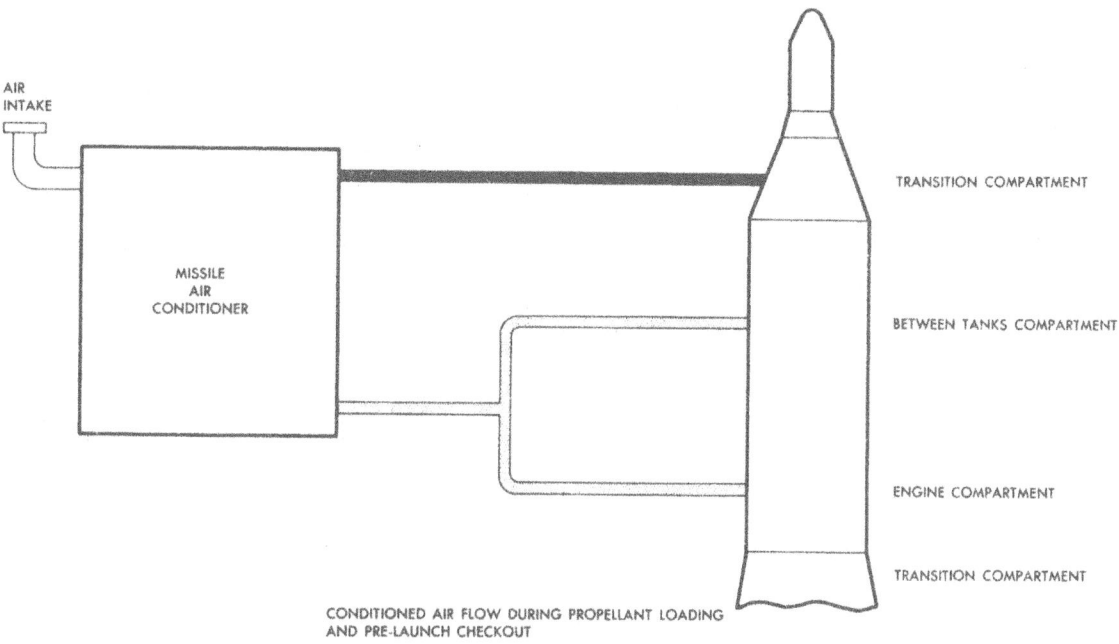
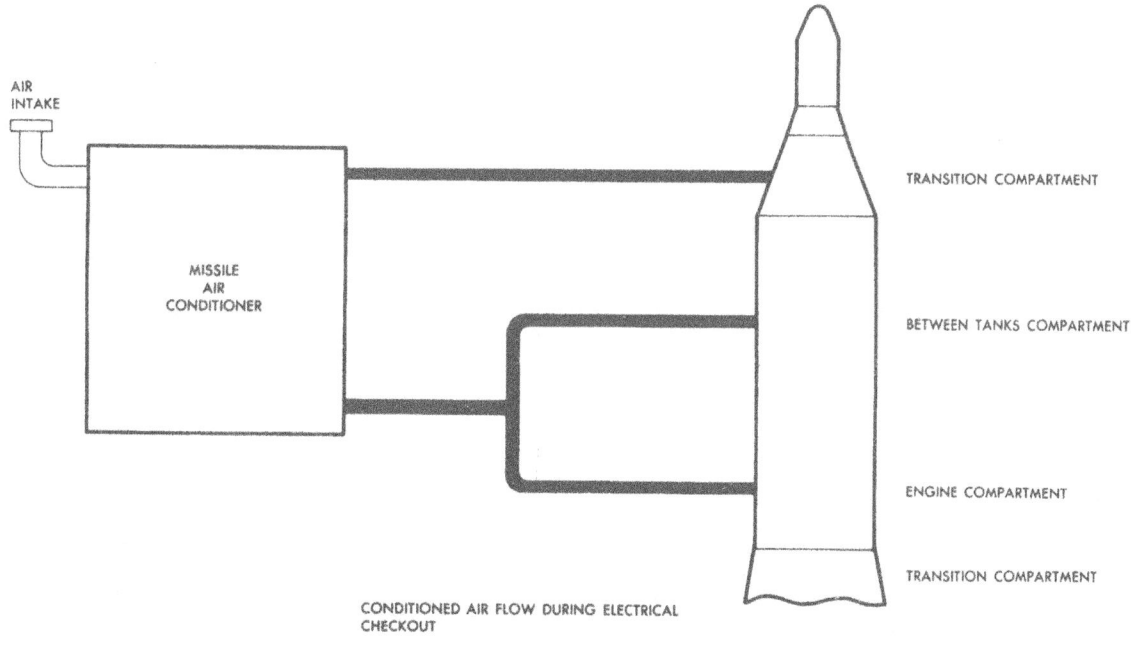

Figure 1-69. Conditioned Air Flow

tracking facilities, and two angle-measuring equipment-correlation tracking and ranging (AME-Cotar) fields.

1-409. The fixed telemetry receiving and recording station monitors pre-launch missile telemetry equipment and receives and records telemetered in-flight missile data. The station also contains sufficient test and auxiliary equipment to assure the proper functioning of the ground telemetry components. In-flight tracking of missiles is performed by an M2 optical tracker. A telemetry receiving antenna is slaved to the M2 optical tracker by a telemetry antenna system operated by remote control.

1-410. MOBILE TELEMETER STATION.

1-411. The mobile telemetry station contains test and auxiliary equipment for checking out the airborne telemetry and destruct equipment and the receiving-recording equipment at the fixed telemetry station. Equipment contained in the mobile station is identical to that of the fixed station plus additional telemetering, recording, and listing facilities.

1-412. COMMAND DESTRUCT FACILITIES.

1-413. The command destruct building and the attached antenna tower houses the standard transmitters, power amplifiers, and antenna equipment. To insure reliability of operation, two 500-watt transmitters (primary and secondary) provide power to the antennas. For transmission of command destruct signals to a missile within a 30-mile radius, the power is supplied to the lower power omnidirectional antenna. As the missile passes the 30-mile radius, a variable timer switches transmitter power to a 10 KW amplifier and the directional antenna. The variable timer is started at the instant missile flight begins. The timer is equipped with a manual override to permit manual operation, if desired.

1-414. RADAR TRACKING FACILITIES.

1-415. Radar tracking facilities consist of an AFMTC MOD III radar set, two AN/MPS-19 radar sets, and a Mark 51 optical gun director for acquisition of initial missile lift-off. Each radar set is equipped with sinecosine potentiometers to convert azimuth, elevation, and range shift position to DC voltages for use with an analog-polar-to-cartesian-converter-plotting board display system.

1-416. AME-COTAR FIELDS.

1-417. There are two AME-Cotar antenna fields located approximately 6 miles apart. A building located near each antenna field contains the Cotar equipment.

1-418. RADAR SURVEILLANCE SYSTEM AN/TPS-39(V).

1-419. PURPOSE.

1-420. The radar surveillance system AN/TPS-39(V) (figure 1-70) provides an audible and visual indication of the presence of an intruder in restricted areas of United States Air Force installations. This surveillance function is accomplished by a combination of components in a configuration suited for a particular installation. The equipment may be arranged to perform four types of radar surveillance. These four types are designated class A, B, C or D surveillance. The class A surveillance detects intrusions around the perimeter of a specific area. The class B type of surveillance detects intrusions within the specific area. Class C surveillance is

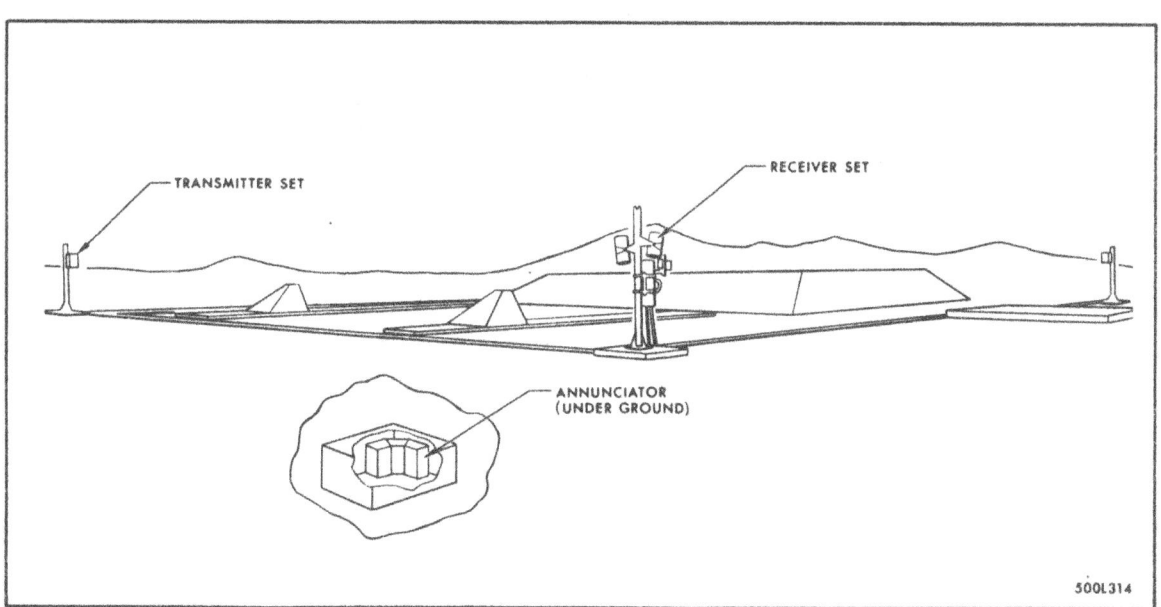

Figure 1-70. Typical Radar Surveillance System AN/TPS-39(v)

accomplished in such a manner that entry through a port is detected. Class D surveillance is similar to class B, except a greater area is under surveillance.

1-421. DESCRIPTION.

1-422. Radar surveillance system AN/TPS-39(V) can detect intrusions in areas where the longest distance between antennas does not exceed 200 feet, and the shortest distance between antennas is not less than 10 feet. Primary power is supplied to receiver and annunciator power supplies, which then provide operating power to the other components of the system through interconnecting cables.

1-423. A continuous wave, unmodulated RF signal is generated by the transmitter (figure 1-71) oscillator, divided into signals of equal magnitude by the power divider (located inside the transmitter), and applied to the transmitting antennas. The outputs from the transmitting antennas are received by the receiver set (figure 1-72) and transferred to the power combiner where they are combined and applied as one signal to the tuner-mixer-detector. The output of the tuner-mixer-detector to the receiver is a steady DC signal. When an intruder moves through the area between a transmitting antenna and a receiving antenna, a portion of the transmitter RF signal is deflected by the intruder and arrives at the receiving antenna slightly out of phase with the transmitter signal, resulting in an RF signal modulated by the movement of the intruder. The tuner-mixer-detector detects the modulation as a sub-audio AC signal. When the AC signal is received, an alarm is initiated by the receiver. The receiver also initiates an alarm any time the RF signal is not received, denoting a transmitter failure. Figure 1-73 illustrates a class A antenna group, and figure 1-74 illustrates the components within a receiver group.

1-424. The alarm signal is transmitted to the annunciator (figure 1-75) by the receiver. The annunciator causes an alarm bell to sound and an indicator, located on its front panel, to light. In addition, an alarm indicator lights on the launch control console. The alarm bell and the indicator on the launch control console inform operating personnel that an intrusion into a designated area has occurred. The indicator on the annunciator panel shows the particular area of intrusion, since it signifies which receiver has transmitted the alarm signal. Figure 1-76 illustrates annunciator power supply and components.

1-425. System and component operating capabilities are contained in figure 1-77.

1-426. MAINTENANCE PLAN.

1-427. The weapon system maintenance plan is designed to provide maximum support through organizational maintenance and depot maintenance. Organizational maintenance is divided into two levels: organizational level, which includes removal and installation of components; and field level, which includes repair of removed components. Depot maintenance consists of maintenance beyond organizational maintenance capabilities such as major modifications and overhaul of equipment.

1-428. ORGANIZATIONAL LEVEL AND FIELD LEVEL MAINTENANCE.

1-429. Organizational level and field level maintenance is that maintenance authorized and performed within the operational squadron on its assigned equipment.

(Text continued on page 1-141)

T.O. 21-SM68-1 Section I

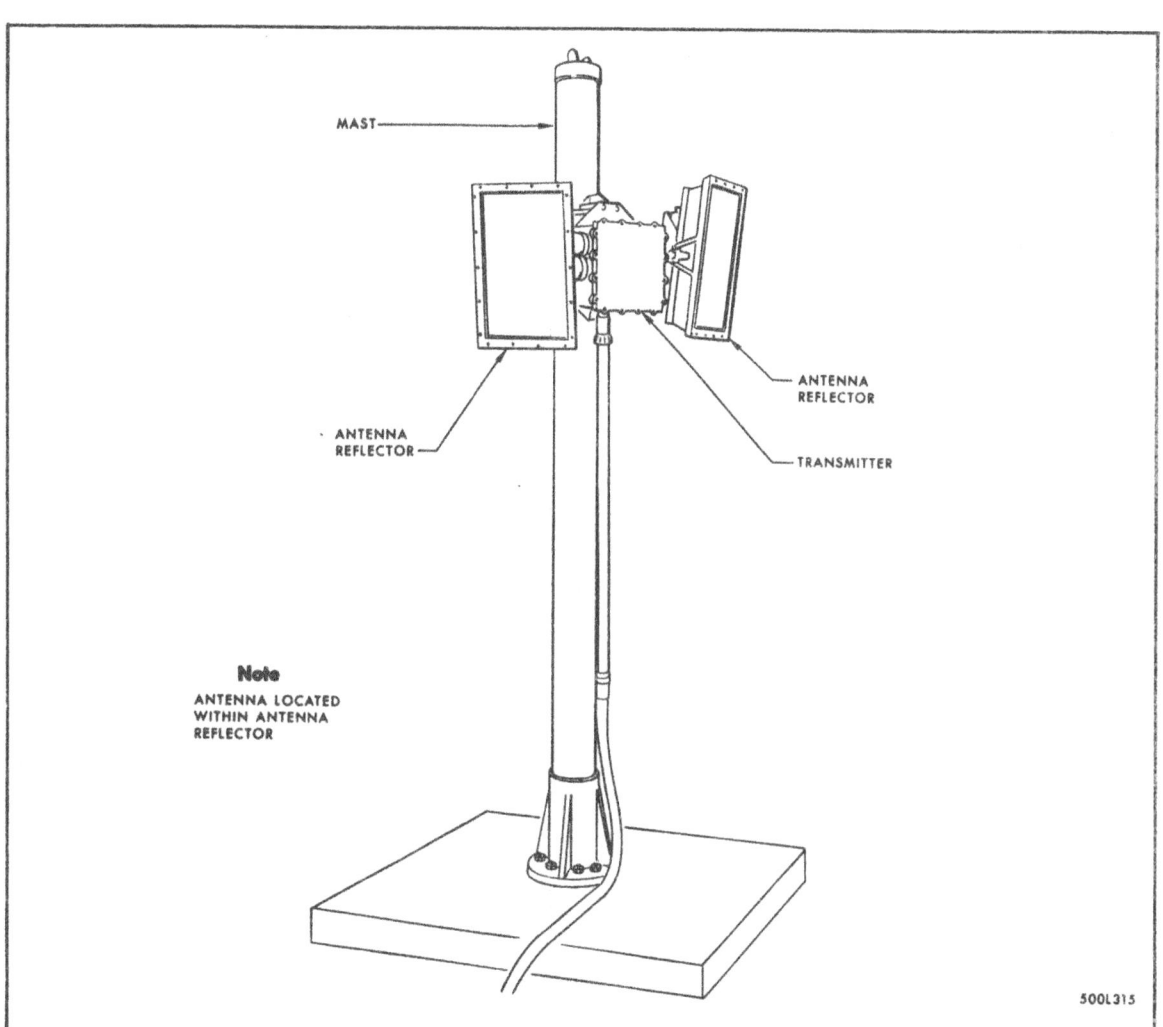

Figure 1-71. Class D Transmitter Set

1-134

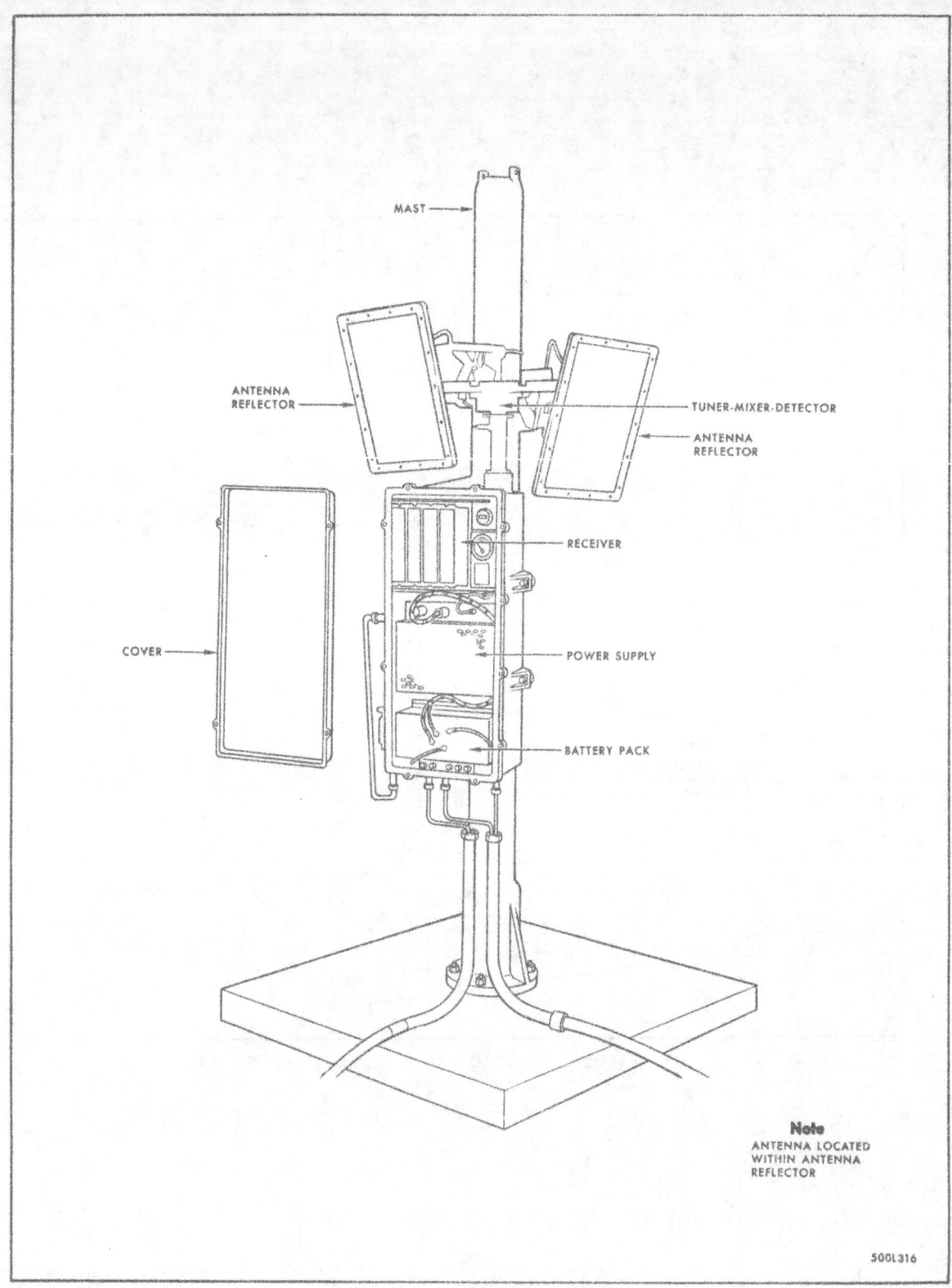

Figure 1-72. Class D Receiver Set (Receiver Group Cover Removed)

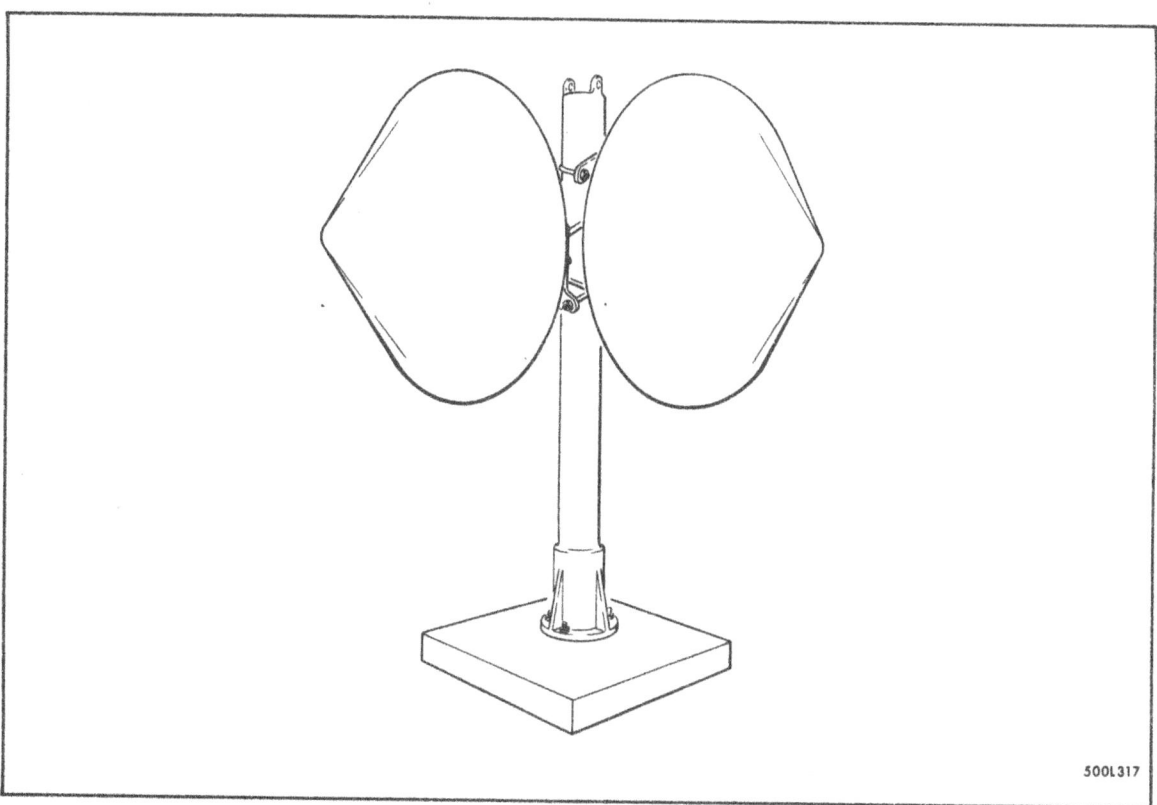

Figure 1-73. Class A Antenna Group (Receiver or Transmitter Set)

T.O. 21-SM68-1　　　　　　　　　　　　　　　　Section I

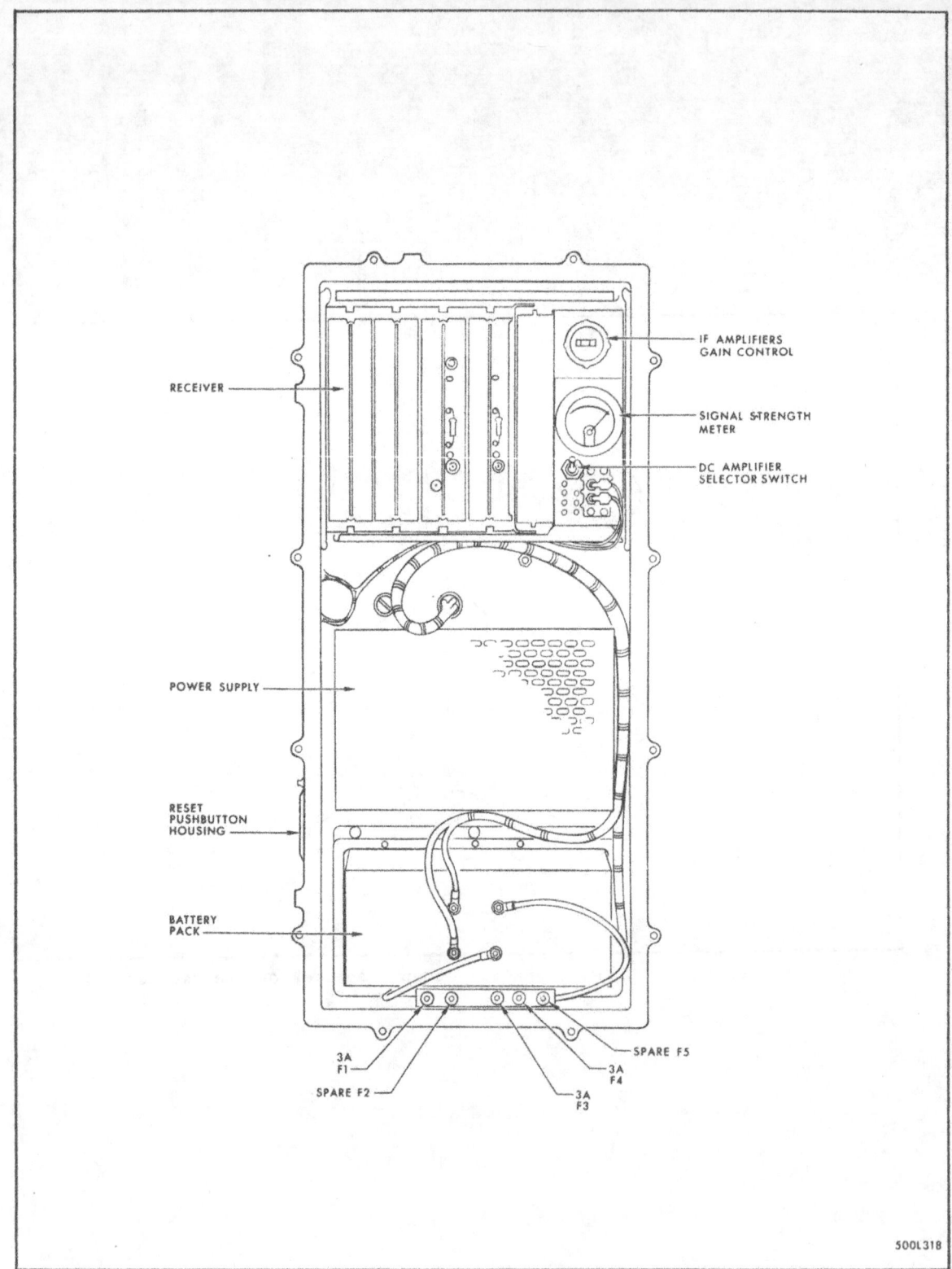

Figure 1-74. Receiver Group

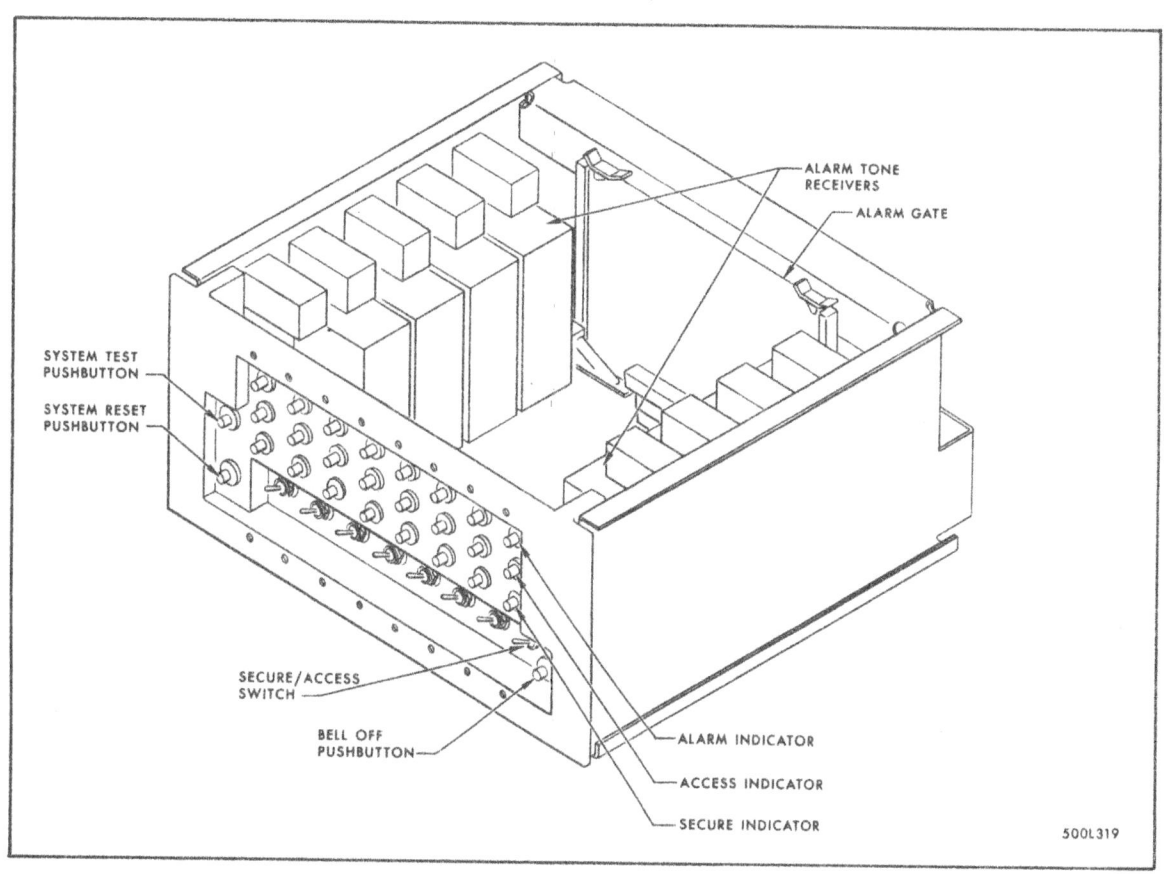

Figure 1-75. Annunciator

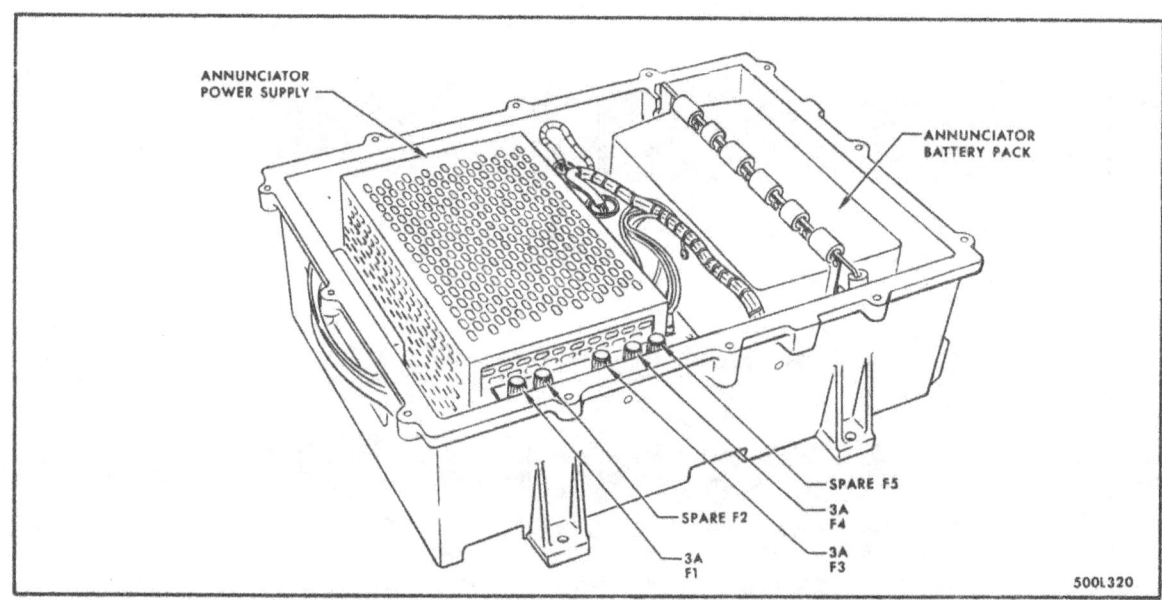

Figure 1-76. Annunciator Power Supply

Frequency range	1710 to 1760 MC
Type of operation	Continuous wave, bistatic detection.
Range and coverage	Detects intrusions in areas where longest dimension between antennas does not exceed 200 feet, and shortest dimension is not less than 10 feet.
Accuracy	Detects human intrusions into sensitive area with 0.1 to 5 CPS variations from the center frequency.
Class A antenna characteristics	Parabolic reflector.
Class B antenna characteristics	Modified corner reflector.
Class C antenna characteristics	Corner reflector.
Class D antenna characteristics	Two class B antenna reflectors.
Sensitivity and selectivity	Detects doppler frequency shifts from 0.1 to 5 CPS from the center frequency within the detection area.
Transmitter power output	0.3 watt to 2 watts per operating system.
Modulation characteristics	Continuous wave, unmodulated.

Figure 1-77. Table of Radar Surveillance System AN/TPS-39(V) Capabilities

(Text continued from page 1-133.)

1-430. Organizational level maintenance includes normal squadron functions such as readiness checkout, daily inspections, storage inspections, routine launch site servicing, preventive maintenance, and the removal and installation of specific components for the purpose of achieving operational readiness.

1-431. Field level maintenance includes functions such as bench maintenance, mobile maintenance, mating of missile stages, mating of re-entry vehicle and missile, periodic inspections, recycle maintenance on repairable items removed from missiles and ground equipment, technical order compliance, and reclamation and repair of components and parts.

1-432. Organizational level and field level maintenance is authorized for components of the airborne and ground equipment. Both levels of maintenance are performed at the launch complex and at the MAMS. Regardless of the area in which the equipment is located, the extent of authorized maintenance is limited by personnel skills, facilities, tools, test equipment, and equipment design.

1-433. Maintenance performed on the airborne and ground equipment at the launch complex consists of the following:

   a. Periodic maintenance and servicing of components.

   b. Testing to insure minimum performance standards.

   c. Performing trouble analysis and isolating faulty components to the smallest replaceable unit, replacing faulty units, aligning and calibrating replacement units, and performance testing components to insure their being in a state of readiness required for all equipment within the complex.

1-434. Maintenance performed on the airborne and ground equipment at the MAMS consists of the following:

   a. Making initial inspections and service checks on the missile and on replacement components.

   b. Isolating malfunctions in items received from the launch complex, repairing the components, if possible, and aligning and calibrating components after repair.

   c. Making periodic inspections and checking shelf (spare) components.

   d. Maintaining test benches used in field level maintenance.

   e. Repairing and calibrating test equipment.

1-435. AIRBORNE EQUIPMENT. Organizational level maintenance of airborne equipment is authorized. Field level maintenance of airborne equipment is authorized if the components are not in the following categories:

   a. A sealed unit (unless maintenance is specifically authorized).

   b. Batteries.

   c. A gyro or some other finely machined, delicate unit.

d. A motor armature or stator that requires winding.

e. An item that becomes uncalibrated during repair, and recalibration requires a static firing or operation under simulated flight conditions.

f. An item that affects engine alignment and positioning.

g. High pressure spheres.

h. Major structural members that affect alignment or structural strength such as stiffener rings, longitudinal members, and braces.

i. Ordnance items.

j. An item requiring elaborate and special testing equipment.

1-436. GROUND OPERATING EQUIPMENT AND GROUND SUPPORT EQUIPMENT. Organizational level maintenance of aerospace operating equipment (AOE) and aerospace ground equipment (AGE) is authorized. Field level maintenance of AOE and AGE is authorized if the components are not in the following categories:

a. A sealed unit (unless maintenance is specifically authorized).

b. A motor armature or stator that requires winding.

c. A component requiring extensive repairs (rebuilding or complete overhaul).

d. A generator armature or stator that requires winding.

e. Gyro checkers.

f. An item that affects calibration of a complete component.

g. An item that requires precision mechanical repairs such as the ground guidance antenna drive equipment components.

h. Batteries.

1-437. DEPOT MAINTENANCE.

1-438. Depot maintenance is that maintenance beyond the capabilities of organizational maintenance personnel and equipment. It includes major modifications, repairs, and overhaul.

1-439. For Martin furnished components, depot level maintenance is accomplished at the Martin-Denver factory. Depot level maintenance on associate contractor items, such as the guidance system, rocket engines, and the re-entry vehicle, is accomplished at the contractor's facility: Bell Telephone Laboratories for guidance, Aerojet-General for the rocket engines, and AVCO for the re-entry vehicle. Repair on vendor and subcontractor items is accomplished at the manufacturer's facility.

1-440. Facility items and other hard-to-transport items are given depot maintenance in the area where they are installed. Teams from the contractor responsible for the equipment perform the maintenance.

1-441. SCHEDULED AND UNSCHEDULED MAINTENANCE.

1-442. Maintenance is divided into two categories: scheduled and unscheduled. Scheduled maintenance includes all periodic maintenance from the initial receipt of the missile at the MAMS to recycle. Unscheduled maintenance is unpredictable maintenance resulting from malfunctions and damage.

1-443. Recycle is the periodic removal of the missile from the silo. In an operational squadron, missiles are stored in the underground silos for several months and periodic recycling is necessary. A missile to be recycled is removed from the silo and towed to the MAMS building. A spare missile stored at the MAMS is towed to the silo to replace the recycled missile.

1-444. At the MAMS building, the recycled missile is given a thorough inspection, and components that have reached the maximum storage time for operational reliability are replaced. The missile is then stored at the MAMS until the next missile is recycled.

1-445. COMMODITY SERVICING.

1-446. DIESEL FUEL.

1-447. Diesel fuel is normally transported to the missile sites by commercial transport carrier. Fuel will be delivered on a prescheduled basis. Caution must be used when servicing fuel so as to not allow below ground tanks to overflow. Fuel is serviced by means of above ground fill pipes.

1-448. LIQUID OXYGEN, LIQUID NITROGEN, GASEOUS NITROGEN, HELIUM AND ROCKET FUEL (RP-1).

1-449. Liquid oxygen, liquid nitrogen, gaseous nitrogen, helium and RP-1 are the primary commodities utilized in the Titan I propellant loading and pressurization system. These commodities are serviced on a necessity basis determined by daily commodity status readings which are reported to the maintenance activity responsible for commodity replenishment. These commodities are transported, when required, and tanks are filled to a specified amount already established in system manuals. RP-1 is replenished only when necessary. Normally RP-1 will require no replenishment after the storage tank has been initially serviced to the desired capacity required for loading three missiles.

SECTION II

RECEIPT THROUGH LAUNCH

2-1. **SCOPE.**

2-2. This section contains a general description of the Titan I Weapon System receipt through launch activity.

2-3. **MISSILE AND RE-ENTRY VEHICLE INSTALLATION AND CHECKOUT.**

2-4. The missile stages and re-entry vehicle are delivered to the complexes on over land trailers. Installation on the launcher is accomplished with a heavy duty mobile crane. As Stage I, Stage II, and the re-entry vehicle are mounted in place, the launcher is lowered a corresponding distance. Upon completion of re-entry vehicle installation the silo doors are closed placing the silo in a hardened condition. Post-installation procedures are performed to bring the two missile stages and re-entry vehicle into a configuration for operational subsystem checkout. After subsystem checkout, the complete system is given a weapon system checkout that is primarily concerned with launcher readiness checks, rocket engine checks, and electrical checks. At this point an optional LOX only exercise may be performed. Then degrease operations, fuel loading, and ordnance installation are performed.

2-5. **ALERT STATUS MONITORING.**

2-6. The complete weapon system is constantly monitored during alert status monitoring for any malfunction or maintenance requirement. Fuel tanks are kept full, guidance facilities are kept in a ready-state, and the complex is in a hardened operational condition.

2-7. **SYSTEM EXERCISES.**

2-8. System exercises consist of combined system exercises (CSE) designed to check out the integrated operation of specific weapon system functions. The three CSE modes are fuel exercise, lox exercise, and dry exercise (without launcher movement). The CSE equipment simulates multiple functions during countdown in each mode to facilitate weapon system exercise and checkout through complete launch countdowns.

2-9. **TACTICAL LAUNCH (EWO).**

2-10. On receipt of a launch order, the combat crews initiate the operations prerequisite to launching. These operations include power house activity, loading of propellant oxidizer, (lox), opening of silo doors, launcher up and locked, guidance lock-on, and final lift-off. The missile's flight is automatically programmed to orient trajectory, in-flight separation of stages at predetermined trajectory positions, and release of re-entry vehicle on a ballistic flight path to the intended target.

2-11. **POST LAUNCH.**

2-12. Post launch operations consist of launcher lowering, silo door closing to a hardened condition, and shutdown of all power and facilities not required for weapon system operation in shutdown condition. Refurbishing activities may then be initiated. However, if the launching was an abortive failure, corrective maintenance may be performed to return the missile and complex to an alert status.

T.O. 21-SM68-1

Section III
Paragraphs 3-1 to 3-12

SECTION III

NORMAL OPERATING PROCEDURES

3-1. SCOPE.

3-2. This section contains the normal operating procedures for the missile combat crew (MCC). Where there is a variance of RPIE systems and equipment parameters between this manual and SAC CEM support manuals, the SAC CEM range of operation will apply. Normal operating procedures consist of crew administrative procedures, alert status monitoring, and launch exercise countdown procedures.

3-3. CREW ADMINISTRATIVE PROCEDURES.

3-4. Crew administrative procedures are the administrative procedures normally performed by the MCC during an alert tour of duty at the launch complex. Also included are procedures utilized in the event of security violations requiring immediate action, and any scheduled special activities. These procedures consist of crew inspection, pre-departure briefing, entry procedures, changeover procedures, operations/special activities briefings, personnel control, contingency actions, wearing of side arms, and exit procedures.

3-5. CREW INSPECTION. (See figure 3-1.)

3-6. The MCCC will perform crew inspection prior to the pre-departure briefing, and will then report the status of his inspection to the unit operations officer or his designated representative of the pre-departure briefing.

3-7. PRE-DEPARTURE CREW BRIEFING.

3-8. The unit operations officer or his designated representative will conduct a general crew briefing, covering operational requirements, general intelligence items, administrative matters, and general unit policies requiring explanation.

3-9. COMPLEX ENTRY PROCEDURES (Operational bases).

3-10. Following the pre-departure crew briefing and after obtaining the key and code, the crew will depart for the complex. At the complex, the crew member with the key and code will call the launch control center from the phone located at the complex entrance. Using approved key and code procedures, the crew member will identify himself to the MCC on duty. The crew will then proceed to the portal entry and request clearance into the control center. The last individual will insure that the portal entrance is properly secured. All crew members will then assemble in the upper level of the control center for the changeover briefing by the duty MCCC.

3-11. CREW SHIFT CHANGE BRIEFING. (See figure 3-2.)

3-12. This briefing will be a formal briefing conducted at the launch complex prior to shift changeover. Both the offgoing and the oncoming crew will attend. The MCCC of the crew being relieved will conduct the briefing, explaining the status of the complex, maintenance being performed and to be performed, the present DEFCON status,

STEP	PROCEDURE
1	Roll call.. Performed
	MCCC ascertains that all crew members are present.
2	Uniform and appearance................................ Checked
	MCCC checks personnel to insure that crew members are in prescribed white coveralls, and that coveralls are clean and in serviceable condition.
3	Security badges and safety accessories................ Checked
	The MCCC inspects crew members for the following items: SAC Form 138, hard hats, dog-tags (on chain), safety shoes, and ear plugs (as applicable).

Figure 3-1. Crew Inspection

STEP	PROCEDURE
1	Launchers status.................................... Briefed
	The duty MCCC will brief the oncoming crew on the status of the launchers, on or off alert, what maintenance was performed, and status of equipment in the launch emplacements.
2	Maintenance... Briefed
	The duty MCCC will brief the oncoming crew on the status of the maintenance in progress and what maintenance is programmed for the oncoming crew.
3	Power house status.................................. Briefed
	The duty MCCC will brief the oncoming crew on the status of the power house and insure that the power house is ready for changeover.
4	DEFCON.. Briefed
	The duty MCCC briefs the oncoming MCC on the present DEFCON status.

Figure 3-2. Crew Changeover Briefing Procedures

and any other items that may affect the normal status of the complex. SACM 50-16 establishes the requirements and contains detailed procedures for this briefing.

3-13. CREW OPERATIONS BRIEFING.

3-14. At the beginning of each alert duty shift, the MCCC will conduct a formal briefing at the launch complex for the purpose of insuring proper crew coordination in the event of an actual EWO execution or a no-advance-notice type exercise. All MCC members will be present. SACM 50-16 establishes the requirement and contains detailed procedures for this briefing. Following this briefing the relief crew is dismissed by the MCCC for individual changeover.

3-15. INDIVIDUAL CHANGEOVER.

3-16. All MCC members perform an individual changeover with their counterparts, transferring and checking documents, reviewing forms, and receiving a more comprehensive briefing on the equipment status than was given at the crew shift change briefing. Figure 3-3 lists the abbreviated procedures for each individual changeover, and figure 3-4 lists the amplified procedures.

3-17. ACTIVITY COORDINATION BRIEFING.

3-18. This is a formal briefing conducted at the launch complex under the supervision of the site commander or his designated representative prior to any operations or maintenance activities other than actual EWO launch operations. Required MCC members and maintenance personnel will be present. Emphasis will be placed on safety, proper operation of systems involved, and emergency procedures. AMF 66-1 and SAC SUP 1 establishes the requirement and contains detailed procedures and responsibilities for this briefing.

3-19. SAFETY. The buddy system will be utilized whenever anyone enters the propellant terminal and missile silo or whenever performing work on hazardous equipment in any area.

3-20. Hard hats are required to be worn in all areas of the complex except the control center, power house, and Levels III and IV of the equipment terminal. In addition, hard hats will be worn in any area where overhead work is being conducted. Chin straps will be fastened whenever loss of hard hat is probable.

3-21. Protective clothing is required when working on hazardous equipment or with any toxic or cryogenic propellants.

3-22. Smoking is allowed in designated areas only. No tobacco or spark producing materials are permitted beyond tunnel junction 10.

3-23. Personnel will be briefed on the location of escape and emergency equipment. SKA-PAKs will be readily available when in the launcher area.

3-24. Headsets are to be checked for proper working order and must be carried or readily available in all areas beyond tunnel junction 10.

(Text continued on page 3-15.)

T.O. 21-SM68-1

STEP	PROCEDURE
	MISSILE LAUNCH OFFICER
1	Equipment status.. Checked
2	Positive control materials............................. Checked
3	Technical orders....................................... Checked
4	Crew changeover checklist completed.................... Reported
5	Control room... Cleared
6	Strike timing sheets................................... Transferred
7	PCE/PCCD... Transferred
8	Command post... Notified
9	Resumption of alert.................................... Announced
	GUIDANCE ELECTRONICS OFFICER
1	Equipment status....................................... Checked
2	Positive control materials............................. Checked
3	Technical orders....................................... Checked
4	Index of refraction.................................... Checked
5	Antenna alignment printout............................. Checked
6	Communication status................................... Checked
7	Inventory trajectory materials......................... Completed
8	GEO ready for PCE/PCCD changeover...................... Reported
9	PCE/PCCD changeover.................................... Completed
10	Command post (MCCC only)............................... Notified
	BALLISTIC MISSILE ANALYST TECHNICIAN
1	Equipment status....................................... Received
2	Positive control materials............................. Checked

Figure 3-3. Individual Changeover, Abbreviated Checklist Procedures
(Sheet 1 of 2)

STEP	PROCEDURE
3	Technical orders.. Checked
4	Changeover complete.. Reported
5	Forms... Reviewed
	MISSILE MAINTENANCE TECHNICIAN
1	Maintenance status... Briefed
2	Launcher and propellant system status.............................. Checked
3	Launcher area access keys.. Available
4	Fire control and safety briefing guides............................ Checked
5	Changeover complete.. Reported
6	AFTO forms.. Reviewed
	ELECTRICAL POWER PRODUCTION TECHNICIAN
	Note
	The offgoing senior EPPT will insure that the power generation equipment, logs, charts, and status boards are properly prepared for crew changeover (if applicable). The oncoming senior EPPT will be responsible for power production crew changeover in the power house.
1	Briefing by offgoing senior EPPT.................................. Accomplished
2	Power house walk-through inspection................................ Accomplished
3	Briefing by power house supervisor................................. Accomplished
4	Crew changeover and equipment status to MLO........................ Reported
5	Facilities personnel... Briefed

Figure 3-3. Individual Changeover, Abbreviated Checklist Procedures
(Sheet 2 of 2)

STEP	PROCEDURE
	MISSILE LAUNCH OFFICER
1	Equipment status.. Checked
	The oncoming MLO, together with the offgoing MLO, checks the equipment status and launch control console for overall status of the weapon system. In addition, a status check of the other complexes is accomplished at the alternate command post.
2	Positive control materials.. Checked
	The MLO checks the copy decode and pre-decode formats and insures that KAA-29 is current and the current 6-hour block is exposed. The following days KAA-29 will be below the current one. KLI 12/TSEC should be located with the KAA-29. The MLO will check the current KAC 65 with the decode side up, as well as the next KAC 65 (below). Cleanliness of the fast reaction checklist will also be insured.
3	Technical orders.. Checked
	The necessary technical orders required to perform missile combat crew duties will be available and current.
4	Crew changeover checklist completed................................. Reported
	All crew members will report the completion of their changeover checklists. The MLO will not proceed to the following task until all crew members have reported in.
5	Control room.. Cleared
	The MLO directs the BMAT to evacuate all unauthorized personnel from the control room, and to prevent entry of unauthorized personnel during PCE/PCCD changeover.
6	Strike timing sheets.. Transferred
	The MLO will inventory the strike timing sheets and sign for their receipt in conjunction with the PCE/PCCD changeover.
7	PCE/PCCD.. Transferred

Figure 3-4. Individual Changeover, Amplified Checklist Procedures
(Sheet 1 of 8)

STEP	PROCEDURE
7 (CONT)	MISSILE LAUNCH OFFICER (Continued) The PCE/PCCD changeover will be accomplished in accordance with SACM 55-2, volume III. Missile combat crew members will wear sidearms whenever the PCE/PCCD is in their possession.
8	Command post.. Notified The MCCC will notify the command post after PCE/PCCD transfer with the following information: Name _____ Crew number _____. The PCE/PCCD has been received, condition is satisfactory, SAC Form 647 has been signed and witnessed at _____Z.
9	Assumption of alert.. Announced Using the public address system, the MLO announces, "Crew _____ relieved. Crew _____ is now on duty." GUIDANCE ELECTRONICS OFFICER
1	Equipment status... Checked GEO checks AFTO forms 207 and 209 for any limitations to system operation and determines what maintenance is in progress or scheduled.
2	Positive control materials..................................... Checked GEO checks copy decode and pre-decode formats, insures that KAA-29 is current and the 6-hour block is exposed, and that the next days KAA-29 is kept under the current one. KLI-12/TSEC should be located with the KAA-29. The GEO also checks current KAC-65 with decode side up and next days KAC-65 under the current one. Fast reaction checklists are spot checked for cleanliness.
3	Technical orders... Checked The necessary technical orders required to perform missile combat crew duties will be available and current.

Figure 3-4. Individual Changeover, Amplified Checklist Procedures
(Sheet 2 of 8)

STEP	PROCEDURE
	GUIDANCE ELECTRONICS OFFICER (Continued)
4	Index of refraction.................................. Checked
	GEO insures that the index of refraction calculator and log is present and that the latest index of refraction is recorded on the missile guidance console.
5	Antenna alignment printout........................... Checked
	GEO insures that the current antenna alignment is posted on the missile guidance console.
6	Communication status................................. Checked
	GEO checks that operational radios are on and set to proper frequency (for HF radio, this includes selecting antenna and upper or lower side band as directed), checks call signs needed and insures that the current voice call sign list (VCSL) is present, and checks status of PAS (SAC and numbered AF) and PAS recorders.
7	Inventory trajectory materials...................... Completed
	The trajectory material listed on the SAC form 151 will be inventoried and the SAC form 151 initialed and signed by GEO.
8	GEO ready for PCE/PCCD changeover.................... Reported
	The GEO will report that he is ready for PCE/PCCD changeover after he has accomplished the preceding steps.
9	PCE/PCCD changeover.................................. Completed
	PCE/PCCD changeover will be accomplished in accordance with SACM 55-2, volume III. Missile combat crew members will wear sidearms whenever the PCE/PCCD is in their possession.
10	Command post (MCCC only)............................. Notified
	If the GEO is the missile combat crew commander, he will be responsible for notifying the unit command post in accordance with SACM 55-18.

Figure 3-4. Individual Changeover, Amplified Checklist Procedures
(Sheet 3 of 8)

STEP	PROCEDURE
	BALLISTIC MISSILE ANALYSIS TECHNICIAN
1	Equipment status.. Received
	The offgoing BMAT will brief the oncoming BMAT on all equipment discrepancies that will adversely affect launch capability. He will identify all discrepancies on safety items, any maintenance in progress, any maintenance that is scheduled, and the reason for any red, amber or abnormal indication on the launch complex facilities console.
2	Positive control materials.. Checked
	The oncoming BMAT will insure that the following materials are available and current: Copy decode formats, KAA 29 (active and next day), KAC 65 (active and next day), pre-decode format, KLI 12/TSEC and fast reaction checklists.
3	Technical orders.. Checked
	The oncoming BMAT will insure that all technical orders required to perform missile combat crew duties are available and current.
4	Changeover complete... Reported
	When the oncoming BMAT has satisfied all the above requirements, he will report his changeover complete to the MCCC.
5	Forms... Reviewed
	As soon as possible after reporting to MLO, the oncoming BMAT will review applicable AFTO Form 209 entries for agreement with status received from the offgoing BMAT. The BMAT will check for correct symbol in AFTO form 207, and will have release signed (if applicable) by MCCC being relieved. After completion of the above items, the oncoming BMAT will brief the MLO on all conditions that could adversely affect a launch. At this time the necessary AFTO forms will be presented to the MCCC for review and exceptional release.

Figure 3-4. Individual Changeover, Amplified Checklist Procedures
(Sheet 4 of 8)

STEP	PROCEDURE
	MISSILE MAINTENANCE TECHNICIAN
1	Maintenance status................................... Briefed
	When maintenance is in progress at the time of changeover, the status of system(s) and launcher area(s) affected will be briefed. Current TCTO/ modification status is checked to determine any new configuration changes to the weapon system.
2	Launcher and propellant system status................. Checked
	The offgoing MMT briefs oncoming MMT on the overall status of each launcher and propellant system. Propellant system commodities will be reviewed for minimum level requirements.
3	Launcher area access keys............................ Available
	The location of the access keys is ascertained in order to perform required alert status monitoring functions.
4	Fire control and safety briefing guides.............. Checked
	MMT will insure that briefing guides are current.
5	Changeover complete.................................. Reported
	The MMT reports to the MLO that his individual changeover is complete. The MLO is advised of discrepancies and recommended corrective actions (if required).
6	AFTO forms... Reviewed
	As soon as possible after changeover, all required forms are reviewed to obtain knowledge of maintenance status. Particular attention is given to red X items. Documented items are compared against briefed items.

Figure 3-4. Individual Changeover, Amplified Checklist Procedures
(Sheet 5 of 8)

STEP	PROCEDURE
6 (CONT)	**MISSILE MAINTENANCE TECHNICIAN** (Continued) Note As soon as possible after reporting to the MLO, the MMT will conduct the fire control and safety briefing. The MMT will insure that the fire control team members are knowledgeable in prescribed team duties. Fire control team members will assist in checking the following equipment: a. Asbestos suits with suspenders/belts (3 pair) and asbestos gloves (3 pair) b. Asbestos hoods (3 each) c. Safety belts (2 each) d. Gox Analyzer (portable) e. Nylon life line (10 feet minimum) (2 each) f. Self contained breathing apparatus (1 per team member) **ELECTRICAL POWER PRODUCTION TECHNICIAN** Note The offgoing senior EPPT will insure that the power generation equipment, logs, charts, and status boards (if applicable) are properly prepared for crew changeover. The senior oncoming EPPT will be responsible for power production crew changeover in the power house.
1	Briefing by offgoing senior EPPT...................... Accomplished The offgoing senior EPPT will insure all required personnel and forms are available for changeover. The offgoing senior EPPT will review with his oncoming counterpart the following items: a. AFTO forms b. Logs

Figure 3-4. Individual Changeover, Amplified Checklist Procedures
(Sheet 6 of 8)

T.O. 21-SM68-1 Section III

STEP	PROCEDURE

1 (CONT)	<u>ELECTRICAL POWER PRODUCTION TECHNICIAN</u> (Continued)
	
	    c. Charts
	    d. Status boards
	    e. Switchgear
	    f. Fuel
	    g. Lubrication
	    h. Vapor phase
	    i. Starting air compressor
	    j. Generator
	    k. Exciters
	    l. Deep well pumps
	    m. Treated water system
	    n. Chillers
	    o. Utility air compressor

2	Power house walk through inspection.................... Accomplished The EPPT and his counterpart will visually check BOI seals and general condition of the power generation equipment.
3	Briefing by power house supervisor..................... Received The power house supervisor will brief the oncoming EPPT on what maintenance is scheduled and how it could affect the operation during a launch or exercise.

4	Crew changeover and equipment status to MLO........... Reported
	
	The EPPT will contact the control center and inform the MLO of the following:
	
	    a. Crew changeover completed
	    b. Power house status

Figure 3-4. Individual Changeover, Amplified Checklist Procedures
(Sheet 7 of 8)

STEP	PROCEDURE
	<u>ELECTRICAL POWER PRODUCTION TECHNICIAN</u> (Continued)
5	Facilities personnel................................... Briefed
	The senior EPPT will brief the missile facilities team as to their duties during EWO countdown.

Figure 3-4. Individual Changeover, Amplified Checklist Procedures
(Sheet 8 of 8)

T.O. 21-SM68-1

Section III
Paragraphs 3-25 to 3-34

(Text continued from page 3-4.)

3-25. Personnel will be briefed on the primary and secondary escape routes. The primary route is through the portal silo. The secondary route is through the escape hatch at tunnel junction 13.

3-26. FIRE TEAM. The fire team is comprised of the launch crew MMT and two facility team members. After the operations/special activities briefing, the MMT will brief the facility team members on fire fighting duties.

3-27. ALERT ASSIGNMENT (EWO). The site commander or MCCC will designate alert assignments as follows:

   a. Maintenance personnel will report to maintenance officer or supervisor in maintenance ready room.

   b. Guards will implement 190 plan.

   c. Cooks remain in mess hall.

3-28. COMMUNICATION PROCEDURES. For any alert, MCC and maintenance monitor will check in on countdown maintenance net. When contacting control center, report name, location, and job assignment of person requiring entry to a specific area. The emergency phones will be used in the event of actual emergencies only.

3-29. CREW PROCEDURES AND COORDINATION. The alert status monitoring will be conducted by designated individuals and directed by the MCCC and in accordance with applicable technical data.

3-30. The maintenance officer or supervisor will brief the personnel on scheduled maintenance and will keep the MCCC informed as to progress of maintenance being performed. During any alert, the maintenance monitor will check in to the MCCC on the maintenance net and give the status of maintenance being performed and personnel involved.

3-31. The complex commander or supervisor will insure that all maintenance personnel have proper technical data, tools, clothing and have been briefed on safety and hazardous conditions prior to dispatch.

3-32. TRAINING. The MCCC or maintenance supervisor will brief crew members on training to be accomplished during the duty shift.

3-33. SPECIAL ACTIVITIES BRIEFING.

3-34. The special activities briefing will only be given when a special activity is scheduled. In this situation the site commander, duty crew and the facilities maintenance personnel will attend. The briefing will be conducted by the site commander with special subjects augmented by other responsible personnel. The special activities briefing will consist of, but not be limited to, the following items:

   a. Sequence of events.

   b. Procedures; the activity to be accomplished and personnel required.

c. Special instructions; controller peculiar items and fast reaction messages.

d. Communications; site net assignments and communications in commission status.

e. Coordination; weather, VIP's expected (if any) and higher headquarters commitments.

f. Technical data available and current.

g. Back out procedures to be utilized in event of malfunctioning equipment during the activity or in event of an EWO commitment.

h. Specialized briefings on safety, standardization, (if applicable), and fire control.

3-35. PERSONNEL CONTROL.

3-36. This procedure is designed to control the movement of personnel within the complex. The MCCC will control the access of all personnel to the alert launchers. The maintenance officer or supervisor will control the access of all personnel to the launchers that are not on alert. A member of the MCC will log movement of personnel in and out of all alert launchers. The maintenance officer or supervisor will assign someone to maintain a log of personnel movement in and out of all launchers not on alert.

3-37. REPORTING PROCEDURES. Each individual will contact the control center prior to entering or departing an alert launch emplacement or the antenna terminal/silo. A supervisor may report for individuals assigned to his team. For movement from one area to another, such as from the missile silo to equipment terminal, each individual will keep the control center advised of his movements (alert launchers only). Individuals will report their name, destination, task to be performed, and effect on the weapon system.

3-38. Whenever personnel enter the missile silo, the control center will be notified and the AUTO FOG DISABLE on the LCFC will be pressed to amber. Personnel will then press FAIL DRY at the missile silo entrance to lighted. When departing the missile silo, personnel will notify the control center, the AUTO FOG DISABLE will be pressed to not lighted, and FAIL WET at the silo entrance will be pressed to lighted.

3-39. CONTINGENCY PROCEDURES.

3-40. Contingency procedures will consist primarily of required actions necessitated by broken arrow, bent spear, and dull sword, seven high/redskin. In the event of an accident or incident involving a nuclear warhead, the MCCC directs appropriate actions as listed in figure 3-5. In an exercise, the MCCC will insure that initial announcements to the agencies concerned identifies the nuclear incident as simulated or practice.

3-41. BROKEN ARROW (nuclear accident). An unexpected event involving nuclear weapons or AEC components that results in detonation (nuclear or non-nuclear), radio-active contamination, loss or destruction of AEC components or a public hazard is defined as broken arrow. T.O. 11-N-4-1 contains definitions of nuclear and non-nuclear components.

STEP	PROCEDURE
	Note
	It is mandatory that no one be permitted to move, test, inspect, change or destroy evidence until the accident investigators arrive, or until a release is given by the accident board president or wing director of safety. The site commander or MCCC may initiate an assessment of the damage.
8	Time of incident (local time)......................... Reported
	After initial emergency actions are completed, the above report and all following reports will be provided to the wing command post (if applicable).
9	Location (site and specific area).................... Reported
10	Access point established (location and time)......... Reported
11	1500 foot cordon established and guards posted....... Verified
12	Name, rank, location of on-scene coordinator......... Reported
13	Personnel injured, degree of injury and disposition (names, if available)................................ Reported
14	Equipment/item(s) involved........................... Reported
15	Degree of damage..................................... Reported
16	EWO capability....................................... Reported
17	Activity in progress at time of incident............. Reported
18	Probable cause such as material deficiency, or human error.. Reported
19	Weather conditions (including wind direction)........ Reported
20	Status of weapon system and present local time....... Reported
	Note
	When problem is resolved and the situation returns to routine status, the complex is returned to normal alert.
21	Return above ground warning system to normal......... Accomplished

Figure 3-5. Broken Arrow, Bent Spear, and Dull Sword Procedures (Sheet 2 of 3)

STEP	PROCEDURE
22	Termination of emergency condition.................... Announced
23	Wing command post...................................... Notified
	Report to wing command post when site has returned to normal alert.

Figure 3-5. Broken Arrow, Bent Spear, and Dull Sword Procedures (Sheet 3 of 3)

T.O. 21-SM68-1

Section III
Paragraphs 3-42 to 3-46

3-42. BENT SPEAR (nuclear incident). An unexpected event that results in damage, malfunction or failure of a nuclear weapon or component to the extent that rework or complete replacement by AEC is necessary to render the weapon safe is defined as bent spear. In addition, bent spear may be an event which requires examination of nuclear weapon(s) or component(s) by the AEC to insure operational capability and nuclear safety.

3-43. DULL SWORD (nuclear safety deficiency). An unexpected event or procedure that could contribute to a nuclear accident/incident as a result of nuclear safety deficiencies is defined as dull sword. These deficiencies are as follows:

   a. Damage to a nuclear weapon that USAF field units are authorized to correct, such as bent fins or scratches.

   b. A deliberate unauthorized act which degrades the reliability, safety, or security of nuclear weapons.

   c. Failure/malfunction of handling, loading, storage, maintenance, transportation, and test equipment.

   d. Damage/malfunction of suspension and release systems when a nuclear weapon is involved.

   e. Lightning strikes on missile, or ground handling equipment loaded with a nuclear weapon; or any time the commander suspects that lightning has degraded the safety or reliability of a nuclear weapon system.

   f. Failure of personnel to adhere to established nuclear safety procedures.

   g. Circumstances affecting nuclear safety that are deemed reportable by the MCCC.

3-44. SEVEN HIGH/REDSKIN NOTIFICATION SYSTEM.

3-45. The initial onset of widespread and coordinated sabotage or covert action could indicate the initiation of a surprise enemy attack of major magnitude against this nation. The most essential item of the notification system is the speed with which valid seven high and redskin reports reach higher headquarters. These reports must be associated strictly and solely with threats to the elements of the retaliatory strike force and its capability to launch. All personnel performing duty at the complex have initial responsibility to report to the MCCC upon detection of an incident that falls within the seven high/redskin category. Personnel will call the MCCC directly, inform him of the condition, and provide a complete description of the incident and its location. The MCCC will then take immediate action in accordance with figure 3-6.

3-46. SEVEN HIGH. Seven high is a spontaneous oral report transmitted with high priority from base or unit level up the chain of command to signify that an extraordinary event has occurred which appears to be capable of adversely affecting the capability to launch, and the person detecting it could not clearly and immediately rule out a possibility of sabotage or covert action.

T.O. 21-SM68-1   Section III

STEP	PROCEDURE

	REPORTING METHODS:
	
	     Primary communications dial _____
	
	     Secondary communications dial _____
	
	     Tertiary communications non-tactical radio net _____ (dial numbers will be written in for easy reference).

1	Seven high or redskin condition................... Received Any individual performing duty at the sites will initially report to the MCCC any incident falling in this category.
2	Launch complex.................................... Alerted The MCCC alerts personnel so they can increase security alertness and perform a thorough search of the area.
3	CSC/command post.................................. Notified The MCCC notifies the CSC/command post of the conditions and events at the complex.
4	Personnel briefed and dispatched.................. Accomplished MCCC briefs personnel and dispatches them to the scene of the incident.
5	Evaluate condition and record findings............ Accomplished MCCC evaluates conditions based on reports, and records all pertinent information.
6	Based on evaluation; cancellation, upgrade condition, or continue condition................... Requested
7	Assistance (if necessary)......................... Requested
8	Action taken under step 6 above, to CSC/command post.. Reported
9	Site personnel advised of action taken under step 6 above.. Notified

Figure 3-6. Seven High/Redskin Notification Procedures

T.O. 21-SM68-1

Section III
Paragraphs 3-47 to 3-57

3-47. REDSKIN. A redskin report signifies one or more of the following:

   a. That an event capable of adversely affecting the capability to launch has been detected and rapid investigation has revealed enemy sabotage action.

   b. That an event capable of adversely affecting the capability to launch has occurred which is of such a serious and suspicious nature, that even without investigation, enemy sabotage or covert action appears highly probable.

   c. That the wing is implementing annex A (sabotage alert) to operations plan 190-____.

3-48. SERIOUS ILLNESS OR INJURY.

3-49. To insure prompt and positive action by responsible personnel in the event of a serious illness or injury at missile sites, it is necessary for the illness or injury to be reported to the MCCC immediately. The MCCC will evaluate the incident and take immediate corrective action in accordance with figure 3-7.

3-50. SEVERE WEATHER REPORT PROCEDURE.

3-51. When severe weather develops at the site, the MCCC on duty will forward all pertinent known information to the unit command post, utilizing figure 3-8 as a guide.

3-52. Deleted.

3-53. Deleted.

3-54. EXIT PROCEDURES (Operational Bases).

3-55. After completion of crew changeover the offgoing crew will assemble in the lower level of the control center and proceed to the revolving portal. When all crew members are at the revolving portal a member of the offgoing crew will call the on-duty crew to have the door unlocked. The offgoing crew will then proceed through the door. The last man through the door will call the on-duty crew to report the portal area is secured and to request permission to depart the area. The off going crew then proceeds to the fence gate where they call the on-duty crew to have the fence gate unlocked. After passing through and locking the gate, the offgoing crew will report to the on-duty crew that exiting is complete, the gate is locked, and the crew is departing the site.

3-56. RADAR SURVEILLANCE SYSTEM (Anti-intrusion) (See figures 1-71 thru 1-76).

3-57. The AN/TPS-39(V) radar surveillance system procedures include starting and stopping procedures, operating procedures, system functions, and security functions required for MCCC radar surveillance.

Changed 3 January 1964 TOCN-1 (DEN-6)

STEP	PROCEDURE
	Note This procedure can be implemented by any responsible person in the control center who receives a report of serious injury or illness. Upon receipt of a report of this nature, dispatch the medically trained first aid man to the scene immediately.
1	Report of findings.................................... Received A report of the findings from the trained first aid man or other person at the scene is received in the control center.
2	Flight surgeon and command post....................... Notified The flight surgeon and the command post are notified of the nature of the injury or illness. **Note** After duty hours call EXT._____. Medical officer of the day.
3	Course of action instructions......................... Received The course of action to be taken for the patient(s) is received from the flight surgeon or medical officer of the day (OD).
4	Action taken or directed.............................. Completed The course of action received is accomplished as outlined by the flight surgeon or medical OD.
5	Contact command post for assistance................... Contacted (Direct line or EXT._____). The command post is contacted and requests made for type of transportation, number of personnel to be transported and the destination (base dispensary or general hospital.)
6	Time of incident...................................... Reported Command post is provided the above information, and all following task reports, after initial actions have been taken to care for and evacuate patient(s).

Figure 3-7. Serious Injury or Illness Checklist Procedure (Sheet 1 of 2)

STEP	PROCEDURE
7	Personnel involved and extent of injuries (name, rank, position)................................ Reported
8	Probable cause (material deficiency, human error).. Reported
9	Replacement personnel (if necessary)................. Requested
10	Estimated effect on EWO capability................... Reported
11	Name, rank, position of replacement individual........ Reported

Figure 3-7. Serious Injury or Illness Checklist Procedure (Sheet 2 of 2)

STEP	PROCEDURE
	WEATHER REPORT CHECKLIST
1	This is_____(CP-SITE)
2	Type of weather (tornado, hail, winds)_____
3	Damage incurred (if any)_____
4	Effect on EWO capability (if known)_____
5	Estimated time to repair damage_____
6	Immediate assistance required and from whom_____
7	Personnel status (casualties)_____
8	Other information, remarks, or requirements_____
9	Command post notified_____

Figure 3-8. Severe Weather Report Procedure

T.O. 21-SM68-1

Section III
Paragraphs 3-58 to 3-64

3-58. STARTING PROCEDURE. To turn on the equipment, insert the proper fuses into their respective holders.

3-59. STOPPING PROCEDURE. To stop the equipment, remove the fuses. See figures 1-72 and 1-75 for fuse locations.

Note

If primary power to the system is turned off, the emergency batteries will automatically continue system operation. Only removal of the fuses will stop the equipment.

3-60. OPERATING PROCEDURES. When an alarm signal is generated, the SYSTEM RESET pushbutton on the annunciator panel is pressed to reset the equipment. If the alarm continues for more than 60 seconds after the system has been reset, the surveillance area will be investigated for intruders. The alarm bell is silenced by pressing the BELL OFF pushbutton on the annunciator panel; however the ALARM indication on the annunciator panel will remain lighted until the equipment is reset. If it is determined that the alarm was not caused by an intruder or other object that by its size and speed of movement could simulate a human intruder, the SYSTEM RESET pushbutton should be pressed again. If the alarm continues for more than 60 seconds after the SYSTEM RESET pushbutton is pressed, assume that there is a malfunction in the equipment, and perform maintenance procedures.

3-61. SYSTEM FUNCTIONS. After an intrusion alarm has been investigated, either one of two reset switches located on the receiver group case and the annunciator panel can be used to reset the system. When the reset switch located on the receiver group is closed, an input signal is supplied to the reset delay circuit. The reset delay circuit delays the system reset long enough to allow the investigating guard to leave the surveillance area. At the end of the delay period (approximately 60 seconds), the reset delay circuit supplies a reset signal to the annunciator. The reset switch on the annunciator provides an instantaneous reset of the system, and is connected to the receiver in such a way that it bypasses the delay circuit. After a system test, it is not necessary to delay a reset. For this reason a long reset period disable circuit is provided in the receiver. The system test relay energizes this circuit at the time a system test is initiated.

3-62. The annunciator circuits and components indicate the condition of the AN/TPS-39(V) system. An annunciator power supply and battery pack provide power for the annunciator. A remote alarm bell and an alarm indicator, located on the control console, are also operated from the annunciator.

3-63. The annunciator contains an alarm tone receiver for each remote receiver in the system. Also included are an alarm gate, a SYSTEM TEST pushbutton switch, a SYSTEM RESET pushbutton switch, a BELL OFF pushbutton switch, a one-shot multivibrator, and relays to control the alarm bell and light.

3-64. A set of three indicators, (red, green, and amber) and a SECURE/ACCESS switch are provided on the front panel of the annunciator for each remote receiver. These indicators are controlled by a relay and the SECURE/ACCESS switch. During the time the tone signal is received from the tone oscillator in the remote receiver, the relay is energized and the green SAFE indicator is lighted signifying a secure condition. When the SECURE/ACCESS switch is set to ACCESS, the green indicator goes out and the amber ACCESS indicator lights amber. If the tone from the remote receiver is interrupted, the relay connected to the tone receiver is de-energized, and the red ALARM indicator lights denoting a possible intrusion.

3-65. A BELL OFF pushbutton on the annunciator panel enables operating personnel to turn off the alarm bell. The indicators, (one on the control console indicating an alarm, and one on the annunciator indicating which receiver caused the alarm) are not affected by the BELL OFF pushbutton.

3-66. The SECURE/ACCESS switch disables the alarm signal from the tone receiver. When the switch is in the ACCESS position, a secure input is provided to the alarm gate regardless of the condition of the remote receiver. This enables operating personnel to enter the surveillance area without causing an alarm.

3-67. The SYSTEM TEST pushbutton located on the annunciator panel initiates a system test. The SYSTEM TEST switch is common to all remote receivers in the system. To check a specific receiver for proper operation, the SECURE/ACCESS switches for the other receivers in the system are set to ACCESS. This disables the alarm inputs from these receivers. Thus, when the SYSTEM TEST pushbutton is pressed, operating personnel can determine that the alarm was caused by the receiver under test. The receiver resets automatically if it is operating properly.

3-68. The SYSTEM RESET pushbutton enables operating personnel to reset the system at the annunciator instead of at the remote receiver.

3-69. SYSTEM FAIL-SAFE CAPABILITY. The AN/TPS-39(V) radar surveillance system is designed to be fail-safe. If a system malfunction occurs, an alarm is indicated requiring guard personnel to investigate and reset the equipment. Thus the restricted area is not left without detection coverage during a system malfunction.

3-70. The receiver utilizes a fail-safe circuit to detect a transmitter malfunction and provide an alarm signal to the annunciator. The annunciator circuits are designed to detect receiver malfunctions. If the tone signal from any remote receiver in the system is not received by the appropriate tone receiver, the tone receiver furnishes an alarm input to the alarm gate. Relays in the annunciator are connected in the normally energized position. In this manner, if the relay fails, it becomes de-energized and provides an alarm input to the alarm gate.

3-71. SECURITY PROCEDURES.

3-72. The monitoring panel for the anti-intrusion alarm system will be under the surveillance and control of the MCCC or his deputy at all times. The MCCC will also control access in accordance with command code control procedures.

3-73. A member of the missile combat crew located in the launch control center will be assigned the responsibility of access controller. This MCC member will monitor the anti-intrusion alarm system, as well as the surface surveillance TV, where it is installed, and will notify CSC at the support base if he needs assistance to determine causes of alarms.

3-74. Upon receiving notification from the access controller at the site, CSC at the support base will inform the MCCC at the site to be visited, the composition, purpose, departure time, and mode of transportation of visitor(s). Upon arrival at the access gate the visitor calls the MCCC to announce his arrival. The MCCC or his designated representative will determine if the individual(s) are those who have been announced by CSC or whether a duress condition exists. Upon favorable completion of this pre-emptory identification the MCCC or his representative will activate the gate unlocking mechanism and monitor the relocking of the access gate after visitor(s) have entered the site.

3-75. During no-notice inspections, the command post controller will advise the MCCC of the name, rank, AFSC and the inspector's SAC form 138 number. The MCCC will authenticate the call from the command post. Upon arrival, the inspector will call the MCCC from the access gate telephone and identify himself. The MCCC will dispatch a crew member to the access gate to check the inspector's credentials and then notify the MCCC that the inspector is as represented. The MCCC will then immediately release the access gate lock to admit the inspector.

3-76. Should an individual requesting access fail to properly identify himself or should the duress code be passed, the MCCC will immediately transmit a seven high report to CSC at the support base. If mobile maintenance team members are close by, the MCCC will direct them to apprehend the individual(s) concerned. Should the seven high report be resolved, the MCCC will call in a cancellation of same to CSC so the mobile strike team (MST) may be recalled.

3-77. Upon departure of an individual from the underground complex, the MCCC will not release the lock on the inner door of the entrapment area until the entrapment area has been viewed by the TV camera to determine that it is unoccupied. Should access control equipment (door controls and TV) be inoperative due to failure of components or loss of power, one of the combat crew members will go the access control station to identify persons desiring access.

3-78. Whenever a site is softened, access to the site will be controlled by a surface guard under the direction of the MCCC.

3-79. Whenever command defense force (CDF) guards are manning a complex, they will maintain radio contact with the MCCC by way of portable radios.

3-80. The MCCC must establish procedures to insure that uncleared contractor personnel do not have access to classified components or information. Pictures of individual utility contractors who have a requirement for frequent access to the complex will be provided so the MCCC can positively identify them prior to authorizing access. MCCC will be responsible for determining the qualifications and/or requirement for access of contractor personnel who do not process through the code control center. The MCCC will notify CSC at the support base of the presence and departure of contractor personnel.

3-81. When the anti-intrusion alarm system initiates an alarm condition, the MCCC or his representative will perform the following procedures:

   a. Press the alarm reset pushbutton to clear the alarm.

   b. Immediately notify CSC at support base of a seven high condition.

   c. Insure all blast doors are closed and locked.

   d. Check the portal entrapment area on the TV monitor to see if anyone is attempting to enter the complex.

T.O. 21-SM68-1

Section III
Paragraph 3-82

e. Where surface TV coverage is available, scan the surface area as a means of determining the cause of the alarm.

f. Notify any mobile maintenance team known to be in the area and request that they ascertain the security status of the surface of the complex.

g. When the MST or mobile maintenance team arrives at the access gate and are properly identified, open the gate on receipt of the code word so they may search the surface.

h. When the MST or mobile maintenance team has searched the surface area and is assured there are no unauthorized persons or obvious sabotage devices, the chief of the MST or mobile maintenance team will contact wht MCCC either by radio or the portal telephone and advise the MCCC the security status of the surface. The MCCC will again identify the caller and if satisfied there is no duress, dispatch a member of the MCC to the surface to technically survey the surface area to insure again that nothing on the surface has been disturbed.

i. Notify CSC that the seven high is cleared.

j. If the alarm condition is determined to be caused by equipment failure the MCCC will:

(1) Turn off the faulty equipment.

(2) Notify CSC of the faulty equipment situation and request surface guards be posted.

(3) Notify communications-maintenance of the equipment failure and request immediate corrective action.

(4) Direct the two man MST that responded to the original alarm that they must remain at the complex until relieved by the CDF guards for surface protection during the alarm maintenance.

(5) Upon re-instatement of the alarm equipment, notify CSC that the equipment is operational and surface guards may be relieved.

3-82. If the person requesting access to the site passes the duress code word to the MCCC during initial identification procedure on the telephone at the access gate, the MCCC will perform the following procedures:

a. Immediately notify CSC that the duress condition exists (seven high).

b. Release the outer access gate lock and request the visitor to proceed to entrapment portal for further identification.

c. When contacted the second time from the outer door to the entrapment area, request verification of the visitor's identity and ask for the code word. If duress code is again passed (if duress still exists) the locking device for the outer door to entrapment area should be released so visitor and anyone with him may enter the entrapment area where they can be seen on the closed circuit TV.

d. Do not release locking device on inner entrapment door until completely satisfied no durress condition exists.

e. Lock the outer door of entrapment area.

f. Offer the visitor some excuse for not opening the inner door.

g. If uncertain as to duress condition, hold the visitor and/or other persons in the entrapment area until MST arrives.

3-83. ALERT STATUS MONITORING.

3-84. To insure immediate launch execution capability and to ascertain complete status of the weapon system, alert status monitoring procedures will be performed on the weapon system by each changeover or shift replacement crew and/or at intervals as directed. In addition to these required procedures, maintenance assistance may be rendered by combat crew personnel when applicable, provided such assistance does not interfere with EWO commitments. Normal console monitoring, equipment status monitoring, and general complex functions will be accomplished during normal tour of duty. Figures 3-9 thru 3-14 list procedures for each combat crew member to perform as an integral part of maintaining alert status. Other data checks included in alert status monitoring are weather information, index of refraction, and launch site targeting.

3-85. WEATHER INFORMATION.

3-86. This procedure provides for transmittal of current weather information from the unit command post to all launch control centers. Current weather information will include sky and cloud condition, visibility, millibar reading, wind particulars, and any other weather hazards. The information will be entered on weather charts (figure 3-15) located at each site. A 24-hour forecast will be provided daily. Current weather information will be provided at the following times:

a. Sunrise plus 1 hour

b. 1200 hours

c. Sunset plus 1 hour

d. 2400 hours

3-87. INDEX OF REFRACTION.

3-88. Provisions are made in the guidance countdown checklist for inserting the current index of refraction. The index of refraction is computed at four specified times daily and it is necessary that the current index of refraction be readily available at the missile guidance console.

3-89. PROCEDURES. (See figure 3-16.) Uncorrected atmospheric pressures will be obtained from the unit command post at one hour after sunrise, noon, one hour after sunset and midnight.

3-90. The correction factor, to be applied to the uncorrected atmospheric pressure, will be maintained at the individual sites. This correction factor will be used to correct the local weather station atmospheric pressure for the difference in elevation of the individual sites.

(Text continued on page 3-89.)

STEP	PROCEDURE
	Note
	Perform this procedure prior to incorporation of TCTO 31X7-2-11-512 or if air conditioning equipment supplying cool air to the guidance system cabinets fail, is removed from the line, or temperature within cabinets exceed recommended limits.
	MISSILE GUIDANCE CONSOLE
1	Launch site targeting...................................... Checked T.O. 21-SM68-1FJ-1-2 Check the launch site targeting log to determine that the appropriate launch site targeting procedures have been accomplished.
2	LAUNCH EXERCISE... Green The LAUNCH EXERCISE pushbutton indicator must be green for a launch.
3	TRAINING.. Green
4	MAINT... Green
5	STBY.. Green
6	ANT LOWER... Green
7	HANDOVER OFF.. Green
8	POWER OFF... Lighted
9	MONITOR ON-OFF switch..................................... ON
10	HV ON-OFF switch.. ON
11	ANTENNA FACILITY SELECT................................... Green
12	ANTENNA FACILITY MAINT.................................... Green
13	ANTENNA FACILITY FAULT.................................... Not Lighted
	POWER SWITCHBOARD (Unit 16)
14	Generator (1 or 2) on line................................ Recorded

Figure 3-9. Guidance Electronics Officer Alert Status Monitoring (Standby) Procedure (Sheet 1 of 2)

T.O. 21-SM68-1　　　　　　　　　　　　　　　　　Section III

STEP	PROCEDURE
15	ADJ PH STBY REG..Not Lighted
16	LINE VOLTS PHASE C...Checked
	If the indication is not in the center of the green segment, press ADJ PH C-INCREASE or DECREASE as required
17	Circuit breakers..ON

Figure 3-9. Guidance Electronics Officer Alert Status Monitoring (Standby) Procedure (Sheet 1A of 2)

Changed 17 January 1964　TOCN-1 (DEN-8)　　　　　　　　　　　3-31A

STEP	PROCEDURE
	MISSILE GUIDANCE CONSOLE
18	BLAST circuit breaker..ON
	COMPUTER CONSOLE
19	STANDBY..Green
20	POWER OFF..Amber
	CONTROL INDICATOR POWER DISTRIBUTION GROUP
21	MOTOR GENERATOR OFF..Amber
22	MOTOR GENERATOR SELECTED...Green
23	AUTO EXC...Green
24	PERIPHERAL A.C. POWER indicators...................................Green
	The CONSOLE, AUX, PRINTER, TAPE READER, and OUTLETS indicators should all be green.
25	EMERGENCY RESET..Green
26	DRUM OFF...Amber
27	60 CYCLE VOLTS...Checked
	Check phase 1-2, phase 1-3, and phase 2-3 by pressing the pushbutton indicators individually. The voltage meter should indicate 120($\pm$6) volts for each phase.
	CONTROL-MONITOR POWER SUPPLY GROUP
28	DC POWER STANDBY SUPPLY..Green
29	MANUAL SEQUENCE rotary switch..OFF
30	SIMULATOR switch...OFF

Figure 3-9. Guidance Electronics Officer Alert Status Monitoring (Standby) Procedure (Sheet 2 of 2)

T.O. 21-SM68-1   Section III

STEP	PROCEDURE
	Note
	Perform this procedure after incorporation of TCTO 31X7-2-11-512.
	The guidance system will be maintained in a power-on configuration during alert monitoring. However, the guidance system will be returned to standby whenever any air conditioning equipment supplying cool air to the guidance system cabinets fail, is removed from the line, or temperature within cabinets exceed recommended limits.
	CAUTION
	Guidance system equipment cabinets must not exceed specified temperature limitations as damage to equipment may result.
	MISSILE GUIDANCE CONSOLE
1	Launch site targeting... Checked T.O. 21-SM68-1FJ-1-2 Check the launch site targeting log to determine that the appropriate launch site targeting procedures have been accomplished.
2	LAUNCH EXERCISE.. Green The LAUNCH EXERCISE pushbutton indicator must be green for a launch.
3	TRAINING... Green
4	MAINT.. Green
5	STBY... Green
6	POWER ON... Green
7	MAG OFF.. Amber
8	ANT LOWER.. Green
9	HANDOVER OFF... Green
10	POWER OFF.. Not Lighted
11	MONITOR ON-OFF switch.. ON

Figure 3-9A. Guidance Electronics Officer Alert Status Monitoring
(Power On) Procedure (Sheet 1 of 5)

Changed 17 January 1964 TOCN-1 (DEN-8)

3-32A

STEP	PROCEDURE
12	HV ON-OFF switch... ON
13	ANTENNA FACILITY SELECT.................................... Green
14	ANTENNA FACILITY MAINT..................................... Green
15	ANTENNA FACILITY FAULT..................................... Not Lighted
16	ANTENNA AZIMUTH LIMIT CW/CCW............................... Green
	POWER SWITCHBOARD (Unit 16)
17	Generator (1 or 2) on line................................. Recorded
18	ADJ PH C STBY REG.. Not Lighted
19	LINE VOLTS PHASE C... Checked
	If the indication is not in the center of the green segment, press ADJ PH C - INCREASE or DECREASE as required.
20	Circuit breakers... ON
	MISSILE GUIDANCE CONSOLE
21	BLAST circuit breaker...................................... ON
	COMPUTER-SIGNAL GENERATOR (Unit 24)
22	OVEN TEMP indicator.. Checked
	Turn METER SELECTOR switch to TEMP (chassis 24A66) and actuate READ METER toggle switch. The temperature indicator should read +60(±5)°F. Temperature will be checked four times daily at six hour intervals.
23	POWER ON... Green
	CONTROL INDICATOR POWER DISTRIBUTION GROUP
24	MOTOR GENERATOR ON... Green
25	MOTOR GENERATOR SELECTED................................... Green
26	AUTO EXC... Green

Figure 3-9A. Guidance Electronics Officer Alert Status Monitoring (Power On) Procedure (Sheet 2 of 5)

T.O. 21-SM68-1 Section III

STEP	PROCEDURE
27	PERIPHERAL A.C. POWER indicators........................ Green
	The CONSOLE, AUX, PRINTER, TAPE READER, and OUTLETS indicators should all be green.
28	EMERGENCY RESET.. Green
29	DRUM ON.. Green
30	60 CYCLE VOLTS... Checked
	Check phase 1-2, phase 1-3, and phase 2-3 by pressing the pushbutton indicators individually. The voltage meter should indicate 120(±6) volts for each phase.
	CONTROL-MONITOR POWER SUPPLY GROUP
31	DC POWER READY... Green
32	MANUAL SEQUENCE rotary switch............................ OFF
33	SIMULATOR switch... OFF
	SIGNAL DATA RECORDER (Unit 22)
34	Events recorder POWER switch............................. ON
	Check LOCAL-REMOTE switch in REMOTE, AUTO-MANUAL switch in MANUAL, RANGE setting at X.1, and CHART SPEEDS at 2. Place POWER ON-OFF toggle switch to ON. The POWER ON, LAMP ON, GRID LINES ON, and MOTOR ON lamps should be lighted green.
	MISSILE GUIDANCE CONSOLE
35	Press GUID X NOT RDY..................................... Not Lighted
36	Press START GUID X....................................... White
	The following indications appear after START GUID X pushbutton indicator is pressed and should be observed:
	a. The digital data printer will print out the contents of the constants register.
	b. A gated pulse will appear on RANGE indicator.
	c. TARGET GATED indicator will light green.

Figure 3-9A. Guidance Electronics Officer Alert Status Monitoring (Power On) Procedure (Sheet 3 of 5)

Changed 17 January 1964 TOCN-1 (DEN-8)

STEP	PROCEDURE
	d. The AGC METER will indicate in the normal segment. If a gated pulse is not obtained reset the guidance exerciser by pressing GUID X NOT RDY pushbutton indicator and then pressing START GUID X pushbutton indicator. During the guidance exerciser coast period, the following indications appear and should be observed: a. COAST indicator will light amber. b. TARGET GATED indicator will go out. c. AGC METER will indicate out of normal segment.
37	MAG RDY... White
38	Press MAG ON.. White, then Green After MAG ON pushbutton indicator is pressed, MAG ON will turn from white to green in 10 to 12 seconds. The following indications appear after pressing MAG ON pushbutton indicator and should be observed: a. MAG RDY will go out. b. MAG OFF will go out. c. The MAG-MOD CUR-VOLT meter should indicate 1.5 to 1.9 MA; press INC-DEC as required. Under no circumstances will the magnetron current be adjusted below 1.5 MA during a guid X run.
39	Magnetron tuning... Accomplished The magnetron switch is held to the COARSE position. The MAG TUNE meter is checked for the approximate segment of the X BAND. The magnetron switch is released to peak. Adjust the frequency control switch as required to peak the MAG TUNE meter.

Figure 3-9A. Guidance Electronics Officer Alert Status Monitoring (Power On) Procedure (Sheet 4 of 5)

STEP	PROCEDURE
	All steps preceded by an asterisk will be coordinated with the MLO upon initiation or completion. CONTROL CENTER WARNING The SYSTEM TEST MODE SELECTOR switch must not be placed in the FULL SYSTEM position until at least 45 seconds have elapsed after the amber indicator has flashed. Between 45 and 55 seconds after the amber light has flashed, the SYSTEM TEST MODE SELECTOR switch must be placed back to the ELECTRONIC position. Failure to observe this warning may result in operation of blast valves.
1	ITT KELLOGG BLAST DETECTOR............................. Checked SAC CEM 21-SM68-2-25-( ) The BMAT checks the blast detection system by observing that all indicators light during one complete cycle of the system (10 minutes). LAUNCH COMPLEX FACILITIES CONSOLE Note Steps 2 through 8 indicate or are checked for the response listed when the complex is in an alert status. All other indicators on the LCFC should indicate not lighted.
2	Lamps... Checked T.O. 21-SM68-2J-15-1 Raise panel of launch complex facility console and activate lamp, flasher, and buzzer switches.
3	Flashers.. Checked
4	Buzzer.. Checked Press and hold buzzer verify switch, then press PUSH TO SILENCE pushbutton. Hold buzzer verify switch until buzzer stops.
5	GROUND GUIDANCE... Green
6	MISSILE AND FACILITY (3)................................ Green

Figure 3-10. Ballistic Missile Analyst Technician Alert Status Monitoring Procedure (Operational Bases) (Sheet 1 of 11)

STEP	PROCEDURE
7	POWER HOUSE GEN(S)..White
	GEN 1, 2, 3, and 4 indicate white only when on the line and supplying power.
8	HAZARD LIGHT (3)..Green
9	PORTAL ACCESS LOCK..Green
	BMAT verifies LOCK pushbutton indicator is lighted green, indicating the portal revolving door is locked.
10	FENCE GATE..Green
	BMAT verifies FENCE GATE pushbutton indicator is lighted green, indicating complex security fence gate is locked.
*11	Press MISSILE AND FACILITY (3)..Red
	LAUNCH CONTROL CONSOLE
12	MISSILE AND FACILITY (3)...Red
	CAUTION
	Prior to raising LCC front panel, press MISSILE AND FACILITY pushbutton indicators on LCFC and verify red indication on LCFC and LCC to prevent accidental initiation of propellant loading during performance of lamp check.
13	Lamps..Checked
	Raise panel on launch control console and actuate lamp verify switch. Verify all indicators are lighted and release switch.
	Note
	Steps 14 thru 17 indicate the responses listed when the complex is in an alert status. All other indicators on the LCC should indicate not lighted.

Figure 3-10. Ballistic Missile Analyst Technician Alert Status Monitoring Procedure (Operational Bases) (Sheet 2 of 11)

T.O. 21-SM68-1   Section III

STEP	PROCEDURE
	CAUTION
	Insure EXERCISE 1, 2, and 3 safety seals are in place and secured to prevent system from being placed in launch mode.
*14	EXERCISE (3)...Green, Seals in Place
15	TARGET SELECTION (3)..Green
	Verify proper target for each launcher is lighted green.
16	GROUND GUIDANCE..Green
17	Press MISSILE AND FACILITY.....................................Green
	When MISSILE AND FACILITY pushbutton indicator is pressed, the MISSILE AND FACILITY indicators on both the LCC and the LCFC must light green.
	AREA SURVEILLANCE AND PORTAL ENTRANCE TV MONITORS
18	Surveillance TV operational.................................Checked
	Verify TV is operational by checking pan, zoom, and tilt.
19	Portal TV operational.......................................Checked
	CONTROL CENTER ALARM PANEL
20	Set ABOVE GROUND RADIATION selector..............................1 SAC CEM 21-SM68-2-25-( )
21	Set WIND VELOCITY PROBE SELECTOR.................................5
22	WIND VELOCITY DETECTOR......................................Checked
	Check WIND VELOCITY DETECTOR then return to HIGH.
23	NUCLEAR BLAST DETECT ALARM DE-ACTIVATING.........................ON
	This switch must be ON to allow blast valves closure in event of a blast.
24	NUCLEAR BLAST INDICATOR NORMAL................................Green
	All other indicators not lighted.

Figure 3-10. Ballistic Missile Analyst Technician Alert Status Monitoring Procedure (Operational Bases) (Sheet 3 of 11)

Changed 17 January 1964 TOCN-1 (DEN-8)   3-35

T.O. 21-SM68-1　　　　　　　　　　　　　　　　　　　　　Section III

STEP	PROCEDURE
	CONTROL CENTER CIRCUITS
25	OPERATING MODE.. Launch T.O. 21-SM68-2J-15-1
26	Lamps... Checked 　　Check LAMP VERIFY and return switch to the OFF position.
27	LOX LEAKAGE OVERRIDE (3)....................................... Not Lighted
28	(After incorporation of TCTO 31X3-10-17-546) CSE control assembly.. Checked 　　BMAT will position the launcher select, mode selector, events recorder, and analog recorder switches as directed at the special activities briefing.
29	TARGET CARD READER AND LOGIC ASSEMBLY (3) lamps.......... Checked
30	TARGETS (9).. Green 　　Target C indicators may be red if guidance is equipped with handover capabilities.
31	TARGETS SELECTED.. Lighted 　　BMAT verifies that TARGET SELECTION A, B, or C on target card reader corresponds with the TARGET SELECTION A, B, or C on the LCC.
32	TARGET SELECT TEST (3)... Not Lighted
33	Color code.. Checked 　　Verify proper chassis to pallet relationship by matching color coding.
34	RECT ON LINE (POWER SUPPLY CONTROL)...................... White
35	LOAD, BUS, RECT, and BATTERY voltages.................... Checked 　　BMAT checks the bus, line, battery and rectifier voltages to insure that the proper voltages exist and that the battery is fully charged (load 29($\pm$3) VDC, battery 30($\pm$3) VDC, and rectifier 28($\pm$3) VDC).

Figure 3-10. Ballistic Missile Analyst Technician Alert Status
Monitoring Procedure (Operational Bases) (Sheet 4 of 11)

T.O. 21-SM68-1 Section III

STEP	PROCEDURE
36	Countdown clocks (3) .... Reset
	Place countdown clock reset switches 1, 2, and 3 in UP position momentarily and verify countdown times set on all three clocks.
37	DISABLE (time display board) .... Red
*38	LSCB .... ENABLE, Green; DISABLE, Red
	BMAT positions LSCB in UP position momentarily and verifies ENABLE indicator lights green. DISABLE indicator will remain red.
39	Hold time indicators (3) 000.00
40	Circuit breakers .... ON
41	Remote gox analyzer .... Checked
	Gox readings are observed to check the operating condition of remote analyzers in all propellant terminals and missile silos to ascertain areas are safe for entry. If any remote gox analyzer(s) is inoperative, the BMAT will have maintenance correct the malfunctioning unit(s).
	EQUIPMENT TERMINAL.
42	MLO .... Notified
	BMAT will notify the MLO that he has arrived at the equipment terminal and will call upon completion of procedures.
	POWER SWITCHGEAR (SUB 1001, MCC 1010, JEU-7/E, and PANEL 1020)
43	GROUNDING INDICATORS (SUB 1001) (3) .... Lighted
	SAC CEM 21-SM68-2-21-( )
44	Circuit breakers .... ON
	All HAND-OFF-AUTO switches will be in the AUTO position except FUEL LINE DRAIN P-112 and FUEL PUMP P-111 which will be in the LOC position.

Figure 3-10. Ballistic Missile Analyst Technician Alert Status Monitoring Procedure (Operational Bases) (Sheet 5 of 11)

Changed 17 January 1964 TOCN-1 (DEN-8) 3-37

STEP	PROCEDURE
	POWER SUPPLY ECU-16
45	MODE SELECTOR.. REMOTE T.O. 21-SM68-2J-10-( ) Positioning MODE SELECTOR on power supply ECU-16 to REMOTE permits unit to be started or stopped remotely.
46	PRIMARY POWER lamp... Lighted
47	Lamps... Checked Verify PRIMARY POWER lamp is lighted and lamps light when checked.
	28 VDC POWER SUPPLY A/E 24A-4
48	PRI POWER INDICATOR.. Lighted
49	LOCAL START-REMOTE START....................................... REMOTE START Positioning LOCAL START-REMOTE START switch on power supply A/E 24A-4 to REMOTE START permits unit to be started or stopped remotely.
	BATTERY POWER SUPPLY A/E 24A-5
50	Lamps... Checked
51	Battery trickle chargers....................................... Green
52	INPUT POWER PHASE A, B, and C.................................. Lighted All other indicators not lighted.
	MOTOR GENERATOR A/E 24A-3
53	LOCAL-REMOTE START... REMOTE START Positioning LOCAL-REMOTE START switch to REMOTE START permits unit to be remotely controlled by control monitor group OA-2438/GJQ-11.
54	LOAD C.B.. ON
55	LINE POWER.. White
56	Circuit Breakers.. ON SAC CEM 21-SM68-2-21-( )

Figure 3-10. Ballistic Missile Analyst Technician Alert Status Monitoring Procedure (Operational Bases) (Sheet 6 of 11)

STEP	PROCEDURE
57	GROUND indicators.. Lighted
	If the system has a GROUND/NORMAL indicator, NORMAL should be lighted. This indicates the system does not contain a ground and the battery charger is capable of maintaining battery pack (BAT 1001) in a charged condition. These batteries supply power for emergency lighting, damage control, and hazard warning units in the launcher area.
58	VOLTAGE... Green, 125($\pm$5) VDC
59	AMMETER... Normal
	ELECTRICAL SYSTEM
*60	All circuit breakers.. ON T.O. 21-SM68-2J-10-( ) During an exercise, all circuit breakers will be positioned as directed by the MLO.
61	OPERATING MODE.. LAUNCH
62	Lamps... Checked Verify lamps and return switch to OFF. Note BMAT notifies MLO that checkout power is being applied. If other personnel are in the launcher area, MLO will announce that power is being applied and to stand clear of all missile and facility valves.
*63	Checkout power (assembly 8A2).................................... Applied Press CHECKOUT POWER pushbutton indicator and verify indicator lights red, then white within 10 seconds.
64	(After incorporation of TCTO 31X3-10-12-543) Press HYDRAULIC REGULATOR STAGE 1 and STAGE 2 PRESS TO READ.. Green When pressed and held, above pushbutton indicators will light green to indicate that the N_2 precharge in the hydraulic regulators is within tolerance.

Figure 3-10. Ballistic Missile Analyst Technician Alert Status Monitoring Procedure (Operational Bases) (Sheet 7 of 11)

STEP	PROCEDURE
65	All other indicators (except CHECKOUT POWER and SYSTEM CHECK).. Green
	CHECKOUT POWER pushbutton indicator will be lighted white and SYSTEM CHECK indicator will be not lighted.
66	DC VOLTS and AC VOLTS selectors........................ OFF
	Selector switches in OFF position prevents meter damage upon application of operating power.
	GUIDED MISSILE TEST SET
67	OPERATING MODE.. LAUNCH T.O. 21-SM68-2J-6-( )
68	ØA, ØB and ØC circuit breakers......................... Pressed
69	TEST SET POWER circuit breakers (2).................... Pressed
	Circuit breakers are checked to insure operating power will be available to the guidance equipment when launch countdown is started.
	ENGINE CONTROL SYSTEM
70	OPERATING MODE.. LAUNCH T.O. 21-SM68-2J-3-( )
71	Lamps.. Checked
	Verify lamps light, and return switch to OFF.
72	ECS GO... Green
73	CHECKOUT SELECTOR..................................... OFF
	LAUNCH SEQUENCER
74	OPERATING MODE.. LAUNCH T.O. 21-SM68-2J-15-1
75	Lamps.. Checked
	Verify lamps light, and return switch to OFF.
	If GO CKT MONITOR is lighted red, press once for a not lighted indication.

Figure 3-10. Ballistic Missile Analyst Technician Alert Status Monitoring Procedure (Operational Bases) (Sheet 8 of 11)

T.O. 21-SM68-1 Section III

STEP	PROCEDURE
	FLIGHT CONTROL SYSTEM
	Note
	IN PROCESS indicator is lighted when CHECKOUT POWER is applied.
76	OPERATING MODE... LAUNCH T.O. 21-SM68-2J-11-( )
77	Lamps.. Checked Verify lamps light, and return switch to OFF.
78	HEATER POWER... White
79	GYRO HEATER GO... Lighted
80	P, Y, and R.. Cycling
	RE-ENTRY VEHICLE SYSTEM
81	OPERATING MODE... LAUNCH T.O. 21-SM68-2J-5-( )
82	Lamps.. Checked Verify lamps light, and return switch to OFF.
83	R/V GOE CONTROL.. MARK 4
84	MARK 4 R/V IDENT... White
85	MARK 4 R/V GOE... Green
86	MARK 4 READINESS MONITOR, W/H SAFETY, A&F SAFETY, AND FUZE SET................................. Green
87	OPERATING MODE... CHECKOUT
	CAUTION
	If any indicator in step 88 is red, do not set MODE SELECTOR to MALFUNCTION.
88	MARK 4 W/H PRESSURE and A&F CONT........................ Green

Figure 3-10. Ballistic Missile Analyst Technician Alert Status Monitoring Procedure (Operational Bases) (Sheet 9 of 11)

STEP	PROCEDURE
89	OPERATING MODE. . . . . LAUNCH
	Notify MLO that checkout power is being removed. If other personnel are in the launcher area, MLO will verify that checkout power is not required before performing step 90.
*90	Checkout power (Assembly 8A2) . . . . Removed
	Press CHECKOUT POWER pushbutton indicator on assembly 8A2 to green. BMAT notifies MLO that he has completed equipment terminal alert status monitoring.

Figure 3-10. Ballistic Missile Analyst Technician Alert Status Monitoring Procedure (Operational Bases) (Sheet 10 of 11)

(Page 3-43, Figure 3-10, Sheet 11 of 11 deleted.)

STEP	PROCEDURE
96	Hydraulic pressures.................................... In Tolerance T.O. 21-SM68-2FJ-7-2 BMAT checks the hydraulic accumulator pressures to insure that they are in tolerance (1850 to 2950 PSI). Note Repeat steps 95 and 96 for other antenna.
97	Supply tank pressure (CC 5030).......................... Normal SAC CEM 21-SM68-2-20-( ) This compressor supplies controlled pneumatic pressure to A/C 2042 valves. Proper operation is necessary for guidance countdowns.
98	Control pressure (CC 5030).............................. Normal This indicator displays output pressure of the regulator unit controlling pneumatics to A/C valves.
99	MLO.. Notified BMAT notifies control center that alert status monitoring procedures have been completed. GEO will replace keys and return guidance equipment to standby.

Figure 3-10. Ballistic Missile Analyst Technician Alert Status Monitoring Procedure (Operational Bases) (Sheet 11 of 11)

STEP	PROCEDURE
	All tasks preceded by an asterisk will be coordinated with the MLO upon initiation or completion. <u>CONTROL CENTER</u> LAUNCH COMPLEX FACILITIES CONSOLE Note Steps 1 through 7 indicate or are checked for the response listed when the complex is in an alert status. All other indicators on the LCFC should indicate not lighted.
1	Lamps.. Checked T.O. 21-SM68-2J-15-1 Raise panel of launch complex facility console and activate lamp, flasher, and buzzer switches.
2	Flashers... Checked
3	Buzzer... Checked Press and hold buzzer verify switch, then press PUSH TO SILENCE pushbutton. Hold buzzer verify switch until buzzer stops.
4	GROUND GUIDANCE... Green
5	MISSILE AND FACILITY (3).................................. Green
6	POWER HOUSE GEN(S).. White GEN 1, 2, and 3, indicate white only when on the line and supplying power.
7	HAZARD LIGHT (3).. Green
8	Press MISSILE AND FACILITY (3)............................ Red LAUNCH CONTROL CONSOLE
9	MISSILE AND FACILITY (3).................................. Red

Figure 3-11. Ballistic Missile Analyst Technician Alert Status Monitoring Procedure (VAFB) (Sheet 1 of 10)

STEP	PROCEDURE
	CAUTION Prior to raising LCC front panel, press MISSILE and FACILITY pushbutton indicators on LCFC and verify red indication on LCFC and LCC to prevent accidental initiation of propellant loading during performance of lamp check.
10	Lamps.. Checked Raise panel on launch control console and actuate LAMP VERIFY switch. Verify all indicators are lighted and release switch. **Note** Steps 11 thru 14 indicate the responses listed when the complex is in an alert status. All other indicators on the LCC should indicate not lighted. **CAUTION** Insure EXERCISE 1, 2, and 3 safety seals are in place and secured to prevent system from being placed in launch mode.
11	EXERCISE (3).. Green, Seals in Place
12	TARGET SELECTION (3).................................. Green Verify proper target for each launcher is lighted green.
13	GROUND GUIDANCE....................................... Green **Note** Press MISSILE AND FACILITY pushbutton indicators on LCFC and verify green indication on LCFC and LCC.
14	Press MISSILE AND FACILITY (LCFC).................... Green When MISSILE AND FACILITY pushbutton indicator is pressed, the MISSILE AND FACILITY indicator on the LCFC and LCC must light green.
15	NUCLEAR BLAST DETECT ALARM DE-ACTIVATING.............. ON SAC CEM 21-SM68-2-25-( )

Figure 3-11. Ballistic Missile Analyst Technician Alert Status Monitoring Procedure (VAFB) (Sheet 2 of 10)

STEP	PROCEDURE
15 (CONT)	This switch must be ON to allow blast valves closure in event of a blast.
16	NUCLEAR BLAST INDICATOR NORMAL...................... Green All other indicators not lighted. CONTROL CENTER CIRCUITS
17	OPERATING MODE.. LAUNCH T.O. 21-SM68-2J-15-1
18	Lamps.. Checked Check LAMP VERIFY and return switch to the OFF position.
19	LOX LEAKAGE OVERRIDE (3)............................. Not Lighted
20	CSE control assembly................................. Checked BMAT will position the launcher select mode selector, events recorder, and analog recorder switches as directed at the special activities briefing.
21	TARGET CARD READER and LOGIC ASSEMBLY (3) lamps....... Checked
22	TARGETS (9).. Green Target C indicators may be red if guidance is equipped with handover capabilities.
23	TARGETS SELECTED..................................... Lighted BMAT verifies that TARGET SELECTION A, B, or C on target card reader corresponds with the TARGET SELECTION A, B, or C on the LCC.
24	TARGET SELECT TEST (3)............................... Not Lighted
25	Color code... Checked Verify proper chassis to pallet relationship by matching color coding.
26	RECT ON LINE (POWER SUPPLY CONTROL).................. White

Figure 3-11. Ballistic Missile Analyst Technician Alert Status Monitoring Procedure (VAFB) (Sheet 3 of 10)

T.O. 21-SM68-1   Section III

STEP	PROCEDURE
27	LOAD, BUS, RECT, and BATTERY voltages....................CHECKED
	BMAT checks the bus, rectifier, and battery voltages to insure that the proper voltages exist and that the battery is in a fully charged condition. (load 29(±3)VDC, battery 30(±3)VDC, and rectifier 28(±3)VDC.)
28	Countdown clocks (3).......................................Reset T.O. 21-SM68-2J-15-1
	Place countdown clock reset switches 1, 2, and 3 in UP position momentarily, and verify countdown times set for applicable launcher.
29	DISABLE (time display board)............................Red
*30	LSCB...ENABLE, Green; DISABLE, Red
	BMAT positions LSCB in UP position momentarily and verifies ENABLE indicator lights green. DISABLE indicator will remain red.
31	Hold time indicators (3)..............................000.00
32	Circuit breakers...ON
33	Remote gox analyzer................................Checked
	Gox readings are observed to check the operating condition of remote analyzers in all propellant terminals and missile silos to ascertain areas are safe for entry. If remote gox analyzer is inoperative, the BMAT will have maintenance personnel insure all analyzers in the missile silos and propellant terminals are operating.
	<u>EQUIPMENT TERMINAL</u>
34	MLO..Notified
	BMAT will notify control center that he has arrived at the equipment terminal.
	SUBSTATION GENERATOR POWER (1404)
35	GROUNDING IND LIGHTS (3)............................Lighted SAC CEM 21-SM68-2-21-( )

Figure 3-11. Ballistic Missile Analyst Technician Alert Status
Monitoring Procedure (VAFB) (Sheet 4 of 10)

3-47

STEP	PROCEDURE
	SUBSTATION COMMERCIAL POWER (1407)
36	GROUNDING IND LIGHTS (3)..................................Lighted
	MOTOR CONTROL CENTER (MCC 1505)
37	All circuit breakers (except FUEL UNLOADING MISSILE SILO)..ON
	MOTOR CONTROL CENTER (MCC 1506)
38	All circuit breakers......................................ON
	POWER SWITCHBOARD JEU-7/E
39	All circuit breakers......................................ON T.O. 21-SM68-2J-10-( )
	POWER SUPPLY ECU-16
40	MODE SELECTOR...REMOTE T.O. 21-SM68-2J-10-( ) Positioning MODE SELECTOR on power supply ECU-16 to REMOTE permits unit to be started or stopped remotely.
41	PRIMARY POWER lamp..Lighted
42	Lamps...Checked Verify PRIMARY POWER LAMP is lighted and lamps light when checked.
	28 VOLT POWER SUPPLY A/E 24A-4
43	PRI POWER INDICATOR.......................................Lighted
44	LOCAL START-REMOTE START..................................REMOTE START Positioning LOCAL START-REMOTE START switch on power supply A/E 24A-4 to REMOTE START permits unit to be started or stopped remotely.
	BATTERY POWER SUPPLY A/E 24A-5
45	Lamps...Checked
46	Battery trickle chargers..................................Green

Figure 3-11. Ballistic Missile Analyst Technician Alert Status Monitoring Procedure (VAFB) (Sheet 5 of 10)

STEP	PROCEDURE
47	INPUT POWER PHASE A, B, and C.......................... Lighted
	All other indicators not lighted.
	MOTOR GENERATOR A/E 24A-3
48	LOCAL-REMOTE START................................... REMOTE START
	Positioning LOCAL-REMOTE START switch to REMOTE START permits unit to be remotely controlled by control monitor group OA-2438/GJQ-11.
49	LOAD C.B. .... ON
50	LINE POWER.. White
	BATTERY CHARGER RECTIFIER (REC 1604)
51	GROUNDING indicators.................................. Lighted
	SAC CEM 21-SM68-2-21-( )
52	VOLTAGE... Green, 125(+5)VDC
53	AMMETER... Green, 0-2 amps
	ELECTRICAL SYSTEM
54	All circuit breakers.................................. ON
	During an exercise all circuit breakers will be positioned as directed by the MLO.
55	OPERATING MODE.. LAUNCH
56	Lamps... Checked
	Verify lamps and return switch to OFF.
	Note
	BMAT notifies MLO that checkout power is being applied. If other personnel are in the launcher area, MLO will announce that power is being applied and to stand clear of all missile and facility valves.

Figure 3-11. Ballistic Missile Analyst Technician Alert Status Monitoring Procedure (VAFB) (Sheet 6 of 10)

STEP	PROCEDURE
*57	Checkout power (assembly 8A2).......................... Applied
	Press CHECKOUT POWER pushbutton indicator and verify indicator lights red, then lights white within 10 seconds.
58	(After incorporation of TCTO 31X3-10-12-543) Press HYDRAULIC REGULATOR STAGE 1 and STAGE 2 PRESS TO READ.. Green
	When pressed and held, above pushbutton indicators will indicate the N_2 precharge in hydraulic regulators are within tolerance.
59	All other indicators (except CHECKOUT POWER and SYSTEM CHECK).. Green
	CHECKOUT POWER pushbutton indicator will be white and SYSTEM CHECK indicator will be not lighted.
60	DC VOLTS and AC VOLTS selectors....................... OFF
	Selector switches in off position prevents meter damage upon application of operating power.
	GUIDED MISSILE TEST SET
61	OPERATING MODE.. LAUNCH
	T.O. 21-SM68-2J-6-( )
62	ØA, ØB and ØC circuit breakers........................ Pressed
63	TEST SET POWER circuit breakers (2)................... Pressed
	Circuit breakers are checked to insure operating power will be available to the guidance equipment when launch countdown is started.
	ENGINE CONTROL SYSTEM.
64	OPERATING MODE.. LAUNCH
65	Lamps.. Checked
	Verify lamps light, and return switch to OFF.
66	ECS GO... Green

Figure 3-11. Ballistic Missile Analyst Technician Alert Status Monitoring Procedure (VAFB) (Sheet 7 of 10)

T.O. 21-SM68-1   Section III

STEP	PROCEDURE
67	CHECKOUT SELECTOR.. OFF
	LAUNCH SEQUENCER
68	OPERATING MODE... LAUNCH T.O. 21-SM68-2J-15-1
69	Lamps... Checked Verify lamps light, and return switch to OFF. If GO CKT MONITOR is lighted red, press once for a not lighted indication. FLIGHT CONTROL SYSTEM Note IN PROCESS indicator is lighted when CHECKOUT POWER is applied.
70	OPERATING MODE... LAUNCH T.O. 21-SM68-2J-11-( )
71	Lamps... Checked Verify lamps light, and return switch to OFF.
72	HEATER POWER.. White
73	GYRO HEATER GO.. Lighted
74	P, Y, and R... Cycling
	RE-ENTRY VEHICLE SYSTEM
75	OPERATING MODE... LAUNCH T.O. 21-SM68-2J-5-( )
76	Lamps... Checked Verify lamps light, and return switch to OFF.
77	R/V GOE CONTROL... MARK 4
78	MARK 4 R/V IDENT... White
79	MARK 4 R/V GOE... Green

Figure 3-11. Ballistic Missile Analyst Technician Alert Status
Monitoring Procedure (VAFB) (Sheet 8 of 10)

STEP	PROCEDURE
80	MARK 4 READINESS MONITOR, W/H SAFETY, A&F SAFETY, AND FUZE SET. . . . . Green
81	OPERATING MODE. . . . . CHECKOUT
	CAUTION
	If any indicator in step 82 is red, do not set MODE SELECTOR to MALFUNCTION.
82	MARK 4 W/H PRESSURE and A&F CONT. . . . . Green
83	OPERATING MODE. . . . . LAUNCH
	Notify MLO that checkout power is being removed. If other personnel are in the launcher area, MLO will verify that checkout power is not required before performing step 84.
*84	Checkout power (assembly 8A2) . . . . Removed
	Press CHECKOUT POWER pushbutton indicator on assembly 8A2 to green. BMAT notifies MLO that he has completed equipment terminal alert status monitoring.

Figure 3-11. Ballistic Missile Analyst Technician Alert Status Monitoring Procedure (VAFB) (Sheet 9 of 10)

(Page 3-53, Figure 3-11 Sheet 10 of 10 deleted.)

STEP	PROCEDURE
88	Gangway... Lowered T.O. 21-SM68-2FJ-7-2 To lower the gangway assembly the hand crank must be connected to the hand operated winch assembly. Gangway assembly pip pin is then removed, and drum lock disengaged.
89	BLOWER... ON BMAT will check antenna BLOWER switch on the third level of the antenna silo.
90	Hydraulic pressures.. In Tolerance BMAT checks the Hydraulic Accumulator pressures to insure that they are in tolerance (1850 to 2950 PSI).
91	Gangway... Raised To raise the gangway assembly, engage the drum lock, turn hand crank as necessary, insert gangway assembly pip pin, and then remove and store the crank.
92	RAILS STORED.. Not lighted RAILS STORED indicator is located in control panel 29A3A2. Note Repeat steps 88 thru 92 for other antenna.
93	Supply tank pressure (CC2601)........................... Green, 70-80 PSI
94	Control pressure (PI 2601).................................. Green, 15 PSI
95	MLO... Notified BMAT notifies control center that alert status monitoring procedures have been completed.

Figure 3-11. Ballistic Missile Analyst Technician Alert Status Monitoring Procedure (VAFB) (Sheet 10 of 10)

T.O. 21M-HGM25A-1-1 (21-SM68-1) Section III

STEP	PROCEDURE
	All tasks preceded by an asterisk will be coordinated with the MLO.
	<u>EQUIPMENT TERMINAL</u>
	LAUNCHER SYSTEM
1	OPERATION SELECTOR. . . . . REMOTE T.O. 21M-HGM25A-2-8-( ) The OPERATION SELECTOR switch determines if the power pack is to be operated remotely by the logic circuitry or locally from the cycling control station. The LOCAL position is used for maintenance only.
2	Lamp test . . . . Performed A lamp test is performed by pressing the LAMP TEST pushbutton on the annunciator panel.
3	Air handler (AC2010) . . . . Operating SAC CEM 21-SM68-2-20-( ) Air handler (AC2010) operates only when the room temperature rises above +75 degrees fahrenheit.
4	Air compressor (CC 5002) External lubricator oil level . . . . Checked Crankcase oil level . . . . Checked Drain tank. . . . . Accomplished SAC CEM 21-SM68-2-26-( ) The plant air compressor (CC 5002) compresses, stores, filters, and dries air. This unit supplies compressed air to the pneumatic sewage ejector and utility air outlets in the missile silo, equipment terminal, and dry filtered air to control devices and valves in the propellant terminal. During a launch this system must be operating and supplying compressed air for control devices in the fuel transfer panel, propellant loading system, blast valve in the propellant terminal, and the damper motor in the missile air conditioning duct.
	HYDRAULIC SYSTEM (C-216)
5	Pump suction pressure . . . . 12(±1) PSI T.O. 21M-HGM25A-2-9-( )

Figure 3-12. Missile Maintenance Technician Alert Status Monitoring Procedure
(Operational Bases) (Sheet 1 of 9)

STEP	PROCEDURE
5 (CONT)	Fluid flows from the reservoir pressurized with dry nitrogen at 12 PSI, and regulated from a K bottle, to provide a positive fluid flow to the main pump inlet.
6	Standby K bottle. . . . . 50 PSI MIN The K bottle provided with this unit supplies regulated dry nitrogen at a constant pressure (50 PSI) to be further regulated to approximately 12 PSI for reservoir pressurization within the unit.
7	Hydraulic reservoir . . . . Within Limits The unit hydraulic reservoir is provided with a sight gage housed inside of the lower right hand access door. This sight gage has an upper and lower marking. The in-limit fluid level is determined by visually observing fluid between these markings.
8	Lamp test . . . . Performed Each lamp located on the face of the A/E27H-2 unit must be individually pressed to test (16 lamps). Burned out lamps must be replaced as soon as possible after discovery.
9	Visual check for excessive leakage. . . . . Performed A visual check for leakage must be performed on the unit by sliding all drip pans out for evidence of fluid. If an excessive leak other than static is discovered, further isolate the cause by opening access doors as required until the source of the leak is found and can be identified for documentation.
10	Air handler (AC2012) Damper linkage connected and unit operating . . . . . . Verified Temperature indicator(s). . . . . Normal SAC CEM 21-SM68-2-20-( ) Air handler (AC2012) supplies heating, cooling, and humidification to the missile silo under normal and launch conditions. If lox spillage occurs, it will automatically purge air from the missile silo.

Figure 3-12. Missile Maintenance Technician Alert Status Monitoring Procedure (Operational Bases) (Sheet 2 of 9)

T.O. 21M-HGM25A-1-1 (21-SM68-1)　　　　　　　　　　　Section III

STEP	PROCEDURE
11	Exhaust fan 2021. . . . . Operating
	Centrifugal air fan 2021 furnishes relief air from all levels of the equipment terminal to the missile silo air handler (AC2012).
12	Air Compressor (CC 5001)
	Supply tank pressure. . . . . Normal
	Control pressure. . . . . Normal
	Oil level . . . . Checked
	Drain tank. . . . . Accomplished
	Air compressor (CC 5001) is located on level II of the equipment terminal and furnishes supply pressure to all air conditioning pneumatic, temperature, humidity, and pressure controllers in the launcher areas.
	PROPELLANT SYSTEM
*13	Checkout power (assembly 8A2) . . . . Applied T.O. 21M-HGM25A-2-10-( )
	MMT presses CHECKOUT POWER pushbutton indicator on control monitor group OA-2438/GJQ-11. The indicator will light red, then white in approximately 10 seconds. This supplies checkout power to the PLPS AGE.
14	Lamps . . . . Checked T.O. 21M-HGM25A-2-12-( )
	Set LAMP VERIFY switch to 1 for red and white check and to 2 for green check. Lamps will be replaced if necessary. Return LAMP VERIFY switch to OFF.
15	INDICATING POWER. . . . . White
	INDICATING POWER lights the valve position pushbutton indicators of the propellant system AGE. When pressed the indicator lights white and remains white until pressed again. It lights green only during lamp verification.
16	PLPS in preset condition. . . . . Verified
	Preset condition for the PLPS is determined by the following indications on control monitor group OA-2440:

Figure 3-12. Missile Maintenance Technician Alert Status Monitoring Procedure (Operatinal Bases) (Sheet 3 of 9)

Changed 13 March 1964　TOCN 1-1 (DEN-11)

T.O. 21M-HGM25A-1-1 (21-SM68-1) Section III

STEP	PROCEDURE
16 (CONT)	a. CHECKOUT switch to OFF. b. MODE switch LAUNCH. c. FCV-218 lower green. d. RESET indicator green. e. Four level sensors green. f. (Prior to incorporation of TCTO 31X3-10-11-627) All valve sensor and pushbutton indicators on assemblies 5A1, 5A2, 5A3, 6A1, and 6A3 upper green, except MISSILE PNEU I, MISSILE PNEU II, and FCV-507 lower green; STAGE I MISSILE FUEL VENT and STAGE II MISSILE FUEL VENT upper red; Stage I and II MISSILE FUEL PRESS REG lower green; Stage I and II MISSILE FILL AND DRAIN upper red; and Stage I and II MISSILE VENT NORMS (3) upper red. g. (After incorporation of TCTO 31X3-10-11-627) All valve sensor and pushbutton indicators on assemblies 5A1, 5A2, 5A3, 6A1, and 6A3 upper green, except FCV-507 lower green; STAGE I MISSILE FUEL VENT and STAGE II MISSILE FUEL VENT upper red; Stage I and II MISSILE FUEL PRESS REG lower green; Stage I and II MISSILE FILL AND DRAIN upper red; and Stage I and II MISSILE VENT NORMS (3) upper red.
17	(After incorporation of TCTO 31X3-10-11-625) KEY switch (assembly 6A5) . . . . Positioned T.O. 21M-HGM25A-2-28-1 Position KEY switch to ON for CSE and OFF for all other modes of operation.
18	(After incorporation of TCTO 31X3-10-11-634) FUEL EXERCISE-OFF switch. . . . . Positioned Verify FUEL EXERCISE-OFF switch is in the FUEL EXERCISE position when conducting a fuel exercise. All other times the FUEL EXERCISE-OFF switch will be in the OFF position.

Figure 3-12. Missile Maintenance Technician Alert Status Monitoring Procedure (Operational Bases) (Sheet 4 of 9)

Changed 13 March 1964 TOCN 1-1 (DEN-11)

STEP	PROCEDURE	
19	(After incorporation of TCTO 31X3-10-11-625) BATTERY switch (assembly 6A5)	Positioned
	Verify BATTERY switch is in the ACTIVATE position during EWO alert monitoring, all other times as briefed.	
*20	Checkout power (assembly 8A2) . . . . T.O. 21M-HGM25A-2-10-( )	Removed
	MMT insures checkout power is no longer required for other subsystem checks, coordinates checkout power removal with MLO, then presses CHECKOUT POWER pushbutton indicator for a green indication which returns the system to an alert status.	
	<u>MISSILE SILO</u>	
	PROPELLANT SYSTEM	
21	Condition of missile and missile silo . . . . T.O. not required	Checked
	MMT, utilizing missile silo elevator, proceeds from level 1 through level 8. A visual inspection of the missile and missile silo is performed checking for RP-1 and hydraulic leaks, expended missile release mechanism explosive bolts, expended Stage I thrust chamber igniters, and condition of the missile silo sump area. If any pyrotechnic(s) is found expended, MMT will record time date in appropriate forms. Upon completion of inspection, MMT will proceed to level 7 1/2 to perform next step.	
22	PI-9321-502 and PI-9321-522 . . . . T.O. 21M-HGM25A-2-12-( )	3000(±100) PSI
	MMT verifies that PI-9321-502 for the NO. 2 bank and PI-9321-522 for the NO. 1 bank of nitrogen start bottles each indicate 3000(±100) PSI. This pressure is utilized to accelerate the Stage I turbopump turbine to pump fuel and lox to the thrust chamber, during initial firing sequence.	
23	CV-9321-505	Positioned

Figure 3-12. Missile Maintenance Technician Alert Status Monitoring Procedure (Operational Bases) (Sheet 5 of 9)

STEP	PROCEDURE
23 (CONT)	MMT verifies that CV-9321-505 is positioned to bank NO. 1. If the NO. 1 bank indicates less than 2900 PSI, the MMT will position CV-9321-505 to bank NO. 2. For the initiation of an exercise, the MMT will be required to position CV-9321-505 to the OFF position.
24	QD-9322-526 . . . . Stored MMT verifies that QD-9322-526 is disconnected and stored free of launcher path. When connected, QD-9322-526 provides the capability for servicing the nitrogen start system to the required pressure.
25	Exhaust fan 2001 . . . . Operating SAC CEM 21-SM68-2-20-( ) Exhaust fan 2001 removes air from the missile silo through the return and exhaust ducts. PROPELLANT TERMINAL PROPELLANT SYSTEM
26	Lox storage tank vacuum . . . . 150 Microns T.O. 21M-HGM25A-2-12-( ) MAX The annular space enclosed by the two walls of the lox storage tank is evacuated for thermal insulation by vacuum pump P-701.
27	PI-701 . . . . 250(±10) PSI PI-701 indicates the working pressure from the instrument air supply system. The pressure indicated on PI-701 operates flow control valves FCV-218, FCV-211, FCV-306, and FCV-207.
28	(LAFB 724TH/725TH SQDN) PI-702 . . . . 40(±1) PSI
29	(EAFB, BAFB, LAFB, MHAFB) PI-702 . . . . 35(±2) PSI PI-702 indicates the regulated working pressure from the instrument air supply system. The pressure indicated on PI-702 is used to operate flow control valves and to supply a working pressure for liquid level indicators.

Figure 3-12. Missile Maintenance Technician Alert Status Monitoring Procedure (Operational Bases) (Sheet 6 of 9)

STEP	PROCEDURE
30	PI-703. . . . . 35(±2) PSI
	PI-703 indicates the regulated working pressure from the instrument air supply system. The pressure indicated on PI-703 is used to operate pressure controllers which subsequently operate diaphragm type valves in the PLPS.
31	PI-601 and PI-602 . . . . 5500 PSI MIN
	PI-601 indicates the stored helium pressure in T-601A, and PI-602 indicates the stored helium pressure in T-601B. This helium pressure is utilized for missile-borne tank pressurization and is transferred to the missile at initiation of the load propellant phase.
32	PI-402. . . . . 740 GAL MIN
	PI-402 indicates the amount, in gallons, of liquid nitrogen present in T-402.
33	PI-503. . . . . 1700 PSI MIN
	PI-503 indicates storage pressure of nitrogen contained in T-503. Gaseous nitrogen stored in T-503 is utilized primarily for utility services.
34	PI-516. . . . . 1900 PSI MIN
	PI-516 indicates pressure contained in T-504. This N_2 provides pneumatic pressure to operate airborne components as well as propellant tank pressurization during unloading.
35	PI-502. . . . . 600 PSI MIN
	PI-502 indicates the pressure available in T-502. This N_2 is utilized to provide a nitrogen blanket for the missile fuel and lox tanks. In addition, this nitrogen is used for the purging of the fuel tanks.
36	PI-303. . . . . 1650 PSI MIN
	PI-303 indicates the pressure available in T-301A, T-301B, and T-301C which are manifold together. This N_2 is utilized during lox transfer for pressurization of the lox storage tank.

Figure 3-12. Missile Maintenance Technician Alert Status Monitoring Procedure (Operational Bases)(Sheet 7 of 9)

T.O. 21M-HGM25A-1-1 (21-SM68-1)　　　　　　　　　　　Section III

STEP	PROCEDURE
37	PI-202. . . . . 22,900 GAL MIN
	PI-202 indicates the amount, in gallons, of liquid oxygen in T-201.
38	PI-401. . . . . 925 GAL MIN
	PI-401 indicates the amount, in gallons, of liquid nitrogen in T-401.
39	PI-515. . . . . 1100 PSI MIN
	PI-515 indicates the pressure in T-505. This N_2 is utilized to provide a blanket pressure for the lox transfer lines at all times during standby. In addition, this pressure is used to purge missile lox tanks.
40	P-303 HAND-OFF-AUTO switch. . . . . AUTO
	P-303 HAND-OFF-AUTO switch is set to AUTO position to provide automatic operation of the exhaust blower in the propellant terminal vent shaft.
41	Helium cooler . . . . 150 Microns MAX
	The annular space enclosed by the two walls of the helium cooler is evacuated for thermal insulation by vacuum pump P-703.
42	Lox subcooler vacuum. . . . . 150 Microns MAX
	The annular space enclosed by the two walls of the lox subcooler is evacuated for thermal insulation by vacuum pump P-703.
43	MCC 1001 circuit breaker. ON SAC CEM 21-SM68-2-21-( )
	MCC 1001 supplies power for lox vacuum pumps P-701, P-702, and P-703, FN 2011, SP 3010, P-303, PNL 1010, LO_2 air conditioning control transformer, and propellant terminal power receptacles.
44	Exhaust fan 2010. . . . . Operating SAC CEM 21-SM68-2-20-( )

Figure 3-12. Missile Maintenance Technician Alert Status Monitoring Procedure
(Operational Bases) (Sheet 8 of 9)

STEP	PROCEDURE
45	PI-707. . . . . 20(±1) PSI T.O. 21M-HGM25A-2-12-( ) PI-707 indicates the regulated pressure from the instrument air system which has been reduced to 20(±1) PSI by PRV-707. This pressure is routed to pressure transducers that control the Stage I and II lox topping valves.
46	PNL 1010 circuit breakers . . . . ON SAC CEM 21-SM68-2-21-( ) PNL 1010 supplies power for operation of control valves for the propellant loading system, PLPS vacuum gages, and gox analyzers.

Figure 3-12. Missile Maintenance Technician Alert Status Monitoring Procedure (Operational Bases) (Sheet 9 of 9)

STEP	PROCEDURE
	All tasks preceded by an asterisk will be coordinated with the MLO.
1 thru 6	Deleted.
	EQUIPMENT TERMINAL
	LAUNCHER SYSTEM
*7	OVERRIDE/EXERCISE (CTL/exercise). . . . . EXERCISE

Figure 3-13. Missile Maintenance Technician Alert Status Monitoring Procedure (VAFB) (Sheet 1 of 9)

STEP	PROCEDURE
*8	OVERRIDE/EXERCISE (EWO)................................ OVERRIDE
9	OPERATION SELECTOR..................................... REMOTE
	The OPERATION SELECTOR switch determines if the power pack is to be operated remotely by the logic circuitry or locally from the cycling control station. The LOCAL position is used for maintenance only.
10	Lamp test... Performed
	A lamp test is performed by pressing the LAMP TEST pushbutton on the annunciator panel.
11	Air handler (A/C 2402)................................ Operating SAC CEM 21-SM68-2-20-( )
	This handler operates only when room temperature rises above 65°F and will operate until temperature drops to 55° F. The operation of the hydraulic power pack increases the heat load.
	HYDRAULIC SYSTEM (C-216)
12	Pump suction pressure................................. 12($\pm$1) PSI T.O. 21-SM68-2FJ-9-( )
	Fluid flows from the reservoir pressurized with dry nitrogen at 12 PSI, and regulated from a K bottle, to provide a positive fluid flow to the main pump inlet.
13	Standby K bottle...................................... 50 PSI (MIN)
	The K bottle provided with this unit is merely to supply regulated dry nitrogen at a constant pressure (50 PSI) to be further regulated to approximately 12 PSI for reservoir pressurization within the unit.
14	Hydraulic Reservoir................................... Within Limits
	The unit hydraulic reservoir is provided with a sight gage housed on the lower right hand access door of the unit. This sight gage has an upper and lower black marking and the in-limits fluid level is determined by visually observing fluid within the two black lines.

Figure 3-13. Missile Maintenance Technician Alert Status Monitoring Procedure (VAFB) (Sheet 2 of 9)

T.O. 21-SM68-1 Section III

STEP	PROCEDURE
15	Lamp test... Performed
	Each lamp located on the face of the A/E27H-2 unit must be individually pressed to test (16 lamps). Burned out lamps must be replaced as soon as possible after discovery.
16	Visual check for excessive leakage.................... Performed
	A visual check for leakage must be performed on the unit by sliding all drip pans out for evidence of fluid. If an excessive leak other than static is discovered, further isolate the cause by opening access doors as required until the source of the leak is found and can be identified for documentation.
17	Air handler A/C 2501
	Damper linkage connected and unit operating.......... Verified
	TI 2506.. Green, 65° F MIN
	TI 2505.. Green, 75° F MAX
	SAC CEM 21-SM68-2-20( ).
	This air handler supplies heating, cooling and humidification to the missile silo under normal and launch conditions. If lox spillage occurs, it will automatically purge air from the missile silo. Ref: SAC CEM.
18	Exhaust fan 2402...................................... Operating
	Centrifugal air fan 2021 furnishes relief air from all levels of the equipment terminal to the missile silo air handler (A/C 2012).
19	Air compressor CC 2401:
	Supply tank pressure gage............................ Green, 70-80 PSI
	Control pressure gage................................ Green, 15($\pm$2) PSI
	This air compressor is located on level 2 of the equipment terminal and furnishes supply pressure to all air conditioning pneumatic temperature, humidity, and pressure controllers in the launcher areas.

Figure 3-13. Missile Maintenance Technician Alert Status Monitoring Procedure (VAFB) (Sheet 3 of 9)

STEP	PROCEDURE
	PROPELLANT SYSTEM (EQUIPMENT TERMINAL)
*20	Checkout power (assembly 8A2).....................Applied T.O. 21-SM68-2J-10-( ) MMT presses CHECKOUT POWER pushbutton indicator on control monitor group OA-2438/GJQ-11. The indicator will light red, then white in approximately 10 seconds. This supplies checkout power to the PLPS AOE.
21	Lamps...Checked T.O. 21-SM68-2J-12-( ) Set LAMP VERIFY switch to 1 for red and white check and to 2 for green check. Lamps will be replaced if necessary. Return LAMP VERIFY switch to OFF.
22	INDICATING POWER....................................White INDICATING POWER lights the valve position pushbutton indicators of the propellant system AOE. When pressed, the indicator lights white and remains white until pressed again. It lights green only during lamp verification.
23	PLPS in preset condition.........................Verified A Preset Condition for the PLPS is determined by the following indications on control monitor group OA-2440: a. CHECKOUT switch OFF. b. MODE SELECTOR switch LAUNCH. c. FCV-218 lower green. d. RESET indicator green. e. Four level sensors green. f. All valve sensor and pushbutton indicators on assemblies 5A1, 5A2, 5A3, 6A1 and 6A3 indicate upper green except FCV-507 lower green, STAGE I MISSILE FUEL VENT and STAGE II MISSILE FUEL VENT upper red; STAGE I

Figure 3-13. Missile Maintenance Technician Alert Status Monitoring Procedure (VAFB) (Sheet 4 of 9)

T.O. 21M-HGM25A-1-1 (21-SM68-1) Section III

STEP	PROCEDURE
23 (CONT)	and II MISSILE FUEL PRESS REG lower green; Stage I and II MISSILE FILL AND DRAIN are upper red; and Stage I and II MISSILE VENT NORMS (3) upper red.
24	KEY switch (assembly 6A5) . . . . Positioned Position KEY switch to ON for CSE and OFF for all other modes of operation.
24.1	(After incorporation of TCTO 31X3-10-11-634) FUEL EXERCISE-OFF switch. . . . . Positioned Verify FUEL EXERCISE-OFF switch is in the FUEL EXERCISE position when conducting a fuel exercise. All other times the FUEL EXERCISE-OFF switch will be in OFF position.
25	BATTERY switch (assembly 6A5) . . . . Positioned Verify BATTERY switch is in the ACTIVATE position during EWO alert status monitoring, all other times as briefed.
*26	Checkout power (assembly 8A2) . . . . Removed MMT insures checkout power is no longer required for other subsystem checks, coordinates checkout power removal with MLO, then presses CHECKOUT POWER pushbutton indicator for a green indication which returns the system to an alert status. PROPELLANT SYSTEM (MISSILE SILO)
27	Condition of missile and missile silo . . . . Checked T.O. not required MMT, utilizing missile silo elevator, proceeds from level 1 through level 8. A visual inspection of the missile and missile silo is performed checking for RP-1 and hydraulic leaks, expended missile release mechanism explosive bolts, expended Stage I thrust chamber igniters, and condition of the missile silo sump area. If any pyrotectnic(s) is found expended, MMT will record time date in appropriate forms. Upon completion of inspection, MMT will proceed to level 7 1/2 to perform next step.

Figure 3-13. Missile Maintenance Technician Alert Status Monitoring
Procedure (VAFB) (Sheet 5 of 9)

Changed 20 February 1964 TOCN 1-1 (DEN-10)

STEP	PROCEDURE
28	PI-502 and PI-522 . . . . 3000(±100) PSI T.O. 21M-HGM25A-2-12-2 MMT verifies that PI-502 for the NO. 2 bank and PI-522 for the NO. 1 bank of nitrogen start bottles each indicate 3000(±100) PSI. This pressure is utilized to accelerate the Stage I turbopump turbine to pump fuel and lox to the thrust chamber during initial firing sequence.

Figure 3-13. Missile Maintenance Technician Alert Status Monitoring Procedure (VAFB) (Sheet 5A of 9)

STEP	PROCEDURE
29	CV-505..Positioned
	MMT verifies that CV-505 is positioned to bank NO. 1. If the NO. 1 bank indicates less than 2900 PSI, the MMT will position CV-505 to bank NO. 2.
30	QD-9322-526...Stored
	The MMT verifies that QD9322-526 is disconnected and stored free of launcher path. When connected, QD-9322-526 provides the capability for servicing the nitrogen start system to the required pressure.
	PROPELLANT SYSTEM (PROPELLANT TERMINAL)
31	Lox storage tank vacuum...150 Microns (MAX)
	The annular space enclosed by the two walls of the lox storage tank is evacuated for thermal insulation by vacuum pump P-701.
32	P-701 Operating...Verified
	The lox storage tank vacuum pump is maintained in an operating condition at all times except for maintenance. The pump is capable of evacuating the annular space in T-201 to 30 Microns.
33	PI-701...250($\pm$10) PSI
	PI-701 indicates the working pressure from the instrument air supply system. The pressure indicated on PI-701 operates flow control valves FCV-218, FCV-211, FCV-306, and FCV-207.
34	PI-702..35($\pm$2.0) PSI
	PI-702 indicates the regulated working pressure from the instrument air supply system. The pressure indicated on PI-702 is used to operate flow control valves and to supply a working pressure for liquid level indicators.

Figure 3-13. Missile Maintenance Technician Alert Status Monitoring Procedure (VAFB) (Sheet 6 of 9)

STEP	PROCEDURE
35	PI-703.. 35($\pm$2.0) PSI
	PI-703 indicates the regulated working pressure from the instrument air supply system. The pressure indicated on PI-703 is used to operate pressure controllers which subsequently operate diaphragm type valves in the PLPS.
36	PI-601 and PI-602...................................... 5500 PSI (MIN)
	PI-601 represents the stored helium pressure in T-601A, and PI-602 represents the stored helium pressure in T-601B. This helium pressure is utilized for missileborne tank pressurization and is transferred to the missile at initiation of the load propellants phase.
37	PI-402.. 740 GAL (MIN)
	PI-402 indicates the amount, in gallons, of liquid nitrogen present in T-402.
38	PI-503.. 1700 PSI (MIN)
	PI-503 indicates storage pressure of nitrogen contained in T-503. Gaseous nitrogen stored in T-503 is utilized primarily for utility service.
39	PI-516.. 1900 PSI (MIN)
	PI-516 indicates pressure contained in T-504. This N_2 pressure provides pneumatic pressure to operate airborne components and also provides pressure to pressurize missile propellant tanks for unloading purposes.
40	PI-502.. 600 PSI (MIN)
	PI-502 indicates the pressure available within T-502. This N_2 is utilized to provide a nitrogen blanket of the missile fuel and lox tanks. In addition, this nitrogen will be used to purge the fuel tanks.
41	PI-303.. 1600 PSI (MIN)
	PI-303 indicates the pressure available within T-301A, T-301B and T-301C which are manifolded together. This N_2 is utilized during pressurization of the lox storage tank.

Figure 3-13. Missile Maintenance Technician Alert Status Monitoring Procedure (VAFB) (Sheet 7 of 9)

T.O. 21-SM68-1   Section III

STEP	PROCEDURE
42	PI-202.. 22,900 GAL (MIN) PI-202 will provide an indication of the amount of liquid oxygen, present within T-201.
43	PI-401.. 925 GAL (MIN) PI-401 indicates the amount, in gallons, of liquid nitrogen present in T-401.
44	PI-515.. 1100 PSI (MIN) PI-515 indicates the pressure available within T-505. This N_2 is utilized to provide a blanket pressure for the lox transfer lines at all times during standby. In addition, this pressure is used to purge missile lox tanks.
45	P-303 HAND-OFF-AUTO....................................... AUTO The HAND-OFF-AUTO switch for P-303 is set to the AUTO position to provide automatic operation of the exhaust blower in the propellant terminal vent shaft.
46	Helium cooler... 150 Microns (MAX) The annular space enclosed by the two walls of the Helium cooler is evacuated for thermal insulation by vacuum pump P-703.
47	P-703 operating... Verified The vacuum pumps at VAFB are maintained in an operating condition at all times except for maintenance. They are capable of evacuating the annular space to 30 microns.
48	Lox subcooler vacuum...................................... 150 Microns (MAX) The annular space enclosed by the two walls of the lox subcooler is evacuated for thermal insulation by vacuum pump P-703.
49	P-702 operating... Verified The vacuum pumps are maintained in an operating condition at all times except for maintenance. They are capable of evacuating the annular space to 30 microns.

Figure 3-13. Missile Maintenance Technician Alert Status Monitoring Procedure (VAFB) (Sheet 8 of 9)

STEP	PROCEDURE
50	MCC 1507 and MCC 1508 circuit breakers................ ON
51	Exhaust fan 2010...................................... Operating
52	PI-707.. 20($\pm$1) PSI
	PI-707 indicates the regulated pressure from the instrument air system which has been reduced to 20 PSI by PRV-707. This pressure is routed to pressure transducers that control the Stage I and II lox topping valves.
53	PNL 1607.. ON

Figure 3-13. Missile Maintenance Technician Alert Status Monitoring Procedure (VAFB) (Sheet 9 of 9)

T.O. 21M-HGM25A-1-1 (21-SM68-1)　　　　　　　　Section III

STEP	PROCEDURE
1	Annunciator panel checkout: SAC CEM 21-SM68-2-21-( ) 　a.　Request control center stand by for annunciator panel test. 　b.　Rotate annunciator panel TEST switch through all 12 positions and return to zero. 　c.　Press annunciator ACKN pushbutton. 　d.　Verify with LCFC operator that POWERHOUSE EMERGENCY indicator and alarm (LCFC) are operating. 　　　　　　　　　Note 　　　Repeat steps b thru d on the remaining four annunciator TEST switches. 　e.　Press annunciator RESET pushbutton. 　f.　Verify with LCFC operator that POWERHOUSE EMERGENCY indicator is not lighted.
2	Operating switchgear inspection: 　　　　　　　　　Note 　　　Operating switchgear inspection will be performed on all operating power generation switchgear connected to the main bus. 　a.　Verify GENERATOR and GENERATOR FIELD circuit breakers are closed and indicators are lighted red. 　b.　Insure DIESEL ENGINE START-RUN switches are set to RUN, and AMMETER selector switch is set to the highest indicating phase. 　c.　Check voltages on all phase on the NO. 1 generator control panel. 　d.　Check instruments on generator and exciter control panel for proper operation. 　e.　Insure voltage REGULATOR CUTOUT switches are set to REG. 　f.　Insure exciter manual field rheostats are turned fully counterclockwise.

Figure 3-13A. Electrical Power Production Technician Alert Status
Monitoring Procedure (LAFB 724TH/725TH SQDN) (Sheet 1 of 7)

Changed 19 March 1964　TOCN 1-1 (DEN-12)

STEP	PROCEDURE
2 (CONT)	g. (Complex 4A only) Insure commercial power selector switch is set to MAN.
3	Standby switchgear inspection:

Note

The standby switchgear inspection will be performed on all power generation switchgear not connected to the main bus and not in a maintenance status

    a. Verify GENERATOR and GENERATOR FIELD circuit breakers are tripped, indicators lighted green, and targets green.

    b. Set DIESEL ENGINE START-RUN switch(es) to START.

    c. Set RESET TRIP relays to RESET.

    d. Insure AMMETER selector switches are set to NO. 1.

    e. Verify flags on safety devices, and generator and exciter control panels are clear.

    f. Insure voltage REGULATOR CUTOUT switches are set to REG.

    g. Insure exciter manual field rheostats are turned fully clockwise.

| 4 | Standby diesel engine(s) checkout: |

Note

Standby diesel engine(s) checkout will be performed on all standby diesel engines. All diesel engines not in a maintenance status will be in a standby configuration.

    a. Check exciter belts for tension and wear.

    b. Insure that all obstructions to the alternator and associated rotating equipment are removed.

    c. Verify switches 1320 through 1323 are closed.

    d. Insure the air manifold drain valve, indicator valves (8), aftercooler drain valve, and turbocharger drain valves are open.

    e. Insure the engine lub oil cooler drain valve is closed.

Figure 3-13A. Electrical Power Production Technician Alert Status Monitoring Procedure (LAFB 724TH/725TH SQDN) (Sheet 2 of 7)

STEP	PROCEDURE
4 (CONT)	f. Insure the prelube oil suction valve and lube oil cooler chilled water supply and return valves are open. g. Insure the cyclonic separator equalizer valve, steam outlet valve, water return valve, and water makeup valves (3) are open. h. Insure the cyclonic separator makeup water bypass valve is closed. i. Insure the starting air supply valve is closed. j. Insure the fuel oil supply valves, turbocharger oil cooler treated water valves, and aftercooler treated water valves are open. k. Insure the lube oil sump tank fill and drain valves are closed. l. Check engine and turbocharger oil level. m. Set engine console power supply switch to ON. n. Rotate indicator light test switch on engine console to test that all indicators light. o. Press engine START pushbutton. CAUTION If engine lube oil pressure gage does not indicate 4 to 5 PSI, set engine console power supply switch to OFF and repeat steps m and o until 4 to 5 PSI is indicated. p. Set engine console power supply switch to OFF. q. Insure starting air supply valve is open. r. Set throttle control lever to STOP. s. Turn governor LOAD LIMIT knob to 0. t. Set SPEED DROOP to 30 or as required. u. Set SYNCHRONIZER indicator so engine will run at approximately 450 RPM.

Figure 3-13A. Electrical Power Production Technician Alert Status Monitoring Procedure (LAFB 724TH/725TH SQDN) (Sheet 3 of 7)

STEP	PROCEDURE
4 (CONT)	CAUTION

 Indicator valves must be observed for moisture and foreign material during engine blow out.

  v. Pull and immediately release starting air valve several times until the engine has completed two revolutions; then pull and hold starting air valve until engine completes six to eight revolutions, then release.

  w. Close indicator valves (8).

  x. Set governor LOAD LIMIT knob to 2.5 or as required.

  y. Set throttle control lever to RUN.

  z. Set engine console power supply switch to ON.

  aa. Press engine START pushbutton.

  Note

 If engine fails to start automatically, set engine console power supply switch to OFF and start manually.

  ab. Close starting air supply valve.

  ac. Perform post diesel engine(s) startup checkout (refer to step 5).

  ad. Set governor LOAD LIMIT knob to 10.

  ae. Press engine STOP pushbutton.

  Note

 After engine stops rotating perform step af.

  af. Set engine console power supply switch to OFF.

  ag. Open starting air supply valve.

  ah. Record time and date standby diesel engine(s) checkout completed.

  Note

 The standby diesel engine(s) checkout must be performed every eight hours.

Figure 3-13A. Electrical Power Production Technician Alert Status Monitoring Procedure (LAFB 724TH/725TH SQDN) (Sheet 4 of 7)

STEP	PROCEDURE
5	Post diesel engine(s) startup checkout: a. Check exciter and generator for vibration and arcing. b. Verify governor oil level is normal. c. Verify engine lube oil sump level is normal. d. Verify turbocharger lube oil sump level is normal. e. Check engine console for proper pressure and temperature indications.
6	Fuel and lube oil transfer system inspection: a. Check fuel and lube oil system for proper valve and control switch position. b. Check fuel oil control panel for proper indications. c. Check lube oil storage tank level indicators for proper indications. Note Step 6d will be performed in conjunction with steps 8 and 9. d. Check fuel and lube oil system for proper valve position.
7	Cyclonic separator checkout: a. Check condensate receiver tank water for normal level. b. Set condensate pump LEAD-LAG switch to opposite position. c. Check condensate tank for normal pressure. d. Check separator water level and steam pressure for normal indications. e. Perform blowdown of separators.
8	AC-2 diesel engine inspection and checkout: a. Verify diesel fuel and lube oil level is normal. b. Set disconnect switch, located at lower left of engine panel, to ON (if applicable).

Figure 3-13A. Electrical Power Production Technician Alert Status Monitoring Procedure (LAFB 724TH/725TH SQDN) (Sheet 5 of 7)

STEP	PROCEDURE
8 (CONT)	c. Set toggle switch, located at lower right of engine panel, to ON. d. Press and hold GLOW PLUGS pushbutton. e. Hold toggle switch on lower left of engine panel to START until engine starts; then release GLOW PLUGS pushbutton and START switch. Note Allow engine to operate for 15 minutes before performing step f. f. Set toggle switch, located on lower right of engine panel, to OFF. g. Set disconnect switch, located at lower left of engine panel, to OFF (if applicable).
9	Starting air system inspection: a. Set starting air compressor HAND-OFF-AUTO switch to OFF. b. Check starting air compressor for normal oil level and proper belt tension. c. Drain condensate from receiver tanks. d. Verify all valves for proper position. e. Set starting air compressor HAND-OFF-AUTO switch to AUTO.
10	Standby diesel engine(s) pre-lube and blow out checkout: a. Set throttle control lever to STOP. b. Turn governor LOAD LIMIT knob to 0. c. Open indicator valves (8). d. Close starting air supply valve. e. Set engine console power supply switch to ON. f. Press engine START pushbutton.

Figure 3-13A. Electrical Power Production Technician Alert Status Monitoring Procedure (LAFB 724TH/725TH SQDN) (Sheet 6 of 7)

STEP	PROCEDURE
10 (CONT)	CAUTION If engine oil pressure gage does not indicate 4 to 5 PSI, set engine console power supply switch to OFF and repeat steps e and f until 4 to 5 PSI is indicated. g. Set engine console power supply switch to OFF. h. Open starting air supply valve. CAUTION Indicator valves must be observed for moisture and foreign material during engine blow out. i. Pull and immediately release starting air valve several times until engine has completed two revolutions; then pull and hold starting air valve until engine completes six to eight revolutions, then release. j. Set throttle control lever to RUN. k. Turn governor LOAD LIMIT knob to 10. l. Close indicator valves (8).

Figure 3-13A. Electrical Power Production Technician Alert Status Monitoring Procedure (LAFB 724TH/725TH SQDN) (Sheet 7 of 7)

T.O. 21M-HGM25A-1-1 (21-SM68-1) Section III

STEP	PROCEDURE
1	Annunciator panel checkout..................................Accomplished SAC CEM 21-SM68-2-21-( ) The EPPT accomplishes the annunciator panel checkout by pressing annunciator TEST pushbutton and verifying all indicators are lighted.
2	Standby switchgear inspection: Note The standby switchgear inspection will be performed on all power generation switchgear not connected to the main bus or not in a maintenance status. a. Verify GENERATOR and GENERATOR FIELD circuit breakers are tripped, indicators lighted green, and targets green. b. Set generator START-RUN switch to START. c. Verify flags on safety devices, and generator and exciter control panels are clear. d. Set FUEL LOCKOUT switch and LOCKOUT circuit breaker switch to the vertical position. e. Set VOLTAGE REGULATOR selector switch to AUTO. f. Insure exciter manual field rheostats are turned fully clockwise.
3	Standby diesel engine(s) checkout: Note Standby diesel engine(s) checkout will be performed on all standby diesel engines. All diesel engines not in a maintenance status will be in a standby configuration. a. Insure engine starting air supply valve is open. b. Insure turbocharger aftercooler drain valves are open. c. Press pre-circulating lube oil pump START pushbutton and verify that oil flows through the turbocharger oil line sight glass and that pressure rises slowly on engine and turbocharger oil pressure gages.

Figure 3-14. Electrical Power Production Technician Alert Status Monitoring Procedure (EAFB, BAFB, LAFB, MHAFB) (Sheet 1 of 8)

Changed 19 March 1964 TOCN 1-1 (DEN-12)

T.O. 21M-HGM25A-1-1 (21-SM68-1)   Section III

STEP	PROCEDURE
3 (CONT)	d. Press CRANKCASE VACUUM pump START pushbutton. e. Press engine JACKET WATER pump START pushbutton. f. Set engine governor LOAD LIMIT knob to MIN FUEL. g. Open indicator valves (8). Note Engage engine barring gear and rotate engine two revolutions; then secure barring gear. CAUTION Indicator valves must be observed for moisture and foreign material during engine blow out. h. Intermittently press AUXILIARY START pushbutton, located under engine governor, until engine has completed two revolutions. i. Close indicator valves (8). j. Set governor LOAD LIMIT knob to MAX FUEL. k. Adjust SPEED and SPEED DROOP as required. CAUTION Before starting engine, check for oil indication in turbocharger sight gage. l. Press pre-circulating lube oil pump START pushbutton and verify oil in turbocharger sight gage. m. Press engine START pushbutton. n. Check engine control console for normal pressure and temperature indications. o. Close turbocharger aftercooler drain valves. p. Check pillow block bearing oil rings for normal indications.

Figure 3-14. Electrical Power Production Technician Alert Status Monitoring Procedure (EAFB, BAFB, LAFB, MHAFB) (Sheet 2 of 8)

STEP	PROCEDURE
4	Post diesel engine(s) startup checkout: a. Check exciter and generator for vibration and arcing. b. Verify governor oil level is normal. c. Verify engine lube oil sump level is normal. d. Check engine console for normal pressure and temperature indications. Note Allow engine to operate for 30 minutes before continuing with procedure. e. Adjust engine speed to 450 RPM. f. Press engine STOP pushbutton. g. Press pre-circulating lube oil pump START pushbutton when turbocharger lube oil pressure has decreased to 20 PSI. Note Allow engine to stop rotating before continuing with procedure. h. Press pre-circulating lube oil pump STOP pushbutton. i. Record time and date that the standby diesel engine(s) checkout is completed. Note The standby diesel engine(s) checkout must be accomplished every eight hours.
5	Operating switchgear inspection: Note Operating switchgear inspection will be performed on all operating power generation switchgear connected to the main bus. a. Verify GENERATOR and GENERATOR FIELD circuit breakers are closed.

Figure 3-14. Electrical Power Production Technician Alert Status Monitoring Procedure (EAFB, BAFB, LAFB, MHAFB) (Sheet 3 of 8)

T.O. 21M-HGM25A-1-1 (21-SM68-1)   Section III

STEP	PROCEDURE
5 (CONT)	b. Verify GENERATOR and GENERATOR FIELD indicators are lighted red. c. Verify FEEDER circuit breakers 1 through 5 are closed. d. Verify FEEDER circuit breakers indicators 1 through 5 are lighted red. e. Verify START-RUN switch is set to RUN. f. Check all instruments on the generator and exciter panel for proper operation. g. Verify VOLTAGE REGULATOR switch is set to AUTO.
6	Distribution panels and motor control centers inspection: a. Verify all circuit breakers and switches on sub-station 1010 are ON. b. Verify GROUND lights on sub-station are lighted. c. Verify all circuit breakers and switches on DC power panels 1042 and 1043 are properly positioned. d. Verify all circuit breakers and switches on all motor control centers are properly positioned. e. Verify circuit breakers and switches on FEEDER panels 6 through 10 are properly positioned.
7	Fuel and lube oil transfer system inspection: a. Check fuel and lube oil system for proper valve and control switch positions. b. (BAFB, LAFB, MHAFB) Check fuel oil control panel for proper indications. c. (BAFB, LAFB, MHAFB) Check lube oil storage tank level indicators for proper indications.
8	Hot water system inspection: SAC CEM 21-SM68-2-24-( ) a. Verify hot water pump(s) operating properly. b. Verify water level and air pressure in hot water compression tank are normal.

Figure 3-14. Electrical Power Production Technician Alert Status Monitoring Procedure (EAFB, BAFB, LAFB, MHAFB) (Sheet 4 of 8)

STEP	PROCEDURE
9	Cyclonic separator checkout: a. Check separator for normal water level and low pressure steam header for normal indications. b. Check control air for normal pressure. c. Verify supply valve is open. d. Verify bypass valve is closed. e. Perform blowdown; then close drain and/or blowdown valve.
10	Heat recovery silencer checkout: a. Verify water level is normal. b. Verify supply valve is open. c. Verify bypass valve is closed. d. Perform blowdown; then close drain and/or blowdown valve.
11	Chilled water system inspection: a. Verify one chilled water pump is operating properly and the other chilled water pump is in standby. b. Verify water level and air pressure in chilled water expansion tank is normal.
12	Battery rectifier inspection: SAC CEM 21-SM68-2-21-( ) a. Verify GROUND indicators are lighted. b. Check voltmeter for proper indication. c. Check ammeter for proper indication.
13	Utility air and starting air systems inspection: SAC CEM 21-SM68-2-26-( ) a. Set starting air compressor HAND-OFF-AUTO switch to OFF. b. Check for normal oil level and proper belt tension. c. Drain condensate from receiver tank.

Figure 3-14. Electrical Power Production Technician Alert Status Monitoring Procedure (EAFB, BAFB, LAFB, MHAFB) (Sheet 5 of 8)

T.O. 21M-HGM25A-1-1 (21-SM68-1) Section III

STEP	PROCEDURE
13 (CONT)	d. Verify supply valves open. e. Set HAND-OFF-AUTO switch to AUTO. f. Set utility air compressor HAND-OFF-AUTO switch to OFF and repeat steps b through e. g. Verify air drier power switch on unit not in service (if applicable) is ON. h. Verify auxiliary diesel engine fuel tank level and auxiliary diesel engine sump lube oil level are normal.
14	Ventilation system inspection: SAC CEM 21-SM68-2-20-( ) a. Verify air intake supply fan(s) operating properly and insure static air pressure is properly maintained. b. Verify exhaust fan(s) operating properly.
15	Domestic water system inspection: SAC CEM 21-SM68-2-24-( ) a. Verify domestic water pumps are operational and pressure is normal. b. Verify water level and air pressure on hydropneumatic tank are normal.
16	Ice bank inspection: a. Verify all ice bank control switches are properly positioned. b. Verify water level in ice banks is normal. c. Verify ice thickness in ice banks is normal.
17	Fire water system inspection: a. Verify jockey water pump is operating and pressure is normal. b. Verify raw water tanks levels are normal. c. (EAFB) Verify FCV 805-1, 805-2, and 805-3 indicators are lighted green. d. (BAFB, LAFB, MHAFB) Verify FCV 805-1, 805-2, and 805-3 indicators are lighted red.

Figure 3-14. Electrical Power Production Technician Alert Status Monitoring Procedure (EAFB, BAFB, LAFB, MHAFB) (Sheet 6 of 8)

Changed 19 March 1964 TOCN 1-1 (DEN-12)

STEP	PROCEDURE
17 (CONT)	e. (EAFB) Verify XFV 802-1, 802-2, and 802-3 indicators are lighted green. f. (BAFB, LAFB, MHAFB) Verify XFV 802-1, 802-2, and 802-3 indicators are lighted red. g. Verify fire water pumps (P3094 and P3095) control switches are properly positioned. h. Set LEAD-LAG switch to opposite position.
18	Raw water system inspection: a. Verify one raw water pump is operating and other raw water pump is in standby.
19	Cooling tower system inspection: a. Verify one cooling tower water pump is operating and other cooling tower water pump is in standby.
20	Standby diesel engine pre-lube and blow out (when required): a. Press pre-circulating lube oil pump START pushbutton. b. Set generator LOAD LIMIT knob to MIN FUEL. c. Verify indicator valves (8) are open. Note Engage engine barring gear and rotate engine two revolutions; then secure barring gear. CAUTION Check for oil indication in turbocharger sight glass before blowing out engine.

Figure 3-14. Electrical Power Production Technician Alert Status Monitoring Procedure (EAFB, BAFB, LAFB, MHAFB) (Sheet 7 of 8)

T.O. 21M-HGM25A-1-1 (21-SM68-1)　　　　Section III

STEP	PROCEDURE
20 (CONT)	d. Intermittently press auxiliary START pushbutton, located under engine governor, until engine has completed two revolutions. e. Close indicator valves (8). f. Set governor LOAD LIMIT knob to MAX FUEL.
21	Diesel fuel storage tanks servicing (if applicable): a. Check level of storage tank by using a sounding tape. CAUTION Do not attempt to service any tank when it has been determined, by sounding, that it will not hold the capacity of the servicing tanker without overflowing. b. Connect fill source to surface receptacle. c. Open fill valve on tank to be serviced. WARNING Do not sound tank during servicing process. d. Start filling from fill source. CAUTION One man will remain near tank being serviced. If any abnormal condition arises such as leakage, overflow, or a line break, shut off fill valve at tank and direct closure of valve at fill source. e. Shut off flow of fuel at fill source. f. Close fill valve on tank that has been serviced. g. Check level of tank after filling is complete by using a sounding tape. h. Record tank level.

Figure 3-14. Electrical Power Production Technician Alert Status Monitoring Procedure (EAFB, BAFB, LAFB, MHAFB) (Sheet 8 of 8)

Changed 19 March 1964　TOCN 1-1 (DEN-12)　　　　3-86

STEP	PROCEDURE
	MECHANICAL EQUIPMENT ROOM
1	Air compressor (CC 5010)
	Supply tank pressure (PI 5064). . . . . Green
	Control pressure (PI 5063). . . . . Green
	Oil level . . . . Checked
	Drain tank. . . . . Accomplished SAC CEM 21-SM68-2-20-( )
	This air compressor located in work area 6J, furnishes supply pressure to pneumatic temperature, humidity and pressure controllers for air conditioning equipment, and pneumatic flow control valves in the control center and fuel storage area.
2	AC2032 thermometer (TI 2207). . . . . Green
	AC2032, located in work area 6J, supplies cool air to all guidance and computer cabinets in the upper level of the control center.
	ELECTRICAL EQUIPMENT ROOM
3	Battery charger (REC 1010)
	GROUND indicating lights. . . . . Same Intensity
	VOLTS . . . . Green
	AMMETER . . . . Green SAC CEM 21-SM68-2-21-( )
	This battery charger supplies charging current to battery bank (BAT 1010) which provides power for the detection system. The battery charger should indicate between 122 and 139 VDC; if below 121 VDC, the high rate light (red or amber) should be lighted. The ammeter high rate indication will be a maximum of 6 amperes, and a trickle rate maximum of 800 MA.
4	Motor control center (MCC 1020)
	All circuit breakers. . . . . ON
	GROUND LIGHTS (3) . . . . ON

Figure 3-14A. Facility Technician Alert Status Monitoring Procedure (Operational Bases) (Sheet 1 of 4)

STEP	PROCEDURE
4 (CONT)	This motor control center contains the main circuit breaker and supplies power to the following units: a. Anemometer panel and radiation probe control unit which supplies power for wind velocity meter and radiation detectors. b. Communication panel which supplies power to provide communications capability from control center to power house. c. Guidance motor A and B which supplies power to guidance motor generator. d. Air conditioning control which supplies power to AC2032. e. Guidance generator which supplies power to guidance generator sets. ANTENNA TERMINAL
5	MLO . . . . Notified T.O. not required Facility technician will report to the MLO that he has arrived at the antenna terminal and requests that the antenna keys be placed in MAINT position.
6	Circuit breakers (MCC 1040) . . . . ON SAC CEM 21-SM68-2-21-( ) Power is supplied through circuit breakers on MCC 1040 to the air conditioning equipment and the air compressor supplying controlled pneumatic pressure for air conditioning valves that are required to operate during a countdown. All HAND-OFF-AUTO switches will be verified in the AUTO position.
7	Circuit breakers (distribution panels 1060/1061). . . . . . ON Power is supplied through these circuit breakers for lights, receptacles, and emergency lights.
8	AC2042 (CTR 2156) . . . . Green SAC CEM 21-SM68-2-20-( )

Figure 3-14A. Facility Technician Alert Status Monitoring Procedure (Operational Bases) (Sheet 2 of 4)

T.O. 21M-HGM25A-1-1 (21-SM68-1) Section III

STEP	PROCEDURE
8 (CONT)	AC2042 supplies cool air to guidance cabinets in the antenna terminal. Proper operation of this unit is necessary for sustained guidance operation.
	ANTENNA SILO A
9	BLOWER. . . . . ON T.O. 21M-HGM25A-2-7-7 Facility technician verifies antenna blower switch, located on the third level of the antenna silo, is in the ON position.
10	Hydraulic pressures . . . . In Tolerance Facility technician checks the hydraulic accumulator pressures to insure they are within tolerance (1850 to 2950 PSI).
11	Air Compressor (CC 5030) Supply tank pressure. . . . . Green Control pressure. . . . . Green Oil level . . . . Checked Drain tank. . . . . Accomplished SAC CEM 21-SM68-2-20-( ) This air compressor supplies controlled pneumatic pressure to AC2042 valves. Operation of this compressor is necessary during all guidance countdowns. The facility technician checks that supply and control pressure is available for AC2042 pneumatic valves, checks oil for proper level, and drains the air tank of water. Note Perform step 12 only if outside air temperature is below +40 degrees F.
12	ENVIRONMENTAL SEAL HEATING SYSTEM Expansion tank. . . . . Checked Circulating pump. . . . . Checked

Figure 3-14A. Facility Technician Alert Status Monitoring Procedure (Operational Bases) (Sheet 3 of 4)

STEP	PROCEDURE
12 (CONT)	The ethlene glycol expansion tank is checked to insure it is at least 3/4 full, and the circulating pump for operation when the outside temperature is below +40 degrees F.

Note

Repeat steps 9 and 10 for antenna B. |
| 13 | MLO . . . . Notified
T.O. not required

Facility technician notifies the control center that alert status monitoring procedures have been completed. |

Figure 3-14A. Facility Technician Alert Status Monitoring Procedure (Operational Bases) (Sheet 4 of 4)

T.O. 21M-HGM25A-1-1 (21-SM68-1)   Section III

STEP	PROCEDURE
	MECHANICAL EQUIPMENT ROOM
1	Air compressor (CC 2001)
	Supply tank pressure. Green
	Control pressure. . . . . Green
	Oil level . . . . Checked
	Drain tank. . . . . Accomplished
	SAC CEM 21-SM68-2-20-( )
	This air compressor located in work area 6K, furnishes supply pressure to pneumatic temperature, humidity and pressure controllers for air conditioning equipment, and pneumatic flow control valves in the operational control centers and fuel storage area.
2	AC2001 thermometer TI 2006. . . . . Green
3	AC2002 thermometer TI 2009. . . . . Green
4	AC2003 thermometer TI 2015. . . . . Green
	AC2001 supplies cool air to equipment in the operational control centers. AC2002 and AC2003 supplies conditioned air to other portions of the control center work area.
	ELECTRICAL EQUIPMENT ROOM
5	Battery charger (REC 1602)
	GROUND indicating lights. . . . . Same Intensity
	DC VOLTS. . . . . Green
	DC AMPERES. . . . . Green
	SAC CEM 21-SM68-2-21-( )
	This battery charger supplies charging current to the battery bank which provides power for the detection system. The DC AMPERES high rate indication will be a maximum of 9 amperes, and a trickle rate maximum of 800 MA.
6	Motor control center (MCC 1509 and MCC 1510) circuit breakers. . . . . ON

Figure 3-14B. Facility Technician Alert Status Monitoring Procedure (VAFB) (Sheet 1 of 3)

STEP	PROCEDURE
	ANTENNA TERMINAL
7	MLO . . . . Notified T.O. not required Facility technician will report to the MLO that he has arrived at the antenna terminal and requests that the antenna keys be placed in MAINT position.
8	Circuit breakers (MCC 1512) . . . . ON SAC CEM 21-SM68-2-21-1
9	AC2602 (TI 2618). . . . . Green SAC CEM 21-SM68-2-20-1 MCC 1512 supplies power, through circuit breakers, to air conditioner AC2602 and air compressor CC 2601.

10	Air compressor (CC 2601)
	
	   Supply tank pressure. . . . . Green
	
	   Control Pressure. . . . . Green
	
	   Oil level . . . . Checked
	
	   Drain tank. . . . . Accomplished
	
	Air compressor CC 2601 supplies controlled pneumatic pressure to AC2602 valves. Operation of this compressor is necessary during all guidance countdowns. The facility technician checks that supply and control pressure is available for AC2602 pneumatic valves, checks oil for proper level, and drains the air tank of water.
	
	ANTENNA SILO A
	
	                      WARNING
	
	   The hand crank socket must be engaged and crank grasped firmly before disengaging the drum lock.

11	Gangway . . . . Lowered T.O. 21M-HGM25A-2-7-7

Figure 3-14B. Facility Technician Alert Status Monitoring Procedure (VAFB) (Sheet 2 of 3)

T.O. 21M-HGM25A-1-1 (21-SM68-1)   Section III

STEP	PROCEDURE
11 (CONT)	To lower the gangway assembly the crank must be connected to the hand operated winch assembly. The gangway assembly pip pin is then removed, and drum lock disengaged.
12	BLOWER. . . . . ON Facility technician verifies antenna blower switch, located on the third level of the antenna silo, is in the ON position.
13	Hydraulic pressures . . . . In Tolerance Facility technician checks the hydraulic accumulator pressures to insure they are within tolerance (1850 to 2950 PSI.)
14	Gangway . . . . Raised To raise the gangway assembly, engage the drum lock, turn hand crank as necessary, insert gangway assembly pip pin, and then remove and store the crank.
15	RAILS STORED. . . . . Not Lighted RAILS STORED indicator is located on control panel 29A3A2. Note Repeat steps 11 through 15 for antenna B.
16	MLO . . . . Notified T.O. not required Facility technician notifies the control center that alert status monitoring procedures have been completed.

Figure 3-14B. Facility Technician Alert Status Monitoring Procedure (VAFB) (Sheet 3 of 3)

T.O. 21-SM68-1   Section III

LOCAL TIMES	SUNRISE + 1:00		1200	SUNSET + 1:00	2400
WEATHER CONDITIONS	FORECAST	CURRENT	CURRENT	CURRENT	CURRENT

SKY CONDITIONS
CLEAR   SCATTERED
  ○   ⊘
BROKEN   OVERCAST
  ⊖ ⊕					

VISIBILITY					
WIND					
HAZARDS					
PRESSURE IN MILLIBARS (UNCORRECTED)					

SEVERE WEATHER ADVISORY _____   VALID TIME _____

ADVISORY AS FOLLOWS _____

Figure 3-15. Typical Weather Chart

3-87

STEP	PROCEDURE
	CALCULATION FOR A TERM
1	Obtain pressure (correct as required to elevation at the complex) and set the cursor over the appropriate number on the PRESSURE-MILLIBARS scale.
2	Obtain dry bulb temperature and adjust center scale so that dry bulb temperature is directly above appropriate figure on PRESSURE-MILLIBARS scale.
3	Read and record the number that appears above A TERM.
	CALCULATION FOR B TERM
1	Obtain dew point temperature and set cursor over appropriate number on DEW POINT TEMPERATURE °F SCALE.
2	Obtain dry bulb temperature and adjust center scale so that dry bulb temperature is directly over appropriate figure on DEW POINT TEMPERATURE °F SCALE.
3	Read and record the number that appears above the B TERM.
	Note
	In the event the value of the B TERM is off scale to the left, the B TERM need not be used in the calculation for the index of refraction constant. This will occur in those cases where the moisture content of the air will not contribute a significant index of refraction error.
	CALCULATION OF INDEX VALUE
1	Add A TERM and B TERM to obtain the index of refraction.
2	Record index of refraction.

Figure 3-16. Index of Refraction Calculation Procedure

T.O. 21-SM68-1

Section III
Paragraphs 3-91 to 3-99

(Text continued from page 3-30.)

3-91. An index of refraction log will be maintained on general purpose worksheets, SAC FORM 210. An entry will be made each time a computation is made and will include the following information: date, name of individual making computation, local time, atmospheric pressure in millibars, correction factor for site elevation, corrected pressure in millibars, dry bulb temperature, wet bulb temperature, A term, B term, and index of refraction.

3-92. A piece of acetate will be affixed near the left end of the missile guidance console for grease pencil recording of the most current index of refraction. This is to insure that the current index is readily available at the missile guidance console for a countdown.

3-93. If the barometric pressure used to calculate index of refraction is obtained from a weather station, the GEO must insure that the necessary elevation correction has been applied. To make the necessary elevation correction, subtract 3.4 millibars from the weather station pressure (not sea level) for each 100 feet that the launch site antenna is above the weather station. If the antenna is below the weather station, add 3.4 millibars for each 100 feet. Elevation of antenna may be found on the missile launch site data sheet.

3-94. LAUNCH SITE TARGETING PROCEDURE. (See figures 3-17 thru 3-28.)

3-95. The launch site targeting contains the necessary functions of launch site targeting for all Titan I squadrons. The retargeting flow diagram (figure 3-17) will be used to determine the course to follow when retargeting the system. Figures 3-18 thru 3-24 are used for normal targeting of the system and are performed whenever time limitations are not a primary concern. Figures 3-25 thru 3-28 contain fast retargeting procedures which are used when it is essential to retarget the system in the shortest possible time and are performed simultaneously by the GEO and MLO. A launch site targeting log will be established utilizing SAC form 210. The log will contain date of installation, control number of the targeting package, signature of the individual performing the installation of the targeting package and any significant remarks. Each time a targeting package, a portion of a targeting package or maintenance tapes are installed in the guidance computer an entry will be made in the launch site targeting log. Figure 3-21 illustrates a typical printed record from digital guidance simulation.

3-96. LAUNCH AND EXERCISE COUNTDOWNS.

3-97. The launch and exercise countdowns consist of alert and fast reaction message procedures prior to launch/exercise, countdown procedures for launch/exercise, post shutdown procedures, and launch countdown system functions.

3-98. ALERT PROCEDURES.

3-99. When an alert is initiated, immediate reaction by all personnel to the alert must be the same, whether the alert is actual, simulated or an exercise. Notification of an alert will be identical in all situations. Upon receipt of a message requiring the alerting of the complex, the MCCC (Deputy MCCC in his absence) will activate the alterting device, or utilizing the PA system, will announce, "ALERT, ALERT, ALERT".

(Text continued on page 3-123.)

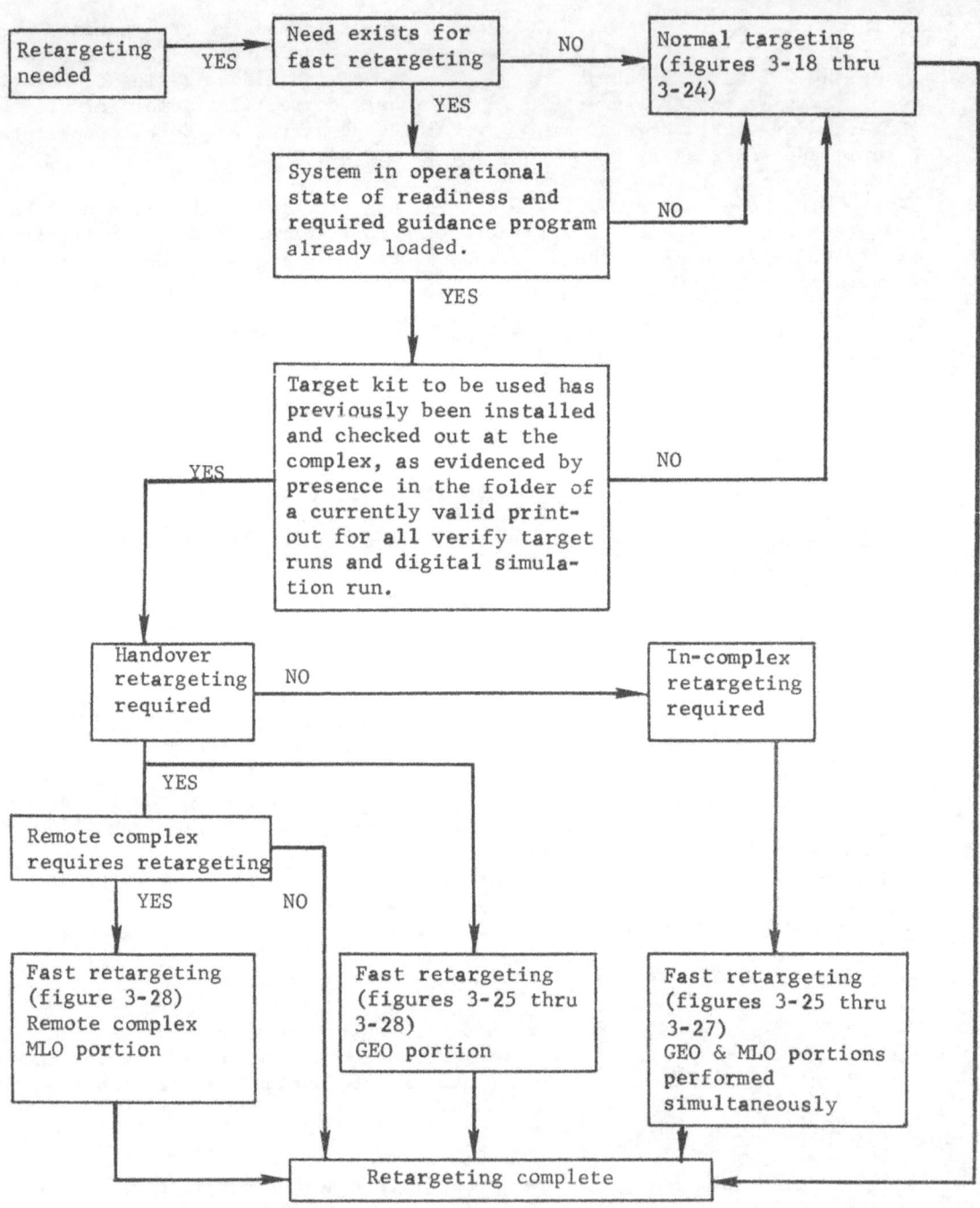

Figure 3-17. Retargeting Flow Diagram

T.O. 21-SM68-1

Section III

STEP	PROCEDURE

1	Check the ground guidance system is in standby condition.
	
	Guidance control target trajectory kit folder.......... Checked
	T.O. 31X7-2-1-151
	
	The GEO checks the guidance control target trajectory kit folder for the following items:
	
	   a. Target kit identification sheet.
	
	   b. Guidance computer tape information sheet.
	
	   c. Target tape contents sheet.
	
	   d. USAF missile launch site data sheets.
	
	   e. Coordinate data table (filled in.)
	
	The GEO will check that the dates listed on lower right of the target and handover target kit identification sheets correspond exactly with the dates on the current USAF missile launch site data sheets and appropriate coordinate data tables. Discrepancies will be referred to the TMCO for resolution. Dates listed for azimuth and range coordinate data on target and handover kit identification sheets will be compared with dates on superseded identification sheets. If the dates for azimuth data differ, an antenna azimuth program alignment must be performed in accordance with T.O. 21-SM68-2J-7-1-2 and T.O. 21-SM68-2J-6-1. If the dates for range data differ, a range program must be performed in accordance with T.O. 21-SM68-2J-7-1-1 and T.O. 21-SM68-2J-6-1 (Refer to AZIMUTH, ELEVATION, and RANGE readout.) These programs must be performed after figures 3-18, 3-19, and 3-20 of this procedure have been completed. The guidance computer tape information sheet control number shall be the same as the target kit identification sheet control number. The target tape contents sheet control number shall be the same as the target kit identification sheet control number.

2	Target tapes... Checked The target tape leader (control number and effective date) shall be the same as the guidance computer tape information sheet.

Figure 3-18. Inventory Targeting Package Procedure (Sheet 1 of 2)

3-91

T.O. 21-SM68-1   Section III

STEP	PROCEDURE
3	Guidance program tapes.................................. Checked The guidance program tape leader (the word GUIDANCE, the effective date, the BN number, and two letters) shall be the same as the guidance computer tape information sheet.
4	Digital simulation tapes................................ Checked The digital simulation tape leader (the word SIMULATION, the effective date, and two letters) shall be the same as the guidance computer tape information sheet.
5	Launch control target trajectory kit folder............ Checked The GEO checks the launch control target trajectory kit folder for the following items: a. One target kit identification sheet b. One re-entry vehicle cards tally sheet c. Two sets R/V cards d. One launch control console labels sheet e. Two sets launch control console labels f. Handover target kit identification sheets (one for each of the other complexes as applicable) The target kit identification sheet control number shall be the same as the control number on the target kit identification sheet of the guidance control target kit folder. The re-entry vehicle cards sheet control number shall be the same as the target kit identification sheet control number. The color coding and the number of R/V cards, the TIN numbers, the DGZ numbers, and control numbers on the R/V cards shall be the same as information on the re-entry vehicle cards sheets. The launch control console label sheet control number shall be the same as the target kit identification sheet control number. The number of launch control console labels and the TIN numbers and DGZ numbers on the labels shall be the same as information appearing on the launch control console labels sheet.

Figure 3-18. Inventory Targeting Package Procedure (Sheet 2 of 2)

T.O. 21-SM68-1

Section III

STEP	PROCEDURE
	MISSILE GUIDANCE CONSOLE
1	STBY.. Green T.O. 21-SM68-2J-7-1-1 T.O. 31X7-2-1-151
2	ANTENNA A or B FACILITY MAINT......................... Green
3	ANTENNA A or B FACILITY SELECT (as applicable)........ Green
4	HANDOVER OFF... Green
	The GEO checks the guidance console to insure that the above indications are displayed prior to pressing POWER ON.
5	Press POWER ON... White
	TAPE READER 2
6	LOAD... Pressed
7	POWER ON... Pressed
8	POWER indicator.. White
9	LOAD indicator... Yellow
10	BULB ON.. Amber
11	Guidance tape.. Mounted and Threaded
	Manually wind tape until all conductive leader is on take-up reel and beginning of program data is at reverse capstan.
12	Control arms at null point............................. Positioned
13	STAND BY... Pressed
14	STAND BY indicator..................................... Blue
15	REMOTE... Pressed
16	REMOTE indicator....................................... Green

Figure 3-19. Install and Verify Guidance Program Tape and Target Tape Procedure (Sheet 1 of 6)

STEP	PROCEDURE
	TAPE READER 1
17	LOAD... Pressed
18	POWER ON... Pressed
19	POWER indicator.................................... White
20	LOAD indicator..................................... Yellow
21	BULB ON.. Amber
22	Target tape.. Mounted and Threaded
	Manually wind tape until all conductive leader is on take-up reel and beginning of program data is at reverse capstan.
23	Control arms at null point......................... Positioned
24	STAND BY... Pressed
25	STAND BY indicator................................. Blue
26	REMOTE... Pressed
27	REMOTE indicator................................... Green
	MISSILE GUIDANCE CONSOLE
28	POWER ON... Green
	POWER ON indicator will indicate green approximately 2 minutes and 30 seconds after pressing POWER ON pushbutton indicator.
29	Press MAINT.. Yellow
	COMPUTER SET CONSOLE
30	POWER ON... Green
31	MAINT.. White
32	Press HOLD MAINT................................... Amber
33	Press NORMAL RATE.................................. Green

Figure 3-19. Install and Verify Guidance Program Tape and Target Tape Procedure (Sheet 2 of 6)

T.O. 21-SM68-1

STEP	PROCEDURE
34	EXECUTE PROGRAM.. White
35	STEP/STOP... Amber
36	READY... White
37	TARGET REF.. White
38	Guidance program TAPE BLOCK NUMBER................... Set
	The TAPE BLOCK NUMBER is listed on the guidance computer tape information sheet.
39	Press LOAD PROGRAM.. White
40	Press TAPE READER 2... White
	No other computer console lower-panel indicators should be lighted except those previously listed. Should any other indicator be lighted, press indicator or position appropriate switch to normal position for a not lighted indication.
41	Press READY... White
42	Press RUN... Green
	TAPE READER 2
43	Guidance tape movement.. Checked
	The guidance tape moves forward and stops near end of tape.
	COMPUTER SET CONSOLE
44	TAPE READER CONTROL STOP.. Lighted
45	TAPE FAULT indicators... Not Lighted
	Guidance data is now loaded on magnetic drum.
46	RUN... Not Lighted
47	STEP/STOP... Amber
48	Target TAPE BLOCK NUMBER.. Set

Figure 3-19. Install and Verify Guidance Program Tape and Target Tape Procedure (Sheet 3 of 6)

T.O. 21-SM68-1

STEP	PROCEDURE	
	The target TAPE BLOCK NUMBER is listed on the target tape contents sheet.	
49	Press TAPE READER 1...	White
50	Press READY...	White
51	Press RUN...	Green
	TAPE READER 1	
52	Target tape movement..	Checked
	The target tape moves forward, and stops near end of tape.	
	COMPUTER SET CONSOLE	
53	TAPE READER CONTROL STOP..	Lighted
54	TAPE FAULT indicators...	Not Lighted
	Targeting data is now loaded on magnetic drum.	
55	RUN...	Not Lighted
56	STEP/STOP...	Amber
57	Press VERIFY PROGRAM..	White
58	Press READY...	White
59	Press RUN...	Green
	TAPE READER 1	
60	Target tape movement..	Checked
	The target tape rewinds, moves forward, then stops near end of tape.	
	COMPUTER SET CONSOLE	
61	TAPE READER CONTROL STOP..	Lighted
62	TAPE FAULT indicators...	Not Lighted
	Target data is now verified.	

Figure 3-19. Install and Verify Guidance Program Tape and Target Tape Procedure (Sheet 4 of 6)

STEP	PROCEDURE
63	RUN.. Not Lighted
64	STEP/STOP... Amber
	TAPE READER 1
65	REVERSE.. Pressed
66	REVERSE indicator..................................... White
67	Target tape... Rewound
68	END OF TAPE... Red
	COMPUTER SET CONSOLE
69	Guidance program TAPE BLOCK NUMBER..................... Set
	The guidance program tape block number is listed on the guidance computer tape information sheet.
70	Press TAPE READER 2................................... White
71	Press READY.. White
72	Press RUN.. Green
	TAPE READER 2
73	Guidance tape movement................................ Checked
	The guidance tape rewinds, then moves forward and stops.
	COMPUTER SET CONSOLE
74	TAPE READER CONTROL STOP.............................. Lighted
75	TAPE FAULT indicators................................. Not Lighted
	Guidance data is now verified.
76	RUN.. Not Lighted
77	STEP/STOP... Amber
	TAPE READER 2
78	REVERSE.. Pressed

Figure 3-19. Install and Verify Guidance Program Tape and Target Tape Procedure (Sheet 5 of 6)

STEP	PROCEDURE	
79	REVERSE indicator	White
80	Guidance tape	Rewound
81	END OF TAPE	Red
	TAPE READER 1	
82	LOAD	Pressed
83	LOAD indicator	Yellow
84	Control arms	Locked
85	Target tape	Removed
86	END OF TAPE	Not Lighted
87	Target tape	Stored
88	POWER OFF	Pressed
89	All indicators	Not Lighted
	TAPE READER 2	
90	LOAD	Pressed
91	LOAD indicator	Yellow
92	Control arms	Locked
93	Guidance tape	Removed
94	END OF TAPE	Not Lighted
95	Guidance tape	Stored
96	POWER OFF	Pressed
97	All indicators	Not Lighted
	COMPUTER SET CONSOLE	
98	Press READY	White
	The guidance program and targeting tapes are now loaded and verified, but guidance computer is not in an operational state of readiness until figure 3-20, digital guidance simulation, has been completed.	

Figure 3-19. Install and Verify Guidance Program Tape and Target Tape Procedure (Sheet 6 of 6)

T.O. 21-SM68-1

Section III

STEP	PROCEDURE
1	Verify that figure 3-19 has been accomplished. DIGITAL DATA PRINTER ON/OFF switch... ON T.O. 21-SM68-2J-6-1 T.O. 21-SM68-2J-7-1-1 T.O. 21-SM68-2J-7-1-2 T.O. 31X7-2-1-151 POWER DISTRIBUTION GROUP
2	PEIRPHERAL A.C. POWER PRINTER......................... Green ELECTRONIC FREQUENCY CONVERTER
3	OPERATE circuit breaker............................... ON
4	STANDBY circuit breaker............................... ON COMPUTER SET CONSOLE
5	POWER ON.. Green
6	HOLD MAINT.. Amber
7	MAINT... White
8	NORMAL RATE... Green
9	STEP/STOP... Amber
10	READY... White POWER SUPPLY GROUP
11	Press CYCLE DC OFF.................................... Amber
12	SIMULATOR selector.................................... ON
13	Press CYCLE DC ON..................................... Amber The CYCLE DC ON will remain amber for approximately one minute and 15 seconds and then becomes not lighted. COMPUTER SET CONSOLE
14	POWER ON.. Green

Figure 3-20. Digital Guidance Simulation Procedure (Sheet 1 of 5)

STEP	PROCEDURE	
	SIMULATOR-VERIFIER	
15	Press OPERATIONAL CONTROLS TEST NORM	TEST White
16	Press NORMAL RATE	Green
17	READY	Pressed
18	CYCLE COUNT	Reset
19	Press OPERATIONAL CONTROLS TEST NORM	NORM Green
20	Press INPUT SELECTION TR1/TR2	TR2 Green
	TAPE READER 2	
21	LOAD	Pressed
22	POWER ON	Pressed
23	POWER indicator	White
24	LOAD indicator	Yellow
25	BULB ON	Amber
26	Digital guidance simulation tape	Mounted and Threaded
	Manually wind the tape until all the conductive leader is on the takeup reel and the beginning of the program data is at the reverse capstan.	
27	Control arms at null point	Positioned
28	STAND BY	Pressed
29	STAND BY indicator	Blue
30	REMOTE	Pressed
31	REMOTE indicator	Green
	ELECTRONIC FREQUENCY CONVERTER	
32	STANDBY	Lighted
33	OPERATE	Lighted

Figure 3-20. Digital Guidance Simulation Procedure (Sheet 2 of 5)

T.O. 21-SM68-1   Section III

STEP	PROCEDURE	
	SIMULATOR-VERIFIER	
34	Press READY	Green
	COMPUTER SET CONSOLE	
35	Press HOLD MAINT	Not Lighted
36	Press SIMULATOR	White
37	Press EXECUTE PROGRAM	White
38	Press NORMAL RATE	Green
39	Press RUN	Green
	SIMULATOR-VERIFIER	
40	Press STEP/RUN	Green
	TAPE READER 2	
41	Simulation tape	Moves Forward
	SIMULATOR-VERIFIER	
42	CYCLE COUNT	Counting
	TAPE READER 2	
43	Simulation tape	Stopped
	The digital guidance simulation tape will stop near the end of the tape.	
	SIMULATOR-VERIFIER	
44	OPERATIONAL CONTROLS ERR STOP/OK STOP	OK STOP Green
	TAPE READER 2	
45	REVERSE	Pressed
46	REVERSE indicator	White
47	Simulation tape	Rewinds
	While digital guidance simulation tape rewinds, continue the procedures.	

Figure 3-20. Digital Guidance Simulation Procedure (Sheet 3 of 5)

STEP	PROCEDURE	
	DIGITAL DATA PRINTER	
48	Printout..	Checked
	Verify that the title word, first seven lines of H constants and last two lines specifying miss distance correspond to the values illustrated in figure 3-21. The sign in the extreme left column of the eighth line will be + if the value set up in the corresponding place at the computer constants register is 0 through 8. The sign will be - if the value set up is 9. The next three values in the eighth line will be 0 and the remaining four values will be the corresponding places at the computer constants register. The last two lines of the printout will be checked against the miss distance printout listed on the guidance computer tape information sheet in the guidance control target trajectory kit. Digital guidance simulation has now been completed.	
	COMPUTER SET CONSOLE	
49	Press HOLD MAINT...	Amber
	POWER SUPPLY GROUP	
50	Press CYCLE DC OFF..	Amber
51	SIMULATOR selector..	OFF
52	Press CYCLE DC ON...	Amber
	The CYCLE DC ON indicator will remain amber for approximately one minute and 15 seconds and then become not lighted.	
	COMPUTER SET CONSOLE	
53	POWER ON..	Green
54	NORMAL RATE...	Green
	Press NORMAL RATE pushbutton indicator if it does not light after POWER ON indicator lights green.	
55	MANUAL POWER SEQUENCE.....................................	Not Lighted

Figure 3-20. Digital Guidance Simulation Procedure (Sheet 4 of 5)

STEP	PROCEDURE
56	Press SIMULATOR.. Not Lighted
57	Press HOLD MAINT....................................... Not Lighted
58	Press READY.. White
	TAPE READER 2
59	Simulation tape.. Rewound
60	END OF TAPE.. Red
61	LOAD... Pressed
62	LOAD indicator... Yellow
63	Control arms... Locked
64	Simulation tape.. Removed
65	END OF TAPE.. Not Lighted
66	Simulation tape.. Stored
67	POWER OFF.. Pressed
68	All indicators... Not Lighted
	MISSILE GUIDANCE CONSOLE
69	Press STBY... Green
	Guidance computer is now in an operational state of readiness.

Figure 3-20. Digital Guidance Simulation Procedure (Sheet 5 of 5)

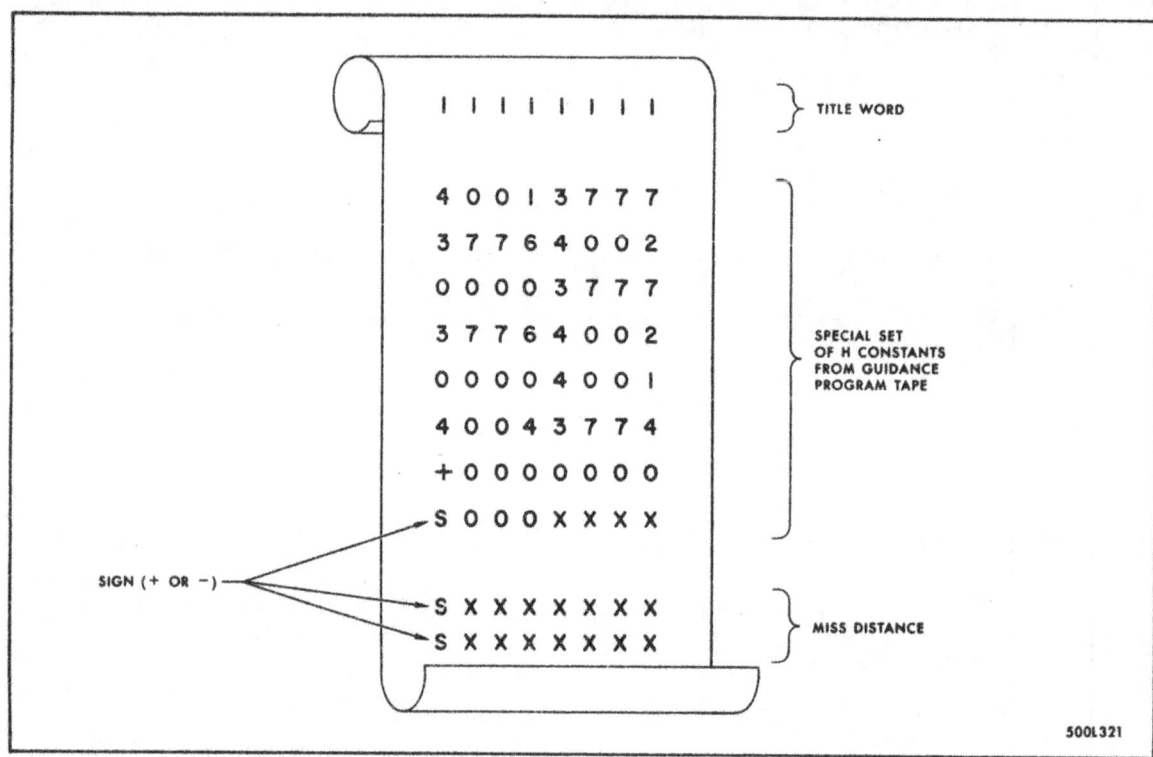

Figure 3-21. Printed Record from Digital Guidance Simulation

T.O. 21-SM68-1 Section III

STEP	PROCEDURE
	Target card reader and logic assemblies key.
	Target selection door panel key.
	Launch control target kit folder.
	Target cards and labels.
	TARGET CARD READER AND LOGIC ASSEMBLIES
1	Lamp verify switches.................................. OFF T.O. 31X7-2-1-151
2	TARGET indicators (as applicable)..................... GREEN
	LAUNCH CONTROL CONSOLE
	CAUTION
	Do not turn any TARGET SELECTION switch to a not used position. Failure to observe this caution may cause serious damage to the re-entry vehicle.
3	TARGET SELECTION LAUNCHER NO. 1, 2 and 3.............. A
	Set all PULL TO TURN switches to position A.
	TARGET CARD READER AND LOGIC ASSEMBLIES
	CAUTION
	Do not open a R/V card holder if it is lighted. Failure to observe this caution may cause serious damage to the re-entry vehicle.
4	R/V card holders....................................... Opened
	Open only the unlighted R/V card holders by inserting key and unlocking.
5	TARGET indicators...................................... Red
	The target indicators will be red for corresponding open R/V card holders.
6	R/V cards.. Removed
	Remove the R/V cards from the open R/V card holders and return to appropriate target kit.

Figure 3-22. R/V Cards and Launch Console Label Installation Procedure (Sheet 1 of 4)

STEP	PROCEDURE
	CAUTION
	To avoid damaging the new R/V cards, insure that card holders are in the full open position.
7	R/V cards.. Inserted
	The R/V card or cards supplied for each launcher are to be inserted as designated on the re-entry vehicle cards sheet. If any R/V cards within the same color group bear the same identification number, the order will be determined by inspecting the hole positions punched in the R/V card. Hole position H-1 is punched for target A, H-2 for target B, and H-3 for target C. The R/V Cards are inserted with cut at lower left corner.
8	Close PUSH TO CLOSE actuators..........................Locked
9	TARGET indicators..................................... Green
	The target indicators for the R/V cards inserted must be green.
	LAUNCH CONTROL CONSOLE
	CAUTION
	Do not turn any TARGET SELECTION switch to a not used position. Failure to observe this caution may cause serious damage to the re-entry vehicle.
10	TARGET SELECTION LAUNCHER NO. 1, 2 and 3.............. B
	Set all PULL TO TURN swithces to target B.
	TARGET CARD READER AND LOGIC ASSEMBLIES
11	R/V card holders A (launchers 1, 2 and 3)............ Opened
	The A R/V card holders will be opened by inserting key and unlocking.

Fig. 3-22. R/V Cards and Launch Console Label Installation Procedure (Sheet 2 of 4)

STEP	PROCEDURE
12	TARGET A (launchers 1, 2 and 3)........................ Red The target A indicators for all three launchers will light red when R/V card holders are opened.
13	R/V cards... Removed Remove the previously installed R/V cards and return to appropriate target kit.
14	R/V cards... Inserted Insert the new R/V Cards for A R/V card holders, launchers 1, 2 and 3.
15	Close PUSH TO CLOSE................................... Locked
16	TARGET indicators..................................... Green Applicable target indicators should be green at this time. LAUNCH CONTROL CONSOLE
17	TARGET SELECTION panel................................ Opened Open TARGET SELECTION panel by unlocking with key and pulling the top of the panel.
18	Console labels.. Removed Remove previously installed launch control console labels and return to appropriate target kit.
19	Console labels.. Installed New launch control console labels will be installed in order given on launch control label sheet.
20	Close TARGET SELECTION panel.......................... Locked Note Check each target by performing steps 22 and 23 in conjunction with step 21.

Fig. 3-22. R/V Cards and Launch Console Label Installation Procedure
(Sheet 3 of 4)

STEP	PROCEDURE
21	TARGET SELECTION (all targets).......................... Green
	As the TARGET SELECTION PULL TO TURN switch is moved to each position, check that TARGET SELECT indicators light green for each launcher and target.
	LAUNCH COMPLEX FACILITIES CONSOLE
22	RE-ENTRY VEHICLE.. Red, Then Not Lighted
	As the TARGET SELECTION PULL TO TURN switch is moved from one target to the other, the RE-ENTRY VEHICLE indicator on LCFC for the appropriate launcher will light red momentarily. If all R/V cards have identical settings, the RE-ENTRY VEHICLE indicators will not light red as the TARGET SELECTION PULL TO TURN switches are positioned from A thru C. However, the RE-ENTRY VEHICLE indicators will light red as the TARGET SELECTION PULL TO TURN switches are positioned from C thru A.
	TARGET CARD READER AND LOGIC ASSEMBLIES
23	Selected R/V card holders............................ Lighted
	The R/V card holder will light for the target selected. Check appropriate R/V card holder for a lighted condition after each movement of PULL TO TURN switch.
	LAUNCH CONTROL CONSOLE
	Note
	After completion of R/V card and launch console label verification, return TARGET SELECTION switches to proper position for alert status monitoring.

Fig. 3-22. R/V Cards and Launch Console Label Installation Procedure
(Sheet 4 of 4)

T.O. 21-SM68-1

Section III

STEP	PROCEDURE
	Verify that figure 3-19 has been accomplished.
	MISSILE GUIDANCE CONSOLE
1	ANT LOWER.. Green T.O. 31X7-2-1-151 T.O. 21-SM68-2J-7-1-1
2	Press SELECT TARGET 1................................... Green
3	Press TARGET VERIFY..................................... White
	Target verify will turn white then green after printout is complete.
4	TARGET VERIFY... Green
	TARGET VERIFY will remain white for not valid targets and TEST FAULT will light yellow. TEST FAULT may be cleared by pressing GUIDE X NOT RDY and HOLD RELEASE pushbuttons.
5	Printout.. Checked
	Digital data printer printout must be identical to printout on target tape contents sheet in guidance control target trajectory kit folder under MGC TGT SELECT.
6	Repeat steps 2 thru 5 for targets 2 thru 10............ Accomplished
7	Press POWER OFF... White
8	Printout.. Stored
	Remove printout from digital data printer Date, initial, and store printout in guidance control target trajectory kit folder.

Figure 3-23. Verify Target Procedure

3-109

STEP	PROCEDURE
1	Handover target kit identification sheets. Guidance control target trajectory kit folder......... Checked T.O. Not Required GEO will check the folder for the following items: a. 1 target kit identification sheet b. 1 guidance computer tape information sheet c. 1 target tape contents sheet
2	Launch control target trajectory kit folder........... Checked GEO will check the folder for the following items: a. 1 target kit identification sheet b. Re-entry vehicle cards sheet c. Launch control console lable sheet
3	Compatibility.. Checked Check that all handover target kit identification sheets are compatible with target kit identification sheets as to control number, effective date, and all targeting information. A compatibility check of handover targets is required. Check control number of handover material with appropriate sites. Any between-complex discrepancies must be noted and resolved with the TMCO. A handover oountdown shall not be performed unless handover targets are compatible.

Figure 3-24. Handover Target Compatibility Procedure

T.O. 21-SM68-1 Section III

STEP	PROCEDURE	
	Check that targeting package contains guidance program tape, target tape, and guidance control target kit folder.	
	MISSILE GUIDANCE CONSOLE	
1	STBY	Green
	T.O. 21-SM68-2J-7-1-1	
	T.O. 31X7-2-1-151	
2	ANTENNA A or B FACILITY MAINT	Green
3	ANTENNA A or B FACILITY SELECT (as applicable)	Green
4	HANDOVER OFF	Green
	The GEO checks the missile guidance console to insure that the above indications are displayed prior to pressing POWER ON.	
5	Press POWER ON	White
	TAPE READER 2	
6	LOAD	Pressed
7	POWER ON	Pressed
8	POWER indicator	White
9	LOAD indicator	Yellow
10	BULB ON	Amber
11	Guidance tape	Mounted and Threaded
	Manually wind tape until all conductive leader is on take up reel and beginning of program data is at reverse capstan.	
12	Control Arms at null point	Positioned
13	STAND BY	Pressed
14	STAND BY indicator	Blue
15	REMOTE	Pressed

Figure 3-25. Fast Retargeting, Install and Verify Target Tape and Verify Guidance Program Tape Procedure (Sheet 1 of 5)

STEP	PROCEDURE
16	REMOTE indicator... Green
	TAPE READER 1
17	LOAD.. Pressed
18	POWER ON.. Pressed
19	POWER indicator... White
20	LOAD indicator... Yellow
21	BULB ON... Amber
22	Target tape.. Mounted and Threaded
	Manually wind tape until all conductive leader is on take-up reel and beginning of program data is at reverse capstan.
23	Control arms at null point............................... Positioned
24	STAND BY... Pressed
25	STAND BY indicator.. Blue
26	REMOTE.. Pressed
27	REMOTE indicator... Green
	MISSILE GUIDANCE CONSOLE
28	POWER ON.. Green
	POWER ON indicator will light green in approximately 2 minutes and 30 seconds after pressing POWER ON pushbutton indicator.
29	Press MAINT... Yellow
	COMPUTER SET CONSOLE
30	POWER ON.. Green
31	MAINT... White
32	Press HOLD MAINT.. Amber

Figure 3-25. Fast Retargeting, Install and Verify Target Tape and Verify Guidance Program Tape Procedure (Sheet 2 of 5)

STEP	PROCEDURE
33	Press NORMAL RATE.. Green
34	EXECUTE PROGRAM.. White
35	STEP/STOP.. Amber
36	READY.. White
37	TARGET REF... White
38	Target TAPE BLOCK NUMBER............................. Set
	The target TAPE BLOCK NUMBER is listed on the Target tape contents sheet.
39	Press LOAD PROGRAM.. White
40	Press TAPE READER 1... White
41	Press READY... White
42	Press RUN... Green
	TAPE READER 1
43	Target tape movement.. Checked
	The target tape moves forward, and stops near end of tape.
	COMPUTER SET CONSOLE
44	TAPE READER CONTROL STOP... Lighted
45	TAPE FAULT indicators.. Not Lighted
	Targeting data is now loaded on magnetic drum.
46	RUN.. Not Lighted
47	STEP/STOP.. Amber
48	Press VERIFY PROGRAM.. White
49	Press READY... White
50	Press RUN... Green

Figure 3-25. Fast Retargeting, Install and Verify Target Tape and Verify Guidance Program Tape Procedure (Sheet 3 of 5)

STEP	PROCEDURE
	TAPE READER 1
51	Target tape movement.................................. Checked
	The Target Tape rewinds, moves forward, then stops.
	COMPUTER SET CONSOLE
52	TAPE FAULT indicators................................. Not Lighted
53	TAPE READER CONTROL STOP.............................. Lighted
54	RUN... Not Lighted
55	STEP/STOP... Amber
56	Guidance program TAPE BLOCK NUMBER.................... Set
	The Guidance Program TAPE BLOCK NUMBER is listed on the Guidance computer tape information sheet.
57	Press TAPE READER 2................................... White
58	Press READY... White
59	Press FORWARD 1....................................... Lighted
60	Press RUN... Green
	TAPE READER 2
61	Guidance tape movement................................ Checked
	The guidance tape moves forward and stops near end of tape.
62	TAPE READER CONTROL STOP.............................. Lighted
63	TAPE FAULT.. Not Lighted
64	RUN... Not Lighted
65	STEP/STOP... Amber
	The target tape is now loaded and verified; the guidance tape has been verified.

Figure 3-25. Fast Retargeting, Install and Verify Target Tape and Verify Guidance Program Tape Procedure (Sheet 4 of 5)

STEP	PROCEDURE
	TAPE READER 1 and TAPE READER 2
66	POWER OFF... Pressed
	POWER OFF pushbutton is pressed at this time. Fast retargeting verify target procedures will be performed at this time, and when time is available the tapes will be rewound, removed from the tape reader, and stored in accordance with post targeting procedures.
67	All indicators.. Not Lighted
	COMPUTER SET CONSOLE
68	Press HOLD MAINT...................................... Not Lighted
69	MAINT... White
70	Press READY... White
	MISSILE GUIDANCE CONSOLE
71	Press STBY.. Green
	Guidance computer is now in an operational state of readiness.

Figure 3-25. Fast Retargeting, Install and Verify Target Tape and Verify Guidance Program Tape Procedure (Sheet 5 of 5)

T.O. 21-SM68-1

STEP	PROCEDURE	
	Verify that Figure 3-21 has been accomplished.	
	MISSILE GUIDANCE CONSOLE	
1	ANT LOWER...	Green
	T.O. 31X7-2-1-151	
	Target verify may be performed with ANT RAISE green if HANDOVER ON is yellow.	
2	Press SELECT TARGET 1...................................	Green
3	Press TARGET VERIFY.....................................	White
	TARGET VERIFY will light white, then green after printout is complete.	
4	TARGET VERIFY...	Green
	TARGET VERIFY will remain white for non-valid targets and TEST FAULT will light yellow. TEST FAULT may be cleared by pressing GUID X NOT RDY and HOLD RELEASE.	
5	Printout..	Checked
	Digital data printout must be identical to printout on target tape contents sheet in guidance control target trajectory kit folder under MGC TGT SELECT.	
6	Repeat steps 2 thru 5 for SELECT TARGETS 2 thru 10.....	Accomplished
7	Printout..	Removed, Stored
	When time is available, date, initial, and store the digital data printout in the guidance control target trajectory kit folder.	

Figure 3-26. Fast Retargeting Verify Target Procedure

T.O. 21-SM68-1 Section III

STEP	PROCEDURE
	This procedure will be performed when time is available. TAPE READER 1 and TAPE READER 2
1	LOAD... Pressed T.O. 31X7-2-1-151 T.O. 21-SM68-2J-7-1-1
2	POWER ON.. Pressed
3	POWER indicators.. White
4	LOAD indicators... Yellow
5	Control arms at null point.............................. Positioned Position the control arms of TAPE READER 1 and perform steps 6 and 7; then position the control arms of TAPE READER 2 and perform steps 6 and 7.
6	STAND BY.. Pressed
7	STAND BY indicators..................................... Blue
8	REVERSE... Pressed
9	REVERSE indicators...................................... White
10	Target tape and guidance tape........................... Rewound The target and guidance tapes rewind and stop near end of tapes.
11	END OF TAPE... Red
12	LOAD.. Pressed Press LOAD pushbutton on TAPE READER 1 when target tape has rewound. Then perform steps 13, 14, 15 and 16. When the guidance tape has rewound, press LOAD pushbutton on TAPE READER 2 and continue steps.
13	Control arms.. Locked
14	POWER OFF... Pressed
15	All indicators.. Not Lighted

Figure 3-27. Fast Retargeting Post Retargeting Procedure (Sheet 1 of 2)

STEP	PROCEDURE
16	Target tape and guidance tape.......................... Removed and Stored
	MISSILE GUIDANCE CONSOLE
17	Press POWER OFF..................................... White

Figure 3-27. Fast Retargeting Post Retargeting Procedure (Sheet 2 of 2)

T.O. 21-SM68-1　　　　　　　　　　　　　　　　　　　　　　Section III

STEP	PROCEDURE
	Verify that the following materials are available: a. Target card reader and logic assemblies key. b. Target selection door panel key. c. Launch control target kit folder. d. Target cards and labels. TARGET CARD READER AND LOGIC ASSEMBLIES
1	LAMP VERIFY switches.................................. OFF T.O. 31X7-2-1-151
2	TARGET indicators (as applicable)..................... Green LAUNCH CONTROL CONSOLE CAUTION 　　Do not turn any TARGET SELECTION switch to a not used position. Failure to observe this caution may cause serious damage to the re-entry vehicle.
3	TARGET SELECTION LAUNCHER NO. 1, 2, and 3............. A Set all PULL TO TURN switches to position A. TARGET CARD READER AND LOGIC ASSEMBLIES CAUTION 　　Do not open R/V holder if it is lighted. Failure to observe this caution may cause serious damage to the re-entry vehicle.
4	R/V card holder....................................... Opened Open only the unlighted R/V card holders by inserting key and unlocking.
5	TARGET indicators..................................... Red The target indicators will be red for corresponding open R/V card holders.
6	R/V CARDS... Removed

Figure 3-28. Fast Retargeting R/V Card and Launch Console Label
Installation Procedure (Sheet 1 of 4)

T.O. 21-SM68-1   Section III

STEP	PROCEDURE
6 (CONT)	Remove the R/V cards from the open R/V card holders and return to appropriate target kit.

CAUTION

To avoid damaging the new R/V cards, insure that card holders are in the full open position.

7	R/V cards... Inserted

The R/V card or cards supplied for each launcher are to be inserted as designated on the re-entry vehicle card sheet. If any R/V cards within the same color group bear the same identification number, the order will be determined by inspecting the hold positions punched in the R/V card. Hole position H-1 is punched for target A, H-2 for target B, and H-3 for target C. The R/V cards are inserted with cut at lower left corner.

8	CLOSE PUSH TO CLOSE actuators.......................... Locked
9	TARGET indicators...................................... Green

The target indicators for the R/V cards inserted must be green.

LAUNCH CONTROL CONSOLE

CAUTION

Do not turn any TARGET SELECTION switch to a not used position. Failure to observe this caution may cause serious damage to the re-entry vehicle.

10	TARGET SELECTION LAUNCHER NO. 1, 2, and 3.............. B

Set all PULL TO TURN switches to target B.

TARGET CARD READER AND LOGIC ASSEMBLIES

11	R/V Card holders A (launchers 1, 2, and 3)............. Opened

The A R/V card holders will be opened by inserting key and unlocking.

12	TARGET A (launchers 1, 2, and 3)....................... Red

Figure 3-28. Fast Retargeting R/V Card and Launch Console Label Installation Procedure (Sheet 2 of 4)

STEP	PROCEDURE
12 (CONT)	The target A indicators for all three launchers will light red when R/V card holders are opened.
13	R/V cards.. Removed Remove the previously installed R/V cards and return to appropriate target kit.
14	R/V cards.. Inserted Insert the new R/V cards for A R/V card holders, launchers 1, 2, and 3.
15	Close PUSH TO CLOSE actuators........................ Locked
16	TARGET indicators....................................... Green Applicable target indicators should be green at this time. LAUNCH CONTROL CONSOLE
17	TARGET SELECTION panel................................. Opened Open TARGET SELECTION panel by unlocking with key and pulling the top of the panel.
18	Console labels.. Removed Remove previously installed launch control console labels and return to appropriate target kit.
19	Console labels.. Installed New launch control console labels will be installed in order given on launch control label sheet.
20	Close TARGET SELECTION panel........................... Locked
21	TARGET SELECTION panel (all targets).................. Green As the TARGET SELECTION PULL TO TURN switch is moved to each position, check that TARGET SELECT indicators light green for each launcher and target. LAUNCH COMPLEX FACILITIES CONSOLE
22	RE-ENTRY VEHICLE....................................... Red, then Not Lighted

Figure 3-28. Fast Retargeting R/V Card and Launch Console Label Installation Procedure (Sheet 3 of 4)

3-121

STEP	PROCEDURE
22 (CONT)	As the TARGET SELECTION PULL TO TURN switch is moved from one target to the other, the RE-ENTRY VEHICLE indicator on LCFC for the appropriate launcher will light red momentarily. If all R/V cards have identical settings, the RE-ENTRY VEHICLE indicators will not light red as the TARGET SELECTION PULL TO TURN switches are positioned from A thru C. However, the RE-ENTRY VEHICLE indicators will light red as the TARGET SELECTION PULL TO TURN switches are positioned from C thru A.
	TARGET CARD READER AND LOGIC ASSEMBLIES
23	Selected R/V card holder............................ Lighted
	The R/V card holder will light for the target selected. Check appropriate R/V card holder for a lighted condition after each movement of PULL TO TURN switch.
	LAUNCH CONTROL CONSOLE
	NOTE
	After completion of R/V card and launch console label verification, return TARGET SELECTION switches to proper position for alert status monitoring.

Figure 3-28. Fast Retargeting R/V Card and Launch Console Label Installation Procedure (Sheet 4 of 4)

(Text continued from page 3-89))

3-100. **MISSILE LAUNCH OFFICER.** If not at launch control console when the alert is sounded, the MLO will report there as soon as possible and complete all actions required by applicable SAC and local fast reaction checklists.

3-101. **GUIDANCE ELECTRONICS OFFICER.** If not at the missile guidance console when the alert is sounded, the GEO will report there as soon as possible and complete all actions required by applicable SAC and local fast reaction checklists.

3-102. **BALLISTIC MISSILE ANALYST TECHNICIAN.** If not at the launch complex facilities console when the alert is sounded, the BMAT will report there as soon as possible and complete all actions required by applicable SAC and local fast reaction checklists.

3-103. **MISSILE MAINTENANCE TECHNICIAN.** If not in the control center when the alert is sounded, the MMT will report to the MLO as soon as possible for instructions. If the MMT is part of a maintenance team, he will react as briefed in the maintenance coordination briefing.

3-104. **ELECTRICAL POWER PRODUCTION TECHNICIAN.** When the alert sounds, one EPPT monitors the briefed communications net while the other EPPT starts the standby generator. If only one EPPT is in the power house, he will proceed immediately to the appropriate checklist, and start and parallel the standby generator.

3-105. **FACILITY CREW MEMBERS.** The facility crew members will immediately report to the EPPT for direction.

3-106. **MAINTENANCE AND SERVICE PERSONNEL.** The maintenance and service personnel will insure equipment is safe and returned to a launch configuration. Personnel will continue maintenance on out-of-commission missiles as briefed. All others will proceed immediately to maintenance ready room and standby for further instructions.

3-107. **COMBAT DEFENSE FORCE.** The combat defense force guards will assemble at the complex gate and await further instructions from the control center. They will be deployed in accordance with current existing directives.

3-108. **TERMINATION OF ALERT.** The MLO will announce the termination of an alert and inform all personnel to resume normal duties. The BMAT will reposition the above ground hazard light to indicate a safe condition. This indication will serve to notify the above ground guards of termination of the alert.

3-109. **FAST REACTION MESSAGE.**

3-110. A fast reaction message is transmitted to alert the MCC for EWO commitments. The requirement for immediate and undivided attention to fast reaction messages is mandatory. Members of the MCC who are required to copy fast reaction messages will cease all other activities and copy the message being transmitted, and will not divert their attention until the required actions have been completed. All fast reaction messages will be handled in accordance with SACM 55-18 and will be logged.

3-111. **LAUNCH, EXERCISE, AND GUIDANCE COUNTDOWN PROCEDURES.**

3-112. The launch, exercise, and guidance countdown procedures consist of capabilities for either an exercise or an actual EWO launch countdown operation. An exercise countdown will be accomplished as an EWO configuration with the exception of

T.O. 21-SM68-1

Section III
Paragraphs 3-113 to 3-116

imposed simulations present in the exercise mode. The countdown will commence upon receipt of a valid execution (actual or exercise) message and will progress from the load propellants phase through the end of guidance phase. Figure 3-29 is the procedure for EWO launch countdown and figure 3-30 is the procedure for an exercise countdown for the MLO/EMAT. Figure 3-31 is the procedure for guidance countdown.

WARNING

Prior to conducting an exercise, the liquid and gaseous oxygen detectors and analyzers must be in an operating condition in accordance with T.O. 21-SM68-CL-12-1, T.O. 21-SM68-CL-24-1, or T.O. 21-SM68-CL-27-1.

3-113. POWER HOUSE COUNTDOWN PROCEDURE.

3-114. The power house countdown procedure (figure 3-32) will be initiated upon receipt of ALERT signal.

3-115. LAUNCH COUNTDOWN SYSTEM FUNCTIONS.

3-116. The launch countdown system functions contain the sequence of all subsystems of the missile weapon system during EWO launch countdown. Figure 3-33 lists functions for operational bases, and figure 3-34 lists function for VAFB. Figure 3-35 lists launcher functions for all bases.

T.O. 21-SM68-1

Section III

STEP	PROCEDURE
	The MLO and BMAT will announce all light indications as they occur on the LCC and LCFC. During combat training launches conducted at VAFB, the MLO must receive clearance from site commander/command post prior to initiation of each countdown phase.
1	Press HAZARD LIGHT (3).................................. Flashing Red Upon receipt of an actual EWO execution message, the BMAT will press the three ABOVE GRD HAZARD LIGHT pushbutton indicators to flashing red for all launchers. For launches other than EWO, press ABOVE GRD HAZARD LIGHT pushbutton indicators to steady red.
2	Guidance and facility status.......................... Received MLO receives reports on equipment status from GEO and BMAT, insuring weapon system status is in an R-O configuration.
3	Power house status..................................... Received MLO receives power house status report from EPPT with any restrictions or exceptions to normal EWO countdown procedures. The load propellants phase is not initiated until receipt of this report.
4	Press LOAD PROPELLANTS ____/ ____/ ____/ .... White MLO presses LOAD PROPELLANTS pushbutton indicator on all three launchers. LOAD PROPELLANTS white indicates that the countdown has started. LOX LOADING indicators will light white, indicating rapid loading is in progress.
5	Go code.. Verified Verification of the go code is normally accomplished after initiating the load propellants phase and must be verified prior to the raise launcher phase.
6	Press EXERCISE____/ ____/ ____/ .... Not Lighted Prior to initiation of the raise launcher phase during an actual launch, the MLO breaks the seals on the EXERCISE pushbutton covers and presses the pushbutton indicators to not lighted.

Figure 3-29. Launch Countdown Procedure (Sheet 1 of 5)

T.O. 21-SM68-1　　　　　　　　　　　　　　　　　　　Section III

STEP	PROCEDURE
7	Launch enable system ENABLE.......................... Verified
	In an actual launch, the launch enable system is enabled prior to initiation of the raise launcher phase. The MLO checks for a green ENABLE on the time display board.
	LOX LOADED indicators will light white signifying missiles are loaded and topping is in effect.
8	RAISE LAUNCHER.. Green
	RAISE LAUNCHER green denotes that all prerequisites to raise launcher phase have been completed.
9	Guidance status...................................... Received
	The MLO must receive a "Guidance go" from the GEO before continuing countdown. Upon receipt of a "Guidance No-Go" the MLO will not proceed until a "Guidance go" is received and handover mode has been initiated as follows:
	a. Communications established with the remote ground guidance station (GGS).
	b. Target compatibility insured between local missiles and the remote GGS.
	c. Handover switch indicator on local LCC and remote GGS actuated.
	RAISE LAUNCHER will not be pressed until remote GGS reports, "Ready to guide." Ready to guide means ANT RAISED and guidance is ready to accept missile.
10	Select target (handover only)........................ Directed Acknowledged
	(Perform after remote GGS antenna is raised.) MLO directs the GEO at the remote GGS to select proper target for missile to be launched. GEO acknowledges and verifies correct target selection.
11	Select launcher (handover only)...................... Directed Acknowledged

Figure 3-29. Launch Countdown Procedure (Sheet 2 of 5)

T.O. 21-SM68-1 Section III

STEP	PROCEDURE
11 (CONT)	MLO directs the GEO at the remote GGS to select the launcher being raised. GEO acknowledges and verifies correct launcher selected.
12	Ready to guide (handover only)......................... Received

Ready to guide means that the remote guidance station has raised antenna, selected applicable target and launcher, pressed ACQ MISSILE, and the antenna has been slewed to the preset coordinates and is standing by for lift off signal. |
| 13 | Press HANDOVER (handover only)......................... White |
| 14 | Press RAISE LAUNCHER ____/ ____/ ____/............... White

The RAISE LAUNCHER white indication denotes that the raise launcher phase is in progress. In addition, the following indications occur:

    a. (After incorporation of TCTO 31X3-10-27-511) FUEL VALVES OPEN white denotes that all fuel storage valves are open.

    b. (Prior to incorporation of TCTO 31X3-10-27-511) CRIB UMB DISC white denotes that the signal to retract the crib umbilical mechanism has been generated.

    c. TARGET SELECT white denotes lockup of target selection.

    d. MISSILE TANKS PRESSURIZED white denotes that missile lox, fuel, and helium tanks are pressurized. |
| 15 | LAUNCH.. Green

LAUNCH green indicates that all launch prerequisites are complete. |

Figure 3-29. Launch Countdown Procedure (Sheet 3 of 5)

T.O. 21-SM68-1   Section III

STEP	PROCEDURE
16 (CONT)	Press LAUNCH ____/ ____/ ____/ .... White

MLO presses the LAUNCH pushbutton indicator from green to white for the applicable launcher. The LAUNCH pushbutton should be pressed as soon as possible after it indicates green. The maximum allowable hold time is 30 seconds. In addition, the following indications occur:

    a. POWER TRANSFERRED white indicates power has been transferred to the missile batteries.

    b. GUIDANCE LOCKED ON white indicates guidance is locked on and ready for start loop check.

    c. GROUND GUIDANCE white indicates that guidance is locked on the missile.

    d. LOOP CHECK COMPLETE white indicates that all guidance and flight control system loop checks are complete. |
| 17 | LIFT OFF.. White

LIFT OFF white indicates the missile is released for flight.

                             Note

Repeat steps 9 thru 17 for remaining launchers when RAISE LAUNCHER lights green. |
| 18 | LOWER LAUNCHER...................................... Green

LOWER LAUNCHER green denotes that the lower launcher phase can be initiated.

                             Note

Lowering the launcher is accomplished as soon as possible after all in-commission missiles have been launched during EWO execution. |
| 19 | Press LOWER LAUNCHER ____/ ____/ ____/ .... White

MLO verifies a lower launcher green indication and presses the LOWER LAUNCHER pushbutton to white. |

Figure 3-29. Launch Countdown Procedure (Sheet 4 of 5)

STEP	PROCEDURE
19.1	Press HANDOVER (handover only). . . . . Not Lighted
20	LOWER LAUNCHER. . . . . Not Lighted
	Note
	Repeat steps 18 thru 20 for remaining launchers.
21	Return power house to alert status monitoring . . . . Directed
	MLO directs EPPT to return the power house to an alert status monitoring configuration.

Figure 3-29. Launch Countdown Procedure (Sheet 5 of 5)

T.O. 21M-HGM25A-1-1 (21-SM68-1)   Section III

STEP	PROCEDURE
	When shutdown occurs, refer to T.O. 21M-HGM25A-12CL-1, T.O. 21M-HGM25A-24CL-1, T.O. 21M-HGM25A-26CL-1, or T.O. 21M-HGM25A-27CL-1 for recycle procedures.
	The MLO and BMAT will announce all light indications as they occur on the LCC and LCFC applicable to the exercise. During exercises conducted at VAFB, the MLO must receive clearance from site commander/command post prior to initiation of each countdown phase.
	WARNING
	All liquid oxygen detectors and gaseous oxygen analyzers must be in an operating condition prior to conducting any lox exercise.
1	Initiate countdown order. . . . . Received
	Upon receipt of the appropriate countdown order, the launch crew will proceed with lox or combined systems exercise countdown.
2	HAZARD LIGHT
	DRY CSE . . . . Green
	LOX CSE, lox only exercise, FUEL CSE, or (After incorporation of TCTO 31X3-10-11-634) FUEL EXERCISE. . . . . Flashing Red
	Upon receipt of the appropriate countdown order, the BMAT will press the ABOVE GRD HAZARD LIGHT pushbutton indicator for appropriate launcher to flashing red for LOX CSE, lox only exercise, FUEL CSE and (after incorporation of TCTO 31X3-10-11-634) FUEL EXERCISE. For a DRY CSE the ABOVE GRD HAZARD LIGHT will be left in the green position.
3	Guidance and facility status. . . . . Received
	MLO receives report on equipment status from GEO and BMAT, insuring weapon system status is in an R-0 configuration.
4	Power house status. . . . . Received
	MLO receives power house status report from EPPT with any restrictions or exceptions to normal exercise countdown procedures. The load propellant phase is not initiated until receipt of this report.

Figure 3-30. Lox or CSE Countdown Procedure (Sheet 1 of 6)

STEP	PROCEDURE
5	EVENTS RECORDER (CSE) switch (10A8) . . . . ON
	When required, MMT will set the CSE events recorder switch located on the launch mode control chassis (assembly 10A8) to ON.
6	Press LOAD PROPELLANTS. . . . . White
	MLO presses LOAD PROPELLANTS pushbutton indicator for the exercising launcher as directed. In addition, LOX LOADING indicator lights white signifying rapid loading is in progress.

Figure 3-30. Lox or CSE Countdown Procedure (Sheet 1A of 6)

STEP	PROCEDURE
7	Go code (simulated) . . . . Verified
	Verification of the go code is normally accomplished after initiating the load propellants phase and must be verified prior to the raise launcher phase. This action is simulated for an exercise countdown.
8	EXERCISE. . . . . White
	Prior to initiation of the raise launcher phase during an exercise countdown, the MLO checks for EXERCISE white on the exercising launcher. This indication assures the MLO that the weapon system is operating in an exercise mode.
9	HANDOVER
	DRY CSE . . . . White
	LOX CSE, lox only exercise, FUEL CSE, or (After incorporation of TCTO 31X3-10-11-634) FUEL EXERCISE. . . . . Not Lighted
	When performing DRY CSE, MLO presses HANDOVER pushbutton indicator (LCC) white to bypass guidance signals not required for a dry exercise countdown. In all other exercise modes of operation, HANDOVER will be left in the not lighted position.
10	Launch enable system DISABLE. . . . . Verified
	CAUTION
	If PLPS NO-GO is received at T-700, a manual shutdown must be initiated immediately to prevent lox overflow from missile vents.
	LOX LOADED indicator will light white and be announced by the MLO. This indication denotes that Stage I and II are at 100%, and that Stage I and II helium spheres are pressurized.
11	RAISE LAUNCHER. . . . . Green
	RAISE LAUNCHER green denotes that all prerequisites to raise launcher phase have been completed.

Figure 3-30. Lox or CSE Countdown Procedure (Sheet 2 of 6)

STEP	PROCEDURE
12	Guidance status .... Received
	The MLO must receive a guidance go report from the GEO before proceeding with the countdown. Upon receipt of a guidance no-go, the MLO will initiate a hold or proceed with handover operations as follows:
	a. Communications established with the remote ground guidance station.
	b. Target compatibility insured between local missile and the remote ground guidance station.
	c. Handover pushbutton indicator on local LCC and remote ground guidance station actuated.
	RAISE LAUNCHER will not be pressed until remote ground guidance station reports, "Ready to guide".
	Note
	Tasks 13 through 16 are performed during LOX CSE, lox only exercise, FUEL CSE, and (After incorporation of TCTO 31X3-10-11-634) FUEL EXERCISE for handover only.
13	Select target .... Directed, Acknowledged
	(Perform after remote GGS antenna is raised) MLO directs the GEO at the remote GGS to select proper target for the missile to be launched. GEO acknowledges and verifies correct target selected.
14	Select launcher .... Directed, Acknowledged
	MLO directs the GEO at the remote GGS to select the launcher being raised. GEO acknowledges and verifies correct launcher selected.
15	Ready to guide. .... Received
	Ready to guide means that the remote GGS has raised antenna, selected applicable target and launcher, pressed the ACQ MISSILE pushbutton, the antenna has slewed to preset coordinates, and is standing by for the lift off signal.

Figure 3-30. Lox or CSE Countdown Procedure (Sheet 3 of 6)

T.O. 21-SM68-1　　　　　　　　　　　　　　　　Section III

STEP	PROCEDURE
16	Press HANDOVER...White
	Handover white enables the countdown to continue without ground guidance.
17	Press RAISE LAUNCHER..White
	MLO presses the RAISE LAUNCHER pushbutton indicator to white. The RAISE LAUNCHER white indication denotes that the raise launcher phase is in progress.
	(Prior to incorporation of TCTO 31X3-10-27-511). The CRIB UMB DISC indicator will light white denoting that the signal to retract the crib umbilical mechanism has been generated.
	(After incorporation of TCTO 31X3-10-27-511) The FUEL VALVES OPEN pushbutton indicator will light white denoting all fuel storage valves are open.
	The TARGET SELECT indicator will light white denoting lock-up of target selection. The MISSILE TANKS PRESS'D indicator will light white denoting that missile lox, fuel, and helium tanks are pressurized.
18	LAUNCH..Green
	This indication denotes that all launch prerequisites are complete.
19	Analog recorder
	Lox exercise and dry CSE.......................................OFF
	Fuel and lox CSE..ON
	When required, the MMT will turn on the analog recorder switch located on the 10A8 assembly.
20	Press LAUNCH..White
	MLO presses the LAUNCH pushbutton from green to white for the applicable launcher. Staging reliability is substantially increased when LAUNCH pushbutton is pressed as soon as possible after it indicates green. LAUNCH white indicates that the launch phase has commenced.
	The POWER TRANSFERRED indicator will light white denoting that power has been transferred to missile batteries.

Figure 3-30. Lox or CSE Countdown Procedure (Sheet 4 of 6)

Changed 18 December 1963　TOCN-1 (DEN-5)　　　　　　　　　　　　　　3-133

T.O. 21M-HGM25A-1-1 (21-SM68-1)　　　　　　　　　　　　　　　　Section III

STEP	PROCEDURE
20 (CONT)	GUIDANCE LOCKED ON indicator will light white denoting that guidance is locked on and ready for start loop check. GROUND GUIDANCE indicator will light white denoting that guidance is locked on the missile. LOOP CHECK COMPLETE indicator will light white denoting that the guidance and flight controls system loop checks are complete and satisfactory. Note For a DRY CSE, lox only exercise, and (After incorporation of TCTO 31X3-10-11-634) FUEL EXERCISE the following indications should occur at T+7: SHUTDOWN red, GROUND POWER red, and EXERCISE green. If shut down does not occur by T+10, MLO will manually press SHUTDOWN (LCC).
21	LIFT OFF DRY CSE, lox only exercise, or (After incorporation of TCTO 31X3-10-11-634) FUEL EXERCISE . . . . Not Lighted LOX CSE or FUEL CSE . . . . White If LIFT OFF lights during DRY CSE, lox only exercise, or (After TCTO 31X3-10-11-634) FUEL EXERCISE, initiate manual shut down at T+10 seconds.
22	LOWER LAUNCHER. . . . . Green This indication denotes that the lower launcher phase may be initiated.
23	SHUTDOWN. . . . . Red During a LOX CSE and FUEL CSE, SHUTDOWN will occur at simulated nose cone release.
24	Analog recorder . . . . OFF The MMT will turn off the analog recorder at completion of CSE.
25	Press LOWER LAUNCHER. White

Figure 3-30. Lox or CSE Countdown Procedure (Sheet 5 of 6)

STEP	PROCEDURE
25 (CONT)	Pressing the LOWER LAUNCHER pushbutton indicator initiates the lower launcher phase. The white indication denotes that the lower launcher phase is in progress.
25.1	Press HANDOVER. . . . . Not Lighted
26	LOWER LAUNCHER. . . . . Not Lighted This indication denotes that the lower launcher phase is complete.
27	Events recorder . . . . OFF The MMT will turn off the events recorder at completion of CSE.
28	Return power house to alert status monitoring . . . . . Directed The MLO directs the EPPT to return the power house to an alert status monitoring configuration.
29	Press HAZARD LIGHT (if applicable). . . . . Amber The BMAT presses the ABOVE GRD HAZARD LIGHT to amber after completion of a LOX CSE, lox only exercise, and (After incorporation of TCTO 31X3 -10-11-634) FUEL EXERCISE. If a hazard indication is present the ABOVE GRD HAZARD LIGHT will be positioned in accordance with T.O. 21M-HGM25A-1 -1CL-4.
30	Post shutdown and unload procedure. . . . . Directed MLO directs the MMT to supervise post shutdown procedures for accomplishment of missile helium and lox unloading utilizing recycle procedures from appropriate functional checklists.
31	Missile helium and lox unloading. . . . . Completed MMT will report to the MLO when missile helium and lox unloading and recycle procedures are complete.

Figure 3-30. Lox or CSE Countdown Procedure (Sheet 6 of 6)

STEP	PROCEDURE
	Anytime the GGS is not in a GO status or cannot meet the time requirements for the next phase in the count down, press the GGS HOLD pushbutton indicator. If the GGS is returned to a GO status after pressing GGS HOLD pushbutton indicator, press HOLD RELEASE pushbutton, and continue the countdown. For handover operation, establish communication with MLO, insure target compatibility, and press HANDOVER ON pushbutton indicator. START LCH EXERCISE indicator will light white when the MLO places the weapon system in the CSE mode. The GEO will press the LAUNCH EXERCISE pushbutton indicator to yellow, and the STBY pushbutton indicator will light red. If the MLO takes the weapon system out of the CSE mode, the STBY pushbutton indicator will change from red to green, the LAUNCH EXERCISE pushbutton indicator will change from yellow to green, and the START LCH EXERCISE indicator will go out. The GGS may be taken out of the CSE mode by pressing STBY pushbutton indicator to green.
1	START CD.. Received The START CD indicator will light white when the LOAD PROPELLANTS pushbutton indicator on the launch control console is pressed. In the handover mode the remitting MLO gives the start countdown command verbally. Note Immediately upon receipt of a message that requires an actual countdown, if the guidance system is in standby, press POWER ON pushbutton indicator.
2	Press POWER ON... White The POWER ON pushbutton indicator will remain white for 2 1/2 minutes to allow the magnetic drum in the computer to reach operating speed. The following indications for the selected antenna must be present: a. ANTENNA FACILITY SELECT, green b. ANTENNA FACILITY MAINT, green c. ANTENNA FACILITY FAULT, not lighted

Figure 3-31. Guidance Countdown Procedure (Sheet 1 of 8)

T.O. 21-SM68-1 Section III

STEP	PROCEDURE
2 (cont)	d. CCW/CW indicator, CCW or CW portion green The following indications appear during power on sequence and should be observed: a. GUIDE X NOT RDY will light amber for approximately one minute while guidance exerciser resets. b. MAG OFF will light amber. c. Range indicator sweep will appear. d. TV monitor raster will appear. e. Constants registers should be enabled in approximately 60 seconds.
3	Index of refraction.. Inserted The index of refraction will be inserted into the right four digits of constants register 6 by first pressing the right-most constants register pushbutton indicator and adjusting the selection knob for the desired numeral. Repeat this procedure for the other three numerals.
4	POWER ON.. Green POWER ON pushbutton indicator will light green when all power feedback prerequisites are met. Note Steps 5 and 6 will be performed only if antennas have been switched during countdown.
5	Press GUIDE X NOT RDY.................................. Not lighted
6	Press START GUID X....................................... White The following indications appear after START GUID X pushbutton indicator is pressed and should be observed: a. The digital data printer will print out the contents of the constants register. b. A gated pulse will appear on the range indicator. c. TARGET GATED indicator will light green. d. The AGC meter will indicate in the normal segment.

Figure 3-31. Guidance Countdown Procedure (Sheet 2 of 8)

Changed 17 January 1964 TOCN-1 (DEN-8)

T.O. 21-SM68-1

Section III

STEP	PROCEDURE	
6 (cont)	If a gated pulse is not obtained, reset the guidance exerciser by pressing GUID X NOT RDY pushbutton indicator and then pressing START GUID X pushbutton indicator. During the guidance exerciser coast period, the following indications appear and should be observed: a. COAST indicator will light amber. b. TARGET GATED indicator will go out. c. AGC meter will indicate out of normal segment.	
7	MAG RDY...	White
	MAG RDY indicator will light white approximately five minutes after POWER ON pushbutton indicator is pressed.	
8	Press MAG ON...	White, then Green
	After the MAG ON pushbutton indicator is pressed, the MAG ON pushbutton indicator will turn from white to green in 10 to 12 seconds. The following indications appear after pressing MAG ON pushbutton indicator and should be observed: a. MAG READY will go out. b. MAG OFF will go out. c. The MAG-MOD CUR-VOLT meter will indicate 1.5 to 1.9 MA; press INC or DEC as required. Under no circumstances will the magnetron current be adjusted below 1.5 MA during a GUID X or after ACQ MISSILE has been pressed.	
9	Magnetron tuning.....................................	Accomplished
	The magnetron switch is held to the COARSE position. The MAG TUNE meter is checked for the approximate segment of the X-band. The MAGNETRON switch is released to PEAK. Adjust the FREQUENCY CONTROL switch as required to peak the MAG TUNE meter.	

Figure 3-31. Guidance Countdown Procedure (Sheet 3 of 8)

Changed 17 January 1964 TOCN-1 (DEN-8)

T.O. 21-SM68-1　　　　　　　　　　　　　　　　　　　　　　　Section III

STEP	PROCEDURE
10	Go code.. Verified
	Verification of the go code must be completed prior to initiation of the RAISE LAUNCHER phase.
10.1	Events recorder POWER switch............................ ON
11	START GUID X.. Green
	START GUID X must be green or a NO-GO exists in the ground guidance system.
	The digital data printer will print out the code for a successful guidance exerciser run. The GUIDE X NOT RDY pushbutton indicator will light while the guidance exerciser resets.

Figure 3-31. Guidance Countdown Procedure (Sheet 3A of 8)

STEP	PROCEDURE	
12	Single sideband antenna...................................	Lowered
13	GGS GO..	Reported
	If a No-Go exists, the GEO will report estimated hold time to MLO or have MLO request handover assistance. If handover is required, the remote GEO will report "ready to raise antenna" to the receiving MLO.	
14	RAISE ANT (verbal in handover)............................	White
	The RAISE ANT indicator will light white when the RAISE LAUNCHER pushbutton indicator on the launch control console is pressed. In the handover mode the remitting MLO gives the raise antenna command verbally. If a blast is detected prior to RAISE ANT indicator white, notify MLO to delay RAISE LAUNCHER phase until a satisfactory guidance antenna level program has been accomplished.	
15	Press ANT RAISE...	White
	If a blast is detected after ANT RAISE pushbutton indicator is pressed, but prior to ACQ MISSILE pushbutton indicator green, the system is automatically placed in the power off condition and the antennas are automatically switched. Notify MLO and restart the countdown. The RAISE LAUNCHER phase will not start until after the antenna is raised and locked, and a successful level program is run.	
16	ANT RAISE...	Green
	A level program is automatically run following ANT RAISE pushbutton indicator green if a blast was detected prior to pressing ANT RAISE pushbutton indicator. The digital data printer will printout if an automatic level program was run. If the TEST FAULT indicator remains not lighted, notify MLO that the RAISE LAUNCHER phase may proceed.	
17	SELECT TARGET (handover only).............................	Received, Accomplished, Acknowledged
	The MLO directs the GEO to select a specified target. The GEO will acknowledge and verify the TARGET SELECTED is green.	

Figure 3-31. Guidance Countdown Procedure (Sheet 4 of 8)

STEP	PROCEDURE
18	SELECT LAUNCHER (handover only).......................... Received; Accomplished; Acknowledged

The MLO directs the GEO to select a specified launcher. The GEO will acknowledge and verify the LAUNCHER SELECT is white. |
| 19 | MISSILE READY.. White

MISSILE READY indicator will light white after the LAUNCH pushbutton indicator on the launch control console is pressed. In handover, MISSILE READY will light white after the GEO has selected target and launcher. Prerequisites for the MISSILE READY indicator lighting white are SELECT TARGET pushbutton indicator green and SELECT LAUNCHER pushbutton indicator white. If the LAUNCH HOLD indicator lights red after MISSILE READY indicator is white but before ACQ MISSILE pushbutton indicator is pressed, then ACQ MISSILE pushbutton indicator must be pressed to enable the recycle function. |
| 20 | ACQ MISSILE.. Pressed

The following occurs after ACQ MISSILE pushbutton indicator is pressed and should be observed:

    a. Antenna slews to preset coordinates.

    b. SELECT LAUNCHER pushbutton indicator will light green.

    c. The digital data printer will print out target verify.

    d. TARGET VERIFY pushbutton indicator will light green.

In the handover mode, the ACQ MISSILE pushbutton indicator will be pressed immediately after selecting target and launcher as directed by the remitting MLO. |
| 21 | ACQ MISSILE.. White

When ACQ MISSILE pushbutton indicator lights white, the following indications appear and should be observed except in handover when they will occur after lift off:

    a. TARGET GATED indicator will light green. |

Figure 3-31. Guidance Countdown Procedure (Sheet 5 of 8)

STEP	PROCEDURE
21 (CONT)	b. AGC meter will indicate in normal segment. c. Gated pulse will appear on the range indicator. In the handover mode, the digital data printer will print out the contents of the constants register.
22	Ready to guide (handover only)..........................Reported
23	LIFT OFF (handover only)..................................White If GGS HOLD indicator lights red after lift off, continue countdown. At a predetermined time after the lift off signal is received, the guidance computer sends a signal to the radar to begin frequency sweep and places the range computer in automatic track. When the radar locks on the missile the following indications occur: a. TARGET GATED indicator will light green. b. AGC meter will indicate in normal segment. c. Gated pulse will appear on the range indicator.
24	ACQ MISSILE..Green The ACQ MISSILE pushbutton indicator will light green after LOOP CHECK complete. The digital data printer will print out the contents of the constants register. If the LAUNCH HOLD indicator lights red after the ACQ MISSILE pushbutton indicator is green, the GGS HOLD pushbutton indicator must be pressed to enable the recycle function. If a blast is detected after ACQ MISSILE pushbutton indicator is green, continue the countdown. In the handover mode the ACQ MISSILE pushbutton indicator will light green when the radar has locked on in automatic track.
25	LIFT OFF..White If the LAUNCH HOLD indicator red or GGS HOLD pushbutton indicator red is received after the LIFT OFF indicator lights white, continue the countdown.
26	Press GUID IN PROGRESS....................................Green

Figure 3-31. Guidance Countdown Procedure (Sheet 6 of 8)

STEP	PROCEDURE
26 (CONT)	The GUID IN PROGRESS pushbutton indicator will be pressed to green after all indicators indicate that the radar is guiding the missile.
27	END OF GUID . . . . White The digital data printer will print out the miss distance; then the END OF GUID indicator lights white.
28	End of guidance . . . . Reported
29	RECYCLE . . . . Pressed The following indications occur after the RECYCLE pushbutton is pressed and should be observed: a. TARGET GATED indicator not lighted b. END OF GUID indicator not lighted c. GUID IN PROGRESS indicator not lighted d. LIFT OFF indicator not lighted e. ACQ MISSILE pushbutton indicator not lighted f. MISSILE READY indicator not lighted g. SELECT TARGET pushbutton indicator not lighted h. SELECT LAUNCHER pushbutton indicator not lighted The recycle function places the GGS in a status just prior to the LAUNCH phase of the next missile. In the handover mode, coordinate with the MLO for further target and launcher selections.
30	Repeat steps 17 through 29 for remaining missiles . . . . . Accomplished Before proceeding, the GEO will confer with the MLO for possible acceptance of handover.
31	Press ANT LOWER . . . . White During the lowering of the antenna, the POWER ON pushbutton indicator may light white.

Figure 3-31. Guidance Countdown Procedure (Sheet 7 of 8)

STEP	PROCEDURE
32	ANT LOWER . . . . Green
	The GGS FAULT pushbutton indicator and ANTENNA FACILITY FAULT indicator may light after ANT LOWER pushbutton indicator is green. If the fault indications appear, wait until the ANTENNA FACILITY FAULT indicator goes out and press the HOLD RELEASE pushbutton.
33	Press MAG OFF . . . . Amber
34	Events recorder POWER switch. . . . . OFF
35	(Prior to incorporation of TCTO 31X7-2-11-512) Press POWER OFF . . . . White
36	GGS alert status monitoring . . . . Reported
	Following a combined systems exercise, perform guidance electronics officer alert status monitoring procedure.
37	Printout. . . . . Analyzed
	The printout will be analyzed for proper computer constants register numbers and flight data.
38	Events recorder records . . . . Analyzed
	The record will be analyzed for the performance of the GGS in accordance with T.O. 21M-HGM25A-2-7-5

Figure 3-31. Guidance Countdown Procedure (Sheet 8 of 8)

T.O. 21-SM68-1　　　　　　　　　　　　　　　　　　　　Section III

STEP	PROCEDURE
1	ALERT.. Received
	When the MLO alerts the complex for a launch or exercise countdown, one EPPT immediately monitors the countdown net while the other EPPT starts the standby generators.
2	Start standby diesel engine............................. Accomplished
	The EPPT starts the standby diesel engine(s) by performing the following procedures:
	(LAFB 724TH/725TH SQDN)
	a. Position engine console power supply switch to ON.
	Note
	If engine fails to start automatically, set engine console power supply switch to OFF and start engine manually.
	b. Press engine START pushbutton. The prelube pump runs for approximately 20 seconds. If engine lube oil pressure gage does not indicate 4 to 5 PSI, set console power switch to OFF and repeat steps a and b. Engine starts at approximately 450 RPM.
	c. Close starting air supply valve.
	d. Close air intake manifold, air intake aftercooler, and turbo charger drain valves.
	(VAFB, BAFB, LAFB, MHAFB)
	a. The EPPT starts the precirculating LUBE OIL, CRANKCASE VACUUM, and ENGINE JACKET WATER pumps by pressing the respective START pushbuttons.
	b. Start engine by pressing engine START pushbutton.
3	Standby generator on line.............................. Accomplished
	The EPPT places the standby generator on the line by performing the following procedures:

Figure 3-32. Power House Countdown Procedure (Sheet 1 of 4)

T.O. 21-SM68-1   Section III

STEP	PROCEDURE
3 (CONT)	a. Remove synchroscope key from running generator SYNCHROSCOPE SWITCH and insert in standby generator panel SYNCHROSCOPE switch. b. Position standby SYNCHROSCOPE switch to on. c. (LAFB 724TH/725TH SQDN) Rotate standby generator manual field rheostat counterclockwise to 35 VDC. d. Close standby GENERATOR FIELD circuit breaker. CAUTION (LAFB 724TH/725TH SQDN) Manual field rheostat must be rotated SLOWLY counterclockwise or to the RAISE VOLTAGE position to prevent damage to incoming voltmeter. e. (LAFB 724TH/725TH SQDN) Rotate standby generator manual field rheostat counterclockwise to the fully raised position. f. Adjust GOVERNOR MOTOR CONTROL until synchroscope pointer is rotating slowly in the fast direction. g. Adjust standby generator regulator pre-set rheostat for required incoming voltage; the incoming voltmeter must indicate the same as the running voltmeter. CAUTION Do not close standby GENERATOR circuit breaker until synchroscope pointer is at the 12 o'clock position. h. Close standby GENERATOR circuit breaker. i. (LAFB 724TH/725TH SQDN) Immediately turn GOVERNOR MOTOR CONTROL to the raise position and hold until on coming generator KW meter indicates approximately 100 K.W. and using pre-set rheostat on voltage regulator adjust KVAR'S. j. Balance K.W. load between operating generators.

Figure 3-32. Power House Countdown Procedure (Sheet 2 of 4)

T.O. 21-SM68-1 Section III

STEP	PROCEDURE
3 (CONT)	k. (LAFB 724TH/725TH SQDN) Adjust KVAR meter. l. (EAFB, BAFB, LAFB, MHAFB) Adjust POWER FACTOR meter. Note During an EWO launch countdown position the START-RUN switch to the START position on all generators connected to the bus, all other times perform step m. m. Position generator START-RUN switch to RUN. n. Return synchroscope switch key to the leading generator or to the lowest numbered operating generator.
4	Communications with control center........................Established EPPT established communications with control center and remains on net until countdown is completed or until he is released by the MLO.
5	Power House status..Reported EPPT informs the MLO of the status of the power house, that the standby generator is on the line, and the powerhouse is in a go condition.
6	Post diesel engine start checkout........................Accomplished (Refer to power house alert status monitoring.)
7	Return power house to alert status monitoring..............Received
8	Standby generator off the line...........................Accomplished The EPPT removes the standby generator from the line by performing the following procedures: a. Position the DIESEL ENGINE START-RUN switch to the START position. b. (LAFB 724TH/725TH SQDN) Remove KW and KVAR load. c. (LAFB 724TH/725TH SQDN) Simultaneously trip GENERATOR circuit breaker and rotate manual field rheostat clockwise to the lower position. If this is not done simultaneously, damage will occur to the DC voltmeter.

Figure 3-32. Power House Countdown Procedure (Sheet 3 of 4)

STEP	PROCEDURE
8 (CONT)	d. (EAFB, BAFB, LAFB, MHAFB) Trip GENERATOR circuit breaker. e. Verify that GENERATOR circuit breaker indicator is lighted green. f. (LAFB 724TH/725TH SQDN) Clear GENERATOR FIELD circuit breaker red target and reposition RESET TRIP relay. g. Trip GENERATOR FIELD circuit breaker and verify indicator lighted green. Note Following an EWO launch countdown, position the START-RUN switch to the RUN position on generators connected to the bus.
9	Shut down standby diesel engine..........................Accomplished The EPPT will shutdown the standby diesel engine by performing the following procedures: (LAFB 724TH/725TH SQDN) a. Allow engine to run at 450 RPM for approximately 30 minutes. b. Press engine STOP pushbutton. c. After engine has completely stopped rotating, position engine console power supply switch to OFF. d. Open starting air valve. e. Open turbocharger, after cooler, and intake air manifold drain valves. (VAFB, EAFB, BAFB, LAFB, MHAFB) a. Press engine STOP pushbutton.

Figure 3-32. Power House Countdown Procedure (Sheet 4 of 4)

T.O. 21-SM68-1 Section III

TIME	REF	ROUTINE COMMAND	SOURCE	DESTINATION	REF	SUB-COMMAND	PREREQUISITES
		Note All T times listed in this procedure are approximate times. (M) designates a momentary signal and (C) designates a continuous signal.					
TSI	001		LCC				LOAD PROPELLANTS pushbutton pressed.
TSI	008	Launch sequence started (M)	LS	LS		Start first timing sequence.	Missile/facility go and item 016 not generated.
				ES		Energize 28 VDC Operating bus to AOE.	First timing sequence started.
						Energize 60 CPS bus to AOE.	
						Start ground 400 CPS motor-generator.	
						Start ground inverter start unit.	
						Start missile air conditioning unit.	

Figure 3-33. Launch Countdown System Functions (Operational Bases) (Sheet 1 of 39)

3-148

T.O. 21-SM68-1 Section III

TIME	REF	ROUTINE COMMAND	SOURCE	DESTINATION	REF	SUB-COMMAND	PREREQUISITES
TSI	008	(Continued)		ES (Cont)		Energize missile 28 VDC buses.	28 VDC operating bus to AOE energized
						Apply standby power to AOE.	
						Energize missile battery heater control circuits.	
				ECS		Energize ECS AOE	
						Energize (1), (2), and (3) TPA heater switches and apply (3) TPA heater preheat.	
					008	Reset Stage II airborne sequencer.	
						Energize re-entry vehicle battery heaters. (Mark 3 R/V)	
			LS	FCS		Freeze RVS go status.	
						Freeze FCS go status.	
TSI	016	Launch sequencer operating (C)		TDB		Start countdown timer.	First timing sequence started and 28 VDC operating bus to AOE energized.

Figure 3-33. Launch Countdown System Functions (Operational Bases) (Sheet 2 of 39)

3-149

T.O. 21-SM68-1　　　　　　　　　　　　　　　　Section III

TIME	REF	ROUTINE COMMAND	SOURCE	DESTINATION	REF	SUB-COMMAND	PREREQUISITES
TSI	016	(Continued)		CCC		LOAD PROPELLANTS white on LCC.	
				LS		Disable manual missile facility no go.	
						Inhibit exercise mode initiation.	
				TCS		Freeze target go status.	First timing sequence started.
TSI	024	Start power pack (M)	LS	LCS		Start launcher power pack pump motors.	First timing sequence started.
TSI	032	Energize RGS (C)	LS	RGS		Energize GMTS	
				GMTS		Energize MGS	
TSI	040	Countdown started (C)	CCC	GGS		START CD white on MGC	Item 016 received.
					040	Press POWER ON pushbutton indicator on MGC (manual).	START CD white.
						POWER ON pushbutton indicator white on MGC.	POWER ON pushbutton indicator pressed.
TSI	052	Start propellant loading (C).	ES				Item 008 received; 28 VDC

Figure 3-33. Launch Countdown System Functions (Operational Bases) (Sheet 3 of 39)

3-150

T.O. 21-SM68-1　　　Section III

TIME	REF	ROUTINE COMMAND	SOURCE	DESTINATION	REF	SUB-COMMAND	PREREQUISITES
TSI	052	(Continued)		PLPS		Energize 750 PSI pneumatic supply valve (FCV 508) open.	
						Close Stage I/II fuel pressure regulators.	
						Open Stage I/II fuel tank vent and relief valves.	
TSI				PLPS	052	Desiccant breather valves.	
						Close missile blanketing nitrogen supply valve.	
						Close lox line blanket valve.	
						Open helium transfer valve and regulate to 3100 PSI.	
						Open Stage I/II lox tank vent and relief valves.	
						Close Stage I/II lox pressure regulator.	
						Open Stage I/II lox fill and drain valves.	Stage I/II lox tank vent and relief valves open.
						Turn on lox vent exhaust blower.	Stage I/II lox tank vent and relief valves open.

Figure 3-33. Launch Countdown System Functions (Operational Bases) (Sheet 4 of 39)

3-151

T.O. 21-SM68-1 Section III

TIME	REF	ROUTINE COMMAND	SOURCE	DESTINATION	REF	SUB-COMMAND	PREREQUISITES
TSI		(Continued)		PLPS	052	Close lox storage tank vent valve.	Lox storage tank above minimum level.
						Open Stage I/II lox fine load valves.	Lox storage tank above minimum level.
						Open Stage I/II lox rapid load valves.	Lox storage tank above minimum level.
						Open Stage I/II lox topping control valves.	
						Open lox transfer pressure valve(s) and regulate to set point 1.	Lox storage tank vent valve closed.
						(After incorporation of TCTO 31X3-10-11-621) Open lox transfer pressure valve(s) and regulate to set point 2.	
						Open Stage I/II lox line end valves.	Stage I/II lox tank vent valves and lox fill and drain valves open.
						Open Stage I/II lox topping line end valves.	Stage I/II lox tank vent valves and lox fill and drain valves open.
						Close warm helium line valve.	

Figure 3-33. Launch Countdown System Functions (Operational Bases) (Sheet 5 of 39)

Changed 18 December 1963 TOCN-1 (DEN-5)

3-152

T.O. 21-SM68-1   Section III

TIME	REF	ROUTINE COMMAND	SOURCE	DESTINATION	REF	SUB-COMMAND	PREREQUISITES
TSI		(Continued)				Open cold helium line valve.	Nitrogen unloading supply valve closed.
						Open Stage I/II primary pressure regulators.	
T-870	072	Apply missile 400 CPS (M)	LS	ES	008	Energize 400 CPS bus to AOE.	400 CPS generator output up to 90 percent of rated voltage.
				ES		Apply 400 CPS ground power to missile AC bus.	
				ES		Energize missile inverter output transfer relay.	
				ES		Initiate monitoring for missile AC and DC.	
				ES	072	Voltages and air conditioning unit on.	
						(After incorporation of TCTO 21-SM68-790) Apply 28 VDC sensor power.	
T-870	076	Transfer gyro monitor (C)	ES	FCS		De-energize 28 VDC gyro standby heaters.	28 VDC and 400 CPS power on missile buses.

Figure 3-33. Launch Countdown System Functions (Operational Bases) (Sheet 6 of 39)

Changed 18 December 1963 TOCN-1 (DEN-5)   3-153

TIME	REF	ROUTINE COMMAND	SOURCE	DESTINATION	REF	SUB-COMMAND	PREREQUISITES
T-870		(Continued)				Reset missile programmer and verify reset. Reset verification readout delayed to item 144.	
T-850	085	Lox loading (C)	PLPS				
				CCC		LOX LOADING white on LCC.	(Prior to incorporation of TCTO 21-SM68-853) Lox storage tank fully pressurized, lox rapid load valves open, and lox in Stage I/II umbilicals.
							(After incorporation of TCTO 21-SM68-853) Lox storage tank fully pressurized and lox rapid load valves open.
				PLPS	052	(Prior to incorporation of TCTO 31X3-10-11-621) Regulate lox transfer pressure valve(s) to set point 2.	(Prior to incorporation of TCTO 21-SM68-853) Lox in Stage I/II fill lines and umbilicals.
						Energize Stage I lox fill and drain valve heater.	Lox in Stage I umbilical.
T-820				GGS	081	Adjust constants register 6 (manual). Enter meteorological data.	Data from latest measurement.

Figure 3-33. Launch Countdown System Functions (Operational Bases) (Sheet 7 of 39)

T.O. 21-SM68-1　　　Section III

TIME	REF	ROUTINE COMMAND	SOURCE	DESTINATION	REF	SUB-COMMAND	PREREQUISITES
T-820	080	Launcher power pack operating (C)	LCS				Launcher power pack operating properly.
				LS		Provide ready to raise prerequisite.	
				GGS	040	POWER ON pushbutton indicator green on MGC.	GGS in full power on condition.
						Press START GUID X pushbutton indicator on MGC.	POWER ON pushbutton indicator green.
						START GUID X pushbutton indicator white on MGC.	START GUID X pushbutton indicator pressed.
T-700	104	Start hydraulics (M)	LS	PLPS		Check 28 VDC sensor power applied.	400 CPS power present on missile bus.
				ES		Start ground hydraulic unit.	

Figure 3-33. Launch Countdown System Functions (Operational Bases) (Sheet 7A of 39)

Changed 18 December 1963　TOCN-1 (DEN-5)　　　3-154A

T.O. 21-SM68-1　　　　　　　　　　　　　　　　　　　　Section III

TIME	REF	ROUTINE COMMAND	SOURCE	DESTINATION	REF	SUB-COMMAND	PREREQUISITES
T-580				GGS	040	MAG RDY indicator white on MGC.	Approximately five minute time delay elapsed.
						Press MAG ON pushbutton indicator on MGC.	MAG RDY indicator white.
						MAG ON pushbutton indicator white on MGC.	MAG ON pushbutton indicator pressed.
						MAG ON pushbutton indicator green on MGC.	Magnetron power on and missing pulses within tolerance.
T-570				FCS	076	Transfer from standby to operating gyro temperature monitor.	Item 076 received and approximately five minute delay expired.
T-470				PLPS	052	Close Stage I/II lox rapid load valves.	Stage I/II lox tanks 95 percent full.
T-360				GGS	040	START GUID X pushbutton indicator green on MGC.	Guidance exercise complete.
T-281	136	Lox loaded (C)	PLPS	CCC		LOX LOADED white on LCC.	Stage I/II lox tanks 100 percent full and Stage I/II helium tanks at normal pressure. (Normal clock jump time is approximately T-420).
				PLPS		Initiate monitoring of Stage I/II lox tanks above 95 percent level.	Stage I/II lox tanks 100 percent full.

Figure 3-33. Launch Countdown System Functions (Operational Bases) (Sheet 8 of 39)

T.O. 21-SM68-1

Section III

TIME	REF	ROUTINE COMMAND	SOURCE	DESTINATION	REF	SUB-COMMAND	PREREQUISITES
T-281	136	(Continued)		PLPS		Close Stage I/II lox fine load valves.	
				PLPS		Close Stage I/II lox line end valves.	
					136	Open Stage I/II lox line vent valves.	Stage I/II lox rapid load and lox fine load valves closed.
				LS		Throttle Stage I/II lox topping control valves.	
						Provide ready to raise prerequisite.	
T-281	144	Check ready to raise (M)	LS	PLPS		Check item 136 initiated and initiate monitoring for helium tanks above minimum pressures.	
				TCS		Unfreeze target go status.	
				TDB		Stop countdown timer clock at first hold position.	
						Start digital hold time indicator.	
				FCS		Unfreeze FCS go status.	

Figure 3-33. Launch Countdown System Functions (Operational Bases) (Sheet 9 of 39)

3-156

T.O. 21-SM68-1 Section III

TIME	REF	ROUTINE COMMAND	SOURCE	DESTINATION	REF	SUB-COMMAND	PREREQUISITES
T-281	144	(Continued)				Check gyro spin motors operating.	
						Check programmer reset.	
						Check gyro temperatures.	
						Check engine nulls.	
				FCS	144	Check missile 25 VDC.	
				RVS		Unfreeze RVS go status.	
						Check R/V fuze setting.	
						Check arming and fuzing safety monitor (Mark 4 R/V only).	
				ES		Initiate monitoring of Stage I/II missile hydraulic reservoir levels.	
T-281	152	Check power pack (M)	LS	LCS		Check launcher power pack operating properly.	
First hold	160	Ready to raise (C)	LS				Launcher power pack operating (item 080), lox loaded (item 136), missile/facility go, first timing sequence completed, and launcher raising enabled from CCC and either launch

Figure 3-33. Launch Countdown System Functions (Operational Bases) (Sheet 10 of 39)

3-157

T.O. 21-SM68-1　　　　Section III

TIME	REF	ROUTINE COMMAND	SOURCE	DESTINATION	REF	SUB-COMMAND	PREREQUISITES
First hold	160	(Continued)					Enabled from LES or exercise enables.
T-279.9	179	Start launcher raising	LC	CCC		RAISE LAUNCHER indicator green on LCC.	RAISE LAUNCHER push-button pressed.
T-279.9	180	Launcher raising started (C)	LS	LS		Start second timing sequence.	Ready to raise (item 160).
				CCC		RAISE LAUNCHER indicator white on LCC.	Second timing sequence started.
						Disable ready to raise on other two missiles.	
						Disable ready to lower on other two missiles.	
				PLPS		Discontinue monitoring lox above 95%.	
						Open Stage I/II missile fuel storage valves.	Not in exercise mode.
						Simulate Stage I/II missile fuel storage valves open.	In exercise mode.

Figure 3-33. Launch Countdown System Functions (Operational Bases) (Sheet 11 of 39)

Changed 18 December 1963　TOCN-1 (DEN-5)　　　　3-158

T.O. 21-SM68-1 Section III

TIME	REF	ROUTINE COMMAND	SOURCE	DESTINATION	REF	SUB-COMMAND	PREREQUISITES
T-279.9	180	(Continued)		ECS		Energize gas generator valve pilot valve open solenoid (GGVPV).	
				TCS		Freeze target go status.	
				TDB	180	Restart countdown timer clock.	
						Stop digital hold time indicator and reset to zero.	
				RVS		Freeze RVS go status.	
				FCS		Freeze FCS go status.	
		(After incorporation of TCTO 21-SM68-859) Fuel storage valves opened.	PLPS	CCC		Turn on white FUEL PRE-VALVES OPEN indicator on LCC.	
T-279.9	184	Raise launcher (M)	LS				Second timing sequence started.
				ES		(After incorporation of TCTO 31X3-10-12-545) Discontinue monitoring of missile AC, DC and air conditioning.	
				LCS		Fill cable equalizer measuring vessel.	
						Insert horizontal crib lock.	

Figure 3-33. Launch Countdown System Functions (Operational Bases) (Sheet 12 of 39)

Changed 18 December 1963 TOCN-1 (DEN-5)   3-159

T.O. 21-SM68-1　　Section III

TIME	REF	ROUTINE COMMAND	SOURCE	DESTINATION	REF	SUB-COMMAND	PREREQUISITES
T-279.9	184	(Continued)					
T-279.9			CCC	LCS	184	Close flame deflector water valve.	
T-279.9						Close engine compartment water valve.	Flame deflector water spray valve closed.
T-279.9	192	Raise antenna (C)		GGS	192	RAISE ANT indicator white on MGC.	Item 180 received.
						Press ANT RAISE pushbutton indicator on MGC (manual).	RAISE ANT indicator white.
						ANT RAISE pushbutton indicator white on MGC.	ANT RAISE pushbutton indicator pressed.
T-250				LCS	184	Insert vertical crib lock.	Horizontal crib lock inserted.
						Insert oblique crib locks.	Horizontal crib lock inserted.
T-250	224	Stop topping (M).	LS	PLPS		Open FCV-201 and FCV-202.	
						(After incorporation of TCTO 31X3-10-11-617) Discontinue monitoring helium pressure switches.	

Figure 3-33. Launch Countdown System Functions (Operational Bases) (Sheet 13 of 39)

Changed 18 December 1963　TOCN-1 (DEN-5)　　3-160

T.O. 21-SM68-1

TIME	REF	ROUTINE COMMAND	SOURCE	DESTINATION	REF	SUB-COMMAND	PREREQUISITES
T-250	224	(Continued)				(After incorporation of TCTO 31X3-10-11-613) Check fuel pre-valves open.	
						Open lox storage tank vent valve.	
						Close lox transfer pressure control valve(s).	
						Close Stage I/II lox topping line end valves. Close Stage I/II lox fill and drain valves.	Stage I/II lox line end valves and lox topping line end valves closed.
						Open Stage I/II lox umbilical drain valves.	Stage I/II lox fill and drain valves closed.
						Open Stage I/II lox umbilical purge valves.	Stage I/II lox fill and drain valves closed.
T-250				PLPS	224	Open lox return line vent valve.	Stage I/II lox umbilical drain valves open.
						Open lox drain line vent valve.	Stage I/II lox umbilical drain valves open.
						Close lox drain blanket valve.	Lox drain line vent valve or lox return line vent valve open.

Figure 3-33. Launch Countdown System Functions (Operational Bases) (Sheet 14 of 39)

T.O. 21-SM68-1 Section III

TIME	REF	ROUTINE COMMAND	SOURCE	DESTINATION	REF	SUB-COMMAND	PREREQUISITES
T-250	224	(Continued)				Close cold helium line valve.	
T-240			PLPS	LCS		Open warm helium line end valve (FCV 604).	
						De-energize Stage I lox fill and drain heater.	No liquid in Stage I umbilical (LS203).
T-235					184	Open upper shelter door.	Crib leveled and locked and measuring vessel filled.
						Activate cable tension equalizer cylinder.	Crib leveled and locked and measuring vessel filled.
						Insert forward spring capsule locks.	
						Insert rear drive base to silo locks.	
T-225	233	Enable umbilicals disconnect (C)	LS	PLPS		(Prior to incorporation of TCTO 31X3-10-11-613) Disconnect Stage I lox fill line (1E1L).	(Prior to incorporation of TCTO 31X3-10-11-613) FCV-215 and FCV-217 open; and either no liquid at the umbilical or no liquid at umbilical drain of each stage; and item 233 received.

Figure 3-33. Launch Countdown System Functions (Operational Bases) (Sheet 15 of 39)

T.O. 21-SM68-1　　　Section III

TIME	REF	ROUTINE COMMAND	SOURCE	DESTINATION	REF	SUB-COMMAND	PREREQUISITES
T-225	233	(Continued)					(After incorporation of TCTO 31X3-10-11-613) FCV-215 and FCV-217 open; no liquid at either umbilical; and item 233 received.
						(Prior to incorporation of TCTO 31X3-10-11-613) Disconnect Stage II lox fill line (3B1L).	(Prior to incorporation of TCTO 31X3-10-11-613) FCV-215 and FCV-217 open; and either no liquid at the umbilical or no liquid at umbilical drain of each stage; and item 233 received.
T-225	235	Start HPC (C)	PLPS	ES		(Prior to incorporation of TCTO 31X3-10-12-545) Discontinue monitoring of missile AC and DC voltages and air conditioning.	(After incorporation of TCTO 31X3-10-11-613) FCV-215 and FCV-217 open; no liquid at either umbilical; and item 233 received.
				LCS		Start launcher raising.	
				ES		Turn off air conditioning.	

Figure 3-33. Launch Countdown System Functions (Operational Bases) (Sheet 16 of 39)

Changed 18 December 1963　TOCN-1 (DEN-5)

T.O. 21-SM68-1 Section III

TIME	REF	ROUTINE COMMAND	SOURCE	DESTINATION	REF	SUB-COMMAND	PREREQUISITES
T-225	235	(Continued)				Start Stage II missile hydraulic pump.	
						Discontinue monitoring of the missile Stage II hydraulic reservoir level for 10 sec minimum.	
T-224				LCS	184	Raise counterweight lifting rod.	
T-215				PLPS	224	(Prior to incorporation of TCTO 31X3-10-11-613) Close Stage I lox umbilical drain valves.	Stage I lox fill line disconnected.
						(Prior to incorporation of TCTO 31X3-10-11-613) Close Stage II lox umbilical drain valves.	Stage II lox fill line disconnected.
						(Prior to incorporation of TCTO 31X3-10-11-613) Close Stage I lox umbilical purge valves.	Stage I lox fill line disconnected.
						(Prior to incorporation of TCTO 31X3-10-11-613) Close Stage II lox umbilical purge valves.	Stage II lox fill line disconnected.
T-214				LCS	184	Open lower shelter door.	Upper shelter door 30 degrees open.
T-209				LCS	184	Release wire rope lock.	Counterweight raised off support.

Figure 3-33. Launch Countdown System Functions (Operational Bases) (Sheet 17 of 39)

Changed 18 December 1963 TOCN-1 (DEN-5)

3-164

TIME	REF	ROUTINE COMMAND	SOURCE	DESTINATION	REF	SUB-COMMAND	PREREQUISITES
T-204				LCS	184	Insert counterweight cylinder (fork).	
T-198				LCS	184	Release counterweights to drive base locks.	
T-197	290	(Prior to incorporation of TCTO 31X3-10-11-613) Umbilicals disconnected (C).	PLPS				Lox lines disconnected.
T-195				LS		Provide retract support mechanisms prerequisite.	Propellant fill lines disconnected (item 290 received).
T-195	304	(Prior to incorporation of TCTO 31X3-10-11-613) Retract support mechanisms (C).	LS	LCS		Retract Stage I lox line (1E1L) support mechanism.	
						Retract Stage II lox line (3B1L) support mechanism.	
T-195	312	(Prior to incorporation of TCTO 31X3-10-11-613) Crib umbilicals disconnected (C).	LS	CCC		CRIB UMB DISC indicator white on LCC.	Item 290 received.

Figure 3-33. Launch Countdown System Functions (Operational Bases) (Sheet 17A of 39)

T.O. 21-SM68-1　　Section III

TIME	REF	ROUTINE COMMAND	SOURCE	DESTINATION	REF	SUB-COMMAND	PREREQUISITES
T-190	318	(Prior to incorporation of TCTO 31X3-10-11-613) Check umbilicals disconnected (M).	LS	PLPS		Check item 290 initiated.	Not in exercise mode.
						Check Stage I/II missile fuel storage valves open.	
						Discontinue monitoring of helium tanks above minimum pressures.	
T-185				LCS	304	Retract launcher platform locks.	Shelter doors opened, crib leveled and locked, counterweight cylinder locks inserted, counterweight support retracted, and umbilical support mechanisms retracted.
						Turn off launcher platform oil pressure.	Launcher platform locks retracted.
T-160	328	Pressurize fuel tanks (M)	LS			Raise launcher platform.	Launcher platform locks retracted.

Figure 3-33. Launch Countdown System Functions (Operational Bases) (Sheet 17B of 39)

T.O. 21-SM68-1

TIME	REF	ROUTINE COMMAND	SOURCE	DESTINATION	REF	SUB-COMMAND	PREREQUISITES
T-160	328	(Continued)		PLPS		Close Stage II fuel tank vent and relief valves.	
						Open Stage I/II fuel secondary pressure regulators.	
						Close Stage I/II lox tank vent valves (two solenoids each vent valve).	Stage I/II lox line end valves and lox topping end valves closed.
T-160				PLPS	328	Turn off lox vent exhaust blower.	Stage I/II lox tank vent and relief valves closed.
						De-energize Stage I/II lox tank vent valve, force close solenoids, and disable force close solenoid control circuit.	Stage I/II lox tank vent and relief valves closed.
T-160			LS	GGS	192	Ant raise pushbutton indicator green on MGC.	Antenna fully raised.
						Initiate level function if required.	Antenna fully raised and blast detected.
T-100	344	Pressurize Stage II lox tank (M)		PLPS		Open Stage II lox secondary pressure regulator.	

Figure 3-33. Launch Countdown System Functions (Operational Bases) (Sheet 18 of 39)

T.O. 21-SM68-1

TIME	REF	ROUTINE COMMAND	SOURCE	DESTINATION	REF	SUB-COMMAND	PREREQUISITES
T-100	352	Activate batteries (m)	LS				System not in exercise mode.
				ES		Start missile 400 CPS inverter.	
				ES		Activate inverter and hydraulic pump batteries.	
T-80	360	Pressurize Stage I lox tank (M)	LS	PLPS	360	Open Stage I lox secondary pressure regulator.	Item 352 received.
				ES		De-energize missile inverter output transfer relay.	
				TCS		Lock up target selection	
				FCS		Change select TARGET number indication from green to white on LCC.	
				FCS		Reset missile programmer.	
T-78	368	Missile tanks pressurized (C)	PLPS	CCC		White MISSILE TANKS PRESS'D white on LCC.	Stage I/II fuel, lox, and helium tanks pressurized.
T-70				LCS	304	Insert launcher platform vertical load locks.	Platform fully raised.

Figure 3-33. Launch Countdown System Functions (Operational Bases) (Sheet 19 of 39)

T.O. 21-SM68-1

TIME	REF	ROUTINE COMMAND	SOURCE	DESTINATION	REF	SUB-COMMAND	PREREQUISITES
T-70		(Continued)				Turn on launcher platform oil pressure.	Platform fully raised.
						Extend flame deflector extension.	Platform fully raised.
T-65				LCS	304	Insert launcher platform lateral load locks.	Vertical load locks inserted.
T-60				LCS	304	Shut off launcher platform drive.	Load locks inserted and flame deflector extended.
T-55	432	Launcher up and locked (c)	LCS				Launcher platform fully up and locked.
				LS		Provide ready to launch prerequisite.	
				LCS		Charge umbilical tower accumulator.	
						Open water supply valve.	Flame deflector and engine compartment water spray valves closed.
				LCS		Replace LCS go signal with launcher ready to fire.	Launcher platform fully up and locked.
T-55	436	Launcher raising completed (c)	LS	CCC		Provide launcher lowering prerequisite.	Item 432 received.

Figure 3-33. Launch Countdown System Functions (Operational Bases) (Sheet 20 of 39)

T.O. 21-SM68-1

TIME	REF	ROUTINE COMMAND	SOURCE	DESTINATION	REF	SUB-COMMAND	PREREQUISITES
T-41 + 30 sec	440	Check launcher up and locked (M)	LS	LCS	440	Check item 432 initiated	T-41 and 30 second time delay elapsed.
T-41	448	Check missile tanks pressurized	LS	FCS		Unfreeze FCS go status	
						Check gyro temperatures	
						Check gyro spin motors operating.	
						Check programmer reset	
						Check missile 25 VDC.	
T-41			LS	GGS	192	Provide missile ready prerequisite.	Antenna level function complete (if run).
Second hold	456	Ready to launch (C)					Launcher up and locked (item 432), missile/facility go, item 548 (GGS operating) not present, second timing sequence completed and ground guidance ready.
				CCC		LAUNCH indicator green on LCC.	
				TDB		Stop countdown timer clock at second hold position.	
						Start digital hold time indicator.	

Figure 3-33. Launch Countdown System Functions (Operational Bases) (Sheet 21 of 39)

T.O. 21-SM68-1　　Section III

TIME	REF	ROUTINE COMMAND	SOURCE	DESTINATION	REF	SUB-COMMAND	PREREQUISITES
T-39.9	464	Start firing sequence.	LCC				LAUNCH pushbutton pressed. Ready to launch.
T-39.9	470	Firing sequence started.	LCC	LS		Start third timing sequence.	
T-39.9	472	Firing sequence started (C)	LS	PLPS	470	Momentarily monitor for Stage I/II fuel, lox, and helium tanks pressure.	Third timing sequence started.
				CCC		LAUNCH indicator white on LCC.	
				TCS		Provide target select prerequisite.	
				TDB		Re-start countdown timer clock.	
				ECS		Stop digital hold time indicator and reset to zero. Arm Stage II airborne sequencer. Open OSBVAP. Close GGVP.	
				FCS		Freeze FCS go status.	

Figure 3-33. Launch Countdown System Functions (Operational Bases) (Sheet 22 of 39)

Changed 18 December 1963　TOCN-1 (DEN-5)　　3-169

T.O. 21-SM68-1   Section III

TIME	REF	ROUTINE COMMAND	SOURCE	DESTINATION	REF	SUB-COMMAND	PREREQUISITES
T-39.9	480	Transfer Power (M)	LS				Third timing sequence started and system not in exercise mode.
				ES		Transfer missile inverter to battery.	Missile inverter battery voltage present.
						Transfer Stage II missile hydraulic pump to battery.	Missile hydraulic battery voltage present.
						Remove ground power from missile battery heater control circuits.	
T-39.9	484	Target select (C)	TCS	GGS		Select designated target program for computer.	Item 472 received.
						SELECT TARGET push-button indicator green on MGC.	Target designated by computer.
T-39.9	488	Missile X ready (1, 2, or 3) (C)	CCC	GGS	488	SELECT LAUNCHER push-button indicator white on MGC.	Item 472 received.
						MISSILE READY indicator white on MGC.	SELECT TARGET push-button indicator green, SELECT LAUNCHER push-button indicator white.

Figure 3-33. Launch Countdown System Functions (Operational Bases) (Sheet 23 of 39)

T.O. 21-SM68-1　　　Section III

TIME	REF	ROUTINE COMMAND	SOURCE	DESTINATION	REF	SUB-COMMAND	PREREQUISITES
T-39.9				GGS	488	Press ACQ MISSILE pushbutton indicator on MGC (manual).	MISSILE READY indicator white.
						SELECT LAUNCHER pushbutton indicator green on MGC.	ACQ MISSILE pushbutton indicator pressed and acquisition in progress.
						ACQ MISSILE pushbutton indicator white on MGC.	Antenna in position and AFC started.
T-35	504	Bleed Stage I lox tank (M)	LS	PLPS		(Prior to incorporation of TCTO 31X3-10-11-617) Open intermittent service pressure regulating valve (FCV 513).	Item 472 received.
						(After incorporation of TCTO 31X3-10-11-617) Open intermittent service pressure regulating valve (FCV-513) and lock PLPS GO.	
				ECS		De-energize GGVPV open Solenoid.	
						Energize GGVPV close solenoid.	

Figure 3-33. Launch Countdown System Functions (Operational Bases) (Sheet 24 of 39)

Changed 18 December 1963　TOCN-1 (DEN-5)　　　3-171

T.O. 21-SM68-1 Section III

TIME	REF	ROUTINE COMMAND	SOURCE	DESTINATION	REF	SUB-COMMAND	PREREQUISITES
T-35	504	(Continued)	ECS			Energize (open) Stage I lox tank bleed valve pilot valve (1 and 2) OSBVPV.	
					488	Energize (open) gas generator oxidizer purge valve (GGOPV).	
						Energize (open) ATPA fuel discharge bleed valve (FDBVAP).	

Figure 3-33. Launch Countdown System Functions (Operational Bases) (Sheet 24A of 39)

T.O. 21-SM68-1   Section III

TIME	REF	ROUTINE COMMAND	SOURCE	DESTINATION	REF	SUB-COMMAND	PREREQUISITES
T-35	504	(Continued)				Energize (open) gas generator valve fuel bleed valve (GGVFBV).	
						Remove arm Stage II airborne sequencer signal.	System not in exercise mode.
T-35	512	Transfer DC bus (M)	LS	ES		Transfer missile DC buses to inverter battery.	
T-35	520	Power transferred (C)	ES	CCC		Arm explosive bolt firing circuits.	Power transfer completed.
						POWER TRANSFERRED indicator white on LCC.	
T-30			GGS	LCS	304	Pre-fill engine and spray lines.	
T-25	536	Guidance locked on (C)		CCC		GUIDANCE LOCKED ON indicator white on LCC.	Missile acquired in frequency, range, azimuth and elevation.
T-25	544	Enable loop check (C)	CCC				Item 536 received.

Figure 3-33. Launch Countdown System Functions (Operational Bases) (Sheet 25 of 39)

T.O. 21-SM68-1 Section III

TIME	REF	ROUTINE COMMAND	SOURCE	DESTINATION	REF	SUB-COMMAND	PREREQUISITES
T-25	544	(Continued)		FCS		Prepare for RGS/FCS loop check.	
T-25	548	GGS Operating (C)	CCC	CCC		Provide initiate loop check prerequisite.	Item 536 received. Note LS monitors item 548 as interlock to prevent generation of enable launcher signal until T + 170.
				LS			
T-25	560	Initiate loop check (C)	CCC	GGS		Initiate guidance commands for loop check: Stage I = pitch up yaw right 2°; Stage II = pitch up yaw right 1.12° verniers = hard over (pitch and yaw).	Item 544 received.
T-18	600	Loop check complete (C)	FCS	CCC		LOOP CHECK COMPL indicator white on LCC.	RGS/FCS loop check completed satisfactorily.
T-18	608	Completed loop check (C)	CCC	GGS		Computer commences guidance program.	Item 600 received.

Figure 3-33. Launch Countdown System Functions (Operational Bases) (Sheet 26 of 39)

3-173

T.O. 21-SM68-1   Section III

TIME	REF	ROUTINE COMMAND	SOURCE	DESTINATION	REF	SUB-COMMAND	PREREQUISITES
T-18	608	(Continued)				Turn ACQ MISSILE pushbutton indicator green on MGC.	Computer commenced guidance program.
T-5	568	Shut off missile nitrogen. (M)	LS	PLPS		Close Stage I/II missile pneumatic nitrogen supply valves.	Item 472 received.
T-5	576	Prepare to fire (M)	LS	LCS		Shut off hydraulic lines to umbilical tower accumulator.	
						Check umbilical tower hydraulic accumulator changed and the main water supply valve open. (if above not accomplished, punch out fault on tape.)	
T-5	584	Check power transferred. (M)	LS	ES		Check item 520 initiated.	System not in exercise mode.
						Check for AC power transferred.	

Figure 3-33. Launch Countdown System Functions (Operational Bases) (Sheet 27 of 39)

3-174

T.O. 21-SM68-1

Section III

TIME	REF	ROUTINE COMMAND	SOURCE	DESTINATION	REF	SUB-COMMAND	PREREQUISITES
T-5	584	(Continued)				Discontinue monitoring of Stage I/II missile hydraulic reservoir levels.	
T-1	624	Check loop check complete. (M)	LS	TCS		Unfreeze target go status.	
				CCC		Provide check ready to guide prerequisites.	
				RVS		Unfreeze RVS go status.	
						Check R/V battery temperature (Mark 3 R/V).	
						Check arming and fuzing continuity (Mark 3 R/V).	
						Check R/V fuze setting.	
						Check arming and fuzing safety monitor (mark 4 R/V).	
						Check warhead safety monitor (mark 4 R/V).	
				FCS		Unfreeze FCS go status.	
						Check item 600 initiated.	

Figure 3-33. Launch Countdown System Functions (Operational Bases) (Sheet 28 of 39)

3-175

T.O. 21-SM68-1

TIME	REF	ROUTINE COMMAND	SOURCE	DESTINATION	REF	SUB-COMMAND	PREREQUISITES
T-1	624	(Continued)				Check gyro temperatures.	
						Check gyro spin motors operating.	
						Check engine nulls.	
						Reset missile programmer.	
						Check missile 25 VDC.	
T-1	632	Check ready to guide (M)	CCC	GGS		Check that computer has commenced guidance program.	Item 624 received.
T-0	640	Firing engines (M)	LS	FCS		Freeze FCS go status.	
						Uncage displacement gyros.	
				RVS		Freeze RVS go status.	
				PLPS		Close helium transfer valve. Close FCV 601/602 and FCV 610.	
						Close intermittent service pressure regulating valve (FCV 513).	

Figure 3-33. Launch Countdown System Functions (Operational Bases) (Sheet 29 of 39)

T.O. 21-SM68-1 Section III

TIME	REF	ROUTINE COMMAND	SOURCE	DESTINATION	REF	SUB-COMMAND	PREREQUISITES
T-0		(Continued)		LS		Interrupt energize RGS signal.	
T-0				CCC		Provide completed launch exercise prerequisite.	
T-0	648	Fire Stage I engines (M)	LS	TCS	640	Freeze target go status.	System not in exercise mode.
				ECS		Remove ground supplied power to Stage II TPA heaters.	
						De-energize (close) Stage I lox bleed valve pilot valve (1 and 2) OSBVPV.	
						De-energize (close) ATPA fuel discharge bleed valve (FDBVAP).	
						De-energize (close) gas generator valve fuel bleed valve (GGVFBV).	
						De-energize Stage I TPA heaters.	

Figure 3-33. Launch Countdown System Functions (Operational Bases) (Sheet 30 of 39)

T.O. 21-SM68-1 Section III

TIME	REF	ROUTINE COMMAND	SOURCE	DESTINATION	REF	SUB-COMMAND	PREREQUISITES
T-0		(Continued)				Energize Stage I thrust chamber igniters (TCIGN).	Power is sensed on GGVPV closed solenoid.
				LS		Energize (open) TPA starter valve (TPAXV).	Power is supplied to TCIGNS.
						Provide internal signal to back up LCS go.	
T-0				ECS	648	De-energize gas generator valve pilot valve close solenoid (GGVPV).	Both TCV 65 percent open (TCV switches actuated).
						Energize Stage I gas generator igniters (GGIGN).	Both TCV 65 percent open (TCV switches actuated).
						Energize GGVPV open solenoid.	Both TCV 65 percent open (TCV switches actuated).
						Close TPA starter valve (TPAXV).	Either GGV 30 percent open (GGV switches actuated).
						De-energize thrust chamber igniters (TCIGN).	Either GGV 30 percent open (GGV switches actuated).
						De-energize (close) gas generator oxidizer de-energize either GGV GGVPV.	Either GGV 30 percent open (GGV switches actuated) either GGV 30 percent open.
						Open solenoid.	(GGV switches actuated).

Figure 3-33. Launch Countdown System Functions (Operational Bases) (Sheet 31 of 39)

T.O. 21-SM68-1

TIME	REF	ROUTINE COMMAND	SOURCE	DESTINATION	REF	SUB-COMMAND	PREREQUISITES
T-0		(Continued)				De-energize Stage I gas generator igniters (GGIGN).	Either GGV 30 percent open (GGV switches actuated).
T+2	656	Start Missile release (C)	ECS				Both thrust chambers up to 440 PSIG (thrust chamber pressure switches actuated for 50 milliseconds).
T+4				ES	656	Fire missile support explosive bolts.	Item 512 received and approximately two seconds time delay 656 received.
T+4						Fire umbilical tower explosive bolts.	Item 512 received and approximately two seconds time delay expired after item 656 received.
T+4	660	Fire bolts (C)	ES	LS		Inhibit automatic shut-down generation.	Item 656 generated.
T+4	664	Lift off (C)		CCC		LIFT OFF indicator white on LCC.	Item 656 received and missile support bolts fired.
T+4			ES	LS	644	Provide enable launcher raising prerequisite.	

Figure 3-33. Launch Countdown System Functions (Operational Bases) (Sheet 32 of 39)

3-179

T.O. 21-SM68-1　　　　　　　　　　　　　　　　　　　　　　　Section III

TIME	REF	ROUTINE COMMAND	SOURCE	DESTINATION	REF	SUB-COMMAND	PREREQUISITES
T+4	672	Missile launched (C)	CCC	GGS		LIFT OFF indicator white on MGC.	Item 664 received.
T+7	680	Check lift off (M)	LS	ES		Check item 664 initiated.	
				GGS		Interrupt item 660.	
T+10				GGS	672	Press GUID IN PROGRESS pushbutton indicator on MGC (Manual).	LIFT OFF WHITE on LCC and missile actually in flight (determined from TV monitor).
T+10	696	Guidance in progress (C)	GGS	CCC		GUID IN PROGRESS pushbutton indicator green on MGC.	GUID IN PROGRESS pushbutton indicator pressed.
				CCC		Provide missile in flight and raise/lower launcher interlock prerequisite.	Guid IN PROGRESS pushbutton indicator pressed.
T+10	704	Missile in flight (C)	CCC	LS		Item 725 locked out until T+170.	Item 696 received.
				PLPS		Close 750 PSI nitrogen supply valve.	

Figure 3-33. Launch Countdown System Functions (Operational Bases) (Sheet 33 of 39)

3-180

T.O. 21-SM68-1 Section III

TIME	REF	ROUTINE COMMAND	SOURCE	DESTINATION	REF	SUB-COMMAND	PREREQUISITES
T+10	712	Ready to lower (C)	LS				Launcher lowering enabled from the CCC (item 436) and launch sequence generates enable lowering signal.
				CCC		LOWER LAUNCHER indicator green on 1CC	
T+170	725	Enable alternate launcher raising (C)	LS				
				CCC		Enable ready to raise on other two missiles of the complex.	
T+XXX				GGS	696	END OF GUID indicator white on MGC.	Guidance satisfactorily completed and 1BDA printed out.
						Press RECYCLE pushbutton indicator on MGC. (Manual)	END OF GUID indicator white.
						RECYCLE pushbutton indicator white on MGC.	RECYCLE pushbutton indicator pressed.
						Drop out launcher and target selections. GGS recycles to prepare for acquisition of next missile.	

Figure 3-33. Launch Countdown System Functions (Operational Bases) (Sheet 34 of 39)

3-181

T.O. 21-SM68-1

TIME	REF	ROUTINE COMMAND	SOURCE	DESTINATION	REF	SUB-COMMAND	PREREQUISITES
T+XXX		(Continued)				RECYCLE pushbutton indicator not lighted on MGC.	Recycle complete.
T+1HR				PLPS	224	Close lox return line vent valve.	Drain line not above minimum vent pressure
						Close lox drain line vent valve.	Drain line not above minimum vent pressure
						Open lox drain blanket valve.	Lox return line vent and drain line vent valves closed.
T+2HR				PLPS	224	Close Stage I/II Lox line vent valves.	Stage I/II fill lines not above minimum vent pressure.
						Open lox line blanket valve	Stage I/II lox line vent valves closed.
H+0	800	Start launcher lowering	LCC	LS		Provide lower launcher prerequisite.	Lower launcher PB actuated.
H+0	808	Launcher lowering started (C)	LS	CCC		Turn on white lower launcher light on LC.	Ready to lower (item 712) and start launcher lowering (item 800).

Figure 3-33. Launch Countdown System Functions (Operational Bases) (Sheet 35 of 39)

T.O. 21-SM68-1

TIME	REF	ROUTINE COMMAND	SOURCE	DESTINATION	REF	SUB-COMMAND	PREREQUISITES
H+0		(Continued)				Disable ready to lower on other launchers.	
						Disable ready to raise on other launchers.	
H+0	816	Launcher lowering started (C)	LS				Ready to lower (item 712) and start launcher lowering (item 800). fire Stage I engines (item 648).
				LCS		Open flame deflector cooling spray valve.	
						Position umbilical tower.	
						Position lower tower umbilical mechanism.	
H+91				LCS	816	Close water supply valve.	
H+101				LCS	816	Retract flame deflector extension.	Engine compartment water spray valve closed.
						Retract launcher platform lateral load locks.	Engine compartment water spray valve closed.

Figure 3-33. Launch Countdown System Functions (Operational Bases) (Sheet 36 of 39)

3-183

T.O. 21-SM68-1

TIME	REF	ROUTINE COMMAND	SOURCE	DESTINATION	REF	SUB-COMMAND	PREREQUISITES
H+117				LCS	816	Drive launcher platform up.	Lateral load locks retracted.
H+122				LCS	816	Retract vertical load locks.	Launcher platform driven up.
H+132				LCS	816	Turn off launcher platform oil pressure.	Vertical load locks retracted.
						Lower launcher platform.	Vertical load locks retracted.
H+252				LCS	816	Pressurize rod end lifting cylinder.	
H+253				LCS	816	Turn on launcher platform oil pressure.	Launcher platform lowered.
						Shut off launcher platform drive.	Launcher platform lowered.
						Close lower shelter door.	Launcher platform lowered.
						Extend Stage I lox vent duct (1C1LV) support mechanism.	Launcher platform lowered.
						Extend Stage II lox vent duct NO. 1 (2B1LV) support mechanism.	Launcher platform lowered.
H+253						Extend Stage II lox vent duct NO. 2 (2B2LV) support mechanism.	Launcher platform lowered.

Figure 3-33. Launch Countdown System Functions (Operational Bases) (Sheet 37 of 39)

T.O. 21-SM68-1

TIME	REF	ROUTINE COMMAND	SOURCE	DESTINATION	REF	SUB-COMMAND	PREREQUISITES
H+254				LCS	816	Open engine compartment water spray valve.	Water supply valve closed.
						Insert counterweight to drive base lock.	
						Close wire rope locks.	Counterweight on support.
H+274				LCS	816	Lower counterweight to seat counterweight.	
H+276				LCS	816	Energize cylinder to introduce slack in cables.	
H+281				LCS	816	Close upper shelter door.	
H+289				LCS	816	Retract foreward spring capsule locks.	Lower shelter door closed.
H+289				LCS	816	Retract rear drive base to silo locks.	
H+294				LCS	816	Release cable equalizer.	Counterweight support lowered.
						Retract horizontal and vertical crib locks.	Counterweight support lowered.
H+324				LCS	816	Retract oblique crib locks.	Horizontal and vertical crib locks retracted.

Figure 3-33. Launch Countdown System Functions (Operational Bases) (Sheet 38 of 39)

T.O. 21-SM68-1　　　　　　　　　　　　　　　　　　　　Section III

TIME	REF	ROUTINE COMMAND	SOURCE	DESTINATION	REF	SUB-COMMAND	PREREQUISITES
H+344	918	Shelter doors closed (C)	LCS				Shelter doors closed and crib fully shock mounted.
				LS		Provide launch sequence complete prerequisite.	Item 918 received subsequent to generation of item 808.
H+344	919	Launch sequence complete (C).	LS	LCS		Shut off power pack pump motors.	
				ES		Turn off operating power to the AOE.	Item 664 initiated and shutdown signal not received.

Figure 3-33. Launch Countdown System Functions (Operational Bases) (Sheet 39 of 39)

Changed 18 December 1963　TOCN-1 (DEN-5)

T.O. 21-SM68-1　　　　　　　　　　　　　Section III

TIME	REF	ROUTINE COMMAND	SOURCE	DESTINATION	REF	SUB-COMMAND	PREREQUISITES
		Note All T times listed in this procedure are approximate times. (M) denotes a momentary signal and (C) denotes a continuous signal.					
TSI	001		LCC				Press PROPELLANTS pushbutton indicator on LCC.
						Start first timing sequence.	Missile/facility go and item 016 not generated.
TSI	008	Launch sequence started (M)	LS	LS			
				ES		Energize 28 VDC operating bus to AOE.	First timing sequence started.
						Energize 60 CPS bus to AOE.	
						Start ground 400 CPS motor-generator.	
						Start ground inverter start unit.	
						Start missile air conditioning unit.	

Figure 3-34. Launch Countdown System Functions (VAFB) (Sheet 1 of 44)

3-187

T.O. 21-SM68-1	Section III

TIME	REF	ROUTINE COMMAND	SOURCE	DESTINATION	REF	SUB-COMMAND	PREREQUISITES
TSI		(Continued)				Energize missile 28 VDC buses.	28 VDC operating bus to AOE energized.
						Apply standby power to the AOE.	
						Energize missile battery heater control circuits.	
				ECS		Energize ECS AOE.	
						Energize (1), (2), and (3) TPA heater switches and apply (3) TPA heater preheat.	
				ECS	008	Reset Stage II airborne sequencer.	
				SECE		Energize SECE.	
				RVS		Energize re-entry vehicle battery heaters (mark 3 R/V only).	
				FCS		Freeze RVS go status.	
						Freeze FCS go status.	

Figure 3-34. Launch Countdown System Functions (VAFB) (Sheet 2 of 44)

3-188

T.O. 21-SM68-1   Section III

TIME	REF	ROUTINE COMMAND	SOURCE	DESTINATION	REF	SUB-COMMAND	PREREQUISITES
TSI	016	Launch sequencer operating (C)	LS				First timing sequence started and 28 VDC operating bus to AOE energized.
				TDB		Start countdown timer clock.	
				CCC		LOAD PROPELLANTS on L.C.	
				LS		Disable manual missile facility no go.	
				TCS		Inhibit exercise mode initiation.	
TSI	024	Start power pack (M)	LS	LCS		Freeze target go status.	First timing sequence started.
				LCS		Start launcher hydraulic.	
TSI	032	Energize RGS (C)	LS	RGS	024	Power pack pump motors.	First timing sequence started.
				GMTS		Energize GMTS.	
						Energize MGS.	

Figure 3-34. Launch Countdown System Functions (VAFB) (Sheet 3 of 44)

3-189

T.O. 21-SM68-1

TIME	REF	ROUTINE COMMAND	SOURCE	DESTINATION	REF	SUB-COMMAND	PREREQUISITES
TSI	040	Countdown started (C).	CCC				
				GGS		START CD indicator white on MGC.	Item 016 received.
TSI				GGS	040	Press POWER ON pushbutton indicator on MGC (Manual).	START CD white.
TSI						POWER ON pushbutton indicator white on MGC.	POWER ON pushbutton indicator pressed.
TSI	052	Start propellant loading (C).	ES				Item 008 received, 28 VDC operating power on AOE buses and missile air conditioning unit on.
				PLPS		Energize 750 PSI pneumatic supply valve (FCV 508) open.	
				PLPS	052	Close Stage I/II fuel pressure regulators.	
						Open Stage I/II fuel tank vent and relief valves.	
						Close Stage I/II lox tank desiccant breather valves.	
						Close missile blanketing nitrogen supply valve.	

Figure 3-34. Launch Countdown System Functions (VAFB) (Sheet 4 of 44)

T.O. 21-SM68-1

Section III

TIME	REF	ROUTINE COMMAND	SOURCE	DESTINATION	REF	SUB-COMMAND	PREREQUISITES
TSI		(Continued)				Close lox line blanket valve.	
						Open helium transfer valve and regulate to 3100 PSI.	Note For aluminum tanks regulate to 550 PSI.
						Open Stage I/II lox tank vent and relief valves.	
						Close Stage I/II lox pressure regulators.	
						Open Stage I/II lox fill and drain valves.	Stage I/II lox tank vent and relief valves open.
						Turn on lox vent exhaust blower.	Stage I/II lox tank vent and relief valves open.
						Close lox storage tank vent valve.	
						Open Stage I/II lox fine load valves.	Lox storage tank above minimum level.
						Open Stage I/II lox rapid load valves.	Lox storage tank above minimum level.
						Open Stage I/II lox topping control valves.	Lox storage tank above minimum level.

Figure 3-34. Launch Countdown System Functions (VAFB) (Sheet 5 of 44)

3-191

T.O. 21-SM68-1   Section III

TIME	REF	ROUTINE COMMAND	SOURCE	DESTINATION	REF	SUB-COMMAND	PREREQUISITES
TSI		(Continued)					
				PLPS	052	Open lox transfer pressure valves and regulate to set point 2.	Lox storage tank vent valve closed.
						Open Stage I/II lox line end valves.	Stage I/II lox tank vent valves and lox fill and drain valves open.
						Open Stage I/II lox topping line end valves.	Stage I/II lox tank vent valves and lox fill and drain valves open.
						Close warm helium line valve.	Nitrogen unloading supply valve closed.
						Open cold helium line valve.	
						Open Stage I/II primary pressure regulators.	
				ES	008	Energize 400 CPS bus to AOE.	400 CPS generator output up to 90 percent of rated voltage.
T-870	072	Apply missile 400 CPS (M)	LS	ES		Apply 400 CPS ground power to missile AC bus.	
						Energize missile inverter output transfer.	

Figure 3-34. Launch Countdown System Functions (VAFB) (Sheet 6 of 44)

T.O. 21-SM68-1 Section III

TIME	REF	ROUTINE COMMAND	SOURCE	DESTINATION	REF	SUB-COMMAND	PREREQUISITES
T-870		(Continued)		ES	072	Relay.	
						Initiate monitoring for missile AC and DC voltages and air conditioning unit on.	
T-870	076	Transfer gyro monitor (C)	ES	FCS		De-energize 28 VDC gyro standby heaters.	28 VDC and 400 CPS power on missile buses.
						Reset missile programmer and verify reset.	
						Reset verification readout delayed to item 144.	
T-850	080	Launcher power pack operating (C).	LCS	LS		Provide ready to raise prerequisite.	
T-850				PLPS	052	Energize Stage I lox fill and drain valve heater.	Launcher power pack operating properly.
T-820				GGS	081	Adjust constants register 6 (manual). Enter meteorological data.	Lox in Stage I umbilical.
							Data from latest measurement.

Figure 3-34. Launch Countdown System Functions (VAFB) (Sheet 7 of 44)

3-193

T.O. 21-SM68-1   Section III

TIME	REF	ROUTINE COMMAND	SOURCE	DESTINATION	REF	SUB-COMMAND	PREREQUISITES
T-820	085	Lox loading (C)	PLPS				Lox storage tank fully pressurized, lox rapid load valves open, and lox in Stage I/II umbilicals.
				CCC		LOX LOADING indicator white on LCC.	
T-730				GGS	040	POWER ON pushbutton indicator green on MGC.	GGS in full power on condition.
				GGS		Press START GUID X pushbutton indicator on MGC.	POWER ON pushbutton indicator green.
				GGS		START GUID X pushbutton indicator white on MGC.	START GUID X pushbutton indicator pressed.
T-700				PLPS	052	Energize Stage II fuel line heater.	Lox in Stage I/II fill lines and umbilicals.
T-700	104	Start hydraulics (M)	LS	ES		Start ground hydraulic unit.	400 CPS power present on missile bus.
				GGS	040	MAG RDY indicator white on MGC.	Approximately 5-minute time delay elapsed.
						Press MAG ON pushbutton indicator on MGC (manual).	MAG RDY white.
						MAG ON pushbutton indicator white on MGC.	MAG ON pushbutton indicator pressed.

Figure 3-34. Launch Countdown System Functions (VAFB) (Sheet 8 of 44)

TIME	REF	ROUTINE COMMAND	SOURCE	DESTINATION	REF	SUB-COMMAND	PREREQUISITES
T-700		(Continued)				MAG ON pushbutton indicator green on MGC.	Magnetron power on and missing pulses within tolerance.
T-570				FCS	076	Transfer from standby to operating gyro temperature monitor.	Item 076 received and approximately 5-minute time delay expired.
T-470				PLPS	052	Close Stage I/II lox rapid load valves.	Stage I/II lox tanks 95 percent full.
						Regulate helium transfer valve to 3000 PSI.	Stage I/II lox tanks 95 percent full. Note sub-command and prerequisite are for aluminum tanks only.
T-360				GGS	040	START GUID X pushbutton indicator green on MGC.	Guidance exercise complete.
T-281	136	Lox loaded (C)	PLPS	CCC		LOX LOADED indicator white on LCC.	Stage I/II lox tanks 100 percent full and Stage I/II helium tanks at normal pressure.
				PLPS	136	Initiate monitoring of Stage I/II lox tanks above 95 percent level.	
						Close Stage I/II lox fine load valves.	Stage I/II lox tanks 100 percent full.

Figure 3-34. Launch Countdown System Functions (VAFB) (Sheet 9 of 44)

T.O. 21-SM68-1　　　　　　　　　　　　　　　　　　Section III

TIME	REF	ROUTINE COMMAND	SOURCE	DESTINATION	REF	SUB-COMMAND	PREREQUISITES
T-281		(Continued)				Close Stage I/II lox line end valves.	
						Open Stage I/II lox line vent valves.	Stage I/II lox rapid load and lox fine load valves closed.
				LS		Throttle Stage I/II lox topping control valves.	
						Provide ready to raise prerequisite.	
T-281	144	Check ready to raise (M)	LS	PLPS		Check item 136 initiated and initiate monitoring for helium tanks and helium accumulators above minimum pressure.	
				TCS		Unfreeze target go status.	
				TDB		Stop countdown timer clock at first hold position.	
				FCS	144	Start digital hold time indicator. Unfreeze FCS go status.	

Figure 3-34. Launch Countdown System Functions (VAFB) (Sheet 10 of 44)

3-196

T.O. 21-SM68-1 Section III

TIME	REF	ROUTINE COMMAND	SOURCE	DESTINATION	REF	SUB-COMMAND	PREREQUISITES
T-281		(Continued)				Check gyro spin motors operating.	
						Check programmer reset.	
						Check gyro temperatures.	
						Check engine nulls.	
						Check missile 25 VDC.	
				RVS		Unfreeze RVS go status.	
						Check R/V battery temperature (mark 3 R/V only).	
						Check arming and fuzing continuity (mark 3 R/V only).	
						Check R/V fuze setting.	
						Check arming and fuzing safety monitor (mark 4 R/V only).	
						Check warhead safety monitor (mark 4 R/V only).	
				A.S.S.		Initiate monitoring of Stage I/II missile hydraulic reservoir levels.	

Figure 3-34. Launch Countdown System Functions (VAFB) (Sheet 11 of 44)

T.O. 21-SM68-1   Section III

TIME	REF	ROUTINE COMMAND	SOURCE	DESTINATION	REF	SUB-COMMAND	PREREQUISITES
T-281		(Continued)		S.E.C.E.		Check temperature of Stage I oxidizer bearings.	
				S.E.C.E.	144	Check temperature of Stage II oxidizer bearings.	
						Check temperature of Stage II auxiliary pump oxidizer bearing.	
T-281	152	Check power pack (M)	LS	L.C.S.		Check launcher power pack operating properly.	
T-281	163		CP	IMLO		Notify MLO clear to continue launch.	
	164	Report range clearance	IMLO	MLO		Report range go to MLO.	
	165		CP/IMLO	MLO		Verify LES enable.	
	166		MLO	MLO		Verify EXERCISE push-button pressed and system in launch mode countdown.	
First hold	167	Initiate raise launcher phase	MLO	PA system		Announce: "Attention all stations, on my mark the raise launcher phase will begin. Mark."	

Figure 3-34. Launch Countdown System Functions (VAFB) (Sheet 12 of 44)

3-198

T.O. 21-SM68-1　　　　　　　　　　　　　　　　　　　　　　　　　　　　　　Section III

TIME	REF	ROUTINE COMMAND	SOURCE	DESTINATION	REF	SUB-COMMAND	PREREQUISITES
First hold	160	Ready to raise (C)	LS				Launcher power pack operating (item 080), lox loaded (item 136), missile/facility go, first timing sequence completed, and launcher raising enabled from CCC and either launch enabled from LES or exercise enabled.
T-279.9 T-280	179	Start launcher raising.	LC	CCC		RAISE LAUNCHER indicator green on LCC.	RAISE LAUNCHER pushbutton pressed.
T-279.9	180	Launcher raising started (C)	LS	LS		Start second timing sequence.	Ready to raise (item 160).
				CCC		RAISE LAUNCHER indicator white on LCC.	Second timing sequence started.
						Disable ready to raise on other two missiles.	
						Disable ready to lower on other two missiles.	

Figure 3-34. Launch Countdown System Functions (VAFB) (Sheet 13 of 44)

T.O. 21-SM68-1　　　　　　　　　　　　　　　　　　　　　　　　Section III

TIME	REF	ROUTINE COMMAND	SOURCE	DESTINATION	REF	SUB-COMMAND	PREREQUISITES
T-279.9		(Continued)		PLPS		Open Stage I/II missile fuel storage valves.	Not in exercise mode.
				ECS		Energize gas generator valve pilot valve open solenoid (GGVPV).	
				TCS		Freeze target go status.	
				TDB		Restart countdown timer clock.	
						Stop digital hold time indicator and reset to zero.	
				RVS		Freeze RVS go status.	
				FCS		Freeze FCS go status.	
T-279.9	182	Fuel storage valves open (C).	PLPS	LS		Enable fuel storage valves opened signal.	Fuel storage valves open.
T-279.9	184	Raise launcher (M)	LS	LCS		Fill cable equalizer measuring vessel.	Second timing sequence started.

Figure 3-34. Launch Countdown System Functions (VAFB) (Sheet 14 of 44)

T.O. 21-SM68-1 Section III

TIME	REF	ROUTINE COMMAND	SOURCE	DESTINATION	REF	SUB-COMMAND	PREREQUISITES
T-279.9		(Continued)				Insert horizontal crib lock.	
T-279.9				LCS	184	Close flame deflector water valve.	Flame deflector water spray valve closed.
T-279.9	192	Raise antenna (C)	CCC	GGS		Close engine compartment water valve.	Item 180 received.
					192	RAISE ANT indicator white on MGC.	RAISE ANT white lamp on.
						Press ANT RAISE pushbutton indicator on MGC (manual).	ANT RAISE pushbutton indicator pressed.
				LCS	184	ANT RAISE pushbutton indicator white on MGC.	Horizontal crib lock inserted.
T-250						Insert vertical crib lock.	Horizontal crib lock inserted.
T-250	224	Stop topping (M).	LS	PLPS		Insert oblique crib locks.	
						Check Stage I/II missile fuel storage valves open. Discontinue	

Figure 3-34. Launch Countdown System Functions (VAFB) (Sheet 15 of 44)

T.O. 21-SM68-1 Section III

TIME	REF	ROUTINE COMMAND	SOURCE	DESTINATION	REF	SUB-COMMAND	PREREQUISITES
T-250		(Continued)				monitoring of helium tanks and helium accumulators above minimum pressures.	
						Open lox storage tank vent valve.	
						Close lox transfer pressure control valve (S).	
						Close Stage I/II lox topping line end valves.	
						Close Stage I/II lox fill and drain valves.	Stage I/II lox line end valves and lox topping line end valves closed.
						Open Stage I/II lox umbilical drain valves.	Stage I/II lox fill and drain valves closed.
						Open Stage I/II lox umbilical purge valves.	Stage I/II lox fill and drain valves closed.
						Open lox return line vent valve.	Stage I/II lox fill and drain valves closed.
						Open lox drain line vent valve.	Stage I/II lox fill and drain valves closed.
						Close lox drain blanket valve.	Lox drain line vent valve or lox return line vent valve open.

Figure 3-34. Launch Countdown System Functions (VAFB) (Sheet 16 of 44)

T.O. 21M-HGM25A-1-1 (21-SM68-1)　　　Section III

TIME	REF	ROUTINE COMMAND	SOURCE	DESTINATION	REF	SUB-COMMAND	PREREQUISITES
T-160		(Continued)		PLPS (CONT)		Close Stage I/II lox tank vent valves (two solenoids each vent valve).	Stage I/II lox line end valves and lox topping line end valves closed.
T-160				PLPS	328	Turn off lox vent exhaust blower.	Stage I/II lox tank vent and relief valves closed.
T-160						De-energize Stage I/II lox tank vent valve, force close solenoids, and disable force close solenoid control circuit.	Stage I/II lox tank vent and relief valves closed.
T-160				GGS	192	ANT RAISE pushbutton indicator green on MGC.	Antenna fully raised.
T-100	344	Pressurize Stage II lox tank (M)	LS	PLPS		Initiate level function if required.	Antenna fully raised and blast detected.
T-100				PLPS		Open Stage II lox secondary pressure regulator.	
T-100	352	Activate batteries (M)	LS	ES	352	Start missile 400 CPS inverter.	System not in exercise mode.

Figure 3-34. Launch Countdown System Functions (VAFB) (Sheet 17 of 37)

T.O. 21M-HGM25A-1-1 (21-SM68-1) Section III

TIME	REF	ROUTINE COMMAND	SOURCE	DESTINATION	REF	SUB-COMMAND	PREREQUISITES
T-100		(Continued)		ES (CONT)		Activate inverter and hydraulic pump batteries.	
T-80	360	Pressurize Stage I lox tank (M)	LS	PLPS		Open Stage I lox secondary pressure regulator.	
				ES		De-energize missile inverter output transfer relay.	Item 352 received.
				TCS		Lock up target selection.	
				FCS		Change TARGET SELECTION number from green to white on LCC.	
						Reset missile programmer.	
T-75	368	Missile tanks pressurized (C)	PLPS	CCC		MISSILE TANKS PRESS'D indicator white on LCC.	Stage I/II fuel, lox, and helium tanks pressurized.
T-62				LCS	304	Insert launcher platform vertical load locks.	Platform fully raised.
						Turn on launcher platform oil pressure.	Platform fully raised.

Figure 3-34. Launch Countdown System Functions (VAFB) (Sheet 18 of 37)

Changed 17 June 1964 TOCN DEN 18 3-204

T.O. 21M-HGM25A-1-1 (21-SM68-1) Section III

TIME	REF	ROUTINE COMMAND	SOURCE	DESTINATION	REF	SUB-COMMAND	PREREQUISITES
T-62		(Continued)		LCS (CONT)		Extend flame deflector extension.	Platform fully raised.
T-52					304	Insert launcher platform lateral load locks.	Vertical load locks inserted.
T-42					304	Shut off launcher platform drive.	Platform fully raised and load locks inserted.
T-40	432	Launcher up and locked (C)	LCS	LS		Provide ready to launch prerequisite.	Launcher platform fully up and locked.
				LCS		Charge umbilical tower accumulator.	
						Open launcher platform water supply valve.	Flame deflector and engine compartment water spray valves closed.
T-40	436	Launcher raising completed (C)	LS	CCC		Pre-fill engine compartment water spray lines.	Launcher platform water supply valve opening.
T-40 (+30 sec.)	440	Check launcher up and locked (M)	LS			Provide launcher lowering prerequisite.	Item 432 received.

Figure 3-34. Launch Countdown System Functions (VAFB) (Sheet 19 of 37)

Changed 17 June 1964   TOCN DEN 18

3-205

T.O. 21M-HGM25A-1-1 (21-SM68-1)　　Section III

TIME	REF	ROUTINE COMMAND	SOURCE	DESTINATION	REF	SUB-COMMAND	PREREQUISITES
T-40		(Continued)		LCS	440	Check item 432 initiated.	
				FCS		Unfreeze FCS go status.	
						Check gyro temperatures.	
						Check gyro spin motors operating.	
						Check programmer reset.	
						Check missile 25 VDC.	
T-40	456	Ready to launch (C)	LS	GGS	192	Provide missile ready prerequisite.	Antenna level function complete (if run).
Second Hold							Launcher up and locked (item 432), missile/facility go, item 548 (GGS operating) not present, second timing sequence completed, and ground guidance go.
				CCC		LAUNCH indicator green on LCG.	
				TDB		Stop countdown timer clock at second hold position.	
						Start digital hold time indicator.	
T-39.9		Check missile tanks pressurized (M)	LS				LAUNCH pushbutton pressed.

Figure 3-34. Launch Countdown System Functions (VAFB) (Sheet 20 of 37)

T.O. 21M-HGM25A-1-1 (21-SM68-1) Section III

TIME	REF	ROUTINE COMMAND	SOURCE	DESTINATION	REF	SUB-COMMAND	PREREQUISITES
T-39.9	464	Start firing sequence.	LCC	PLPS		Momentarily monitor for Stage I/II fuel, lox, and helium tanks pressures.	
				LS		Start third timing sequence.	Ready to launch.
T-39.9	472	Firing sequence started (C).	LS	CCC		LAUNCH indicator white on LCC.	Third timing sequence started.
				TCS		Provide target select prerequisite.	
				TDB		Re-start countdown timer clock.	
						Stop digital hold time indicator and reset to zero.	
				ECS		Arm Stage II airborne sequencer.	
				FCS		Freeze FCS go status.	
T-39.9	480	Transfer power (M)	LS	ES		Transfer missile inverter to battery.	Third timing sequence started and system not in exercise mode. Missile inverter battery voltage present.

Figure 3-34. Launch Countdown System Functions (VAFB) (Sheet 21 of 37)

Changed 17 June 1964 TOCN DEN 18   3-207

T.O. 21M-HGM25A-1-1 (21-SM68-1) Section III

TIME	REF	ROUTINE COMMAND	SOURCE	DESTINATION	REF	SUB-COMMAND	PREREQUISITES
T-39.9		(Continued)		ES (CONT)		Transfer Stage II missile hydraulic pump to battery.	Missile hydraulic battery voltage present.
						Remove ground power from missile battery heater control circuits.	
T-39.9	484	Target select (C)	TCS	GGS		Select designated target program for computer.	Item 472 received.
						SELECT TARGET pushbutton indicator green on MGC.	Target designated by computer.
T-39.9	488	Missile X ready (1, 2, or 3) (C)	CCC	GGS		SELECT LAUNCHER pushbutton indicator white on MGC.	Item 472 received.
T-39.9					488	MISSILE READY indicator white on MGC.	SELECT TARGET pushbutton indicator green and SELECT LAUNCHER pushbutton indicator white.
						Press ACQ MISSILE pushbutton indicator on MGC (manual).	MISSILE READY white.
						SELECT LAUNCHER pushbutton indicator green on MGC.	ACQ MISSILE pressed and acquisition in progress.

Figure 3-34. Launch Countdown System Functions (VAFB) (Sheet 22 of 37)

T.O. 21-SM68-1 Section III

TIME	REF	ROUTINE COMMAND	SOURCE	DESTINATION	REF	SUB-COMMAND	PREREQUISITES
T-41	432	Launcher up and locked (C)	LCS				Launcher platform fully up and locked.
				LS		Provide ready to launch prerequisite.	
				LCS		Charge umbilical tower accumulator.	
						Open water supply valve.	Flame deflector and engine compartment water spray valves closed.
T-41	436	Launcher raising completed (C)	LS	CCC		Provide launcher lowering prerequisite.	Item 432 received.
	174	Check IRSS ready	PMR/MFSO	O&C		REPORT and COMMAND RSOA green.	
	175	Clear to launch	PMR/MFSO	MLO		Report clear to launch, RANGE green and LAUNCH green.	
						WARNING	
						Maximum hold time is 30 SEC on digital hold time clock.	
	440	Check launcher up and locked	LS				T-41 and 30-second time delay elapsed.

Figure 3-34. Launch Countdown System Functions (VAFB) (Sheet 23 of 44)

TIME	REF	ROUTINE COMMAND	SOURCE	DESTINATION	REF	SUB-COMMAND	PREREQUISITES
T-41		(Continued)			440	Check item 432 initiated.	
T-41	448	Check missile tanks pressurized (M)	LS	LCS			
				PLPS		Initiate monitoring for Stage I/II fuel, lox and helium tanks and helium accumulators above minimum pressures.	
						Initiate monitoring of Stage I/II helium tank and accumulator over-pressure switches.	
				FCS		Unfreeze FCS go status.	
						Check gyro spin motors operating.	
						Check programmer reset.	
						Check missile 25 VDC.	
T-41				GGS	192	Provide missile ready prerequisite.	Antenna level function complete (if run).
Second Hold	456	Ready to launch (C)	LS				Launcher up and locked (item 432), missile/facility go, item 548 (GGS operating) not present, second timing sequence completed and ground guidance go.

Figure 3-34. Launch Countdown System Functions (VAFB) (Sheet 24 of 44)

T.O. 21-SM68-1 Section III

TIME	REF	ROUTINE COMMAND	SOURCE	DESTINATION	REF	SUB-COMMAND	PREREQUISITES
Second Hold		(Continued)		CCC		LAUNCH indicator green on LCC.	
				TDB		Stop countdown timer clock at second hold position.	
						Start digital hold time indicator.	
T-39.9	464	Start firing sequence.	LCC	LS		Start third timing sequence.	Launch PB actuated. Ready to launch.
T-39.9	472	Firing sequence started (C)	LS	CCC		LAUNCH indicator white on LCC.	Third timing sequence started.
				TCS		Provide target select prerequisite.	
				TDB		Re-start countdown timer clock.	
					472	Stop digital hold time indicator and reset to zero.	
				ECS		Arm Stage II airborne sequencer.	
				FCS		Freeze FCS go status.	

Figure 3-34. Launch Countdown System Functions (VAFB) (Sheet 25 of 44)

3-211

T.O. 21-SM68-1 Section III

TIME	REF	ROUTINE COMMAND	SOURCE	DESTINATION	REF	SUB-COMMAND	PREREQUISITES
T-39.9	480	Transfer power (M)	LS				Third timing sequence started and system not in exercise mode.
				ES		Transfer missile inverter to battery.	Missile inverter battery voltage present.
						Transfer Stage II missile hydraulic pump to battery.	Missile hydraulic battery voltage present.
						Remove ground power from missile battery heater control circuits.	
T-39.9	484	Target select (C)	TCS	GGS		Select designated target program for computer.	Item 472 received.
T-39.9	488	Missile X ready (1, 2, or 3) (C)	CCC			SELECT TARGET pushbutton indicator green on MGC.	Target designated by computer.
						SELECT LAUNCHER pushbutton indicator white on MGC.	Item 472 received.
T-39.9				GGS	488	MISSILE READY indicator white on MGC.	SELECT TARGET pushbutton indicator green and SELECT LAUNCHER pushbutton indicator white.

Figure 3-34. Launch Countdown System Functions (VAFB) (Sheet 26 of 44)

T.O. 21-SM68-1   Section III

TIME	REF	ROUTINE COMMAND	SOURCE	DESTINATION	REF	SUB-COMMAND	PREREQUISITES
T-39.9				GGS	488	Press ACQ MISSILE pushbutton indicator on MGC (manual).	MISSILE READY white.
						SELECT LAUNCHER pushbutton indicator green on MGC.	ACQ MISSILE pressed and acquisition in progress.
						ACQ MISSILE pushbutton indicator white on MGC.	Antenna in position and AFC started.
T-35	504	Bleed Stage I lox tank (M)	LS	PLPS		Open intermittent service pressure regulating valve (FCV 513).	Item 472 received.
				ECS		De-energize GGVPV open solenoid.	
						Energize GGVPV close solenoid.	
						Energize (open) Stage I lox tank bleed valve pilot valve (1 and 2) OSBVPV.	
						Energize (open) gas generator oxidizer purge valve (GGOPV).	
						Energize (open) ATPA fuel discharge bleed valve (FDBVAP).	

Figure 3-34. Launch Countdown System Functions (VAFB) (Sheet 27 of 44)

3-213

T.O. 21-SM68-1   Section III

TIME	REF	ROUTINE COMMAND	SOURCE	DESTINATION	REF	SUB-COMMAND	PREREQUISITES
T-35		(Continued)				Energize (open) gas generator valve fuel bleed valve (GGVFBV).	
						Remove arm Stage II airborne sequencer signal.	
T-35	512	Transfer DC bus (M)	LS	SECE		Check Stage I thrust chamber and gas generator igniter continuities.	
				ES		Transfer missile DC buses to inverter battery.	System not in exercise mode.
						Arm explosive bolt firing circuits.	
T-35	520	Power transferred (C)	A.S.S.	CCC		POWER TRANSFERRED pushbutton indicator white on LCC.	
T-30				LCS	304	Pre-fill engine and spray lines.	Power transfer completed.

Figure 3-34. Launch Countdown System Functions (VAFB) (Sheet 28 of 44)

3-214

T.O. 21-SM68-1 Section III

TIME	REF	ROUTINE COMMAND	SOURCE	DESTINATION	REF	SUB-COMMAND	PREREQUISITES
T-25	536	Guidance locked on (C)	GGS				Missile acquired in frequency, range, azimuth and elevation.
T-25	544	Enable loop check (C)	CCC	CCC		GUIDANCE LOCKED ON indicator white on LCC.	Item 536 received.
				FCS		Prepare for RGS/FCS loop check.	
				CCC		Provide initiate loop.	
				CCC	544	Check prerequisite.	Item 536 received. Note LS monitors item 548 as interlock to prevent generation of enable launcher signal until T+170.
T-25	548	GGS operating (C)	CCC	LS			
T-25	560	Initiate loop check (C)	CCC	GGS		Initiate guidance commands for loop check.	Item 544 received.
T-18	562	Loop check complete (C)	FCS	CCC		LOOP CHECK COMPL indicator white on LCC.	RGS/FCS loop check completed satisfactorily.

Figure 3-34. Launch Countdown System Functions (VAFB) (Sheet 29 of 44)

3-215

T.O. 21-SM68-1 Section III

TIME	REF	ROUTINE COMMAND	SOURCE	DESTINATION	REF	SUB-COMMAND	PREREQUISITES
T-18	564	Completed loop check (C)	CCC				Item 564 received.
				GGS		Computer commences guidance program.	Computer commenced guidance program.
T-5	568	Shut off missile nitrogen (M)	LS			ACQ MISSILE pushbutton indicator green on MGC.	Item 472 received.
				PLPS		Close Stage I/II missile pneumatic nitrogen supply valves.	
T-5	576	Prepare to fire (M)	LS	LCS		Shut off hydraulic lines to umbilical tower accumulator.	
					576	Check umbilical tower hydraulic accumulator charged and the main water supply valve open. Replace LCS go signal with launcher ready to fire.	
T-5	584	Check power transferred (M)	LS	ES		Check item 520 initiated.	System not in exercise mode.
						Check for AC power transferred.	

Figure 3-34. Launch Countdown System Functions (VAFB) (Sheet 30 of 44)

3-216

T.O. 21-SM68-1　　　　　　　　　　　　　　　　　　　　　　　　Section III

TIME	REF	ROUTINE COMMAND	SOURCE	DESTINATION	REF	SUB-COMMAND	PREREQUISITES
T-5		(Continued)				Discontinue monitoring of Stage I/II missile hydraulic reservoir levels.	
T-1	624	Check loop check complete (M)	LS	TCS	624	Unfreeze target go status.	
				CCC		Provide check ready to guide prerequisites.	
				RVS		Unfreeze RVS go status.	
						Check R/V battery temperature (mark 3 R/V only).	
						Check arming and fuzing continuity (mark 3 R/V only).	
						Check R/V fuze setting.	
						Check arming and fuzing safety monitor (mark 4 R/V only).	
						Check warhead safety monitor (mark 4 R/V only).	

Figure 3-34. Launch Countdown System Functions (VAFB) (Sheet 31 of 44)

3-217

T.O. 21-SM68-1

TIME	REF	ROUTINE COMMAND	SOURCE	DESTINATION	REF	SUB-COMMAND	PREREQUISITES
T-1		(Continued)		FCS		Unfreeze FCS go status.	
						Check item 600 initiated.	
						Check gyro temperatures.	
						Check gyro spin motors operating.	
						Check engine nulls.	
						Reset missile programmer.	
						Check missile 25 VDC.	
T-1				FCS	624	Reset missile programmer check missile 25 VDC.	
				SECE		Check temperature of Stage I oxidizer bearings.	
						Check temperature of Stage I oxidizer suctions.	
						Check temperature of Stage II auxiliary pump oxidizer bearing.	

Figure 3-34. Launch Countdown System Functions (VAFB) (Sheet 32 of 44)

T.O. 21-SM68-1

TIME	REF	ROUTINE COMMAND	SOURCE	DESTINATION	REF	SUB-COMMAND	PREREQUISITES
T-1		(Continued)				Check Stage II helium starter bottle above minimum pressure (PGXTAP).	
T-1	632	Check ready to guide (M)	CCC	GGS		Check that computer has commenced guidance program.	Item 624 received.
T-0	640	Firing engines (M)	LS	FCS		Freeze FCS go status.	
						Uncage displacement gyros.	
				RVS		Freeze RVS go status.	
						De-energize re-entry vehicle battery heaters (mark 3 R/V).	
T-0				PLPS	640	Close helium transfer valve.	
						Close warm helium line.	
						De-energize Stage II fuel line heater.	

Figure 3-34. Launch Countdown System Functions (VAFB) (Sheet 33 of 44)

T.O. 21-SM68-1 Section III

TIME	REF	ROUTINE COMMAND	SOURCE	DESTINATION	REF	SUB-COMMAND	PREREQUISITES
T-0		(Continued)				Discontinue monitoring of Stage I/II helium tank and accumulator overpressure switches.	
						Discontinue monitoring of Stage II fuel and lox tanks and Stage I/II helium tanks and helium accumulators above minimum pressures.	
						Close intermittent service pressure regulating valve (FCV 513).	
						Discontinue monitoring of Stage I/II lox tanks above 95 percent level.	
				LS		Interrupt energize RGS signal.	
				CCC		Provide completed launch exercise prerequisite.	
T-0				TCS	640	Freeze target go status.	
T-0				ECS		Remove ground supplied power to Stage II TPA heaters.	System not in exercise mode.
T-0	648	Fire Stage I engines (M)					

Figure 3-34. Launch Countdown System Functions (VAFB) (Sheet 34 of 44)

3-220

TIME	REF	ROUTINE COMMAND	SOURCE	DESTINATION	REF	SUB-COMMAND	PREREQUISITES
T-0		(Continued)				De-energize (close) Stage I lox bleed valve pilot valve (1 and 2) (OSBVPV).	
						De-energize (close) ATPA fuel discharge bleed valve (FDBVAP).	
						De-energize (close) gas generator valve fuel bleed valve (GGVFBV).	
						De-energize Stage I TPA heaters.	
						Energize Stage I thrust chamber igniters (TCIGN).	Power is sensed on GGVPV closed solenoid.
						Energize (open) TPA starter valve (TPAXV).	Power is supplied to TCIGNS.
				LS		Provide internal signal to back up LCS go.	
T-0				ECS	648	De-energize gas generator valve pilot valve close solenoid (GGVPV).	Both TCV 65 percent open (TCV switches actuated).
						Energize Stage I gas generator igniters (GGIGN).	Both TCV 65 percent open (TCV switches actuated).

Figure 3-34. Launch Countdown System Functions (VAFB) (Sheet 35 of 44)

T.O. 21-SM68-1 Section III

TIME	REF	ROUTINE COMMAND	SOURCE	DESTINATION	REF	SUB-COMMAND	PREREQUISITES
T-0				ECS	648	Energize GGVPV open solenoid.	Both TCV 65 percent open (TCV switches actuated).
						Close TPA starter valve (TPAXV).	Either GGV 30 percent open (GGV switches actuated).
						De-energize thrust chamber igniters (TCIGN).	Either GGV 30 percent open (GGV switches actuated).
						De-energize (close) gas generator oxidizer.	Either GGV 30 percent open (GGV switches actuated).
						De-energize GGVPV open solenoid.	Either GGV 30 percent open (GGV switches actuated).
						De-energize Stage I gas generator igniters (GGIGN).	Either GGV 30 percent open (GGV switches actuated).
T+2	656	Start missile release (C)	ECS				Both thrust chambers up to 440 PSIG (thrust chamber pressure switches actuated for 50 milliseconds).
T+4				ES	656	Fire missile support explosive bolts.	Item 512 received and approximately 2-second time delay expired after item 656 received.

Figure 3-34. Launch Countdown System Functions (VAFB) (Sheet 36 of 44)

T.O. 21-SM68-1   Section III

TIME	REF	ROUTINE COMMAND	SOURCE	DESTINATION	REF	SUB-COMMAND	PREREQUISITES
T+4		(Continued)				Fire umbilical tower explosive bolts.	Item 512 received and approximately 2-second time delay expired after item 656 received.
T+4	660	Fire bolts (C)	ES	LS		Inhibit automatic shutdown generation.	Item 656 generated.
			ES	PLPS	660	Discontinue monitoring of Stage I fuel and lox tanks above minimum pressures.	
T+4	664	Lift off (C)		CCC		LIFT OFF indicator white on LCC.	Item 656 received and missile support bolts fired.
				LS		Provide enable launcher raising prerequisite.	
				IRSS		Provide lift off signal to ICC (range safety officer).	
T+4	672	Missile launched (C)	CCC	GGS		LIFT OFF indicator white on MGC.	Item 664 received.

Figure 3-34. Launch Countdown System Functions (VAFB) (Sheet 37 of 44)

T.O. 21-SM68-1

Section III

TIME	REF	ROUTINE COMMAND	SOURCE	DESTINATION	REF	SUB-COMMAND	PREREQUISITES
T+7	680	Check lift off (M)	LS	ES		Check item 664 initiated interrupt item 660.	
T+10				GGS	672	Press GUID IN PROGRESS pushbutton indicator on MGC (manual).	LIFT OFF white and missile actually in flight (determined from TV monitor).
T+10	696	Guidance in progress (C)	GGS			GUID IN PROGRESS pushbutton indicator green on MGC.	GUID IN PROGRESS pushbutton indicator pressed.
T+10	704	Missile in flight (C)	CCC	CCC		Provide missile in flight and raise/lower launcher interlock prerequisite.	GUID IN PROGRESS pressed.
T+10				LS		Item 725 locked out until T+170.	Item 696 received.
T+10	712	Ready to lower (C)	LS	PLPS		Close 750 PSI nitrogen supply valve.	Launcher lowering enabled from the CCC (item 436) and launch sequence generates enable lowering signal.

Figure 3-34. Launch Countdown System Functions (VAFB) (Sheet 38 of 44)

3-224

T.O. 21-SM68-1 Section III

TIME	REF	ROUTINE COMMAND	SOURCE	DESTINATION	REF	SUB-COMMAND	PREREQUISITES
T+10		(Continued)		CCC		LOWER LAUNCHER indicator green on LCC.	
T+170	725	Enable launcher raising (C)	LS	CCC		Enable ready to raise on other two missiles of the complex.	
T+XXX				GGS	696	END OF GUID indicator white on MGC.	Guidance satisfactorily completed and IBDA printed out.
						Press RECYCLE pushbutton indicator on MGC (manual).	END OF GUID white.
						RECYCLE pushbutton indicator white on MGC.	RECYCLE pushbutton indicator pressed.
						Drop out launcher and target selections. GGS recycles to prepare for acquisition of next missile.	
						RECYCLE pushbutton indicator not lighted on MGC.	Recycle complete.
T+1HR				PLPS	224	Close lox return line vent valve.	Drain line not above minimum vent pressure.
						Close lox drain line vent valve.	Drain line not above minimum vent pressure.

Figure 3-34. Launch Countdown System Functions (VAFB) (Sheet 39 of 44)

T.O. 21-SM68-1 Section III

TIME	REF	ROUTINE COMMAND	SOURCE	DESTINATION	REF	SUB-COMMAND	PREREQUISITES
T+1HR		(Continued)				Open lox drain blanket valve.	Lox return line vent and drain line vent valves closed.
T+2HR				PLPS	224	Close Stage I/II lox line vent valves.	Stage I/II fill lines not above minimum vent pressure.
H-0	800	Start launcher lowering.	LC			Open lox line blanket valve.	Stage I/II lox line vent valves closed. LOWER LAUNCHER pushbutton pressed.
H-0	808	Launcher lowering started (C)	LS	LS		Provide lower launcher prerequisite.	Ready to lower (item 712) and start launcher lowering (item 800).
				CCC		LOWER LAUNCHER indicator white on LCC.	
H-0	816	Lower launcher (C)	LS			Disable ready to lower on other launchers.	
						Disable ready to raise on other launchers.	Ready to lower (item 712) and start launcher lowering (item 800). Fire Stage I engines (item 648).

Figure 3-34. Launch Countdown System Functions (VAFB) (Sheet 40 of 44)

T.O. 21-SM68-1   Section III

TIME	REF	ROUTINE COMMAND	SOURCE	DESTINATION	REF	SUB-COMMAND	PREREQUISITES
H+0		(Continued)		LCS		Open flame deflector cooling spray valve.	
H+10	176	IRSS shutdown	O&C			Position umbilical tower.	
						Position lower tower umbilical mechanism. De-energize O&C console.	
H+90	177	Inspect above ground and silo areas	CSO	CSO/CST/MAET		Dispatch MAET teams to missile silo and above ground area.	
H+91				LCS	816	Close water supply valve.	
H+101				LCS	816	Retract flame deflector extension.	Engine compartment water spray valve closed.
H+101				LCS	816	Retract launcher platform lateral load locks.	Engine compartment water spray valve closed.
H+117				LCS	816	Drive launcher platform up.	Lateral load locks retracted.
H+122				LCS	816	Retract vertical load locks.	Launcher platform driven up.
H+132				LCS	816	Turn off launcher platform oil pressure.	Vertical load locks retracted.

Figure 3-34. Launch Countdown System Functions (VAFB) (Sheet 41 of 44)

3-227

TIME	REF	ROUTINE COMMAND	SOURCE	DESTINATION	REF	SUB-COMMAND	PREREQUISITES
H+132		(Continued)				Lower launcher platform.	Vertical load locks retracted.
H+150	178	Report area safe	CSO	LCS		Report missile silo and above-ground area clear for limited access.	
H+253					816	Turn on launcher platform oil pressure.	Launcher platform lowered.
						Shut off launcher platform drive.	Launcher platform lowered.
						Close lower shelter door.	Launcher platform lowered.
						Rotate launcher platform counterweight support.	Launcher platform lowered.
						Extend Stage I lox vent duct (1C1LV) support mechanism.	Launcher platform lowered.
						Extend Stage II lox vent duct no. 1 (2B1LV) support mechanism.	Launcher platform lowered.
						Extend Stage II lox vent duct NO. 2 (2B2LV) support mechanism.	Launcher platform lowered.
H+254				LCS	816	Open engine compartment water spray valve.	Water supply valve closed.

Figure 3-34. Launch Countdown System Functions (VAFB) (Sheet 42 of 44)

T.O. 21-SM68-1 Section III

TIME	REF	ROUTINE COMMAND	SOURCE	DESTINATION	REF	SUB-COMMAND	PREREQUISITES
H+262				LCS	816	Pressurize rod end slacking cylinder.	Counterweight support rotated.
H+264				LCS	816	Release counterweight cylinder locks.	Rod end slacking cylinder pressurized.
H+274				LCS	816	Lower counterweight cylinder.	Counterweight cylinder locks released.
H+280				LCS	816	Close wire rope locks.	Counterweight on support.
						Rotate counterweight support lock.	Counterweight on support.
H+281				LCS	816	Close upper shelter door.	Lower shelter door closed.
H+304				LCS	816	Release cable equalizer.	Counterweight support lowered.
						Retract horizontal and vertical crib locks.	Counterweight support lowered.
H+334				LCS	816	Retract oblique crib locks.	Horizontal and vertical crib locks retracted.
H+354	920	Shelter doors closed (C)	LCS	LS		Provide launch sequence complete prerequisite.	Shelter doors closed and crib locks retracted.
				LCS		Shut off power pack pump motors.	

Figure 3-34. Launch Countdown System Functions (VAFB) (Sheet 43 of 44)

T.O. 21-SM68-1   Section III

TIME	REF	ROUTINE COMMAND	SOURCE	DESTINATION	REF	SUB-COMMAND	PREREQUISITES
H+354	928	Launch sequence complete (C)	LS				Item 920 received subsequent to generation of item 808.
H+354	928	Complete (C)	LS	ES		Power to the AOE.	and shutdown signal. Subsequent to generation.

Figure 3-34. Launch Countdown System Functions (VAFB) (Sheet 44 of 44)

3-230

T.O. 21-SM68-1

STEP	PROCEDURE		
A	L+0		Start launcher lowering
B	L+0		Open flame deflector cooling valve
	Note:		After T-O and with no lift-off occuring, any shutdown will result in engine compartment water spray.
C	L+0		Erect umbilical tower
D	L+90		Close main water supply valve
E	L+91		Retract flame deflector extension
F	L+91		Retract lateral load locks
G	L+101		Retract vertical load locks
H	L+120		Shut off launcher platform oil pressure
I	L+121		Lower launcher platform
			The following times will be approximate for an empty launcher and will be different for a DPL, a lox, only and a fuel only exercise; however, the sequence of events will be the same.
J	L+606		Turn on launcher platform oil pressure
K	L+606		Shut off launcher drive
L	L+606		Close lower silo door
M	L+606		(LAFB 724TH/725TH SQDN, EAFB, BAFB, LAFB, MHAFB) Raise counterweight lifting cylinder
N	L+606		(VAFB) Rotate counterweight support
O	L+614		(LAFB 724TH/725TH SQDN, EAFB, BAFB, LAFB, MHAFB) Insert CWT to drive base locks
P	L+616		(VAFB) Pressure CWT lift cylinder raise
Q	L+618		(VAFB) Release CWT cylinder locks
R	L+619		(LAFB 724TH/725TH SQDN, EAFB, BAFB, LAFB, MHAFB) Deenergize CWT lift cylinders.
S	L+621		(LAFB 724TH/725TH SQDN, EAFB, BAFB, LAFB, MHAFB) lower tension equalizer cylinders.

Figure 3-35. Launch Countdown System Functions Launcher Control System Lower Launcher (Sheet 1 of 2)

STEP	PROCEDURE
T	L+628 (VAFB) Lower CWT lift cylinders.
U	L+636 Close upper door
V	L+643 (LAFB 724TH/725TH SQDN, EAFB, BAFB, LAFB, MHAFB) Unlock spring capsules
W	L+648 (LAFB 724TH/725TH SQDN, EAFB, BAFB, LAFB, MHAFB) Retract stub rail latch
X	L+653 (LAFB 724TH/725TH SQDN, EAFB, BAFB, LAFB, MHAFB) Retract rear drive base lock
Y	L+658 (VAFB) Extend tension equalizer cylinders.
Z	L+658 (LAFB 724TH/725TH SQDN, EAFB, BAFB, LAFB, MHAFB) Retract Horizontal crib locks
AA	L+673 (LAFB 724TH/725TH SQDN, EAFB, BAFB, LAFB, MHAFB) Retract oblique crib locks
BB	L+678 (VAFB) Rotate CWT support lock
CC	L+683 (VAFB) Extend tension equalizer cylinders.
DD	L+683 (VAFB) Retract horizontal crib locks
EE	L+694 (LAFB 724TH/725TH SQDN, EAFB, BAFB, LAFB, MHAFB) Retract vertical crib locks
FF	L+704 (LAFB 724TH/725TH SQDN, EAFB, BAFB, LAFB, MHAFB) System hard: doors closed, crib on shock mounts
GG	L+704 (LAFB 724TH/725TH SQDN, EAFB, BAFB, LAFB, MHAFB) Shut off power pack
HH	L+713 (VAFB) Retract oblique crib locks
II	L+733 (VAFB) Retract vertical crib locks
JJ	L+743 (VAFB) System hard: crib on shock mounts, doors closed
KK	L+743 (VAFB) Shut off power pack

Figure 3-35. Launch Countdown System Functions Launcher Control System Lower Launcher (Sheet 2 of 2)

T.O. 21-SM68-1

Section IV
Paragraphs 4-1 to 4-6

SECTION IV

EMERGENCY PROCEDURES

4-1. **GENERAL**.

4-2. This section contains procedures to be accomplished when an emergency condition occurs during weapon system operation and alert status monitoring. The emergencies that may be encountered at the launch complex are many and varied in nature. The primary concern is to protect personnel and equipment in order to complete a countdown or maintain the complex in an alert status.

4-3. During weapon system operation, the missile and facility is considered to be in an emergency condition if a shutdown occurs (with the exception of normal shutdown at completion of all exercise). Shutdown may be manually initiated any time during weapon system operation or shutdown will be automatically initiated if equipment malfunction occurs subsequent to initiation of raise launcher phase. The missile and facility is also considered to be in an emergency condition any time a hazard indication occurs during weapon system operation or alert status monitoring.

4-3A. When a gox hazard occurs, personnel will not be allowed to enter or remain in any area where the gox content is above 35 percent except to effect the rescue of personnel. When performing appropriate gox/lox hazard functions in T.O. 21-SM68-CL-21-1, portable gox analyzer readings will be taken frequently to insure that the 35 percent level is not exceeded. Clearance to perform essential corrective or safing actions in the affected area when gox concentration is above 35 percent must be obtained from the headquarters of the using command.

4-4. If a shutdown occurs, proceed with countdown on remaining launchers before performing post shutdown procedures. If a shutdown occurs during a PLX, perform post shutdown procedures immediately. (Refer to T.O. 21-SM68-CL-24-1 or T.O. 21-SM68-CL-27-1).

WARNING

If missile APS and HPS batteries have been activated they must be removed and discharged within 8 hours or they may rupture. In remote instances, they may pressure explode causing damage to equipment and injury to personnel. (Refer to T.O. 21-SM68-2J-10-1 or -2).

4-5. **BOIL-OFF PROCEDURE**.

4-6. Boil-off procedure is performed after post shutdown missile and facility safing has been accomplished and it has been verified that the launcher is in the intermediate position. However, other situations may arise that would require use of boil-off procedure. If the launcher is up and locked and **LOWER LAUNCHER** pushbutton on the LCC has been pressed and launcher does not lower, OSBV lox dump cannot be performed and boil-off procedure will have to be used. (Refer to T.O. 21-SM68-2J-12-2 or -5.)

Changed 3 January 1964 TOCN-1 (DEN-6)

4-1

4-7. **OSBV LOX DUMP.**

4-8. OSBV lox dump is performed after post shutdown missile and facility safing has been accomplished and it has been verified that the launcher is up and locked. If LOWER LAUNCHER pushbutton on LCC has been pressed and launcher does not lower, OSBV lox dump cannot be performed and boil-off procedure will have to be used. Approximately 10 hours are required to dump missile lox and approximately 3 minutes are required to dump missile helium. (Refer to T.O. 21-SM68-2J-12-2 or -5.)

Note

OSBV lox dump is performed only when launcher platform is up and locked and a shutdown is in effect. If OSBV lox dump cannot be accomplished, perform boil-off procedure immediately. If launcher is up and locked and EMERGENCY UNLOAD STAGE 1 or 2 indicator (assembly 6A2) is lighted white, press EMERGENCY UNLOAD STAGE 1 or 2 pushbutton immediately and verify green indication.

4-9. After OSBV lox dump has been accomplished and malfunction has been corrected, perform lower launcher procedures. After launcher has been lowered, extend maintenance platforms and connect probes, recycle electrical system and PLPS, and verify that lox tanks are empty.

Note

If launcher should move during OSBV lox dump, the dump operation will be stopped automatically.

4-10. RECYCLE OF ELECTRICAL SYSTEM AND PLPS.

4-11. Recycle of electrical system and PLPS is performed after OSBV lox dump or boil-off procedure has been performed, launcher is down and locked, and probes have been connected. This procedure is provided to recycle the electrical and propellant systems out of shutdown condition. This procedure also provides for manual control of propellant system valves in the checkout mode. After recycle of electrical system and PLPS has been accomplished, verification of lox tanks empty is performed. (Refer to T.O. 21-SM68-2J-10-1 and -2; and T.O. 21-SM68-2J-12-2 and -5.)

4-12. VERIFICATION OF LOX TANKS EMPTY.

4-13. Verification of lox tanks empty is performed to verify that the missile lox tanks are empty after OSBV lox dump or boil-off procedure has been accomplished, launcher is down and locked, probes have been connected, and recycle of electrical system and PLPS has been accomplished. (Refer to T.O. 21-SM68-2J-12-2 and -5.)

4-14. HAZARD PROCEDURES.

4-15. Hazard procedures are performed as various situations arise during weapon system operation or launch readiness monitoring. Figures 4-1 through 4-15 are guides for the MLO and are not to be used as a substitute for good judgment. Figures 4-16 through 4-30 contain procedures for power house emergency conditions.

4-16. RADAR SURVEILLANCE SYSTEM (ANTI-INTRUSION).

4-17. ALARM INDICATION.

4-18. Either failure of critical components or a moving object in the surveillance area will cause an alarm to be indicated on the annunciator panel. Since it is impossible to determine without investigating the area whether an alarm is the result of an intrusion or is caused by an equipment failure, first initiate whatever actions are necessary to protect the secured area. If the surveillance area is clear of moving objects and the system cannot be reset, maintenance is to be performed on the system using the performance tests in T.O. 31P7-2TPS39-2.

4-19. PRIMARY POWER FAILURE.

4-20. In the event of a primary AC power failure, the battery packs supplied with the system will automatically furnish emergency power to the system components for up to 2 hours. No emergency procedures are necessary.

4-21. JAMMING AND ANTI-JAMMING.

4-22. Attempts to jam the AN/TPS-39(V) system by any known method of electronic deception will cause an alarm indication; therefore, no anti-jamming procedures are necessary.

HAZARD CONDITION	ALERT STATUS MONITORING	PROPELLANT LOADING PHASE	RAISE LAUNCHER PHASE	LAUNCH PHASE	LOWER LAUNCHER PHASE
Equipment terminal hydraulic fire	NO-GO: See figure 4-9.	Manual shutdown: Continue countdown on remaining launchers, then see figure 4-9.	GO: After missiles have been launched, see figure 4-9.	GO: After missiles have been launched, see figure 4-9.	NO-GO: See figure 4-9.
Equipment terminal fire	NO-GO: See figure 4-8.	Manual shutdown: Continue countdown on remaining launchers, then see figures 3-22 and 4-8.	Manual shutdown prior to vent disconnect: Continue countdown on remaining launchers, then see figures 3-22 and 4-8. Go after vent disconnect.	GO: After missiles have been launched, see figure 4-8.	NO-GO: See figure 4-8. If launcher contains missile, see figures 3-22 and 4-8
Gox hazard in missile silo	NO-GO: See figure 4-2.	Manual shutdown if above 40%: Continue countdown on remaining launchers, then see figure 4-2.	Manual shutdown prior to vent disconnect if above 40%: Continue countdown on remaining launchers, then see figure 4-2.	GO: After missiles have been launched, see figure 4-2.	NO-GO if above 40% and launcher contains missile: See figure 4-2.
Gox hazard in propellant terminal	NO-GO: See figure 4-3.	Manual shutdown if rapid rise: Continue countdown on remaining launchers, then see figure 4-3.	GO: After missiles have been launched, see figure 4-3.	GO: After missiles have been launched, see figure 4-3.	GO: After launcher is lowered, see figure 4-3.
Propellant terminal fire	NO-GO: See figure 4-7.	Manual shutdown: See figure 4-7.	GO: After missiles have been launched, see figure 4-7.	GO: After missiles have been launched, see figure 4-7.	NO-GO: See figure 4-7
Power house emergency	NO-GO: See figure 4-18.	GO: See figure 4-18.	GO: See figure 4-18.	GO: See figure 4-18.	NO-GO: See figure 4-18
Missile silo fire	NO-GO: See figure 4-6.	Manual shutdown: Continue countdown on remaining launchers, then see figure 4-6.	Manual shutdown prior to vent disconnect: Continue countdown on remaining launchers, then see figure 4-6. Go after vent disconnect.	GO: After remaining missiles have been launched, see figure 4-6.	NO-GO: See figure 4-6

Figure 4-1. Hazard Condition Chart (Sheet 1 of 2)

HAZARD CONDITION	ALERT STATUS MONITORING	PROPELLANT LOADING PHASE	RAISE LAUNCHER PHASE	LAUNCH PHASE	LOWER LAUNCHER PHASE
Fire in fuel terminal	NO-GO: See figure 4-11.	GO: After missiles have been launched, see figure 4-11.	GO: After missiles have been launched, see figure 4-11.	GO: After missiles have been launched, see figure 4-11.	NO-GO: See figure 4-11.
Lox spillage in missile silo	NO-GO: See figure 4-5.	GO: After missiles have been launched, see figure 4-5. If gox content rises, refer to gox hazard in missile silo.	GO: After missiles have been launched, see figure 4-5.	GO: After missiles have been launched, see figure 4-5.	NO-GO: See figure 4-5.
Missile silo explosion	NO-GO: See figure 4-13.	See figure 4-13.	See figure 4-13.	See figure 4-13.	NO-GO: See figure 4-13.

Figure 4-1. Hazard Condition Chart (Sheet 2 of 2)

T.O. 21-SM68-1

Section IV

STEP	PROCEDURE
	Note
	All hazard actions and procedures will be at the discretion of the MLO.
	All tasks preceded by an asterisk will be coordinated with the MLO.
1	MISSILE SILO GOX (LCFC)..................................Flashing Red
	Gox indicator flashes red indicating a gox hazard in the missile silo.
2	Buzzer...Silenced
	The buzzer sounds indicating a hazard exists, providing the buzzer was not silenced from a prior hazard. BMAT will press PUSH TO SILENCE pushbutton on LCFC.
	Note
	If corrective action has not started turn applicable silo air purge switch on.
3	Corrective Action..Started
	Gox indicator flashes red and white indicating that silo air conditioner is operating in purge condition.
4	MLO..Notified
	Upon observing the hazard, BMAT notifies the MLO.
	Note
	If countdown is in progress, perform only step 5; all other times perform steps 6 thru 21.
5	Countdown...Continued
	MLO will evaluate the hazard and determine if it will be feasible to continue countdown or initiate shutdown. If shutdown is initiated, perform steps 6 thru 21.

Figure 4-2. Gox Hazard in Missile Silo (Sheet 1 of 3)

4-6

STEP	PROCEDURE
6	"Attention all personnel in launcher ____, gox hazard in missile silo. Team chief call control center immediately" (if applicable.)............................Announced
	BMAT or MLO makes above announcement over P.A. system to alert all personnel of hazard.
7	Press HAZARD LIGHT((LCFC).................................Red
	BMAT presses ABOVE GRD HAZARD LIGHT pushbutton indicator for affected launcher to red to indicate an unsafe condition in that launcher.
8	Press MISSILE AND FACILITY (LCFC).......................Red
	BMAT presses MISSILE AND FACILITY pushbutton indicator to insure that a countdown will not be inadvertently started with a hazard in the launcher area.
9	Command post..Notified
	MLO notifies command post of hazard and all pertinent facts, and requests assistance, if necessary.
10	Gox readout (control center)............................Logged
	BMAT will take readings of gox content in the missile silo and propellant terminal and records them for later reference. At intervals determined by the MLO, readings will be taken to determine if gox content is rising or falling.
11	Personnel to missile silo................................Directed
	MLO directs personnel into missile silo to investigate and evaluate the hazard. Personnel will silence horns and report conditions to the MLO.
12	HORN SILENCER (MSAP).......................................Pressed
*13	Gox content (missile silo)................................Reported
	MMT uses a portable analyzer to measure actual gox content.
*14	Condition of missile silo.................................Reported

Figure 4-2. Gox Hazard in Missile Silo (Sheet 2 of 3)

STEP	PROCEDURE
15	Maintenance...Performed
	Necessary maintenance will be performed to return system to normal operation.
16	Gox alarm RESET...Pressed
	After maintenance has been performed, system will be reset to normal.
17	MSAP..Normal
18	MISSILE SILO GOX (LCFC).................................Not Lighted
19	"Attention all personnel, gox hazard in launcher _____ has been corrected"..Announced
	BMAT or MLO will make above announcement over P.A. system after maintenance is completed and system is returned to alert status monitoring.
20	Press HAZARD LIGHT (LCFC)...................................Green
	When hazard has been corrected, BMAT will press ABOVE GRD HAZARD LIGHT pushbutton indicator to green signifying hazard has been cleared. Absence of a red indication above ground indicates hazard has been corrected and area is clear for normal operation.
21	Press MISSILE AND FACILITY (LCFC).........................Green
	BMAT presses MISSILE AND FACILITY pushbutton to green, releasing the hold, which allows a launch countdown to be initiated.

Figure 4-2. Gox Hazard in Missile Silo (Sheet 3 of 3)

T.O. 21-SM68-1   Section IV

STEP	PROCEDURE
	Note
	All hazard actions and procedures will be at the discretion of the MLO.
	All tasks preceded by an asterisk will be coordinated with MLO.
1	PROP TERM GOX (LCFC)..........................Flashing Red
	GOX indicator flashes red whenever gox content in propellant terminal is above or below limits set on the analyzer. (High gox only at VAFB).
2	Buzzer......................................Silenced
	If buzzer was not silenced from a prior hazard, buzzer sounds indicating a hazard exists. BMAT presses PUSH TO SILENCE pushbutton on the LCFC.
3	MLO..Notified
	Upon observing the hazard, BMAT notifies MLO immediately.
	Note
	If countdown is in progress perform only step 4; at all other times perform steps 5 thru 20.
4	Countdown..................................Continued
	MLO will evaluate hazard and determine if it will be feasible to continue countdown. If shutdown is initiated, perform steps 5 thru 20.
5	Press HAZARD LIGHT (LCFC).............................Red
	BMAT presses ABOVE GRD HAZARD LIGHT pushbutton indicator for affected launcher to red to indicate an unsafe condition in that launcher.
6	Press MISSILE AND FACILITY (LCFC)....................Red
	BMAT presses MISSILE AND FACILITY pushbutton to insure that a countdown will not be inadvertently started with a hazard in launcher area.

Figure 4-3. Gox Hazard in Propellant Terminal (Sheet 1 of 3)

T.O. 21-SM68-1   Section IV

STEP	PROCEDURE
7	Command post..Notified
	MLO notifies command post of hazard and all pertinent facts, and requests assistance, if necessary.
8	"Attention all personnel in launcher _____, gox hazard in propellant terminal. Team chief call control center immediately." (if applicable)................Announced
	BMAT or MLO makes above announcement over P.A. system to alert all personnel of the hazard.
9	Gox Readout (Control Center)...........................Logged
	BMAT takes a reading of gox content in missile silo and propellant terminal and records them for later reference. At intervals determined by MLO, readings will be taken to determine if gox content is rising or falling.
10	Personnel to propellant terminal......................Directed
	MLO directs personnel to propellant terminal to investigate and evaluate hazard. Personnel will silence horns, make gox readings, and report conditions to MLO.
11	HORN SILENCER (PTAP).......................................Pressed
*12	Gox content (propellant terminal)....................Reported
*13	Condition of propellant terminal.....................Reported
14	Maintenance..Performed
	Maintenance will be performed as necessary to return system to normal operation.
15	Gox alarm RESET..Pressed
	After maintenance has been performed, system will be reset to normal.
16	PTAP...Normal
17	PROP TERM GOX (LCFC)....................................Not Lighted
	After system is reset, PTAP and PROP TERM GOX (LCFC) will be checked for normal operation.

Figure 4-3. Gox Hazard in Propellant Terminal (Sheet 2 of 3)

STEP	PROCEDURE
18	"Attention all personnel in launcher _____, gox hazard in propellant terminal has been corrected".......Announced
	BMAT or MLO makes announcement over P.A. system to inform personnel that hazard has been corrected.
19	Press HAZARD LIGHT (LCFC)................................Green
	When hazard has been corrected, BMAT will press the ABOVE GRD HAZARD LIGHT pushbutton indicator to green signifying hazard has been cleared. Absence of a red indication above ground indicates hazard has been corrected and area is clear for normal operation.
20	Press MISSILE AND FACILITY (LCFC).......................Green
	BMAT presses MISSILE AND FACILITY pushbutton indicator to green releasing the hold, which allows a launch countdown to be initiated.

Figure 4-3. Gox Hazard in Propellant Terminal (Sheet 3 of 3)

STEP	PROCEDURE
	All hazard actions and procedures will be at the discretion of the MLO. All tasks preceded by an asterisk will be coordinated with MLO. Note If this hazard occurs during lox unloading, MLO will direct MMT to stop unloading immediately.
1	TUNNEL LOX P.T. VENT (LCFC).................................Flashing Red LOX P.T. VENT indicator will flash red whenever liquid oxygen is in the vent shaft. Indicator will also flash for approximately 10 seconds when checkout power is applied or LOAD PROPELLANTS is pressed.
2	MLO...Notified BMAT will notify the MLO upon observing LOX P.T. VENT indication. Note If countdown is in progress, perform only step 3; all other times perform steps 4 thru 14.
3	Countdown...Continued MLO will evaluate hazard and determine if it will be feasible to continue the countdown. If shutdown is initiated, perform steps 4 thru 14.
4	"Attention all personnel in launcher _____, lox in propellant terminal vent. Team chief call control center." (if applicable)..............................Announced BMAT or MLO makes above announcement over P.A. system to alert personnel of hazard.
5	Press HAZARD LIGHT (LCFC)..................................Red BMAT presses ABOVE GRD HAZARD LIGHT pushbutton indicator for the affected launcher to red to indicate an unsafe condition in that launcher.

Figure 4-4. Lox Hazard in Propellant Terminal Lox Vent
(Operational Bases) (Sheet 1 of 2)

T.O. 21-SM68-1 Section IV

STEP	PROCEDURE
6	Press MISSILE AND FACILITY (LCFC)..........................Red
	BMAT presses MISSILE AND FACILITY pushbutton indicator to insure that a countdown will not be inadvertently started with a hazard in the launcher area.
7	Command post..Notified
	MLO notifies command post of hazard and all pertinent facts, and requests assistance, if necessary.
8	Gox readout (control center)...............................Logged
	BMAT will take readings of gox content in missile silo and propellant terminal and records them for later reference. At intervals determined by the MLO, further readings will be taken to determine if gox content is rising or falling.
9	MISSILE SILO AIR PURGE......................................ON
	BMAT places silo in 100% purge to clear silo of gox.
10	Personnel to propellant terminal..........................Directed
	MLO directs personnel to propellant terminal to investigate and evaluate hazard.
*11	Condition of propellant terminal vent shaft...............Reported
	Note
	If shutdown was initiated, perform past shutdown procedures. If lox unloading was in progress restart of lox unloading will be at the discretion of the MLO.
12	Press HAZARD LIGHT (LCFC)..................................Green
	When hazard has been corrected, BMAT will press ABOVE GRD HAZARD LIGHT pushbutton indicator to green, signifying hazard has been cleared.
13	Press MISSILE AND FACILITY (LCFC)..........................Green
	BMAT presses MISSILE AND FACILITY pushbutton indicator to green, releasing the hold, which allows launch countdown to be initiated.

Figure 4-4. Lox Hazard in Propellant Terminal Lox Vent
(Operational Bases) (Sheet 2 of 2)

STEP	PROCEDURE
14	MISSILE SILO AIR PURGE..................................OFF

Figure 4-4. Lox Hazard in Propellant Terminal Lox Vent (Operational Bases) (Sheet 2A of 2)

STEP	PROCEDURE
	All hazard actions and procedurds will be at the descretion of the MLO.
	All steps preceded by an asterisk will be coordinated with the MLO.
1	MISSILE SILO LOX SUMP (LCFC).................................Flashing Red
2	Buzzer..Silenced
	If buzzer was not silenced from a prior hazard, the buzzer will sound indicating a hazard exists. BMAT presses PUSH TO SILENCE pushbutton on LCFC.
3	MLO...Notified
	Upon observing hazard, BMAT will notify MLO immediately.
	WARNING
	If gross lox spillage occurs during lox unloading, MLO will direct MMT to stop unloading and immediately perform steps 14 thru 19.
4	MISSILE SILO AIR PURGE..ON
	BMAT places missile silo in 100 percent purge to clear silo of gox. At VAFB, if purge is not automatic, accomplish as part of step 12.
	Note
	If countdown is in progress perform only step 5, all other times perform steps 6 thru 29.
5	Countdown...Continued
	MLO will evaluate hazard and determine if it will be feasible to continue countdown. If shutdown is initiated, perform steps 6 thru 29.
6	"Attention all personnel in launcher area _____, lox spillage hazard in missile silo. Team chief call control center immediately" (if applicable)..........Announced
	BMAT or MLO makes above announcement over P.A. system to alert personnel of the hazard.

Figure 4-5. Lox Spillage in Missile Silo (Sheet 1 of 4)

T.O. 21-SM68-1   Section IV

STEP	PROCEDURE
7	Press HAZARD LIGHT (LCFC).....................................Red
	BMAT presses ABOVE GRD HAZARD LIGHT pushbutton indicator for the affected launcher to red to indicate an unsafe condition in that launcher.
8	Press MISSILE AND FACILITY (LCFC)............................Red
	BMAT presses MISSILE AND FACILITY pushbutton to insure that a countdown will not be inadvertently started with a hazard in launcher area.
9	Command post...Notified
	MLO notifies command post of hazard and all pertinent facts, and requests assistance if necessary.
10	Gox readout (control center).................................Logged
	BMAT takes a reading of gox content in missile silo and propellant terminal and records for later reference. At intervals determined by the MLO, readings will be taken to determine if gox content is rising or falling.
11	Personnel to missile silo....................................Directed
	WARNING
	If extreme pressure is necessary to open blast lock doors, do not attempt entry. This is an indication that gross lox spillage has occurred, resulting in pressure buildup in the launcher area.
12	HORN SILENCER (MSAP)..Pressed
*13	Condition of missile silo....................................Reported
	Portable analyzer will be used to measure actual gox content.
	WARNING
	If gross lox spillage has occurred in the missile silo, perform steps 14 thru 19 immediately.
*14	MODE selector (assembly 6A2)..................................CHECKOUT
	MLO directs MMT or BMAT to set MODE selector on PLPS chassis to CHECKOUT.

Figure 4-5. Lox Spillage in Missile Silo (Sheet 2 of 4)

Changed 17 January 1964 TOCN-1 (DEN-8)

T.O. 21-SM68-1

Section IV

STEP	PROCEDURE
*15	CV-3123, CV-3102, or CV-3113 main water valve (affected launcher)..Closed
	MLO directs EPPT to close the applicable main water valve located upstream from excess flow control valves at the entrance to blast lock of affected launcher.
*16	BATTERY LOCKOUT (A/E 24A) switch............................OFF
	MLO directs the BMAT or MMT to remove standby batteries off the line to insure that all electrical power is removed from the missile.
*17	IPS and AGE 28 VDC rectifier circuit breakers...............OFF
	MLO directs MMT or BMAT to turn off IPS and AGE 28V DC rectifier to remove all electrical power.
*18	CB1, 2, 3, and 4 (PNL 1021) (level IV, equipment terminal)..OFF
	MLO directs MMT or BMAT to turn off above circuit breakers to remove power from emergency lights in equipment terminal, missile silo, propellant terminal and alarm panel 1022.
*19	SWITCHGEAR FEEDER circuit breaker (affected launcher)..OFF
	MLO directs EPPT to turn off SWITCHGEAR FEEDER circuit breaker to remove all power to the affected launcher.
	WARNING
	Steps 20 through 22 are performed only if gross lox spillage has occurred.
20	Press LAUNCHER AIR FILTRATION BLAST VALVES OVERRIDE CONTROLS CLOSED (unaffected launchers)....................Amber
	BMAT presses above pushbutton indicator for the unaffected launchers, forcing maximum air into the affected launcher which will partially equalize pressure on the blast lock door and aid in personnel escape.
21	Air filtration system main tunnel vent....................Covered

Figure 4-5. Lox Spillage in Missile Silo (Sheet 3 of 4)

T.O. 21-SM68-1 Section IV

STEP	PROCEDURE
21 (CONT)	BMAT or any available personnel covers tunnel vent to force maximum air into affected launcher. Note After all personnel are clear of the affected area, perform step 22.
22	Press LAUNCHER AIR FILTRATION BLAST VALVES OVERRIDE CONTROLS OPEN (unaffected launchers)..................Not Lighted BMAT presses above pushbutton indicator for the unaffected launchers, allowing maximum escape of air from affected launcher. WARNING Step 23 will not be accomplished until gox content is within safe limits.
23	Maintenance...Perform
24	MSAP...Normal
25	"Attention all personnel, lox spillage hazard in missile silo _____, has been corrected"........................Announced
26	Press HAZARD LIGHT (LCFC)......................................Green When hazard has been corrected, BMAT will press ABOVE GRD HAZARD LIGHT pushbutton indicator to green, signifying hazard has been cleared. The absence of a red indication above ground indicates hazard has been corrected and area is clear for normal operation.
27	Press MISSILE AND FACILITY (LCFC)..............................Green BMAT presses MISSILE AND FACILITY pushbutton indicator to green, releasing hold, which allows a launch countdown to be initiated.
28	MISSILE SILO AIR PURGE...OFF
29	Air filtration system main tunnel vent (if applicable)..Uncovered

Figure 4-5. Lox Spillage in Missile Silo (Sheet 4 of 4)

T.O. 21-SM68-1

Section IV

STEP	PROCEDURE
	Note
	All hazard actions and procedures will be at the discretion of the MLO.
	All tasks preceded by an asterisk will be coordinated with the MLO.
1	MISSILE SILO FIRE (LCFC).....................................Flashing Red
2	Buzzer...Silenced
	If buzzer was not silenced from a prior hazard, buzzer sounds indicating a hazard exists. BMAT presses PUSH TO SILENCE pushbutton on LCFC.
3	MLO...Notified
	Upon observing hazard, BMAT will notifies MLO immediately.
4	Corrective action...Started
	When corrective action starts, MISSILE SILO FIRE indicator will be flashing red and white. The FOG ON indicator will be flashing white.
	Note
	If corrective action has not started:
	(Except VAFB) Check AUTO FOG DISABLE indicator. (VAFB) Check EMERGENCY WATER OFF indicator.
	If indicator is amber, press to not lighted.
	Note
	If countdown is in progress, perform only step 5; at all other times perform steps 6 thru 26.
5	Countdown...Continued
	MLO will evaluate hazard and determine if it will be feasible to continue countdown. If shutdown is initiated, perform steps 6 thru 26.

Figure 4-6. Missile Silo Fire (Sheet 1 of 4)

4-18

T.O. 21-SM68-1

Section IV

STEP	PROCEDURE
6	"Attention all personnel in launcher ____, fire in missile silo. Team chief contact control center immediately" (if applicable)..........................Announced
	BMAT or MLO makes above announcement over P.A. system.
7	Command post...Notified
	MLO notifies command post of hazard and all pertinent facts, and requests assistance, if necessary.
8	Press HAZARD LIGHT (LCFC)...............................Red
	BMAT presses ABOVE GRD HAZARD LIGHT pushbutton indicator for affected launcher to red to indicate an unsafe condition in that launcher.
9	Press MISSILE AND FACILITY (LCFC).....................Red
	BMAT presses MISSILE AND FACILITY pushbutton indicator to insure that a countdown will not be inadvertently started with a hazard in launcher area.
10	(Except VAFB) Press LAUNCHER AIR FILTRATION BLAST VALVES OVERRIDE CONTROLS CLOSE (applicable launcher)....Amber
	BMAT checks control center alarm panel to see if the AIR FILTRATION BLAST VALVES have closed. If valves did not close, he presses the CLOSE pushbutton for applicable launcher.
11	Terminate corrective action............................Directed
	MLO will direct BMAT to terminate corrective action at discretion of BMAT.
12	Press AUTO FOG DISABLE..................................Amber
	BMAT presses AUTO FOG DISABLE pushbutton indicator which lights amber and provides part of circuit which turns off fog in the missile silo.
13	FOG ON..Pressed
	Note
	In approximately 30 seconds, FOG ON will be not lighted and MISSILE SILO FIRE will be flashing red.

Figure 4-6. Missile Silo Fire (Sheet 2 of 4)

STEP	PROCEDURE
13 (CONT)	BMAT presses FOG ON pushbutton indicator. At this time a short delay is required for the water valve to close. After the delay, FOG ON indicator will be not lighted and MISSILE SILO FIRE indicator will flash red only. This indicates that water fog is off and corrective action has terminated. At this time BMAT will notify MLO of corrective action status.
*14	Corrective action terminated..........................Reported After corrective action has been terminated and MISSILE SILO FIRE indicator is flashing red, corrective action may be restarted by pressing AUTO FOG DISABLE pushbutton indicator to not lighted.
15	Personnel to missile silo.............................Directed At his discretion, MLO will direct personnel to missile silo.
16	HORN SILENCER (MSAP)..................................Pressed
17	MANUAL RESET (MSAP)...................................Pressed Note If alarm fails to silence after MANUAL RESET has been pressed, sensors have not cooled sufficiently to be reset. Repeat steps 16 and 17 until normal indication on MSAP is achieved.
*18	MSAP..Normal Personnel at MSAP will notify MLO that fire sensors have been reset and all indications are normal.
19	MISSILE SILO FIRE (LCFC).........................Not Lighted When MANUAL RESET is pressed on MSAP, MISSILE SILO FIRE indicator will be not lighted on LCFC.
*20	Condition of missile silo............................Reported Personnel will proceed with caution to missile silo to observe damage caused by the fire. Personnel will not proceed into any area that has been damaged by fire. Condition of the missile silo is reported to MLO.

Figure 4-6. Missile Silo Fire (Sheet 3 of 4)

STEP	PROCEDURE
21	"Attention all personnel, fire in missile silo _____ has been extinguished".......................... Announced
	BMAT or MLO will make above announcement over P.A. system to inform personnel that hazard has been corrected.
22	(Except VAFB) Press LAUNCHER AIR FILTRATION BLAST VALVES OVERRIDE CONTROLS OPEN (applicable launcher).. Not Lighted
23	Air conditioner (AC 2012) and fans (FN 2001 and FN 2021).. Started
	MLO directs personnel to start missile silo air conditioner and fans at the discretion of MMT.
*24	Maintenance... Performed
	Necessary maintenance will be performed to return missile silo to normal operation.
25	Press HAZARD LIGHT (LCFC)............................... Green
	When hazard has been corrected, BMAT will press ABOVE GRD HAZARD LIGHT pushbutton indicator to green, signifying hazard has been cleared. Absence of a red indication above ground indicates hazard has been corrected and area is clear for normal operation.
26	Press MISSILE AND FACILITY (LCFC)..................... Green
	BMAT presses the MISSILE AND FACILITY pushbutton indicator to green, releasing the hold which allows a launch countdown to be initiated.

Figure 4-6. Missile Silo Fire (Sheet 4 of 4)

T.O. 21-SM68-1 Section IV

STEP	PROCEDURE
	Note
	All hazard actions and procedures will be at the discretion of the MLO.
	All tasks preceded by an asterisk will be coordinated with the MLO.
1	PROP TERM LOX FIRE (LCFC)..............................Flashing Red
	PROP TERM LOX FIRE indicator on LCFC will light flashing red.
2	Buzzer...Silenced
	If buzzer was not silenced from a prior hazard, the buzzer sounds indicating a hazard exists. BMAT presses the PUSH TO SILENCE pushbutton on LCFC.
3	MLO..Notified
	BMAT notifies MLO immediately upon observing hazard.
	Note
	If countdown is in progress perform only step 4; all other times perform steps 5 thru 20.
4	Countdown..Continued
	MLO will evaluate hazard and determine if it will be feasible to continue countdown. If shutdown is initiated, perform steps 5 thru 20.
5	Press HAZARD LIGHT (LCFC)..............................Red
	BMAT presses ABOVE GRD HAZARD LIGHT pushbutton indicator for the affected launcher to red to indicate an unsafe condition in that launcher.
6	Press MISSILE AND FACILITY (LCFC)......................Red
	BMAT presses MISSILE AND FACILITY pushbutton indicator to insure that a countdown will not be inadvertently started with a hazard in launcher area.

Figure 4-7. Propellant Terminal Fire (Sheet 1 of 3)

T.O. 21-SM68-1

Section IV

STEP	PROCEDURE
7	Command post..Notified
	MLO notifies command post of hazard and all pertinent facts, and requests assistance, if necessary.
8	"Attention all personnel. Fire in propellant terminal _____. Team chief call control center immediately" (if applicable)............................Announced
	BMAT or MLO makes above announcement over P.A. system to alert personnel of hazard.
9	(Except VAFB) Press LAUNCHER AIR FILTRATION BLAST VALVES OVERRIDE CONTROLS CLOSE (applicalbe launcher)...Amber
	BMAT checks control center alarm panel to see if the AIR FILTRATION BLAST VALVES have closed. If valves did not close he presses CLOSE pushbutton for the applicable launcher.
10	Personnel to propellant terminal.......................Directed
	At his discretion, MLO directs personnel to propellant terminal.
11	HORN SILENCER (PTAP)....................................Pressed
	Personnel will not open propellant terminal door if there is any indication that fire is not out. If fire appears to be out, open propellant terminal door and proceed with caution to PTAP and press HORN SILENCE.
*12	Propellant terminal condition..........................Reported
	Personnel will investigate and evaluate condition of propellant terminal and report findings to MLO.
13	LOX FIRE RESET (PTAP)...................................Pressed
	If no fire is present or sensors have cooled, press LOX FIRE RESET ON PTAP.
14	PTAP..Normal

Figure 4-7. Propellant Terminal Fire (Sheet 2 of 3)

4-23

STEP	PROCEDURE
15	PROP TERM LOX FIRE (LCFC)..............................Not Lighted
16	"Attention all personnel, propellant terminal _____ is now open for normal work."................Announced
	BMAT will make above announcement after all conditions are found to be normal.
17	(Except VAFB) Press LAUNCHER AIR FILTRATION BLAST VALVES OVERRIDE CONTROLS OPEN (applicable launcher)...Not Lighted
18	Maintenance..Performed
	Maintenance will be performed as necessary to return propellant terminal to normal operation.
19	Press HAZARD LIGHT (LCFC)..............................Green
	When hazard has been corrected, BMAT will press ABOVE GRD HAZARD LIGHT pushbutton indicator to green, signifying hazard has been cleared. Absence of a red indication above gound indicates hazard has been corrected and area is clear for normal operation.
20	Press MISSILE AND FACILITY (LCFC).....................Green
	BMAT presses MISSILE AND FACILITY pushbutton indicator to green, releasing the hold, which allows a launch countdown to be initiated.

Figure 4-7. Propellant Terminal Fire (Sheet 3 of 3)

STEP	PROCEDURE
	All hazard actions and procedures will be at the discretion of the MLO. All tasks preceded by an asterisk will be coordinated with the MLO.
1	EQUIP TERM FIRE (LCFC)..Flashing Red FIRE indicator will flash red whenever a fire sensor has been activated by excessive heat in equipment terminal.
2	Buzzer...Silenced If buzzer was not silenced from a prior hazard, buzzer sounds indicating a hazard exists. BMAT will press PUSH TO SILENCE pushbutton on LCFC.
3	MLO..Notified BMAT will notify MLO immediately upon observing hazard. Note If countdown is in progress, perform only step 4; all other times perform steps 5 thru 20.
4	Countdown..Continued MLO will evaluate hazard and determine if it will be feasible to continue countdown. If shutdown is initiated, perform steps 6 thru 20.
5	Press HAZARD LIGHT (LCFC)...Red BMAT presses ABOVE GRD HAZARD LIGHT pushbutton indicator for the affected launcher to red to indicate an unsafe condition in that launcher.
6	Press MISSILE AND FACILITY (LCFC)...................................Red BMAT presses MISSILE AND FACILITY pushbutton indicator to insure that a countdown will not be inadvertently started with a hazard in launcher area.

Figure 4-8. Equipment Terminal Fire (Sheet 1 of 3)

T.O. 21-SM68-1

STEP	PROCEDURE
7	"Attention all personnel in launcher _____, fire in equipment terminal. Team chief call control center immediately." (if applicable)..Announced BMAT or MLO makes above announcement to alert personnel of hazard.
8	(Except VAFB) Press LAUNCHER AIR FILTRATION BLAST VALVES OVERRIDE CONTROLS CLOSE (applicable launcher)...Amber BMAT checks control center alarm panel to see if AIR FILTRATION BLAST VALVES have closed. If valves did not close, he presses the CLOSE pushbutton for applicable launcher.
9	Command post..Notified MLO notifies command post of hazard and all pertinent facts, and requests assistance, if necessary.
10	Personnel to equipment terminal.........................Directed MLO directs personnel to equipment terminal to investigate and evaluate hazard. Personnel will silence horns, if possible, and report condition of equipment terminal to MLO. After fire has been extinguished, maintenance will be performed and fire sensors reset.
11	HORN SILENCER (ETAP).......................................Pressed
*12	Condition of equipment terminal..........................Reported
13	FIRE SENSOR RESET...Pressed
14	ETAP..Normal
15	EQUIP TERM FIRE (LCFC)................................Not Lighted
16	"Attention all personnel, fire in equipment terminal _____ has been extinguised"......................Announced

Figure 4-8. Equipment Terminal Fire (Sheet 2 of 3)

STEP	PROCEDURE
16 (CONT)	After system is reset, ETAP and FIRE indicator (LCFC) will be checked for normal indications and BMAT or MLO will make an announcement over P.A. system to inform personnel that hazard has been corrected.
17	(Except VAFB) Press LAUNCHER AIR FILTRATION BLAST VALVES OVERRIDE CONTROLS open (applicable launcher)...Not Lighted BMAT opens air filtration blast valves on control center alarm panel.
18	Maintenance...Performed
19	Press HAZARD LIGHT (LCFC)................................Green When hazard has been corrected, BMAT will press ABOVE GRD HAZARD LIGHT pushbutton indicator to green, signifying hazard has been cleared. Absence of a red indication above ground indicates hazard has been corrected and area is clear for normal operation.
20	Press MISSILE AND FACILITY (LCFC).......................Green BMAT presses MISSILE AND FACILITY pushbutton indicator to green, releasing the hold, which allows a launch countdown to be initiated.

Figure 4-8. Equipment Terminal Fire (Sheet 3 of 3)

STEP	PROCEDURE
	Note All hazard actions and procedures will be at the discretion of the MLO. All tasks preceded by an asterisk will be coordinated with the MLO.
1	EQUIP TERM HYDRAULIC FIRE (LCFC)......................Flashing Red
2	Buzzer..Silenced If buzzer was not silenced from a prior hazzard, buzzer sounds indicating a hazard exists. BMAT will press PUSH TO SILENCE pushbutton on LCFC.
3	Corrective action.....................................Started Hydraulic fire indicator flashes red and buzzer will sound indicating that a fire has started in the hydraulic unit on Level II of equipment terminal. When indicator flashes red and white, it indicates corrective action has started.
4	MLO...Notified BMAT will notify MLO immediately upon observing hazard. Note If countdown is in progress perform only step 5; at all other times perform steps 6 thru 22.
5	Countdown...Continued MLO will evaluate the hazard and determine if it will be feasible to continue countdown or initiate shutdown. If a shutdown is initiated, perform steps 6 thru 22.
6	"Attention all personnel in launcher _____, hydraulic fire on level II of equipment terminal. Team chief call control center immediately." (if applicable)......................Announced BMAT or MLO makes above announcement over P.A. system to alert all personnel of hazard.

Figure 4-9. Hydraulic Fire, Equipment Terminal (Sheet 1 of 4)

T.O. 21-SM68-1 Section IV

STEP	PROCEDURE
7	Press HAZARD LIGHT (LCFC).................................Red
	EMAT presses ABOVE GRD HAZARD LIGHT pushbutton indicator for affected launcher to red to indicate an unsafe condition in that launcher.
8	Press MISSILE AND FACILITY (LCFC).......................Red
	EMAT presses MISSILE AND FACILITY pushbutton indicator for the affected launcher to red to indicate an unsafe condition in that launcher.
9	Command post..Notified
	MLO notifies command post of hazard and all pertinent facts, and requests assistance, if necessary.
10	(Except VAFB) Press LAUNCHER AIR FILTRATION BLAST VALVES OVERRIDE CONTROLS CLOSE (applicable launcher)...Amber
	EMAT checks control center alarm panel to see if AIR FILTRATION BLAST VALVES are closed. If valves did not close, he presses the CLOSE pushbutton for the applicable launcher.
11	Personnel to level II of equipment terminal..............Directed
	MLO directs MMT to level II to investigate and evaluate condition of hydraulic pumping unit (C-216). MMT silences alarm horn (hydraulic fire) on ETAP before proceeding to level II, and reports condition to MLO.
	Note
	If corrective action was initiated, continue with step 12. If corrective action was not initiated, MLO will direct team chief to fight fire with portable CO_2 bottles. When fire is extinguished, continue with step 12.
12	HORN SILENCER (ETAP).....................................Pressed

Figure 4-9. Hydraulic Fire, Equipment Terminal (Sheet 2 of 4)

T.O. 21M-HGM25A-1-1 (21-SM68-1) Section IV

STEP	PROCEDURE
*13	Condition of A/E27A-2 (C-216).........................Reported
14	Press DISCHARGE CO_2 RESET (C-216)..................Not Lighted
	When the carbon dioxide has been discharged within the pumping unit the high temperature red indicator and buzzer will be deenergized and the DISCHARGE CO_2 indicator will be lighted white. Team chief presses DISCHARGE CO_2 RESET for a DISCHARGE CO_2 indicator not lighted. Carbon dioxide bottle must be recharged.
15	EQUIP TERM HYDRAULIC FIRE (LCFC).......................Not Lighted
16	ETAP..Normal
17	"Attention all personnel in launcher _____, hydraulic fire on level II of equipment terminal is extinguished"......................................Announced
	After system is reset, ETAP and FIRE indicator (LCFC) will be checked for normal indications and BMAT or MLO will make an announcement over P.A. system to inform personnel that hazard has been corrected.
18	(Except VAFB) Press LAUNCHER AIR FILTRATION BLAST VALVES OVERRIDE CONTROLS OPEN (applicable launcher)..Not Lighted
	BMAT opens AIR FILTRATION BLAST VALVES on control center alarm panel.
19	Press HAZARD LIGHT (LCFC).............................Green
	When hazard has been corrected, BMAT will press above ground hazard light pushbutton indicator to green, signifying hazard has been cleared. Absence of a red indication above ground indicates hazard has been corrected and area is clear for normal operation.
20	Press MISSILE AND FACILITY (LCFC).....................Green
	BMAT presses MISSILE AND FACILITY pushbutton indicator to green, releasing hold, which re-enables the weapon system launch countdown capability.

Figure 4-9. Hydraulic Fire, Equipment Terminal (Sheet 3 of 4)

T.O. 21-SM68-1

STEP	PROCEDURE
21	Maintenance..Performed
22	Pneumatic control..Reset

Figure 4-9. Hydraulic Fire, Equipment Terminal (Sheet 4 of 4)

(Pages 4-32 through 4-34, Figure 4-10 deleted.)

T.O. 21-SM68-1

Section IV

STEP	PROCEDURE
	Note
	All hazard actions and procedures will be at the discretion of the MLO.
	All tasks preceded by an asterisk will be coordinated with the MLO.
1	FUEL TERM FUEL FIRE (LCFC).................................Flashing Red
	FIRE indicator flashes red whenever a fire sets off a sensor in fuel terminal.
2	Buzzer...Silenced
	If the buzzer was not silenced from a prior hazard, buzzer sounds indicating a hazard exists. BMAT will press the PUSH TO SILENCE pushbutton on the LCFC.
3	Corrective action..Started
	FUEL FIRE indicator on LCFC lights flashing red and white. At this time fuel terminal CO_2 system is activated.
	Note
	If corrective action did not start, MLO must dispatch personnel to the fuel terminal to initiate corrective action manually.
4	MLO..Notified
	BMAT notifies MLO immediately upon observing hazard.
	WARNING
	If fueling or defueling is in progress, operations will cease immediately. Only personnel in fuel terminal will evacuate to control center. All other personnel will remain at their stations.

Figure 4-11. Fire in Fuel Terminal (Sheet 1 of 3)

STEP	PROCEDURE
5	"Attention all personnel, fire in fuel terminal. All personnel in fuel terminal evacuate to control center immediately. Team chief call control center." (if applicable)..Announced
6	Press HAZARD LIGHT (3) (LCFC).........................Red BMAT presses all three ABOVE GRD HAZARD LIGHT pushbutton indicators to red, indicating entire complex is in a hazardous condition.
7	Command post..Notified MLO notifies command post of hazard, and all pertinent facts, and requests assistance, if necessary.
8	Personnel to fuel terminal............................Directed MLO directs personnel to fuel terminal to investigate and evaluate hazard. Personnel will silence horns, reset system, and report conditions to MLO.
9	HORN SILENCER (FTAP)..................................Pressed Note If alarm bell fails to silence after RESET has been pressed, sensors have not cooled sufficiently to be reset. Repeat steps 9 and 10 until normal indication on FTAP is noted.
10	SENSOR RESET (FTAP)...................................Pressed
11	FTAP..Normal
*12	Conditions of fuel terminal..........................Reported
13	FUEL TERM FUEL FIRE (LCFC)...........................Not Lighted After system is reset, the FTAP and FUEL TERM FUEL FIRE (LCFC) will be checked for normal operation.

Figure 4-11. Fire in Fuel Terminal (Sheet 2 of 3)

T.O. 21-SM68-1

Section IV

STEP	PROCEDURE
14	"Attention all personnel, fuel terminal fuel fire has been corrected"..................................Announced BMAT or MLO makes announcement over the P.A. system to inform personnel that hazard has been corrected.
15	Press HAZARD LIGHT (3) (LCFC)............................Green When hazard has been corrected, BMAT will press ABOVE GRD HAZARD LIGHT pushbutton indicators (3) to green, signifying hazard has been cleared. Absence of a red indication above ground indicates hazard has been corrected and area is clear for normal operation.
16	Maintenance...Performed Maintenance will be performed as necessary to return system to an alert status monitoring condition.

Figure 4-11. Fire in Fuel Terminal (Sheet 3 of 3)

(Pages 4-38 through 4-39, Figure 4-12 deleted.)

STEP	PROCEDURE
	Note
	All hazard actions and procedures will be at the discretion of the MLO.
	All tasks preceded by an asterisk will be coordinated with the MLO.
1	MISSILE SILO EXPLOSION (LCFC)..........................Flashing Red
	MISSILE SILO EXPLOSION indicator will be flashing red whenever one or more explosion detectors mounted on wall of missile silo detect an explosion. Automatic corrective/containing action is as follows: Blast valves located in propellant terminal and tunnel entrance to applicable launcher will close; blast valves in remaining two launchers will close for 3 seconds to prevent shock waves and blast effect from reaching remote portions of complex.
2	Buzzer..Silenced
	If buzzer was not silenced from a prior hazard, buzzer sounds indicating a hazard exists. BMAT presses PUSH TO SILENCE pushbutton on the LCFC.
3	MLO...Notified
	BMAT notifies MLO immediately upon observing hazard.
4	Gox content (missile silo)...................................Checked
	BMAT visually checks remote gox indicator for affected launcher.
5	Press HAZARD LIGHT (LCFC)..Red
	BMAT presses ABOVE GRD HAZARD LIGHT pushbutton indicator for affected launcher to red to indicate an unsafe condition in that launcher.
6	Press MISSILE AND FACILITY (LCFC)................................Red
	BMAT presses MISSILE AND FACILITY pushbutton indicator to insure that a countdown will not be inadvertently started with a hazard in the launcher area.

Figure 4-13. Missile Silo Explosion (Sheet 1 of 2)

T.O. 21-SM68-1 Section IV

STEP	PROCEDURE
7	Command post..Notified
	MLO notifies command post of hazard, and all pertinent facts, and requests assistance if necessary.
8	Personnel to missile silo tunnel entrance.................Directed
	Following a reasonable length of time during which no other hazard indications occur, personnel proceed to missile silo tunnel entrance upon direction of MLO.
9	HORN SILENCER (MSAP)..Pressed
	Alarm horns in missile silo are silenced by pressing pushbutton PB9 on MSAP.
10	RESET (MSAP)..Pressed
	Pressing RESET pushbutton deactivates explosion sensors in missile silo and opens all blast valves in affected launcher area.
*11	Condition of missile silo...................................Reported
	Personnel inspect missile silo and report to MLO cause and effects of explosion encountered.
12	Press HAZARD LIGHT (LCFC).....................................Green
	BMAT presses ABOVE GRD HAZARD LIGHT pushbutton indicator to green signifying hazard has been cleared. Absence of a red indication above ground indicates that affected launcher is in a normal condition.
13	Press MISSILE AND FACILITY (LCFC)............................Green
	BMAT presses MISSILE AND FACILITY pushbutton indicator to green, releasing hold, which allows a launch countdown to be initiated.
14	Maintenance...Performed
	Required maintenance will be performed to return weapon system to normal operation.

Figure 4-13. Missile Silo Explosion (Sheet 2 of 2)

STEP	PROCEDURE
	Note
	All hazard actions and procedures will be at the discretion of the MLO.
1	LOX EMPTY (LCFC)..Red
	LOX EMPTY red indication denotes that quantity of liquid oxygen in lox storage tank (T-201) is approximately 900 gallons or below.
2	MLO..Notified
	BMAT notifies MLO of indication received on LCFC.
	LOX EMPTY signal, if received during a countdown, causes automatic closure of FCV-301 and/or FCV-307 and opening of FCV-302.
	MLO initiates a manual shutdown if LOX LOADING or LOX LOADED is not received due to a valid LOX EMPTY signal. If LOX EMPTY signal is generated by the PLPS during the first hold period, MLO must initiate RAISE LAUNCHER phase immediately.
3	Countdown..Continued
	MLO will evaluate the hazard and determine if it will be feasible to continue countdown.

Figure 4-14. Lox Empty Propellant Terminal

STEP	PROCEDURE
	Note
	All hazard actions and procedures will be at the discretion of the MLO.
1	EQUIP TERM BATTERY POWER..............................Red
	BATTERY POWER red indicator lights steady red indicating that first end cell of standby batteries has been activated. This indicates that 28 VDC rectifier A/E24A-4 has failed.
2	MLO...Notified
	Upon observing hazard, BMAT notifies MLO immediately.
	Note
	If countdown is in progress and has not proceeded past first hold, perform steps 3 and 4. If countdown has progressed beyond first hold, perform only step 3.
3	Countdown...Continued
4	Personnel to level IV of equipment terminal............Directed
	Note
	Refer to Section V for malfunction isolation.
	BMAT will refer to malfunction chart to troubleshoot indication and attempt to return rectifier to proper operation.

Figure 4-15. Battery Power, Equipment Terminal

T.O. 21-SM68-1

Section IV

STEP	PROCEDURE
	Note
	All hazard actions and procedures will be at the discretion of the MLO.
	All tasks preceded by an asterisk will be coordinated with the MLO.
1	POWER HOUSE EMERGENCY (LCFC)..........................Flashing Red
	The POWER HOUSE EMERGENCY indicator flashes red and buzzer sounds indicating an emergency in power house. BMAT silences buzzer, notifies MLO of emergency indication, and then contacts power house to inquire as to nature of emergency. Power house will advise control center of condition.
2	Buzzer..Silenced
3	MLO...Notified
4	Power house..Contacted
*5	Condition..Reported
	Note
	If countdown is in progress, perform only step 6; at all other times perform steps 7 thru 14.
6	Countdown..Continued
	MLO will evaluate hazard and determine if it will be feasible to continue countdown or initiate shutdown. If shutdown is initiated, perform steps 7 thru 14.
7	"Attention all personnel, emergency in the power house; standby for further instructions."...............Announced
	Personnel are directed to power house by MLO to assist as necessary.
8	Press HAZARD LIGHT (3) (LCFC)...............................Red
	BMAT presses all three HAZARD LIGHTS pushbutton indicators indicating entire complex is in a hazardous condition.

Figure 4-16. Power House Emergency (Sheet 1 of 2)

STEP	PROCEDURE
9	Command post..Notified
	MLO notifies command post of hazard, all pertinent facts, and request assistance if necessary.
10	POWER HOUSE EMERGENCY (LCFC)..........................Not Lighted
11	Final status..Reported
	EPPT notifies the control center of final outcome of condition that caused power house emergency indication.
12	"Attention all personnel, power house emergency has been corrected"..Announced
13	Press HAZARD LIGHT (3) (LCFC)...........................Green
	When hazard has been corrected, BMAT will press the ABOVE GRD HAZARD LIGHT pushbutton indicators to green, signifying hazard has been cleared. Absence of a red indication above ground indicates hazard has been corrected and area is clear for normal operation.
14	Maintenance..Performed
	EPPT supervises and assists maintenance personnel in performing maintenance, if required.

Figure 4-16. Power House Emergency (Sheet 2 of 2)

T.O. 21-SM68-1 Section IV

STEP	PROCEDURE
	All hazard actions and procedures will be at the discretion of the MLO.
	This procedure outlines the steps required of the EPPT for restoring AC power to the complex in the event of loss of all AC power.
1	Locate, isolate, troubleshoot, and correct system malfunction..Accomplished
	EPPT visually checks annunciator panel, switchgear, and safety devices to determine the cause of power failure.
2	Feeder circuit breakers 2 thru 5...........................Tripped
	EPPT manually trips feeder circuit breakers to isolate feeders from bus bar.
3	Fire water pumps switches...................................OFF
	EPPT directs facility personnel to turn off fire water pumps.
4	Standby generator on the line...........................Accomplished
	EPPT starts standby generator and connects generator to the bus.
5	Fire water jockey pump.......................................Started
	EPPT directs facility personnel to start fire water jockey pump.
6	Raw water pump..Started
	EPPT directs facility personnel to start raw water pump.
7	(VAFB, EAFB, BAFB, LAFB, MHAFB) Cooling tower pumps...Started
	EPPT directs facility personnel to start cooling tower pumps.

Figure 4-17. Loss of All AC Power (Sheet 1 of 3)

Changed 17 January 1964 TOCN-1 (DEN-8)

4-46

STEP	PROCEDURE
8	Chilled water pump...Started
	EPPT directs facility personnel to start chilled water pump.
9	Hot water pump...Started
	EPPT directs facility personnel to start the hot water pump.
10	Exhaust fan..Started
	EPPT starts exhaust fan by closing circuit breaker and pressing START pushbutton, or by setting START switch to START.
11	(LAFB 724TH/725TH SQDN) Condenser water pump...Started
	EPPT directs facility personnel to start condenser water pump.
12	Water pressure on all systems............................Checked
	EPPT and facility personnel visually check all water pressure systems.
13	Second diesel engine...Started
	EPPT accomplishes the above by starting the diesel engine.
14	Parallel second generator..................................Accomplished
	EPPT accomplishes the above by paralleling generator to the bus.
15	Power house intake air supply fan........................Started
	EPPT starts the intake fan by closing circuit breaker and setting START switch to START, or by pressing START pushbutton.
16	Water chiller..Started
	EPPT directs facility personnel to start water chiller.

Figure 4-17. Loss of All AC Power (Sheet 2 of 3)

T.O. 21-SM68-1

STEP	PROCEDURE
17	Post diesel engine start checkout..........................Accomplished EPPT will accomplish the above by using the post diesel engine start checkout checklist.
18	Communication between the power house and control center...Established EPPT contacts control center to report status of power house by using applicable communication net.
19	Feeder circuit breakers 2 thru 5 when directed by control center...Closed EPPT contacts the control center to obtain status of the affected launchers before closing feeder circuit breakers.
20	Fire water pumps switches....................................ON EPPT directs facility personnel to place fire water pumps HAND-OFF-AUTO switches in AUTO position.
21	All systems within the power house......................Checked EPPT and facility personnel check all systems for proper pressures, temperatures, and levels.
22	Applicable logs and forms.................................Annotated

Figure 4-17. Loss of All AC Power (Sheet 3 of 3)

Changed 17 January 1964 TOCN-1 (DEN-8)

STEP	PROCEDURE
	All hazard actions and procedures will be at the discretion of the MLO.
	This procedure applies when it is necessary for two generators to be on the line during alert status monitoring.
1	Power house intake air supply fan . . . . OFF
	EPPT secures intake air supply fan by setting STOP switch to STOP, or by pressing STOP pushbutton.
2	(EAFB, LAFB, MHAFB) Electrical heater hot water system. . . . . OFF
	EPPT secures electrical heater hot water system in accordance with SAC CEM 21-SM68-2-24-( ).
3	Inform control center of emergency. . . . . Accomplished
4	Standby engine. . . . . Started
	EPPT accomplishes above by starting the standby diesel engine.
5	Parallel standby generator on the line. . . . . Accomplished
	EPPT accomplishes the above by paralleling generator to the bus.
6	Power house intake air supply fan . . . . Started
	EPPT starts intake air supply fan by setting START switch to START, or by pressing START pushbutton.
7	(EAFB, LAFB, MHAFB) Electrical heater hot water system. . . . . Started
	EPPT starts electrical heater hot water system in accordance with SAC CEM 21-SM68-2-24-( ).
8	Post diesel engine start checkout . . . . Accomplished
	EPPT accomplishes above by using post diesel engine start checkout checklist.

Figure 4-18. Loss of One of Two Generators During Alert Status Monitoring (EAFB, BAFB, LAFB, MHAFB) (Sheet 1 of 2)

STEP	PROCEDURE
9	All systems within the power house......................Checked
	EPPT and facility personnel will check all systems for proper pressures, temperatures, and levels.
10	Inform control center emergency corrected...............Accomplished
11	Locate, isolate, troubleshoot, and correct system malfunction......................................Accomplished
	EPPT accomplishes above by using portions of Section V and applicable SAC CEM manuals.
12	Applicable logs and forms...............................Annotated

Figure 4-18. Loss of one of Two Generators During Alert Status Monitoring (EAFB, BAFB, LAFB, MHAFB) (Sheet 2 of 2)

STEP	PROCEDURE
	Note All hazard actions and procedures will be at the discretion of the MLO.
1	Operating water chiller STOP pushbutton..................Pressed EPPT directs facility personnel to stop operating water chiller.
2	Inform control center of emergency.......................Accomplished EPPT contacts control center to report status of power house by using applicable communication net.
3	Standby engine...Started EPPT accomplishes above by starting the standby diesel engine.
4	Parallel standby generator...............................Accomplished EPPT accomplishes above by paralleling generator to the bus.
5	Water chiller START pushbutton...........................Pressed EPPT directs facility personnel to start water chiller.
6	Post diesel engine start checkout........................Accomplished EPPT accomplishes above by using post diesel engine start checkout checklist.
7	All systems within the power house.......................Checked EPPT and facility personnel check all systems for proper pressures, temperatures, and levels.
8	Inform control center emergency corrected................Accomplished
9	Locate, isolate, and troubleshoot system.................Accomplished EPPT accomplishes above by using portions of Section V and applicable SAC CEM manuals.
10	Applicable forms and logs................................Annotated

Figure 4-19. Loss of One of Two Generators During Alert Status Monitoring (LAFB 724TH/725TH SQDN)

STEP	PROCEDURE
	Note
	All hazard actions and procedures will be at the discretion of the MLO.
1	Operating water chiller STOP pushbutton..................Pressed
	EPPT or facility personnel immediately stop operating water chiller by pressing STOP pushbutton.
2	Inform control center of emergency and to continue countdown.......................................Accomplished
3	First ice bank...On Line
	EPPT directs facility personnel to place first ice bank on line.
4	Monitor chilled water temperature, ice bank water level, and add ice banks as required................Accomplished
5	Applicable logs and forms...............................Annotated

Figure 4-20. Loss of One of Three Generators During Countdown
(LAFB 724TH/725TH SQDN)

STEP	PROCEDURE
	Note
	All hazard actions and procedures will be at the discretion of the MLO.
1	Alert signal..Received
2	Operating water chiller STOP pushbutton................Pressed
	EPPT directs facility personnel to stop operating water chiller by pressing STOP pushbutton.
3	"Power house GO to control center"....................Reported
	EPPT will be on the communication net and after all meters have been monitored, will report power house GO to the control center.
4	First ice bank..On Line
	EPPT directs facility personnel to place first ice bank on line.
5	Monitor chilled water temperature, ice bank water level, and add ice banks as required.............Accomplished

Figure 4-21. Two Generator Countdown (LAFB 724TH/725TH SQDN)

STEP	PROCEDURE
	Note
	All hazard actions and procedures are at the discretion of the MLO.
1	Inform control center of emergency....................Accomplished
2	Locate, isolate, troubleshoot, and correct system malfunction........................Accomplished
	EPPT visually checks the annunciator panel and feeder (a) safety devices to determine the cause of power failure.
	CAUTION
	Do not restore power to launcher areas until directed by control center. Failure to heed this caution may result in damage to equipment.
3	Power to affected launcher areas.....................Restored
	EPPT contacts control center to determine status of affected launcher (a) before closing launcher feeder air circuit breaker.

Figure 4-22. Loss of Launcher Feeder AC Power

STEP	PROCEDURE
	Note
	All hazard actions and procedures are at the discretion of the MLO.
1	Locate, isolate, troubleshoot, and correct system malfunction..............................Accomplished
2	Powerhouse feeder air circuit breaker...................Closed
3	Applicable logs and forms...............................Annotated

Figure 4-23. Loss of Power House Feeder AC Power

T.O. 21-SM68-1   Section IV

STEP	PROCEDURE
	Note
	All hazard actions and procedures are at the discretion of the MLO.
1	Inform control center of emergency.....................Accomplished
2	Locate, isolate, troubleshoot, and correct system malfunction..Accomplished
	EPPT visually checks annunciator panel and feeder safety devices to determine cause of power failure.
	CAUTION
	Do not restore power until directed by control center. Failure to heed this caution may result in damage to equipment.
3	Control center feeder air circuit breaker...............Closed
	EPPT contacts control center to determine status of control center before closing control center air circuit breaker.

Figure 4-24. Loss of Control Center Feeder AC Power

STEP	PROCEDURE
	Note
	All hazard actions and procedures are at the discretion of the MLO.
1	Inform control center of emergency....................Accomplished
2	(LAFB 724TH/725TH SQDN only) Dampers in intake air facility..................................Blocked Open
	EPPT will accomplish above by placing blocks in intake air facility dampers to open position.
3	Locate, isolate, troubleshoot, and correct system malfunction.......................................Accomplished
	EPPT will accomplish above by using portions of Section V of this manual and applicable SAC CEM manuals.
4	(LAFB 724TH/725TH SQDN only) Blocks in dampers..Removed
	EPPT will accomplish above by removing blocks from intake air facility dampers.
5	Intake fan START pushbutton..........................Pressed
	EPPT starts intake fan by pressing START pushbutton.

Figure 4-25. Loss of Power House Intake Fan

STEP	PROCEDURE
	Note
	All hazard actions and procedures are at the discretion of the MLO.
1	Inform control center of emergency.................... Accomplished
2	Vanes on exhaust fan.................................. Locked Open
	EPPT facility personnel accomplish the above by locking exhaust fan vanes in open position.
3	Locate, isolate, troubleshoot, and correct system malfunction.. Accomplished
	EPPT will accomplish the above by using portions of section V of this manual and applicable SAC CEM manuals.
4	Vanes on exhaust fan.................................. Unlocked
	EPPT facility personnel will accomplish the above by unlocking exhaust fan vanes.
5	Exhaust fan... Started
	EPPT/Facility personnel start exhaust fan by closing circuit breaker and setting START switch to START or pressing START pushbutton.

Figure 4-26. Loss of Power House Exhaust Fan

STEP	PROCEDURE
	All hazard actions and procedures are at the discretion of the MLO.
1	(LAFB 724TH/725TH SQDN) Manual throttle control lever..STOP
	EPPT manually places throttle control lever to stop position.
2	EMERGENCY STOP pushbutton...................................Pressed
	EPPT manually presses EMERGENCY STOP pushbutton on engine control console and visually checks fuel control linkage to insure fuel rack is in the decreased fuel position.
	Note
	Step 3 is to be performed only if step 2 does not effect an immediate decrease in engine RPM.
3	CO_2 into air intake...Injected
	As a last resort, EPPT will use an ax to chop a hole in engine intake flex duct near the turbocharger intake and inject CO_2 from a fire extinguisher. It will take a minimum of three CO_2 bottles to effect engine shutdown.
	WARNING
	If all prerequisites for stopping runaway engine are complied with an engine has not reduced speed, evacuate the power house.
4	Engine stopped...Verified
	EPPT visually verifies that engine has stopped.
5	Inform control center of emergency......................Accomplished
6	Locate system malfunction................................Accomplished
7	Damage to engine and generator............................Evaluated
	EPPT will visually analyze extent of damage to affected equipment but will not disturb any equipment until directed by investigating personnel.

Figure 4-27. Diesel Engine Run-Away (Sheet 1 of 2)

T.O. 21-SM68-1

Section IV

STEP	PROCEDURE
8	Applicable logs and forms..................................Annotated

Figure 4-27. Diesel Engine Run-Away (Sheet 2 of 2)

Changed 18 December 1963 TOCN-1 (DEN-5)

STEP	PROCEDURE
	Note All hazard actions and procedures are at the discretion of the MLO.
1	Inform control center of power house fire..................Accomplished The EPPT/facility personnel contact control center using quickest method possible.
1.1	Power house intake fan OFF................................Accomplished
2	Locate source of fire....................................Accomplished EPPT/facility personnel determine what type of fire (A, B, or C) has occurred, and take immediate action to combat fire.
3	Isolate all equipment to affected area....................Accomplished EPPT/facility personnel accomplish above by isolating affected area.
4	Corrective action..Started Control center dispatches fire control team to assist in combating fire.
5	Damage to equipment..Evaluated EPPT/facility personnel visually analyze extent of damage to affected area/equipment but will not disturb any equipment until directed by investigating personnel.
6	Power to all operating equipment............................Restored EPPT/facility personnel restore power to any operating equipment that was not damaged by fire.
7	Control center informed of status........................Accomplished EPPT contacts control center and reports status of power house/associated equipment by using applicable communication net.
8	Applicable logs and forms....................................Annotated

Figure 4-28. Power House Fire

STEP	PROCEDURE
	Note
	All hazard actions and procedures are at the discretion of the MLO.
1	GENERATOR and EXCITER air circuit breaker checkout......Accomplished
2	Standby diesel engine...................................Started
3	Insert synchroscope key and position to ON.............Accomplished
4	Manual field rheostat to 35 VDC........................Rotated CCW
5	Field circuit breaker..................................Closed
	CAUTION
	Manual field rheostat must be rotated slowly to prevent damage to oncoming voltmeter.
6	Manual field rheostat full CCW.........................Rotated
7	Governor motor control to 60 CPS.......................Adjusted
8	Regulator preset rheostat to 2400 volts................Adjusted
9	Generator circuit breaker..............................Closed
10	Frequency and voltage..................................Adjusted
11	START-RUN switch.......................................RUN

Figure 4-29. Single Generator Operation

STEP	PROCEDURE
	Note
	All hazard actions and procedures are at the discretion of the MLO.
1	Throttle control lever..................................OIL
	CAUTION
	Hold throttle control lever as required to prevent engine from accelerating too fast when starting air valve is pulled.
2	Starting air valve....................................Pulled
	Note
	Engine starts at approximately 450 RPM and governor takes over.
3	Throttle control lever..................................RUN
4	Engine console power supply switch......................ON

Figure 4-30. Standby Diesel Engine Manual Start (LAFB 724TH/724TH SQDN)

SECTION V

COMBAT CREW MALFUNCTION ISOLATION

5-1. SCOPE.

5-2. This section contains missile combat crew procedures for isolating, to the component level, those malfunctions that may occur during the countdown. Most of the malfunctions listed are those which the combat crew will be able to isolate and take positive corrective action during the first first hold period (T-280). This analysis is based on the following assumptions:

   a. All situations cannot be covered by procedure and corrective action because malfunction isolation of various situations depends on the combat crew's weapon system knowledge. The malfunction procedures are guides only and are not a substitue for good judgement.

   b. Corrective action may differ between an exercise mode of operation and an EWO mode of operation.

   c. Manual operating procedures override automatic operation and are provided as an emergency means of operating a system if the automatic mode fails during a launch countdown.

   d. The system configuration will not be changed.

5-3. MALFUNCTION ISOLATION.

5-4. This section presents the procedures to be used in analyzing malfunction indications which may appear on the launch complex facility console and/or the launch control console. During a countdown without TV monitoring, the first indication of a malfunction will appear on these consoles. This section also contains the necessary corrective actions to be taken for finding and correcting the malfunction. The more common subsystem malfunctions are analyzed, where an automatic subsystem checkout can be performed during a hold time, and the correction procedures are indicated in the corrective action column. Where corrective action is indicated, complete if possible and resume countdown.

5-5. MALFUNCTION ISOLATION OF PROPELLANT LOADING AND PRESSURIZATION SYSTEM.

5-6. Figure 5-1 through 5-7 cover malfunctions and analysis of the propellant loading and pressurization system.

5-7. MALFUNCTION ISOLATION OF ELECTRICAL SYSTEM.

5-8. Figures 5-8 through 5-11 cover malfunctions and analysis of the electrical system.

5-9. MALFUNCTION ISOLATION FLIGHT CONTROL SYSTEM.

5-10. Figure 5-12 covers malfunctions and analysis of the flight control system.

5-11. MALFUNCTION ISOLATION OF RVS AND GMTS.

5-12. Figure 5-13 covers malfunctions and analysis of the RVS and GMTS.

5-12A. MALFUNCTION ISOLATION FOR LAUNCHER.

5-12B. Figure 5-13A covers malfunction and analysis for enabling the two remaining launchers when one launcher has malfunctioned and stopped in an intermediate position.

5-13. MALFUNCTION ISOLATION FOR GUIDANCE.

5-14. Figures 5-14 through 5-37 cover malfunctions and analysis of the ground guidance system. If a malfunction occurs that is not covered or cannot be corrected by the malfunction analysis procedures, the GEO will report an indefinite hold to the MLO and proceed to the following technical orders for further analysis and troubleshooting:

   a. T.O. 21-SM68-2J-7-1-1, countdown trouble analysis.

   b. T.O. 21-SM68-2J-7-1-1, handover countdown trouble analysis.

   c. T.O. 21-SM68-2J-6-3, computer power trouble analysis.

5-15. MALFUNCTION OF POWER HOUSE.

5-16. Figures 5-38 covers malfunction analysis of the power house.

MALFUNCTION INDICATION	IMMEDIATE ACTION		POSSIBLE CAUSES	CORRECTIVE ACTION	
	EXERCISE	EWO		EXERCISE	EWO
PLPS red (LCFC) at TSI.	Shut down.	Shut down.	Stage I or II lox probe disconnected.	Reconnect lox probe, recycle ES, and re-initiate countdown.	Same as EXERCISE.
	Shut down.	Shut down.	(Prior to incorporation of TCTO 31X3-10-11-621) Airborne point sensors prematurely armed.	Unload helium and lox if necessary, recycle, and troubleshoot to determine malfunction.	Same as EXERCISE.

Figure 5-1. PLPS Red (LCFC) at TSI

T.O. 21-SM68-1　　　　Section V

MALFUNCTION INDICATION	IMMEDIATE ACTION		POSSIBLE CAUSES	CORRECTIVE ACTION	
	EXERCISE	EWO		EXERCISE	EWO
No LOX LOADING white (LCC).	Continue countdown.	Continue countdown.	CV-311 closed.	Open CV-311 immediately.	Same as EXERCISE.
	Continue countdown.	Continue countdown.	(Prior to incorporation of TCTO 31X3-10-11-621) CV-538 closed.	Open CV-538 immediately.	Same as EXERCISE.
	Continue countdown.	Continue countdown.	FCV-211 and/or FCV-212 not open.	Continue to lox loaded.	Same as EXERCISE.
	Shut down.	Shut down.	(Prior to incorporation of TCTO 31X3-10-11-621) SOV-310 closed.	Recycle.	Same as EXERCISE.
	Shut down.	Shut down.	(Prior to incorporation of TCTO 31X3-10-11-621) ROV-801 or ROV-803 not closed.	Recycle.	Same as EXERCISE.
	Continue countdown.	Continue countdown.	PC-311 not regulating properly.	Readjust PC-311. If not possible by T-500 shut down.	Same as EXERCISE.
	Shut down.	Shut down.	(Prior to incorporation of TCTO 31X3-10-11-621). Missile fill and drain or vent valve fail to open.	Recycle.	Same as EXERCISE.

Figure 5-2. No LOX LOADING White (LCC)

Changed 18 December 1963　TOCN-1 (DEN-5)　Page 5-5, Figure 5-3 deleted　　5-4

T.O. 21-SM68-1 Section V

MALFUNCTION INDICATION	IMMEDIATE ACTION		POSSIBLE CAUSES	CORRECTIVE ACTION	
	EXERCISE	EWO		EXERCISE	EWO
(After incorporation of TCTO 31X3-10-11-621) PLPS red at T-700.	Shut down.	Shut down.	Airborne point sensors failed to arm.	Unload and recycle ES in accordance with T.O. 21-SM68-CL-24-1 or T.O. 21-SM68-CL-27-1. Run PLPS checkout.	Same as EXERCISE.

Figure 5-4. PLPS Red at T-700

Changed 18 December 1963 TOCN-1 (DEN-5) 5-6

T.O. 21M-HGM25A-1-1 (21-SM68-1) Section V

MALFUNCTION INDICATION	IMMEDIATE ACTION		POSSIBLE CAUSES	CORRECTIVE ACTION	
	EXERCISE	EWO		EXERCISE	EWO
LOX EMPTY red (LCFC).	Attempt corrective action.	Attempt corrective action.	Pressure switch P-206 failure.	Unload missile helium and lox if necessary. Recycle. Replace or repair pressure switch P-206.	Same as EXERCISE.
	Attempt corrective action.	Attempt corrective action.	Liquid level indicator LLI-201 failure. Failure of CC-2 compressor. Lox storage tank empty.	Replace or calibrate liquid level indicator LLI-201. Correct CC-2 compressor malfunction. Replenish lox storage tank.	Same as EXERCISE.

Figure 5-5. LOX EMPTY Red (LCFC)

Changed 19 March 1964 TOCN 1-1 (DEN-12)

T.O. 21-SM68-1 Section V

MALFUNCTION INDICATION	IMMEDIATE ACTION		POSSIBLE CAUSES	CORRECTIVE ACTION	
	EXERCISE	EWO		EXERCISE	EWO
PLPS red (LCFC) at T-280.	Attempt corrective action.	Attempt corrective action.	Helium storage tank T601A depleted below 4000 PSI.	Verify sufficient helium in T601B for loading. Close CV-607 and CV-608. Check system for leaks and repair. Open CV-607 and CV-608. Cycle ES circuit breaker 59.	Same as EXERCISE.
	Attempt corrective action.	Attempt corrective action.	Low transfer regulator pressure on PI-603 below 3200 (±50) PSI.	Adjust pressure controller PC-602 to 3200 (±50) PSI.	Same as EXERCISE.
	Shut down.	Attempt corrective action.	Stage I or II helium accumulator burst disc ruptured.	Install new burst disc in missile burst disc exhaust port. Unload helium and lox. Recycle.	Close CV-607 and CV-608. Verify helium storage tank T601B pressure sufficient for loading. Replace ruptured burst disc and primary regulator if available. Open CV-607 and CV-608. Cycle circuit breaker 59. Verify that PI-603 reaches 3200 (±50) PSI. Resume count.

Figure 5-6. PLPS Red at T-280 (Sheet 1 of 3)

T.O. 21-SM68-1 Section V

MALFUNCTION INDICATION	IMMEDIATE ACTION		POSSIBLE CAUSES	CORRECTIVE ACTION	
	EXERCISE	EWO		EXERCISE	EWO
	Attempt corrective action.	Attempt corrective action.	Quick disconnect QD-9322-635 not connected. (Stage I and II HELIUM SPHERE SAFE indicators not lighted on assembly 6A3. PI-603 indicating 3200 (±50) PSI.	Close CV-9321-631. Close CV-9322-633. Open CV-9321-634. Open CV-9322-632. Connect QD-9321-635. Close BV-9321-632 and BV-9322-634. Open CV-9321-631 and CV-9322-633. Hold for 10 minutes to insure helium loaded.	Same as EXERCISE.
	Attempt corrective action.	Attempt corrective action.	Stage I or II helium umbilical not connected. (Applicable stage helium sphere safe indicator not lighted).	Verify sufficient helium in T601A or T601B to reload missile. Close CV-607 and CV-608. Open CV-604. Press and hold FCV-605 and LS-212 until PI-603 indicates zero. Connect helium umbilical. If FCV-601 is open and T601B must be used, cycle circuit breaker 59 on ES to OFF, then ON.	Same as EXERCISE.
	Attempt corrective action.	Attempt corrective action.	Helium filter (F-9322-638) crushed or clogged.	Close CV-607, CV-608, and CV-9321-631. Open CV-9322-632. Verify PI-603 indicates zero. Remove or replace filter. Close CV-9322-632. Open CV-607, CV-608, and CV-9321-631.	Same as EXERCISE.

Figure 5-6. PLPS Red at T-280 (Sheet 2 of 3)

T.O. 21-SM68-1 Section V

MALFUNCTION INDICATION	IMMEDIATE ACTION		POSSIBLE CAUSES	CORRECTIVE ACTION	
	EXERCISE	EWO		EXERCISE	EWO
	Continue countdown.	Continue countdown.	Stage I or II lox tanks not loaded.	If no malfunction indicated, wait for LOX LOADED white.	Same as EXERCISE.

Figure 5-6. PLPS Red at T-280 (Sheet 3 of 3)

Changed 18 December 1963 TOCN-1 (DEN-5) (Page 5-11, figure 5-7 deleted.) 5-10

T.O. 21-SM68-1

MALFUNCTION INDICATION	IMMEDIATE ACTION		POSSIBLE CAUSES	CORRECTIVE ACTION	
	EXERCISE	EWO		EXERCISE	EWO
GROUND POWER red at T-870.	Continue countdown.	Continue countdown.	Missile air conditioner failed to start.	Check for tripped circuit breaker or blown fuse in A/C panel on JEU-7/E. If resetting breaker or replacing fuse starts A/C unit, lox loading will start. If breaker of fuse continues to blow, shut down. If circuit breaker is not tripped and fuse not blown, press CHECKOUT POWER and A/C pushbuttons on assembly 8A2. If A/C unit starts, leave on and continue count.	Same as EXERCISE.

Figure 5-8. GROUND POWER Red at T-870

Changed 17 January 1964   TOCN-1 (DEN-8)

T.O. 21-SM68-1　　　　Section V

MALFUNCTION INDICATION	IMMEDIATE ACTION		POSSIBLE CAUSES	CORRECTIVE ACTION	
	EXERCISE	EWO		EXERCISE	EWO
GROUND POWER red prior to T-280.	Continue countdown.	Continue countdown.	Missile A/C unit stopped.	Check JEU-7/E A/C panel for tripped circuit breaker or blown fuse. If breaker or fuse blows again, shut down.	Same as EXERCISE.
			Missile DC power not applied (Missile DC indicator assembly 8A2 not upper white).	Check ES circuit breaker 82 and if tripped, reset. If it trips again, shut down. If circuit breaker 82 is not tripped, shut down and troubleshoot ES and missile shut down relay circuit.	Same as EXERCISE.
			Missile AC power not applied. (Missile 400 CPS indicator assembly 8A2 not upper white).	Check ES circuit breaker 101 and reset if tripped. If it trips again, shut down. Check 9510 motor generator set for proper output and adjust if necessary. If output breaker tripped, reset. If it trips again, shut down. If none of the above actions correct the problem, ES chassis is defective; shut down.	Same as EXERCISE.

Figure 5-9. GROUND POWER Red Prior to T-280

Changed 18 December 1963　TOCN-1 (DEN-5)　　　　5-13

MALFUNCTION INDICATION	IMMEDIATE ACTION		POSSIBLE CAUSES	CORRECTIVE ACTION	
	EXERCISE	EWO		EXERCISE	EWO
BATTERY POWER red.	Shut down.	Continue countdown.	Power supply A/E 24A-4, 28-volt rectifier failure.	Attempt restarting unit by switching local remote switch to local and pressing start pushbutton. (If overcurrent or over voltage indicators are lighted, the reset pushbutton inside cabinet SW-6 must be pressed before restarting). If unit cannot be repaired and restarted, turn off all ES DC circuit breakers except 1, 10, 50, 59 thru 70, and 250. If primary power circuit breaker is tripped, reset and attempt to restart.	If countdown must be held at T-280, attempt to restart power supply A/E 24A-4. If a hold is not in effect, continue the count on battery power. If primary power to launcher is lost and cannot be reapplied, shut down and turn off all DC circuit breakers except 1, 10, 50, 59 thru 70, and 250.

Figure 5-10. BATTERY POWER Red

T.O. 21-SM68-1

MALFUNCTION INDICATION	IMMEDIATE ACTION		POSSIBLE CAUSES	CORRECTIVE ACTION	
	EXERCISE	EWO		EXERCISE	EWO
GROUND POWER red at T-280.	Hold.	Hold.	Stage I or II hydraulic umbilical not connected. (Applicable reservoir level indicator on hydraulic pumping unit C-216 red.)	On hydraulic pumping unit, open bypass valve. Close pressure outlet valves and connect quick disconnect. Open pressure outlet valves and close bypass valve.	Same as EXERCISE.
			Hydraulic pumping unit C-216 not running.	Check primary power circuit breaker on JEU-7/E. Reset if tripped. If it trips again, shut down. Check C-216 panel on JEU-7/E for blown fuse and replace if necessary. If fuse blows again, shut down.	Same as EXERCISE.

Figure 5-11. GROUND POWER Red at T-280

T.O. 21-SM68-1 Section V

MALFUNCTION INDICATION	IMMEDIATE ACTION		POSSIBLE CAUSES	CORRECTIVE ACTION	
	EXERCISE	EWO		EXERCISE	EWO
FLIGHT CONTROLS red (LCFC) at T-280 and a readout on any of the 10 channel lights on OA-2441/GJQ-11.					Note *Denotes: If malfunction is not corrected, replace FCS assemblies in the following order: Turn off ES circuit breakers 6, 56, 109, and 203. 1. 3A4 PROGRAMMER CHECK 2. 3A2 SIGNAL ANALYZER 3. 3A6 SIGNAL GENERATOR 4. 3A8 POWER SUPPLY 5. 3A5 COMPARATOR 6. 3A7 SIGNAL SELECTOR & CONDITIONER

Figure 5-12. FLIGHT CONTROLS Red on LCFC (T-280) and Assembly 3A2 (Sheet 1 of 6)

Changed 17 January 1964 TOCN-1 (DEN-8)   5-16

T.O. 21-SM68-1   Section V

MALFUNCTION INDICATION	IMMEDIATE ACTION		POSSIBLE CAUSES	CORRECTIVE ACTION	
	EXERCISE	EWO		EXERCISE	EWO
FLIGHT CONTROLS red (LCFC) at T-280 and a readout on any of the 10 channel lights on OA-2441/GJQ-11.	Hold.	Hold.	Channel 1 - ACT. 1_1 6 - ACT. 3_2 8 - ACT. 4_2 9 - ACT. 5_2 10 - ACT. 6_2 Channel 2 - ACT. 2_1 or jato fire timer, staging bolts timer, or sustainer start timer. Channel 3 - ACT. 3_1 or nose cone release timer. Channel 4 - ACT. 4_1 or jato jettison timer.	Record all indications on assembly 3A2 of OA-2441/GJQ-11 and then shut down.	Channel 1, 9, or 10: Adjust applicable trimpot (T.O. 21-SM68-2J-11 -1 or -2) or *. Channel 6 or 8: *. Channel 2: Check voltage at 14TB5-61, 62, 60, and 63. If 28 VDC, shut down. If not: Adjust 2_1 trimpot (21-SM68-2J -11-1 or -2) or *. Channel 3: Check voltage at 2014TB5-63. If 28 VDC, shut down. If not: Adjust 3_1 trimpot (21-SM68-2J-11-1 or -2) or *. Channel 4: Check voltage at 2014TB5-71. If 28 VDC, shut down. If not: Adjust 4_1 trimpot (21-SM68-2J-11-1 or 2) or *.

Figure 5-12. FLIGHT CONTROLS Red on LCFC (T-280) and Assembly 3A2 (Sheet 2 of 6)

T.O. 21-SM68-1   Section V

MALFUNCTION INDICATION	IMMEDIATE ACTION		POSSIBLE CAUSES	CORRECTIVE ACTION	
	EXERCISE	EWO		EXERCISE	EWO
			Channel 5 - ACT. 2_2 or Stage II FTPR cut off timer.		Channel 5: Check voltage at 14TB5-64. If 28 VDC, shut down. If not: *
			Channel 7 - ACT. 1_2 or programmer not reset.	Channel 7: Set MODE SELECTOR switch to CHECKOUT for minimum of 5 seconds, then to LAUNCH. If malfunction is not corrected, record all indications on assembly 3A2 of OA-2441/GJQ-11 and then shut down.	Channel 7: Set MODE SELECTOR switch to CHECKOUT for minimum of 5 SEC, then to LAUNCH or *.

Figure 5-12. FLIGHT CONTROLS Red on LCFC (T-280) and Assembly 3A2 (Sheet 3 of 6)

Changed 17 January 1964 TOCN-1 (DEN-8)

T.O. 21-SM68-1 Section V

MALFUNCTION INDICATION	IMMEDIATE ACTION		POSSIBLE CAUSES	CORRECTIVE ACTION	
	EXERCISE	EWO		EXERCISE	EWO
T-280: FLIGHT CONTROL red (LCFC) assembly 3A2 malfunction window; SPIN MOTORS and any one of the following: 3-AXIS. REF. PKG. RATE GYRO STAGE II. RATE GYRO STAGE I.	Hold.	Hold.	Bad spin motor. Bad spin motor detector package. Bad signal analyzer assembly.	Shut down.	Refer to 21-SM68-2J-11 -1 or -2 for troubleshooting and possible replacement of bad unit.

Figure 5-12. FLIGHT CONTROLS Red on LCFC (T-280) and Assembly 3A2 (Sheet 4 of 6)

T.O. 21-SM68-1　　　Section V

MALFUNCTION INDICATION	IMMEDIATE ACTION		POSSIBLE CAUSES	CORRECTIVE ACTION	
	EXERCISE	EWO		EXERCISE	EWO
T-280: FLIGHT CONTROL red on LCFC (T-280) assembly 3A2 FCS malfunction window: 25 VDC POWER SUPPLY.	Hold.	Hold.	Bad airborne 25 VDC power supply. Bad FCS power supply assembly.	Shut down.	Set LOCAL-REMOTE switch to LOCAL on hydraulic pumping unit C-216. Turn off CB82 and CB101 on circuit breaker panel 33. Replace power supply assembly.
T-280: FLIGHT CONTROL red on LCFC (T-280) assembly 3A2 GOE malfunction window: POWER SUPPLY.	Hold.	Hold.	CB109 on circuit breaker panel 33 OFF.	Reset CB109 on circuit breaker panel 33.	Same as EXERCISE.
			Blown fuse(s) on power supply assembly.	Replace blown fuse(s) on power supply assembly.	Same as EXERCISE.
			Power supply out of tolerance.	Shut down.	Turn off CB6, CB56, CB109, and CB203 on circuit breaker panel 33. Replace power supply assembly.
			Signal analyzer assembly malfunction.	Shut down.	Turn off CB6, CB56, CB109, and CB203 on circuit breaker panel 33. Replace signal analyzer assembly.

Figure 5-12. FLIGHT CONTROL Red on LCFC (T-280) and Assembly 3A2 (Sheet 5 of 6)

MALFUNCTION INDICATION	IMMEDIATE ACTION		POSSIBLE CAUSES	CORRECTIVE ACTION	
	EXERCISE	EWO		EXERCISE	EWO
T-280: FLIGHT CONTROL red (LCFC) assembly 3A2 READINESS MONITOR window; GYRO HTR NO-GO.	Hold.	Hold.	Bad power supply assembly.	Shut down.	Set MODE SELECTOR to MALFUNCTION or turn off CB-6, CB-56, CB-109, and CB-203, on circuit breaker panel 33. Replace power supply assembly.
			Bad 3-axis REF. PKG.	Shut down.	Set LOCAL-REMOTE switch to LOCAL on hydraulic pumping unit C-216 and turn off CB82 and CB101 on circuit breaker panel 33. GROUND POWER red will appear on LCFC. Replace 3-AXIS REF. PKG.

Figure 5-12. FLIGHT CONTROL Red on LCFC (T-280) and Assembly 3A2 (Sheet 6 of 6)

T.O. 21-SM68-1 Section V

MALFUNCTION INDICATION	IMMEDIATE ACTION		POSSIBLE CAUSES	CORRECTIVE ACTION	
	EXERCISE	EWO		EXERCISE	EWO
RVS red (LCFC) T-280.	Hold.	Hold.	Loss of fuse set.	Select new target on LCC. Cycle from MARK 4 to MARK 3 and back to MARK 4 on control monitor group OA-2440/GJQ-11.	Same as EXERCISE.
RVS red (LCFC) T-280 and CONTROL CENTER CIRCUIT red.	Hold.	Hold.	Loss of target go.	Select new target on LCC.	Same as EXERCISE. Note When replacing assembly 11A1 for launcher NO. 1, set CB3 and CB19 to OFF on control monitor group OA-2439/GJQ-11. When replacing assembly 11A2 for launcher NO. 2, set CB9 and CB24 to OFF on control monitor group OA-2439/GJQ-11. When replacing assembly 11A3 for launcher NO. 3, set CB15 and CB29 to OFF on control monitor group OA-2439/GJQ-11.

Figure 5-13 RVS Red (LCFC) T-280 or RVS Red (LCFC) T-280 and CONTROL CENTER CIRCUITS Red (Sheet 1 of 2)

5-21

T.O. 21-SM68-1   Section V

MALFUNCTION INDICATION	IMMEDIATE ACTION		POSSIBLE CAUSES	CORRECTIVE ACTION	
	EXERCISE	EWO		EXERCISE	EWO
					Following replacement of any of the above assemblies, return applicable circuit breakers to ON and recycle MODE SELECTOR switch (assembly 4A2) from LAUNCH to CHECKOUT to LAUNCH.

Figure 5-13 RVS Red (LCFC) T-280 or RVS Red (LCFC) T-280 and CONTROL CENTER CIRCUITS Red (Sheet 2 of 2)

5-22

T.O. 21-SM68-1   Section V

MALFUNCTION INDICATION	IMMEDIATE ACTION		POSSIBLE CAUSES	CORRECTIVE ACTION	
	EXERCISE	EWO		EXERCISE	EWO
LOWER LAUNCHER pressed white and launcher remains in the intermediate position.	Attempt corrective action.	Attempt corrective action.		Refer to T.O. 21-SM68-CL-24-1 or T.O. 21-SM68-CL-27-1.	(Malfunctioning launcher, equipment terminal) Turn circuit breaker CB57 (9A1) OFF. Note When the malfunctioning launcher circuit breaker CB57 (assembly 9A1) is turned to the OFF position, 28 VDC operating power is removed from launch sequence controller #2 (assembly 2A3) and the applicable launch lowering started signal relay in the common control center circuit (assembly 10A2).

Figure 5-13A. LOWER LAUNCHER Pressed White and Launcher Remains in the Intermediate Position

MALFUNCTION INDICATION	TROUBLE INDICATION	POSSIBLE CAUSES	CORRECTIVE ACTION	
			EXERCISE	EWO
TSI to T-280 Guidance red.	Hold.	Loss of phase A, B, or C because circuit breakers in GMTS tripped.	Reset tripped circuit breakers.	Same as EXERCISE.

Figure 5-14. TSI to T-280 GUIDANCE Red

MALFUNCTION INDICATION	TROUBLE INDICATION	POSSIBLE CAUSES	CORRECTIVE ACTION	
			EXERCISE	EWO
LAUNCHER red, power pack not operating at T-281.	Hold.	Loss of AC power to launcher system.	Reset launcher system main circuit breaker to ON (PNL-1001). Reset all circuit breakers and overloads ON A15A2, A15A3, A11A1, A12A1, A13A1 and, A14A1. Check voltage on both sides of fuses in A15A2, A15A3, A11A1, A12A1, A13A1 and, A14A1.	Same as EXERCISE.
		Loss of DC power to launcher logic.	Cycle normal supply selector to ALTERNATE SUPPLY (A18A1). If indicators on A18A1 are out, reset CB01 and CB02 (A18A1). Reset all OFF circuit breakers to ON (5A3A1). Check voltage on both sides of fuses for supplies 1 and 2 (A18A1).	Same as EXERCISE.
		Poor contact in operation selector.	Cycle operation selector from REMOTE to LOCAL, and back to REMOTE.	Same as EXERCISE.

Figure 5-15. LAUNCHER Red, Power Pack Not Operating at T-281

MALFUNCTION INDICATION	TROUBLE INDICATION	POSSIBLE CAUSES	CORRECTIVE ACTION	
			EXERCISE	EWO
All guidance indicators not lighted.	Hold.	Motor generator stopped.	Start alternate motor generator as follows: Press GEN 1 or GEN 2 START pushbutton indicator green, LINE VOLTS switch to C, and adjust LINE VOLTS as required.	Same as EXERCISE.
		-28V STBY RELAY PWR CB tripped (unit 16).	Reset 28V STBY RELAY PWR CB.	Same as EXERCISE.
		-28 volt standby power supply.	Check -28 volt standby power supply (unit 15). Replace power supply if inoperative.	Same as EXERCISE.

Figure 5-16. All Guidance Indicators Not Lighted

T.O. 21M-HGM25A-1-1 (21-SM68-1) Section V

MALFUNCTION INDICATION	TROUBLE INDICATION	POSSIBLE CAUSES	CORRECTIVE ACTION	
			EXERCISE	EWO
CONSTANTS REGISTER 6 inoperative.		Magnetic clutch inoperative.	Continue countdown if index of refraction is within ±1000 of value contained in CONSTANTS REGISTER 6.	Same as EXERCISE.

Figure 5-17. CONSTANTS REGISTER 6 Inoperative

T.O. 21-SM68-1 Section V

MALFUNCTION INDICATION	TROUBLE INDICATION	POSSIBLE CAUSES	CORRECTIVE ACTION	
			EXERCISE	EWO
POWER ON not white.		-28 volt operating power supply.	Check -28 volt operating power supply (unit 15). Replace power supply if inoperative.	Same as EXERCISE.

Figure 5-18. POWER ON Not White

5-27

T.O. 21M-HGM25A-1-1 (21-SM68-1)   Section V

MALFUNCTION INDICATION	TROUBLE INDICATION	POSSIBLE CAUSES	CORRECTIVE ACTION	
			EXERCISE	EWO
GUID X NOT RDY does not go out (before START GUID X green).	POWER ON not green (unit 25).	Circuit breaker CB10 tripped.	Reset to ON.	Same as EXERCISE.
	LOCAL POWER FAILURE red (unit 25).	Circuit breaker CB1 thru CB9 tripped.	Reset to ON.	Same as EXERCISE.
	PLATE VOLTS ON and SERVOS ON not green (unit 25).	Interlock open (unit 25).	Securely fasten drawers and swinging frames. If PLATE VOLTS ON and SERVOS ON do not indicate green, pull out interlock override.	Same as EXERCISE.
	STANDBY not green (unit 25).	GROUND RANGE and/or SLANT RANGE servos not reset (CAB. 23).	Manually position servo dials to approx 20,000 feet and release.	Same as EXERCISE.

Figure 5-19. GUID X NOT RDY Does Not Go Out (Before START GUID X Green)

Changed 31 January 1964   TOCN 1-1 (DEN-9)   5-28

MALFUNCTION INDICATION	TROUBLE INDICATION	POSSIBLE CAUSES	CORRECTIVE ACTION	
			EXERCISE	EWO
GUID X NOT RDY does not go out (after START GUID X green).			Continue countdown.	Same as EXERCISE.

Figure 5-20. GUID X NOT RDY Does Not Go Out (After START GUID X Green)

MALFUNCTION INDICATION	TROUBLE INDICATION	POSSIBLE CAUSES	CORRECTIVE ACTION	
			EXERCISE	EWO
START CD indicator does not light.			Continue countdown.	Same as EXERCISE.

Figure 5-21. START CD Indicator Does Not Light

T.O. 21M-HGM25A-1-1 (21-SM68-1) Section V

MALFUNCTION INDICATION	TROUBLE INDICATION	POSSIBLE CAUSES	CORRECTIVE ACTION	
			EXERCISE	EWO
POWER ON not green.	GGS FAULT yellow.			
	ANTENNA FACILITY FAULT red.	Antenna hydraulic pressure below normal.	Select alternate antenna: Press POWER OFF white, press ALTERNATE ANTENNA green, press POWER ON white, and continue countdown.	Same as EXERCISE.
	COMP FAULT yellow and COMPUTER POWER ON not green.	DC POWER SUPPLY circuit breakers tripped.	Reset indicator circuit breakers to ON: Press MAINT (unit 13) yellow, press HOLD MAINT (computer) amber, press CLEAR FAULT (computer), press CYCLE DC ON (computer), press HOLD MAINT (computer) not lighted, and press STBY green.	Same as EXERCISE.
	BREAKER OPEN IN-LINE red (unit 16).	Circuit breakers tripped (unit 16).	RESET to ON.	Same as EXERCISE.

Figure 5-22. POWER ON Not Green (Sheet 1 of 3)

Changed 31 January 1964 TOCN 1-1 (DEN-9) 5-31

MALFUNCTION INDICATION	TROUBLE INDICATION	POSSIBLE CAUSES	CORRECTIVE ACTION	
			EXERCISE	EWO
	POWER ON (computer) not green. MOTOR GENERATOR ON not green.	MOTOR GENERATOR not running.	Press MOTOR GENERATOR MANUAL START. If selected motor generator does not start, select ALTERNATE GENERATOR as follows: Press MOTOR GENERATOR STOP, set MOTOR GENERATOR SELECTOR to ALTERNATE GENERATOR, press MOTOR GENERATOR MANUAL START green, and verify MOTOR GENERATOR ON indication.	Same as EXERCISE.
	DC POWER-DC READY not green.	AUTOMATIC SEQUENCER switch malfunctioning.	MAINT (unit 13) yellow, press HOLD MAINT (computer) amber, press CYCLE DC OFF amber, press SELECT MANUAL SEQUENCE amber, press CLEAR FAULT, rotate MANUAL SEQUENCE rotary switch clockwise A through M, press HOLD MAINT (computer), and press STBY (unit 13) green.	Same as EXERCISE.

Figure 5-22. POWER ON Not Green (Sheet 2 of 3)

T.O. 21M-HGM25A-1-1 (21-SM68-1) Section V

MALFUNCTION INDICATION	TROUBLE INDICATION	POSSIBLE CAUSES	CORRECTIVE ACTION	
			EXERCISE	EWO
	Operations room INTLK OPEN (unit 15) red.	Interlock open on unit 7, 8, 15, 21, or 22.	Secure fasteners, drawers, and swing frames. If operations room INTLK OPEN (unit 15) indication does not extinguish, pull out interlock override.	Same as EXERCISE.
	Antenna terminal INTLK OPEN (unit 15) red.	Interlock open on a unit in antenna terminal.	Select alternate antenna: Press POWER OFF white, press ALTERNATE ANTENNA FACILITY SELECT green, press POWER ON white, and continue countdown.	Same as EXERCISE.

Figure 5-22. POWER ON Not Green (Sheet 3 of 3)

T.O. 21-SM68-1   Section V

MALFUNCTION INDICATION	TROUBLE INDICATION	POSSIBLE CAUSES	CORRECTIVE ACTION	
			EXERCISE	EWO
TARGET GATED Not Green and no gated pulse when START GUID X is initiated.		Guidance exerciser did not reset properly.	Press GUID X NOT RDY and RESTART GUID X.	Same as EXERCISE.

Figure 5-23. TARGET GATED Not Green and No Gated Pulse When START GUID X is Initiated

5-34

T.O. 21-SM68-1

MALFUNCTION INDICATION	TROUBLE INDICATION	POSSIBLE CAUSES	CORRECTIVE ACTION	
			EXERCISE	EWO
MAG RDY not white.		MAG RDY lamp defective.	Press MAG ON and continue countdown.	Same as EXERCISE.
			Select alternate antenna: Press POWER OFF white, press alternate ANTENNA FACILITY SELECT green, press POWER ON white, and continue countdown.	Same as EXERCISE.

Figure 5-24. MAG RDY Not White

T.O. 21M-HGM25A-1-1 (21-SM68-1) Section V

MALFUNCTION INDICATION	TROUBLE INDICATION	POSSIBLE CAUSES	CORRECTIVE ACTION	
			EXERCISE	EWO
MAG ON not green (before LIFT OFF white).	MAG I not indicating 1.2 to 1.9 MA.		Select alternate antenna: Press POWER OFF white, press ALTERNATE ANTENNA FACILITY SELECT green, press POWER ON white, and continue countdown.	Same as EXERCISE.
	MAG I indicating 1.5 to 1.9 MA.		Continue countdown.	Same as EXERCISE.

Figure 5-25. MAG ON Not Green (Before LIFT OFF White)

T.O. 21-SM68-1 Section V

MALFUNCTION INDICATION	TROUBLE INDICATION	POSSIBLE CAUSES	CORRECTIVE ACTION	
			EXERCISE	EWO
START GUID X not green. (Disregard if after a successful GUID X or a successful launch.)			Select alternate antenna: Press POWER OFF white, press alternate ANTENNA FACILITY SELECT green, press POWER ON white, and continue countdown.	Same as EXERCISE.

Figure 5-26. START GUID X Not Green

5-37

T.O. 21-SM68-1　　　Section V

MALFUNCTION INDICATION	TROUBLE INDICATION	POSSIBLE CAUSES	CORRECTIVE ACTION	
			EXERCISE	EWO
RAISE ANT not white.			Continue countdown.	Same as EXERCISE.

Figure 5-27. RAISE ANT Not White

T.O. 21M-HGM25A-1-1 (21-SM68-1) Section V

MALFUNCTION INDICATION	TROUBLE INDICATION	POSSIBLE CAUSES	CORRECTIVE ACTION	
			EXERCISE	EWO
ANT RAISE not green.	ANTENNA FACILITY FAULT red, GGS HOLD red, GGS FAULT lighted.	Slow operation of the antenna protective and elevating system (APES).	Notify MLO of antenna status and continue countdown.	Same as EXERCISE.
			Select alternate antenna: Press POWER OFF white, press ALTERNATE ANTENNA FACILITY SELECT green, press POWER ON white, and continue countdown.	Same as EXERCISE.

Figure 5-28. ANT RAISE Not Green

T.O. 21-SM68-1   Section V

MALFUNCTION INDICATION	TROUBLE INDICATION	POSSIBLE CAUSES	CORRECTIVE ACTION	
			EXERCISE	EWO
MISSILE READY not white.	SELECT LAUNCHER white and SELECT TARGET green.	Defective lamp.	Press ACQ MISSILE.	Same as EXERCISE.
	SELECT LAUNCHER not white.	Open interface.	Press appropriate SELECT LAUNCHER pushbutton.	Same as EXERCISE.
	SELECT TARGET not green.	Open interface.	Refer to T.O. 21-SM68-2J-7-1-1.	On subsequent missiles prior to initiation of raise launcher phase: Press HANDOVER ON yellow, press appropriate SELECT TARGET green, press HANDOVER OFF green, press appropriate SELECT LAUNCHER white, and press ACQ MISSILE white.

Figure 5-29. MISSILE READY Not White

5-40

T.O. 21-SM68-1   Section V

MALFUNCTION INDICATION	TROUBLE INDICATION	POSSIBLE CAUSES	CORRECTIVE ACTION	
			EXERCISE	EWO
ACQ MISSILE not green (in complex only).	GGS HOLD red, TARGET VERIFY green, TARGET GATED green.	Failure to receive loop check COMP signal	Proceed to Figure 3-5 of T.O. 21-SM68-2J-7-1-1	Same as EXERCISE.
	GGS HOLD red, TARGET VERIFY green, TARGET GATED not lighted, no gated pulse.	Failure to acquire missile.	Check for correct address and missile frequency. Check launcher coordinates. Refer to T.O. 21-SM68-2J-7-1-1.	Same as EXERCISE.

Figure 5-30. ACQ MISSILE Not Green

5-41

T.O. 21-SM68-1　　　　Section V

MALFUNCTION INDICATION	TROUBLE INDICATION	POSSIBLE CAUSES	CORRECTIVE ACTION	
			EXERCISE	EWO
LIFT OFF not white.		Defective lamp.	Continue countdown.	Same as EXERCISE.

Figure 5-31. LIFT OFF Not White

MALFUNCTION INDICATION	TROUBLE INDICATION	POSSIBLE CAUSES	CORRECTIVE ACTION	
			EXERCISE	EWO
GUID IN PROGRESS not green		Defective lamp.	Continue countdown.	Same as EXERCISE.

Figure 5-32. GUID IN PROGRESS Not Green

T.O. 21-SM68-1　　　　　　　　　　　　　　　　　　　　　　Section V

MALFUNCTION INDICATION	TROUBLE INDICATION	POSSIBLE CAUSES	CORRECTIVE ACTION	
			EXERCISE	EWO
GGS FAULT lighted (accompanied by GGS HOLD lighted after ANT RAISE white).	POWER ON not green.	Transients.	Press HOLD RELEASE and continue countdown.	Same as EXERCISE.
	ANTENNA FACILITY FAULT red (prior to ACQ MISSILE green).	Circuit breaker open in antenna terminal cabinets.	Proceed to figure 5-22. Select alternate antenna: Press POWER OFF white, Press alternate ANTENNA FACILITY SELECT green, press POWER ON white, and continue countdown.	Same as EXERCISE. Same as EXERCISE.
	ANTENNA FACILITY FAULT red (after ACQ MISSILE green).	Circuit breaker open in antenna cabinets.	Recycle, select alternate antenna: Press POWER OFF white, press alternate ANTENNA FACILITY SELECT green, press POWER ON white, and continue countdown.	Same as EXERCISE.
	CTU ALARM red.	Transients.	Reset CTU, press HOLD RELEASE, and continue countdown.	Same as EXERCISE.

Figure 5-33. GGS FAULT Lighted

Changed 17 January 1964　TOCN-1 (DEN-8)　　　　　　　　　　　　　5-44

T.O. 21-SM68-1

Section V

MALFUNCTION INDICATION	TROUBLE INDICATION	POSSIBLE CAUSES	CORRECTIVE ACTION	
			EXERCISE	EWO
ABORT red (during GUID X run).			Select alternate antenna: Press POWER OFF white, press alternate ANTENNA FACILITY SELECT green, press POWER ON white, and continue countdown.	Same as EXERCISE.

Figure 5-34. ABORT Red (During GUID X Run)

5-45

T.O. 21-SM68-1　　　Section V

MALFUNCTION INDICATION	TROUBLE INDICATION	POSSIBLE CAUSES	CORRECTIVE ACTION	
			EXERCISE	EWO
ABORT red (during missile flight).			Select alternate antenna: Press POWER OFF white, press alternate ANTENNA FACILITY SELECT green, press POWER ON white, and continue countdown.	Same as EXERCISE.

Figure 5-35. ABORT Red (During Missile Flight)

5-46

T.O. 21M-HGM25A-1-1 (21-SM68-1) Section V

MALFUNCTION INDICATION	TROUBLE INDICATION	POSSIBLE CAUSES	CORRECTIVE ACTION	
			EXERCISE	EWO
MAG I not indicating 1.5 to 1.9 MA.			Increase or decrease as required. Prior to the raise launcher phase, select alternate antenna: Press POWER OFF white, press alternate ANTENNA FACILITY SELECT green, press POWER ON white, and continue countdown. After raise launcher phase, continue countdown if MAG ON green.	Same as EXERCISE.

Figure 5-36. MAG I Not Indicating 1.5 to 1.9 MA

Changed 31 January 1964   TOCN 1-1 (DEN-9)   5-47

T.O. 21M-HGM25A-1-1 (21-SM68-1) Section V

MALFUNCTION INDICATION	TROUBLE INDICATION	POSSIBLE CAUSES	CORRECTIVE ACTION	
			EXERCISE	EWO
Erratic MAG I indication.	More than 10 deflections in a 5-second period on MAG-MOD CUR-VOLT meter.	High voltage arcing.	Decrease or increase until reading is stable between 1.5 to 1.9 MA and continue countdown. If reading cannot be stabilized prior to the raise launcher phase, select alternate antenna: Press POWER OFF white, press alternate ANTENNA FACILITY SELECT green, press POWER ON white, and continue countdown. After raise launcher phase, continue countdown if MAG I reading is stable and MAG ON is green.	Same as EXERCISE.

Figure 5-37. Erratic MAG I Indication

Changed 31 January 1964 TOCN 1-1 (DEN-9) 5-48

T.O. 21-SM68-1   Section V

MALFUNCTION INDICATION	AFFECT ON COUNTDOWN	PROBABLE CAUSES	CORRECTIVE ACTION	
			ALERT STATUS MONITORING	EWO/EXERCISE
Annunciator.	None.	Defective lamps.	Replace lamp(s).	None.
Indicators fail to light and horn fails to sound.		No DC voltage.	Check circuit breakers and fuses.	
		Defective annunciator circuitry.	Check circuitry.	
Engine and turbo charger low lube oil pressure.	Yes.	Clogged filter(s).		Bypass engine lube oil filter(s).
		Defective safety circuit(s)/switch(s).		Bypass safety circuit(s)/switch(s).
		High lube oil temperature.	If malfunction occurs during the initial starting procedure, reaccomplish start sequence. If engine is on the line and malfunction occurs, start and parallel standby engine.	(EAFB, BAFB, LAFB, MHAFB) Switch engine lube oil from filters to strainers and set START-RUN switch to START.
Cyclonic separator low level.	Yes.	Defective control valve.	Start and parallel standby engine.	Manually operate control valves.
		Low utility air pressure.	Stop malfunctioning engine. Check utility air system.	Bypass controllers/safety circuit(s).
Engine overspeeds.	Yes.	Defective governor.	Start and parallel standby engine.	Continue launch with remaining generator(s).
Fuel oil day tank low level.	No.	Day tanks not serviced.	Service fuel oil day tank.	Service fuel oil day tank.
		Defective liquid level indicator.		

Figure 5-38. Table of Power House Malfunction Isolation (Sheet 1 of 6)

Changed 17 January 1964   TOCN-1 (DEN-8)   5-49

T.O. 21-SM68-1 Section V

MALFUNCTION INDICATION	AFFECT ON COUNTDOWN	PROBABLE CAUSES	CORRECTIVE ACTION	
			ALERT STATUS MONITORING	EWO
Generator 1, 2, 3, or 4 air circuit breaker tripped.	Yes.	Safety circuits activated.	Start and parallel standby engine.	Verify safety circuits are de-activated.
		Defective air circuit breaker.		Re-energize generator air circuit breaker.
Launcher 1, 2, or 3 feeder air circuit breaker tripped.	Yes.	Safety circuits activated.	Refer to Section IV.	Re-energize launcher feeder air circuit breaker as directed by control center.
		Defective air circuit breaker.		
Chiller 1, or 2 feeder air circuit breaker tripped.	Yes.	Condenser temperature high or low.	Inform facility personnel of malfunction.	Direct facility personnel to place ice tanks on line (if applicable).
Powerhouse feeder air circuit breaker tripped.	Yes.	Safety circuits activated or defective air circuit breaker.	Refer to emergency procedure (loss of power house feeder AC power).	Re-energize feeder air circuit breaker.
Control center feeder air circuit breaker tripped.	Yes.	Safety circuits activated.	Refer to emergency procedure (loss of control center feeder AC power).	Re-energize feeder air circuit breaker as directed by control center.

Figure 5-38. Table of Power House Malfunction Isolation (Sheet 2 of 6)

Changed 5 November 1963 TOCN-1 (DEN-3) 5-50

T.O. 21-SM68-1 Section V

MALFUNCTION INDICATION	AFFECT ON COUNTDOWN	PROBABLE CAUSES	CORRECTIVE ACTION	
			ALERT STATUS MONITORING	EWO/EXERCISE
Intake air supply fan circuit breaker tripped.	No.	Defective circuit breaker.	Obtain combustible air from outside source. Refer to emergency procedure. (Loss of power house intake fan).	None.
Exhaust fan(s) circuit breaker tripped.	No.	Defective circuit breaker.	Refer to emergency procedure (loss of power house exhaust fan).	None.
Battery bank low voltage.	No.	Defective rectifier.	Check battery bank and rectifier and set HI-LO charge switch to HI.	Check circuit breaker and fuse. Check battery bank and rectifier and set HI-LO charge switch to HI.
		Defective battery bank.	Check battery bank and rectifier.	
Loss of all DC power (LAFB 724TH/725TH SQDN).	No.	Circuit breaker tripped or blown fuse.	Check fuse/circuit breaker.	Manually operate governor controls.
Loss of all DC power (LAFB, BAFB, EAFB, MHAFB).	Yes.	Defective fuse and circuit breaker.	Refer to emergency procedure (loss of all AC power).	Refer to emergency procedure (loss of all AC power).
Water storage tank low level.	No.	Defective controller.	Set pump HAND-OFF-AUTO switch to HAND.	Set pump HAND-OFF-AUTO switch to HAND.

Figure 5-38. Table of Power House Malfunction Isolation (Sheet 3 of 6)

Changed 17 January 1964 TOCN-1 (DEN-8)

MALFUNCTION INDICATION	AFFECT ON COUNTDOWN	PROBABLE CAUSES	CORRECTIVE ACTION	
			ALERT STATUS MONITORING	EWO/EXERCISE
Starting air pressure low.	No.	Defective controller.	Bypass controller by manually operating switch.	(EAFB, BAFB, LAFB, MHAFB) Bypass controller by manually operating switch and/or remove shutdown arm from fuel rack.
Engine fails to start automatically (LAFB 724TH/725TH SQDN).	No.	Defective HAND-OFF-AUTO switch. Centrifugal switch stuck closed; TR-3 defective; R-1/SU defective. Starting air valve stuck closed.	Refer to emergency procedure (standby diesel engine manual start, LAFB 724TH/725TH SQDN). Free air valve.	Same. Free air valve.
Engine fails to stop automatically (LAFB 724TH/725TH SQDN).	No.	Loss of DC power. Defective circuitry in engine console.	Shutoff power switch on engine console. Set manual throttle lever to STOP. Set LOAD LIMIT knob on governor to 0.	Shut off power switch on engine console. Set manual throttle lever to STOP. Set LOAD LIMIT knob on governor to 0.
Engine high water temperature (VAFB, EAFB, BAFB, LAFB, MHAFB).	No.	Circulating pump circuit breaker tripped. Restricted supply/return line.	Check circuit breaker. Check supply/return valves.	Same. Same.

Figure 5-38. Table of Power House Malfunction Isolation (Sheet 4 of 6)

T.O. 21-SM68-1

MALFUNCTION INDICATION	AFFECT ON COUNTDOWN	PROBABLE CAUSES	CORRECTIVE ACTION	
			ALERT STATUS MONITORING	EWO/EXERCISE
Engine and turbo high lube oil temperature (VAFB, EAFB, BAFB, LAFB, MHAFB).	Yes.	Defective coolant system.	Check temperature controller.	Refer to procedure for low lube oil pressure.
		Low lube oil level.	Check coolant system pumps/valves. Check lube oil level.	

Figure 5-38. Table of Power House Malfunction Isolation (Sheet 4A of 6)

T.O. 21-SM68-1   Section V

MALFUNCTION INDICATION	AFFECT ON COUNTDOWN	PROBABLE CAUSES	CORRECTIVE ACTION	
			ALERT STATUS MONITORING	EWO
Prelube pump fails to operate.	No.	Blown fuse.	Check fuse.	None.
		Circuit breaker tripped.	Check circuit breaker.	
		Defective circuitry.	Check circuitry.	
Prelube circulating pump fails to start (VAFB, EAFB, BAFB, LAFB, MHAFB).	No.	Reset relay tripped.	Open engine console control panel and press reset relay.	None.
		Blown fuse.	Replace fuse.	
Generator and exciter circuit breaker fails to close/tripped.	Yes.	Defective mechanical linkage.	Start and parallel standby engine. Adjust mechanical linkage.	If time permits, accomplish the following: Adjust mechanical linkage/replace fuse.
		Blown fuse.	Replace fuse.	
		Defective closing/tripping mechanism.	Replace defective closing/tripping mechanism.	
Loss of utility air pressure (LAFB 724TH/725TH SQDN).	Yes.	Defective controller. Circuit breaker tripped.	Manually switch to starting air pressure.	Refer to emergency procedure (loss of all AC power).
		Defective air drier.	Inform facility personnel of defective air drier.	

Figure 5-38. Table of Power House Malfunction Isolation (Sheet 5 of 6)

Changed 5 November 1963 TOCN-1 (DEN-3)   5-53

T.O. 21-SM68-1   Section V

MALFUNCTION INDICATION	AFFECT ON COUNTDOWN	PROBABLE CAUSES	CORRECTIVE ACTION	
			ALERT STATUS MONITORING	EWO
No Remote engine speed control on generator panel/engine control console.	No.	Defective governor motor control switch. Governor friction clutch slipping.	Replace defective governor motor control switch. Adjust friction clutch.	Manually operate governor speed control.
		Open control circuit in governor motor control.	Replace fuse(s).	
Voltage regulator inoperative (VAFB, EAFB, BAFB, LAFB, MHAFB).	No.	Voltage dividers resistors out of tolerance.	Adjust voltage dividers resistors.	Manually operate exciter field rheostat.
		Burned/dirty contacts.	Clean contacts.	
		Defective pre-set rheostat.	Replace pre-set rheostat.	
Voltage regulator inoperative (LAFB 724TH/ 725TH SQDN).	No.	Defective voltage regulator circuit.	Troubleshoot/replace regulator.	Manually operate exciter field rheostat.
Synchroscope inoperative.	No.	Blown fuse.	Replace fuse.	Synchronize using synchronizing indicators.
Synchronizing indicators fail to light.	No.	Defective lamp(s). Open circuit.	Replace lamp(s).	Synchronize using synchroscope.

Figure 5-38. Table of Power House Malfunction Isolation (Sheet 6 of 6)

T.O. 21-SM68-1

Section VI
Paragraphs 6-1 to 6-8

SECTION VI

OPERATING LIMITATIONS

6-1. SCOPE.

6-2. This section describes procedural limitations to pre-launch, launch, and post-launch operations as imposed by equipment design. The equipment design limitations make it mandatory in some areas to adhere strictly to prescribed procedures, while in other areas certain deviations are permissible in view of the flexibility of design. In future issues of this manual, the scope of this section will be enlarged as information becomes available.

6-3. WEATHER LIMITATIONS.

6-4. Launcher system operation should not be attempted under any of the following weather conditions due to launcher limitations:

   a. Launcher platform motion with wind in excess of 60 MPH at 10 feet above ground level for an EWO launch. For peacetime exercises, maximum allowable wind velocity is 50 MPH including a maximum gust factor of 20 MPH.

   b. Opening of missile silo doors with ice in excess of 2 feet thick on doors.

   c. Opening of missile silo doors with snow in excess of 15 feet deep on doors.

6-5. Launcher system operation may be erratic if exercise is attempted under conditions beyond the following design requirements:

   a. Rain in excess of 5 inches per hour.

   b. Rain in excess of 3 inches per hour with wind in excess of 40 MPH at 10 feet above ground level.

   c. Temperature in excess of 125°F (in silo).

   d. Temperature below -35°F (in silo).

WARNING

Prior to lowering of launcher during winter months after extended periods of an up and locked condition, all excessive ice and snow must be removed from the flame deflector area, corner lock area, and closure door areas.

6-6. POWER HOUSE.

6-7. ONE GENERATOR OPERATION.

6-8. In the event there is only one operational generator available for an EWO launch, coordination is essential between the EPPT and MLO before starting or ending a function to insure the following:

   a. Starting amperage within operating limits.

b. Isolation of non-essential operating equipment from the system.

6-9. DIESEL FUEL OIL SUPPLY.

6-10. Due to the configuration of the fuel oil storage tanks, it is mandatory that a minimum of 5000 gallons of fuel oil be maintained in one of the tanks to assure a successful EWO launch.

6-11. ICE BANKS.

6-12. If water chillers cannot maintain the desired temperature, the ice banks will supplement for a period of approximately 12 hours of continuous operation.

6-13. COUNTDOWN LIMITATIONS.

6-14. FIRST HOLD PERIOD.

6-15. The permissible duration of the first hold period is primarily determined by time requirements of lox boil-off and lox handling facilities. The design limit of one hour for the maximum hold makes allowance for lox recycle and for variations in the time elapsed since the last refilling of the lox storage tank. It has been determined that after loading and unloading lox, and after a one-hour delay, there is still enough lox available for reloading and for a successful launch even if 10 days have elapsed since the los storage tank was last refilled. Therefore, extensions beyond the one-hour time limit for the first hold are permissible under favorable circumstances.

6-16. Figure 6-1 presents chart-form data for computing maximum hold time for the first hold. Plots are provided for hold times with and without recycle. In this case, lox and nitrogen remaining in the storage facilities are the primary limiting factors. The sample shown depicts a condition where 10 days have elapsed since the storage facilitess were last refilled. Entering this 10-day figure in the chart results in approximately 170 minutes of hold time available and still retains the recycle capability. In this case, lox is the limiting factor. The sample alos shows that if recycle was not required, the hold could be extented to 210 minutes. In this case, nitrogen is the limiting factor.

6-17. SECOND HOLD PERIOD.

6-18. The second hold period is limited to a much shorter time delay than the first hold. In this case, the missile is above ground without air conditioning or lox topping and the missile lox tanks are pressurized. This hold period has been given a maximum time limit of 30 seconds, is based on a reliability confidence factor of the particular missile being launched, and is related to the net positive suction head pressure available at the Stage II lox pump when the Stage II engine is fired. Any delay in pressing LAUNCH from green to white, at the moment LAUNCH indicates green, tends to decrease this confidence factor by causing a possible decrease of net positive suction head pressure at Stage II lox turbine pumps. This delay could cause cavitation of the turbine when the engine is fired.

6-19. If the launcher is not up and locked within 30 seconds after T-41, an automatic shutdown will occur.

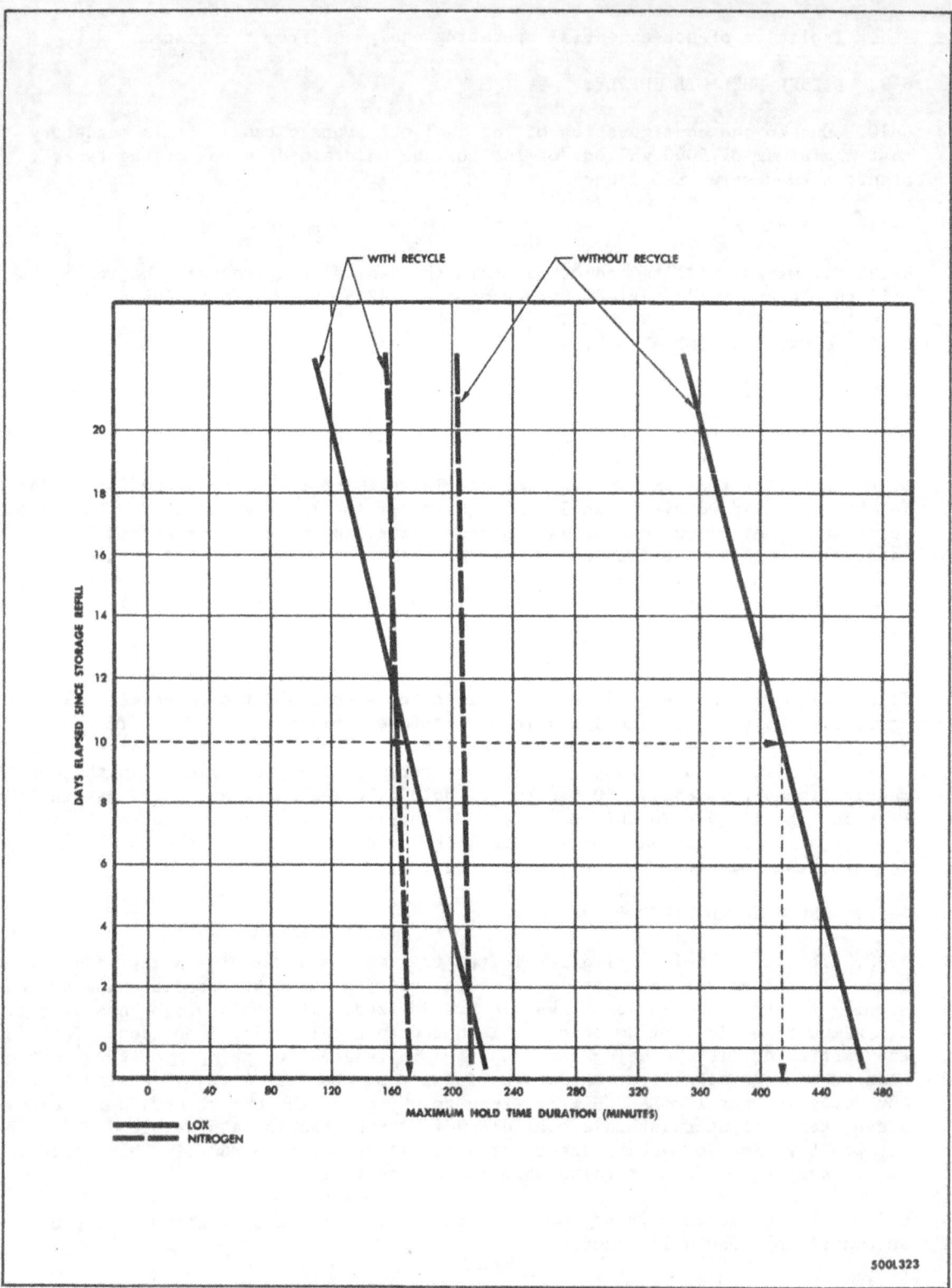

Figure 6-1. Maximum Allowable Hold Time, First Hold

6-20. **LAUNCH PLATFORM RAISING AND LOWERING.**

Note

All T times referenced in this section are approximate times.

6-21. If RAISE LAUNCHER or LOWER LAUNCHER pushbutton on launch control console (LCC) is pressed for one of the three launchers, the two remaining launchers of the complex are disabled; that is, neither one can be raised or lowered until re-enabled by an automatically sequenced signal.

6-22. Therefore when launch countdown is initiated simultaneously on all three launchers and carried through the load propellants phase to the first hold, only one of the three launchers can enter the raise launcher phase. After RAISE LAUNCHER pushbutton is pressed for the first launcher, the second launcher can enter the raise launcher phase only after a minimum first hold period of 450 to 480 seconds. First hold varies depending on the length of time the missile being launched remains in second hold. The third launcher will be held in first hold for an additional minimum period of 450 to 480 seconds before entering the raise launcher phase.

6-23. If, during simultaneous propellant loading on all three launchers, a malfunction imposes an extended first hold on any one of the three launchers, the raise launcher phase on one of the two remaining launchers can be initiated immediately after termination of the load propellants phase. The raise launcher phase on the second remaining launcher can be started 450 seconds thereafter. If the malfunction on the first launcher is eliminated in less than 900 seconds, this launcher will have to remain in the hold position until 900 seconds have elapsed. However, the minimum total period of launching all three missiles will remain the same.

6-24. If lower launcher phase is initiated, after firing the first of three missiles, the raise launcher capability of the other two launchers is disabled until the lowering of the empty launcher is complete. This delays initiation of the raise launcher phase for the next missile by approximately 11 minutes beyond the normal delay.

6-25. If lower launcher phase on the first launcher is not initiated prior to T+170 the raising of the two remaining launchers is enabled, provided both have gone through the load propellants phase.

6-26. If shutdown occurs between first hold and second hold, the launcher is lowered automatically. If launcher is up and locked and shutdown occurs between second hold and prior to lift off (explosive bolts not fired) the LOWER LAUNCHER pushbutton must be pressed to transfer the shutdown signal to the launcher control system to lower the launcher.

6-27. If shutdown occurs after the Stage I engine has been fired but prior to missile in flight, the engine compartment water spray signal is generated. This signal will be interrupted to turn off the water spray upon receipt of start LOWER LAUNCHER command from the LCC or the water spray will be turned off automatically at T+303 signal from the launch sequencer.

6-28. LAUNCHER PLATFORM OPERATING WEIGHT LIMITS.

6-29. The following is a summary of launcher platform gross weight conditions. If these maximum weight limits are exceeded, operation of the launcher platform is considered unsafe.

    a. Raising launcher platform with lox or dual propellant loads between 70,000 and 160,000 pounds.

Note

Step b does not apply after incorporation of CSE equipment.

    b. Raising launcher platform with fuel load only.

    c. Lowering launcher platform with lox or dual propellant loads between 140,000 and 160,000 pounds. Under emergency conditions only, the launcher platform may be lowered with either lox only or dual propellant load conditions, and total weight in the range from 20,000 to 140,000 pounds.

Note

Step d does not apply after incorporation of CSE equipment.

    d. Under emergency condition only, the launcher platform may be lowered within th 20,000 to 140,000 pound range for fuel load condition.

6-30. All possible missile propellant loadings and the safety features for raising and lowering the launcher platform are shown in figure 6-2.

WARNING

Those conditions marked EMERGENCY ONLY (figure 6-2) produce high motor pressures. Insure that the condition is an actual emergency before operating with these loadings. Do not operate launcher platform in the area marked UNSAFE.

6-31. Weight will be determined by the length of time a missile is maintained in a HOLD condition. If missile contains lox only, maximum hold time is 45 minutes. If this time is exceeded missile must be held until the overall weight is reduced to 70,000 pounds or less. Since there is no way to actually determine a weight of 70,000 pounds, the missile should be held until all lox has boiled off. If missile contains dual propellants, maximum hold time is 8 hours. If this time is exceeded, all lox must be boiled off before lowering launcher platform. Since it is impossible to determine exactly what weight of lox is aboard the missile, a complete unloading if lox must be performed before lowering launcher platform.

T.O. 21-SM68-1　　Section VI

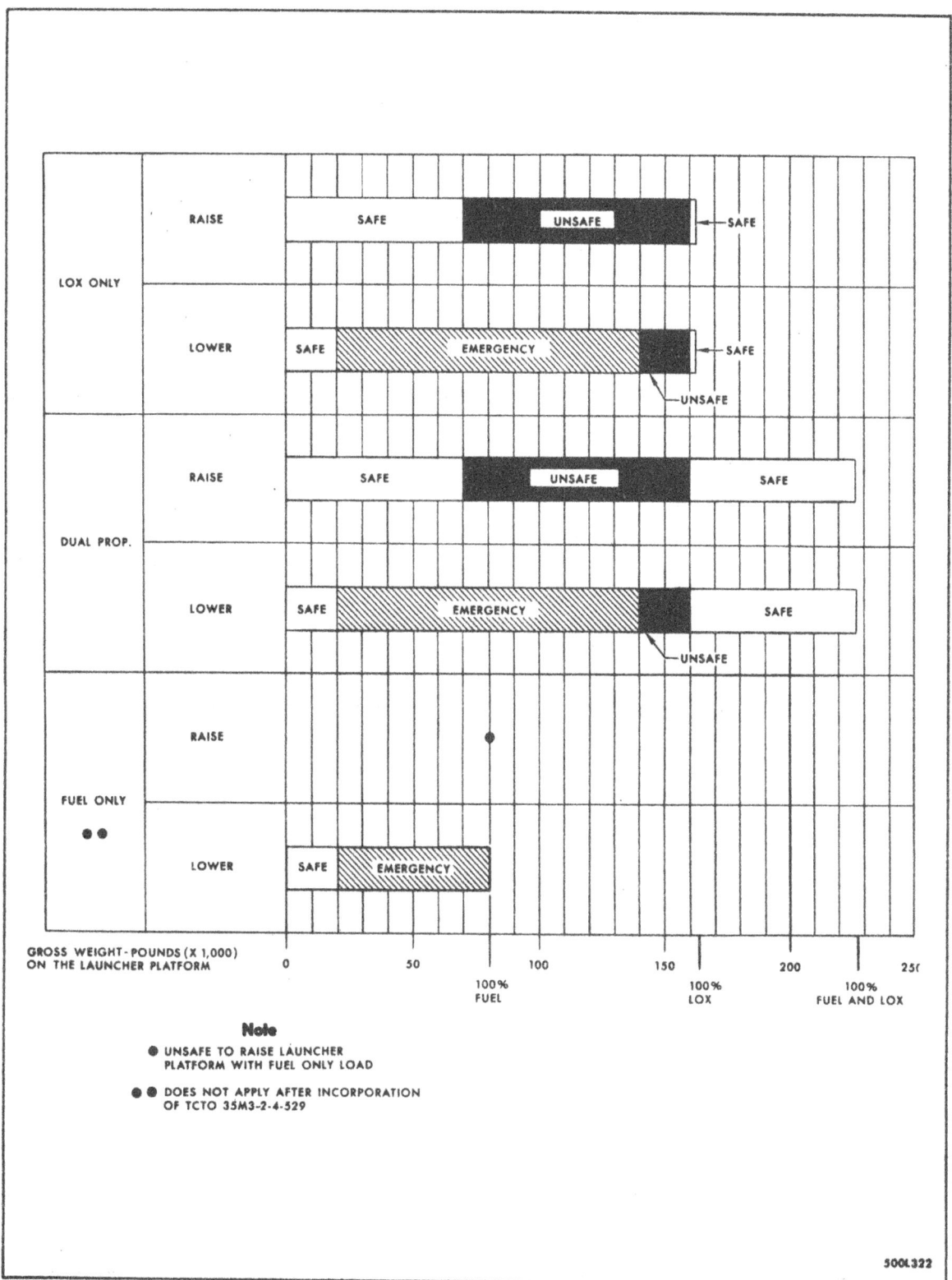

Figure 6-2. Launcher Platform Operating Weight Limits

CAUTION

> For a topside hold exceeding one hour, the inclined locks must be checked to verify that lock drift has not exceeded one-half inch. If this drift value has been exceeded, the lox load must be dumped or allowed to boil off prior to lowering of the launcher platform. With fuel load only remaining, lowering will be accomplished under emergency conditions. This check is required to preclude excessive movement of the crib with possible attendant damage to launcher platform and facility equipment.

6-32. TARGET SELECTION.

6-33. Target selection cannot be changed after T-80 during the countdown. Therefore, it is recommended that all target selection be completed prior to initiation of the raise launcher phase.

6-34. GGS MALFUNCTION OR NOT-READY.

6-35. GGS malfunction, or not-ready, does not immediately affect the ability to initiate 2 countdown. However, launch countdown cannot proceed beyond the second hold until the guidance malfunction is corrected, or unless handover has been initiated. A GGS not-ready indication after pressing of the LAUNCH pushbutton automatically initiates 2 shutdown.

6-36. HANDOVER OR SHUTDOWN.

6-37. The decision as to whether shutdown or handover action is to be initiated depends on the particular countdown phase at which GGS malfunction occurs, on the time delay required for establishing backup guidance availability, and on the average time delay to be allotted to verbal communication via voice link with the backup GGS. As a general limitation, it has been established that no handover procedures should be attempted on any launcher which has advanced past the first hold stage of its countdown when GGS malfunction occurs.

6-38. RADAR SURVEILLANCE SYSTEM.

6-39. System and component climatic and environment limitations for the radar surveillance system anti-intrusion equipment operations are as follows:

    a. Ambient operating temperatures   -40 to +140 degrees F (-40 to +60 degrees C)

    b. Humidity   Refer to Military Standard

    c. Barometric pressure (in operation)   As prevelant from sea level to 6000 feet (altitude)

    d. Wind loading   52 knots with ice, 75 knots without ice

    e. Ice loading   2 inches of ice, measured radially

SECTION VII

CREW DUTIES

7-1. SCOPE.

7-2. This section contains a description of the responsibilities of each missile combat crew member in operating and maintaining the missile complex. The duties of each crew member include a discussion of their primary and secondary functions.

7-3. GENERAL.

7-4. The Titan I missile combat crew is comprised of a missile combat crew commander (missile launch officer or guidance electronics officer, depending upon seniority), missile launch officer (MLO), guidance electronics officer (GEO), ballistic missile analyst technician (BMAT), missile maintenance technician (MMT), and two electrical power production technicians (EPPT). The six crew members of the missile combat crew have certain specific duties that must be performed in maintaining and operating the launch complex. A crew member may be called on to perform other than his normal duties if an emergency arises during standby, countdown or abort; or if a malfunction occurs during a tactical countdown.

7-5. MISSILE COMBAT CREW COMMANDER (MCCC).

7-6. The MCCC is the senior officer of the missile combat crew. He is responsible for conducting the crew coordination, crew changeover, and when necessary, safety briefings. He will make EWO assignments and insure daily performance of the weapon system verification checklist. The MCCC controls access to the launch complex, launch emplacements, and the upper level of the launch control center. He will assume the responsibilities of the complex commander during his absence. He will direct all combat crew activities, verify complex configuration, and insure adequacy, currency and adherence to operational technical orders and checklists. He is responsible for insuring immediate EWO reaction capability, adherence to the two man policy, and compliance with JCS weapon system safety rules. The MCCC is also responsible for insuring timely completion of crew training requirements and for maintaining a high degree of crew professionalism.

7-7. MISSILE LAUNCH OFFICER (MLO).

7-8. The MLO is responsible for copying, decoding and authenticating fast reaction messages and determining if a launch exercise countdown is authorized to proceed. The missile launch officer will always assume the responsibilities of the MCCC during performance of weapon system verification, launch countdowns and exercises. In addition the MLO is responsible for the following tasks:

 a. Manning the launch control console during countdown.

 b. Reviewing logs, charts, status boards, and other information applicable to the status of the complex.

 c. Reviewing applicable AFTO 200 series forms.

 d. Coordinating all required maintenance actions/functions with the maintenance officer/supervisor.

e. Reviewing operational checklists/technical data applicable to his crew station for currency and completeness.

f. Performing and coordinating his portion of the positive control changeover with the GEO.

g. Coordinating with command post on effective changeover and applicable countdown times.

h. Announcing his assumption of command over the public address system after crew changeover.

i. Adhering to JCS safety rules.

j. Participating in all crew briefings.

7-9. GUIDANCE ELECTRONICS OFFICER (GEO).

7-10. The GEO is responsible for copying, decoding and authenticating fast reaction messages. He will insure the guidance countdown is started at the proper time and the correct trajectory kits are inserted for launch/exercise. In addition the GEO is responsible for the following tasks:

a. Manning the missile guidance console during countdowns and readiness monitoring.

b. Performing weapons system verification checklist and insures the guidance system is maintained in a readiness condition.

c. Reviewing operational checklists/technical data applicable to his crew station for currency and completeness.

d. Performing and coordinating his portion of the positive control changeover with the MLO.

e. Manning the launch control console in absence of the MLO.

f. Performing malfunction analysis as required.

g. Reviewing applicable AFTO 200 series forms and coordinates with maintenance for necessary corrective action.

h. Jointly responsible with the MLO for adhering to JCS safety rules.

i. Participating in all crew briefings.

7-11. BALLISTIC MISSILE ANALYST TECHNICIAN (BMAT).

7-12. The BMAT monitors the launch complex facilities console during alert status monitoring and launch countdown. The BMAT is also responsible for the following tasks:

a. Visual monitoring of countdown sequence and performing malfunction analysis on the missile systems and all associated AGE and AOE.

T.O. 21-SM68-1

Section VII
Paragraphs 7-13 to 7-16

b. Operating and assisting in maintaining AOE during alert status monitoring.

c. Performing weapon system status verification.

d. Coordinating checklist functions.

e. Reviewing AFTO series 200 Forms and coordinating with maintenance for necessary corrective action.

f. Copying, decoding and authenticating fast reaction messages.

g. Acting as back-up operator for the launch control console (LCC).

h. Troubleshooting all sub-systems as required.

i. Performing sub-system checkouts and providing maintenance assistance as a secondary function when directed by the MCCC.

7-13. MISSILE MAINTENANCE TECHNICIAN (MMT).

7-14. The MMT monitors AGE during alert status monitoring. He follows the countdown sequence and assists in malfunction analysis as required. In addition the MMT is responsible for the following tasks:

a. Acting as back up operator for the LCFC, and assisting the electrical power production technicians as required.

b. Monitoring the PLPS on TV surveillance cameras during propellant loading exercises.

c. Supervising post shutdown procedures for accomplishment of missile helium and lox unloading, utilizing recycle procedures from appropriate functional checklists.

d. Performing sub-system checkouts and provides maintenance assistance as a secondary function when directed by the MCCC.

7-15. ELECTRICAL POWER PRODUCTION TECHNICIANS (EPPT).

7-16. The two EPPT are responsible to the MCCC for the operation of the power generation, distribution, and associated equipment. In addition, the EPPT are responsible for the following tasks:

a. When an exercise is directed by the MLO, the senior power production technician will immediately take control of all activities and functions in the power house. He will remain in control until the exercise has been terminated or until returned to normal status by direction of the MLO.

b. Advising the MLO on status of equipment throughout the power house.

c. Maintaining and completing applicable forms as directed by AFM-66-1, T.O. 00-20E-1, AFR-91-4, applicable SAC supplements, and applicable SAC CEM manuals.

d. Assisting maintenance dispatched personnel in accomplishing maintenance, when these duties do not interfere with his alert duties and after coordinating with the MLO.

7-3

GLOSSARY

A

ABORT:	Stopping a missile countdown sequence.
AEC:	Atomic energy commission.
AEROSPACE GROUND EQUIPMENT (AGE):	The equipment other than operational which is required to inspect, test, adjust, calibrate, appraise, gage, measure, repair, overhaul, assemble, disassemble, transport, record, store, actuate, or otherwise maintain the operating status of the airborne vehicle AOE, and guidance station equipment.
AEROSPACE OPERATING EQUIPMENT (AOE):	The ground equipment which is the functional part of the weapon system of support system and which operates with the missile in the performance of the latter's mission as a major operational element of the weapon system or support system.
AFC:	Automatic frequency control.
AFM:	Air Force manual.
AFSC:	Air Force specialty code.
AIRFRAME:	The assembled structural and aerodynamic components of a missile which support the various systems and subsystems.
ALERT STATUS MONITORING:	A monitoring condition from which a launch countdown can be initiated immediately.
AME-COTAR:	Angle measuring equipment-correlation tracking and ranging.
APS:	Airborne power supply.
ARMING:	Process of changing a fuze or warhead from a safe condition to a state of readiness for initiation.
ATTITUDE:	The position of an airborne missile about its pitch, roll, and yaw axes to some frame of reference.
ATPA:	Auxiliary turbine pump assembly.
AZIMUTH:	A direction expressed as a horizontal angle measured clockwise from north.

B

BACKOUT:	Performing procedures to return the missile and associated AGE to a safe condition.

BEACON SIGNAL:	An RF pulse on which directional receiving antennas are locked.
BI-APS:	Battery inverter-accessory power supply.
BLANKET:	A term used to denote the use of low pressure gaseous nitrogen in propellant lines and tanks to replace air or gox.
BLAP:	Blast lock alarm panel.
BMAT:	Ballistic missile analyst technician.
BOI:	Break of inspection.
BOIL-OFF:	The vaporization of any volatile liquid.
BUDDY SYSTEM:	A system by which at least two men are together at all times when in designated areas that require the system.

C

CASSEGRAINIAN REFLECTOR (MODIFIED):	A parabolic reflector that reflects RF energy to receiving horns. The horns are in the focal point of the reflector and direct the RF energy through the center of the reflector.
CCAP:	Control center alarm panel.
CCC:	Control center circuits.
CDF:	Combat defense force.
CHECKOUT:	The test procedure that determines the capability of a device to perform a desired operation or function.
CO_2:	Carbon dioxide.
COMBINED SYSTEM EXERCISE (CSE):	A countdown used for crew training and weapon system checkout.
COMBUSTION CHAMBER:	The area where the burning of the fuel/oxidizer mixture occurs in any internal combustion engine. In rocket engines, the combustion chamber is the enclosed area between the injector face and an imaginary plane across the throat of the nozzle.
COMMAND DESTRUCT SIGNAL:	Radio signal used to initiate the destruction device carried in the missile.
COMMUTATION:	A time-sequenced sampling of instrumentation data for transmission on one telemetering channel to a receiving station.

CORRELATION TRACKING AND RANGING (COTAR):	A system that determines missile position by phase comparison of an RF signal received by two or more separate antennas.
COUNTDOWN:	The step-by-step procedure performed prior to missile launching in accordance with a predesignated schedule and measured in terms of T-time.
CP:	Command post.
CSO:	Control system officer.
CST:	Control system technician.
CWT:	Counterweight.

D

DEFCON:	Defense condition.
DELUGE:	A method of cooling a flame deflector with water to prevent damage from a rocket blast.
DIAPHRAGM, BURST:	A dividing wall in a pipe or tube designed to burst at a given pressure.
DIGITAL COMPUTER:	A calculating machine that solves complex problems relating to the missile flight path and presents the result in digits of the decimal system.
DUAL PROPELLANT LOADING (DPL):	A countdown in which fuel and oxidizer are loaded.

E

ECS:	Engine control system.
EPPT:	Electrical power production technician.
ERROR SIGNAL:	In servo mechanisms, a signal voltage applied to a control circuit.
ES:	Electrical system.
ETAP:	Equipment terminal alarm panel.
EWO:	Emergency war order.
EXERCISE MODE:	Mode of operation of the weapon system used to verify the weapon system operation without launching the missile and for training purposes. In the exercise mode, missile fuel tanks are empty and the operation and activation of certain missile system functions are simulated.

F

FAIL-SAFE:	A control for the automatic selection of an alternative action in case of malfunction.
FCS:	Flight control system.
FCV:	Flow control valve.
FDBVAP:	Fuel discharge bleed valve.
FTAP:	Fuel terminal alarm panel.
FUEL:	In a rocket engine, any matter that is mixed with an oxidizer to maintain combustion.
FUZE:	A device for initiating a detonation.

G

GAS GENERATOR:	The component of a rocket engine which provides hot pressurized gas products for driving the turbine of a turbopump assembly.
GEO:	Guidance electronics officer.
GGIGN:	Gas generator igniter.
GGS:	Ground guidance station.
GGVFBV:	Gas generator valve fuel bleed valve.
GGVPV:	Gas generator valve pilot valve.
GIMBAL:	A device consisting of a pair of rings pivoted on axis that are at right angles to each other so that one is free to swing within the other.
GMTS:	Guided missile test set.
GN_2:	Gaseous nitrogen.
GO STATUS SIGNAL:	A signal signifying that a system is in operating condition and ready to perform its particular function.
GYRO:	An electromechanical device whose qualities to maintain rigidity in space and precision are used to furnish steering commands and to stabilize the guidance platform.

H

HARDENED CONDITION:	The hardened condition of a building or structure when it is protected against overpressure.

HEAT EXCHANGER:	A device which transfers heat from one fluid or substance to another.
HF:	High frequency.
HOLD:	A condition initiated during a launch countdown wherein the countdown is interrupted and is not allowed to proceed until the condition is resolved.
HPS:	Hydraulic power supply.
HR:	Hour.
H_2SO_4:	Sulphuric acid.

I

ICC:	Instrumentation control center.
IGNITER:	A pyrogenic device to initiate burning of the fuel mixture in the combustion chamber.
IMLO:	Instructor missile launch officer.
INITIATOR:	An electrical device used to detonate primacord.
INJECTOR:	A device through which the fuel and oxidizer are sprayed into the combustion chamber.
IRSS:	Instrumentation range and safety system.
INSTRUMENTATION:	All equipment that senses, transmits, processes, indicates, or records the performance of components and systems during missile captive or flight tests.

K

KOH	Potassium hydroxide.

L

LAUNCH COMPLEX	The area encompassing the launch stands, guidance stations, and control centers.
LAUNCHER:	Structural device designed to physically support and hold missile in position for firing.
LAUNCHER SITE:	A launcher site consists of a missile silo, equipment terminal, a propellant terminal, and related equipment.
LCC:	Launch control console.

LCFC:	Launch complex facilities console.
LCS:	Launch control system.
LES:	Launch enable system.
LONGERON:	Lengthwise structural member.
LN_2:	Liquid nitrogen.
LS:	Launch sequencer.

M

MAET:	Missile accident emergency team.
MCC:	Missile combat crew.
MCCC:	Missile combat crew commander.
MFSO:	Missile flight safety officer.
MGC:	Missile guidance console.
MGS:	Missile guidance set.
MLO:	Missile launch officer.
MMT:	Missile maintenance technician.
MODULATION:	The result of varying some characteristic of a wave in accordance with another wave. In radio communications, carrier wave is varied to convey intelligence. The intelligence is called the modulating signal and the modulated carrier is called the modulated waved
MSAP:	Missile silo alarm panel.

N

N/A:	Not applicable.
NAOH:	Sodium hydroxide.
NAUTICAL MILE:	A distance equal to 6076.1033 feet.

O

O&C:	Operations and checkout console.
OSBVAP:	ATPA oxidizer pump suction line bleed valve.
OSBVPV:	Oxidizer suction bleed valve pilot valve.

OXIDIZER:	A substance such as liquid oxygen which supports combustion when combined with fuel.

P

PACKAGE:	A complete unit made up of sub-units.
PITCH:	The angular displacement about the lateral axis of an airframe.
PLPS:	Propellant loading and pressurization system.
PMR:	Pacific missile range.
POWER PACK:	An electric motor driven hydraulic power unit used to provide hydraulic power for operation of the missile launcher.
PRIMACORD:	The explosive cord that ruptures the propellant tanks upon receipt of a command destruct signal.
PROPELLANT:	The fuel and/or oxidizer used in a propulsion system.
PTAP:	Propellant terminal alarm panel.
PURGE:	The act of removing gaseous oxygen from lox loading lines and missile lox tanks, and replacing with gaseous nitrogen.
PUSHBUTTON:	A device that closes an electrical circuit when pressed and opens the circuit when released or pressed a second time.

R

RECYCLE:	Performing procedures to return the missile and associated AGE to alert status monitoring.
RGS:	GMTS plus MGS.
R-0:	Missile state of readiness preparatory to launch wherein all system checks have been completed, fuel has been loaded, and the weapon system is ready to begin the terminal countdown.
ROLL:	The angular displacement of an airframe about its longitudinal axis.
RP-1:	Rocket propellant (fuel).
RPIE:	Real property installed equipment.
R/V:	Re-entry vehicle.

RVS:	Re-entry vehicle system.

S

SAC CEM:	Strategic Air Command civil engineering manual.
SACM:	Strategic Air Command manual.
SAC SUP:	Strategic Air Command supplement.
SECE:	Supplemental engine control equipment.
SERVOAMPLIFIER:	An electronic device which converts and amplifies an electrical input signal to direct current for actuating electrohydraulic servovalves.
SERVOVALVE:	Electrohydraulic valve which acts in response to electrical control signals.
SHUTDOWN:	The act of terminating the launch countdown prior to lift off, usually because of a malfunction. Shutdowns are automatically initiated by system or component malfunction or manually initiated by means of a pushbutton on the LCC.
SKA-PAKS:	Portable oxygen packages to be used in emergencies.
SM:	Strategic missile.
	A condition of a missile or facility when openly exposed to overpressure, heat, radiation, penetration, or other effects of enemy attack.
STAGING:	The transition from booster phase to sustainer phase.
STAGING ROCKET:	The auxiliary solid propellant units attached to Stage II of the misssle to assist in stage separation.
SQUIB:	Small explosive device used to activate batteries.

T

TCIGN:	Thrust chamber igniter.
TCTO:	Time compliance technical order.
TCS:	Targeting control system.
TDB:	Time display board.
T/M:	Telemetering.
TMCO:	Target material control officer.

TOPPING:	An act accomplished near the completion of the launch countdown wherein the missile lox tanks receive an additional amount of sub-cooled liquid oxygen to replace lox which has boiled off following lox loading.
TPA:	Turbine pump assembly.
TPAXV:	TPA starter valve.
TRAJECTORY:	The path of the missile from launch to impact.
TRANSDUCER:	A data gathering sensing device that gathers and converts physical variations into corresponding voltages.
TSI:	Time sequence 1.

U

UMBILICAL CABLE:	A cable with a quick disconnect plug through which missile equipment is powered, controlled, and checked out while the missile is still attached to the launching equipment.
UMBILICAL TOWER:	A steel structure that supports servicing lines and cables that must remain attached to the missile when it is raised out of the silo.

V

VIP:	Very important person.

W

WARHEAD:	The portion of the missile intended to be lethal or incapacitating; normally includes the warhead casing with an explosive, chemical, or incendiary agent.

Y

YAW:	An angular displacement from the vertical axis of a missile. Looking forward, a positive yaw is clockwise.

ALPHABETICAL INDEX

*Denotes figure number

Paragraph

A

AC failures (See Power failures)

Administrative procedures, MCC...3-3
   Activity coordination briefing...3-17
   Complex entry (operational bases)..3-9
   Crew operations briefing..3-13
   Individual changeover (crew member)...................................*3-3, *3-4, 3-15
   Inspection..*3-1, 3-5
   Pre-departure briefing...3-7
   Shift change briefing...*3-2, 3-11

Air conditioning
   Antenna terminal silo..1-122
   Control center..1-121
   Equipment terminal..1-118
   Fuel terminal...1-120
   Missile..*1-68, *-169, 1-397
   Missile silo..1-118
   Propellant terminal...1-119

Air supply system, compressed
   Filtered..1-146
   Plant...1-145
   Utility...1-142

Alert procedures..3-98
   Combat defense force...3-107
   Missile combat crew member (See Crew member title)
   Termination..3-108

Arms, small (Procedures)..3-51, 3-53

Atmospheric pressure..*3-16, 3-87

B

Ballistic missile analyst technician
   Alert procedure..3-102
   Alert status monitoring..*3-10, *3-11
   Individual changeover...*3-3, *3-4

Barometric pressure..3-93

Battery power failure in equipment terminal..*4-15

Paragraph

Bent spear...*3-5, 3-42

Bolts
    Missile release...1-27
    Staging separation..1-24

Briefing, special activities..3-33
    (See also Administrative Procedures)

Broken arrow..*3-5, 3-41

C

Cable conduits, external..1-18

Checkout, missile and re-entry vehicle....................................2-3

Combat defense force (See Alert procedures)

Complex, launch...1-30
    Leading particulars...*1-4, *1-5, 1-31
    Facilities console...*1-26, *1-27, 1-74

Configuration, missile..*1-1

Console
    Launch complex..*1-26, *1-27, 1-74
    Launch control..*1-23, *1-24, 1-67
    Missile guidance..*1-25, 1-73

Control panel, fuel transfer..*1-33, *1-34, 1-94

Control station
    Local...*1-36, 1-106
    Tunnel entrance...*1-37, 1-109

Countdown
    Description...1-6
    Exercise procedure - CSE or lox...................................*3-30, 3-111
    Guidance procedure..*3-31, 3-111
    Launch and exercise...3-96
    Launch procedure (MLO/BMAT).......................................*3-29, 3-111
    Power house...*3-32, 3-113
    System functions (See System functions, launch countdown)

Combined system exercise (CSE)
    Dry...1-11
    Fuel..1-12
    Lox...1-13

D

Description, general - SM68 Missile.......................................1-3

Diesel engine manual start, standby..*4-30

Doors, missile silo..1-36

Drive system, launcher platform..*1-11, 1-46

Dull sword..*3-5, 3-43

Duties, crew..7-1 thru 7-16

E

Electrical power production technician
    Alert procedure..3-104
    Alert status monitoring..*3-13A, *3-14
    Individual changeover..*3-3, *3-4
    Countdown procedures (See Countdown)

Electrical room, equipment terminal..*1-14

Elevator
    Antenna silo personnel..1-153
    Instrument and TV camera mount..1-151

Emergency procedures
    Boil-off..4-5
    OSBV lox dump..4-7
    Recycle of electrical system and PLPS..4-10

EWO
    Alert assignment..3-27
    Communication procedures..3-28
    Crew procedures and coordination..3-29
    Training..3-32

Exercise, system..2-7

Explosion, missile silo..*4-13

F

Facility crew members
    Alert procedures..3-105

Facility technician
    Alert status monitoring..*3-14A, *3-14B

Fan failures
    Power house exhaust..*4-26
    Power house intake..*4-25

Index
Fire

Paragraph

Fire combating procedures..*4-1
  Equipment terminal...*4-8
  Equipment terminal hydraulics..*4-9
  Fuel terminal...*4-11
  Missile silo..*4-6
  Propellant terminal...*4-7

	Paragraph
Fuel oil supply, diesel	6-9

G

Generator failures
  Loss of one of two generators during alert status monitoring (EAFB, BAFB, LAFB, MHAFB) ... *4-18
  Loss of one of two generators during alert status monitoring (LAFB 724TH/725TH SQDN) ... *4-19
  Loss of one of three generators during countdown (LAFB 724TH/725TH SQDN) ... *4-20

Generator operating procedures (special)
  Single generator operation ... *4-29
  Two generator countdown (LAFB 724TH/725TH SQDN) ... *4-21

Gox hazards
  Gox in missile silo ... *4-2
  Gox in propellant terminal ... *4-3

Guidance electronics officer
  Alert procedure ... 3-101
  Alert status monitoring ... *3-9
  Countdown procedures (See Countdown, guidance)
  Individual changeover ... *3-3, *3-4

Guidance program tape installation and verification
  Fast retargeting ... *3-25
  Normal procedure ... *3-19

Guidance simulation procedure, digital ... *3-20

Guidance system ... *1-41, 1-158
  Ground equipment ... *1-22, 1-160
  Missileborne ... *1-42 thru *1-48, 1-165

H

Hazards ... *4-1 thru *4-30, 4-14
  AC power (See Power)
  Battery power (See Battery power failure)
  Explosion in missile silo (See explosion)
  Fire (See Fire combating procedures)
  Generator failures (See Generator failures)
  Gox (See Gox hazards)
  Lox (See Lox hazards)
  Vapor (See Vapor hazards)

Heating
  Antenna terminal silo ... 1-122
  Control center ... 1-121
  Enviornmental seal ... 1-123
  Equipment terminal ... 1-118

	Paragraph
Fuel terminal	1-120
Missile	*1-68, *1-69, 1-397
Missile silo	1-118
Propellant terminal	1-119

Hold period limits during countdown..................*6-2, 6-20, 6-23

Hydraulic system, portal..1-148

I

Illness or injury...*3-7, 3-47

Installation, missile and re-entry vehicle..........................2-3

L

Launch and shutdown, post operation................................1-14

Launch console label installation and verification
    Fast retargeting..*3-28
    Normal procedures...*3-22

Launch platform raising and lowering................................6-3

Launch, tactical (EWO)...2-9

Limitations, operating...6-1
    Countdown..6-19
    Power house..6-37
    Radar surveillance system....................................6-35
    Weather..6-16

Lox hazards
    Propellant terminal lox vent..................................*4-4
    Spillage in missile silo......................................*4-5

Lox tank empty verification.......................................4-12

M

Maintenance
    Depot..1-437
    Field level..1-428
    Ground operating equipment...................................1-436
    Ground support equipment.....................................1-436
    Organizational level...1-428
    Scheduled..1-441
    Unscheduled..1-441

Maintenance and service personnel alert procedures................3-106

Malfunction isolation
  Electrical system..*5-8 thru *5-11
  Flight control system..*5-12
  Guided missile test set...*5-13
  Guidance system...5-13, *5-14 thru *5-37
  Launch complex facility console...5-3
  Launch control console..5-3
  Power house...*5-38
  Propellant loading and pressurization system.........................*5-1 thru *5-7
  Re-entry vehicle system...*5-13

Manual start of standby diesel engine..*4-30

Message, fast reaction..3-109

Missile launch officer
  Alert procedure..3-100
  Individual changeover..*3-3, *3-4

Missile maintenance technician
  Alert procedure..3-103
  Alert Status Monitoring...*3-12, *3-13
  Individual changeover..*3-3, *3-4

Monitoring, alert status...2-5, *3-9 thru *3-14, 3-83

N

Nozzle, vernier...1-28

O

Operating weight limits, launch platform..*6-1, 6-11

P

Panels, access..*1-3, 1-20

Particulars, leading
  Launch complex..*1-4, *1-5, 1-31
  SM68 missile..*1-2, 1-4

Platform, launcher..*1-9, 1-42

Post retargeting procedures, fast retargeting..*3-27

Power failures
  Loss of all AC..*4-17
  Loss of control center feeder AC..*4-24
  Loss of launcher feeder AC..*4-22
  Loss of power house feeder AC...*4-23

Power house emergency..*4-16

Paragraph

Power pack, equipment terminal...*1-14

Printout data, digital data printer RO-144/GSK-1...*1-56

Procedures (See Emergencies or hazards)

R

Raising and lowering launch platform (See Launch platform)

Redskin...*3-6, 3-44, 3-46

Refraction, index of (See Atmospheric pressure)

Release bolts, missile...1-27

Release squibs, staging rocket...1-25

Rocket engine...1-236
    Operation...1-262
    Stage I...*1-58, *1-60, 1-243
    Stage II..*1-59, *1-61, 1-247

Rockets, staging..1-22

Run away diesel engine...*4-27

R/V card fast retargeting installation...*3-28

S

Separation bolts, staging...1-24

Servicing, commodity...1-445

Seven high...*3-6, 3-44, 3-45

Shutdown or handover..6-28

Silo, antenna..1-86
    Equipment functions..*1-47
    Equipment locations..*1-46

Silo, missile..*1-6, 1-34

Spray ponds and pump house...*1-38, 1-111

Station
    Local control..*1-36, 1-106
    Tunnel entrance control..*1-37, 1-109

Structure, crib...*1-8, 1-38

```
                        T.O. 21-SM68-1                                Index
                                                               Support/Target

                                                          Paragraph
```

Support mechanism, umbilical lines..................................*1-12, 1-47

Surveillance radar (anti-intrusion).........*1-71 thru *1-78, 1-418, 3-56, 4-16, 6-35
    Alarm indication...4-17
    Jamming and anti-jamming...4-21
    Primary power failure..4-19
    Starting procedures..3-58
    Stopping procedures..3-59
    Operating procedures...3-60
    System functions...3-61
    Fail-safe capability...3-69
    Security procedures..3-71

System
    Communication...1-405
    Electrical..1-212
    Engine...*1-58, *1-59, *1-60, 1-236
    Facility air conditioning, heating and ventilating............................1-116
    Fire fighting..1-95
    Flight control...*1-57, 1-192
    Hydraulic...*1-66, *1-67, 1-369
    Instrumentation and range safety (VAFB).......................................1-407
    Missile air conditioning...............................*1-68, *1-69, 1-397
    Missile launcher..1-302
    Non-sanitary waste..1-138
    Plant compressed air..1-144
    Portal hydraulic..1-148
    Power distribution..1-127
    Power generation..1-125
    Propellant..*1-62, *1-63, 1-282
    Re-Entry vehicle..1-334
    Sensing, warning, and blast protection................................*1-39, 1-140
    Sewage, sanitary..1-136
    Surveillance radar (anti-intrusion)..4-16
    Utility compressed air..1-142
    Water, raw..1-130
    Water supply, distribution and waste..1-129

System functions
    Ground guidance equipment...1-169
    Missileborne guidance equipment..........................*1-52 thru 1-55, 1-182
    Missile guidance set..*1-49
    Launch countdown...*3-33, *3-34, *3-35, 3-115

                                                T

Tank
    Fuel storage...1-92
    Nitrogen blanket...1-93

Target tape installation and verification
    Fast retargeting...*3-25, *3-26
    Normal procedure..*3-19

Paragraph

Targeting procedures, launch site..........................*3-17 thru *3-28, 3-94
    Fast retargeting (See Target tape installation)
    Inventory targeting..*3-18
    Retargeting..*3-17
    R/V Card (See R/V card fast retargeting)
    Launch console label (See Launch console)

Terminal, antenna.....................................*1-31, *1-32, 1-82
    Equipment functions..*1-45
    Equipment location...*1-44

Terminal, equipment..1-49
    Electrical room..*1-14
    Level I..*1-13, 1-51
    Level II...*1-15, 1-56
    Level III..*1-16, 1-57
    Level IV...*1-17, 1-58
    Power pack room..*1-14

Terminal, fuel..*1-33, *1-34, 1-87

Terminal, propellant..1-60
    Lower level..*1-18, 1-62
    Upper level..*1-19, 1-63

Test set, guided missile..1-211

Tower, umbilical..*1-10

Tunnel
    Liquid oxygen (lox)..1-105
    Utilities..1-104

V

Valve box, ground level...1-89

Vapor hazards
    Fuel vapor in fuel terminal..*4-12
    Fuel vapor in missile silo...*4-10

Velocity, wind..6-32

Ventilating
    Antenna terminal silo..1-122
    Control center...1-121
    Equipment terminal...1-118
    Fuel terminal..1-120
    Missile silo...1-118
    Propellant terminal..1-119

Paragraph

W

Waste
  Non-sanitary...1-138
  Water...1-129

Water
  Distribution..1-129
  Raw...1-130
  Supply..1-129
  Waste...1-129

Weather report procedure - severe weather.....................*3-8, 3-49

LMA 790-1

PROJECT APOLLO

lem
LUNAR EXCURSION MODULE

NOW AVAILABLE!

FIRST MANNED LUNAR LANDING
FAMILIARIZATION MANUAL

GRUMMAN AIRCRAFT ENGINEERING CORPORATION • BETHPAGE, L. I., N. Y.

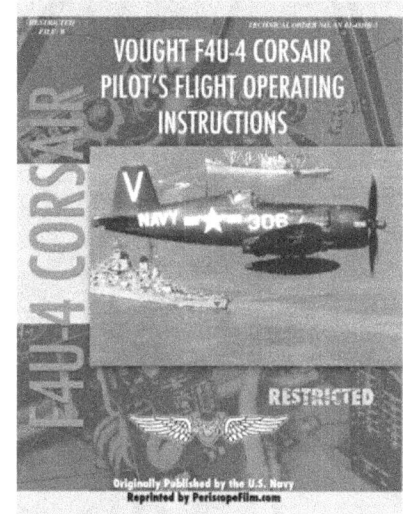
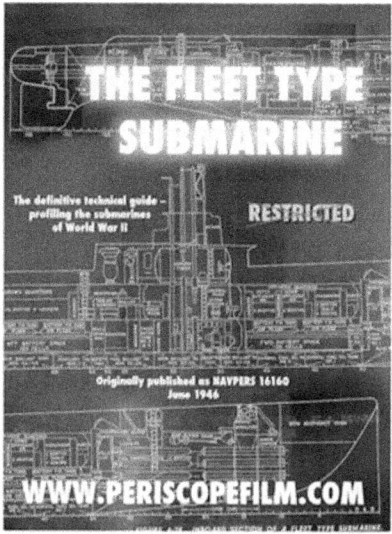

ALSO NOW AVAILABLE
FROM PERISCOPEFILM.COM

©2011 Periscope Film LLC
ISBN #978-1-937684-94-5
All Rights Reserved
www.PeriscopeFilm.com

www.ingramcontent.com/pod-product-compliance
Lightning Source LLC
Chambersburg PA
CBHW081753300426
44116CB00014B/2104